HARDENING
Network Infrastructure

Wesley J. Noonan

MCGRAW-HILL/OSBORNE

New York   Chicago   San Francisco
Lisbon   London   Madrid   Mexico City   Milan
New Delhi   San Juan   Seoul   Singapore   Sydney   Toronto

The McGraw·Hill Companies

McGraw-Hill/Osborne
2100 Powell Street, 10th Floor
Emeryville, California 94608
U.S.A.

To arrange bulk purchase discounts for sales promotions, premiums, or fund-raisers, please contact **McGraw-Hill**/Osborne at the above address. For information on translations or book distributors outside the U.S.A., please see the International Contact Information page immediately following the index of this book.

Hardening Network Infrastructure

1234567890 CUS CUS 01987654

ISBN 0-07-225502-1

Publisher
Brandon A. Nordin
Vice President & Associate Publisher
Scott Rogers
Acquisitions Editor
Tracy Dunkelberger
Project Editor
Mark Karmendy
Acquisitions Coordinator
Athena Honore
Technical Editor
Eric Seagren
Copy Editors
Bart Reed, Lisa Theobald,
Mark Karmendy

Proofreaders
Linda and Paul Medoff
Indexer
Jack Lewis
Composition
Kelly Stanton-Scott, John Patrus
Illustrators
Kathleen Edwards, Melinda Lytle
Cover Series Design
Theresa Havener
Series Design
Kelly Stanton-Scott, Peter F. Hancik

This book was composed with Corel VENTURA™ Publisher.

To my wife Norma for her support.
To my dogs Loki and Odin for keeping me company
on those long days and nights of writing.
To Dwaine for being a father, even though he didn't need to be.

About the Author

Wesley J. Noonan (Houston, Texas) has been working in the computer industry for over 11 years, specializing in Windows-based networks and network infrastructure design and implementation. He is a Senior Network Consultant for Collective Technologies, LLC (www.colltech.com) a company that specializes in storage, server and network design, architecture, implementation, and security. Wes got his start in the United States Marine Corps working on its Banyan VINES network, and has since worked on building and designing secure networks ranging in size from 25 to 25,000 users. Most recently Wes has been working on designing and implementing a 100-location secure VPN internetwork, implementing a global secure Citrix installation, and performing numerous security audits and security design consultations for Collective Technologies, LLC customers. Wes previously worked in R&D for BMC Software, Inc., on their PATROL management solutions, architecting and testing their network and application management products. Previous engagements have included designing a secure network infrastructure for a company that provided 24/7 in-flight airplane status and information, as well as working with a number of Houston-based finance and petrochemical companies in the design and implementation of their security and network infrastructure solutions. Wes is also an active trainer, developing and teaching his own custom, Cisco-based routing and switching curriculum. He has spoken at a number of technical conferences and user groups, including MCTCON2002 and the Associate of IT Professionals–Houston, on the subject of network security and methods to secure a corporate network infrastructure from exploits and intruders. He is an active participant on the SecurityFocus and Firewall-Wizards mailing lists. His certifications include MCSE, CCNA, CCDA, NNCSS, and Security+, of which he was a subject matter expert. This is the second book that Wes has written, previously authoring a chapter on network security and design for *The CISSP Training Guide* by QUE Publishing. Wes is fortunate in the sense that he manages to get paid for what he considers a hobby and continues to be entertained by all aspects of network design and security.

About the Series Editor

Roberta Bragg (Grain Valley, MO), CISSP, MCSE:Security, MVP, Security+, ETI-Client Server, Certified Technical Trainer, IBM Certified Trainer, DB2-UDB, Citrix Certified Administrator, has been a Security Advisor columnist for *MCP* magazine for six years, is a Security Expert for searchWin2000.com, and writes for the *Security Watch* newsletter, which has over 55,000 subscribers. Roberta designed, planned, produced, and participated in the first Windows Security Summit, held in Seattle, WA in 2002. Roberta is the author and presenter of the "Windows Security Academy," a three-day hands-on secure network-building workshop. She has taught for SANS and MIS. She was selected by Microsoft to present the IT Professional advanced track for their 2004 Security Summits. Roberta is a Security Evangelist, traveling all over the world consulting, assessing, and training in network and Windows security issues. She is featured in the *Cool Careers for Girls* book series by Ceel Pasternak and Linda Thornburg. Roberta has served as adjunct faculty member at Seattle Pacific University and the Johnson County Community College, teaching courses on Windows 2000 Security Design and Network Security Design. Roberta is the author of *MCSE Self-Paced Training Kit (Exam 70-298): Designing Security for a Microsoft Windows Server 2003 Network*. Roberta is the lead author of McGraw-Hill/Osborne's *Network Security: The Complete Reference*. She has written on SQL Server 2000, CISSP, and Windows Security for QUE and New Riders.

About the Technical Reviewer

Eric S. Seagren (Missouri City, TX), CISSP, SCNP, CCNA, CNE, MCP+i, MCSE, has eight years of experience in the computer industry, with the last five years spent in the financial industry for a Fortune 100 company. Eric's computer career began running cables and performing general network and server troubleshooting for a small Houston-based company. His experience in the financial industry has involved Novell and Microsoft server administration, disaster recovery responsibilities, and Y2K remediation efforts. He has spent the last couple of years as an IT Architect, designing secure, scalable, and redundant networks, including extensive DMZ design, and evaluating and auditing the security of various network designs and products including routers, switches, firewalls, and intrusion detection and prevention systems.

Contents

PART I   Do This Now!

PART II   Take It from the Top: The Systematic Hardening Process

PART III   Once Is Never Enough!

Foreword

Today's information technology professional has to deal with security events as a matter of course—from worms and viruses to rogue users, down to the stereotypical black t-shirt–clad intruder. This book contains valuable here's-what-to-type information—not just theory—and that's very handy for an administrator who has to do real work. The examples in the book are all helpful for using at the command prompt.

The more proactively you set up your security, the less reactively you'll have to patch, update, and recover from security events. One mindset that may help to ease the transition to proactive security is to think in terms of reducing risk, instead of increasing security. Ask questions like "how can I reduce the most risk?" often, and the reward will be more security. Remember that "perfect" is the enemy of "good enough." Don't worry about putting in the perfect solution, but rather concentrate on the most practical one.

When it's all said and done, an effective and sustainable security strategy is not possible without the help of your network's users. Tackling management and resource issues can often be more challenging than tackling IPsec configuration issues. Fortunately, Wes has covered both sets of issues in this book.

Finally, know that you're not alone. We defenders must all work together if we're to have a greater effect on the security of our networks, users, and data. Forums like the Firewall-Wizards Mailing List allow helpful folks like the author of this book to assist people with specific problems. It may not be our fault that things weren't set up correctly, that someone did something they shouldn't have, or that someone attacks our systems. But it is our responsibility to do what we can to make our networks safe and to help others do the same.

Paul D. Robertson
Director of Risk Assessment, TruSecure® Corporation
Moderator, Firewall-Wizards® Security Mailing List

Paul Robertson has been in information technology and security over 20 years; highlights include being stationed at The White House while in the United States Army and putting *USA Today*'s website on the Internet. Paul currently helps manage risk for hundreds of corporate clients at TruSecure®, and he participates in computer forensics, advocating www.personalfirewallday.org and moderating the Firewall-Wizards Mailing List.

Acknowledgments

This book would not have been possible without the help and assistance of numerous people. First, thank you Roberta for providing me this opportunity. Second, I have to thank the editors who took the words I wrote and invariably made them sound so much better. Tracy, Athena, Mark, Bart, and Lisa, thank you all. I also could not have done this without the assistance of my technical editor, Eric Seagren, for collaborating with me far more than he was required to and taking the cheesy Visio diagrams I created and making them look sharp. This book would also not have been possible without the assistance of numerous vendors and technical contributors who provided me access to hardware, software, documentation, resources, and good old-fashioned advice: MaryEtta Morris for her assistance with obtaining Cisco wireless equipment; Anne Camden, Public Relations Manager for Dell portable and wireless products for her assistance with obtaining Dell wireless products; Roger Billings of Nortel Networks for going above and beyond the call in getting me access to Nortel Equipment (Roger, other vendors could learn from you about customer service); and Ben Thomas of Cisco Systems, Inc., for getting me access to Cisco IDS technologies. Thank you also to Chuck Cook for getting me started so many years ago, being one of my mentors, and for giving me free reign in his lab during this endeavor.

Introduction

If you know the enemy and know yourself, you need not fear the result of a hundred battles. If you know yourself but not the enemy, for every victory gained you will also suffer a defeat. If you know neither the enemy nor yourself, you will succumb in every battle.

A general is skillful in attack whose opponent does not know what to defend; and he is skillful in defense whose opponent does not know what to attack.

Sun Tzu, *The Art of War*

Why would a book on hardening network infrastructure open with a couple of quotes on warfare by Sun Tzu? The answer is that today's networks are under attack. It is nothing less than digital warfare. On one side, you have hackers, crackers, and script kiddies who are attempting to gather information and gain access to protected resources. They are the enemy, and you need to know who they are and what they do. You need to understand the methods of attack and the types of exploits they use. An excellent resource for understanding the existing threats to your network is the *Hacking Exposed* series (McGraw-Hill/Osborne). These books contain examples and explanations of the types of tactics that hackers employ. Knowing the enemy, however, is only part of the equation.

On the other side of the digital battlefield, you have the security professionals. We are the folks who attempt to prevent the hackers, crackers, and script kiddies from exploiting our systems. It is not good enough just to know what kinds of threats exist to your network. You must know not only the enemy, but also yourself and your network. You must know what resources exist on your network, from firewalls to routers to switches and everything in between. Once you are familiar with these, you need to know how to harden those network resources. For example, if you know that hackers will employ spoofing in an attempt to gain access to resources, how do you configure your firewalls and routers to protect against that threat? This book adds to the valuable information in *Hacking Exposed* by detailing the specific methods and procedures that you can implement to harden your network resources. I will show you what to defend so that your enemy's attacks will be in vain.

I have been frustrated with many technical books and whitepapers I have read because they rarely provide specific examples of what to do. They provide a great depth of conceptual information and explanations, but I often find myself asking, "OK, so now that I understand the issue, what exactly should I do about it?" When I was approached about writing this book, the one thing that intrigued me most was the publisher's desire to answer the question, "What should I *do* about it?" I decided to write this book from the perspective of a consultant. Instead of explaining the details of how various exploits work and then telling you that you need to fix the problems, I will tell you what you can do to harden your resources to *prevent* attacks, providing specific configuration examples as much as I can. I want you to be able to take this book and use it as a pocket consultant or procedural manual to guide you through the steps and procedures to follow in order to harden your network infrastructure.

We will look at all aspects of hardening network infrastructure, separated into four distinct parts. In Part I, "Do This Now!", we will start with an examination of six things that you should do right now, if you aren't doing them already.

In Part II, "Take It from the Top—The Systematic Hardening Process," we will start by performing an examination of a security policy, and then we will provide guidelines that you can follow to develop a good security policy. You cannot bring all your network devices into a consistent hardened state unless you have clearly defined what that state looks like, and this is why writing a security policy must be the first step to hardening your network. Then we will examine the specific network infrastructure hardware that needs to be hardened. We will look not only at what you can do to protect that hardware, but also at how you can use that hardware to protect your network. For example, we will investigate not only the steps to take to protect the firewall itself from being compromised, but also the steps needed to use the firewall to protect your network infrastructure. Part II will wrap up with a look at all of the various technologies and concepts, and integrate them into a systematically hardened network infrastructure design.

Part III, "Once Is Never Enough," will explore how to address changes that will occur with your network infrastructure. From security policy changes to patches and updates, we will cover how to effectively address the changes that need to occur without compromising your network security posture.

Finally, Part IV, "How to Succeed at Hardening Your Network Infrastructure," will address the soft-skills aspects of hardening your network. Issues covered will range from how to justify expenses to the powers that be to staffing and training concerns. We will wrap up with a look at the hard reality of network security: what to do when your best efforts fail and your network is compromised.

It is my sincere desire that after reading this book and implementing its suggestions, you will not only know your enemy but you will know yourself and your network, and by extension, you will know what to defend and how to defend it.

NOTE   At the end of some code lines throughout this book (as in the example below), you'll see a right-pointing arrow (→). This signifies that the single-line command, which really should fall on one line, must break due to width limitations of the printed page.

```
iptables -A INPUT -I eth0 -p tcp -m tcp -s 192.168.1.100 -d →
192.168.1.1 --dport 443 --syn -j ACCEPT
```

Part I

Do This Now!

Chapter 1

Do These Six Things Before You Do Anything Else

- Review Your Network Design
- Implement a Firewall
- Implement Access Control Lists
- Turn Off Unnecessary Features and Services
- Implement Virus Protection
- Secure Your Wireless Connections

ardening your network infrastructure is a process, not a task. It is something that, once started, does not end. You must remain constantly vigilant to the threats against your network and continuously undertake actions to prevent any compromises. Because of the scale of the undertaking, hardening your network infrastructure is not an endeavor you should undertake lightly. Depending on the size and complexity of your environment, you might spend weeks or even months planning before you make any changes. At the same time, if you are looking at how to harden your network, you probably recognize that you have security issues that need to be addressed, even if you aren't sure exactly what those issues are or how to fix them. This can put you in a bind in that you may have issues that really need to be addressed immediately, before the full-scale hardening process begins. So what are some things you should do immediately, right now, without any hesitation? I'm glad you asked. Chapter 1 looks at six things you should do right now, before you do anything else.

There are many tasks you can perform as part of the systematic hardening process. These are all generally big-ticket items—for example, hardening your routers and switches or implementing DMZs and perimeter network devices. These tasks take time, sometimes months from the initial planning and design phase to the implementation. Although all these tasks are necessary, you should undertake six tasks, in particular, before you do anything else on your network. I consider these six tasks to be the biggest impact undertakings you should evaluate. At the same time, I don't want to mislead you into thinking, "OK, if I do these six things, I am probably pretty safe." You aren't. However, what you will have is an excellent foundation from which to start the systematic hardening process of your network infrastructure. This foundation consists of the following elements:

- *Review your network design.* If you don't know what your network design looks like, how your devices are interconnected, how the data flows in your enterprise, you will never be able to successfully protect your network. The first step to hardening your network is to understand it.

- *Implement a firewall.* If you don't have a firewall, stop reading this book right now and go buy or build one and implement it on your network. I'm deadly serious here. You can pick this book back up afterward and continue where you left off. Implementing a firewall has the most impact of any task you can perform for hardening your network infrastructure because it allows you to define a perimeter.

- *Implement access control lists (ACLs).* You should be restricting and controlling all traffic entering and exiting your network from the outside world. At the same time, you should be restricting traffic between internal network segments. If there isn't a business justification for the traffic, block it. You should be filtering traffic with ACLs not only on your external firewalls and routers, but on your internal firewalls and routers as well.

- *Turn off unnecessary features and services.* Although traditionally the realm of servers and applications, unnecessary services equally plague your network infrastructure devices. If you don't have a reason to be running a particular service on your network equipment, don't do it.

- *Implement virus protection.* Today's worms and viruses, though directed at applications and computers, have the uncanny side effect of often causing Distributed Denial of Service (DDoS) attacks against routers and switches because of how they attempt to replicate. The easiest way to protect against these kinds of attacks is to ensure that every system from Windows to Unix, desktop to server, runs virus protection. Don't forget to implement virus protection on your gateway devices, such as SMTP gateways, to prevent e-mail–based viruses and worms as well.

- *Secure your wireless connections.* Wireless connectivity presents a unique problem to securing your network. If you aren't sure why you are running wireless, turn it off. Revisit the issue once you know why you are implementing a wireless network. If you have to run wireless, ensure that you implement encryption and authentication to prevent unauthorized users from connecting and/or intercepting and reading your wireless communications.

Review Your Network Design

Someone once told me, "In order to know where you are going, you have to know where you came from." This is true for hardening your network infrastructure. In order to effectively protect your resources, you must know how your network is designed. You must know how your routers are interconnected, where your network ingress points are, where your various resources are located, and so on. Only once you know this information can you effectively protect those resources. In addition, if your network does become compromised, knowing how everything is connected will help you in determining how to recover from it or how to isolate the problem to specific network segments. At the same time, I'm not proposing that the first thing you should do is redesign you network. Remember, we are looking at things you can do right now to make an immediate impact on the security of your network.

Because every network is different, it is impossible for me to provide you a comprehensive review of a network design. I can, however, provide you with 21 questions you should be asking as you review your network design. These questions will help you better understand where and how your network can be hardened.

- *Where are your Internet connections?* Today's networks commonly have multiple Internet connections. Review your network design and identify all your Internet connections. These can range from your enterprise Internet connection to a backup/redundant connection for your company, all the way down to a DSL or cable modem connection used as a temporary backup exclusively for your sales force. Be prepared to locate "surprises," such as unauthorized connections to your network in executive suites. Identify these ingress points because those are where you will implement your firewalls.

■ *Where are your external connections?* External connections range from traditional frame relay and ATM connections to dedicated serial T1/T3 lines to the Internet connections addressed previously. They are typically used to connect remote offices or external business partners. These are all potential ingress points on your network. Consequently, you need to implement firewalls at those connections as well as potentially employ encryption for the data traversing them.

■ *What networks/subnets are you using?* Identify the IP addressing scheme and the location of all your subnets. Are you using dynamic addressing products and protocols such as VitalQIP and DHCP? DHCP networks, although they provide significant ease of resource addressing, create a security issue. Anyone can connect to your DHCP network and immediately begin attempting to gain access to your network resources by exploiting weak security that might exist elsewhere on your network.

■ *What routing protocols are you employing?* The routing protocols you use will identify the methods you can implement to protect those protocols. The steps you take to harden Routing Information Protocol (RIP), for example, are not necessarily the same as the steps to harden Open Shortest Path First (OSPF). Are you redistributing routes between protocols? Knowing what protocols you are running, where they are running, and how they are configured will dictate how to harden the protocols.

■ *Are you running Spanning Tree Protocol?* Spanning Tree Protocol, like your routing protocols, contains a tremendous amount of information about your network that any hacker would give his two front teeth to get. Identify where you are running Spanning Tree Protocol so that you can decide whether you need to be running it in that location.

■ *Where is your Intrusion Detection/Protection System (IDS/IPS) located?* You need to know what you are monitoring for and where you are monitoring. Are you only monitoring with network-based intrusion detection systems (NIDSs) or are you also using host-based intrusion detections systems (HIDSs)? Where are you performing these functions, and more important, where are you not?

■ *Where are you performing content filtering?* Knowing where and how you are performing content filtering is critical in preventing web-based exploits from entering your network. This is commonly done at your Internet connections, but it might make sense for you to do this in other locations, such as between extranet partners.

Content Filtering and Redundant Internet Connection

I worked at a company that implemented content filtering at their primary Internet connection, but somehow overlooked implementing it at their backup/secondary Internet connections. One day their primary Internet connection failed, and everything failed over to the secondary location in another state, as designed. Unfortunately, because they were not performing content filtering on that connection, this failover exposed them not only to inappropriate work content but also to malicious code and websites. Although this situation was quickly remedied, had they reviewed their network design at some point, they would have recognized that they had overlooked content filtering on their backup connections and prevented this entire situation.

- *Are you implementing NAT, and where are you implementing NAT?* Network Address Translation (NAT) is commonly implemented at your Internet connections; however, with growth and acquisitions, companies are using NAT on their internal network segments more and more. NAT can present problems with IPsec encryption as well as increased network complexity. Knowing where you are implementing NAT can illustrate areas of your network that you need to keep an eye on, in particular, to make sure NAT is working securely and properly.

- *What VLANs are in use?* Virtual Local Area Networks (VLANs) can be a saving grace to large networks, making it much easier to logically separate resources. At the same time, VLANs can dramatically increase the complexity of a network, consequently allowing security problems to be hidden by the complexities of the VLAN. A common example of this is having VLANs for networks of different security levels (that is, inside and outside or inside and DMZ) running on the same switch fabric. This is a bad thing because switches have historically shown a propensity to allow traffic to traverse between VLANs when it shouldn't. Knowing where you have VLANs will help you harden those VLANs.

- *Where are your server resources located?* If your server resources are located on a dedicated subnet away from your users, it's much easier to implement ACLs or similar filters to protect those resources. Knowing where your critical server resources are located will allow you to strategize a method to protect those resources.

- *Do you provide VPN/remote access connectivity?* VPN/remote access connectivity is one of the biggest threats to your network's security posture. This is due in large part to the fact that you rarely have control of the equipment that is connecting via your VPN connections. Employee's home networks are rarely protected as they should be, and when those systems connect via VPN to your corporate network, it becomes susceptible to compromise. Knowing where your VPN/remote access connectivity occurs allows you to focus on where to protect against remote exploits.

- *What vendor's equipment are you using?* Different vendors are susceptible to different exploits. Likewise, different vendors implement different methods to secure their equipment. Knowing what vendor's equipment you have on your network will allow you to develop a reasonable policy for hardening that equipment.

- *What network devices are you using?* Routers require different security measures than switches do. Switches require different security measures than hubs do. By identifying the devices employed on your network, you can develop a security policy that addresses the specific issues of each device type on your network.

- *What are your device naming conventions?* Although a relatively mundane item, device naming conventions can be a real problem in large environments where you need to figure out what a device is or where it might be located by name alone. Using names of *fish* and *trees*, as one company I worked at did, serves only to make identifying where a problem or security issue is occurring much more difficult than it needs to be. At the same time, using names that lead people to critical or sensitive servers or resources can also be an issue. You need to strike a balance between function and anonymity.

- *What circuit types do you employ?* Point-to-point connections and frame relay connections require different methods of hardening. Identifying the various circuit types you are using will allow you to define a policy that doesn't overlook a circuit type.

- *What network protocols and standards are in use?* Are you using Hot-Swap Router Protocol (HSRP)? What about Data-Link Switching (DLSw)? Do you still need to run Internetwork Packet Exchange/Sequenced Packet Exchange (IPX/SPX)? By examining the network protocols and standards in use on your network, you can identify security issues unique to each protocol or standard.

- *Do you have dedicated management segments?* Using dedicated management segments is one of the best methods to protect your devices from remote management exploits. Where are these segments, and most important, who has access to them? Knowing this information will help ensure that people do not inadvertently gain management access to your equipment.

- *Where are your critical segments?* Backbone connections, critical Line of Business (LOB) segments, human resources (HR) segments, and so on, need to be identified so that you can ensure not only that the data on those segments is protected, but that those segments are reliable and redundant. Connections between subnets and segments—particularly critical subnets and segments—represent locations where filtering and access lists should be implemented to protect those subnets and segments.

- *What kind of AAA mechanism are you using on your network?* Are you using common passwords (for example, enable secret passwords) or are you performing user-based authentication? Do you have RADIUS or TACACS+ for authentication, authorization, and accounting?

- *What kind of enterprise monitoring/management products are you using?* Many management protocols such as SNMP and Syslog transmit their data in an unencrypted and therefore insecure fashion. Identifying what management products you are using, where they are located, and what devices they communicate with will allow you to determine the most effective method for securing the traffic.

- *Where are your wireless connections?* Wireless represents a significant security issue on a corporate network. Know where you have wireless access points set up so that you can identify and secure that access.

Implement a Firewall

If you can do nothing else to harden your network, you need to implement a firewall. The reason for this is simple: a firewall is the single device that can do more to keep unauthorized traffic from entering a network than any other device. Now you might have heard that firewalls aren't effective anymore because so many things use port 80 to pass traffic; however, those situations are a small, small portion of all the threats that exist from which a firewall can protect you. In addition, when implementing an application-filtering firewall, you can gain the ability to filter application content, identifying legitimate web requests from illegitimate web requests. Finally, remember that a firewall, although the best single choice you can make, is most effective as a component of security, being complemented by an intrusion detection/prevention system (IDS/IPS) and content filters.

Although many folks think of a firewall as something used to protect their network from Internet-based threats, do not overlook the value of using firewalls at other locations on your network. For example, you can use a firewall on your WAN perimeter to filter traffic to and from frame relay or point-to-point circuit connections across a public internetwork. Likewise, you can implement a firewall to filter traffic between internal LAN segments, protecting critical business resources such as HR servers and application servers from unauthorized traffic. There are a few types of firewalls to consider:

- Application proxies
- Stateful packet-inspecting/filtering gateways
- Hybrid firewalls

Application Proxies

Application proxies are identified by their ability to read and process an entire packet to the application level and make filtering decisions based on the actual application data, not just the packet header. Application proxies receive all incoming packets and completely decode them to the Application layer. The actual application data can then be scrutinized to determine whether it is legitimate data. If this data is legitimate, the firewall will rebuild the packet and forward it accordingly. Because of this capability, application proxy firewalls can apply a significant amount of intelligence before making a filtering decision. One drawback is that this type of filtering introduces latency to network communications and requires significant amounts of processing power. Another drawback is that unless the firewall has the proxy capability for a given protocol or service, it might not be able to facilitate communications with the given protocol or service. Secure Computing Sidewinder G2, Microsoft's Internet Security & Acceleration (ISA) Server 2000, CyberGuard firewall/VPN appliances, and Symantec Enterprise Firewall are examples of application proxy firewalls.

Stateful Packet-Inspecting/Filtering Gateways

Packet-inspecting/filtering gateways are generally not able to process the packet to the application level to make a filtering decision. Instead, packet-inspecting/filtering gateways tend to process the data to the Network/Transport layer and make filtering decisions based on the protocol and port numbers contained in the packet header only. Packet-inspecting/filtering gateways also typically implement a stateful packet inspection model, which allows the firewall to maintain a record of the state of all conversations occurring through the firewall, automatically permitting responses for legitimate outbound requests. IPtables, IPchains, SonicWALL, Clavister, and many of your SOHO firewalls such as Linksys and D-Link are examples of packet-inspecting/filtering gateways.

Hybrid Firewalls

More and more today, most firewalls fall into the hybrid category. Although they typically perform stateful packet filtering/inspecting for making most filtering decisions, they may have some application proxy functionalities built in for specific high-risk protocols and services such as HTTP and FTP. Most of the firewalls on the market today are hybrid firewalls. Examples of hybrid firewalls are Check Point Firewall-1 NG, Cisco Secure PIX, and Netscreen Deep Inspection Firewall.

Which Firewall Should You Implement?

There is no one right answer as to which firewall to use for your environment. This is one of the rare cases when I really can't give you a definitive answer. You will need to make a decision based on your requirements and your environment. For example, if you require extremely high throughput, a packet-filtering firewall would be a good choice to implement. If you are using standard protocols and require the most rigorous application inspection, an application proxy would be a good choice to implement. In some environments, you might even need both—a packet-filtering firewall to perform initial packet inspection on all traffic, and an application proxy behind that to perform the more detailed application filtering. Regardless of which type of firewall you decide is best for your environment, however, if you do not currently have a firewall, make sure you get one. Any of the firewalls mentioned are better than having none at all.

Implement Access Control Lists

Properly implemented access control lists (ACLs) on your routers provide packet-filtering capabilities without the stateful functionality of a full-featured firewall. Consequently, I think of ACLs on routers as being part of a firewall system, where the router is performing initial packet-filtering functionality in front of a firewall that is providing the full-bore stateful filtering or application proxy functionality. Implementing ACLs, including specific examples, will be covered in much more detail in Chapter 6. However, here are some types of access you should filter with your ACLs immediately:

- Block RFC1918 addresses at your perimeter, including the following:
    - 0.0.0.0/8
    - 10.0.0.0/8
    - 169.254.0.0/16
    - 172.16.0.0/20
    - 192.168.0.0/16
- Block bogon addresses. The term *bogon* refers to packets addressed to/from a bogus network. Bogons represent the addresses that have not been allocated by the Internet Assigned Numbers Authority (IANA) and Regional Internet Registries (RIRs) to Internet service providers (ISPs) or organizations for use. A current list of bogon networks can be found at http://www.iana.org/assignments/ipv4-address-space. Any entry with the term "reserved" or "unallocated" should be blocked as a bogon. You will need to periodically update the bogons you are blocking because those addresses get assigned to legitimate ISPs and organizations for use.
- Implement spoof protection.
- Implement TCP SYN attack protection.
- Implement LAND attack protection.
- Implement Smurf attack protection.
- Implement ICMP filtering.

- Block multicast traffic if it is not needed.
- Implement ACLs to control Virtual Type Terminal (VTY) access (Telnet and SSH).
- Implement ACLs to control who can manage the router via SNMP.

Turn Off Unnecessary Features and Services

One point of security that has been hammered on within the desktop/server world is the need to turn off unnecessary services. Unfortunately, people commonly overlook the fact that it is not just the desktops and servers that are potentially running unnecessary services—your network devices are also likely doing this. Detailed configuration examples of how to turn off services will be covered in the device-specific chapters of this book (for example, Chapter 6 for your routers and switches). However, here is a list of services you should look for on your network equipment and turn off if you are not actively using them:

- Cisco Discovery Protocol (CDP)
- TCP and UDP small servers
- Finger server
- HTTP server
- Bootp server
- Network Time Protocol (NTP) service
- Simple Network Management Protocol (SNMP) services
- Configuration auto-loading
- IP source routing
- Proxy ARP
- IP directed broadcast
- IP unreachable, redirects, and mask replies
- Router name and DNS name resolution services

Implement Virus Protection

Virus protection and implementing virus protection typically fall within the realm of the server/desktop administrator. Indeed, in large environments, if you are responsible for the network infrastructure, you may never be involved in any virus-protection discussions. Unfortunately, today's worms and viruses are having a larger impact on the network infrastructure, which means you need to become concerned with the status of virus protection on your network. In addition, you can install virus-protection gateway devices and virus-protection applications in conjunction with your existing firewalls and gateways to prevent viruses from entering your network. You should be involved in advocating these systems being implemented.

The methods that many of the worms use to self-replicate (for example, by scanning an entire subnet and attempting to connect to every IP address on that subnet) have the uncanny ability to result in a denial of service (DoS) on many routers. The reason for this is pretty straightforward. When a router receives a packet destined for a subnet that it is directly connected to, the router will generate an ARP request for the destination MAC address. In the case of these worms, often the destination is not online, but the router has no way of knowing this and issues the ARP request anyway. The router then must wait for a response, or wait for the ARP request to time out before it can drop the packet in question. As the router gets hit with thousands of these requests, it fills its buffers and input/output queues with these packets waiting for the timeout periods to occur. Often this consumes the entire free RAM on a router. The end result is that the router starts dropping legitimate traffic because it cannot queue the traffic, and/or the router will no longer accept VTY sessions because it does not have enough free RAM to house those sessions. Both of these circumstances result in a DoS against the router. In fact, when you think about it, the way that these worms work is a great example of just how effective a distributed denial of service (DDoS) attack can be.

ONE STEP FURTHER

I know of a number of companies that have invested heavily in virus protection for their Windows-based systems but run no virus protection on their Unix and Linux systems. As Linux, in particular, continues to gain market share, it is only a matter of time before more Linux-based viruses are written and distributed. Do not overlook the risk of not protecting your Unix/Linux systems. Viruses are not uniquely a Windows problem.

If you are not running virus protection on all your systems—Windows, Unix, Linux, and Macintosh based—you need to be.

Don't forget your gateway virus protection when talking about implementing virus protection on all your systems. This allows you to catch and stop a significant amount of viruses attempting to enter your network at your network ingress points. TrendMicro, Network Associates, and Symantec all have gateway virus protection you can implement. Don't overlook the value of implementing virus protection on your gateways and firewalls.

The only way to effectively prevent your network from being susceptible to virus- and worm-based DDoS attacks is to keep the systems that propagate the worms from being infected in the first place and to attempt to prevent the viruses from entering your network to begin with.

Secure Your Wireless Connections

Hardening your wireless network will be covered in much more detail in Chapter 8. However, what you can do right now is to locate and remove all wireless access points that you do not need or did not plan properly. This may sound like a little bit of overkill, but it isn't. If you have not developed a wireless security plan and implemented your wireless network by restricting IP addresses and implementing encryption and authentication, you need to unplug everything and start all over again building a secure wireless network. If you must run wireless, you can do the following four tasks to harden your wireless network against attack:

- Require a written wireless security policy that allows only IT supported wireless products that are only implemented by IT. If an employee goes out and buys the latest, cheapest personal wireless access point or router, that should be grounds for dismissal.

- Only allow authorized MAC addresses to connect to your wireless network.

- Require Wired Equivalent Privacy (WEP), WiFi Protected Access (WPA), or 802.11i for encryption. Be aware that WEP has been compromised, but is better than clear text.

- Require authentication via shared secret key, 802.1x, RADIUS authentication, or certificates as supported by your devices.

Summary

Hardening your network infrastructure is going to be a long process that involves examining all your network infrastructure equipment and evaluating what vulnerabilities exist as well as identifying how to harden your equipment against those vulnerabilities. However, you can undertake six tasks to start making an immediate impact on the security of your network.

First, you must review your network design so that you know what you are dealing with. This will serve as a roadmap of what needs to be done. Next, you need to implement a firewall. A firewall is the best thing you can introduce into your environment to address security. After that, you should implement ACLs on your equipment. Restrict not only the traffic that can pass through the system, but also who has access to the system. At the same time, review all your network equipment and ensure that any unnecessary services and features have been turned off or disabled. Protocols like Spanning Tree Protocol are very good at what they do, but if you do not need that functionality, turn those features off. Although likely not in the realm of the network infrastructure engineer, virus protection can make your life much easier. Insist that virus protection be installed and configured on all systems in your enterprise. Also, make sure there is a regular schedule for updating the virus signatures and scanning engine to protect against new viruses. Last but not least, secure your wireless connections. Wireless today is really just an open door to your network, inviting unauthorized access to anyone who happens to be in range of your wireless access point. If you don't need wireless access, don't use it. If you do, make sure you have properly secured your wireless access points. If you aren't sure whether your wireless access points are secured, turn them off and start again.

Security is a complex process; however, these six tasks are all relatively easy to perform and will make an immediate and noticeable impact on your overall security posture.

Part II

Take It from the Top: The Systematic Hardening Process

Chapter 2

Write a Security Policy

- The Role of a Security Policy
- Security Policy Components
- Security Policy Recommendations
- Why Security Policies Fail and How to Ensure Yours Won't

I opened Chapter 1 by saying, "Hardening your network infrastructure is a long process that, if done properly, never really ends; rather, it becomes part of your routine." A well-designed and well-written security policy is the guide you will use along that process to ensure that hardening your network becomes a part of your daily routine. A popular self-help book called *The 7 Habits of Highly Effective People: Powerful Lessons in Personal Change* (Stephen R. Corey, Fireside, 1989) details how effective folks form habits that contribute to their success. These aren't tasks or actions they just do some of the time; rather, they incorporate these ideals into their daily lives and make it a habit to do these things.

Your security policy should be approached from that perspective. It should become habit for you to design and implement technologies and processes on your network using the guidelines defined in your security policy. In fact, a well-written security policy should become a standard operating procedure of sorts that can be used by anyone in the organization as a reference of what to do and how to do it.

Before you make any changes to your network—be it adding new devices or simply rearranging devices—you should review your security policy to make sure that whatever you are undertaking is in compliance with it. If it isn't, either the security policy needs to be updated or the changes you are making need to be reviewed.

In this chapter, we are going to look at the following aspects of a security policy:

- What the role of a security policy is
- What the components of a security policy are
- What specific points your security policy should addresses
- Why security policies fail and how to ensure yours won't

In addition to this chapter, you should read RFC 2196, "Site Security Handbook," located at http://www.ietf.org/rfc/rfc2196.txt, and RCF 2504, "Users' Security Handbooks," located at http://www.ietf.org/rfc/rfc2504.txt. In addition, ISO 17799 is a detailed standard covering ten sections that provide detailed information about what your security policy should contain. Unfortunately, like many ISO standards, this document is only available by purchase at www.iso.org. Virtually all security policy concepts have a foundation and basis in the concepts and recommendations of these two RFCs and the ISO standard.

The Role of a Security Policy

All too often, corporate technology initiatives fail due in large part to a lack of planning and consideration of the impact such changes will make on a network. A corporate security initiative is no different. When I was in the Marine Corps, they used to talk about the seven P's: Proper prior planning prevents pretty poor performance. This holds true for networking. You need to plan and prepare before you implement anything. As they say, "an ounce of prevention is worth a pound of cure." Your security is part of that prevention. The reason why most initiatives fail is because no one has taken the time to define exactly what the goals of these initiatives are; therefore, no one truly knows what they are working toward. Without that knowledge, you can't possibly know what to do to accomplish your goal. For example, it isn't good enough to simply say that you need a firewall to be more secure. You must define precisely what you want to secure and how you want to secure it. What kind of filtering do you want to put in place? What kind of access do you want to grant users? Do you want to authenticate and log user Internet usage? Only by answering these and other questions and defining explicitly what the goals and objectives are can you truly identify, purchase, and implement a firewall that will actually do what you want it to do.

Two predominant schools of thought exist regarding what a security policy should contain. The first school of thought is that a security policy is an all-encompassing document that should contain the simple commandments and recommendations as well as the detailed specifications and configuration examples. In essence, the security policy is not only the policy but the procedures as well. The second school of thought differs in that it holds that a security policy should contain the simple commandments and recommendations and leave the detailed specifications and configuration examples to additional procedural documentation that may or may not be referred to in the security policy. Both approaches have their pros and cons, and the truth is that either approach will work depending on your environment. The benefit of the "all-encompassing security policy" is that all your information regarding security and implementation is contained in a single document, thus making it easier to keep track of. A downside of this, however, is that your security policy is much more susceptible to change, because the policy itself must be updated for simple procedural changes. The benefit of the "security policy is only the policy" method is that your security policy can effectively be written in stone because it leaves the details of how to perform the various tasks to other documents, simply stating what must be done. The downside of this method, however, is that you can wind up having multiple documents containing all your security implementation information, making it more difficult to keep track of everything.

I am going to approach the security policy largely from the "all-encompassing" method. The reason for this is simple: You have to detail your procedures at some point. Whether you do it in the security policy itself or in additional documents, it must occur. By addressing those points from the "all-encompassing" perspective, I can make sure we talk about them, and you can decide whether you want to keep them as part of the security policy itself or you want to break the procedures out into other documents. In practice, the "all-encompassing" approach is better suited for smaller organizations, whereas the "separated" approach is better suited for large organizations where changing the security policy is a very laborious task.

ONE STEP FURTHER

For you to properly understand the role of a security policy, we need to define some of the terminology used:

- **Policies**   Policies simply state what should occur. For example, a policy might state that all traffic traversing a public infrastructure (such as the Internet) must be encrypted.

- **Standards**   Standards define how something works. For example, as part of the preceding policy, we may require 3DES and IPsec as the standards used.

- **Procedures**   Procedures define how a device will be configured, in accordance to the policies and standards defined for the device. For example, you might have a procedure that defines how to configure 3DES and IPsec on a router that is used to pass data over the Internet so that the data is encrypted.

The Purpose of a Security Policy

At its most fundamental, a security policy exists to convey the corporate vision and commitment to security and to define the standards and procedures regarding what is considered acceptable while working with or on corporate resources. Your security policy needs to specify what your corporate standards are. Should all systems be implemented to authenticate against a TACACS+ server? If so, your security policy should mandate that this must occur. Your security policy should also lay out what your corporate security goals are. Is your organization trying to reduce the impact of viruses and worms? Are they trying to mitigate external access threats? If so, don't leave these statements as assumptions or common sense. Write them out and define them. Having a stated corporate security objective can be critical in cases where corporate politics come into play and you have folks who don't want to adhere to the security policy. It allows you to point to a written document signed off by your CEO that tells the user, "This is why you need to do what we are asking."

This last point brings up another important element of your security policy—the fact that for a security policy to have any chance at success, it must have upper management's support, including C-level support. Security is constantly at odds with usability. In some cases, usability is going to win over security. In other cases, security is more important than usability. Without upper management's support, you stand virtually no chance at making changes with users or departments that do not want to sacrifice any usability for increased security.

Security Policies and Problem Users

I once worked at a company that had a particularly problematic user when it came to running virus protection. This individual saw the computer that he used as "his" computer, and he wasn't interested in anyone telling him what he could do with "his" computer. According to him, running virus protection per the corporate standards made compiling take too long to perform, so he wasn't going to do it. Because the company lacked any kind of written and enforceable policy, the security team and this individual went round and round on a monthly basis with no progress ever being made, up until the time I left the company. Having the buy in from the R&D director could have put a quick end to the discussion, but no one bothered to get that. Do not underestimate the influence that an executive or director has in ensuring that employees adhere to the corporate security policy.

Security Policy Components

People often refer to a corporate security policy as if it is a single document. Even in this book I have done that. The truth, however, is that much like TCP/IP is a combination of a number of different protocols, your security policy is actually a combination of any number of specific policies, such as a wireless access policy and an ingress filtering policy. There are common components to all security policies, however, as well as a common methodology to developing your security policies. We are going to look at these components and methodologies.

Where to Start?

As previously mentioned, one of the big reasons to have a security policy is to define where you are and where you want to go. This is a three-step cycle that involves the following components:

- Security policy design
- Security policy implementation and enforcement
- Security policy monitoring and review

Security Policy Design

The first step involves designing your security policy. For all intents and purposes, this is the beginning of the security policy design process. This is where a security policy design committee works to develop the overall policy strategy.

Your security policy design committee should consist of representatives from every aspect of your organization. Upper and middle management, local and remote users, human resources, legal, information technology, the corporate security team, and any relevant data owners and stakeholders should all be represented in the design committee. The reason for this is that whether we like it or not, politics will play a role in virtually all security policies. Ensuring that everyone is represented and has input in the policy design will make it easier politically to enforce the policy down the road.

Designing your security policy begins with a high-level overview that gradually gets more granular as the policy is formulated. To initiate the design of a security policy, you should address the following points:

- *Identify the critical business resources.* For example, you should identify the servers and networks your human resources or financial data is located on.

- *Identify the critical business policies.* Are there any general corporate policies that exist in regard to the resources you have identified?

- *Identify the threats to the resources.* Is unauthorized access an issue for the resources? Could the resources provide access to sensitive or proprietary data? Do you need to secure your wireless access and, by extension, your wireless access hardware and software?

- *Determine the roles and responsibilities of key personnel in the company or organization.* Who is responsible for the resources being addressed by the security policy? Who are the users of the resources being addressed by the security policy? What are the administrators of the resources expected to do? What are the users expected to do?

- *Determine the type of policies to create.* Do you need a wireless access policy? Do you need a remote access policy?

An important aspect of designing a security policy is to conduct a risk analysis. A risk analysis is the process of identifying the threats to your company's assets and the likelihood of those threats being realized (in other words, the risks) as well as identifying cost-effective measures to minimize those risks.

You need to identify where your risks are—risks to the network, to the resources, and to the data. Risk analysis doesn't mean you need to be a hacker, though. You don't need to identify every single possible method of attack there is. However, you do need to identify the portions of the network that exist, assign a threat rating to each portion, and then apply a level of security to address the threat level. Many security administrators fail to grasp this concept. Not everything needs to be defended like Fort Knox.

The most basic method of risk analysis is to assign one of three levels of risk (sometimes called *threat ratings)* to your network resources:

- **Low risk**   These are systems or data that if compromised would not disrupt the business, cause legal issues, or result in any financial ramifications. The targeted system can be easily rebuilt and cannot be leveraged to provide further access to systems. In many cases, contrary to popular opinion, devices such as bastion hosts could fall into this category.

- **Medium risk** These are systems that if compromised would cause a moderate disruption to the business, minor legal or financial ramifications, or that could be used to provide access to other resources. These systems require moderate effort to restore, and the restoration, too, could be disruptive to the system.

- **High risk** These are systems that if compromised could cause significant disruption to the business and could result in significant legal or financial ramifications. In extreme cases, they could even threaten the safety of personnel. These systems would take significant effort to restore, at a significant disruption and cost to the business.

Assign one of these three risk levels to each network resource, including core network devices, distribution network devices, access network devices, network monitoring devices, network security devices, e-mail systems, network file and print servers, network applications servers (such as DNS or DHCP), data application servers (such as Oracle or SQL), desktop computers, and other network devices not already covered.

When you go to assign risk levels, make sure you think outside of the box. For example, what is the risk level of a DHCP server being compromised? Not high, you say? Consider that it contains a mapping of every single in-use IP address and MAC address on your network. Sounds like spoofing made easy in the wrong hands to me. Once hackers know your IP address scheme and/or the MAC addresses of important systems, it becomes much easier for them to masquerade as that system and potentially compromise your data.

Once you have assigned the risk levels, the next thing to do is identify the types of users you have and then assign what privileges they will have on each system. There are generally five types of users:

- **Administrators** These are *trusted* internal users responsible for network access. I remember a customer one time asking me what could be done to restrict what the administrators could do on the network. I replied, "Better hiring practices." These are your administrators. If you don't trust them, they shouldn't be your administrators.

- **Privileged internal users** These are users with a need for greater access (for example, technicians and help desk staff).

- **Users** These are your general access users.

- **Partners** These are external users with a need to access some resources. This may be access to Enterprise Resource Planning (ERP) systems, websites, or other data. This could also be vendors who provide support.

- **Others** This is everyone else.

Once you have identified and assigned the threat level to your various network resources and then identified the types of users you have and the privileges those users require on your network resources, you can begin writing and building your security policy in preparation of implementing it on your network.

Security Policy Implementation and Enforcement

Once a policy has been designed, it should be implemented and enforced. This last part is particularly critical to the success of any security policy. A security policy is only effective if it can be enforced, including the need to have appropriate repercussions in the event that the policy is not adhered to.

To ensure that you can successfully implement and enforce a security policy, you should ensure that the security policy enhances the business process, not interferes with it. Your security policy should be usable, not only for you but for your users. The quickest way to ensure that your users will attempt to undermine or otherwise not adhere to your security policy is if it makes their daily jobs so difficult that they don't feel like they can effectively perform them. By getting your users involved in the security policy design, you can help prevent this situation from occurring.

Another aspect of ensuring that your security policy can be enforced is to make sure it takes into account local, state, and federal laws. This is where your legal department comes into play. Make sure your legal department reviews all the policies that make up your security policy to ensure not only that they are enforceable but that your organization is not legally liable as a result of anything contained in these policies.

Finally, you absolutely must have upper management's support in order to implement and enforce your security policy. In many cases, the punishment for violating the security policy is termination of employment. You have to have upper management's support in these cases. If people know that violating the security policy has no real punishment attached to it, they will quickly start dismissing the need to adhere to the policy.

Security Policy Monitoring and Review

Finally, you should continuously monitor the performance and effectiveness of the security policy to ensure it is addressing the issues it was designed to address. Remember how I said that your security policy has a beginning? That statement does not imply that there is an end. Once your policy has been designed and implemented, you will need to periodically review it and make changes to it according to the information discovered while monitoring the policy's performance and effectiveness, thus starting the cycle anew.

The review process should include allowing all stakeholders and members of your security policy design committee to provide input on the process. In particular, you should make it a point to pay special attention to the information and feedback your user representatives provide. A measure of just how effective a policy is can often be determined by whether your user community is actively trying to find ways around the policy because it makes their life too difficult.

The Characteristics of a Good Security Policy

All good security policies contain a number of common characteristics. A good security policy must be implemented through the use of system administration procedures, published acceptable-use policies, and other methods as defined in your organization. Your security policy must also be enforceable with security tools, where possible, and with repercussions when actual prevention is not possible. Finally, your security policy must clearly define who is responsible for all aspects of the security policy and the business resources identified in the security policy.

In order for your security policy to adhere to these characteristics, it should consist of the following seven sections:

- Overview
- Purpose
- Scope
- Policy
- Enforcement
- Definitions
- Revision History

Security Policy: Overview Section

The overview section should contain a brief explanation of what the security policy addresses and what the problems are. The overview section could also include background information regarding the technology or resources the security policy will address. Details of the security policy are left for further explanation in the other sections. This section is where you briefly explain what the security policy will do.

Security Policy: Purpose Section

The purpose section should explain exactly why the security policy is being created and what the goals of the security policy are. You should be as clear and concise in this explanation as possible to ensure that everyone who reads the security policy will clearly understand the purpose and function of the security policy. This section is where you clearly explain the reason for the security policy.

Security Policy: Scope Section

The scope section should define who the security policy applies to, as well as who is responsible for creating and maintaining the security policy. The scope section should also define *what* the security policy applies to. This is the section where you identify the resources the security policy was written for.

Security Policy: Policy Section

The policy section is where the actual policy details are addressed. This is the section that clearly explains what the security policy is and what to do to ensure compliance with the security policy. Items such as guidelines, configuration examples, education, training and awareness, backups, and business continuity plans should all be addressed in the policy section. Here are some specific points to address in the security policy section:

- **Threat definition**   You should identify what the threats are that exist for the resources the security policy addresses. Identifying the threats ensures that you address how to protect against or deal with those threats.

- **Resource configuration and guidelines**   You should provide information about how to configure your resources, including specific configuration examples as much as you can. Also provide specific recommendations and guidelines as well as references to any standards or external documentation and best practices.

- **User training and education**   In many cases, the security policy may require that users learn new ways of doing tasks. The security policy should address these training and education needs by identifying the issues and defining the appropriate training and education mechanisms to address these needs.

- **Administrator training and education**   Like users, your administrators may require training and education to address learning new technologies or products that may be required by your security policy.

- **Security notices and warnings (logon banners, and so on)**   You should have security notices and warnings for all your resources that, at a minimum, establish that there is no expectation of privacy, that unauthorized access is prohibited, and that monitoring of the resources will occur and the use of the resources is consent to monitoring. Ensure that all your security notices and warnings have been reviewed and signed off on by your legal department.

- **Notification processes**   You need to define who should be notified and what the notification and escalation process is in the event that a security exploit or event occurs.

- **Backup and recovery procedures**   Regardless of how well you plan and attempt to prevent a security incident, it will occur. Your security policy needs to define what your backup and recovery procedures are in the event of a security violation, device failure, or natural disaster.

- **Business continuity or disaster-recovery plans**   One of the most important things a security policy can address is how to make sure the business can keep running in the event of a catastrophe or natural disaster. Your security policy should address what to do to ensure that the business gets running as soon as possible after a catastrophe or disaster. Your business-continuity or disaster-recovery plan usually complements the information in your backup and recovery procedures plans.

- **Physical security requirements**   Your security policy should also address the physical security of the resources, such as air regulation, temperature, and fire-safety equipment and measures.

- **Security incident response**   Practice makes perfect, and planning how to respond to a security violation will make your response much more effective. Let's face it, when it has hit the fan, things are hectic enough that you need something to guide you in your actions. By making the decisions on how to react to security violations *before* a violation has occurred, you are going to make it that much easier to deal with when a violation happens. In a sense, having the plan ahead of time is like doing fire drills. It makes it that much easier to find the door in all the smoke.

The policy section is where you clearly explain what must be done to comply with the security policy and how to respond in the event that a security incident occurs.

Security Policy: Enforcement Section

The enforcement section is where you define how you plan on enforcing the rules and recommendations from the policy section. This includes defining what software or other mechanisms exist to ensure that the threats identified in the policy do not occur as well as defining the repercussions of violating the security policy. This section is where you define how to make sure the policy is adhered to. Something not to be overlooked in the enforcement section is that a social or administrative method can sometimes be much more cost effective than a technical method. For example, it might be more cost effective to log the websites a user has visited and provide that report to the user's manager than to try to filter out those websites via a technical solution. Often, the best solution to a people problem is not a technical one.

Security Policy: Definitions Section

The definitions section is where you define any terms or concepts you used in the security policy to ensure that everyone understands what was meant. You should also use this section to clarify any acronyms used in the policy.

Security Policy: Revision History Section

The revision history section is where you track all updates and changes made to the security policy. Not only should you document the current date and version of the security policy, but you also need to provide a brief explanation of the changes made to the security policy.

Security Policy Recommendations

Although it is impossible to make a one-size-fits-all security policy for all environments, most environments should have a few types of security policies in common and, at a minimum, should address or contain some specific points. Because this book is about hardening your network infrastructure, I am going to focus on security policies that are particularly relevant to your network infrastructure. These are not exhaustive security policies, but they highlight specific details that each policy should address in some way. For information about applications and operating system security policies, see the counterpart books in this series, *Hardening Windows Systems* by Roberta Bragg and *Hardening Linux* by John Terpstra. In addition, SANS maintains a list of sample security policies that you can review for use in your environment at http://www.sans.org/resources/policies/.

Encryption Policy

Your encryption security policy should define not only the supported encryption standards you will use to protect data across your network, but the encryption mechanisms and standards you will use to protect the data on your servers or with your applications (for example, encrypting e-mail messages). Your encryption policy should also define the types of data that require encryption to ensure that everyone knows what must be encrypted regardless of circumstances. Finally, your encryption policy should provide configuration information and examples to ensure compliance.

Analog/ISDN Policy

Your analog/ISDN security policy should define the various analog line devices such as modems, fax machines, and computer connections. It should contain a procedure that defines how this type of access should be requested and how this type of access should be protected from exploit or compromise. Ensure that all analog or ISDN connections have a justified business case for their existence, because analog lines often represent a significant security threat due to them commonly being used for dial-in purposes. Finally, your security policy should require that any network diagrams and documentation be updated prior to any new devices being implemented.

Antivirus Policy

Your antivirus policy should address running virus protection on all your desktops and servers as well as your e-mail servers and gateway systems. In addition to defining where to run virus protection, your antivirus policy should provide specific configuration requirements, including requiring on-demand scanning, regularly scheduled scanning operations, and periodic updates and upgrades. Your antivirus policy should also provide information regarding blocking e-mail attachments as well as a statement preventing disk sharing and downloading of unauthorized files.

Audit, Vulnerability Assessment, and Risk Assessment Policy

Your audit, vulnerability assessment, and risk assessment policy should define the procedures and tools that will be used for auditing and testing your network. It should address questions regarding obtaining the consent to perform testing and the liability from outages and interruptions that may be related to the testing. You should require that client points of contact be established for all systems that will be tested as well as ensure that the scanning period of the testing is well defined prior to testing.

Dial-in Policy

Your dial-in policy should require that all users explicitly request dial-in access and that all requests provide a business justification for the access. The security policy should ensure that no one other than the authorized user connects to the network and assign the responsibility of ensuring this occurs with the user. Your security policy should also require callback or caller ID verification, where possible, and authentication in all cases. Your dial-in policy should define a procedure for disabling dial-in access that has not been used in a certain amount of time. Finally, your security policy should require that any network diagrams and documentation be updated prior to any new devices being implemented.

DMZ Policy

Your DMZ policy should define the configuration requirements of all systems that exist in the DMZ, including disabling services and defining the types of equipment that can be placed in the DMZ. Your DMZ policy should require that systems in the DMZ be patched in a more rapid fashion than other systems, due to their close proximity to external threats, and identify who is responsible for the equipment to ensure this occurs. Your DMZ policy should also define how remote administration will be performed, if it is permitted at all, to ensure that only secure remote administration occurs. All communications between systems on the internal network and the DMZ should also be defined in this policy, requiring secure content updates, and so on. Your DMZ policy should define an exhaustive and extensive logging policy, allowing you to better monitor your DMZ resources. Finally, your security policy should require that any network diagrams and documentation be updated prior to any new devices being implemented.

Extranet Policy

Your extranet policy should define that all extranet connections require a security review and business case to justify them. Your extranet connections should also require a point of contact for all remote connections and should grant access only to the specific resources required for the extranet users to perform their jobs. All traffic traversing the extranet connections should be encrypted to prevent eavesdropping on the data. Finally, your security policy should require that any network diagrams and documentation be updated prior to any new devices being implemented.

Wireless Communications Policy

Your wireless communications policy should define the equipment that will be used and require that all wireless equipment be registered with the information technology (IT) department to allow for easier tracking of these resources. Your wireless communications policy should require not only explicit authorization from IT for all wireless access, but also a business case and justification for granting access. It should also define the encryption and authentication requirements of all wireless connections. Your service set identifier (SSID) should not contain any organizational information because SSIDs are easily read by external users, which would allow them to know that they found an access point on your network. Because wireless networks are so inherently insecure and pose such a substantial threat to your network, your wireless communications policy should clearly state that implementing an unauthorized wireless access point or wireless connection is grounds for employment termination. Finally, your security policy should require that any network diagrams and documentation be updated prior to any new devices being implemented. We will look at hardening wireless access in much more detail in Chapter 8.

VPN Policy

Your VPN policy should specify the permitted hardware, software, technologies, and protocols used to provide VPN access to your network. It should define the encryption and authentication mechanisms that will be used to secure the VPN. In addition, it should clearly state that only authorized users are allowed to use the VPN connection, and it should assign the responsibility of ensuring this occurs with the users. The policy should also define how the VPN connection will be established, identifying whether split tunneling is permitted, what the idle timeouts are, and whether the user can access local resources and VPN resources at the same time. Your VPN policy should also require that all remote systems adhere to any relevant corporate security policies and run virus protection and firewall software in accordance with the appropriate security policies. Finally, your security policy should require that any network diagrams and documentation be updated prior to any new devices being implemented. We will look at hardening VPN connectivity in much more detail in Chapter 5.

Firewall Security Policy

Your firewall security policy should define the network- and software-based firewalls that should be implemented on your network. It should also define the types of firewalls that will be implemented and how they should be configured, including what services and protocols will be run. Details regarding ingress and egress filtering, including configuration examples, should also be defined in the policy. In addition, your policy needs to define how remote administration should be performed and what authentication mechanisms and logon banners should be used. Finally, your security policy should require that any network diagrams and documentation be updated prior to any new devices being implemented. We will look at hardening firewalls in much more detail in Chapter 3.

Router and Switch Security Policy

Your router and switch security policy should define how your routers and switches should be configured and deployed throughout your network. The types of remote administration and authentication mechanisms, including logon banners, should be defined. In addition, permitted protocols and services should be identified with configuration requirements, and disallowed protocols and services should be identified to be disabled. Any access control lists (ACLs) should also be defined. Finally, your security policy should require that any network diagrams and documentation be updated prior to any new devices being implemented. We will look at hardening routers and switches in much more detail in Chapter 6.

Remote Access Policy

Your remote access policy should define the types and methods of remote access that will be permitted on your network. It should not replace your dial-in and VPN policies but rather should complement them by defining the process of requesting remote access and the types of remote access a given scenario requires. It should also define the kind of access that remote users will have on your network. In other words, can remote users access the entire network or only specific segments and resources? Finally, your remote access policy should define who is qualified to connect via a remote access connection.

Password Policy

Your password policy should define the requirements not only of passwords but for SNMP community strings, preshared keys, and any other manual/text-based authentication mechanism that exists on your network. The password policy should define the minimum lengths of passwords, how often passwords must change, whether passwords can be reused, whether a user must log on to change their password, and how many incorrect passwords are required for an account lockout. It should also stipulate what the password requirements are (for example, requiring letters, numbers, and mixed case). The process of notifying a user what their password is should also be clarified (for example, prohibiting the sending of the password via electronic means). The policy should also prohibit using "password remember" functions of any application as well as prohibit the user from writing down their password or sharing their password with anyone, including IT or their boss.

Intrusion Detection/Prevention System Policy

Your IDS/IPS security policy should define how your IDS/IPS should be deployed as well as where it should be located. It should also define the types of traffic you are going to monitor for and what actions will be taken when a specified traffic pattern has been identified. Your IDS/IPS security policy should also address remote administration and authentication of users authorized to manage the system. In addition, the security policy should define how often the signatures are updated and provide a mechanism for implementing high-risk signatures in a rapid fashion. The policy should also address what type of auditing and reporting will be performed on the system and who is authorized to view the reports and what is done with the data. Finally, your security policy should require that any network diagrams and documentation be updated prior to any new devices being implemented. We will look at hardening IDS/IPS in much more detail in Chapter 4.

Content-Filtering/Internet Policy

Your content-filtering/Internet policy should define who is allowed to access the Internet and what types of access are permitted. In addition, the policy should identify the vendors of any content-filtering software you will be using and define the method for updating the lists of websites being permitted/blocked. Your security policy should also identify the categories of websites that exist and whether those websites are acceptable for a work environment. The policy should define how users can request access and what the policy is for logging and reporting violations. The policy should also define the level of privacy the users can expect while using the Internet. Finally, your security policy should require that any network diagrams and documentation be updated prior to any new devices being implemented. We will look at hardening content filtering in much more detail in Chapter 7.

Enterprise-Monitoring Policy

Your enterprise-monitoring policy should define the monitoring and management protocols and technologies that will be used on your network, including SNMP, RMON, NetFlow, and Syslog. The policy should require that all management occur using secure and authenticated sessions, where possible, and IPsec encapsulation in all other cases. The policy should also define the logging policy for all resources on your network, including who can review the logs and what gets done with the information in the logs. The policy should identify the types of network events that may occur and what to do when an event is triggered. The management stations that are allowed to monitor your network should also be defined in your policy as well as who has access to those management stations and the information collected. Finally, your security policy should require that any network diagrams and documentation be updated prior to any new devices being implemented. We will look at hardening an enterprise-monitoring solution in much more detail in Chapter 10.

Acceptable-Use Policy

The acceptable-use policy (AUP) is one of the most important policies on your network because it defines what the acceptable usage of organizational resources is. The policy should define, among other things, whether users can share passwords; install applications; copy data for archiving or other purposes; use instant messaging clients; store sensitive data on their laptops, floppy disks, or pen drives; and read, view, or change data that they did not create or are not common files. Every aspect of what a user can and, more important, cannot do should be addressed in your acceptable-use policy. The acceptable-use policy should also set the levels of privacy the user can expect while using organization resources. This policy should also require the user to sign the AUP as part of their hiring process to ensure the user understands not only the policy but the repercussions of not adhering to the policy.

Network Connection Policy

Your network connection policy should address the connectivity of devices on the network, including what types of devices can be connected to the network, who can connect the devices to the network, and what the process is to request a device be connected to your network. The policy should also define what to do in the event that a network device is down or causing a problem on the network, and what the process is for addressing unauthorized network connections. Finally, your security policy should require that any network diagrams and documentation be updated prior to any new devices being implemented.

Network Documentation Policy

Your network documentation policy should define who is responsible for keeping your network documentation and diagrams up to date. It should also define where and how the diagrams are stored and who has access to the information. It should also define the data classification that all your network documentation and diagrams should be considered as. For example, your network diagrams are as valuable as a map in the hands of a hacker in terms of identifying what and where to attempt to compromise your network. You should classify the data accordingly, with it being considered at least a confidential document.

Why Security Policies Fail and How to Ensure Yours Won't

Four weaknesses exist with virtually all security policies that cause many of them to collapse under their own weight. By not addressing these issues, you can virtually ensure that your security policy will be unenforceable and unusable by most if not all your users. The four reasons why security policies fail are as follows:

- Security is viewed as a barrier to progress.
- Security is a learned behavior.
- Security is rife with unexpected events and occurrences.
- Your security policy is never finished.

Security Is Viewed as a Barrier to Progress

This is perhaps the biggest barrier to a successful security policy and should not be underestimated. Because security policies are designed to secure resources and mitigate threats, they are often at odds with the users and the resources they are trying to protect. There is an old joke about how securing a network is a triangle with three choices—security, functionality, and usability—and you can only choose two of the three. Although it probably isn't quite that bad, it isn't that far from the truth either. In some cases, these are technical issues that can be addressed by technical solutions (for example, implementing a different method to perform a task that doesn't interfere with the usability of the resource). In other cases, this is simply a people issue for which technical solutions are often not appropriate. Such cases require tact and communication to work through the issues, and this includes the necessity for you and your users to make compromises in many cases. Your users will only accept so many interferences to how they need to work, or think they need to work, before they will give up and stop paying attention to the security policy, ultimately dooming it to failure. One method to address this, however, is training and education.

Security Is a Learned Behavior

Security is not instinctual. Securing resources is something that needs to be taught to your users, and it needs to be periodically reinforced through training to ensure that your users are kept up to date on methods to secure their resources in accordance with your network security policy. You need to teach your users to understand the value of the network resources so that they understand the value in protecting them. In educating your users, you can eliminate the perception that security in general is a barrier to progress.

Security Is Rife with Unexpected Events and Occurrences

You have to be able to expect the unexpected; the more complex a security policy is, the greater the likelihood that the security policy will fail. There is simply no way you can address every user's every need and still provide a secure environment. You have to expect certain failures (as well as certain disasters) to occur, remaining constantly vigilant so that you can react accordingly and update and change your security policy as required. This leads us to the next section.

Your Security Policy Is Never Finished

No matter how much effort you put in, your security policy is never finished. A security policy is a living document, and you must constantly review and update the policy to address changes in technology, system failures, and even policy issues that cause the security policy to become ineffective. Don't wait for your security policy to stop being functional before you decide to review it.

Preventing the Failure

So how do you prevent your security policy from failing? It's relatively straightforward if you always remember that there is no perfect policy. Here are the steps you should follow:

1. Identify and plan for the natural weaknesses that exist in your security policy.

2. Educate your users to ensure that they understand the value of protecting the resources and why they play an integral role in the security process.

3. Perform regular reviews and audits of your security policy to ensure function and compliance.

4. Most important of all, make corrections when needed. Don't be afraid to say, "Well, that didn't work," and make changes accordingly.

Summary

The security policies that exist on your network provide the stable foundation upon which the details of hardening your network are built. Your security policies define not only what can be done with your network resources, but what cannot be done.

Security policies should be written and developed by a security committee, which should first conduct a risk analysis and then use that information to develop effective security policies. Your security policies should provide information regarding how to prevent a security incident from occurring as well as defining what to do in the event that a security incident occurs. You can ensure that your security policies cover the needs of your enterprise by addressing seven sections in all your security policies: the overview section, purpose section, scope section, policy section, enforcement section, definitions section, and revision history section.

Finally, you should identify and address the issues that commonly cause a security policy to fail to ensure that your security policies avoid those pitfalls.

Chapter 3

Hardening Your Firewall

Firewalls are arguably the most important component that can be implemented to harden a network. Historically firewalls have been implemented on the perimeter of a network, providing protection and defenses against external threats. Firewalls allow you to define a protected network. In other words, you want to control the traffic that can enter and exit the network and protect the network from traffic that originates from an external source. Today, however, the role of a firewall in a network is evolving as administrators recognize that many threats to a network come from internal sources. As a result, firewalls are now being implemented within networks to segment and protect resources in the same manner that they have traditionally been used for segmenting and protecting against external threats. A great example of this is using a firewall between the network containing HR resources (the protected network) and the rest of the network (the unprotected network), thus controlling which systems, if any, can access those protected resources.

At the same time, the role of the firewall in hardening a network is not simply a case of "How do I use the firewall to protect my resources?" Your firewall must also be protected, intrusions must be detected, statistics must be gathered for management, and reliable logs must be created for post-mortem analysis or to pursue legal actions. As a result, this chapter looks at methods to harden your firewall and protect it from exploits and unauthorized access. Utilizing the firewall to harden your network perimeter and interior networks will be covered later in Chapters 11 and 12, respectively.

Many, many different firewall vendors are out there, and the concepts conveyed in this chapter are relevant for all of them. However, I have limited space I can devote to providing specific command syntax and examples, so I cannot cover them all. In deciding which firewalls to cover, I selected the top two market share leaders in commercial firewalls, as well as an open-source firewall solution. As a result, I will provide specific command examples for the following firewalls, where possible:

- **Cisco Secure PIX Firewall Operating System 6.3(1)**   A hardware-based firewall that is the current market share leader of all firewalls

- **Check Point SecurePlatform NG with Application Intelligence Build 142**   A software-based firewall that is currently the number-two market share leader

- **Iptables 1.2.7a running on Red Hat Linux 9.0**   An open-source software-based firewall that is popular in Linux/Unix shops

Hardware-Based and Software-Based Firewalls

Two types of firewalls are predominantly used today: *application proxies* and *packet-inspecting/filtering gateways*. Application proxies are identified by their ability to read and process an entire packet to the Application level and make filtering decisions based on the actual application data, not just the packet header. Packet-inspecting/filtering gateways are generally not able to process a packet to the Application level to make a filtering decision. Instead, packet-inspecting/filtering gateways tend to process the data to the Network/Transport layer and make filtering decisions based on the protocol and port numbers contained in the packet header only. Many packet-inspecting/filtering gateways are becoming hybrids, offering some basic application-filtering capabilities for specific commonly used applications, such as HTTP/Web traffic. Much debate exists about which firewall system is better for which environment. However, regardless of the type of firewall you have, you can perform some common tasks to harden your firewall against compromise.

One of the nice things about firewalls is that because they are expressly designed for security, they often come fairly well hardened from the vendors. After all, if a firewall is going to spend the majority of its life under attack and threat, it doesn't make much sense to design it and not focus on hardening the system. So you might be thinking "OK, great, so there isn't anything I need to do then." Well, that's not quite correct either. No matter how hard the vendors try to harden their systems out of the box, they really can't know what you specifically need. Software firewalls, although often well hardened by their vendors, have the unique issue of needing to rely on an underlying operating system to provide bootstrapping functionality. As a result, the underlying operating system of a software firewall often requires extensive hardening in addition to whatever hardening might be required for the firewall application itself. Even hardware firewalls, where the vendor controls every aspect of the firewall and operating system, have common issues and vulnerabilities that can be hardened in many environments. As a result, you can do a number of things to further harden your firewalls and protect them from being compromised. We are going to look at the following common tasks you can perform to further harden your hardware-based and software-based firewalls:

- Hardening remote administration
- Implementing authentication and authorization
- Hardening the operating system
- Hardening firewall services and protocols
- Providing redundancy and fault tolerance
- Hardening routing protocols

Hardening Remote Administration

Remote administrating presents a unique quandary to a firewall administrator. On one hand, the best solution to hardening your firewall against remote administration exploits is to simply not allow any remote administration. On the other hand, not having remote administration capabilities can make an administrator's job much more difficult. Security is always a struggle between providing the best security and providing the required level of functionality. In environments that require remote administration, you can perform specific steps that can mitigate the risks involved with remote administration by providing secure remote administration functionality. In this section, we look at how to provide both options.

Preventing Remote Administration

Most firewalls provide remote administration capabilities through the use of web-based (HTTP/HTTPS), Telnet, or SSH sessions, although Check Point uses a proprietary management console known as the Windows/X-Motif GUI client. To prevent remote administration exploits, simply turn the web-based, Telnet, and SSH services off. In the case of Check Point GUI clients, the most effective method of preventing remote administration is to not grant any hosts remote administration access through the use of a ruleset.

For example, with the Cisco PIX firewall, you can use the PIX Device Manager for web-based management. This access can be disabled by running the following command at the CLI:

```
firewall(config)# no http server enable
```

Likewise, if you want to disable Telnet and SSH access for a PIX firewall, you can run the following commands at the CLI for all IP addresses that have been granted Telnet or SSH access:

```
firewall(config)# no telnet <local_ip> [<mask>] [<if_name>]
firewall(config)# no ssh <local_ip> [<mask>] [<if_name>]
```

The syntax *<local ip>* refers to the IP address of the remote management system. Make sure you run the preceding commands for every local IP address that has been granted access.

Because iptables is an open-source firewall solution, a number of open-source web-based management tools can be used for remote administration. However, most of them rely on Apache or a similar web server to be running on the Linux host that is running the firewall. Telnet and SSH access for iptables works in a similar fashion, relying on the underlying operating system or a third-party vendor to provide Telnet and SSH services. The actual service names will vary depending on the vendor that supplies the software. For example, the service that runs Apache is sometimes called "httpd" and other times is called "apache." You can stop and prevent most services from running by entering the following commands at the CLI (you will need to be logged on as root to run these commands):

```
chkconfig 'service_name' off
service 'service_name' stop
```

The first command prevents a service from running at startup. The second command stops the service. For more information regarding how to stop and start services on Linux, see *Hardening Linux* by John Terpstra.

Removing remote administration capabilities for Check Point is a little more tricky than it is for the PIX and iptables because Check Point uses HTTPS and SSH for certain configuration tasks and uses a proprietary GUI client for the majority of the actual ruleset and firewall administration tasks. You can turn off HTTPS server functionality by running the following command at the CLI:

```
[cpfirewall]# webui disable
```

Because SecurePlatform runs on a hardened version of the Linux operating system, you can disable the SSH service similar to how it is done for iptables. First, however, you must enter the expert mode at the CLI. The expert mode grants access to the underlying operating system on SecurePlatform:

```
[cpfirewall]# expert
Enter expert password: <expertpassword> <enter>
You are in expert mode now.
[Expert@cpfirewall]# chkconfig sshd off
```

The Check Point Management Interface (CPMI) that enables remote GUI clients to connect cannot be turned off like Telnet and SSH can. However, you can prevent the Check Point firewall from accepting any GUI client connections by removing the permitted GUI client hosts using the **cpconfig** command from the CLI as follows:

```
[cpfirewall]# cpconfig
This program will let you re-configure
your VPN-1 & FireWall-1 configuration.
Configuration Options:
----------------------
(1)  Licenses
(2)  Administrators
(3)  GUI Clients
......
(12) Exit
Enter your choice (1-12) :3
```

Here you would select option 3 (GUI Clients).

```
Configuring GUI Clients...
==========================
GUI Clients are trusted hosts from which
Administrators are allowed to log on to this SmartCenter Server
using Windows/X-Motif GUI.
you have selected the following hosts to be GUI Clients:
192.168.173.107
```

```
Do you want to modify this list (y/n) [y] ? y
Do you want to [C]reate a new list, [A]dd or [D]elete one?: d
Enter the host you wish to delete: 192.168.173.107
192.168.173.107 will be deleted. Are you sure? (y/n) [y] ? y
192.168.173.107 was deleted successfully!
Configuration Options:
---------------------
(1)   Licenses
(2)   Administrators
(3)   GUI Clients
......
(12) Exit
Enter your choice (1-12) :3
```

Here again you would select option 3 (GUI Clients).

```
Configuring GUI Clients...
==========================
GUI Clients are trusted hosts from which
Administrators are allowed to log on to this SmartCenter Server
using Windows/X-Motif GUI.
No GUI Clients defined
Do you want to add a GUI Client (y/n) [y] ?
```

You will need to remove all the GUI clients listed until the firewall specifies "No GUI Clients defined."

Granting Secure Remote Administration

So far we have looked at how to disable remote management access to harden your firewall. Now you are no doubt thinking, "Yeah, that sounds great, but let's get back to the real world where I need to be able to remotely manage my firewall." Although disabling remote management access is indeed the best way to prevent a remote management exploit, the reality is that most of us need that remote management capability. The good news is that you can perform the following tasks to harden remote management access while still allowing yourself to take advantage of the benefits that remote management access provides:

- Allow only secure remote management access, such as SSH, HTTPS, or the Check Point GUI client

- Restrict remote management access only to permitted hosts.

- If possible, require all remote management to occur over a management segment.

- Implement authentication and authorization to control who can log on and what they can do when logged on.

One of the most common methods of providing remote access to firewalls is through the use of Telnet. As we all know, however, Telnet uses an unencrypted session for the transmission of data. As a result, if you use Telnet to manage your firewall, you are taking what should be one of your most secure devices and making it extremely insecure. How insecure? Anyone with a packet sniffer can read everything that goes between your management system and the firewall, including every password you type. For example, using Ethereal, I can capture and play back a captured Telnet session by right-clicking any frame in the Telnet capture and selecting Follow TCP Stream. This gives me the following results:

```
Contents of TCP stream
. . . . . . . . . . . .
User Access Verification
Password: . . . . . . . . . . . . . .P. . . . . . . . . . . . . .vt100..tooeasytosniff
local-rtr>
```

As you can clearly see, the password is too easy to sniff. HTTP, being unencrypted just like Telnet, has the same vulnerabilities. Consequently, you should never use Telnet or HTTP to manage your firewalls. Turn it off, as referenced in the preceding examples.

If you need to remotely manage your firewalls, use either SSH for command-line access or HTTPS for web-based management—both protocols encrypt the data being transmitted. In addition, you should restrict management access to specific interfaces and allow traffic from specified addresses only. For example, you might want to permit management traffic only on the inside interface of a firewall and only from your management system's IP address.

Enabling SSH management for the Cisco PIX is a three-step process. First, you must configure the hostname and domain name for the firewall. Second, you must configure an RSA key for the SSH server to use. Third, you grant access for specific hosts to connect to specific interfaces using SSH. This is accomplished by running the following commands at the CLI:

```
firewall(config)# hostname firewall
firewall(config)# domain-name yourcompany.com
firewall(config)# ca generate rsa key 1024
For <key_modulus_size> >= 1024, key generation could
   take up to several minutes. Please wait.
Keypair generation process begin.
..Success.
firewall(config)# ca save all
firewall(config)# ssh <local_ip> [<mask>] [<if_name>]
```

CAUTION You must run the command *ca save all* because RSA keys are not saved when you copy the running configuration to the startup configuration. If you do not run this command, when you reboot the PIX firewall, it will lose any unsaved RSA keys, thus preventing SSH connections from being established.

One nice thing about the Cisco PIX is that it only allows HTTPS access, so if you enable the HTTP server on it, you are only granting HTTPS access. This is a two-step process that includes first enabling the HTTP server and then granting specific IP addresses or networks access to the HTTP server service. These commands supersede any ACLs, so you don't need to explicitly permit this traffic via an ACL. This can be done by entering the following commands at the CLI:

```
firewall(config)# http server enable
firewall(config)# http <local_ip> [<mask>] [<if_name>]
```

Because iptables relies on the underlying operating system to provide SSH and web server functionality, you will need to configure the relevant SSH or web server service in the operating system. In general, all services can be enabled at the CLI with the following commands:

```
chkconfig 'service_name' on
service 'service_name' start
```

The first command configures the service to start automatically upon reboot. The second command causes the service to start running immediately.

Web management of iptables is a much more complex process in that it requires an extensive knowledge of Apache in order to properly implement it. Consequently, I advise against using web management of iptables, instead relying on SSH to perform command-line configuration. If you find yourself requiring web management, however, you need to configure Apache as follows:

- Implement mod_SSL and OpenSSL to provide for HTTPS encryption. (See http://httpd.apache.org/docs-2.0/ssl/ for configuration examples.)

- Implement authentication, requiring all connected users to authenticate prior to being permitted to perform any configuration functions. (See http://httpd.apache.org/docs-2.0/howto/auth.html for configuration examples.)

- Configure iptables to allow HTTPS connections to the firewall system. For example, if you wanted to permit a management system at 192.168.1.100 to access the firewall at 192.168.1.1 on interface eth0, you would run the following command:

NOTE   At the end of some code lines throughout this book, you'll see a right-pointing arrow (→). This signifies that the single-line command, which really should fall on one line, must break due to width limitations of the printed page.

```
iptables -A INPUT -I eth0 -p tcp -m tcp -s 192.168.1.100 -d →
192.168.1.1 --dport 443 --syn -j ACCEPT
```

Providing remote administrative capabilities for Check Point is similar to the Cisco PIX in that Check Point only allows SSH, HTTPS, and their proprietary GUI client. By default, SSH is enabled on the Check Point system, so no further configuration is required. Similarly, you can enable HTTPS by selecting to enable it during the installation or by running the following command at the CLI after installation:

```
[cpfirewall]# webui enable 443
```

NOTE Make sure you have configured your firewall rules to permit SSH or HTTPS access from the management systems you want to grant access to.

Configuring the GUI client for Check Point is a relatively straightforward process. By default, Check Point supports the use of the GUI client. You simply need to specify the management stations to be permitted. You can grant GUI client access by running the following commands at the CLI:

```
[cpfirewall]# cpconfig
This program will let you re-configure
your VPN-1 & FireWall-1 configuration.
Configuration Options:
(1)   Licenses
(2)   Administrators
(3)   GUI Clients
......
(12) Exit
Enter your choice (1-12) :3
```

Here you would select option 3 (GUI Clients).

```
Configuring GUI Clients...
GUI Clients are trusted hosts from which
Administrators are allowed to log on to this SmartCenter Server
using Windows/X-Motif GUI.
you have selected the following hosts to be GUI Clients:
192.168.173.107
Do you want to modify this list (y/n) [y] ? y
Do you want to [C]reate a new list, [A]dd or [D]elete one?: a
You can add GUI Clients using any of the following formats:
1. IP address.
2. Machine name.
3. "Any" - Any IP without restriction.
4. A range of addresses, for example 1.2.3.4-1.2.3.40
5. Wild cards - for example 1.2.3.* or *.checkpoint.com
Enter GUI Client: 192.168.173.109
192.168.173.109 will be added as a GUI Client. →
```

```
Are you sure? (y/n) [y] ? y
192.168.173.109 was added successfully!
```

Regardless of the firewall you are running, when you decide to enable remote administration, you should follow these general recommendations:

- Provide only secure remote administration. Do not allow native HTTP or Telnet connections.

- Grant access only to specific administrative workstations.

- If possible, require all remote administration to occur on a dedicated administration segment. If that is not possible, only allow remote administration to occur on trusted interfaces.

Implementing Authentication and Authorization

The next step in hardening the firewall is to allow only authorized users to connect to and manage the firewall. In addition, those users should only be able to perform the specific tasks they have been authorized to perform. This section is a subset of Authentication, Authorization, and Accounting (AAA), which covered in more detail, including providing configuration examples, in Chapter 9.

Hardening Authentication

One of the biggest authentication flaws that occurs on a network is the use of common user accounts and passwords. People use the administrator account to log on to Windows, they use the root account to access Unix/Linux, they use telnet and enable or enable secret passwords for Cisco equipment, and they use the admin account for Check Point. The problem with this is that it removes all accountability from the system. Instead of using common accounts and passwords to access your firewall, you should create unique users for performing management tasks.

Generally, two methods are used to provide unique usernames and passwords for management tasks. The first method is to create unique local accounts on every firewall in your environment. The obvious flaw with this method is that it does not scale very well. However, if you are in a small environment, this method is still better than using common usernames and passwords and worth the effort to implement. The other method is to use an authentication server to validate the user's identity. The benefits to this type of system are centralized user account management and greater scalability. When a user needs to be added or deleted, you can do so at the authentication server instead of needing to make the changes on multiple firewalls. The two most widely used authentication servers available for use are RADIUS and TACACS/TACACS+.

Regardless of whether you choose to go with local users or centralized authentication through the use of authentication servers, you will want to ensure that you use a hard password policy for all the users, as specified in Chapter 2. One of the things I like most about Check Point is that it enforces a password policy that requires the user to use passwords that are not based on dictionary words so that they are more difficult to crack. At a minimum, you should require that all your users adhere to the following policy:

- Do not allow the use of a password that is based on a dictionary word.
- Require the use of letters, numbers, and special characters in the password.
- Do not require passwords to be so complex or difficult that people have to write them down to remember them. At that point, you have defeated your entire password policy.

Hardening Authorization

In concert with hardening authentication, hardening authorization is the process of specifying what tasks an authenticated user is authorized to perform. Authorization allows you to define different levels of access for your users, as opposed to simply having an all-or-nothing system where someone is either an administrator or isn't an administrator. For example, you may want to have certain users who need to be able to manage the security policy or the access lists on a firewall, but don't need to change IP addresses or update the software on the firewall. Authorization allows you to control who can do what on your firewall, thus further hardening your firewall against attack.

Using Logon Banners

Logon banners should be implemented to set the appropriate expectations of privacy and acceptable use of the system, resources, data, and network access capabilities. Your logon banner should include a notice stating that the monitoring of users' activities while they are using the system is authorized and permitted. Your logon banner should also include a warning that legal action may be taken should the monitoring reveal that any illegal activities or violations of the security policy have occurred.

It is important to include logon banners on your systems because the lack of logon banners can make the prosecution of violations much more difficult. In fact, in some legal cases defendants have been acquitted of charges of system tampering because there was no explicit notice that prohibited such activities. Other cases exist where companies have been taken to court for violating an individual's privacy because no notice was given acknowledging that the monitoring of users' activities was occurring.

Your legal department should review your logon banners to ensure that they comply to the legal requirements of your state and jurisdiction, as well as to ensure that they are legally sound and without loopholes or flaws. A number of templates are available that you can use as the basis for your logon banner. My favorite, shown here, is located at the CERT website (http://www.cert.org/security-improvement/implementations/i034.01.html):

> This system is for the use of authorized users only. Individuals using this computer system without authority, or in excess of their authority, are subject to having all of their activities on this system monitored and recorded by system personnel. In the course of monitoring individuals improperly using this system, or in the course of

system maintenance the activities of authorized users may also be monitored. Anyone using this system expressly consents to such monitoring and is advised that if such monitoring reveals possible evidence of criminal activity, system personnel may provide the evidence of such monitoring to law enforcement officials. Report suspected violations to the system security officer.

Hardening the Underlying Operating System

One of the drawbacks of using iptables, Check Point, Microsoft ISA Server, or any other firewall that does not run on top of a dedicated operating system is that you need to harden the underlying operating system in addition to hardening the actual firewall application. The sister publications to this book, *Hardening Windows Systems* by Roberta Bragg and *Hardening Linux* by John Terpstra, contain detailed hardening procedures for those operating systems. However, in general, you should approach hardening the operating system of any system that will function as a firewall from the following perspectives:

- *Disable any and all unnecessary services.* If the service is not expressly required for the firewall to function, disable it.

- *Remove any and all unnecessary applications and registry entries.* This may seem excessive; however, if your firewall doesn't need an application such as a calculator on it, you should remove it. Once again, unless the application is required for the firewall to function, remove it. Any applications left on the system could allow a hacker to use them to gain further control of the system. Although there may not be a root-level exploit for applications such as a calculator today, there could be one tomorrow. And that is what you are protecting against—the unknown potential exploits of the future.

- *Restrict the file system, registry, and services permissions to be run only by authorized users.* Any applications that can be executed by an unknown system can be used to exploit a back door. For example, a common way to gain administrative access is to run an application as the localsystem on Windows, thus gaining an unauthorized increase in privileges. Similarly, the default file system in Windows often grants the Everyone group permission to change and execute files. This access should be removed and replaced with much more restrictive NTFS settings.

HEADS UP!

When changing the default NTFS permissions, be very careful that you do not unintentionally remove system access to files that are required for operation. For example, preventing the system from being able to read ntoskrnl.exe is a bad thing.

Hardening Firewall Services and Protocols

Now that you have restricted management access, implement authentication and authorization, and hardened the underlying operating system where applicable, the last step is to harden your firewall's services and protocols. The philosophy here is the same through this book: turn off anything you don't need and harden that which you do need. For most appliance-based firewalls, there aren't a lot of unnecessary services that need to be addressed. Likewise, for most OS-based firewalls, once the OS has been hardened, there aren't a lot of services that need to be addressed. Therefore, in this section we will take a look at four common services/protocols used with many firewalls and consider how to harden them:

- Simple Network Management Protocol (SNMP)
- Network Time Protocol (NTP)
- syslog
- Trivial File Transfer Protocol (TFTP)

Encapsulating Insecure Traffic in IPsec

A common theme with all the services mentioned in the preceding list is the fact that they all use an unencrypted transmission method for the delivery of data. You will likely find that many of the network protocols and applications you may want to run on your firewall perform in this manner. In that case, the only viable alternative to securing the traffic is to encapsulate the original data in IPsec and use the encryption of IPsec to protect the data's integrity.

Configuring IPsec on the management station is outside of the scope of this book. However, you can find a good whitepaper for doing this for Microsoft servers at http://support.microsoft.com/default.aspx?scid=http://support.microsoft.com:80/support/kb/articles/Q252/7/35.ASP&NoWebContent=1. For further information about how to configure IPsec on Windows or Red Hat Linux systems, see *Hardening Windows Systems* by Roberta Bragg or *Hardening Linux* by John Terpstra.

Configuring the Cisco PIX to encapsulate the data in IPsec is a relatively straightforward process. The first step is to configure an access list that will be used to define which hosts require IPsec to communicate. This can be done at the CLI as follows:

```
firewall(config)# access-list secure permit ip interface inside →
host 192.168.1.109
```

In this case, I configured the access list between the inside interface and the management station located at IP address 192.168.1.109. Next, you must configure the IPsec policy for the PIX, as follows:

```
firewall(config)# sysopt connection permit-ipsec
firewall(config)# crypto ipsec transform-set ESP-3DES-SHA esp-3des →
esp-sha-hmac
```

```
firewall(config)# crypto map secure 30 ipsec-isakmp
firewall(config)# crypto map secure 30 match address secure
firewall(config)# crypto map secure 30 set peer 192.168.1.109
firewall(config)# crypto map secure 30 set transform-set ESP-3DES-SHA
firewall(config)# crypto map secure interface inside
firewall(config)# isakmp enable inside
firewall(config)# isakmp key ******** address 192.168.1.109 →
netmask 255.255.255.255
firewall(config)# isakmp policy 10 authentication pre-share
firewall(config)# isakmp policy 10 encryption 3des
firewall(config)# isakmp policy 10 hash sha
firewall(config)# isakmp policy 10 group 1
firewall(config)# isakmp policy 10 lifetime 28800
```

Once this has been done, the PIX will only communicate with the host at 192.168.1.109 via IPsec. This means that if that host is your SNMP, NTP, syslog, or TFTP server, the insecure data will be encapsulated with IPsec and securely transmitted between the firewall and remote host.

iptables relies on the underlying operating system to provide IPsec functionality. Contact your operating system vendor regarding their specific IPsec offerings. Another option is to use FreeS/WAN for Linux (http://www.freeswan.org). FreeS/WAN configuration is covered in *Hardening Linux* by John Terpstra.

Check Point uses the Windows/X-Motif GUI to configure and manage IPsec/VPN connections. Configuring a VPN consists of defining the network to be protected, creating objects that specify the firewall and remote host, assigning the appropriate IPsec/IKE settings to the VPN community, and defining a rule to permit the traffic. The steps to configure IPsec between the firewall and a management station are as follows:

1. Create a network object for the interface IP address of the firewall by right-clicking Network Objects in the tree pane and selecting New | Network.

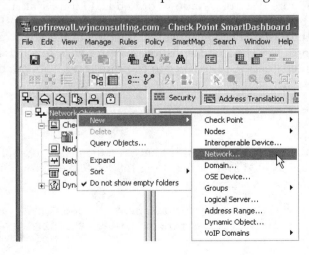

2. Add a network to identify the IP address of the firewall. Configure an appropriate name and specify the network address as the IP address of the firewall interface you want to connect to. For the subnet mask, specify a full "/32 mask" (255.255.255.255). Click OK when you're finished.

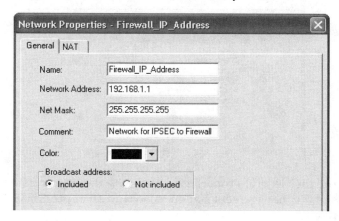

3. Repeat step 2, creating a network to identify the IP address of the management station. Click OK when you're finished.

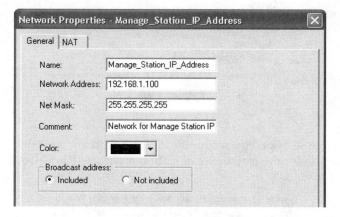

4. Add a new interoperable device by right-clicking Network Objects in the tree pane and selecting New | Interoperable Device.

5. Configure the General Properties section with the appropriate name and IP address of the management station. Also, add an appropriate comment for future reference.

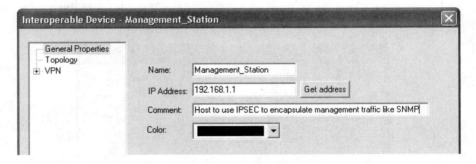

6. Configure the Topology section by clicking Add and entering the network information for the management station interface IP address. Click OK when you're finished.

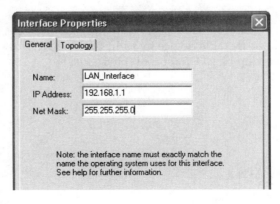

7. This step is very important. Under the VPN Domain section, select Manually Defined and specify the network you created for the IP address of the management station in step 3. This will tell the firewall what traffic should be protected by IPsec/VPN. If you do not do this, the firewall will not properly encrypt/decrypt packets, even though it will allow the IPsec/VPN tunnel to be established. Once you are finished, click OK to close the Interoperable Device configuration pages.

8. Open the new object up again by double-clicking it in the tree pane. Select the VPN section and click Add. Select the appropriate VPN community and click OK. The object should appear similar to the following. Click OK to close the Interoperable Device configuration pages.

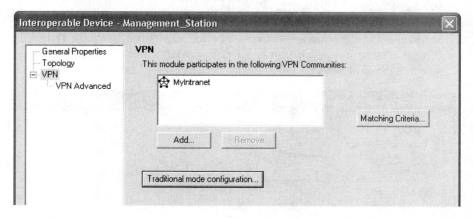

9. Right-click the firewall object and select Edit. Select the Topology section. In the VPN Domain section, select Manually Defined and select the firewall IP address network object you created in step 2.

10. Select the VPN section and click Add to specify the appropriate VPN community. This should match the community you specified in step 8. When you are finished configuring the firewall, click OK to close the firewall configuration pages.

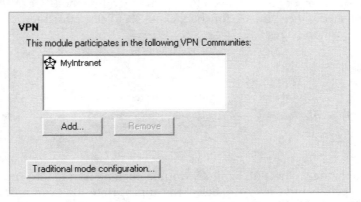

11. Now it is time to configure the VPN community you specified earlier. In the right pane, select the padlock to bring up the VPN Community section. Locate the VPN community you specified earlier, right-click it, and select Edit.

12. Select the VPN Properties section and configure the IKE (Phase 1) and IPsec (Phase 2) settings appropriately for your environment. I recommend that you select 3DES and SHA1 for maximum security, as shown here:

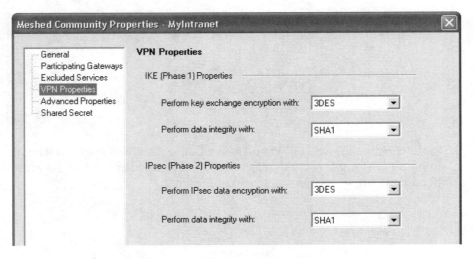

13. Select the Advanced Properties section and configure the IKE (Phase 1) and IPsec (Phase 2) settings appropriately for your environment. These settings must exactly match on both IPsec/VPN endpoints.

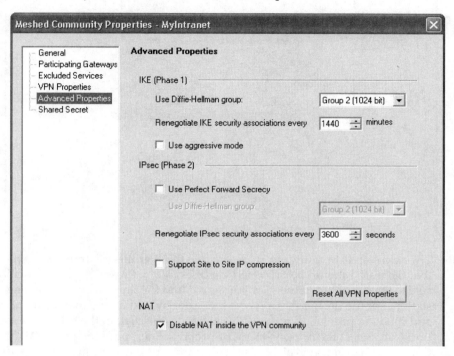

14. Select the Shared Secret section. Highlight the peer and click Edit. Enter the shared secret value and click OK. The key will be hidden by asterisks on the configuration page for security reasons. Click OK when you're finished to close the VPN Community configuration screens.

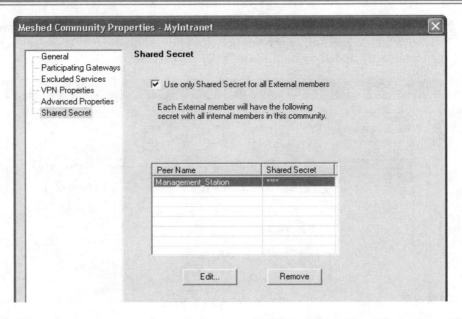

15. The next step is to configure an access rule that permits the traffic and specifies that the traffic should be protected via IPsec/VPN. Press CTRL-ALT-T to add the rule to the top of the ruleset. For the source, add the firewall and the management station. For the destination, reverse the order by adding the management station and then the firewall. For the VPN section, right-click in the cell and select Edit Cell. Select the option Only Connections Encrypted in Specific VPN Communities and then click Add. Select the VPN community you specified previously and click OK.

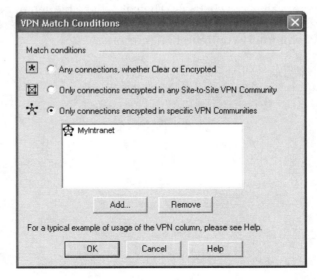

For the service, leave the default setting of Any. Right-click in the Action cell and select Accept. In the Track cell, right-click and select Log. Right-click in the Install On cell, select Add | Targets, and then specify the firewall. When completed, your rule should look something like rule 1:

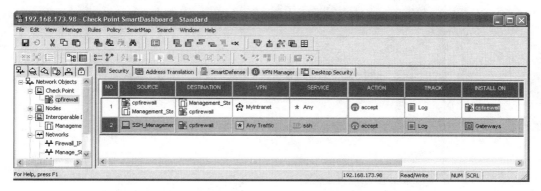

16. The last step is to install the policy on the firewall. You can do this by selecting the Policy menu, selecting Install, and then specifying the target. Click OK.

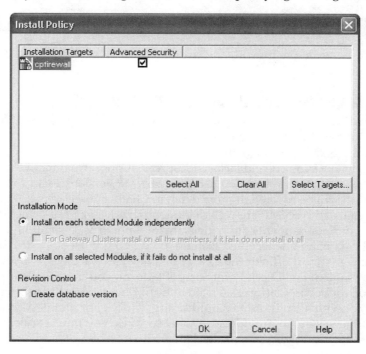

17. When this is completed, you should be presented with the following screen:

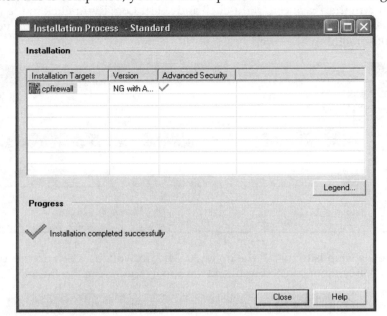

The traffic between the firewall and the management station should be protected by IPsec at this point.

Hardening Simple Network Management Protocol (SNMP)

SNMP is a particularly problematic protocol because although it can provide significant benefits to your network, by design it is a highly insecure protocol, particularly SNMP versions 1 and 2. SNMP version 3 mitigates many of these security issues; however, it is a relatively new protocol and lacks widespread support from many vendors. Consequently, I am going to focus on hardening SNMP versions 1 and 2 in this chapter. SNMP version 3 will be covered in more detail in Chapter 10.

The problems with SNMP are well documented; however, the principal issues are that it uses a common authentication mechanism (known as *community strings*) and transmits all data in an unencrypted fashion. If you do not need SNMP, then by far the best solution is to turn it off. For the Cisco PIX, SNMP is disabled by default and must be explicitly enabled. For Check Point SecurePlatform, you must explicitly install the SNMP add-on for SecurePlatform, located at http://www.checkpoint.com/techsupport/downloadsng/utilities.html#snmp_addon. For iptables, because it relies on the operating system to provide additional services, you must explicitly install SNMP on the operating system in order to have it available.

If you want to disable SNMP on a Cisco PIX firewall, you can do so by running the following command at the CLI:

```
firewall(config)# no snmp-server
```

For iptables, you can disable SNMP as you would any other service, as shown here:

```
chkconfig 'service_name' off
service 'service_name' stop
```

For Check Point, you can disable SNMP by running the following commands at the expert CLI:

```
[Expert@cpfirewall]# snmp service disable
Stopping snmpd: [  OK  ]
```

If you decide that you need to use SNMP on your firewall, here are some steps to follow to harden the protocol:

1. Ensure that you are using good community strings. I once got into a discussion with a developer about whether SNMP community strings were passwords. Although the developer was technically correct that they are not passwords, practically speaking they are every bit as valuable as passwords and therefore should be protected accordingly. You should ensure that your community strings, at a minimum, meet the requirements of your password security policy.

2. Protect the integrity of the data. Because SNMP transmits the data in the clear, there is really only one viable option to protecting the data—to encapsulate the SNMP communications within an IPsec tunnel. In fact, I recommend that all communications between the firewall and the management system be encapsulated in IPsec, just for good measure.

3. The final step to hardening SNMP is to only allow SNMP requests from specific hosts.

For the Cisco PIX, you can specify the hosts you want to allow to connect via SNMP by running the following command at the CLI:

```
firewall(config)# snmp-server host [if_name>] <local_ip>
```

For iptables, SNMP access is controlled by the use of the ruleset. In order to permit SNMP traffic, configure a rule that allows traffic from the management system to the firewall interface from which you want to perform SNMP administration (in this case, interface eth0):

```
iptables -A INPUT -I eth0 -p udp -m udp -s 192.168.1.100 -d →
192.168.1.1 --dport 161 -j ACCEPT
```

For Check Point, SNMP access is controlled by the rulebase. In order to permit SNMP traffic, configure a rule that allows traffic from the management system to the firewall interface from which you want to perform SNMP administration, as shown here:

| 3 | 🗔 Manage_Station | 🖼 cpfirewall | ✴ Any Traffic | UDP snmp | 🌐 accept | − None | 🗔 Gateways |

Hardening Network Time Protocol (NTP)

Network Time Protocol (NTP) is used to synchronize time between systems. It is particularly valuable on firewalls for use in the date/timestamping of log files. I strongly recommend the use of NTP because it not only makes troubleshooting easier but can be invaluable when trying to do forensics in terms of determining when something occurred. Like SNMP, however, NTP transmits data in an unencrypted fashion that makes it particularly vulnerable to man-in-the-middle attacks. In addition, until recently, NTP did not use any kind of authentication method. That is no longer the case, however. The current version of NTP supports authentication through the use of an MD5 hash and a pre-shared key. As a result, if you are going to use NTP on your firewall, you should always configure it to use authentication. In addition, like with SNMP, you should encapsulate NTP in IPsec to protect the data integrity. To configure NTP with authentication on the PIX, you can run the following commands at the CLI:

```
firewall(config)# ntp authenticate
firewall(config)# ntp authentication-key 1 md5 authenticationkey
firewall(config)# ntp trusted-key 1
firewall(config)# ntp server 192.168.1.109 key 1 source inside
```

iptables relies on the native operating system to provide NTP functionality. Because different OS vendors can implement NTP differently, you should contact your OS vendor for information about how to configure NTP with authentication for their OS. For Check Point, you can configure NTP at the CLI as follows:

```
[cpfirewall]# ntp MD5secret 5 192.168.1.109
```

This will configure the firewall to poll a server at 192.168.1.109 with an MD5 secret of MD5secret.

Hardening syslog

syslog is another protocol that was never designed for security. Like SNMP and NTP, syslog does not encrypt the data being transmitted. Unlike SNMP and NTP, though, there is no method for authenticating syslog connections. With that said, I firmly believe that syslog should be required when implementing any firewall. The reason for this is simple: syslog has the ability to show you everything that is happening on your firewall at any given time.

Using syslog as a Troubleshooting Tool

During the week I was writing this chapter, I walked into a customer location, installed and configured syslog in their environment, and isolated a routing problem and a VPN problem that they were unaware were the causes of some other issues, within minutes of having syslog configured and operational.

I cannot stress enough how valuable syslog is in managing and maintaining firewalls. However, we still have a problem with the fact that syslog is sending data in the clear. This presents a *huge* security risk because, for the same reasons that syslog is invaluable as a troubleshooting tool, it is equally invaluable for use by a hacker to gain all sorts of information about how the firewall is configured, what rulesets are in use, and so on. The good news is that we already know how to secure this traffic by encapsulating it in IPsec.

Because syslog utilizes a timestamp for all events, I recommend that you configure NTP prior to configuring syslog. This will ensure that all your logs contain accurate timestamps for forensic and troubleshooting usage. On the Cisco PIX firewall, you can configure syslog by running the following commands at the CLI:

```
firewall(config)# logging on
firewall(config)# logging timestamp
firewall(config)# logging host inside 192.168.1.109
firewall(config)# logging trap debugging
```

The last line configures what level of logging to syslog you want to perform. Logging at debug level causes the maximum amount of information to be logged. However, this can cause a significant amount of traffic to be logged as well as create a processor bottleneck, so you should be careful about setting the logging level to debug. The next highest level of logging is informational, and I recommend that you always log either at this level or debug if your equipment can handle the load.

Another option for syslog you should be aware of on the PIX firewall is the ability to log via TCP instead of UDP (the default for syslog). The benefit of using TCP instead of UDP is that if the PIX is for some reason unable to send events to the syslog server, it will stop accepting *any* traffic. The downside to this, obviously, is that the PIX will stop accepting any traffic. If your environment requires that if the PIX is for some reason unable to send syslog information it must stop passing traffic, then this is probably an acceptable risk. Other environments should seriously consider whether implementing this configuration will create a larger support issue than the security issue it addresses. If you want to configure the PIX to send syslog via TCP, you can run the following command at the CLI:

```
firewall(config)# logging host inside 192.168.1.109 tcp/1740
```

The port number must be between 1025 and 65535. In this case, I selected port 1740 as the port to use.

iptables relies on the underlying operating system for the configuration of syslog. Once the underlying operating system is configured to properly log to a remote host, you can configure iptables to log matching packets by specifying the LOG target extension. For example, if you wanted to log all HTTP packets, you would do that by entering the following command:

```
iptables -A INPUT -p tcp -m tcp --dport 80 --syn -j LOG
```

An unfortunate drawback of logging with iptables is that if you want to log packets you are rejecting, you must specify two rules. The first rule should be your logging rule. The second rule would be your reject rule.

Check Point uses a proprietary logging format and logging servers known as *Enterprise Log Servers*. Although it is possible to configure Check Point to send its logs to a syslog server via the Unix **logger** command, this generally requires extensive modification of the underlying operating system and I therefore advise against doing it. The biggest reason I advise against doing this is that the procedure is not documented very well by Check Point and really constitutes what is little more than a hack. Until Check Point decides to provide native syslog functionality, the only other supported option for syslog on Check Point is to implement a third-party log-monitoring solution such as NetIQ Security Manager for FireWall-1.

Hardening Trivial File Transfer Protocol (TFTP)

Trivial File Transfer Protocol (TFTP) is susceptible to all the vulnerabilities that syslog is, specifically, no authentication, no encryption, and the use of UDP as a transport protocol. Like syslog, TFTP should be encapsulated in IPsec to ensure data integrity. This is especially important with TFTP because it is often used to transmit configuration files to and from the firewall, allowing anyone with a packet sniffer to capture the TFTP traffic and gain the entire firewall configuration file in clear text. Also like syslog, TFTP traffic should only be allowed to a designated server. You can accomplish this on the Cisco PIX by running the following command at the CLI:

```
firewall(config)# tftp-server [<if_name>] <ip> <directory>
```

TFTP is not used with iptables. For Check Point, you manage what systems can act as a TFTP server by configuring the ruleset to permit TFTP traffic from the firewall to the TFTP server.

Using Redundancy to Harden Your Firewall

Today's companies realize that the Internet is a critical business resource that they cannot operate efficiently without. From e-mail, to VPNs, to extranet connections between business partners, to using the Internet as a research tool, the need for redundancy for Internet connectivity has become a requirement at many companies. By that same token, having redundancy with your firewall is an excellent method of hardening your system against hardware failures.

Redundancy and Cisco PIX Firewalls

The Cisco PIX supports hardware redundancy on all models except the PIX 501 and PIX 506. Implementing redundancy is simply a matter of getting identical hardware and software in every way, obtaining the appropriate license, and then configuring the firewalls accordingly. The PIX supports two primary methods of configuring redundancy:

- Failover via the use of a failover cable
- LAN-based failover

The major difference between the two failover methods is that LAN-based failover supports stateful failover, thus allowing the replication of the following information between units:

- TCP connection table, including timeout information
- Port allocation table information for PAT
- Translation table and status
- Negotiated H.323 UDP ports

In addition, because the failover is LAN based, the 6-foot distance limitation on the use of a failover cable is no longer an issue. The drawback of LAN-based failover is that you can have delayed detection of peer power loss.

Configuring the PIX for failover is a relatively straightforward procedure, with the difference between failover methods being a couple of commands. To configure stateful failover (LAN based), run the following commands at the CLI on the primary PIX:

```
firewall(config)# nameif ethernet2 fo security20
firewall(config)# interface ethernet2 100full
firewall(config)# ip address fo 192.168.2.1 255.255.255.0
firewall(config)# ip address outside 192.168.3.1 255.255.255.0
firewall(config)# ip address inside 192.168.4.1 255.255.255.0
firewall(config)# failover ip address fo 192.168.2.2
firewall(config)# failover lan unit primary
firewall(config)# failover lan interface fo
firewall(config)# failover lan key yourpresharekey
firewall(config)# failover lan enable
firewall(config)# failover
```

On the secondary PIX, you need to run the following commands, at minimum:

```
firewall(config)# nameif ethernet2 fo security20
firewall(config)# interface ethernet2 100full
firewall(config)# ip address fo 192.168.1.1 255.255.255.0
firewall(config)# ip address outside 192.168.3.1 255.255.255.0
firewall(config)# ip address inside 192.168.4.1 255.255.255.0
firewall(config)# failover ip address fo 192.168.1.2
firewall(config)# failover lan unit secondary
firewall(config)# failover lan interface fo
firewall(config)# failover lan key yourpresharekey
firewall(config)# failover lan enable
firewall(config)# failover
```

NOTE If you're implementing LAN-based failover in a switched environment, ensure that you enable portfast on your switches to prevent them from taking up to 30 seconds to transition between listening to forwarding.

Configuring the PIX for nonstateful failover is a much simpler process, requiring only the **failover** command to be run on both firewalls.

Redundancy and iptables Firewalls

iptables has no direct redundancy support; rather, because it is an application running on top of an operating system, it requires the operating system to be configured to support clustering in order to provide redundancy. Your operating system vendor can provide you with information regarding clustering solutions. For example, Red Hat has a cluster offering about which you can find more information at http://www.redhat.com/software/rha/cluster.

Redundancy and Check Point Firewalls

Check Point has an additional product that can be installed with FireWall-1 called ClusterXL. It provides not only high-availability cluster support to the firewall, but also load balancing of traffic between cluster nodes. The installation and configuration of ClusterXL is outside of the scope of this chapter; however, you can find the Check Point documentation that covers this information at http://www.checkpoint.com/products/accelerate/clusterxl.html.

Hardening Routing Protocols

As networks have become more complex, the need for routing protocols to effectively define how data should be routed throughout a network has become a requirement. At the same time, firewalls are finding themselves more and more in environments where they need to be able to route between multiple networks. This is especially true when you consider the requirements of implementing a firewall between internal networks instead of in the traditional firewall role on the perimeter. This creates a potential problem however. Like many services and protocols, routing protocols have not always been designed with security in mind. Certain routing protocols (for example, RIP) are particularly vulnerable to attacks such as RIP spoofing. Hackers who are able to gain access to your routing tables have a map that shows them exactly how your network is laid out. Additionally, they can insert routes into your routing table and reroute traffic to a location of their choosing, or stop the flow of traffic completely as a denial of service (DoS). Obviously, the need to harden your routing protocols at your firewall is a critical business need.

Using Static Routes

As a general rule, I recommend that you only configure static routes on your firewalls. This ensures that your firewalls are not susceptible to poisoned updates and such. The drawback, of course, is that maintaining static routes in an enterprise environment can be all but impossible to do. For the Cisco PIX firewall, entering static routes is a straightforward process that involves running the following command at the CLI:

```
firewall(config)# route <if_name> <foreign_ip> <mask> →
<gateway> [<metric>]
```

HEADS UP!

The Cisco PIX cannot be used as a router between multiple networks on the same interface. This is due to the fact that the Cisco PIX will not route traffic back on an interface that it originated from. For example, if you have two internal networks connected to the same PIX interface and you have a host on network A attempting to connect to a host on network B, either host cannot use the PIX to route that data because the data originated on the same interface that the PIX needs to route it back on. However, if you have a request that originates from an external host, the PIX will route the data to either network because the packet originated on an interface different from the one it needs to exit from. If you need to route between multiple networks on the same interface, you must implement a router and configure your hosts to send the data to the router that will route the data accordingly.

Replace the variables with the corresponding information for your network. For example, if you wanted to add a route to the 192.168.100.0/24 network on your inside interface using a gateway of 192.168.1.254, you would enter the following:

```
firewall(config)# route inside 192.168.100.0 255.255.255.0 →
192.168.1.254
```

iptables relies on the operating system to provide routing information. On Red Hat Linux 9.0, you can add static routes by editing the /etc/rc.local file and adding route lines according to the syntax of the **route** command:

```
route add -net 192.168.100.0 netmask 255.255.255.0 gw →
192.168.1.254 dev eth0
```

Check Point allows for the configuration of static routes via the expert CLI through the use of the **route** command:

```
[Expert@cpfirewall]# route add -net 192.168.100.0/24 gw 192.168.1.254
[Expert@cpfirewall]# route --save
```

Notice that the **route** command on Check Point requires the use of */prefix* to define the subnet mask. Once you have added all the static routes, make sure that you run the last command to make the route changes persistent.

When it comes to hardening routing protocols on a firewall, you have three primary routing protocols to take into consideration:

- Routing Information Protocol (RIP)
- Open Shortest Path First (OSPF)
- Border Gateway Protocol (BGP)

Regardless of the protocol you have to support, you should make sure there is some sort of encryption and authentication mechanism to ensure that the routing protocol data has not been compromised. Although many of them support some sort of authentication (generally utilizing an MD5 hash and pre-shared key), the routing data itself is generally not encrypted and not capable of being encrypted (unless you encapsulate it within IPsec). As a result, although authentication will protect your firewall from receiving routes from untrusted hosts, without encryption of the routing protocol you are still vulnerable to a hacker sniffing those packets off the wire and gaining access to your routing information, even if they can't hijack your routing protocols and make any changes. Because of these insecurities, you should not use routing protocols on untrusted networks such as your DMZ or external networks, except as required (for example, using BGP to connect to multiple upstream providers). Even in those required cases, you should never allow your internal routing tables to be transmitted across those untrusted networks.

Hardening RIP on Your Firewalls

Although I do not recommend using RIP because it has historically proven to be particularly vulnerable to attack, if you must use it on your Cisco PIX firewall, you should configure it to use MD5 authentication at the CLI, as follows:

```
firewall(config)# rip inside passive version 2 authentication →
md5 ripkey 2
```

This configures RIP version 2 on the inside interface in passive mode with an MD5 hash key of "ripkey" and a key ID of "2." The firewall will only exchange RIP routing information with other routers that exchange the appropriate hash and key ID.

As previously mentioned, iptables relies on the underlying operating system to provide routing protocol information and configuration. Check Point also relies on the underlying operating system to provide for routing protocol information and configuration. Although a number of different third-party routing daemons can be installed on these systems, because both ship with a version of Zebra, I am going to focus on how to configure Zebra to harden RIP.

Zebra uses a command set based on the Cisco IOS command set for configuration. The benefit to this is that the commands required for configuring RIP to use an MD5 hash for authentication are virtually identical to those you would use on a Cisco router. First, you must specify the key chain to use. Next, you must configure the interface to use RIP authentication and specify the key chain to be used for that interface. After that, you configure the RIP routing protocol to use RIP version 2 as well as specify what networks to use RIP with. Finally, you need to make sure you permit RIP traffic in your firewall access rules; otherwise, the firewall will prevent any RIP updates from occurring. You can configure Zebra by running the command **vtysh** at the CLI. You should be logged in as root on Linux/Unix or you should be in the Check Point expert mode to run the command. A sample configuration is shown here:

```
key chain rip2
 key 2
  key-string ripkey
!-- This assigns a key chain name of rip2 with a rip key string
!-- of "ripkey"
interface eth0
 ip rip authentication mode md5
 ip rip authentication key-chain rip2
!-- This assigns the key chain of "rip2" and specifies to use an MD5
!-- hash instead of passing the actual key string.
router rip
 network 192.168.1.0/24
 network 192.168.2.0/24
!-- This configures RIP routing on the specified network. RIP version
!-- 2 is the default version, and thus is not shown in the config
```

Make sure you save your configuration before exiting Zebra by running the command *write memory* to make the configuration changes persistent. This will cause the configuration to be saved in the file /etc/Zebra.conf.

Hardening OSPF on Your Firewalls

Configuring OSPF for authentication follows the same basic principles as for RIP. You will configure a pre-shared key that is used for authentication and then use MD5 to create a hash that is exchanged between the systems. This ensures that only authenticated systems can communicate with and exchange routing information with each other.

For the Cisco PIX, you have a number of commands to run to configure OSPF to use MD5 authentication. In this example, we are configuring MD5 authentication with a pre-shared key of "ospfkey" and a network of 192.168.1.0. You would run the following commands using CLI:

```
firewall(config)# router ospf 10
firewall(config-router)# network 192.168.1.0 255.255.255.0 area 0
firewall(config-router)# area 0 authentication message-digest
firewall(config-router)# routing interface inside
firewall(config-routing)# ospf message-digest-key 1 md5 ospfkey
```

For iptables and Check Point, you can enable OSPF with MD5 authentication by running the command *vtysh* at the CLI and configuring Zebra as follows:

```
interface eth0
 ip ospf message-digest-key 1 md5 ospfkey
!-- This configures the interface to create an MD5 hash of the
!-- pre-share key for authentication
router ospf
 network 192.168.1.0/24 area 0
 network 192.168.2.0/24 area 0
 area 0 authentication message-digest
!-- This configures the OSPF networks and specifies the OSPF area
```

Hardening BGP on Your Firewalls

Border Gateway Protocol (BGP) presents a unique problem as it relates to firewalls. Some firewalls, such as the Cisco PIX, do not support running BGP and therefore aren't relevant to this discussion. For iptables and Check Point running Zebra for BGP routing services, the problem is that Zebra does not support BGP authentication, even though it does support running BGP. Consequently, regardless of what BGP configuration options Zebra does support, I recommend that you do not run BGP with Zebra. So what can you do if you have to run BGP? I recommend that you implement routers in front of the firewalls, letting the routers handle the BGP functionality, and that you harden BGP on the routers accordingly. Hardening BGP on your routers is covered in Chapter 6. Once you have your routers configured for BGP, use either static routes or RIP/OSPF to communicate between the firewalls and the routers to exchange routing information.

Summary

One of the most dangerous things administrators can think is that because the device they are implementing is a firewall, it must already be hardened by the vendor and therefore they don't need to do anything else to further protect the firewall from being compromised. This is patently incorrect. Every firewall can be hardened beyond what the vendors do to protect the system against being compromised. As you saw in this chapter, a basic template for hardening your firewalls consists of the following steps:

- *Harden remote administration.* Prevent remote administration where possible, and permit only secure remote administration if you must allow it.

- *Implement authentication and authorization.* Implement unique usernames and hard-to-guess passwords, and only allow users to run the commands required.

- *Harden the operating system.* If you are using a software-based firewall, you must harden the underlying operating system because it is the biggest vulnerability to your firewall.

- *Harden firewall services and protocols.* Allow only the services that are required, encrypt insecure traffic by encapsulating it with IPsec, and only allow specific hosts to connect to any services.

- *Implement syslog.* syslog is critical for auditing, forensics, and troubleshooting purposes. Protect your syslog traffic by encapsulating it with IPsec.

- *Provide redundancy and fault tolerance.* A firewall is only effective if it is running. Providing redundancy allows your company to continue to function in the event of a hardware failure.

- *Harden routing protocols.* If possible, use only static routes. If you must use dynamic routing protocols, only use those protocols that provide for some kind of authentication mechanism.

Chapter 4

Hardening Your Network with Intrusion Detection and Prevention

- IDS/IPS Technologies
- IDS/IPS Components
- IDS/IPS Device Hardening
- IDS/IPS Deployments
- IDS/IPS Tuning
- IDS/IPS Logging, Alerting, and Blocking

73

A couple of years ago I made the decision to purchase an alarm system for my house. My reasoning was pretty simple: I thought that I had reached a point where I had acquired some decent stuff that I didn't want to lose. Now, I knew that the alarm system wouldn't necessarily keep someone from breaking into my house and taking everything, but I hoped that it would at least serve as some kind of early warning system that might help alert the police and thus allow them to arrive sooner, perhaps even enabling them to show up fast enough to actually stop anyone who might be in the act of breaking in. I went hunting last year, and my wife set the alarm off one morning while I was gone. The police showed up within two minutes of the initial phone call when unfortunately my wife could not recall the passphrase to use. Although she was quick to point out upon my return that this was my fault <grin>, I liked the knowledge that my investment in a home security alarm was not in vain.

Intrusion Detection Systems (IDS) are different from many of the other topics discussed in this book because, by and large, they serve not as something we can do to prevent a security occurrence, but rather, much like a home alarm, they serve to alert the relevant authorities that something is occurring that requires attention. Intrusion Prevention Systems (IPS) build upon this foundation and attempt to take the detection a step further and prevent a security occurrence from happening, preferably without user intervention.

Because IDS/IPS serves more of a role as an alarm system on a network than anything else, I approach this chapter a little differently than the rest. Whereas routers and firewalls, for example, have a number of tasks that can be performed to harden and secure them, IDS/IPS serves more to passively monitor the network environment. Consequently, this chapter focuses more on how IDS/IPS functions, how to design an IDS/IPS infrastructure, and how you can use IDS/IPS throughout your network environment to increase your security posture. For this chapter, I will focus on the following IDS products:

- Demarc Security PureSecure version 1.6 (www.demarc.com), a network IDS (NIDS) based on Snort (www.snort.com) running on Microsoft Windows (runs on Linux as well)

- Cisco IDS 4210 Sensor version 4.1(3)S78 and Cisco VPN/Security Management Solution version 2.2 (www.cisco.com)

IDS/IPS Technologies

As mentioned earlier, intrusion detection is largely a process of setting up alarms to notify you in the event of an incident. Even intrusion prevention, with its ability to stop an incident, adheres to this same operating philosophy. In order to understand which IDS or IPS solution is the best solution for a given scenario, you have to understand the technologies used in most IDS/IPS solutions. The two predominant types of IDS/IPS are host based and network based. We will look at each of these technologies and examine the pros and cons to determine where each technology best fits into your network. Finally, we will look at the different components of an IDS/IPS to help you understand how to deploy an IDS/IPS in the most effective manner.

This section is more "educational" and less "how to" than sections in other chapters of this book because I have found that one of the biggest problems people encounter in dealing with IDS/IPS is a general confusion as to exactly what IDS/IPS is and how it works. Sure, people know that they want an IDS to detect unauthorized access, but they often don't understand what that really means. This confusion is compounded by the IDS/IPS vendors who have spent more time on marketing a concept than defining what that concept means and does. Making sure you understand these technologies will help you establish realistic expectations and thus increase the likelihood that the IDS/IPS you select will accomplish the goals and objectives you've defined when you deploy it in your environment.

Host-Based Intrusion Detection/Prevention

Host-based IDS/IPS (HIDS/HIPS) entails software to be run on the hosts you want to protect in the first place. The defining difference between host-based and network-based IDS/IPS is that host-based IDS/IPS monitors from the host's point of view, whereas network-based IDS/IPS monitors from the network's point of view. HIDS/HIPS software functions by monitoring not only the traffic that is entering and exiting the host, but also by monitoring the user and operating system activity to detect an incident. HIDS/HIPS is generally able to monitor to a much greater level of detail than a network-based IDS/IPS because it can focus exclusively on monitoring the host upon which it is installed. This allows HIDS/HIPS to detect attacks that might be overlooked by a network-based solution and also to analyze data that may have been encrypted over the network (and thus undetected by the network-based IDS/IPS) after it has been decrypted on the host.

ONE STEP FURTHER

The two broad categories of alarms are false positives (also known as *false alarms*) and true positives. False positives refer to situations where the IDS/IPS has failed to accurately report on what has occurred. False positives refer to alarms that are generated for normal traffic, and they are the biggest problem with IDS/IPS because they waste time and resources and can desensitize your network administrators to incident alarms. False negatives, on the other hand, are the worst-case scenario, because they represent real attacks that were missed by the IDS/IPS. True positives are the opposite of false positives, representing the IDS/IPS accurately reporting what is happening. True positives are what you want to tune your IDS/IPS to report. These represent attacks that the IDS/IPS recognized and reported properly. True negatives, although they sound bad, actually represent the IDS/IPS not generating an alarm when it is observing normal traffic.

The most time-consuming part of IDS/IPS deployment that I have encountered is the time it takes to tune the IDS/IPS to generate the appropriate alarm for a given situation. The objective is to generate 100-percent true positive alarms.

Although this may make HIDS/HIPS sound like a perfect solution, it does have some drawbacks. First, because the HIDS/HIPS resides on the host, if the host is compromised, the HIDS/HIPS can no longer be considered reliable. In addition, HIDS/HIPS requires that the software be installed on all the hosts to be monitored, which results in the use of processing and memory resources on those hosts. HIDS/HIPS is also generally ineffective at addressing denial of service attacks because it can only detect a DoS once the host is under attack.

A number of different HIDS/HIPS software is available to you, including the following:

- Cisco Security Agent (http://www.cisco.com/en/US/customer/products/sw/secursw/ps5057/index.html)
- Tripwire for Servers (http://www.tripwire.com/products/servers/)
- ISS BlackICE (http://blackice.iss.net/product_server_protection.php)
- Symantec Host IDS (http://enterprisesecurity.symantec.com/products/products.cfm?ProductID=48&EID=0)

Host-based intrusion detection and prevention products are beyond the scope of this book; however, you should employ them on any critical servers at a minimum and on all your systems if possible. Refer to *Hardening Windows Systems* by Roberta Bragg and *Hardening Linux* by John Terpstra for more information about server hardening and HIDS/HIPS.

Network-Based Intrusion Detection/Prevention

Network-based IDS/IPS (NIDS/NIPS) includes devices that are deployed to monitor the traffic on a network segment and report on any suspicious traffic. Most NIDS/NIPS function in a fashion similar to a packet sniffer, using a network interface operating in promiscuous mode to sniff the packets traversing a network segment. One of the biggest benefits of a NIDS/NIPS is this ability to monitor an entire segment, allowing a single NIDS/NIPS that has been strategically placed in your network to provide a deep breadth of resource coverage. For example, an NIDS/NIPS that monitors your Internet uplink segment to the firewall allows you to see all traffic entering or exiting your network. Other benefits of NIDS/NIPS are stealth and the minimal impact on your network. Because NIDS/NIPS passively monitors traffic, the traffic is passed at wire speed as if the NIDS/NIPS were not even there.

However, NIDS/NIPS has some significant drawbacks. First, NIDS/NIPS is unable to monitor encrypted traffic, so attacks that are encapsulated in encrypted packets will be undetected by the NIDS/NIPS. Also, because the NIDS/NIPS must potentially monitor a huge amount of traffic, there can be latency in alarming and even missed incidents due to an inability of the NIDS/NIPS to process the amount of data it is observing. For example, the Cisco 4250 IDS sensor has a rated performance of 500 Mbps, assuming conditions of 5,000 TCP connections per second, 5,000 HTTP transactions per second, and an average packet size of 445 bytes. This does not mean that the NIDS/NIPS is not useful for monitoring links that are faster than that; it simply means that the NIDS/NIPS will be dropping packets, and you should be aware of this limitation.

In addition to the NIDS we will be covering in this chapter, the following systems are available to you:

- Fortinet (http://www.fortinet.com/)
- Sourcefire (http://www.sourcefire.com/)
- Enterasys Dragon (http://www.enterasys.com/products/ids/)

Detection Technologies

There are two primary IDS/IPS detection technologies, anomaly detection and misuse detection.

Anomaly detection–based IDS/IPS use profiles that define the behavior characteristics for the group of users and thus establish the baseline that the traffic is compared against to identify a deviation. Anomaly detection essentially learns what the normal traffic is, and alerts if it sees an anomaly. These systems require a tremendous amount of configuration however to "teach" the system what is normal. While these systems are not as susceptible to zero-day exploits like a misuse detection is, I recommend that you employ them only where you think you are susceptible to zero-day exploits due to the complexities involved in the system.

Misuse detection is also known as *signature-based* or *pattern matching*, and it uses a database of known attack signatures to identify suspicious traffic. Misuse detection is the traditional method of IDS/IPS. Because the signatures are based on known activity, the attacks that are detected are well defined and easy to identify. This makes for a much simpler system than an anomaly-based system. I recommend signature-based IDS/IPS in most environments where the risk of being susceptible to a zero-day exploits is minimal.

IDS/IPS Components

Something that was initially very confusing for me when I first learned about IDS/IPS technologies was how it all came together. When I heard the term "intrusion detection system," I kept expecting to see something that did it all. Inevitably I was disappointed because an IDS is not a single device; rather, it is a system made up of two components:

- **The network sensor**   For all intents and purposes, in a network-based solution, sensors tend to be beefed-up network sniffers that are deployed strategically throughout the network to monitor the traffic. In host-based solutions, the sensor is the software that is installed on the host that is being monitored.

- **The management console**   The management console is the central data repository that all the sensors report back to. This allows you to manage your entire environment from a single location as well as provides a central data repository from which you can run reports.

IDS/IPS Device Hardening

Like all your network devices, your IDS/IPS can and should be hardened against attack before you use it to harden your network. The reason is quite simple: if the attacker can disable your alarm system, they have free reign on your network.

Hardening PureSecure and hardening a Cisco IDS require two dramatically different techniques. As a result, I am going to cover the hardening process for each product individually.

Hardening PureSecure on Microsoft Windows

Because PureSecure runs on top of an underlying operating system, the most important thing you can do is to harden the HTTP server it uses for the console (for example, IIS on Windows) and the operating system itself, as prescribed in *Hardening Windows Systems* by Roberta Bragg (or *Hardening Linux* by John Terpstra, if you decided to run PureSecure on Linux).

Beyond those general instructions, however, are a few tasks that should be performed to harden the IDS. These tasks include the following:

- Implementing HTTPS
- Hardening remote access
- Hardening network interfaces

Implementing HTTPS

PureSecure is managed through a web-based interface running on Microsoft IIS. As a result, one of the first tasks is to implement HTTPS to ensure that all management traffic is encrypted and protected accordingly. The following steps detail this process:

1. Open the Internet Information Services administrative tool, connect to the web server, right-click the website, and select Properties.

2. Select the Directory Security tab and click Server Certificate. This will start the Web Server Certificate Wizard. At the Welcome screen, click Next.

3. At the Server Certificate screen, select "Create a new certificate" and click Next.

4. At the Delayed or Immediate Request screen, if you have implemented a public key infrastructure, select "Send the request immediately to an online certification authority." (If you have not implemented PKI on your network, you must obtain a certificate from a public certificate authority [CA] by creating a request file and following their instructions to obtain the server certificate.) When you're finished, click Next.

5. At the Name and Security Settings screen, enter the appropriate name and select a bit length of at least 1024 bits. When you're finished, click Next.

6. At the Organization Information screen, enter the appropriate organization and organizational unit. When you're finished, click Next.

7. At the Your Site's Common Name screen, enter the name you want to use to connect to the server (for example, the fully qualified domain name). When you're finished, click Next.

8. At the Geographical Information screen, enter the appropriate country/region, state/province, and city/locality information and click Next.

9. At the Choose a Certification Authority screen, enter the appropriate certification authority server for your environment and click Next.

10. At the Certificate Request Submission screen, click Next.

11. Once the certificate has been obtained and installed, click Finish to complete the wizard.

12. At the Directory Security tab under Secure Communications, click Edit. Check the boxes to require secure channel (SSL) and 128-bit encryption, as shown next, and then click OK. Click OK to close the website properties and exit the Internet Information Services administrator tool.

At this point, the server should only accept HTTPS/SSL connections.

Hardening Remote Access

The next step is to harden remote access by implementing users and IP address restrictions concerning who is permitted to log onto the management console. You do this by clicking Configure in the top bar and selecting PureSecure Console Users from the configuration menu. This will present you with the user configuration screen:

Add User			
New Username	**Password**	**Email**	**IP Restrictions**
Super User	**NIDS Admin**	**ESM Admin**	**SIV Admin**
■	■	■	■
Add User			

Modify/Delete User		
Username	**Select**	**Input**
- Select - ▾	Change Password To: ▾	
Update		

Current User List							
Username	**Email**	**SU**	**NIDS Admin**	**ESM Admin**	**SIV Admin**	**IP Restrictions**	**Last Login**
admin		YES	YES	YES	YES	192.168.173.114	2004-03-12 16:45:39 from 192.168.173.114
wnoonan	wnoonan@wjnconsulting.com	YES	YES	YES	YES	192.168.173.114	2004-03-12 16:49:36 from 192.168.173.114

One of the nicer features is the ability to add an IP address restriction for the user account. If the user does not connect from a permitted IP address, they will not be allowed to log in. You can use a semicolon to separate IP addresses (for example, 192.168.1.25;192.168.1.26). In addition, you can use wildcards, such as entering 192.168.1.1-254 to permit all hosts on this subnet. You can also combine the two methods (for example, 192.168.0.1-254;192.168.1.1-254).

You can also specify five user roles:

- **Super User**   This type of user has full administrative privileges, including the ability to add, edit, and delete other users (with the exception of the original admin account specified during installation).

- **NIDS Admin**   This type of user has the ability to administer the NIDS portion of the PureSecure console, including editing the Snort ruleset.

- **ESM Admin**   This type of user has the ability to administer the Extensible Service Monitoring portion of the PureSecure console, including the ability to add, modify, or delete any monitored services.

- **SIV Admin**   This type of user has the ability to administer the System Integrity Verification portion of the PureSecure console, including the ability to add, modify, and delete the rules for the files and web pages being monitored.

- **Regular users**   Regular users have none of the check boxes checked and can only view the PureSecure console, with the exception of adding new alert rules for themselves.

Hardening Sensor Network Interfaces

One of the problems that you have to address in deploying a sensor is that one of its network interfaces will frequently be connected to an unsecured network segment. For example, it is very common to deploy a sensor outside of the firewall to monitor the attack attempts that are hitting the firewall. This creates an obvious security issue: if the network interface is outside of the firewall, it is largely unprotected. For this reason, most sensors have two network interfaces. One network interface is known as the *management interface* and is connected to your protected network, typically on your management subnet. The other network interface is known as the *monitoring interface* and, as the name implies, is the interface that the sensor uses to monitor network traffic.

The most effective method of hardening this interface is to remove any and all protocol bindings from the interface. You can unbind the network protocols and services by accessing the network interface properties and unchecking all the components. This will prevent anyone from being able to communicated or connect to this interface because no protocols are bound to it.

Hardening Cisco IDS

Like all your other network devices, the Cisco IDS sensor should be hardened before it is deployed in your environment. You need to be sure that the IDS is secure and protected before you can expect it to adequately protect your network. We are going to look at the following hardening tasks:

- Restricting remote access
- Specifying users
- Configuring NTP

Restricting Remote Access

The first task in hardening your Cisco IDS sensor is to restrict which IP addresses can connect for remote administration. Remote access is controlled by the **accesslist** command. You can permit remote access by running the following commands at the CLI while consoled into the sensor:

```
cisco-ids# configure terminal
cisco-ids(config)# service host
cisco-ids(config-Host)# networkParams
cisco-ids(config-Host-net)# accesslist ipAddress 192.168.1.105 →
netmask 255.255.255.255
```

Once you have done this, you should be able to connect to the sensor via HTTPS/ TLS, SSH, and the Management Center for IDS Sensors from the permitted IP address.

Specifying Users

The Cisco IDS sensor supports four user roles that define what operations can be performed:

- **Administrator** This role can perform all administrative functions on the sensor.
- **Operator** This role can view everything and can modify the following items:
  - Signature tuning
  - Assignment of virtual sensor configuration to interface groups
  - Managed routers
  - The Operator user's own password
- **Viewer** This role can view the configuration and any events but cannot modify anything other than the Viewer user's own password.
- **Service** This is a special role that can only be assigned to one account. This role allows the user to log into the underlying Linux operating system with a bash shell instead of using the CLI. This account should only be created at the direction of the Cisco TAC for troubleshooting purposes only.

Like many Cisco devices, the IDS sensor has a default username of "cisco," which should be removed (the username cannot be changed) at the first opportunity. This can be done by first creating a new administrator-level user, logging in as that user, and then removing the "cisco" user.

You can add a new user via the GUI at the Device | Sensor Setup | Users screen by clicking Add, entering a username and password, and selecting the appropriate user role, as shown next. One of the nice security requirements of the IDS sensor is that it will not allow you to use a password based on a dictionary word. You must use letters and numbers or special characters. When you are finished, click Apply to Sensor.

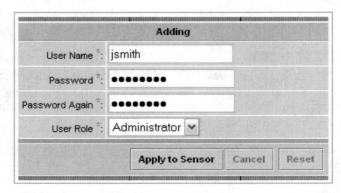

You can then remove the "cisco" username by checking the user at the Device | Sensor Setup | Users screen and clicking Delete.

Configuring NTP

A critical component of your IDS logs is ensuring that they contain accurate timestamps of the activity being logged. You can configure the time settings for the IDS sensor at the Device | Sensor Setup | Time screen, as shown here:

Time Settings		
Time (hh:mm:ss) *:	11 11 01	
Date (mm/dd/yyyy) *:	March ▾ 16 2004	
Current Zone Name / Offset:	CST -360	
Standard Timezone		
Zone Name *:	CST	
UTC Offset (minutes) *:	-360	
NTP Server		
Server IP:	192.168.1.34	
Key:	ticktock	
Key ID:	10	
Daylight Savings Time		
Enabled:	☑	
DST Zone Name *:	CDT	

The IDS sensor requires that you use NTP authentication, which is another nice security requirement that Cisco has implemented.

IDS/IPS Deployments

The most critical part of intrusion detection and prevention is the proper deployment and placement of your sensors. An IDS/IPS is only going to be effective if it is deployed in such a manner that it can monitor the traffic that is of concern.

Figure 4-1 illustrates how you would connect two IDS sensors to your network to monitor the traffic entering and exiting your Internet DMZ segment as well as the traffic in front of your firewall. The monitoring interfaces are connected to switches, which mirror the traffic from the ports that the firewall is connected on to the ports that the IDS is connected on. The management interfaces are connected back to the internal network (preferably on a management subnet), allowing the IDS sensors to be managed by a central management console.

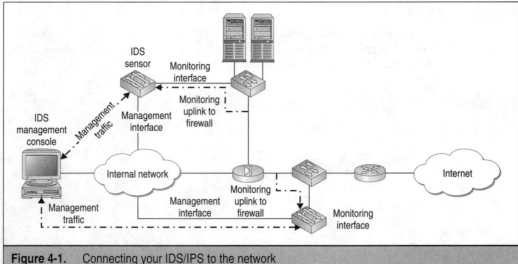

Figure 4-1.   Connecting your IDS/IPS to the network

Detection vs. Prevention

Throughout this chapter, I have referred to intrusion detection and intrusion prevention as almost the same thing. In truth, there are many similarities between the two; however, they are two distinct products with unique roles in your environment.

Intrusion detection is just that, detection. As mentioned earlier in this chapter, intrusion detection is largely a process of implementing an alarm system throughout your network to notify you of situations that warrant further investigation. Intrusion detection is best suited for application throughout your network to monitor traffic at specific choke points, such as backbone segments.

Intrusion prevention takes detection a step further and follows the mantra, "If we have detected suspicious traffic, let's prevent it from accessing the network or host." Intrusion prevention seeks to actively stop an intrusion from occurring, as opposed to passively alarming as to its occurrence. On the surface, this sounds like a great thing. In practice, however, IPS often misses the mark because the detection process is not a perfect science. There are still far too many false positives that can occur in the detection process, and a misconfigured IPS can take a false positive and create one of the very same things it is trying to prevent—a denial of service by preventing legitimate traffic from being permitted.

Sensor Placement

Attacks originate from both internal and external sources. As a result, it is important to locate your intrusion detection and prevention systems where they can monitor not only external traffic, but internal traffic as well. Because of this requirement, you need to plan on IDS/IPS being a system of devices, not a singular device. The following locations are recommended locations for IDS/IPS sensors:

- **In front of your external firewall** Although there is some debate as to the value of placing a sensor outside your firewall, I recommend it so that you can gain some kind of insight as to what is happening that your firewall is protecting you from. The sensor should be configured to monitor the traffic on the switch port that the firewall is connected to. When you implement the IDS/IPS in this location, I recommend that you significantly tune down the alerts because much of this traffic should be blocked by the firewall.

- **Behind your firewalls that provide access to DMZ or internal networks** This is the most common location for sensor placement because these network connections represent choke points where all traffic between network modules must pass. The sensor should be configured to monitor the traffic on the switch port that the firewall is connected to. When you implement the IDS/IPS in these locations, I recommend that you configure the sensor to monitor and alarm on any suspicious traffic, because an alarm at this point means that the traffic has bypassed the firewall in some way.

- **Integrated into your gateway devices** Many gateway devices, such as firewalls, have IDS and in particular IPS functionality built in. This is the location where I recommend most IPSs be implemented, because the firewall is already providing blocking functionality, and the IPS function merely extends that functionality.

- **Behind your VPN concentrators** VPNs represent an easy way for harmful traffic to enter your network. This is due to the fact that often the remote connection does not implement the same degree of security that your internal network enjoys (for example, due to a laptop user who hasn't patched their laptop). You should place the IDS/IPS sensor behind the VPN concentrators so that it can monitor the unencrypted traffic as it passes to and from the VPN connections. This is important because if you place the IDS/IPS in front of the concentrator, you will not be able to gather any valid information because the data is encrypted.

- **In front of your server segments** Because your servers generally contain the most valuable data in your environment, you should implement an IDS/IPS in front of your server segment to monitor the traffic passing to and from the server segment. The easiest way to do this is to configure the monitoring interface to monitor the traffic on the switch port that connects the server segment to the rest of the network.

■ **Behind your WAN connections**   With the nature of worms, WAN connections represent an easy point for them to spread. As a result, I recommend that you implement an IDS/IPS to monitor the traffic that is passing through your WAN connections. You should configure the monitoring interface to monitor the traffic on the switch port that connects the WAN router to the internal network.

■ **On your extranet connections**   Because extranet connections imply a connection to a remote network that you probably do not have administrative control over, you should make extensive use of IDS/IPS sensors. The first location to implement a sensor is between the extranet partner and the shared resources, typically monitoring the traffic on the switch port that connects the extranet segment to the external partner network. The second location to implement a sensor is between the internal network and the extranet segment. This is typically done by monitoring the traffic on the switch port that connects the extranet segment to the internal network.

■ **On any segment that contains or connects to critical resources**   This is the generic catchall bullet. You should implement sensors anywhere else in your network where you have valuable resources or want a more granular idea of the kinds of traffic being passed.

Network diagrams illustrating sensor placement are provided in Chapters 11 and 12.

Sensor Placement in a Switched Network Infrastructure

One of the most confusing aspects of sensor placement is implementing them in a switched network. As you know, the whole purpose of a switched network is to prevent systems on one port from receiving traffic destined for systems on another port. This creates a problem because the sensor needs to be able to monitor all traffic passing for a given segment if you want it to be effective. You can address this, however, by connecting the sensor monitoring interface to a switch port that is configured to receive mirrored traffic from the switch ports that you want to monitor traffic on. This is referred to as a *Switched Port Analyzer (SPAN)* by Cisco; other vendors simply refer to it as *port mirroring*.

You can implement SPAN on a CATOS-based switch by running the following command at the CLI:

```
switch03> (enable) set span 1/1 2/1
```

In this example, SPAN is configured to mirror the traffic from interface 1/1 to the destination interface 2/1, where the sensor is connected.

You can implement SPAN on IOS-based switches by running the following command at the CLI:

```
switch02(config)#monitor session 1 source interface Fa0/1
switch02(config)#monitor session 1 destination interface Fa0/5
```

In this example, SPAN is configured to mirror the traffic from interface Fa0/1 to interface Fa0/5, where the sensor is connected. Although this example shows a one-to-one mirror, it is common to mirror multiple ports to a single monitoring port.

Another issue with implementing sensors on a switched network occurs when you want the sensor to be able to block unauthorized traffic. Many switches prevent a monitoring port from being able to send traffic. The sensor, however, needs to be able to transmit the countermeasure packet (typically, a spoof of the original source MAC address) in order to block the session. In addition, because the sensor is going to spoof the MAC address of the system that it is trying to protect, the switch needs to be configured to disable MAC learning on the monitoring port. If you do not do this, the switch will send all traffic for the destination system to the sensor until the server transmits and causes the switch to relearn the port that it is connected to. You can configure this on your CATOS-based switches by running the following command at the CLI:

```
switch03> (enable) set span 1/1 2/1 inpkts enable learning disable
```

IDS/IPS Tuning

The most time-consuming and, in my opinion, biggest reason why IDS/IPS deployments fail or fail to live up to expectations is the time and effort required in tuning an IDS/IPS. Regardless of whether you implement an anomaly detection or misuse detection system, it is going to require significant long-term effort to configure the IDS/IPS to minimize the occurrence of false positives and negatives.

The need for tuning is simple: without it, the sensor is going to generate alerts for all traffic that matches a given criteria, regardless of whether the traffic is indeed something that should generate an alert. For example, by default, Cisco generates alerts for traffic that uses RFC1918 addresses. Because many networks are designed using the RFC1918 address space, if the sensor is monitoring internal network segments, this is a false positive that should be tuned accordingly. False positives are a lot like the boy who cried wolf. Given enough false positives, even the most diligent of IT personnel will begin to ignore the sensor.

There are six steps to tuning your sensors:

1. *Identify where you are going to locate the sensor.* You need to identify where you are going to be placing the sensor because monitoring different network segments and modules will require a different amount of tuning, and tuning of different traffic.

2. *Apply an initial configuration.* You want to configure the sensor with the initial basic configuration that monitors and alarms on all traffic. From this starting point, you will work backward to tune the sensor accordingly.

3. *Monitor the sensor during the tuning period.* During this time, you need to monitor the sensor as you begin the tuning process to ensure that the amount of false alarms is decreasing. One thing not to underestimate is the amount of time that this step will require. Depending on your environment and the number of sensors, the initial tuning period could easily take a week or more.

4. *Analyze the alarms, tune out false positives, and implement signature customization during the tuning period.* This is the most tedious part of the tuning period because it requires extensive legwork. You have to analyze every alarm that is generated by the sensor to determine whether the alarm is a false positive or not. It is difficult to tell you whether a given alarm is a false positive because each network is unique, both in traffic and in what traffic is permitted by security policies. To assist you in this, you can verify the meaning of the alarm by checking it against a known database of alarm meanings. For example, Cisco maintains a Network Security Database (NSDB) on all of its sensors that can be accessed at the web GUI by following the URL /protected/nsdb/html/ all_sigs_index.html; for example, if your IDS was named "sensor," you would enter **https://sensor/protected/nsdb/html/all_sigs_index.html**. Snort rules can be checked against an online database at http://www.snort.org/snort-db/ sid.html?sid=1317.

   When you are tuning the alarms, make sure you do not assume that the proper response is to prevent the sensor from generating the alarm. For example, if the sensor is generating alarms due to NETBIOS traffic, verify whether NETBIOS is indeed needed on the system in question. If it isn't, disable it on that system instead of tuning the alarm out. You also need to be as granular as possible when tuning alarms. For example, rather than removing a signature or rule because of legitimate systems engaging in that traffic, configure the sensor not to generate an alarm only when the traffic is from those legitimate systems, but continue to alarm for all other systems.

5. *Implement response actions (if required).* Only once you have tuned out false positives can you implement response actions such as e-mails, pages, TCP resets, shunning, or IP logging.

6. *Update the sensor with new signatures.* Because the sensor is only as effective as the signatures it contains, you should make sure you regularly update the signature or rule database. When you do this, you will need to take a day or two to tune the new signatures accordingly.

Tuning PureSecure Sensors

PureSecure runs Snort as the underlying IDS mechanism. As a result, PureSecure can be largely tuned using the underlying Snort methodologies through the PureSecure console interface.

Adding or Removing Rulesets

The first thing to tune on your sensor are the rulesets that are going to be used, as specified in the snort.conf file. The rulesets can be edited by performing the following steps:

1. Log into your PureSecure console and click Configure.

2. In the PureSecure Configuration Menu, click Network IDS Rules in the Network Intrusion Detection section.

3. At the Sensor Details screen, click the sensor you want to modify.

4. In the Sensor Rulesets section, click the Go button on the line Edit Snort Configuration File, as shown here:

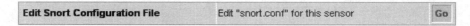

| **Edit Snort Configuration File** | Edit "snort.conf" for this sensor | Go |

5. Scroll down to the ruleset section and include/exclude the appropriate rulesets by using "#" to ignore an entry or removing "#" to implement an entry, as shown next. For example, if I wanted to use the DNS_RULES ruleset, I would remove "#" from the line. When you are finished editing the configuration file, select Update and click Go.

```
#     Brian Caswell <bmc@mitre.org>


#------------------------------------------------------------
# PureSecure Note:
# To make a ruleset inactive, simply comment out
# the appropriate lines below that correspond with
# the name of the ruleset defined through the PureSecure
# Console. Likewise, only rulesets defined with an
# "include" statement below will be active on this Sensor
#
# Please use "_" in place of any spaces in the ruleset name
#------------------------------------------------------------

include ATTACK_RESPONSES
include BACKDOOR_RULES
include BAD_TRAFFIC_RULES
include CHAT_RULES
include DDOS_RULES
#include DNS_RULES
```

Editing Rules

Editing the rules on PureSecure sensors follows the Snort syntax and rule format. The syntax and format can be found at http://www.snort.org/docs/snort_manual/ under the "How to Write Snort Rules and Keep Your Sanity" section. You can access the rules-editing feature by returning to the Sensor Ruleset screen, as previously detailed, and selecting the ruleset you want to modify and then clicking Go, as shown next.

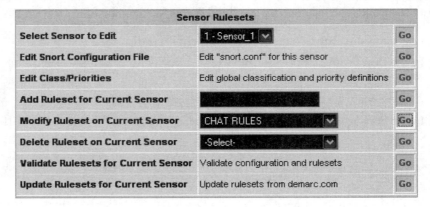

ONE STEP FURTHER

A more efficient way of maintaining your signature files is to use variables to define the various source and destination addresses. If you do not do this when a given address changes, you might need to update multiple signature files. It is much easier to use variables in the signatures and update these variables in a single location. The variables are stored in the snort.conf file on the sensor.

Tuning Cisco IDS Sensors

Tuning the Cisco IDS sensor is a little bit more complex than tuning and customizing PureSecure (or other Snort-based IDSs) because Cisco signatures are based on a proprietary format. You have a number of different ways to reduce the amount of false positives on your sensor, including the following:

- Defining internal networks
- Disabling signatures
- Signature filtering
- Customizing prebuilt signatures
- Writing custom signatures

Defining Internal Networks

Because Cisco assumes that the internal network is more trusted, one method of reducing false positives is to define the internal network, which can then be used for filters to reduce the signatures processed for the internal network. You can define the internal network by connecting to the IDS Device Manager and navigating to the Configuration | Sensing Engine | Alarm Channel Configuration | System Variables screen. Check the box that you want to assign to the variable "IN" and click Edit. At the next screen, enter the network or networks you want to define and then click OK. When you are finished, commit the changes by saving the configuration using the Save Changes button on the activity bar.

Disabling Signatures

Some signatures you are not going to want to have the IDS process and use. The most efficient way of addressing this is to disable these signatures on the sensor. You can do this using the IDS Device Manager by accessing the Configuration | Sensing Engine | Virtual Sensor Configuration | Signature Configuration Mode screen and navigating through the signature groups to locate the signature you want to disable. For example, if you wanted to disable the RFC1918 addresses signature, you would navigate to the OS | General OS screen and check the box next to the signature, as shown next. Then you would click Disable. Disabled signatures will have a white circle in the Enabled column, whereas enabled signatures have a blue circle.

General OS								
							Showing 11-20 of 390	
#	Enabled	ID	SubSig ID	Name	Type	Severity	Action	More
11. ☐	⬤	1005	0	SATNET ID	Tuned	informational		▽
12. ☐	⬤	1006	0	Strict Src Rte	Tuned	high		▽
13. ☐	⬤	1101	0	Unknown IP Proto	Tuned	informational		▽
14. ☐	⬤	1102	0	Impossible IP packet	Tuned	high		▽
15. ☐	⬤	1104	0	Localhost	Tuned	high		▽
16. ☑	⬤	1107	0	RFC1918 address	Tuned	informational		▽
17. ☐	⬤	1108	0	IP Packet with Proto 11	Tuned	high		▽

Signature Filtering

Signature filtering is used to allow the sensor to analyze the data while preventing it from generating an alarm (with the exception of inclusive filters). You can perform filtering based on the source address, destination address, or signature. You can do this using the IDS Device Manager by navigating to the Configuration | Sensing Engine |

Alarm Channel Configuration | Event Filters screen and clicking Add. At the Adding screen, enter the following information:

Sigid	The signature ID.
SubSig	The subsignature ID.
Exception	This check box defines whether it is an exclusion filter (unchecked) or an inclusion filter (checked).
SrcAddrs	The source IP address to filter.
DestAddrs	The destination IP address to filter.

For example, let's assume you have a DHCP server you want to filter alarms for because it is a legitimate DHCP server, but you want to generate alarms for all other DHCP servers that may attempt to provide IP addresses to clients on the network. You would enter a Sigid of 4605 (the DHCP offer signature) and a SrcAddrs value of the legitimate DHCP server and then click Apply to Sensor. When you are finished, commit the changes to make them permanent.

Customizing Prebuilt Signatures

Although it is not possible to customize Cisco signatures to the same degree of granularity as you can Snort rules, you can still undertake a number of tasks to tune and customize the prebuilt signatures on the sensor.

You can customize any signature by accessing the Configuration | Sensing Engine | Virtual Sensor Configuration | Signature Configuration Mode screen and navigating the signature groups to locate the signature you want to edit. For example, let's say you want to customize the HTTP authorization failure signature (signature ID 6256). Once you have located the signature in question, check the box next to the signature and click Edit.

				All signatures				
								Showing 981-990 of 1126
#	**Enabled**	**ID**	**SubSig ID**	**Name**	**Type**	**Severity**	**Action**	**More**
981.	☐ ●	6253	0	POP3 Authorization Failure	Tuned	informational		▽
982.	☐ ●	6255	0	SMB Authorization Failure	Tuned	informational		▽
983.	☑ ○	6256	0	HTTP Authorization Failure	Built-in	informational		▽
984.	☐ ●	6275	0	SGI fam Attempt	Tuned	low		▽
985.	☐ ●	6275	1	SGI fam Attempt	Tuned	low		▽
986.	☐ ●	6276	0	TooltalkDB overflow	Tuned	high		▽

Let's assume you want to change the severity from informational to high, and you want to change the minimum number of matches (minhits) to 2. Edit the appropriate fields and click OK when you're finished, as shown next. In the case of this signature, because it is disabled by default, you will also need to enable it as previously described.

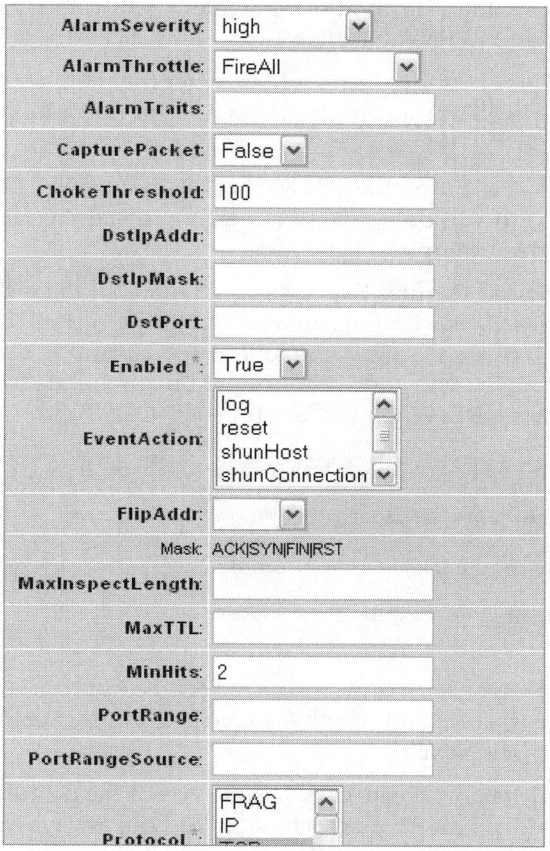

AlarmSeverity:	high
AlarmThrottle:	FireAll
AlarmTraits:	
CapturePacket:	False
ChokeThreshold:	100
DstIpAddr:	
DstIpMask:	
DstPort:	
Enabled:	True
EventAction:	log reset shunHost shunConnection
FlipAddr:	
Mask:	ACK|SYN|FIN|RST
MaxInspectLength:	
MaxTTL:	
MinHits:	2
PortRange:	
PortRangeSource:	
Protocol:	FRAG IP

NOTE   Each signature contains unique fields and values that you can customize, so if you follow these procedures with a different signature, you may see different options.

Writing Custom Signatures

Custom signatures are particularly valuable in situations where you have unique traffic in your environment that you want to be able to monitor. The IDS sensor has a wizard to help you build custom signatures. Let's assume you want to create a new signature that generates an alarm any time someone goes to an online forum. The following steps detail the process:

1. Navigate to the Configuration | Sensing Engine screen and click Signature Wizard. At the introduction screen, click Start the Wizard.

2. At the Signature Type screen, select the appropriate signature type. In this case, select Web Server Signature. When you are finished, click Next.

3. At the Signature Identification screen, enter a valid signature ID and signature name. When you're finished, click Next.

4. At the Web Server Service Ports screen, enter the ports on which you want to be looking for web traffic. I recommend leaving the default values and clicking Next.

5. At the Web Server Buffer Overflow Checks screen, enter the appropriate values and click Next. If you do not want to perform these checks (for instance, for the signature in this example), click Next.

6. At the Web Server Regular Expressions screen, edit the HTTP Header URI Regular Expression section to contain [/\\][Ff][Oo][Rr][Uu][Mm], as shown next. This will cause the signature to look for \forum in the HTTP header information, which will allow it to trigger on any online forums that use \forum in their URL. When you are finished, click Next.

Web Server Regular Expressions		
HTTP Request Regular Expression:		
Minimum HTTP request length:		
HTTP Header Regular Expression:		

7. At the Alert Response Actions screen, select the appropriate alert level, what action to take (if any), and whether to include the packet in the alert. When you are finished, click Next.

8. At the Alert Behavior screen, click Next to accept the default alert behavior or click Advanced to edit the alert behavior. You can always tune the alert behavior later by customizing the signature, as described previously.

9. At the Ready to Create the New Signature screen, click Create.

10. The last step is to click OK to close the wizard and save the changes to cause the sensor to start using the new signature.

IDS/IPS Logging, Alerting, and Blocking

The logging and alerting functions of many IDS/IPS products are perhaps the most confusing part of intrusion detection and prevention. This is due, in part, to the disparity between what the various IDS/IPS vendors mean by "alerting" and what most of us expect. For many IDS/IPS vendors, alerting simply means that an event will be logged, and it is up to you to review the logs to identify the event. For most of us, alerting means that we are getting a page or e-mail telling us that we need to investigate something in more detail. This disparity is what I am going to try to address by offering some examples of how you can perform more effective logging and alerting.

Logging with PureSecure

PureSecure uses a MySQL database as the logging destination for all network events that are triggered. This functionality and the respective web GUI for event review are two of the biggest reasons I recommend it over a plain-vanilla Snort installation. You can review the events that have been logged into the database by clicking the Events button in the PureSecure console, shown here:

P	Signature	Classification	Type	Source	Destination	Sensor	Time Stamp »
			Event List				
2	MS-SQL Worm propagation attempt	misc-attack	UDP			Sensor_1	10:54 AM - 3/15
2	DDOS shaft client to handler	attempted-dos	TCP			Sensor_1	10:48 AM - 3/15
2	DDOS shaft client to handler	attempted-dos	TCP			Sensor_1	10:48 AM - 3/15
2	DDOS shaft client to handler	attempted-dos	TCP			Sensor_1	10:48 AM - 3/15
2	DDOS shaft client to handler	attempted-dos	TCP			Sensor_1	10:48 AM - 3/15
2	DDOS shaft client to handler	attempted-dos	TCP			Sensor_1	10:48 AM - 3/15
2	DDOS shaft client to handler	attempted-dos	TCP			Sensor_1	10:48 AM - 3/15
2	DDOS shaft client to handler	attempted-dos	TCP			Sensor_1	10:48 AM - 3/15
2	DDOS shaft client to handler	attempted-dos	TCP			Sensor_1	10:48 AM - 3/15

The default event list provides a general view of all events that have been logged over time, including the signature, classification, traffic type, source, destination, sensor that logged the entry, and time stamp. You can view a specific event in more detail by clicking the signature value. For example, if I click "MS-SQL Worm propagation attempt," I am presented with this signature information screen:

Signature Information			
Signature	**Sensor**	**Event ID**	**Time Stamp**
MS-SQL Worm propagation attempt More Info - Find in Rules	Sensor_1 (1)	3089	2004-03-15 10:54:54
Classification Description	**Priority**	**Classification**	**Time Since Event**
Miscellaneous Attack	2	misc-attack	28 min 47 sec Ago

Basic Information								
Src IP	**Src Host**	**Src Port**	**Src Service**	**Dst IP**	**Dst Host**	**Dst Port**	**Dst Service**
		1060	-			1434	ms-sql-m

From this screen, I can perform basic network diagnostics, such as running a whois, trace route, ping, or DNS lookup against a given source or destination. I can also scroll down and view the raw data payload that triggered the event.

A benefit of logging to a MySQL database is that the data can be accessed and reports can be built using any standard database reporting tool, such as Crystal Reports. Although configuring Crystal Reports and designing the reports are beyond the scope of this book, if you have DBAs in your organization, they can greatly enhance the logging functionality of PureSecure by designing custom reports and queries that allow you to be very specific about what data you want to view, and so on.

Configuring PureSecure to Log to a syslog Server

As I have mentioned in other chapters, logging to syslog is a valuable way of correlating events throughout your network. In addition to logging to MySQL, you can configure PureSecure to log data to a syslog server. This allows you to leverage an exiting syslog infrastructure as well as take advantage of any reporting or alert-generation functionality that you have built into your syslog infrastructure.

Configuring PureSecure to log to a syslog server is a two-step process. The first step is to edit the file psd.conf, located in the c:\puresecure\sensor\conf directory (assuming you installed to the default locations). Locate the line that begins with snort_options and modify it as follows, adding **–s** to the value:

```
snort_options = " -o -N -s "
```

The next step is to edit the snort.conf file as previously described in this chapter. Edit the file, as shown next, by entering the following value:

```
output alert_syslog: host=<SyslogServerIP>, LOG_AUTH LOG_ALERT
```

When you are finished, select Update and click Go. The last step is to restart the PureSecure service on the sensor. The sensor will now log to the syslog server you defined. For more information about how to customize your syslog server to generate e-mails on events, and so on, see Chapter 10. For additional security, you should also remember to encrypt your syslog traffic as outlined in Chapter 10.

Logging with Cisco IDS

Cisco provides a very extensive logging and reporting functionality for their IDS with their Monitoring Center for Security (Security Monitor), which is part of the CiscoWorks VPN/Security Management Solution (VMS) product.

You can launch the Security Monitor by clicking Security Monitor from the Table of Contents under VPN/Security Management Solution | Monitoring Center.

The first step is to add the devices you want the Monitoring Center to monitor. You can do this by clicking the Devices tab and then clicking Add. This will take you through a wizard that prompts you for the device configuration information.

When you have successfully added the sensor, you can monitor it by clicking the Monitor tab. Cisco takes a nice approach to the logging in that they use a pull-based methodology. This ensures that the Security Monitor is always ready to accept events and doesn't miss them because it is busy processing other items.

Although Cisco does not support exporting to syslog, the built-in logging is more than an effective equivalent to syslog. You can view the log in real time by navigating to the Monitor | Events screen and selecting the event type you want to view as well as the event start and stop time. Once you have selected the event options you want to display, click Launch Event Viewer. This will cause the specified event criteria to be displayed in the monitor for further review, as shown here:

Count	IDS Alarm Type	Sig Name	Severity	Sensor Name	OS Family	OS	Attack Type	Service	Prot
216		IIS DOT DOT EXECUTE Attack	Medium	cisco-ids	Windows	General Windows NT/2K/XP	Code Execution	HTTP	IP
198		IIS DOT DOT VIEW Attack	Info	cisco-ids	Windows	General Windows NT/2K/XP	Files Access	HTTP	IP
130		Inbalance-of-Requests	Info	cisco-ids	General OS	<n/a>	General Attack	General Service	ARP
24		Long HTTP Request	Medium	cisco-ids	General OS	<n/a>	Code Execution	HTTP	IP
1		Long WebDAV Request	High	cisco-ids	Windows	General Windows NT/2K/XP	Code Execution	HTTP	IP
4		MSN Messenger Activity	Low	cisco-ids	<n/a>	<n/a>	<n/a>	<n/a>	<n/a>
27		NbtStat Query	Low	cisco-ids	Windows	General Windows	Reconnaissance	NETBIOS/SMB	IP
5		Net Sweep-Echo	Low	cisco-ids	General OS	<n/a>	Reconnaissance	General Service	IP
1		Netsky Virus Activity	High	cisco-ids	<n/a>	<n/a>	<n/a>	<n/a>	<n/a>
1		Outlook mailto Quote Attack	High	cisco-ids	<n/a>	<n/a>	<n/a>	<n/a>	<n/a>
1		PHP File Inclusion Remote Exec	Info	cisco-ids	General OS	<n/a>	Code Execution	HTTP	IP
138		RFC1918 address	Info	cisco-ids	General OS	<n/a>	Informational	General Service	IP
36		Root.exe access	High	cisco-ids	Windows	General Windows	Code Execution	HTTP	IP
1		SMTP Suspicious Attachment	Low	cisco-ids	General OS	<n/a>	Viruses/Worms/Trojans	SMTP	IP
15		TCP SYN Host Sweep	Info	cisco-ids	General OS	<n/a>	Reconnaissance	General Service	IP

You can expand or collapse the rows to display individual events that match a certain event category (for example, you could expand the Root.exe access row to view the 36 unique occurrences of the event).

Reporting on Events

Cisco provides some extensive reporting capabilities with the Security Monitor. You can access the reporting features by clicking the Reports tab. There are three options:

- **Generate Report**   This choice presents a wizard for generating the various reports.

- **Scheduled**   This choice will show you the status of the reports that have been generated.

- **View**   This choice will allow you to view the reports that have been generated.

Generating a report is a straightforward process. Follow these steps:

1. Click Generate Reports to begin the wizard.

2. At the Select Report screen, select the type of report you want to generate (for example, IDS Alarms by Day report). When you are finished, click Select.

3. At the Report Filtering screen, specify the filtering options you want to use. This allows you to build reports on as many or as few events as you choose. When you are finished, click Next.

4. At the Schedule Report screen, specify the scheduling options you want to configure. One of the nicest features is the ability to schedule the report to run on a regular basis and to e-mail the report to a list of e-mail addresses. This allows you to preconfigure all the standard and routine reports that management may require, as shown next. You can select to export the HTML report to a file by entering the exact filename in the Export To text field. This could be used to export the report to a directory that allows it to be viewed from a website, for example. You can also set the scheduling options as well as define who the report should be e-mailed to. When you are finished, click Finish.

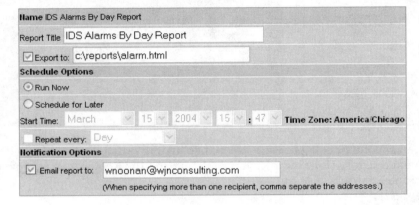

The report will be listed at the Reports | View screen when it has been generated. This may take several minutes, however, depending on how much data needs to be processed. When the report is displayed in the Completed Report section, simply check the report you want to view and click Open in Window.

Alerting with PureSecure

PureSecure is one of the few IDS/IPS vendors that provides a relatively intuitive mechanism for configuring the system to generate e-mails on specific events. E-mail alerts can be generated for the following situations:

Network IDS alerts	For IDS events
Service alerts	For service events that are being monitored
System integrity alerts	For system integrity verification events
General alerts	For any general events that are logged

You can configure all the alerts by clicking the appropriate alert notification at the PureSecure Configuration Menu screen. For example, if I wanted to generate an e-mail alert for specific IDS events, I would click Network IDS Event Notification and be presented with the Define Network IDS Alert Notification Rule screen (the other alert notification methods use a similar intuitive interface for configuring e-mail notification), as shown next. For this screen, I can enter the e-mail recipient and signature that I want to generate an alert on (for example, WEB-IIS cmd.exe access). I would then specify the notification period, priority level, and e-mail detail level and then click Add Event.

Define Network IDS Alert Notification Rule				
Email Recipient	Priority Level	Email Detail Level	Notify From	Notify Through
wnoonan@wjnconsultinç	Any	High	12 AM	11 PM
Existing Signature			Signature Contains	
WEB-IIS cmd.exe access				
Add Event				

Alerting with Cisco IDS

Alerting with Cisco IDS is handled by the Security Monitor program, much like logging is. There are two methods of generating e-mail alerts. The first method is relatively simple but does not provide as much detail in the e-mail as you will probably require. The second method is more complex and requires writing some scripts as well as the use of some third-party utilities; however, it provides much more detail in regard to the details contained in the e-mail. We will look at both methods.

Configuring Simple E-mail Alerting

Configuring the Security Monitor to send e-mail alarms is a multistep process. The first step is to configure an SMTP server to be used at the Admin | System Configuration | Email Server screen. The second step is to configure an event rule at the Admin | Event Rules screen. The following steps detail how to configure the event rule:

1. At the Event Rules screen, click Add.

2. At the Identify the Rule screen, enter an appropriate name and description and click Next.

3. At the Specify the Event Filter screen, enter the filtering rules you want to apply. For example, if you want to generate an e-mail whenever an exploit using the WWW WinNT cmd.exe flaw is attempted, you could select Signature

Name for the first filtering rule and select (5081) WWW WinNT cmd.exe access, as shown next. When you are finished defining the event filter rules, click Next.

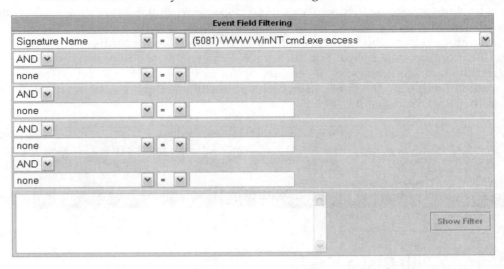

4. At the Choose the Actions screen, select the rule action you want to apply. For example, if you want an e-mail to be generated, you can check Notify via Email and enter the recipient of the e-mail, as shown next. The message body will display only what is shown on this screen, so unfortunately there is no mechanism to provide more comprehensive details, such as the source and destination address, and so on. That will need to be located by viewing the event log, as previously described. When you are finished, click Next.

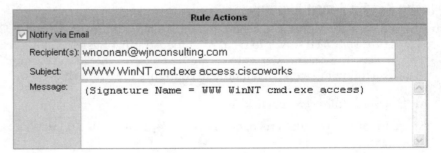

5. At the Specify the Thresholds and Intervals screen, enter thresholds that will prevent you from being inundated by e-mail alarms, but will still provide you with adequate notice of a potential security incident. When you are done, click Finish.

6. The final step is to activate the new rule by selecting the rule and clicking Activate. When you are finished, the value for Active will change to "yes."

Configuring Complex E-mail Alerting

You can configure more complex e-mail alerting by using a third-party SMTP client utility called "blat," which is provided as part of VMS. The following steps detail the procedures for implementing e-mail alerting using blat:

1. The first step is to ensure that blat is installed and configured properly. Blat needs to be in the path of the VMS server. You can verify whether blat is in the path by opening a command prompt and typing **blat** and then pressing ENTER. If you receive the error "file not found," you will need to place the blat executable in a directory that is in the path. By default, blat is located in the $BASE\CSCOpx\bin directory.

2. Next you need to install and configure blat. You can do this by running the following command at a command prompt on the VMS server:

   ```
   blat -install <SMTP server IP address> <sender's email address>
   ```

3. Next you need to write a script that will handle the parsing of the event and building the information that will be e-mailed. An alternative to writing the script from scratch is to download the following script from Cisco and copy it to the $BASE\CSCOpx\MDC\etc\ids\scripts directory on the VMS server:

   ```
   http://www.cisco.com/en/US/customer/products/sw/cscowork/ps3991/
   products_configuration_example09186a00801fc770.shtml#foursensor
   ```

   These procedures will assume that you named the file emailalert.pl. You may need to modify these instructions if you use a different name.

4. The script from Cisco is extensively documented internally with descriptions of the various sections. You may need to edit certain values to match your environment. One value that does need to be edited is the $EmailRcpt value near the top of the script. This variable represents the e-mail address of the person to whom the alarm should be e-mailed. Edit it to reflect the e-mail address you want to receive the alarm. Once you have finished editing the script, save it and open the Security Monitor.

HEADS UP!

Make sure you escape the @ symbol in the e-mail address by putting a backslash in front of it; otherwise, you'll get a Perl syntax error when the script attempts to run. For example, if you wanted to send the e-mail to user@yourco.com, you would enter it as user\@yourco.com.

5. Navigate to the Admin | Event Rules screen and click Add to build a new event rule, as described previously.

6. At the Identify the Rule screen, enter a rule name and description and then click Next.

7. At the Specify the Event Filter screen, select the filtering rules you want to use. For example, if you wanted to generate an e-mail alert for all high-severity events, you could select Severity and specify that it must be equal to a value of High. When you are finished, click Next.

8. At the Choose the Actions screen, check the box Execute a Script and then select the e-mail script file you defined in step 3. In the Arguments section, enter **"${Query}"** exactly as it is shown next. When you are finished, click Next.

9. At the Specify the Thresholds and Intervals screen, enter the appropriate values and click Finish.

10. The last step is to activate the event rule by selecting the rule and clicking Activate.

ONE STEP FURTHER

If you do not receive e-mail alerts, you can test blat to make sure it is working by typing the following:

```
Blat <filenamewithtext> -t <email address> -s "Test Message"
```

Blat will attempt to send the contents of the filename to the specified e-mail address. If this does not work, blat is not functioning properly. If it does work, you can test the Perl script by opening a command prompt and running the following command while in the $BASE\CSCOpx\MDC\etc\ids\scripts directory:

```
Emailalert.pl ${Query}
```

If you receive any path or Perl errors, verify that the script does not contain any typos. For example, verify that you entered the e-mail address using the backslash character (\) in front of the @ symbol.

Blocking Traffic Using Cisco IDS and Cisco PIX Firewalls

A nice feature that the Cisco IDS supports is the ability to integrate with Cisco devices and configure routers, switches, and PIX firewalls to block traffic that generates alarms on the IDS. This allows the IDS to provide some intrusion prevention functionality. Configuring blocking is a three-step process. The first step is to configure a logical device to provide the authentication parameters to use. You can do this by using the IDS Device Manager and navigating to the Configuration | Blocking | Logical Devices screen and clicking Add. At the Adding screen, enter the appropriate authentication values and click Apply to Sensor.

The second step is to configure blocking at the Configuration | Blocking | Blocking Devices screen by clicking Add to add a new blocking device. At the Adding screen, enter the IP address of the device you want to configure blocking on. Select the proper device type and communication method. When you are finished, click Apply to Sensor.

HEADS UP!

Although 3DES/SSH is more secure than Telnet, using 3DES/SSH requires that you configure a known host key for the remote device. To do this, you can run the command **ssh host-key <ipaddressofremotehost>** at the sensor CLI.

The third step is to configure the signatures on which you want to enable the block action by customizing them using the procedure previously described in this chapter. Navigate to the Configuration | Sensing Engine | Virtual Sensor Configuration | Signature Configuration Mode screen and edit the signature you want to modify. In the EventAction field, select shunHost or shunConnection, as shown next. When you are finished, click OK and commit the changes to the sensor.

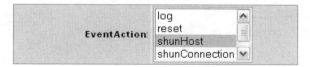

HEADS UP!

Be aware that configuring blocking using the shunHost option can result in a self-imposed denial of service in the event that the alarm is a false positive.

ONE STEP FURTHER

You can configure blocking with routers and Catalyst 6000 series switches as well by following most of these same procedures. In addition to the just process detailed, you will need to configure the blocking interface for the router or Catalyst 6000 series switch.

Summary

Intrusion detection and prevention, if implemented properly, has the ability to provide significant insight into what is happening on your network. If not implemented properly, however, it stands to be one of the largest wastes of money in your IT budget. The key to a successful IDS/IPS deployment is a realistic expectation of what the IDS/IPS is capable of and, most important, what it is not capable of.

To help ensure the success of your IDS/IPS deployment, we took a look at the IDS/IPS technologies and defined what each technology is and what it is capable of to ensure that you deploy it in accordance with its actual capabilities—not the marketing hype surrounding it.

Next, we took a look at how to harden your IDS/IPS sensors and management consoles to ensure that they cannot be used to exploit your network. Once the IDS/IPS devices had been properly secured, we took a look at how to effectively deploy the sensors throughout the network, including looking at the difference between detection and prevention. After that we examined the most time-consuming part of any IDS/IPS deployment—the tuning of the IDS/IPS to reduce the likelihood of false alarms. We finished up the chapter with a look at logging, alerting, and blocking with an IDS/IPS.

Chapter 5

Hardening VPN and Dial-in Remote Access

- Hardening VPN Connectivity
- Different VPN Connection Types and Technologies
- VPN Device-Hardening Methods
- Hardening IPsec-Based VPNs
- Hardening VPN Clients
- Hardening Dial-in Remote Access

Granting external access to a network has gone from the realm of the sporadic use of pcAnywhere and a modem on a desktop and dial-in remote access to run corporate applications to fully integrated enterprise networks using VPN connections across the Internet to grant full remote office connectivity.

A Virtual Private Network (VPN) involves the use of a public network infrastructure, such as the Internet, to provide remote user and remote site access to a corporate network via a secure connection. Security is provided through authentication and encryption techniques such as RADIUS, TACACS+, PPTP, L2TP, SSL, and IPsec to protect the data. A VPN typically involves taking the original data and encapsulating it within IP packets that are secured by the given VPN technology, such as IPsec.

As these external access technologies have matured, many companies have turned in particular to VPNs as a method to provide all manner of remote connectivity—from individual user access, to remote office networks' access to the corporate internetwork, to initial connections between companies after an acquisition, and even access between strategic business partners' resources and systems.

At the same time, this creates a security issue that must be addressed—namely, how can we provide the kinds of external access that our users require while ensuring that our network remains as hardened as possible. We are going to look at the unique issues of VPN connectivity and how it can be hardened. After that, we are going to look at providing traditional dial-in remote access connectivity and how those connections can be hardened.

Here are the hardware and software I provide specific configuration examples for in this chapter:

- A Cisco Secure VPN 3005 concentrator running Cisco Systems, Inc./VPN 3000 concentrator version 4.0.4.Rel Dec 4, 2003
- A Nortel Contivity 1100 extranet switch running version 4.80.124

Hardening VPN Connectivity

VPN connectivity is commonplace on most corporate networks today. The reason for this is simple. In many cases, the remote client or office already has an Internet connection, and this connection is often at broadband speeds or faster. As a result, instead of putting in an additional and more costly packet switched or dedicated point-to-point connection to provide access to the remote location, the company can establish a VPN connection across the Internet connection that they are already paying for and enjoy many of the same benefits that a packet switched or dedicated connection would provide. Sure, a downside exists in that there is no guaranteed service level for Internet-based connections, but in many cases the cost saving justifies the risk of downtime due to Internet-related outages.

At the same time, providing connections across the Internet introduces a huge security risk—namely that you are now passing private corporate data across the very public Internet. This allows an eavesdropper to potentially view or change your private data.

The technologies that define how VPNs operate address many of these risks through the use of authentication, encryption, and data integrity protocols; however, you can do certain things to ensure your data is as hardened as it possibly can be when traveling across a VPN. At the same time, you also have the risk associated with the need to place the device accepting the VPN connections in a position where it is exposed to the Internet. As with firewalls, this means that you must not only harden the VPN traffic itself from compromise, you also have to harden the VPN devices themselves. In our effort to harden our VPN connectivity, we are going to examine the following topics:

- Different VPN connection types and technologies
- VPN device-hardening methods
- Hardening IPsec-based VPNs
- Hardening VPN clients

Different VPN Connection Types and Technologies

Before we can explore how to harden VPNs, we must first take a look at the types of VPN connections and the VPN technologies that exist. Doing so will allow you to understand not only how you should implement your VPN connections from a design perspective, but will show you which VPN technologies provide you the most security.

Different VPN Connection Types

The two predominant VPN connection types are remote access VPNs and site-to-site VPNs. Remote access VPNs refer to connections that provide individual remote users access to the corporate network via their PC. For example, a user at a hotel using the hotel Internet connection may establish a tunnel over that Internet connection to the corporate network, allowing that user to access corporate resources. Another example, as shown in Figure 5-1, is a user at home telecommuting to the local office via a VPN connection through their dial-up or broadband Internet service provider.

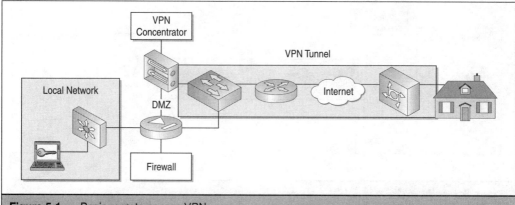

Figure 5-1.   Basic remote access VPN

Site-to-site VPNs refer to connections that provide access from an entire remote network, such as a small office or remote branch, to the corporate network through the use of gateway devices. Figure 5-2 shows a network diagram of a site-to-site VPN connection between a local and remote office.

Site-to-site VPN connections can be further broken down into intranet and extranet VPN connections. Intranet VPN connections refer to connections that are part of the same company (for example, a remote branch office). Extranet VPN connections refer to connections between a company and its business partners (for example, between a manufacturing company and their supplier). Extranet VPN connections are generally much more restrictive than intranet VPN connections, and they should only provide remote access to the specific resource or resources that the remote location requires.

Different VPN Technologies

Most devices today support four primary VPN technologies: Point-to-Point Tunneling Protocol (PPTP), Layer 2 Tunneling Protocol (L2TP), IPsec, and Secure Socket Layer (SSL) VPNs.

PPTP is considered a Layer 2 tunneling protocol because it operates at the Data Link layer of the OSI model. The benefit this provides is the ability to tunnel multiple protocols within the VPN tunnel. This allows you to tunnel IPX/SPX and TCP/IP within the same tunnel, for example. PPTP has some drawbacks, however. First, it is not based on an open standard but rather is a proprietary system developed in large part by Microsoft. Second, and more important, PPTP does not provide data encryption by itself, although later versions of PPTP provide some rudimentary data-encryption methods through the use of Microsoft Point-to-Point Encryption (MPPE). Third, PPTP has historically had security problems and has been exposed to significant security vulnerabilities. PPTPv1 was cracked in 1998 and, as a result, should not be used in any circumstances. PPTPv2, although it's much more secure than PPTPv1 and addresses

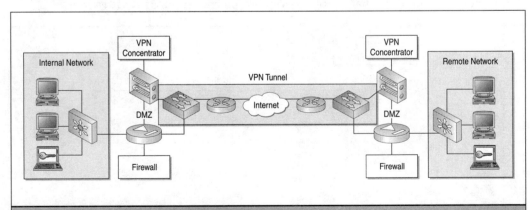

Figure 5-2.   Basic site-to-site VPN

many of the security flaws of PPTPv1, is still susceptible to password crackers such as L0phtcrack because key values in PPTP are a function of the user password. This allows a malicious user to gain access to the key values used to protect the data, and thus the data itself, by simply monitoring the network and then executing a dictionary hack using L0phtcrack against the challenge and response data. As a result, although PPTP is generally easier to deploy than other technologies due to being built into many Microsoft operating systems, I do not recommend implementing PPTP-based VPNs. Instead, to harden PPTP, you should use L2TP or IPsec for reasons I will explain in a moment.

L2TP is also considered a Layer 2 tunneling protocol and, in fact, is based on Microsoft's PPTP and Cisco's Layer 2 Forwarding (L2F) protocol, combining the best of both. L2TP provides for multiprotocol VPN tunnels, much like PPTP does, and is based on IETF open standards. Where L2TP differs, and is thus a better solution than PPTP, is the fact that it uses IPsec ESP for data encryption as well as supports more robust authentication methods. If you have to provide a multiprotocol VPN solution, you should use L2TP instead of PPTP.

IPsec is the de facto standard for providing purely IP-based VPN connections. IPsec is a Layer 3 protocol and, as a result, can only be used to tunnel TCP/IP-based traffic in a VPN. IPsec supports a couple of different methods of providing for data encryption, either using Authentication Header (AH) or Encapsulating Security Payload (ESP). IPsec supports multiple authentication and key protocols, although the most commonly used key protocol is the ISAKMP/Oakley protocol. IPsec also supports much more secure encryption methods, including 160-bit 3DES and 256-bit Advanced Encryption Standard (AES) encryption. In environments that do not require multiprotocol VPN support, you should only use IPsec for your VPN connections due to the increased security, better encryption, more robust authentication, and better scalability over PPTP and L2TP. The rest of this chapter will focus on IPsec because it provides the greatest security for our environments and is being used to harden L2TP.

The use of SSL VPNs is an emerging method of providing secure remote access to applications without deploying client VPN software. Most SSL VPNs use a web browser's built-in SSL functionality and Java or ActiveX controls to provide the remote application access. The obvious benefit to this is that you generally do not need to install any kind of client VPN software on the remote system. Your users can connect to your network from public kiosks or wireless hotspots and access the application while still enjoying data security and privacy. A drawback of this type of VPN is that most SSL VPNs require web-based applications in order to be used effectively. Although many companies are working at utilizing proxy servers to provide expanded access to legacy or client/server-based applications, this technology is still in its relative infancy.

Now, you might be reading this and thinking, "OK, but this sounds like what we do to provide secure e-mail access via a web-based e-mail interface," and in many ways you are correct. Some of the hype surrounding SSL VPNs is simply a new marketing spin of an old concept. However, as these application proxies as well as web-based remote access applications, such as Citrix and Microsoft Terminal Server, gain maturity, SSL VPNs will continue to expand beyond the traditional definitions and implementations.

VPN Device-Hardening Methods

Before we can look to harden the VPN tunnels themselves, we must first look at how to harden our VPN devices. The areas to focus on include the following:

- Hardening remote administration
- Implementing authentication and authorization
- Restricting services and protocols
- Providing redundancy and fault tolerance
- Hardening routing protocols

Hardening Remote Administration

Like firewalls, many VPN devices support multiple management protocols, including Telnet, SSH, HTTP, and HTTPS. As was demonstrated with firewalls, you should not use insecure protocols such as Telnet and HTTP to manage your devices. This is also true for your VPN devices. Only use SSH, HTTPS, or a similar encrypted protocol to manage your equipment. For example, with your Cisco VPN 3005, you can disable any management protocol via the web GUI by selecting the appropriate protocol from the Configuration | System | Management Protocols | HTTP/HTTPS screen and unchecking the Enable button.

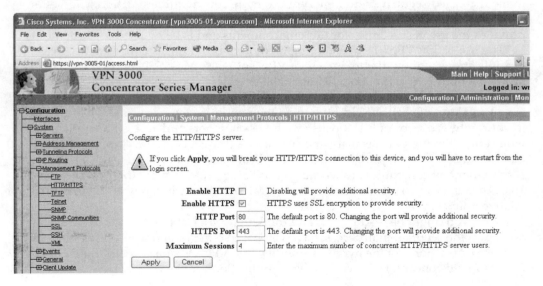

In this case, we have disabled HTTP access, only allowing HTTPS management access. You should enable only the secure management protocols you will use.

Your Nortel Contivity has similar functionality. A Nortel Contivity extranet switch supports HTTP, HTTPS, SNMP, FTP, and Telnet as management protocols. One notable protocol that it does not support is SSH. As a result, if you want to access the device via a CLI, you must use Telnet. Although this may sound like a drawback, the Contivity was designed around a web GUI, so most if not all the functionality you will need is in the GUI. Consequently, you should only manage your Contivity device via the secure web-based administration methods. On your Nortel Contivity VPN, you can configure your remote management protocols at the Services | Available | Services screen, as shown here:

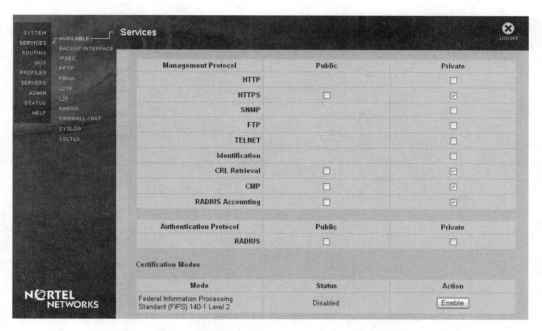

You can configure which protocols to support by checking or unchecking the appropriate check box. Because the public interface is inherently insecure, you cannot enable an insecure management protocol, which is a nice feature.

Configuring HTTPS support on your Nortel Contivity is a little bit more complex a process than on the Cisco VPN 3005 due to the fact that Cisco uses an internally generated certificate by default to allow HTTPS access. For the Nortel Contivity, you will need to configure certificates on the device before HTTPS access is allowed. The following steps detail this process:

1. In addition to checking HTTPS, as previously detailed, you must first ensure that the device name and DNS servers are configured properly at the System | Identity | System Identity screen, as shown here:

System Identity

| Management IP Address | 192.168.173.102 | (Web Management, FTP, etc. Subnet:255.255.255.224) |

Domain Identity

| DNS Host Name | norconvpn01 |
| DNS Domain Name | wjnconsulting.com |

DNS Server Configuration

DNS Proxy	☑ ENABLED	
Split DNS	☐ ENABLED	
Primary	192.168.173.100	Operational
Second Server	192.168.173.101	*Optional	Server not configured
Third Server	0.0.0.0	*Optional	Server not configured
Fourth Server	0.0.0.0	*Optional	Server not configured

2. Next, make sure your Contivity is configured with the appropriate date and time. You can do this at the System | Date & Time | Date and Time screen, as shown here:

Date	01/08/2004	(mm/dd/yyyy)
Time	12:58:06	(hh:mm:ss)
Day	THURSDAY	
Time Zone	(GMT -06:00) US Central	

[OK] [Cancel]

Configure Network Time Protocol

3. I also recommend that you configure the Network Time Protocol (NTP) to allow the Contivity to automatically update its time. You can do this by clicking Configure Network Time Protocol at the System | Date & Time | Date

and Time screen. At the System | Date & Time | Network Time Protocol screen, check the Enable box and add the appropriate NTP servers for your environment, as shown next:

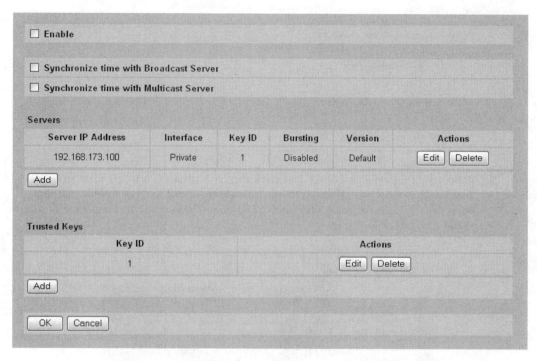

Ensure that you enable NTP authentication by configuring the appropriate key ID for increased security.

4. The next step is to configure the Contivity with a certificate authority trusted CA certificate. Using Microsoft Certificate Services, you can obtain the trusted CA certificate by selecting the Retrieve the CA Certificate or Certificate Revocation List radio button, as shown here:

Microsoft Certificate Services — furyondy.wjnconsulting.com   **Home**

Welcome

You use this web site to request a certificate for your web browser, e-mail client, or other secure program. Once you acquire a certificate, you will be able to securely identify yourself to other people over the web, sign your e-mail messages, encrypt your e-mail messages, and more depending upon the type of certificate you request.

Select a task:
  ⦿ Retrieve the CA certificate or certificate revocation list
  ○ Request a certificate
  ○ Check on a pending certificate

[Next >]

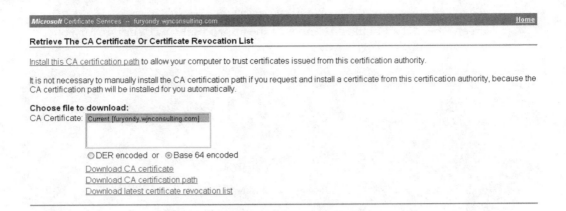

5. Then select Base 64 Encoded and click the Download CA Certificate button. You will be prompted to save the certificate to your local hard disk. After that, open the file using a text editor such as Microsoft Notepad and copy the contents of the file, as shown here:

6. Next, go to the System | Certificates | Certificate Configuration screen and click Import Tunnel or Transport Certificate, as shown here:

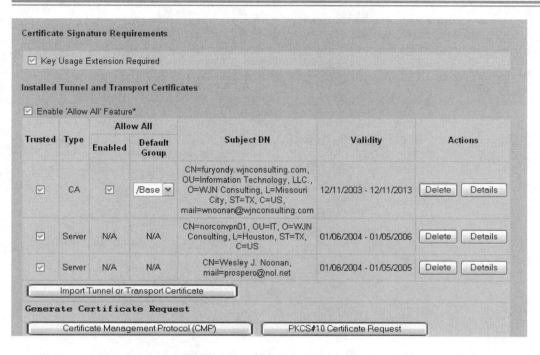

Certificate Signature Requirements

☑ Key Usage Extension Required

Installed Tunnel and Transport Certificates

☑ Enable 'Allow All' Feature*

Trusted	Type	Allow All		Subject DN	Validity	Actions	
		Enabled	Default Group				
☑	CA	☑	/Base ▾	CN=furyondy.wjnconsulting.com, OU=Information Technology, LLC., O=WJN Consulting, L=Missouri City, ST=TX, C=US, mail=wnoonan@wjnconsulting.com	12/11/2003 - 12/11/2013	Delete	Details
☑	Server	N/A	N/A	CN=norconvpn01, OU=IT, O=WJN Consulting, L=Houston, ST=TX, C=US	01/06/2004 - 01/05/2006	Delete	Details
☑	Server	N/A	N/A	CN=Wesley J. Noonan, mail=prospero@nol.net	01/06/2004 - 01/05/2005	Delete	Details

Import Tunnel or Transport Certificate

Generate Certificate Request

Certificate Management Protocol (CMP)   PKCS#10 Certificate Request

7. At the System | Certificates | Import Tunnel or Transport Certificate screen, paste the contents of the certificate file into the dialog box, select Trusted CA Certificate, and then click OK, as shown here:

Paste PKCS#7 Base-64 Certificate encoding into input box below

○ Server Certificate
◉ Trusted CA Certificate

```
UkxEaXNOcmlidXRpb25Qb21udDBRoE+gTYZLaHROcDovL2Z1cn1vbmR5LndqbmN
v
bnN1bHRpbmcuY29tL0N1cnRFbnJvbGwvZnVyeW9uZHkud2puY29uc3VsdGluZy5
j
b20uY3JsMBAGCSsGAQQBgjcVAQQDAgEAMA0GCSqGSIb3DQEBBQUAA0EA2nkDTQA
4
OhcMTcJUpcc5c6lomfD4ZmoMaKdKo6eJf1G/C5SIGjMWUScJqVz1AiDBFwg+f6R
e
MGhM06DrniVwWg==
-----END CERTIFICATE-----|
```

LDAP (SSL) CA certificate are installed via: Servers LDAP

OK   Cancel

Make sure that the Trusted and Enabled check boxes are selected for your CA certificate.

8. The next step is to generate a certificate for the Contivity using the CA you added. You can do this by clicking PKCS#10 Certificate Request at the System | Certificates | Certificate Configuration screen. This will take you to the System | Certificates | Certification Request – PKCS#10 screen, as shown here:

Create New Key and Certificate Request

Common Name (e.g. Entrust Reference #)	norconvpn01.wjnconsul
Organizational Unit (e.g. Finance)	IT
Organization (e.g. ACME Networks)	WJN Consulting, LLC.
Locality (e.g. Norfolk County)	Houston
State/Province (e.g. MA)	TX
Country (e.g. US)	US
Public Key Size	1024

OK   Cancel

Fill in the request with the appropriate information. Make sure that you use the correct system name and use a public key size of at least 1024 for security purposes. When this screen is complete, click OK.

9. You will be presented with the System | Certificates | Certification Request screen, as shown here:

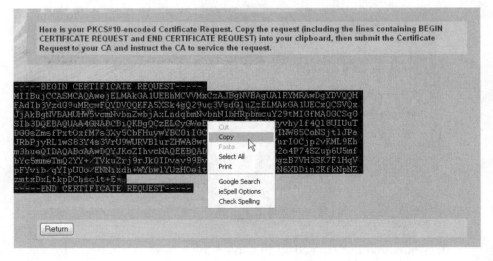

Here is your PKCS#10-encoded Certificate Request. Copy the request (including the lines containing BEGIN CERTIFICATE REQUEST and END CERTIFICATE REQUEST) into your clipboard, then submit the Certificate Request to your CA and instruct the CA to service the request.

Highlight the certificate request data and copy it. Click the Return button to return to the System | Certificates | Certificate Configuration screen.

10. The next step is to request a new certificate from your CA. For Microsoft Certificate Services, you can do this by selecting Request a Certificate, as shown here:

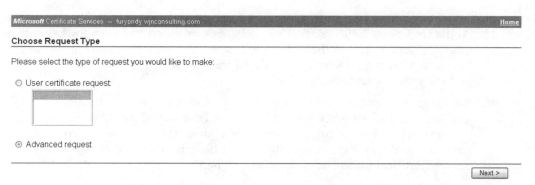

11. At the Choose Request Type screen, select the Advanced Request radio button and click next.

12. At the Advanced Certificate Requests screen, select the option Submit a Certificate Request Using a Base 64 Encoded PKCS #10 File or a Renewal Request Using a Base 64 Encoded PKCS #7 File. Then click Next.

13. At the Submit a Saved Request screen, paste the certificate data into the Saved Request section, select Web Server from the Certificate Template drop-down list, and click Submit, as shown here:

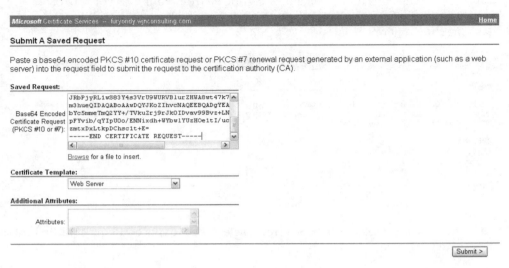

14. At the Certificate Issued screen, select Base 64 Encoded and click the Download CA Certificate button. When prompted, save the certificate to an appropriate location. After that, open the file using a text editor such as Microsoft Notepad and copy the contents of the file.

15. Return to the Contivity and, at the System | Certificates | Certificate Configuration screen, click Import Tunnel or Transport Certificate. At the System | Certificates | Import Tunnel or Transport Certificate screen, paste the contents of the certificate request file into the text field, select Server Certificate, and click OK, as shown here:

At this point, your certificate configuration should appear as follows:

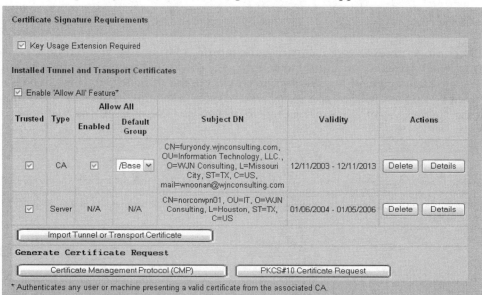

Make sure your CA certificate has the Trusted and Enabled boxes checked. Make sure that your server certificate has the Trusted box checked.

16. The final step is to configure SSL/TLS to use the certificate for authentication. This is performed at the Services | SSLTLS | SSL screen, as shown here:

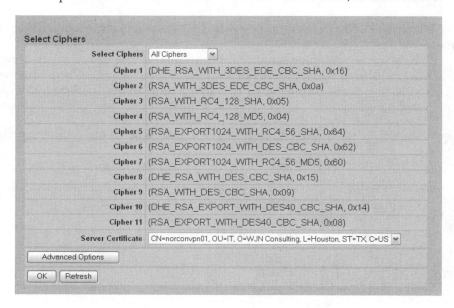

Simply select the server certificate from the drop-down list, enable your ciphers, and click OK. You should be able to connect to the Contivity using HTTPS at this time.

In addition to restricting the management protocols allowed, you should also restrict what systems can connect to and manage the VPN device by permitting only designated management workstations to connect to the VPN device. This can be done on your Cisco VPN 3005 by specifying a manager workstation in the Administration | Access Rights | Access Control List screen of the web GUI, as demonstrated here:

Administration | Access Rights | Access Control List

Save Needed

This section presents administrator access control list options. Only those IP addresses listed will have access to manage this VPN 3000 Concentrator. If no addresses are listed, then anybody with the proper username/password combination can access this VPN 3000 Concentrator. If you do not add your IP address to the list first, you will be unable to access this VPN 3000 Concentrator.

Manager Workstations

192.168.173.107/255.255.255.255 Group=5

Actions

Add
Modify
Delete
Move Up
Move Down

The Nortel Contivity lacks the ability to restrict management workstations in this manner.

Another aspect of hardening remote administration is to specify a session timeout value as well as the maximum number of sessions allowed. You can configure these on the Cisco VPN 3005 at the Administration | Access Rights | Access Settings screen, as demonstrated here:

Administration | Access Rights | Access Settings

This section presents General Access options.

Session Idle Timeout 300   (seconds) Enter the administrative session idle timeout. Limit is 1800 seconds.

Session Limit 2   Enter the maximum number of administrative sessions.

⊙ RC4
Config File Encryption ○ None Select configuration file encryption.
○ DES

Apply   Cancel

In this case, I have specified a Session Idle Timeout value of 300 seconds (5 minutes). I also specified two administrative sessions so that if, for some reason, an administrative session locks up, I can connect via a different session. I recommend that you allow only two administrative sessions to reduce the likelihood of multiple administrators interfering with each other. Finally, I have specified that the config file should be encrypted for an additional measure of security.

For the Nortel Contivity, you can specify idle timeout configuration at the Admin | Administrator | Administrator screen, as shown here:

The default is 15 minutes. In this example, I have configured a 5-minute timeout value and applied that timeout to the serial (hard console) connection as well as the remote administrative connections.

Implementing Authentication and Authorization

Another aspect of hardening your VPN devices is to only allow authenticated users to manage each device and to ensure that they are only authorized to run the appropriate commands. Avoid using common usernames and passwords and instead implement individual usernames. For example, Cisco and Nortel both ship with a default username of "admin." You should change this username for the same reasons you change the administrator account name on Microsoft Windows. If someone is trying to hack your VPN device, they are always going to start by using default usernames. In addition, your passwords should conform to your environment's password security policy, requiring at a minimum the use of alphanumeric characters, special characters, and upper- and lowercase characters.

For additional scalability and security, you can implement an AAA server to authenticate your users and authorize the commands they can run. We will discuss AAA mechanisms in more detail in Chapter 9.

For a Cisco VPN 3005 concentrator, this is a two-step process that requires you to first specify what the AAA access level is for a user at the Administration | Access Rights | Administrators | Modify Properties screen, as demonstrated here:

Administration | Access Rights | Administrators | Modify Properties

This section lets you modify the properties for administrators. Any changes you make take effect immediately.

Username admin	
Password ●●●●●●●●●●●●	A password is required.
Verify ●●●●●●●●●●●●	The password must be verified.
Access Rights	
Authentication Modify Config ⌄	
General Modify Config ⌄	
SNMP Modify Config ⌄	
Files Read/Write Files ⌄	Includes Configuration Files
AAA Access Level 15 ⌄	Select the Privilege Level for this administrator. An administrator logging in using AAA will need to have a Privilege Level equal to one of the administrators.

[Apply] [Default] [Cancel]

In this case, we have granted the user full command authorization by specifying access level 15. The next step is to specify the appropriate TACACS+ server to use for administrative user authentication at the Administration | Access Rights | AAA Servers | Authentication | Add screen, as demonstrated here:

Administration | Access Rights | AAA Servers | Authentication | Add

Configure and add a TACACS+ administrator authentication server.

Authentication Server 192.168.1.100		Enter IP address or hostname.
Server Port 0		Enter the server TCP port number (0 for default).
Timeout 4		Enter the timeout for this server (seconds).
Retries 2		Enter the number of retries for this server.
Server Secret ●●●●●●●		Enter the server secret.
Verify ●●●●●●●		Re-enter the server secret.

[Add] [Cancel]

The Nortel Contivity does not support using any kind of external authentication for administrative users. Instead, you can define additional administrators as a function of the user properties at the Profiles | Users | User Management --> Edit User screen, as shown here:

Locality
State/Province
Email Address

○ Full   Full Distinguished Name

Subject Alternative Name   **Subject Alternative Name Type** Email Name

Local Identity
   Server Certificate
   (Inherit server certificate from group)

Administration Privileges

	User ID	Password	Confirm Password
Admin	wnoonan	••••••••••••••••	••••••••••••••••

Admin Rights   Manage Switch Manage ∨ Manage Users Manage ∨ /Base ∨

[OK]   [Cancel]

A note of caution when configuring external AAA for your device: Where possible, you should have at least one emergency local account with some impossibly difficult password that only a few select people know in case the AAA server is unavailable (failure, DoS, network problems, and so on). This is to be used only as a last resort, not for day-to-day activities. This will prevent a situation where a network problem is keeping you from getting to the AAA server and being able to get into your own routers to fix the problem because you can't authenticate.

Restricting Services and Protocols

Restricting the services and protocols running on your VPN device is one of the best methods for hardening it, especially if you have a dedicated VPN device. Your VPN device should only run the minimum protocols required for it to be able to accept and terminate VPN connections, especially on the external interfaces.

Removing Unnecessary Tunneling Protocols   Many VPN devices are configured to accept all three connection methods—PPTP, L2TP, and IPsec—by default. If you only require IPsec, you should disable the other connection types. To disable PPTP on your Cisco

VPN 3005, you can uncheck Enabled at the Configuration | System | Tunneling Protocols | PPTP screen, as shown here:

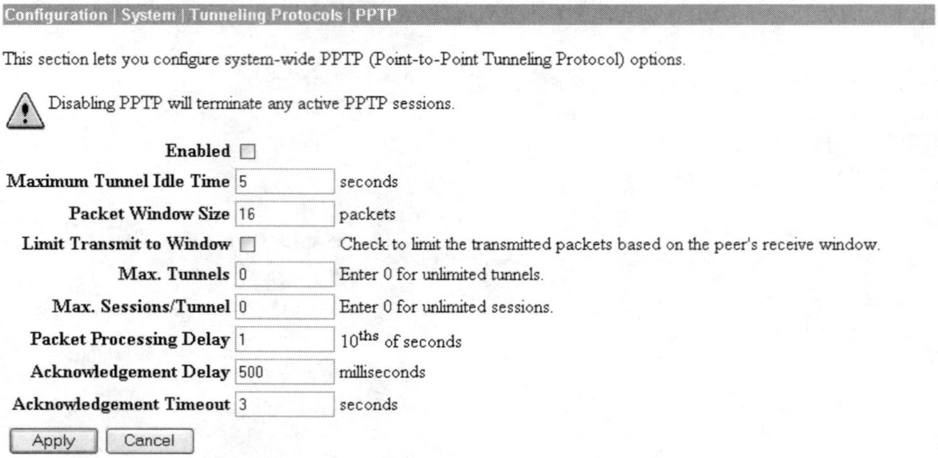

Configuration	System	Tunneling Protocols	PPTP

This section lets you configure system-wide PPTP (Point-to-Point Tunneling Protocol) options.

⚠ Disabling PPTP will terminate any active PPTP sessions.

Enabled	☐	
Maximum Tunnel Idle Time	5	seconds
Packet Window Size	16	packets
Limit Transmit to Window	☐	Check to limit the transmitted packets based on the peer's receive window.
Max. Tunnels	0	Enter 0 for unlimited tunnels.
Max. Sessions/Tunnel	0	Enter 0 for unlimited sessions.
Packet Processing Delay	1	10^{ths} of seconds
Acknowledgement Delay	500	milliseconds
Acknowledgement Timeout	3	seconds

[Apply] [Cancel]

Repeat this step for L2TP if you want to disable it as well.

The Nortel Contivity uses a central screen for enabling and disabling many protocols and services. You can remove a tunneling protocol from being supported on an interface by unchecking the relevant protocol at the Services | Available | Services screen, as shown here:

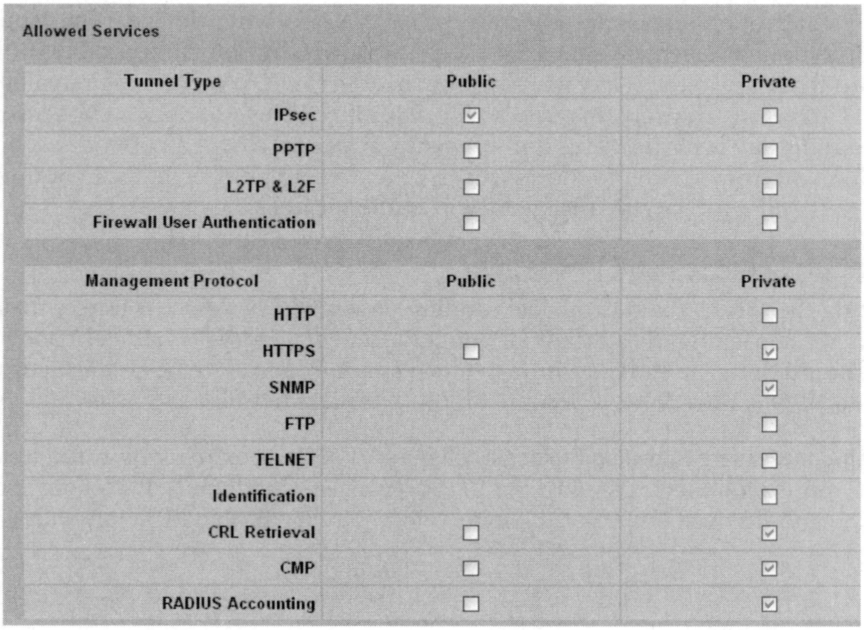

Allowed Services

Tunnel Type	Public	Private
IPsec	☑	☐
PPTP	☐	☐
L2TP & L2F	☐	☐
Firewall User Authentication	☐	☐

Management Protocol	Public	Private
HTTP		☐
HTTPS	☐	☑
SNMP		☑
FTP		☐
TELNET		☐
Identification		☐
CRL Retrieval	☐	☑
CMP	☐	☑
RADIUS Accounting	☐	☑

In this case, I am allowing only IPsec, and only on the external interface.

Removing Unnecessary Security Associations and IKE Proposals   In addition to disabling unnecessary tunneling protocols, you should also disable or remove any security associations (SAs) and IKE proposals you are not actively using. This allows you to limit your connections to the more secure connection options, such as using 3DES and SHA-1, as well as to prevent someone from inadvertently connecting using a protocol that you do not want to permit. You can remove unnecessary SAs on your Cisco VPN 3005 at the Configuration | Policy Management | Traffic Management | Security Associations screen, as shown here:

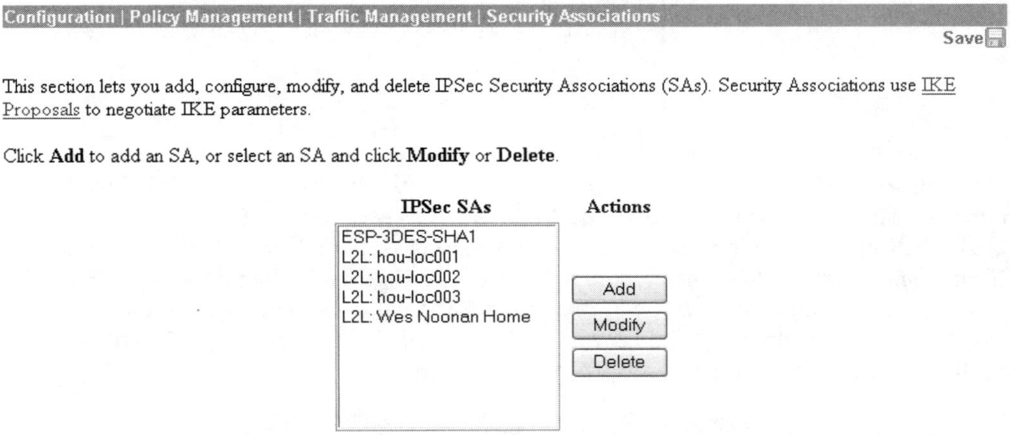

Configuration | Policy Management | Traffic Management | Security Associations

Save🖫

This section lets you add, configure, modify, and delete IPSec Security Associations (SAs). Security Associations use IKE Proposals to negotiate IKE parameters.

Click **Add** to add an SA, or select an SA and click **Modify** or **Delete**.

                              IPSec SAs   **Actions**

                    ESP-3DES-SHA1
                    L2L: hou-loc001
                    L2L: hou-loc002   Add
                    L2L: hou-loc003   Modify
                    L2L: Wes Noonan Home   Delete

In this example, I am only allowing the SAs associated with active VPN connections that are in use or will be in use. You can add or remove SAs by clicking the appropriate button.

To remove unnecessary IKE proposals on your Cisco VPN 3005, go to the Configuration | System | Tunneling Protocols | IPSec | IKE Proposals screen and deactivate any unnecessary proposals, as demonstrated next.

Save 🖫

Add, delete, prioritize, and configure IKE Proposals.

Select an **Inactive Proposal** and click **Activate** to make it **Active**, or click **Modify**, **Copy** or **Delete** as appropriate.
Select an **Active Proposal** and click **Deactivate** to make it **Inactive**, or click **Move Up** or **Move Down** to change its priority.
Click **Add** or **Copy** to add a new **Inactive Proposal**. IKE Proposals are used by Security Associations to specify IKE parameters.

Active Proposals	Actions	Inactive Proposals
IKE-3DES-MD5	<< Activate	IKE-DES-MD5
IKE-3DES-SHA1	Deactivate >>	IKE-3DES-MD5-RSA
	Move Up	IKE-3DES-SHA-DSA
	Move Down	IKE-3DES-MD5-DH1
	Add	IKE-3DES-MD5-RSA-DH1
	Modify	IKE-3DES-MD5-DH7
		IKE-DES-MD5-DH7
		CiscoVPNClient-3DES-MD5-RSA
		CiscoVPNClient-3DES-SHA-DSA
		CiscoVPNClient-3DES-MD5

In this example, I am only allowing two IKE proposals that support MD5 for legacy interoperability purposes only because MD5 is not as secure as SHA-1.

The Nortel Contivity refers to security associations as *encryption* and IKE proposals as *IKE encryption and Diffie-Hellman group*. Both can be configured at the Services | IPSec | IPSec Settings screen shown next. Simply uncheck the values you do not want to use. In this case, I am only allowing AES 128 and 3DES with SHA-1 for my encryption protocol and 3DES with Diffie-Hellman group 2 for my IKE proposal.

Encryption

ESP - AES 128 with SHA1 Integrity	☑
ESP - Triple DES with SHA1 Integrity	☑
ESP - Triple DES with MD5 Integrity	☐
ESP - 56-bit DES with SHA1 Integrity	☐
ESP - 56-bit DES with MD5 Integrity	☐
ESP - 40-bit DES with SHA1 Integrity	☐
ESP - 40-bit DES with MD5 Integrity	☐
ESP - NULL (Authentication Only) with SHA1 Integrity	☐
ESP - NULL (Authentication Only) with MD5 Integrity	☐
AH - Authentication Only (HMAC-SHA1)	☐
AH - Authentication Only (HMAC-MD5)	☐

IKE Encryption and Diffie-Hellman Group

56-bit DES with Group 1 (768-bit prime)	☐
Triple DES with Group 2 (1024-bit prime)	☑
Triple DES with Group 7 (ECC 163-bit field)	☐
AES 128 with Group 5 (1536-bit prime)	☐
AES 128 with Group 8 (ECC 283-bit field)	☐

Assigning Filtering Rules to Interfaces   Among the most important hardening steps you can perform with your VPN devices is to filter the traffic that is permitted on any given interface. Your VPN devices exist for one purpose—to accept and terminate VPN tunnels using only the protocols you have defined. As a result, you should permit only the traffic directly related to tunnel establishment and termination and deny every other protocol and port number. Many VPN devices ship with HTTP, ICMP, and every VPN tunnel protocol enabled by default on the external interface. This is a security oversight on the part of the vendors. It is what I like to call "lowest common denominator" development. The vendors have no idea what protocols you require, so they permit anywhere from a few protocols to all protocols to make it easy to connect. You should review what protocols your vendor has enabled by default and filter out all unnecessary protocols. You can do this for your Cisco VPN 3005 at the Configuration | Policy Management | Traffic Management | Assign Rules to Filter screen, as demonstrated next.

Configuration | Policy Management | Traffic Management | Assign Rules to Filter

Save 💾

Add, remove, prioritize, and configure rules that apply to a filter.

Filter Name: Public (High Security)

Select an **Available Rule** and click **Add** to apply it to this filter.
Select a **Current Rule in Filter** and click **Remove, Move Up, Move Down,** or **Assign SA to Rule** as appropriate.
Select an **Available Rule,** then select a **Current Rule in Filter,** and click **Insert Above** to add the available rule above the current rule.

Current Rules in Filter	Actions	Available
L2L: hou-loc001 In (IPSec/L2L: hou-loc001/in)	<< Add	GRE In (forward/in)
L2L: hou-loc002 In (IPSec/L2L: hou-loc002/in)	<< Insert Above	GRE Out (forward/out)
L2L: Wes Noonan Home In (IPSec/L2L: Wes Noonan Home/in)	<< Insert Above	PPTP In (forward/in)
L2L: hou-loc003 In (IPSec/L2L: hou-loc003/in)	Remove >>	PPTP Out (forward/out)
IPSEC-ESP In (forward/in)	Remove >>	L2TP In (forward/in)
IKE In (forward/in)	Move Up	L2TP Out (forward/out)
NAT-T In (forward/in)	Move Up	ICMP In (forward/in)
L2L: hou-loc001 Out (IPSec/L2L: hou-loc001/out)	Move Down	ICMP Out (forward/out)
L2L: hou-loc002 Out (IPSec/L2L: hou-loc002/out)	Move Down	RIP In (forward/in)
L2L: Wes Noonan Home Out (IPSec/L2L: Wes Noonan Home/out)	Assign SA to Rule	RIP Out (forward/out)
L2L: hou-loc003 Out (IPSec/L2L: hou-loc003/out)		OSPF In (forward/in)

In this example, I am permitting only the traffic from my remote LAN-to-LAN VPN sites as well as IPsec, IKE, and NAT-T (to support IPsec NAT traversal) to support my remote access VPN connections. If any other protocol is used to connect to the external interface, it will be dropped by the VPN device. You can add or remove the permitted protocols by selecting each protocol and using the appropriate button.

The Nortel Contivity uses a slightly different filtering methodology than the Cisco VPN 3005. The Cisco VPN 3005 filters based on protocol rules for all protocols. The Nortel Contivity, however, only supports basic port filtering rules using TCP, UDP, ICMP, and IP by default.

The Nortel Contivity also supports two types of filters: a tunnel filter and an interface filter. You can configure your filters in either location, as you deem appropriate, and can copy a filter between the two filtering types with the click of a button. You can configure additional ports and protocols to be supported for filtering at the Profiles | Filters | Interface Filters --> Rules --> Create screen by selecting to modify the protocol or port, as shown here:

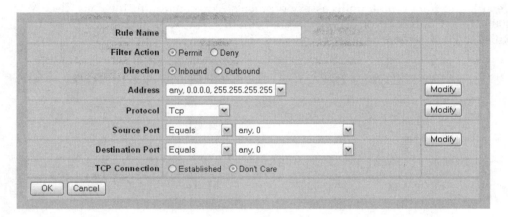

By default, the Nortel Contivity will accept all protocols. Because of the way the Nortel Contivity is designed, you would need to add individual "permit" and "deny" rules for all protocols other than TCP, UDP, ICMP, and IP that you want to control. For example, if you only wanted to allow ESP (protocol 50) and IKE (UDP port 500), you would need to create a permit rule allowing ESP and IKE, then a deny protocol rule for all the other (254) protocols, with the exception of TCP, UDP, ICMP, and IP, which are created by default. It is impractical to demonstrate the adding of all the protocols that would need to be denied, but a high-security filter that allows only ESP and IKE might be configured to only permit ESP and IKE and deny every other protocol that you added, including the default protocols of IP, TCP, UDP, and ICMP.

Providing Redundancy and Fault Tolerance

As with many devices, you can harden your VPN devices against failure by implementing a redundant and fault-tolerant configuration. The benefit of this type of implementation is the ability to continue to accept incoming VPN tunnels in the event of a device failure. This is done by implementing multiple VPN devices in a pool on your network, as shown in Figure 5-3.

Cisco utilizes Virtual Router Redundancy Protocol (VRRP) to provide VPN redundancy. VRRP can be configured at the Configuration | System | IP Routing | Redundancy screen of your VPN device, as shown here:

Configuration | System | IP Routing | Redundancy

Configure the Virtual Router Redundancy Protocol (VRRP) for your system. **All interfaces that you want to configure VRRP on should already be configured**. If you later configure an additional interface, you need to revisit this screen.

Enable VRRP	☑	Check to enable VRRP.
Group ID	1	Enter the Group ID for this set of redundant routers.
Group Password	vrrppassword	Enter the shared group password, or leave blank for no password.
Role	Master ▾	Select the Role for this system within the group.
Advertisement Interval	1	Enter the Advertisement interval (seconds).
Group Shared Addresses		
1 (Private)	192.168.1.124	
2 (Public)	192.168.198.171	

[Apply] [Cancel]

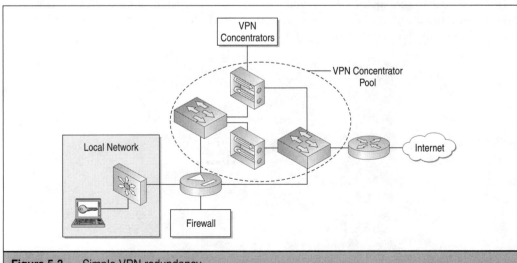

Figure 5-3.   Simple VPN redundancy

In this case, I have defined this system as the master role in the VRRP group. I would configure the remaining systems as backup roles, ensuring that the rest of the settings are the same on all systems. Although the password is displayed in clear text in the management console—which is not a very secure implementation on Cisco's part—you should use a password to ensure that only VPN devices that share a common password will join the VRRP pool.

The Nortel Contivity also supports VRRP for redundancy. The first step is to create an interface group at the Routing | Interface GRP | Interface Group --> Add, screen as shown here:

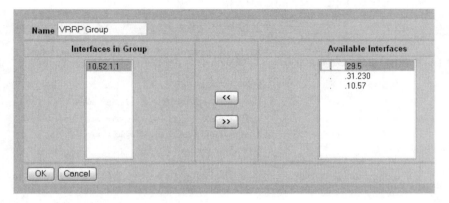

The next step is to enable and configure VRRP at the Routing | VRRP | VRRP screen by checking to enable VRRP and adding the relevant address. When you click Create for the IP address, you will be taken to the Routing | VRRP | VRRP --> Create VRRP IP Address screen, as shown next. Select the appropriate VRID, select to use simple authentication, and enter the authentication data. Notice how Nortel, unlike Cisco, masks this data onscreen.

The final step is configure VRRP on the interface by going to the Routing |
Interfaces | Routing Interfaces screen and clicking Configure. This will take you to the
Routing | Interfaces | Routing Interfaces --> Configure VRRP screen, as shown next.
Configure your system to enable VRRP, and with the appropriate master status. If this
is the master device, make sure you have selected the appropriate group, selected to
serve as the master, and enabled the administrative state.

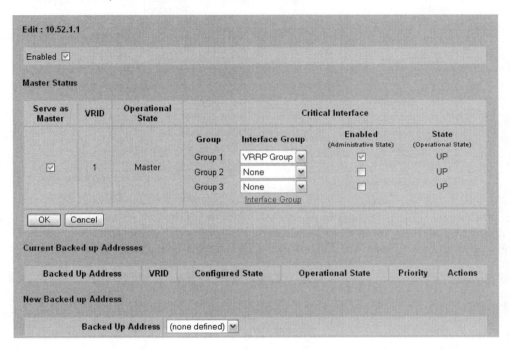

Hardening Routing Protocols

Like your routers, it may be necessary for your VPN device to be able to route data.
As we previously discussed with firewalls, static routing is the most secure method to
provide routing information due to the fact that the device is not susceptible to invalid
route statements. If you do require the use of a routing protocol, however, you should
only use routing protocols that support authentication, such as RIP version 2, OSPF,
and BGP, to ensure that they only accept route updates from authorized partners. The
Cisco VPN 3005 only supports OSPF as an authenticated routing protocol; therefore, I
recommend that you only use OSPF. You can configure OSPF for the interface at the

Configuration | Interfaces | Interface screen (in this case, the Ethernet 1 interface), as demonstrated here:

Configuring Ethernet Interface 1 (Private).

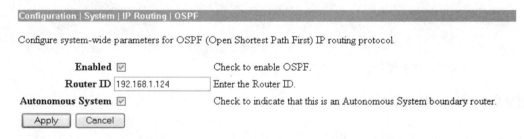

| General | RIP | OSPF | Bandwidth |

OSPF Parameters		
Attribute	**Value**	**Description**
OSPF Enabled	☑	Check to enable OSPF on this interface.
OSPF Area ID	0.0.0.0	Enter the OSPF Area ID for this interface. The format is the same as an IP address.
OSPF Priority	1	Enter the OSPF Priority for this interface.
OSPF Metric	1	Enter the OSPF Metric for this interface.
OSPF Retransmit Interval	5	Enter the OSPF Retransmit Interval for this interface.
OSPF Hello Interval	10	Enter the OSPF Hello Interval for this interface.
OSPF Dead Interval	40	Enter the OSPF Dead Interval for this interface.
OSPF Transit Delay	1	Enter the OSPF Transit Delay for this interface.
OSPF Authentication	MD5	Select the OSPF Authentication method to use.
OSPF Password	ospfkey	Enter the OSPF Password when *Simple Password* or *MD5* is selected above.

In this case, I have selected to use an MD5 hash with the key value "ospfkey" to authenticate with my other OSPF-enabled devices. The next step is to enable OSPF at the Configuration | System | IP Routing | OSPF screen, as demonstrated here:

Configuration | System | IP Routing | OSPF

Configure system-wide parameters for OSPF (Open Shortest Path First) IP routing protocol.

Enabled ☑   Check to enable OSPF.

Router ID 192.168.1.124   Enter the Router ID.

Autonomous System ☑   Check to indicate that this is an Autonomous System boundary router.

[Apply]   [Cancel]

In this case, I have configured the VPN device as an autonomous system boundary router so that it will update the OSPF routing tables with the remote LAN-to-LAN subnets. Note that Cisco displays the password in clear text in the console, so you should ensure that no one is looking over your shoulder while you configure this.

The Nortel Contivity supports RIP and OSPF as routing protocols. Configuring RIP is a two-step process. First, you need to enable RIP. This can be done at the Routing | RIP | RIP screen, as shown next.

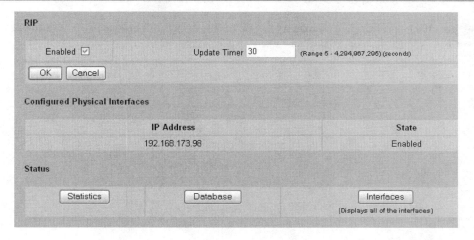

The next step is to configure RIP on the interface at the Routing | Interfaces | Routing Interfaces screen. Click Configure and you will be taken to the Configure RIP screen. You should make sure that you only use RIP version 2 and that you select to use MD5 authentication and specify the appropriate secret, as shown here:

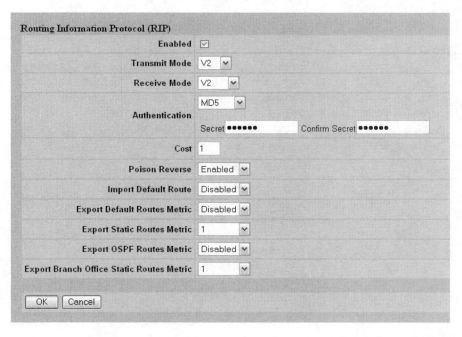

Configuring OSPF on your Nortel Contivity is very similar to configuring RIP. First you want to enable OSPF at the Routing | OSPF | OSPF screen, as shown next.

Make sure that you add the necessary OSPF areas, configure the appropriate router ID, and set the AS-Boundary-Router value as appropriate for your environment.

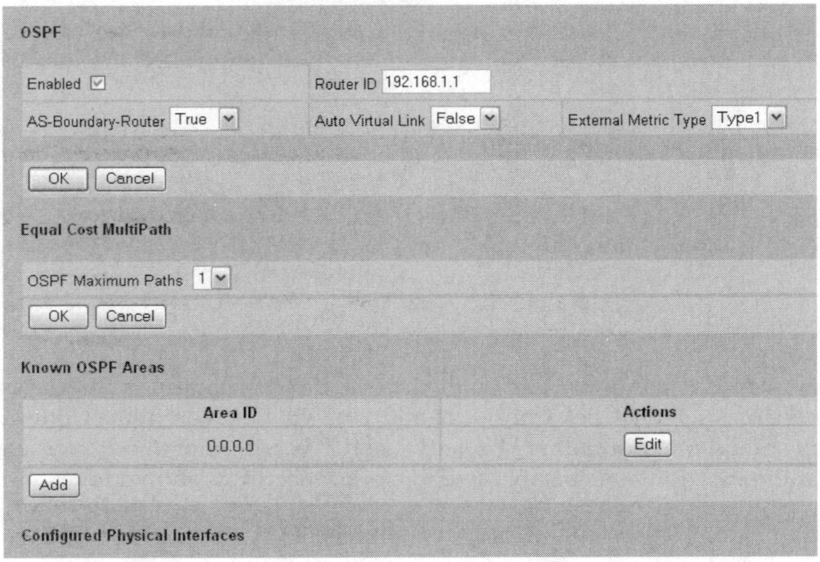

The next step is to configure OSPF on the interface at the Routing | Interface | Routing Interfaces screen. Click Configure and you will be taken to the Configure OSPF screen. Configure OSPF, as shown next, making sure that you select MD5 authentication and enter the appropriate key ID and key value as well as any other configuration requirements for your environment.

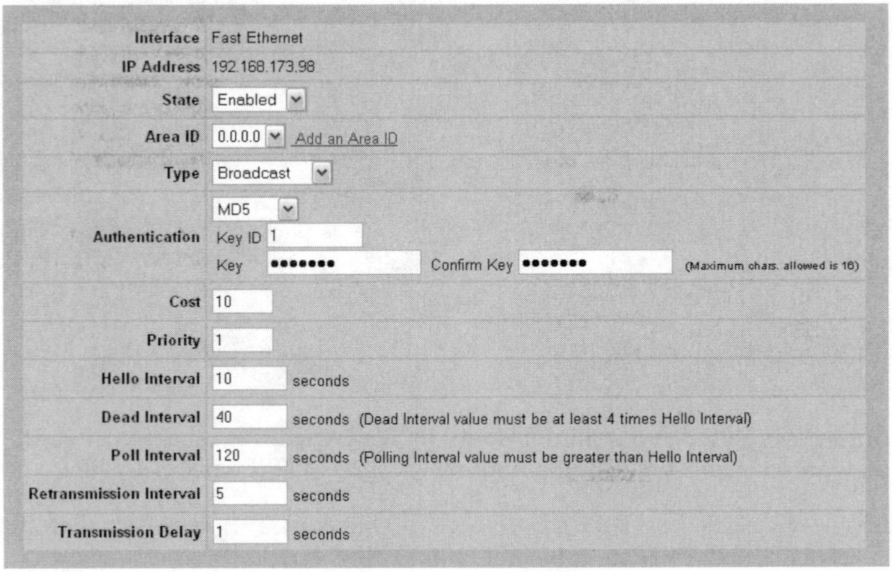

Hardening IPsec-Based VPNs

As previously mentioned, you should not implement PPTP-based VPNs because they are not as secure as the alternatives. If you need to support multiple protocols across your VPN, you should use L2TP. Although L2TP is more secure than PPTP, it is less secure than an IPsec-based VPN can be configured, as shown previously. The nice thing about this, however, is that L2TP supports IPsec ESP encapsulation, thereby providing all the functionality of L2TP with all the encryption and security of IPsec. L2TP is encapsulated with an IPsec ESP session/tunnel. You can enable this on your Cisco VPN 3005 concentrator at the Configuration | User Management | Groups | Modify <Group or Username> screen on the General tab in the "Tunneling Protocols" section, as shown next:

Secondary WINS		☑	Enter the IP address of the secondary WINS server.
Tunneling Protocols	☐ PPTP ☐ L2TP ☐ IPSec ☑ L2TP over IPSec	☐	Select the tunneling protocols this group can connect with.
Strip Realm	☐	☑	Check to remove the realm qualifier of the username during authentication.

On your Nortel Contivity, you can enable L2TP over IPsec as a part of your group configuration settings. The first step is to configure IPsec to provide transport mode connections. This is enabled by default, but it can be configured at the Profiles | Groups | Groups --> Edit --> IPSec screen, as shown here:

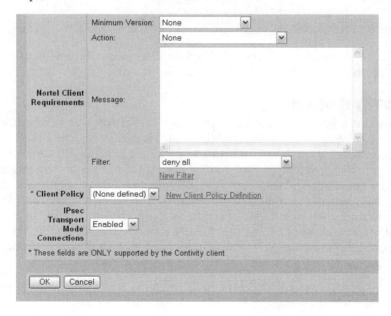

The next step is to configure your L2TP settings to use IPsec. This can be done at the user or group configuration screen. The benefit of configuring these settings at the group level is the ability to effectively modify the functionality of multiple users. This can be done at the Profiles | Groups | Groups --> Edit --> L2TP screen, as shown next. Select the appropriate IPsec data protection level (I recommend Triple DES due to the increased security) and make sure that the appropriate group is selected for the Require IPsec Transport Mode Connections From data field.

Field	Value
Authentication	MS-CHAP: ☐V1 ☑V2 ☐Not Encrypted ☐RC4-40 ☑RC4-128 CHAP: ☑ PAP: ☐ (NOTE: PAP passwords are sent in the clear)
Compression	Enabled ▾
Use Client Specified Address	Disabled ▾
Primary DNS	
Secondary DNS	
Primary WINS	
Secondary WINS	
Minimum IPsec Data Protection Level	Triple DES ▾
Require IPsec Transport Mode Connections from	/Base ▾

Because L2TP supports being tunneled within IPsec, we will now focus on hardening IPsec-based VPNs to protect your environment.

Traffic Security Protocols

IPsec uses two traffic security protocols to provide data security: Authentication Header (AH) and Encapsulating Security Payload (ESP). AH is defined in RFCs 1826 and 2402 and provides authentication, integrity, and anti-replaying functionality. Figure 5-4 shows the format of an AH-formatted packet. Notice that AH simply splits the original IP header and transport header and inserts the AH information between them. A major drawback of AH, however, is that it does not encrypt the data contents and therefore provides no data confidentiality. AH also does not support functioning in a NAT environment because when NAT changes the IP header, it invalidates the AH signature checksum. You should not use AH because it does not encrypt the original data.

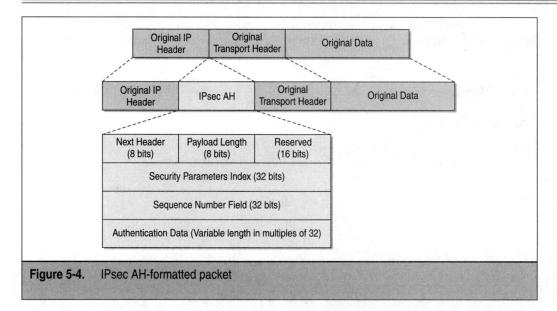

Figure 5-4.   IPsec AH-formatted packet

ESP, on the other hand, provides for authentication, integrity, and anti-replaying functionality as well as for data confidentiality by encrypting the original packet's data contents. As you can see in Figure 5-5, ESP actually encapsulates the original transport header and data between an ESP header and trailer. This causes the original data to be encrypted as an encapsulated payload within the ESP header and trailer. ESP also functions within a NAT environment through the use of NAT Transparency (sometimes referred to as *NAT Traversal).*

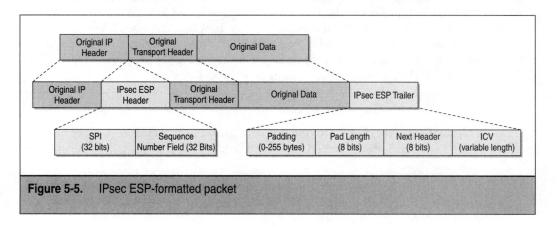

Figure 5-5.   IPsec ESP-formatted packet

You can enable NAT Traversal functionality on your Cisco VPN 3005 at the Configuration | System | Tunneling Protocols | IPSec | NAT Transparency screen, as shown here:

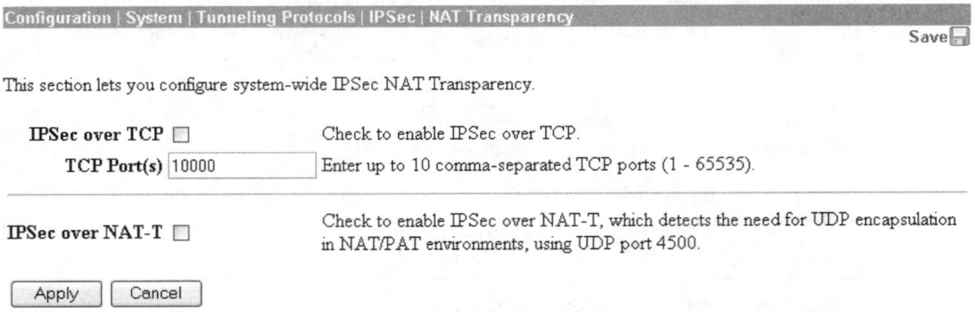

Configuration | System | Tunneling Protocols | IPSec | NAT Transparency

Save 🖫

This section lets you configure system-wide IPSec NAT Transparency.

IPSec over TCP ☐   Check to enable IPSec over TCP.
     TCP Port(s) `10000`   Enter up to 10 comma-separated TCP ports (1 - 65535).

IPSec over NAT-T ☐   Check to enable IPSec over NAT-T, which detects the need for UDP encapsulation in NAT/PAT environments, using UDP port 4500.

[Apply] [Cancel]

ONE STEP FURTHER

Cisco has an excellent whitepaper on NAT Traversal and how it works located at http://www.cisco.com/univercd/cc/td/doc/product/software/ios122/122newft/122t/122t13/ftipsnat.htm.

Specifically, it is important to understand that although NAT Traversal can help you tremendously in dealing with IPsec traffic, there are some items you need to be aware of. If an IP address is used as a search key to find a pre-shared key, you will not be able to use NAT Traversal because the NAT function will result in a mismatch between the IP address and pre-shared key. In addition, any protocols that use embedded IP addresses will not function with NAT Traversal. These protocols include File Transfer Protocol (FTP), Internet Relay Chat (IRC), Simple Network Management Protocol (SNMP), Lightweight Directory Access Protocol (LDAP), H.323, and Session Initiation Protocol (SIP).

For the Nortel Contivity, NAT Traversal is configured as a property of IPsec at the Services | IPSec | IPSec Settings screen, as shown next.

NAT Traversal

Enabled	☑
Disable Client IKE Source Port Switching	☐
UDP Port	4500

Authentication Order

Order	Server	Type	Associated Group	Action
1	LDAP	Internal		
2	RADIUS	MS-CHAP-V2, MS-CHAP, CHAP, PAP	/Base	Delete

Add LDAP Proxy

Fail-Over

Fail-Over	Enabled	Public IP Address
Host 1	☐	
Host 2	☐	
Host 3	☐	

You should use ESP for your IPsec-based VPNs due to the increased security that the data encryption provides; in fact, the Cisco VPN 3000 concentrator does not even support AH.

AH and ESP both use two modes of operation that define how they function: transport mode and tunnel mode. In transport mode, the original packet header and data are separated, and the original IP header is used for the new packet, followed by the AH and the original data (unencrypted) or the ESP header and encrypted data, as shown in Figures 5-6 and 5-7.

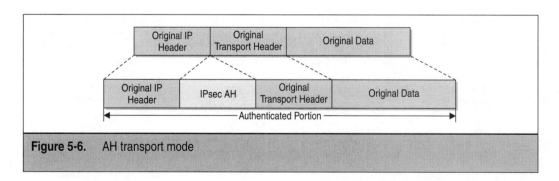

Figure 5-6. AH transport mode

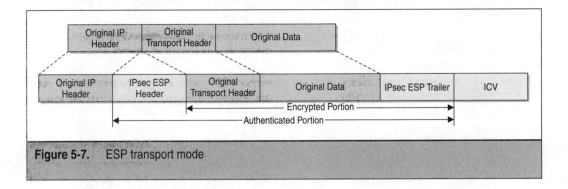

Figure 5-7. ESP transport mode

In tunnel mode, the original packet is completely encapsulated in a new IP header, including the AH or ESP header information, as shown in Figures 5-8 and 5-9. Transport mode is typically used for end-to-end connections between hosts, whereas tunnel mode is used for pretty much everything else. In most cases, you will use tunnel mode.

Security Associations

Security associations are simply a combination of the protocols, rules, and policies that two hosts use to negotiate their security service relationship. These security associations define the encryption protocols, the message integrity methods, and the authentication methods to be used by the hosts. The IETF has established a standard method of security association and key exchange resolution combining the Internet Security Association and Key Management Protocol (ISAKMP) and the Oakley key-generation protocol. ISAKMP centralizes security association management, thus reducing connection time. Oakley generates and manages the authenticated keys used to secure the information.

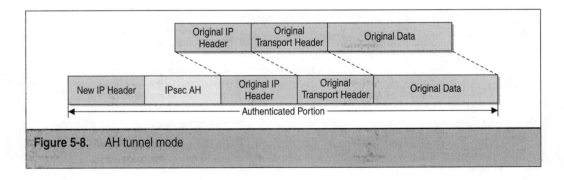

Figure 5-8. AH tunnel mode

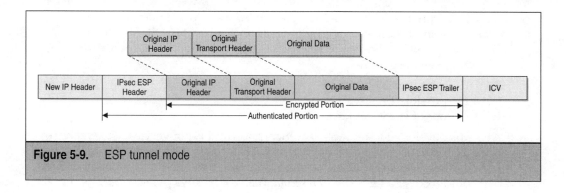

Figure 5-9.   ESP tunnel mode

A benefit of this process is that not only are the computer-to-computer communications protected, but remote computers that are requesting secure access to a corporate network or any situations in which the negotiation for the final destination computer (or endpoint) is actually performed by a security router or other proxy server are also protected. This latter situation is known as *ISAKMP client mode,* and the identities of the endpoints are hidden to further protect the communication and provide transparency to the client.

Encryption Protocols

You can use many different encryption protocols to encrypt your data and ensure confidentiality. Although they all fundamentally function in the same manner, the difference between them is the strength of the encryption. Some of the more common encryption protocols are listed here:

- **DES**   Data Encryption Standard (DES) uses a 56-bit key that it applies to every 64 bits of data to provide encryption. This provides 72 quadrillion possible encryption keys, which sounds really good until you realize that DES was cracked in a mere 22 hours and 15 minutes in 1999. Since then, DES has been cracked within similar times using relatively inexpensive equipment. If one is willing to invest a million dollars in equipment, DES can be cracked in under an hour. As a result, you should not use DES encryption.

- **3DES**   3DES is a more robust method of DES, performing three 56-bit encryption operations on the data (hence the name 3DES). This provides an aggregate 168-bit key providing much stronger data encryption, although in actuality it is a 112-bit key. 3DES has not been cracked . . .yet. Some estimates say that it would take trillions of years using today's technology to crack it. At the same time, people made similar claims about DES cracking, and we know what the results were. Keep this in mind any time someone tells you that something is "impossible to crack." You should use 3DES at a minimum for your data encryption.

- **AES-128, AES-192, and AES-256**   Advanced Encryption Standard is an encryption method developed by the National Institute of Standard and Technology (NIST). The three key sizes—128, 192, and 256—provide the following key possibilities:

  3.4×10^{38} possible 128-bit keys
  6.2×10^{57} possible 192-bit keys
  1.1×10^{77} possible 256-bit keys

  AES was developed to replace DES encryption and is not very easy to crack. To put this in perspective, according to the NIST website (http://www.nist.gov/public_affairs/releases/aesq&a.htm), "assuming that one could build a machine that could recover a DES key in a *second* (i.e., try 2^{55} keys per second), then it would take that machine approximately 149 thousand-billion (149 trillion) years to crack a 128-bit AES key. To put that into perspective, the universe is believed to be less than 20 billion years old."

3DES and any of the AES encryption protocols should be adequate for most environments. A benefit that 3DES has is very widespread support through all vendors, whereas AES is relatively new and not as widely supported. You can specify the encryption method to use at numerous screens for your Cisco VPN 3005 concentrator. For example, if you were adding a LAN-to-LAN VPN connection, you would specify the encryption from the Encryption drop-down list at the Configuration | System | Tunneling Protocols | IPSec | LAN-to-LAN | Add screen, as shown at right.

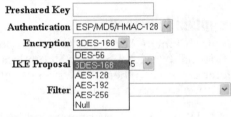

You can specify the encryption method for your IKE proposals at the Configuration | System | Tunneling Protocols | IPSec | IKE Proposals | Modify screen, as shown here:

Configuration | System | Tunneling Protocols | IPSec | IKE Proposals | Modify

Modify a configured IKE Proposal.

Proposal Name	IKE-3DES-SHA1	Specify the name of this IKE Proposal.
Authentication Mode	Preshared Keys	Select the authentication mode to use.
Authentication Algorithm	SHA/HMAC-160	Select the packet authentication algorithm to use.
Encryption Algorithm	3DES-168	Select the encryption algorithm to use.
Diffie-Hellman Group	DES-56 / 3DES-168 / AES-128 / AES-192 / AES-256 -bits)	Select the Diffie Hellman Group to use.
Lifetime Measurement		Select the lifetime measurement of the IKE keys.
Data Lifetime		Specify the data lifetime in kilobytes (KB).
Time Lifetime	86400	Specify the time lifetime in seconds.

Apply   Cancel

You can specify the encryption method for your security associations at the Configuration | Policy Management | Traffic Management | Security Associations | Modify screen, as shown here:

| Configuration | Policy Management | Traffic Management | Security Associations | Modify |

Modify a configured Security Association.

SA Name	ESP-3DES-SHA1	Specify the name of this Security Association (SA).
Inheritance	From Rule	Select the granularity of this SA.

IPSec Parameters

Authentication Algorithm	ESP/SHA/HMAC-160	Select the packet authentication algorithm to use.
Encryption Algorithm	3DES-168	Select the ESP encryption algorithm to use.
Encapsulation Mode	DES-56 / 3DES-168	Select the Encapsulation Mode for this SA.
Perfect Forward Secrecy	AES-128 / AES-192 / AES-256	Select the use of Perfect Forward Secrecy.
Lifetime Measurement		Select the lifetime measurement of the IPSec keys.
Data Lifetime	Null	Specify the data lifetime in kilobytes (KB).
Time Lifetime	28800	Specify the time lifetime in seconds.

IKE Parameters

IKE Peer	0.0.0.0	Specify the IKE Peer for a LAN-to-LAN IPSec connection.
Negotiation Mode	Main	Select the IKE Negotiation mode to use.
Digital Certificate	None (Use Preshared Keys)	Select the Digital Certificate to use.
Certificate Transmission	○ Entire certificate chain ◉ Identity certificate only	Choose how to send the digital certificate to the IKE peer.

Message Integrity

Hashing algorithms are used to provide message integrity of the transmitted data. This works by the source system generating a fixed-length message digest that is a condensed representation of the message or data file. This message digest is transmitted with the data to the destination host, which runs the same hashing algorithm on the data to generate its own message digest. The source and destination message digests are then compared, and any deviation means that the data has been altered since the original message digest was created. Most vendors support two primary message digest algorithms: Message Digest 5 (MD5) and Secure Hash Algorithm 1 (SHA-1). Both use hash-keyed message authentication code (HMAC) as their keyed hashing mechanism. HMAC is defined in RFC 2104.

MD5 was developed by Ronald Rivest of MIT and RSA Data Security Corporation. It creates a 128-bit message digest of the data by using a 128-bit secret key. SHA-1 was developed by the NIST and produces a 160-bit message digest using a 160-bit secret key. Because SHA-1 uses a larger secret key, it is considered more secure than MD5. However, this comes at the expense of performance. You should use SHA-1 unless you have a performance issue that precludes its use.

You can configure the message integrity method for your LAN-to-LAN VPN connection at the Configuration | System | Tunneling Protocols | IPSec | LAN-to-LAN | Add screen by selecting the Authentication drop-down list, as shown here:

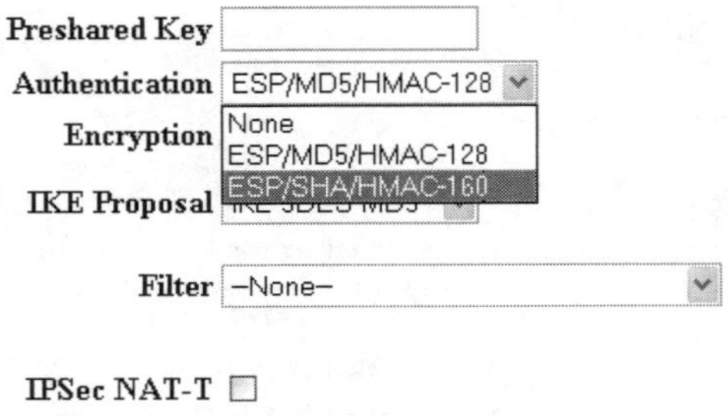

Preshared Key	
Authentication	ESP/MD5/HMAC-128
Encryption	None ESP/MD5/HMAC-128 ESP/SHA/HMAC-160
IKE Proposal	IKE 3DES-MD5
Filter	–None–

IPSec NAT-T ☐

You can configure the message integrity method for your IKE proposals at the Configuration | System | Tunneling Protocols | IPSec | IKE Proposals | Modify screen by selecting the Authentication Algorithm drop-down list, as shown here:

Authentication Mode	Preshared Keys
Authentication Algorithm	SHA/HMAC-160
Encryption Algorithm	MD5/HMAC-128 SHA/HMAC-160
Diffie-Hellman Group	Group 2 (1024-bits)
Lifetime Measurement	Time

You can configure the message integrity method for your security associations at the Configuration | Policy Management | Traffic Management | Security Associations | Modify screen by selecting the Authentication Algorithm drop-down list, as shown here:

IPSec Parameters

Authentication Algorithm	ESP/SHA/HMAC-160
Encryption Algorithm	None ESP/MD5/HMAC-128 ESP/SHA/HMAC-160
Encapsulation Mode	
Perfect Forward Secrecy	Disabled
Lifetime Measurement	Time
Data Lifetime	10000
Time Lifetime	28800

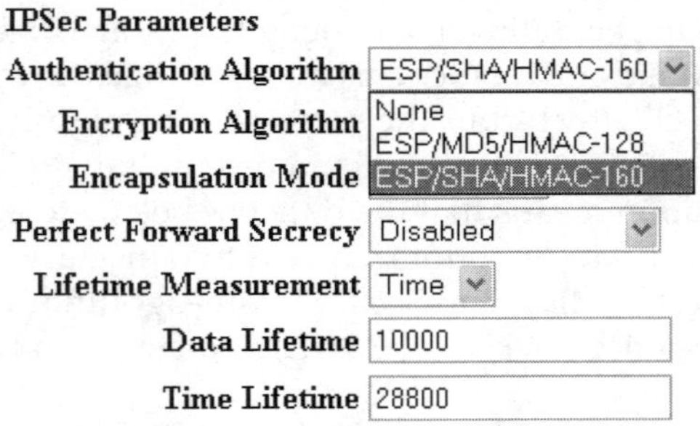

The Nortel Contivity takes a much simpler approach to configuring your encryption protocols and message integrity by using a single global-configuration setting for both. Nortel combines the encryption protocol and message integrity method into a single configuration setting (for example, by specifying 3DES and SHA-1 in a single encryption setting). You can define the supported encryption protocols and message integrity to use at the Services | IPSec | IPSec Settings screen, as shown next.

Encryption

ESP - AES 128 with SHA1 Integrity	☑
ESP - Triple DES with SHA1 Integrity	☑
ESP - Triple DES with MD5 Integrity	☐
ESP - 56-bit DES with SHA1 Integrity	☐
ESP - 56-bit DES with MD5 Integrity	☐
ESP - 40-bit DES with SHA1 Integrity	☐
ESP - 40-bit DES with MD5 Integrity	☐
ESP - NULL (Authentication Only) with SHA1 Integrity	☐
ESP - NULL (Authentication Only) with MD5 Integrity	☐
AH - Authentication Only (HMAC-SHA1)	☐
AH - Authentication Only (HMAC-MD5)	☐

IKE Encryption and Diffie-Hellman Group

56-bit DES with Group 1 (768-bit prime)	☐
Triple DES with Group 2 (1024-bit prime)	☑
Triple DES with Group 7 (ECC 163-bit field)	☐

You can configure your IKE proposals at the same screen by scrolling down to the "IKE Encryption and Diffie-Hellman Group" section, as shown here:

IKE Encryption and Diffie-Hellman Group

56-bit DES with Group 1 (768-bit prime)	☐	
Triple DES with Group 2 (1024-bit prime)	☑	
Triple DES with Group 7 (ECC 163-bit field)	☐	
AES 128 with Group 5 (1536-bit prime)	☐	Only valid with Branch Office
AES 128 with Group 8 (ECC 283-bit field)	☐	Only valid with Branch Office

NAT Traversal

Enabled	☐
Disable Client IKE Source Port Switching	☐
UDP Port	

Authentication Order

Order	Server	Type	Associated Group	Action
1	LDAP	Internal		
2	RADIUS	MS-CHAP-V2, MS-CHAP, CHAP, PAP	/Base	Delete

Add LDAP Proxy

Authentication

IKE provides for the authentication of peers during IKE phase 1 by using one of three possible key types:

- Preshared keys
- RSA digital signatures
- RSA encrypted nonces (This key type is rarely used and will not be covered in this book.)

The use of pre-shared keys is the most common method of authenticating users. This is due to the fact that it is a relatively simple and straightforward process, even though it is not as secure as the other methods. Pre-shared keys use an authentication mechanism based on both nodes sharing a common key value (the pre-shared key). This key value must be manually entered and, for all intents and purposes, should be treated in the same manner you would treat a password. Because both nodes must be configured with the same key, the same administrator should configure both systems. Alternatively, if the key must be provided to another user to implement, it should be delivered using a secure out-of-band method. For example, you should send the key via certified mail to the remote administrator as opposed to sending it via clear-text e-mail. Once both peers have been configured with a common key value, they use this key to generate authentication hashes that are transmitted to authenticate that both peers are who they claim to be.

Using pre-shared keys does have some drawbacks. As previously mentioned, pre-shared keys are more insecure than digital signatures or nonces. The use of pre-shared keys also does not scale to large environments because the key updates and changes must be manually performed on all equipment. Another drawback is the fact that because pre-shared keys are human generated, they tend to use a much smaller set of bits for the key generation, as compared to a computer-generated method, which might use in excess of 100 bits for the key-generation process. In addition, because the more people who know a secret, the less secret something is, it can be very difficult to update all your systems if one of the trusted users who knows your key values leaves. Finally, Microsoft stores pre-shared keys in an unencrypted format in the Registry, which is a horrible method of key storage quite frankly.

You can specify to use a pre-shared key for your LAN-to-LAN VPN connections on your Cisco VPN 3005 at the Configuration | System | Tunneling Protocols | IPSec | LAN-to-LAN | Add screen by selecting "None (Use Preshared Key)" in the Digital Certificate drop-down list and then entering the key value in the Preshared Key box, as shown next.

Digital Certificate | None (Use Preshared Keys) ▾

Certificate Transmission | ○ Entire certificate chain ◉ Identity certificate only

Preshared Key | keydata

Authentication | ESP/SHA/HMAC-160 ▾

You can specify to use a pre-shared key with your IKE proposals at the Configuration | System | Tunneling Protocols | IPSec | IKE Proposals | Modify screen by selecting Preshared Keys in the Authentication Mode drop-down box, as shown here:

Authentication Mode | Preshared Keys ▾
| | Preshared Keys
| | RSA Digital Certificate
Authentication Algorithm | DSA Digital Certificate
Encryption Algorithm | Preshared Keys (XAUTH)
Diffie-Hellman Group | RSA Digital Certificate (XAUTH)
Lifetime Measurement | DSA Digital Certificate (XAUTH)

You can specify to use a pre-shared key with your security associations at the Configuration | Policy Management | Traffic Management | Security Associations | Modify screen by selecting "None (Use Preshared Keys)" in the Digital Certificates drop-down box, as shown here:

IKE Parameters

IKE Peer | 0.0.0.0

Negotiation Mode | Main ▾

Digital Certificate | None (Use Preshared Keys) ▾

Certificate Transmission | ○ Entire certificate chain ◉ Identity certificate only

For your Nortel Contivity, you can specify to use pre-shared keys for your branch office profile configuration. You can specify the pre-shared key at the Profiles | Branch Office | Connection Configuration screen in the "Authentication" section by selecting Text or Hex Pre-Shared Key from the drop-down box and entering the key value, as shown here:

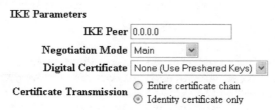

RSA digital signatures are more complex to initially set up and configure because they require the use of a certificate authority to provide digital certificates for hosts that register with that CA. They are much more secure than pre-shared keys, however, because they use a greater number of bits to generate the hash that is used, and they generally remove the human element from the validation, configuration, and distribution of the signatures by using certificate authorities to validate and distribute certificates.

A certificate authority (CA) is a server or host that has been authorized to issue and manage security credentials and public keys for encryption. Certificate authorities can be either external (for example, VeriSign) or internal (for example, Microsoft Certificate Services). The only requirement to use a certificate authority is for all the hosts to trust the certificate authority. For external certificate authorities, the list of trusted certificate authorities is generally handled by the OS vendor and is installed and updated periodically through Windows Update or similar functions. For internal certificate authorities, you will need to manually configure your hosts to recognize the CAs. For more information on how to configure a host operating system to recognize certificate authorities, see the counterpart publications in this series, *Hardening Windows Systems* by Roberta Bragg and *Hardening Linux* by John Terpstra.

Obtaining a certificate is a relatively straightforward process. First, you need to ensure that your VPN device trusts the certificate authority from which you want to obtain a certificate. Next, you will need to generate a certificate request, typically making a manual certificate request using the Public Key Cryptography Standards (PKCS) 10 message format. This typically generates output that looks like the following:

```
-----BEGIN NEW CERTIFICATE REQUEST-----
MIIBKTCB1AIBADB0MSYwJAYDVQQDEx1pZGx1LXZwbjMwMDUtMDEuNGlkbGV0aW1l
LmNvbTELMAkGA1UECxMCSVQxETAPBgNVBAoTCElkbGVaW1lMRAwDgYDVQQHEwdI
b3VzdG9uMQswCQYDVQQIEwJUWDELMAkGA1UEBhMCVVMwWTANBgkqhkiG9w0BAQEF
AANIADBFAkBRnk0aLy6N1681wsSvCnPd63u/N30PYZ6jxNexWIwqUoFwzfBnF3V+
8Js163SEmjfuMUdfLiG+NkHCHcw8KPPpAgEFMA0GCSqGSIb3DQEBBAUAA0EAQRxG
R/Oirun8nKrv/gS0wgNqLCje7frfR7RsBp7pW5gGA59b8+OBgmikdGZOqClxMg7c
xPShKUGAqJbnoelvYw==
-----END NEW CERTIFICATE REQUEST-----
```

You can either copy and paste this information into your certificate request form or save the output into a text file and upload the text file for your certificate request. The next step is actually to request the certificate using the certificate request information you previously generated. The exact method of doing this depends on whether you are using an external certificate authority such as VeriSign or are using an internal certificate server such as Microsoft Certificate Services. Typically, however, your certificate authority will request that you either upload or paste the certificate request into an online form of some sort. Once your certificate request has been acted upon, you will be provided with a certificate file. The last step is then to install the certificate on your device. This can typically be done by either copying and pasting the certificate data or uploading the certificate to your device. A certificate will typically looks like this:

```
-----BEGIN CERTIFICATE-----
MIIGRTCCBe+gAwIBAgIKIxBNWgAAAAAAETANBgkqhkiG9w0BAQUFADCBwTEoMCYG
CSqGSIb3DQEJARYZd25vb25hbkB3am5jb25zdWx0aW5nLmNvbTELMAkGA1UEBhMC
VVMxCzAJBgNVBAgTAlRYMRYwFAYDVQQHEw1NaXNzb3VyaSBDaXR5MR0wGwYDVQQK
ExRXSk4gQ29uc3VsdGluZywgTExDLjEfMB0GA1UECxMWSW5mb3JtYXRpb24gVGVj
aG5vbG9neTEjMCEGA1UEAxMaZnVyeW9uZHkud2puY29uc3VsdGluZy5jb20wHhcN
MDMxMjIxMjAzNTE2WhcNMDQxMjIwMjAzNTE2WjA8MR8wHQYJKoZIhvcNAQkBFhBw
cm9zcGVyb0Bub2wwubmV0MRkwFwYDVQQDExBXZXNsZXkgSi4gTm9vbmFuMFkwDQYJ
KoZIhvcNAQEBBQADSAAwRQJAUZ5NGi8ujZevNcLErwpz3et7vzd9D2Geo8TXsViM
K1KBcM3wZxd1fvCbJet0hJo37jFHXy4hvjZBwh3MPCjz6QIBBaOCBE4wggRKMB0G
A1UdDgQWBBTVb+a9lue8520gKltcQ+SAPuZZYTCB/QYDVR0jBIH1MIHygBSphpyM
Pg8DhZn3jD1k/0mlfmqiUaGBx6SBxDCBwTEoMCYGCSqGSIb3DQEJARYZd25vb25h
bkB3am5jb25zdWx0aW5nLmNvbTELMAkGA1UEBhMCVVMxCzAJBgNVBAgTAlRYMRYw
FAYDVQQHEw1NaXNzb3VyaSBDaXR5MR0wGwYDVQQKExRXSk4gQ29uc3VsdGluZywg
TExDLjEfMB0GA1UECxMWSW5mb3JtYXRpb24gVGVjaG5vbG9neTEjMCEGA1UEAxMa
ZnVyeW9uZHkud2puY29uc3VsdGluZy5jb22CEF+e6bUtBwGvRERM2h8jpSUwggE0
BgNVHR8EggErMIIBJzCB0aCBzqCBy4aByGxkYXA6Ly8vQ049ZnVyeW9uZHkud2pu
Y29uc3VsdGluZy5jb20sQ049ZnVyeW9uZHksQ049Q0RQLENOPVB1YmxpYyUyMEtl
eSUyMFNlcnZpY2VzLENOPVNlcnZpY2VzLENOPUNvbmZpZ3VyYXRpb24sREM9d2pu
Y29uc3VsdGluZyxEQz1jb20/Y2VydGlmaWNhdGVSZXZvY2F0aW9uTGlzdD9iYXNl
P29iamVjdGNsYXNzPWNSTERpc3RyaWJ1dGlvblBvaW50MFGgT6BNhktodHRwOi8v
ZnVyeW9uZHkud2puY29uc3VsdGluZy5jb20vQ2VydEVucm9sbC9mdXJ5b25keeS53
am5jb25zdWx0aW5nLmNvbS5jcmwwggFIBggrBgEFBQcBAQSCATowggE2MIG/Bggr
BgEFBQcwAoaBsmxkYXA6Ly8vQ049ZnVyeW9uZHkud2puY29uc3VsdGluZy5jb20s
Q049QUlBLENOPVB1YmxpYyUyMEtleSUyMFNlcnZpY2VzLENOPVNlcnZpY2VzLENO
PUNvbmZpZ3VyYXRpb24sREM9d2puY29uc3VsdGluZyxEQz1jb20/Y0FDZXJ0aWZp
Y2F0ZT9iYXNlP29iamVjdGNsYXNzPWNlcnRpZmljYXRpb25BdXRob3JpdHkwcgYI
KwYBBQUHMAKGZmh0dHA6Ly9mdXJ5b25keeS53am5jb25zdWx0aW5nLmNvbS9DZXJ0
RW5yb2xsL2Z1cnlvbmR5LndqbmNvbnN1bHRpbmcuY29tX2Z1cnlvbmR5LndqbmNv
bnN1bHRpbmcuY29tLmNydDAMBgNVHRMBAf8EAjAAMAsGA1UdDwQEAwIFoDApBgNV
HSUEIjAgBgorBgEEAYI3CgMEBggrBgEFBQcDBAYIKwYBBQUHAwIwFwYJKwYBBAGC
NxQCBAoeCABVAHMAZQByMEYGA1UdEQQ/MD2gKQYKKwYBBAGCNxQCA6AbDBl3bm9v
bmFuQHdqbmNvbnN1bHRpbmcuY29tgRBwcm9zcGVyb0Bub2wwubmV0MA0GCSqGSIb3
DQEBBQUAA0EAHgrIiOJiDNjhBudDXWJ5McTq/3ZT9zpPfb2abzsVldtpxVRvvVvA
dVVl8EptaAu7d5BAKf5RZDbH9TYEZ7a02Q==
-----END CERTIFICATE-----
```

Once this initial effort of configuring an internal certificate authority or using an external certificate authority, updating your systems to trust the chosen certificate authority, and obtaining a certificate has been made, however, peers using RSA digital certificates can authenticate with one another without user intervention. This allows digital certificates to scale much better in large environments due to the reduced user intervention. Because the infrastructure has been previously implemented, you simply generate a new certificate for the system in question and configure the system to use the certificate.

Configuring your devices to use a digital certificate is generally no different from configuring them to use a pre-shared key. Simply select the certificate from the drop-down list that you want to use instead of selecting "None (Use Preshared Key)" for your Cisco VPN 3005.

For your Nortel Contivity, you would simply select Certificates for the branch office authentication method and specify the appropriate identity information, as shown here:

Hardening VPN Clients

One area that is often overlooked in hardening VPNs is the need to harden the client that is accessing your network. A client accessing your network over a VPN is for all intents and purposes on your network. That means that any security problems that client may have just become a security problem on your network.

One simple thing you can do to harden the VPN client is to ensure that all VPN clients are running virus protection per corporate standards. In addition, your remote clients should all run personal firewall software that prevents unauthorized access to these remote clients without the users granting explicit permission to connect. In some cases, you will need to use third-party personal firewall software such as ZoneAlarm to protect the client. However, many vendors are building basic stateful firewall functionality into the VPN client software itself that you can enable.

In addition, many VPN vendors are building enforcement technologies into their VPN client software, or as add-ons to the VPN client software. These technologies will detect whether the client is running the required software (for example, a certain version and signature file for virus protection) and will update the client if it is out of compliance before allowing it to connect to your production network. For example, Nortel has an add-on for their VPN client software called TunnelGuard that can be used to ensure that the client is running the required software. Otherwise, the tunnel is placed in a restricted mode that prevents all traffic other than the TunnelGuard traffic from passing.

Another method of hardening your VPN clients is to restrict the kinds of access the clients will have to other networks while connected to the corporate network. For example, can the clients access the Internet or the local network at the same time they are connected to the corporate network? This is commonly known as *split tunneling*. Although this is certainly convenient for the user, it introduces a security hole in that a client could potentially be used to provide access to your network to other systems by functioning as a router. As a result, you should disable local LAN access while the VPN is connected to your corporate network and require that the VPN client use the VPN and, by extension, your Internet gateway for Internet access.

Some VPN devices support specifying a client policy that can be used to control the types of applications a system connected to the VPN concentrator can run. For your Nortel Contivity, this is known as the Client Policy feature. Client Policy acts in a fashion similar to a personal firewall by shutting down a VPN tunnel if a nonpermitted application is launched. It does this by monitoring the protocols and ports that are active while the tunnel is running.

Finally, your VPN client operating system should be hardened according to your security policy—for example, removing or disabling unnecessary services (Internet Information Services and the Microsoft Server service are two I can think of that should probably be disabled). For more information on hardening Windows and Linux-based clients, see *Hardening Windows Systems* by Roberta Bragg and *Hardening Linux* by John Terpstra.

Hardening Dial-in Remote Access

Dial-in remote access presents a particularly sticky situation regarding the hardening of your network infrastructure. One of the biggest problems is how hard it can be to truly control dial-in access. Even though your security policy should expressly prevent anyone from doing this, people may install modems on their desktops to use pcAnywhere, and suddenly you go from having a couple of highly controlled ingress points on your network to dozens of uncontrolled and largely unprotected ingress points on your network. This problem, as well as the popularity of VPN connections, has caused a marked decline in the use of dial-in connections on corporate networks.

Today you are better served to *not* provide any dial-in access but rather to provide your users with a global Internet dialer and VPN software, allowing them to connect via VPN to your network over their dial-in Internet connection. This allows you to control all your remote access connections at your VPN devices, thus simplifying the management of dial-in users because they effectively become just another VPN connection. In the event that you require dial-in remote access, however, you can do three things to harden that access:

- *Centralize your dial-in access.* By locating your dial-in access to a centralized location, such as a DMZ, you can filter and control the types of traffic you want to allow from your dial-in connections in a much easier fashion using your firewalls and routers for traffic filtering as well as IDS/IPS hardware to detect unauthorized traffic. For example, Figure 5-10 shows how you could locate your dial-in concentrator in a DMZ, allowing you to filter and control the kinds of traffic your remote users can pass to your internal network through your firewall and intrusion-detection system.

- *Require authentication of all connections.* Ensure that every dial-in connection has been authenticated, preferably using RADIUS, TACACS+, Active Directory, NDS, or local user databases, similar to how you configure your VPN connections to only allow authorized users to connect. Authentication will be covered in more detail in Chapter 9.

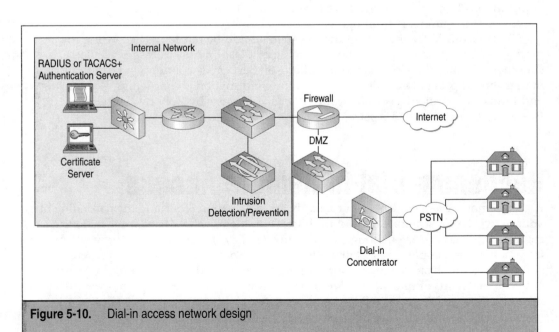

Figure 5-10. Dial-in access network design

■   *Require callback or caller ID verification of as many connections as possible.*
Unfortunately, because most of your dial-in connections will be traveling users
without a designated callback number, this might prove to be an impossible task.
However, if you know that a dial-in connection is always going to be initiated
from the same phone number, your dial-in access should be configured to drop
the initial phone call and dial the user back at the specified location in order to
establish a connection. Configuring callback or caller ID verification is typically
done on the device, although many authentication servers, such as TACACS+
and Windows Authentication, provide callback and caller ID verification to be
configured for the user. For example, if you are using a Windows server to
provide dial-in access, you can configure the callback options as part of the
user settings in the Active Directory Users and Computers MMC snap-in.

Summary

VPN and dial-in connections provide a means to extend your corporate network to
remote users and locations, allowing those remote users and locations to access your
corporate resources as if they were local. With this access comes the need to harden
these connections to ensure that you maintain the desired level of security on your
infrastructure while providing the kind of functionality required by your users and
business.

If you are providing VPN connectivity, you should use IPsec for your VPN
connection protocol. If you require multiprotocol support, you should use L2TP
tunneled within IPsec to provide connectivity. You should not use PPTP.

In providing IPsec VPN connections, you should use the most secure protocols and
authentication methods available. Do not use AH as a traffic security protocol due to
the fact that it does not encrypt the data. Instead, implement ESP to ensure that the
data is encrypted as it is transmitted. For your encryption protocol, you should not
use DES but rather should use 3DES or any of the AES encryption protocols. Message
integrity should be provided by SHA-1 instead of MD5 because SHA-1 uses a large bit-
key and therefore is more secure than MD5. Finally, make sure you authenticate all
your connections via the use of pre-shared keys or RSA digital signatures to ensure
that only authenticated peers can connect to your network.

Your VPN devices should also be hardened against threats to the devices themselves.
You should only allow secure protocols for remote administration, such as SSH and
HTTPS. Only authorized users should be able to connect to and manage a device, and
these users should not use common passwords. Instead, they should use individual local
accounts or RADIUS or TACACS+ to be authenticated and authorized. Any unnecessary
services and protocols should be disabled or filtered from the device, providing the
minimum required services and protocols. If all you support are IPsec VPN connections,
you should disable PPTP and L2TP as unnecessary services. You should also implement
redundant devices to address hardware failure scenarios, ensuring that your users obtain

the maximum uptime as required by your environment. Finally, ensure that you only support authenticated routing updates with your routing protocols.

Instead of providing dedicated dial-in access, you should implement a global Internet dialer and use VPN connections to provide remote user access. If, however, you are required to provide dial-in access, ensure that all connections are authenticated and that your dial-in access is centralized and managed to make it easier to control and filter that external traffic. Where possible, implement callback against authenticated users to ensure that the connection attempt is coming from an authorized location.

Although providing remote access can invite a multitude of security problems in your environment, if it's done properly, you can ensure that your security posture is fundamentally unchanged after providing the kind of functionality your users and company require.

Chapter 6

Hardening Your Routers and Switches

- Hardening Management Access
- Hardening Services and Features
- Hardening Router Technologies
- Hardening Switch Technologies
- Configuring IPsec on Your Routers

Routers and switches make up the core of the network infrastructure. Indeed, it's not a far claim to say that routers and switches *are* the network infrastructure. Consequently, if you want your network infrastructure to be as secure as possible, you have to harden your routers and switches.

This chapter takes a look at hardening routers and switches from two perspectives. First, we will look at how to harden the device itself. Second, we will look at how to use the device to harden the network. I will be covering the following devices/ software in this chapter:

- IOS C1700 Software (C1700-ADVSECURITYK9-M), version 12.3(3)
- IOS 2500 Software (C2500-JK8OS-L), version 12.2(1d)
- WS-C5505 Software, version McpSW: 4.5(9) NmpSW: 4.5(9)
- IOS C2950 Software (C2950-I6K2L2Q4-M), version 12.1(20)EA1
- Catalyst 6500 Series CatOS version 8.2

Although these are all Cisco devices, the concepts and recommendations in this chapter are valid for all vendors. In addition, many of the commands that run on the IOS-based devices will be valid for all vendors that implement an IOS-based CLI.

Hardening Management Access

Before you can implement a network device and expect to be able to use it to secure your network, you must first configure the device for secure management access. There are four primary methods of interactive management access:

Console access	Requires physical console connectivity to the device
VTY access	Uses the network to establish virtual console access through the use of protocols such as Telnet and SSH
Web-based GUI	Uses a web-based GUI over HTTP or HTTPS to manage the device
Auxiliary access	Uses a modem connection for out-of-band console access

You can implement a couple common items for all the access types that will increase the security of remote management access.

The first item you can implement is service password encryption on the device. You can do this on your IOS-based equipment by running the following command at the global configuration mode of execution:

```
rtr-1721(config)#service password-encryption
```

Although the encryption method implemented can be cracked in a matter of seconds, this will protect your system from casual observation hacks (for example, someone looking over your shoulder while you are viewing the system configuration).

The second item you can implement is exec timeouts. This will cause the remote management session to terminate automatically after a period of inactivity. The ensures that people are not able to connect to the device and gain access that they shouldn't have. It also ensures that if someone forgets to log off of the system, the session is not left connected.

You can implement exec timeouts on your IOS-based devices by running the following command while in the line configuration mode of execution:

```
rtr-1721(config-line)#exec-timeout 5 0
```

This configures the exec timeout to log off any idle session after five minutes and zero seconds. You will need to run this command for each line type, console, auxiliary, and VTY. For example, if you wanted to implement an exec timeout on all line types, you could run the following commands:

```
rtr-1721(config)#line con 0
rtr-1721(config-line)#exec-timeout 5 0
rtr-1721(config)#line vty 0 4
rtr-1721(config-line)#exec-timeout 5 0
rtr-1721(config-line)#line aux 0
rtr-1721(config-line)#exec-timeout 5 0
```

For your CatOS-based devices, you can implement exec timeouts by running the following command:

```
Console> (enable) set logout 5
```

This will configure the device to log out inactive sessions after five minutes.

Implement Exec Timeouts for Console Connections

Implementing exec timeouts is particularly valuable for console connections because if someone disconnects from the console without logging out while in a privileged mode of execution, the next person who connects to the console port will automatically be in whatever mode of execution the device was left at. For example, if you disconnect while in the privileged mode of execution, the next person who connects will be in the privileged mode of execution without needing to enter a password.

Securing Console Access

The first step of securing console access actually has nothing to do with configuring the device; rather, it relates to physical access. Console access requires that someone be able to physically connect to the console port on the device, typically using a PC serial connection. With physical access to the device, a hacker can do anything they want, including gaining access to the device configuration. Consequently, the first step of securing console access is to provide for the physical security of the device. The device should be placed in a locked and secured area to restrict individuals from gaining access to it.

The next step is to configure the device to require authentication of any console connections through the use of console passwords. This can be performed on your IOS-based devices by running the following commands from the global configuration mode of execution:

```
rtr-1721(config)#line con 0
rtr-1721(config-line)#login
rtr-1721(config-line)#password <enterpassword>
```

For your CatOS-based devices, you can run the following command to enable a console password:

```
Console> (enable) set password
Enter old password: <enteroldpassword>
Enter new password: <enternewpassword>
Retype new password: <enternewpassword>
```

This will require all users who connect via the console port to enter the password you defined. The drawback of this type of system is that all users share a common password. You can avoid this drawback by implementing Authentication, Authorization, and Accounting (AAA) or by using individual usernames and passwords for each user who may need to connect. We will discuss how to implement usernames and AAA in a moment.

Preventing Reverse Telnet Console Access

Reverse Telnet is sometime referred to as *direct Telnet*. Reverse Telnet is when the host computer initiates a Telnet session instead of accepting one, and it's a security issue for your IOS-based devices. You can prevent Reverse Telnet on your console port by running the following command at the console line configuration mode of execution:

```
local-rtr(config-line)#transport input none
```

NOTE   Not all devices support this command.

Securing VTY Access

VTY access is the traditional network-based management access using Telnet or SSH. Unlike console access, there are two aspects to securing your VTY access. The first aspect is implementing authentication. The second aspect is controlling management access to the device.

ONE STEP FURTHER

Some IOS-based devices support more than five VTY lines. In those cases, you will need to repeat the commands for all VTY lines. For example, if your device supports 16 VTY lines, you would need to run **line vty 5 16** and repeat the **password** command. This is true for all the line commands covered in this chapter.

Implementing Authentication

Securing your VTY access for authentication is virtually the same as for your console, with one difference—you must enable login before you define a password for authentication. You can do this by running the following commands from the global configuration mode of execution:

```
rtr-1721(config)#line vty 0 4
rtr-1721(config-line)#login
rtr-1721(config-line)#password <enterpassword>
```

Like with console access, however, this system relies on shared passwords. We will discuss how to implement usernames and AAA in a moment.

Controlling Access

Controlling VTY access is as important as authentication, because if a system is not permitted to connect, it doesn't matter whether the user knows the password or not. You can control VTY access through the use of access lists that define what IP addresses are allowed to connect to the device.

The first step is to build the actual access control list. You can do this by running the following commands from the global configuration mode of execution:

```
rtr-1721(config)#access-list 70 remark ACL for VTY Access
rtr-1721(config)#access-list 70 permit host 192.168.173.114
rtr-1721(config)#access-list 70 deny any log
```

This will create an ACL that permits 192.168.173.114 and denies all other IP addresses while logging the denial. The next step is to apply the ACL to the VTY line through the use of the **access-class** commands:

```
rtr-1721(config)#line vty 0 4
rtr-1721(config-line)#access-class 70 in
```

This will prevent all hosts that are not 192.168.173.114 from being able to establish a VTY connection.

ONE STEP FURTHER

You can also prevent any remote administration of certain devices either by creating an ACL that denies all traffic and applying it to the VTY interface or by running the following commands on the VTY line:

```
rtr-1721(config-line)#transport input none
rtr-1721(config-line)#exec-timeout 0 1
rtr-1721(config-line)#no exec
```

For your CatOS-based devices, you can restrict VTY access with the **set ip permit** command, as follows:

```
Console> (enable) set ip permit enable
Console> (enable) set ip permit 10.20.20.20 255.255.255.255
```

This will permit only the host at 10.20.20.20 to establish a VTY connection.

Telnet vs. SSH

As you know from other chapters, Telnet is less secure than SSH because Telnet does not encrypt the data being transmitted. Because of this, instead of using Telnet for VTY access, you should use SSH. You can configure SSH access on your IOS-based devices by running the following commands:

```
rtr-1721(config)#ip domain-name wjnconsulting.com
rtr-1721(config)#crypto key generate rsa
The name for the keys will be: rtr-1721.wjnconsulting.com
Choose the size of the key modulus in the range of 360 to 2048 for your
  General Purpose Keys. Choosing a key modulus greater than 512 may take
  a few minutes.
How many bits in the modulus [512]: 1024
% Generating 1024 bit RSA keys ...[OK]
rtr-1721(config-line)#transport input ssh
```

The first command assigns a domain name to the device, which is required for RSA key generation. The second command generates the RSA keys needed to provide SSH access. After these two commands have been run, the device is prepared to run SSH. The final command requires that all VTY connections be established using SSH. Any other VTY connections, including Telnet connections, will be rejected.

You can configure SSH on CatOS-based devices that are running 6.0 mainline code or newer. The following commands will enable SSH connections:

```
Console> (enable) set ip dns domain wjnconsulting.com
Default DNS domain name set to wjnconsulting.com
Console> (enable) set crypto key rsa 1024
RSA keys were generated at: Tue Mar 16 2004, 17:43:30 1024
65537 15144146953605773328536717047857098506066347687468697
…
16963940352440620678575338701550888525699691478330537B
Console> (enable) set ip permit enable
Console> (enable) set ip permit 10.20.20.20 255.255.255.255
10.20.20.20 with mask 255.255.255.255 added to IP permit list.
```

Securing Web-Based Management Access

Web-based management is certainly the direction that most devices are headed in. Unfortunately, Cisco has had some significant security issues related to their web-based management. In addition, currently web-based management is just not at a point where it can replace the CLI. As a result, I recommend that you disable web-based management using the following commands on your IOS-based devices:

```
rtr-1721(config)#no ip http server
rtr-1721(config)#no ip http secure-server
```

For your CatOS-based devices, you can disable web-based management using the following command:

```
Console> (enable) set ip http server disable
```

If you require web-based management, you should only use HTTPS because HTTP does not encrypt the data. You can enable HTTPS on your IOS-based devices by running the following commands:

```
rtr-1721(config)#ip http secure-server
rtr-1721(config)#ip http access-class 70
rtr-1721(config)#ip http timeout-policy idle 300 life 3600 requests 1
```

These commands will enable HTTPS connections to the device that are permitted by ACL 70. In addition, they configure a number of timeout variables to further secure the access.

Securing Auxiliary Access

The auxiliary port is one of the most overlooked ports for device hardening. Although it is typically used for connecting a modem to provide out-of-band management to the device, it can also be used as a secondary console port. That means that if you overlook it, no matter how much you harden the console access, an attacker can potentially circumvent it.

The best recommendation I can make for hardening your auxiliary port is to simply disable it unless you are going to be using a modem. You can do this on your IOS-based devices by running the following commands at the global configuration mode of execution:

```
rtr-1721(config)#line aux 0
rtr-1721(config-line)#transport input none
rtr-1721(config-line)#login local
rtr-1721(config-line)#exec-timeout 0 1
rtr-1721(config-line)#no exec
```

If you are going to use the auxiliary port for out-of-band management, it should be secured in the same manner as your VTY lines.

Securing Privileged Mode Access

The privileged access mode is the mode of access that allows users to begin making changes. It is analogous to root in Linux/Unix or administrator in Microsoft Windows. Consequently, you want to secure who can access the privileged mode through the use of password authentication.

For your IOS-based devices, there are two methods of authenticating privileged mode access. The first method is through the use of the **enable password** command. This is a deprecated method, however, and should never be configured. The recommended method is through the use of the **enable secret** command. This method is recommended because it uses a more secure encryption method (the **enable password** method was hacked years ago, and a wealth of online password crackers are available that can crack **enable password** in less than a second). You can configure the **enable secret** password by running the following command at the global configuration mode:

```
rtr-1721(config)#enable secret <enterpassword>
```

The enable secret is stored in the configuration as an MD5 hash, and many password-cracking tools are available out there to perform dictionary attacks against an MD5 hash, such as Cain and Abel. This is why you should follow good password guidelines and not use a password that is susceptible to a dictionary attack.

Also, because the enable secret is the most secure method to encrypt your passwords, you should not use the same password anywhere else in the router configuration. Because the rest of the passwords are not encrypted as well, you could be throwing away the security you had for the MD5 hash by having the same password used and stored for some other type of authentication on your router.

You can configure your CatOS-based devices with an enable password to protect the privileged mode of execution by running the following command:

```
Console> (enable) set enablepass
Enter old password: <enteroldpassword>
Enter new password: <enternewpassword>
Retype new password: <enternewpassword>
```

Although this will secure the privileged EXEC mode, this method has the same drawback as the previous authentication methods, namely the use of shared passwords. To address this drawback, however, you can implement usernames and AAA as described in the next section.

Implementing Usernames and AAA

By default, and as most of us were taught, logon and enable secret passwords are how to implement authentication on your network devices. Although they are better than nothing, the truth is that shared passwords are really pretty insecure. Because multiple people have the password, no accountability is available to determine who may have made a change to the device. In addition, anytime someone leaves the organization, you have to change all shared passwords throughout the enterprise. A much better solution is to implement usernames or, even more preferably, AAA on your network devices.

Implementing local usernames on your IOS-based devices is a pretty straightforward process. The first step is to create the usernames on the device by running the following command:

```
rtr-1721(config)#username <entername> privilege 15 password →
<enterpassword>
```

You can specify a privilege level from 0 to 15 for each user you have created. The second step is to configure the various access methods to use the local user accounts for authentication. You can do this by running the following command at all of the line configuration modes of operation for the device:

```
rtr-1721(config-line)#login local
rtr-1721(config-line)#no password
```

The last line removes any shared password that may have been configured.

An even better solution is to implement AAA on the device. AAA on IOS-based devices is covered in exhaustive detail in Chapter 9.

Your CatOS-based devices can also be configured with AAA authentication. You can enable AAA authentication by running the following commands to enable authentication using TACACS+:

```
Console> (enable) set authentication enable tacacs enable primary
Console> (enable) set authentication enable local enable
Console> (enable) set authentication login tacacs enable primary
Console> (enable) set authentication login local enable
Console> (enable) set tacacs server 10.20.20.20 primary
Console> (enable) set tacacs key <enterkey>
```

If you wanted to configure the device to use RADIUS, you would simply replace "tacacs" with "radius".

Implementing Banners

As mentioned in Chapter 3, logon banners should be implemented to set the appropriate expectations of privacy and acceptable use of the system, resources, data, and network access capabilities.

You can enable banners on your IOS-based devices by running the command **banner motd ^**. This will configure the device to use a caret (^) as a delimiting character. All data you enter until you type another "^" will be made the banner text. For example, to implement the sample banner text from Chapter 3, you would type the following:

```
rtr-1721(config)#banner motd ^
Enter TEXT message.  End with the character '^'.
This system is for the use of authorized users only.
Individuals using this computer system without authority,
or in excess of their authority, are subject to having all
of their activities on this system monitored and recorded
by system personnel. In the course of monitoring
individuals improperly using this system, or in the course
of system maintenance the activities of authorized users
may also be monitored. Anyone using this system expressly
consents to such monitoring and is advised that if such
monitoring reveals possible evidence of criminal activity,
system personnel may provide the evidence of such monitoring
to law enforcement officials.
Report suspected violations to the system security officer^
```

For your CatOS-based devices, you can implement a banner in a similar fashion by running the command **set banner motd ^** followed by the banner text. End the text by repeating the delimiter, in this case the "^" character.

Hardening Services and Features

We all know how important it is to harden the services that are running on our servers and workstations. Often overlooked areas of services, however, are the ones running on our routers and switches. For the same reasons that you disable unnecessary services on your servers and workstations, you want to disable unnecessary services on your routers and switches. Any services that are required you want to harden through whatever built-in security mechanism is supported. The following services and features are going to be reviewed:

Cisco Discovery Protocol (CDP)	TCP and UDP small servers
Finger	Network Time Protocol (NTP)
Bootp server	Dynamic Host Configuration Protocol (DHCP)
Configuration autoloading	Name resolution
Proxy ARP	Directed broadcasts

IP source routing	ICMP Redirects, Unreachables, and Mask replies
Syslog	Simple Network Management Protocol (SNMP)
Implement loopback address	Disable unused interfaces
Configure core dumps	

Cisco Discovery Protocol (CDP)

Cisco Discovery Protocol is a proprietary management protocol. Although it can be useful for troubleshooting personnel, it also creates additional network traffic and can provide an attacker with useful network information. Therefore, it should probably be disabled. You can disable CDP on your IOS-based devices in one of two ways: You can disable it completely on the switch, or you can disable it on certain interfaces (for example, an external interface on a perimeter router). The same command is used in either method to disable CDP; however, it is run at a different mode of execution. To disable CDP completely, run the following command at the global configuration mode:

```
rtr-1721(config)#no cdp run
```

To disable CDP on a specific interface, simply run the command at the interface configuration mode. For example, if you wanted to disable it on interface FastEthernet 0, you would run the following commands:

```
rtr-1721(config)#interface fastethernet 0
rtr-1721(config-if)#no cdp run
```

You can disable CDP for the entire device or for individual interfaces on your CatOS-based devices, too. Here is the command to disable CDP for the device:

```
Console> (enable) set cdp disable all
```

If you wanted to disable CDP for a specific interface (for example, interface 3/1), you would run the following command:

```
Console> (enable) set cdp disable 3/1
```

TCP and UDP Small Servers

TCP and UDP small servers run a series of servers that, in theory, provide some diagnostic and informational types information, but in practice these are largely worthless features—and in some cases they can be exploited by attacks such as the fraggle attack, which uses a UDP echo.

You can disable TCP and UDP small servers on your IOS-based devices by running the following commands at the global configuration mode:

```
rtr-1721(config)#no service tcp-small-servers
rtr-1721(config)#no service udp-small-servers
```

CatOS-based devices do not support TCP or UDP small servers.

finger

The finger server is used by the finger protocol to gain information about the currently logged-on users from a network location. Because you can log onto the device and view the currently logged-on users by running the command **show users**, there is no reason to run a server that allows unauthenticated users to gain access to that same information.

You should disable finger on your IOS-based devices by running the following commands at the global configuration mode:

```
rtr-1721(config)#no ip finger
rtr-1721(config)#no service finger
```

CatOS-based devices do not support finger.

Network Time Protocol (NTP)

As mentioned in previous chapters, NTP is used to synchronize time throughout your environment. This is a critical component of logging because you need accurate timestamps for all events if you want to be able to accurately determine what happened with your device in the event of an exploit or security incident.

You can approach NTP in two ways. The first way is to simply disable it on all interfaces on your IOS-based devices. You can do this by running the following command on every interface on the device:

```
rtr-1721(config-if)#ntp disable
```

You can disable NTP on your CatOS-based devices by running the following command:

```
Console> (enable) set ntp client disable
```

A better solution than simply disabling NTP—because it does serve a valid purpose in your environment—is to configure NTP to operate in a secure fashion. You can configure NTP to operate in a secure fashion by running the following commands on your IOS-based device:

```
rtr-1721(config)#service timestamps log datetime localtime msec
rtr-1721(config)#service timestamps deb datetime localtime msec
rtr-1721(config)#clock timezone CST -6
rtr-1721(config)#clock summer-time CDT recurring
rtr-1721(config)#access-list 20 remark ACL for Remote NTP Server
rtr-1721(config)#access-list 20 permit 192.168.173.99
rtr-1721(config)#ntp access-group peer 20
rtr-1721(config)#ntp authenticate
rtr-1721(config)#ntp authentication-key 1 md5 ntpkey
rtr-1721(config)#ntp trusted-key 1
rtr-1721(config)#ntp server 192.168.173.99 key 1
```

This configures the system to debug and log timestamps using the local date and time format. Next, it configures the appropriate time zone values based on U.S. standards. The remaining lines establish an ACL that specifies who the permitted NTP servers are and configures NTP to use authentication to ensure that the NTP host is who it claims to be. Once you have run these commands, you should disable NTP on any external interfaces, as previously described.

Configuring NTP on your CatOS-based devices requires you to run the following commands:

```
Console> (enable) set ntp timezone CST -6
Console> (enable) set ntp summertime enable CDT
Console> (enable) set ntp summertime recurring
Console> (enable) set ntp key 1 trusted md5 ntpkey
Console> (enable) set ntp server 10.20.20.20 key 1
Console> (enable) set ntp client enable
Console> (enable) set ntp authentication enable
```

The first three commands enable the time zone–related information based on U.S. standards. The last four commands define the NTP key that should be used, define the NTP server that should be used, and enable the NTP client and authentication.

bootp Server

bootp is used by hosts to load their operating system over the network, typically by diskless workstations. You can use a Cisco router as a bootp server to provide IOS software to other Cisco equipment. In theory, this can be used as part of a deployment strategy for configuring your routers; however, in practice, there are a multitude of better deployment strategies. Consequently, you should disable bootp server on your IOS-based devices by running the following command from the global configuration mode:

```
rtr-1721(config)#no ip bootp server
```

CatOS-based devices do not support bootp.

Dynamic Host Configuration Protocol (DHCP)

DHCP is used to provide IP addresses to clients that request them. Cisco routers can act as a DHCP server to provide IP addresses to clients that request them. In most environments, however, a local server can provide DHCP services, or the router can be configured to support the forwarding of DHCP broadcasts (DHCP relay agent) to a centralized DHCP server with the **ip helper-address** command.

By default, the router should not be running a DHCP server; however, you can ensure that is the case by running the following command:

```
rtr-1721(config)#no ip dhcp pool <poolname>
```

CatOS-based devices do not support DHCP.

ONE STEP FURTHER

The **ip helper-address** command actually forwards a number of broadcasts types by default. If want your routers to only forward DHCP broadcasts, you should restrict the protocols that will be broadcast by using the **ip forward-protocol udp bootpc** and **ip forward-protocol udp bootps** commands.

Configuration Autoloading

Many Cisco devices are capable of pulling their configuration from a network device through a process known as configuration autoloading. This is a completely insecure process however as the device will pull the configuration from any server that offers one. In fact, some buddies and I used to use this to mess with each other in the lab by causing the devices to pull invalid configurations (geek humor is great <g>).

You can disable this functionality on you IOS-based devices by running the following commands from the global configuration mode of execution:

```
rtr-1721(config)#no boot network
rtr-1721(config)#no service config
```

CatOS-based devices do not support configuration autoloading.

Name Resolution

Name resolution is used by IOS-based devices to support the entering of hostnames instead of IP addresses. However, if you have every mistyped a command on a device, you know that you will have to wait 20–30 seconds for the name resolution to fail because, by default, the device attempts to broadcast the name query, and I have never encountered a name server that responds to this type of request. There are two methods in which you can approach name resolution. The first method is to disable name resolution completely. You can do this on your IOS-based devices by running the following command at the global configuration mode of execution:

```
rtr-1721(config)#no ip domain-lookup
```

You can perform the same thing on your CatOS-based devices by entering the following command:

```
Console> (enable) set ip dns disable
```

If you want to use name resolution and have trusted DNS servers that you can use, you can enable DNS by running the following commands on an IOS-based device:

```
rtr-1721(config)#ip domain-lookup
rtr-1721(config)#ip name-server 192.168.173.100
rtr-1721(config)#ip domain-name wjnconsulting.com
```

For your CatOS-based devices, you can run the following commands:

```
Console> (enable) set ip dns enable
Console> (enable) set ip dns server 10.20.20.20
Console> (enable) set ip dns domain wjnconsulting.com
```

Proxy ARP

Proxy ARP is used to allow systems on two different subnets that would not normally be able to communicate with each other to do so. Proxy ARP is typically implemented for dial-in PPP users. For a host to use proxy ARP, it is configured with its own IP address for its default gateway. This causes the host to ARP for all remote hosts. By default, Cisco routers will respond to this broadcast and then route the remote packets to the destination on behalf of the client. Outside of the very specific scenario of implementing proxy ARP to support dial-in users, however, you should disable proxy ARP. You can do this on your IOS-based devices by running the following command at the interface configuration mode for all interfaces on your device:

```
rtr-1721(config-if)#no ip proxy-arp
```

Proxy ARP is not supported in the CatOS.

Directed Broadcasts

Directed broadcasts allow a remote host to initiate a broadcast on a different LAN segment. As a result, directed broadcasts are typically used for generating a denial of service (DoS) attack by inundating a segment with broadcast traffic. Although most IOS-based devices disable directed broadcasts by default, you can explicitly disable them by running the following command at the interface configuration mode for all the interfaces on your device:

```
rtr-1721(config-if)#no ip directed-broadcast
```

Directed broadcasts are not supported in the CatOS.

IP Source Routing

IP source routing is used to allow the source to define the route a packet should take in the network (hence, the name *source routing*). Source routing is used most commonly for token ring networks, and because it can be used for a number of different attacks, you should disable it unless you explicitly require it. You can disable IP source routing by running the following command at the global configuration mode of execution:

```
rtr-1721(config)#no ip source-route
```

IP source routing is not supported in the CatOS.

ICMP Redirects, Unreachables, and Mask Replies

Although ICMP messages provide a wealth of troubleshooting information, they can also be used by a malicious user to map and diagnose a network. Three ICMP messages in particular are commonly used for this purpose: redirects, unreachables, and mask reply messages. You should disable all these protocols by running the following commands at the interface configuration mode for all the interfaces in your device:

```
rtr-1721(config-if)#no ip redirects
rtr-1721(config-if)#no ip unreachable
rtr-1721(config-if)#no ip mask-reply
```

Your CatOS-based devices support redirects and unreachables, and you disable them by running the following commands:

```
Console> (enable) set ip redirect disable
Console> (enable) set ip unreachable disable
```

syslog

As mentioned in previous chapters, syslog is used to provide a central repository of logging data that can be used for auditing and troubleshooting. You can configure syslog to send all events of a certain level or lower to a syslog server. For example, if you set the logging level at informational, all events from emergency events to informational events are sent to the syslog server. Because debugging should not be routinely occurring on your devices, I recommend that you do not send debugging events to the syslog server by default and instead use informational as the default syslog logging severity level. You can configure syslog on your IOS-based devices by running the following commands at the global configuration mode:

```
rtr-1721(config)#logging trap informational
rtr-1721(config)#logging 192.168.173.114
```

You can enable syslog logging on your CatOS-based devices by running the following commands:

```
Console> (enable) set logging server enable
Console> (enable) set logging server 10.20.20.20
Console> (enable) set logging server severity 6
```

ONE STEP FURTHER

Note that syslog is transmitted in clear text. Although this is not a good thing, you are better off to configuring logging in clear text than to not use syslog at all. You can provide encryption to syslog data by configuring IPsec on the device and using IPsec to encapsulate the syslog data. IPsec configuration is covered later in this chapter.

Simple Network Management Protocol (SNMP)

SNMP can be used to manage your network devices, providing configuration mechanisms as well as the monitoring of performance and device configuration. Although a low-level discussion of SNMP is beyond the scope of this book, it is important to understand the pros and cons of SNMP and how to securely implement SNMP on your network infrastructure devices. It is important to understand that if you are not actively using SNMP, you should disable it by running **set snmp disable** on your CatOS-based devices and **no snmp-server** on your IOS-based devices.

SNMP has three versions: SNMP v1, SNMP v2c. and SNMP v3. Both SNMP v1 and SNMP v2c are largely insecure protocols. Although they support the use of community strings as a rudimentary authentication mechanism, the data transported (including the community string) is done so in clear text, so it requires very little effort to compromise. SNMP v3 was implemented with authentication and privacy in the form of usernames, passwords, and the use of 56-bit DES encryption. Unfortunately, many vendors still do not support SNMP v3 for their devices. As a result, we are going to look at how to implement SNMP v1 and SNMP v2c and then at how to implement SNMP v3 separately.

Securing SNMP v1 and SNMP v2c

The only truly secure way to implement SNMP v1 and SNMP v2c is to encapsulate the data in an IPsec tunnel to prevent eavesdropping. We will cover how to implement IPsec later in this chapter. You can, however, undertake a number of steps to mitigate the insecurity of SNMP v1 and SNMP v2c through the use of ACLs and community strings. First, you should treat your community strings in the same manner as you would passwords. Second, you should review what you are using SNMP for and only grant SNMP access that is required. For example, if you are not using SNMP to configure devices, implement SNMP in a read-only mode.

You can configure SNMP on your IOS-based devices by running the following commands at the global configuration mode:

```
rtr-1721(config)#access-list 15 remark ACL to Permit SNMP
rtr-1721(config)#access-list 15 permit host 192.168.173.114
rtr-1721(config)#snmp-server community <enterrostring> ro 15
rtr-1721(config)#snmp-server community <enterrwstring> rw 15
rtr-1721(config)#snmp-server host 192.168.173.114 traps →
<entercommstring>
```

The first two lines define an ACL that is used to specify what hosts are permitted to use SNMP to connect to the device. The next two lines define read-only and read-write community strings and assign the previously defined ACL to permit access. You should use different community strings for different degrees of access. The final line configures the device to send SNMP traps to a management station on IP address 192.168.173.114 using the specified community string.

You can enable SNMP v1 or SNMP v2c by running the following commands on your CatOS-based device:

```
Console> (enable) set snmp enable
Console> (enable) set snmp access-list 1 10.20.20.20
Console> (enable) set snmp community read-only <enterrostring>
Console> (enable) set snmp community read-write <enterrwstring>
Console> (enable) set snmp trap 10.20.20.20 <entercommstring>
Console> (enable) set snmp trap enable all
```

Again, if you do not require read-write access, you should disable it.

Securing SNMP v3 on Your IOS-Based Devices

Configuring SNMP v3 is more secure than SNMP v1 and SNMP v2c; however, it is also a much more complex process to implement. The following steps are required to implement SNMP v3 on your IOS-based devices:

1. Configure the SNMP-server engineID.
2. Configure the SNMP-server views.
3. Configure the SNMP-server group names.
4. Configure the SNMP-server hosts.
5. Configure the SNMP-server users.

Configure the SNMP-Server EngineID   The SNMP server engineID is used to identify the local and remote SNMP entities. By default, your IOS-based device has a local engineID based on the MAC address of the device. You can enter a different SNMP-server engineID by running the following command at the global configuration mode of execution:

```
rtr-1721(config)#snmp-server engineid local <idstring>
```

You can also configure the remote entity engineID using the following command (this is optional):

```
rtr-1721(config)#snmp-server engineid remote 192.168.173.114 <idstring>
```

Configure SNMP-Server Views   SNMP-server views define what part of the SNMP MIB tree will be accessible. For example, if you wanted to make all of the Internet MIB as well as all the sub-branches available, you could run the following command to create a view named "readview":

```
rtr-1721(config)#snmp-server view readview internet included
```

Configure the SNMP-Server Group Names   The next step is to configure the SNMP-server group names. This maps SNMP users to SNMP views, allowing you to control who can view what SNMP information. For example, you could create a group named "readonly" that has the ability to read the view you previously created (readview) and uses authentication and privacy by running the following command:

```
rtr-1721(config)#snmp-server group readonly v3 priv read readview
```

Configure SNMP-Server Hosts   SNMP-server hosts define the destination for SNMP traps. You can configure SNMP traps by running the following command line:

```
rtr-1721(config)#snmp-server host 192.168.173.114 traps →
version 3 priv privpass
```

Configure SNMP-Server Users   The last step is to configure the SNMP-server users who are allowed to connect. You can do this by running the following command:

```
rtr-1721(config)#snmp-server user wnoonan readonly v3 auth md5 →
<enterpassword> priv des56 <passphrase>
```

In this case, I created a user named wnoonan and made that user a member of the group readonly that was previously configured. I have also specified the use of MD5 authentication and, to ensure privacy, the use of 56-bit DES encryption.

Securing SNMP v3 on Your CatOS-Based Devices

Implementing SNMP v3 on your CatOS-based devices is largely the same process as on your IOS-based devices, but instead you use the CatOS-specific command syntax. You can enable SNMP v3 by running the following commands:

```
Console> (enable) set snmp engineid <engineID>
Console> (enable) set snmp view readview internet included
Console> (enable) set snmp access readonly security-model v3 →
privacy read readview
Console> (enable) set snmp user wnoonan authentication md5 <authpass> →
privacy <privpass>
Console> (enable) set snmp group readonly user wnoonan →
security-model v3
```

Implementing Loopback Address

You should configure the loopback address of the router to provide a stable and secure method of managing the device because the loopback interface is fixed. In addition, you can use the loopback interface as the source interface for a number of services and routing protocols, allowing you to configure the security of other devices more tightly because you need only grant access from the loopback address as opposed to one of the interfaces. Configuring the services in this manner means that packets sourced from the router are sourced from the IP address of the loopback interface.

Creating the loopback interface is a relatively straightforward process. Simply assign it an IP address as you would any other interface. One important note is that the loopback address cannot be an IP address in use anywhere else on the router, nor can it be a part of the same network as any other interface. Consequently, if you want to be able to access the loopback address from any other network, you will need to configure the appropriate routing functionality.

Setting a loopback ensures that all the traffic the router creates will be sourced from the same IP, thus facilitating better management and control. You can run the following commands from the global configuration mode of execution to implement a loopback address:

```
local-rtr(config)#interface loopback 0
local-rtr(config-if)#ip address 192.168.250.1 255.255.255.255
```

You can then reference the loopback address throughout the router configuration. For example, you can assign the loopback address as the source for FTP, TFTP, syslog, SNMP, and NTP, just to name a few, by running the following commands at the global configuration mode:

```
local-rtr(config)#ip ftp source-interface loopback 0
local-rtr(config)#ip tftp source-interface loopback 0
local-rtr(config)#logging source-interface loopback 0
local-rtr(config)#snmp-server trap-source loopback 0
local-rtr(config)#ntp source loopback 0
```

For more information about commands that support the loopback as a source interface, see the "Cisco IOS Command Reference" for your version of IOS software.

Disabling Unused Interfaces

As a standard practice, you should disable any unused interfaces. This will prevent someone from being able to locate an open jack and plugging something into the network—in particular technicians who are adding network devices for which they may not have followed the appropriate change control procedures. You can disable interfaces on your IOS-based devices by running the following command at the interface configuration mode of all the device interfaces that need to be disabled:

```
rtr-1721(config-if)#shutdown
```

Disabling ports is much simpler on your CatOS-based devices because you can disable multiple ports with a single command:

```
Console> (enable) set port disable 3/1
Console> (enable) set port disable 3/1-3/10
Console> (enable) set port disable 3/1,3/3,3/5
```

The first command disables a single port, port 3/1. The second command disables ports 3/1 through 3/10. The third command disables ports 3/1, 3/3, and 3/5.

Configuring Core Dumps

We all like to joke about the blue screen of death on Microsoft Windows systems, but the truth is that all systems have the ability to core dump (I had at least 30 core dumps while I wrote just this chapter because the routers I was using did not have enough RAM to run OSPF and attempt to obtain a PKI certificate). To help in diagnosing the cause of router crashes, you can configure the router to offload the core memory to an external server. The most secure method of performing this is through the use of the FTP protocol:

```
remote-rtr01(config)#ip ftp source-interface loopback 0
remote-rtr01(config)#ip ftp username routeruser
remote-rtr01(config)#ip ftp password routerpass
remote-rtr01(config)#exception protocol ftp
remote-rtr01(config)#exception dump 192.168.173.100
```

In this case, I have configured the router to perform a core dump to the FTP server at 192.168.173.100.

Hardening Router Technologies

Now that you have performed the fundamental device-hardening measures, the next step is to harden router-specific technologies. The four primary tasks to undertake in hardening your router technologies are as follows:

- Implementing redundancy
- Hardening routing protocols
- Implementing traffic management
- Implementing IPsec

Implementing Redundancy

One of the most important things you can do to provide infrastructure security is to provide redundancy of critical devices. This ensures that if one device fails, the redundant device can transparently fill the void left behind.

Cisco uses Hot Standby Routing Protocol (HSRP) to provide device redundancy between two or more routers. HSRP functions by using a virtual IP address and MAC address that are shared between the routers, although only one router can be using the virtual addresses at any given time. If the router that owns the virtual addresses fails for any reason, the backup router will assume the role of responding on the virtual addresses. For end clients, the entire process is transparent because they are assigned the virtual IP address for their default gateway. In most cases, any service interruption lasts less than ten seconds.

HSRP configuration has two primary steps. First, you must configure HSRP on the primary router. Second, you must configure HSRP on the secondary router. To prevent HSRP spoofing or hijacking, you should also implement authentication. Once you implement authentication, the router will only participate in using HSRP with other routers that provide the correct authentication string (the string uses an MD5 hash for security).

To configure the primary router, enter the following commands at the interface configuration mode for the interface on which you want to enable HSRP:

```
local-rtr(config-if)#interface Ethernet0
local-rtr(config-if)#ip address 192.168.1.1 255.255.255.0
local-rtr(config-if)#standby priority 200 preempt
local-rtr(config-if)#standby preempt
local-rtr(config-if)#standby ip 192.168.1.3
local-rtr(config-if)#standby authentication <authstring>
```

To configure the backup router, enter the following commands at the interface configuration mode for the interface on which you want to enable HSRP:

```
remote-rtr(config-if)#interface Ethernet0
remote-rtr(config-if)#ip address 192.168.1.2 255.255.255.0
remote-rtr(config-if)#standby priority 101
remote-rtr(config-if)#standby ip 192.168.1.3
```

In this example, all clients use 192.168.1.3 as their default gateway. If, for some reason, the primary router fails, the secondary router will take over. As soon as the primary router is brought back online, it will preempt the secondary router and reassume the virtual addresses.

Hardening Routing Protocols

All the hardening steps you have taken on your routers lead to this section, because running routing protocols is why you implement routers in the first place. You have four primary routing mechanisms available to you:

- **Direct connections**   Although direct connections are often overlooked as routing functions, they are included in the routing table. They represent the subnets that the router has an interface connected to.

- **Static routing**   Static routing is simply the manual entry of all routes on a device. Static routing generally takes precedence over other routing methods and is the most secure method of routing because the router will only route if it is explicitly configured to do so. Static routing should be employed on all insecure network segments, such as DMZ segments.

- **Dynamic routing**   Dynamic routing makes use of routing protocols to exchange routing information between routers. Dynamic routing is the most flexible routing choice because the routers can dynamically update and change according to network changes. The rest of this section will focus on how to secure dynamic routing protocols.

- **Default routing**   Default routing is a form of static routing that is used to route a packet to another router when no explicit route to the destination network is known.

Generally speaking, there is not a whole lot we can do about securing the way the routing protocols function. For example, most (if not all) routing protocols were written so that the data is not encrypted, and there isn't much you or I can do about that. Similarly, most (if not all) routing protocols use multicast or broadcast traffic to locate other routers, and, again, there isn't much you or I can do about that.

The problem with all this, of course, is that we do not want our routers to be able to be poisoned with invalid routes or to have routes hijacked and data sent to remote locations. This we can do something about—through the use of authentication, as you saw in Chapter 3. This section will exclusively focus on IOS-based devices and will look at how to implement authentication, as well as any routing protocol–specific security functions that are available.

Router Information Protocol (RIP)

Three steps are involved in configuring RIP authentication. The first step is to configure the key chain that will be used by RIP. You can do this by running the following commands from the global configuration mode of execution:

```
rtr-1721(config)#key chain ripchain
rtr-1721(config-keychain)#key 1
rtr-1721(config-keychain-key)#key-string ripkeystring
```

This example configures a key chain named ripchain, with a key string of ripkeystring. The next step is to configure RIP by running the following commands from the global configuration mode of execution:

```
rtr-1721(config)#router rip
rtr-1721(config-router)#version 2
rtr-1721(config-router)#network 192.168.2.0
```

ONE STEP FURTHER

All hash-based authentication mechanisms are only as strong as the length of the key used to generate the hash. Consequently, I recommend that you use long key values (22 characters or longer), containing upper- and lowercase, numeric, and special characters.

The last step is to configure RIP authentication from the interface configuration mode of execution for all the interfaces on which you want to enable RIP authentication:

```
rtr-1721(config-if)#ip rip authentication key-chain ripchain
rtr-1721(config-if)#ip rip authentication mode md5
```

Open Shortest Path First (OSPF)

OSPF uses a similar authentication mechanism, although the commands are a little different. The following commands will configure OSPF:

```
rtr-1721(config)#router ospf 10
rtr-1721(config-router)#log-adjacency-changes
rtr-1721(config-router)#area 10 authentication message-digest
rtr-1721(config-router)#network 192.168.1.06 0.0.0.255 area 10
rtr-1721(config-router)#network 192.168.254.0 0.0.0.3 area 10
```

In this case, I have configured OSPF with an area of 10, assigned two networks for routing, and defined area 10 to use authentication. The second line configures the router to generate a syslog message anytime a neighbor router goes up or down to provide a means of alerting as to a potential routing problem. Finally, you need to configure the OSPF authentication key from the interface configuration mode of execution for all the interfaces on which you want to run OSPF:

```
rtr-1721(config-if)#ip ospf message-digest-key 1 md5 ospfkey
```

Enhanced Interior Gateway Router Protocol (EIGRP)

EIGRP is a proprietary Cisco routing protocol that can be used instead of RIP or OSPF. As with RIP, there are three steps to configuring EIGRP authentication. The first step is to create a key chain by running the following commands from the global configuration mode of execution:

```
rtr-1721(config)#key chain eigrp-key-chain
rtr-1721(config-keychain)#key 1
rtr-1721(config-keychain-key)#key-string eigrpkey
```

The next step is to configure the EIGRP routing process by running the following commands from the global configuration mode of execution:

```
rtr-1721(config)#router eigrp 100
rtr-1721(config-router)#network 192.168.2.0 255.255.255.0
rtr-1721(config-router)#network 192.168.254.4 255.255.255.252
```

The final step is to configure authentication from the interface configuration mode for all the interfaces on which you want to use EIGRP:

```
rtr-1721(config-if)#ip authentication mode eigrp 100 md5
rtr-1721(config-if)#ip authentication key-chain eigrp 100 →
eigrp-key-chain
```

Border Gateway Protocol (BGP)

BGP is an exterior gateway protocol that is typically implemented on Internet-connected gateways. BGP is a fairly complex routing protocol. Although the details of its implementation are beyond the scope of this book, you can take a couple fundamental hardening steps: using authentication to protect against route injection attacks and simple TCP resets and protecting against potential denial of service attacks due to route flapping.

BGP, like the other routing protocols, uses an MD5 hash for authentication. One important aspect to clarify is that configuring authentication is required on both neighbor routers. In most cases, this is no big deal because the same administrator is responsible for both devices. With BGP, however, the neighbor router is commonly managed by the service provider; therefore, you need to ensure that the service provider configures their router accordingly. You can configure BGP authentication by running the following commands at the BGP router configuration mode of execution:

```
local-rtr(config-router)#neighbor 192.168.254.1 remote-as 12345
local-rtr(config-router)#neighbor 192.168.254.1 password <password>
```

In this case, I configured neighbor router entries for the router at 192.168.254.1, adding the appropriate password. The ISP would configure their router in a similar fashion.

BGP Route Flap Dampening   Route flapping occurs when BGP networks are converging and can cause network instability and high CPU utilization. A route flap occurs when a route is constantly changing from an up to a down state, or from a down to an up state. Every time the router makes this transition, it sends a route update message to propagate around the network (in this case, the Internet). Although your ISP will typically implement BGP route flap dampening, you can also do it by running the following command at the BGP router configuration mode of execution:

```
local-rtr(config-router)#bgp dampening
```

You can implement additional BGP dampening options with the command to provide more granular control over things such as timing. One method is to define the half-life, reuse, suppress-limit, and max-suppress-time. There is no good answer as to what these values should be; rather, you should start with the default values (15 minutes, 750, 2000, and four times the half-life parameter, respectively) and then monitor your network to see whether route flapping is a problem.

The other method is to employ route-maps. This is a much more granular, but complex, method, allowing you to define different time values for different subnet sizes. See the Secure BGP IOS template located at http://www.cymru.com/Documents/secure-bgp-template.html for more information about how to configure the route-map entries.

ONE STEP FURTHER

The BGP section of this chapter focuses exclusively on BGP authentication and flap dampening. This is due to the fact that both configurations are relatively straightforward, whereas route distribution and other BGP functionality require a much more exhaustive discussion than is practical for a single chapter. For more information about how to configure route distribution and a more concise filtering list for Internet-connected routers, see the Secure BGP IOS template located at http://www.cymru.com/Documents/secure-bgp-template.html.

Implementing Passive Interfaces

In addition to configuring authentication for your routing protocols, you can configure certain interfaces to not participate in routing by running the command **passive-interface** in the router configuration mode and assigning the interface on which to disable the routing protocol. For example, if you wanted to configure interface FastEthernet 0 as a passive interface, you would run the following commands:

```
rtr-1721(config)#router ospf 10
rtr-1721(config-router)#passive-interface FastEthernet 0
```

Filtering Routing Updates

You can also configure the router to filter what network information will be shared between devices. The **distribute-list** command can be used to apply access control lists that will perform the filtering.

There are two methods of filtering. The first method is to suppress the networks that will be advertised by running the **distribute-list out** command. The second method is to filter the networks that will be learned with the **distribute-list in** command.

You can use the **distribute-list in** command to protect against invalid routes being inserted into the routing table. To do this, you must first configure an access list containing the list of valid networks; for example, if you only wanted to permit networks 192.168.1.0/24 and 192.168.254.0/30, you would run the following commands from the global configuration mode of execution:

```
local-rtr(config)#access-list 34 remark ACL for Routing Filter
local-rtr(config)#access-list 34 permit 192.168.1.0 0.0.0.255
local-rtr(config)#access-list 34 permit 192.168.254.0 0.0.0.3
```

The second step is to configure the distribute list for the routing protocol. You can configure distribute lists for RIP, OSPF, and EIGRP. For example, if I wanted to configure the distribute list for the EIGRP network I previously configured, I would run the following commands from the global configuration mode of execution:

```
local-rtr(config)#router eigrp 100
local-rtr(config-router)#distribute-list 34 in
```

This will prevent the router from learning about any networks other than the 192.168.1.0/24 and 192.168.254.0/30 networks, even if a neighbor router advertises those networks. This is an excellent method of ensuring that your routers will only learn about actual subnets that you have defined and created on your network.

If you wanted to prevent a router from advertising a network, you would follow the same general process. The first step is to create an ACL, except that instead of defining the networks to permit, you define the networks to deny and then permit everything else, as shown here:

```
rtr-1721(config)#access-list 37 remark ACL to Deny Routing
rtr-1721(config)#access-list 37 deny 192.168.1.0
rtr-1721(config)#access-list 37 permit any
```

The last step is to simply configure the distribute list, this time using the **out** operator:

```
rtr-1721(config-router)#distribute-list 37 out
```

This configuration could be used, for example, to prevent the subnet containing HR resources from being advertised in your environment.

Using Black-Hole Routes and Null Routing

Although distribute lists and access control lists provide a much more granular method of controlling the traffic that can pass in and out of a router, they can impose a performance degradation on the device because it has to inspect all packets. Although most routers will not have a problem with this, in large networks and, in particular, on backbone devices, this can be an issue.

As an alternative to configuring distribute lists and ACLs, you can implement what is known as *null routing,* or using black-hole routes. Null routing functions by configuring the router to route all packets for a given network to the null interface, effectively preventing any traffic from going to that network. Null routing uses static route entries to define the black-holed networks. You can configure null routing by running the following commands at the global configuration mode of execution:

```
rtr-1721(config)#interface null0
rtr-1721(config-if)#no ip unreachables
rtr-1721(config-if)#exit
rtr-1721(config)#ip route 10.0.0.0 255.0.0.0 null0
rtr-1721(config)#ip route 192.168.1.0 255.255.255.0 null0
```

You want to ensure that you disable IP unreachables on the null interface because the router could potentially flood the upstream neighbor with unreachables due to the fact that packets destined to the network will never reach there. You can then add static route entries for each network you want to black hole (in this case, network 10.0.0.0/8 and network 192.168.1.0/24).

Implementing Traffic Management

In addition to routing of traffic, our routers can be used to perform traffic management, defining what traffic will be permitted, and how much of any given traffic type will be allowed. We have already looked at how to filter traffic to the router (for example, filtering SNMP or VTY access), and in this section we are going to look at how to filter traffic through the router. We will examine the following traffic management mechanisms:

- Unicast Reverse-Path Forwarding (RPF) verification
- Access Control Lists (ACLs)
- Context Based Access Control (CBAC)
- Flood management

Unicast Reverse-Path Forwarding (RPF) Verification

Unicast RPF is a feature that allows you to configure your router to perform a reverse-path verification on all packets it receives. The packets are compared against the router's routing table to see if a valid router to the source network exists. If it does, the router will forward the packets. If it does not, the router assumes the source has been spoofed and drops the packets.

Unicast RPF is typically implemented on border routers to ensure that internal hosts are not spoofing addresses to the Internet (for example, a host that may be infected with a Trojan to execute a DDoS). The only real caveat to unicast RPF is that Cisco Express Forwarding must be enabled on the router in order to perform the "look backward" function. In addition, you cannot use unicast RPF if your router uses asymmetric routes because the packets will be incorrectly dropped on the receive leg of the asymmetric route.

You can configure unicast RPF by running the following commands from the global configuration mode of execution:

```
rtr-1721(config)#ip cef
rtr-1721(config)#interface Serial 0
rtr-1721(config-if)#ip verify unicast reverse-path
```

In this example, I have applied the unicast RPF to the serial 0 interface. You will need to do this for all interfaces on which you want to perform unicast RPF. As long as a route exists for the traffic, it will be permitted. If it doesn't exist, the traffic will be denied. For example, if this was your Internet gateway and you wanted to use unicast RPF, you could add a default route by running the command **ip route 0.0.0.0 0.0.0.0 Serial 0**. This would allow all traffic from the Internet into the serial 0 interface connected to the ISP while dropping all traffic that may have a source IP address of the internal network because the internal network is directly connected to a different interface.

NOTE If your device uses a Versatile Interface Processor (VIP), you need to run the command **ip cef distributed**.

A new feature for IOS versions 12.1(2)T and later is the inclusion of access lists in the commands. This allows you to configure an ACL to permit traffic in the event that the source address check fails. You can apply the ACL to the command by running the following at the interface configuration mode:

```
rtr-1721(config-if)#ip verify unicast reverse-path 101
```

In this case, I have configured unicast RPF to check ACL 101 before rejecting a packet that fails the initial source check.

Using Access Control Lists to Filter Traffic

ACLs represent the most functional method of controlling traffic because they offer a high degree of configuration granularity. Although ACL syntax, formats, and concepts are beyond the scope of this book (if you are not familiar with them, I strongly suggest

that you review them before you undertake this section of the book), we will look at
how to apply ACLs in various scenarios to protect your network from attack. We will
look at how to use ACLs for both inbound (ingress) and outbound (egress) filtering on
your network, including the following scenarios:

- Implementing spoof protection
- Implementing TCP SYN attack filtering
- Implementing Land attack filtering
- Implementing Smurf attack filtering
- Implementing ICMP message type filtering
- Implementing Bogon filtering

NOTE   A potential source of confusion will be the repeated use of the terms *internal* and *external*
network. This does not necessarily refer to your internal subnet in your protected enterprise LAN/
WAN. Instead, it refers to internal and external from the perspective of the router. For example, on
a perimeter router that connects to your ISP, the internal network is the subnet between the router
and the firewall, not the protected networks behind the firewall.

ONE STEP FURTHER

In all these ACL scenarios, you should consider using Turbo ACLs. Turbo ACLs
compile all suitable ACLs into fast lookup tables, reducing the performance
impact of ACL processing on the router. In general, any ACL with more than five
entries is a candidate for turbo ACLs. You can configure turbo ACLs by running
the following command at the global configuration mode of execution:

```
Router#(config) access-list compiled
```

Implementing Spoof Protection   Spoof protection with ACLs allows you to prevent inbound
traffic that claims to be from the inside or to prevent outbound traffic that claims to be from
the outside. If you are using unicast RPF, you should not implement spoof protection with
ACLs because unicast RPF is a lesser load on the router than processing ACLs.

The first type of spoof protection to implement is inbound spoof protection. With
inbound spoof protection, you want to configure an ACL that denies any traffic with a
source IP address of your internal network. In addition, you should deny the RFC1918
private address ranges and multicast traffic if you do not need to permit them. You can
configure a basic inbound spoof-protection ACL by running the following commands
at the global configuration mode of execution:

```
rtr-1721(config)#access-list 111 deny ip 7.7.7.0 0.0.0.255 any log
rtr-1721(config)#access-list 111 deny ip 127.0.0.0 0.255.255.255 any log
rtr-1721(config)#access-list 111 deny ip 10.0.0.0 0.255.255.255 any log
rtr-1721(config)#access-list 111 deny ip 0.0.0.0 0.255.255.255 any log
```

```
rtr-1721(config)#access-list 111 deny ip 172.16.0.0 0.15.255.255 any log
rtr-1721(config)#access-list 111 deny ip 192.168.0.0 0.0.255.255 any log
rtr-1721(config)#access-list 111 deny ip 192.0.2.0 0.0.0.255 any log
rtr-1721(config)#access-list 111 deny ip 169.254.0.0 0.0.255.255 any log
rtr-1721(config)#access-list 111 deny ip 224.0.0.0 15.255.255.255 any log
rtr-1721(config)#access-list 111 deny ip host 255.255.255.255 any log
rtr-1721(config)#access-list 111 permit ip any 7.7.7.0 0.0.0.255
rtr-1721(config)#interface s0
rtr-1721(config-if)#description External Connection to Internet
rtr-1721(config-if)#ip access-group 111 in
```

This ACL will prevent the specified IP addresses from being able to send packets inbound with the final line or the ACL permitting all other IP traffic to the internal network of 7.7.7.0/24. The ACL is then applied to the external interface on the router.

Implementing outbound spoof protection is considerably simpler than implementing inbound spoof protection. Simply create an ACL that permits traffic from the internal network and denies everything else, as shown here:

```
rtr-1721(config)#access-list 115 permit ip 7.7.7.0 0.0.0.255 any
rtr-1721(config)#access-list 115 deny ip any any log
```

The next step is to apply the ACL to the internal interface on the router:

```
rtr-1721(config-if)#ip access-group 115 in
```

Implementing TCP SYN Attack Filtering   TCP SYN attacks function by partially establishing a volume of connections on a router that causes connection queues to fill up, thus preventing subsequent connection methods. There are two approaches to providing TCP SYN attack filtering.

The first method is to implement a filter that allows connections that are sourced from the internal network out and their subsequent responses back in while preventing all traffic from the external network from establishing a connection at all. Be advised that this will prevent all external hosts from being able to connect to internal resources, so use care when implementing this method. You can configure the ACL by running the following commands at the global and interface configuration modes of execution:

```
rtr-1721(config)#access-list 117 permit tcp any 7.7.7.0 0.0.0.255 →
established
rtr-1721(config)#access-list 117 deny ip any any log
rtr-1721(config-if)#ip access-group 117 in
```

This allows any external host to respond on an established connection to hosts on the 7.7.7.0/24 subnet. The ACL should be applied to the external interface of the router.

A more effective method of protecting against TCP SYN attacks, though at the cost of more performance degradation, is to implement the TCP intercept feature on your router. This feature will intercept the inbound SYN requests and respond with an ACK and SYN on behalf of the destination. If it receives an ACK, the session is established between the source and destination. If it does not receive an ACK, the session is dropped, thus protecting the server from the SYN attack. You can configure TCP intercept to use ACLs to define the traffic that it should be intercepting by running the following commands at the global configuration mode of execution:

```
local-rtr(config)#ip tcp intercept mode intercept
local-rtr(config)#ip tcp intercept list 121
local-rtr(config)#access-list 121 permit tcp any 7.7.7.0 0.0.0.255
local-rtr(config)#access-list 121 deny ip any any log
local-rtr(config)#interface s0
local-rtr(config-if)#desc External Interface
local-rtr(config-if)#ip access-group 121 in
```

In this case, I have configured TCP intercept to use ACL 121, which has been subsequently applied to the external interface to define what traffic is permitted inbound.

Implementing Land Attack Filtering   A Land attack is when a device receives a packet that has the same source and destination IP address and the same source and destination port number. These types of attacks can cause a denial of service or inflict performance degradation on the router and therefore should be filtered by using ACLs. Land attack defense simply involves applying an ACL that denies all traffic with the same source and destination IP address of the interface it is being applied to. For example, if the serial 0 interface has an IP address of 7.7.7.1, you would build and apply the ACL by running the following commands at the global configuration mode of execution:

```
rtr-1721(config)#access-list 141 deny ip host 7.7.7.1 host 7.7.7.1 log
rtr-1721(config)#access-list 141 permit ip any any
rtr-1721(config)#interface serial0
rtr-1721(config-if)#ip access-group 141 in
```

Implementing Smurf Attack Filtering   A Smurf attack entails sending ICMP echoes at a subnet's broadcast address while using a spoofed source address for that subnet, causing the entire subnet to send an ECHO-REPLY to the spoofed IP address. You can filter Smurf attacks either by not forwarding broadcasts (**no ip directed-broadcast**) or by denying all traffic from external hosts to the internal broadcast addresses. For example, if your internal network is 7.7.7.0/24, you could run the following commands at the global configuration mode of execution:

```
rtr-1721(config)#access-list 151 deny ip any host 7.7.7.255 log
rtr-1721(config)#access-list 151 deny ip any host 7.7.7.0 log
rtr-1721(config)#access-list 151 permit ip any any
rtr-1721(config)#interface serial 0
rtr-1721(config-if)#ip access-group 151 in
```

Implementing ICMP Message Type Filtering   As mentioned previously in this chapter, ICMP can be used by an attacker to gain information about the network they are trying to attack. To mitigate this, you should implement ICMP message filtering at your router.

You will filter ICMP differently depending on whether you are controlling inbound or outbound traffic.

For inbound traffic, you should deny the Echo, Redirect, and Mask-Request message types. You can permit all other message types. You can do this by building an ACL, as follows, and applying it to the external router interface as an inbound ACL:

```
rtr-1721(config)#access-list 161 deny icmp any any echo log
rtr-1721(config)#access-list 161 deny icmp any any redirect log
rtr-1721(config)#access-list 161 deny icmp any any mask-request log
rtr-1721(config)#access-list 161 permit icmp any 7.7.7.0 0.0.0.255
```

This will deny the three message types we want to prevent while permitting any other ICMP traffic from external hosts to the internal network.

You should also filter the ICMP messages that are permitted from the internal network to external destinations. As a general rule, you should permit the Echo, Parameter-Problem, Packet-Too-Big, and Source-Quench message types while denying all other outbound ICMP traffic. You can do this by building an ACL, as follows, and applying it to the internal router interface as an inbound ACL:

```
rtr-1721(config)#access-list 164 permit icmp any any echo
rtr-1721(config)#access-list 164 permit icmp any any parameter-problem
rtr-1721(config)#access-list 164 permit icmp any any packet-too-big
rtr-1721(config)#access-list 164 permit icmp any any source-quench
rtr-1721(config)#access-list 164 deny icmp any any
```

In addition to filtering ICMP message types, you will also filter inbound traceroute packets because they can map a network as easily as an ICMP echo can. You can prevent inbound traceroute by adding the following line to an ACL that is assigned to an external interface as in inbound ACL (for example, the previous ICMP ACL 161):

```
rtr-1721(config)#access-list 161 deny udp any any range 33434 →
33434 log
```

You can permit outbound traceroute by simply adding a permit rule similar to the preceding deny:

```
rtr-1721(config)#access-list 164 permit udp any any range 33434 →
33434 log
```

Implementing Bogon Filtering   I think the question I have received from the editors the most on this book is, What the heck is a bogon <g>? Bogons are network address spaces that have not been assigned to anyone yet. The term is a bit of slang that means "bogus network," in the sense that because the IP address space has not been assigned to anyone, if someone claims they own that address space, it is a bogus claim.

Bogon filtering is predominantly applied for use with BGP routing to prevent your router from accepting routing entries to these bogus network. Bogon filtering can also be used as a component of null routing or spoof protection.

An obvious implementation issue with bogon filtering is the fact that periodically these addresses are going to be properly assigned to organizations, at which point they are not bogus anymore. This means that bogon filtering is not a one-time thing. You need to regularly and routinely update your bogon lists. To help stay on top of bogons, I recommend that you bookmark and check http://www.cymru.com/ Bogons/ for the latest bogon list and compare it to your list. Now, you might be thinking at this point, "OK, this seems like an awful lot of effort," and I'm not going to mislead you—it is a lot of effort. However, when you consider that some studies have identified that over 60 percent of the "naughty" traffic roaming around the Internet comes from these bogons, blocking them at your router is a good step toward protecting your internal users.

As of March 18, 2004, the following is the list of bogons (in Cisco ACL format so that you can see how they would be applied in your configuration). This is an aggregated list of the bogons, which simply means that any bogon entries that could be combined into a single entry have been:

0.0.0.0 1.255.255.255	2.0.0.0 0.255.255.255	5.0.0.0 0.255.255.255
7.0.0.0 0.255.255.255	10.0.0.0 0.255.255.255	23.0.0.0 0.255.255.255
27.0.0.0 0.255.255.255	31.0.0.0 0.255.255.255	36.0.0.0 1.255.255.255
39.0.0.0 0.255.255.255	41.0.0.0 0.255.255.255	42.0.0.0 0.255.255.255
49.0.0.0 0.255.255.255	50.0.0.0 0.255.255.255	58.0.0.0 1.255.255.255
71.0.0.0 0.255.255.255	72.0.0.0 7.255.255.255	85.0.0.0 0.255.255.255
86.0.0.0 1.255.255.255	88.0.0.0 7.255.255.255	96.0.0.0 31.255.255.255
169.254.0.0 0.0.255.255	172.16.0.0 0.15.255.255	173.0.0.0 0.255.255.255
174.0.0.0 1.255.255.255	176.0.0.0 7.255.255.255	184.0.0.0 3.255.255.255
189.0.0.0 0.255.255.255	190.0.0.0 0.255.255.255	192.0.2.0 0.0.0.255
192.168.0.0 0.0.255.255	197.0.0.0 0.255.255.255	198.18.0.0 0.1.255.255
223.0.0.0 0.255.255.255	224.0.0.0 31.255.255.255	

Implementing Context Based Access Control

Context Based Access Control (CBAC) is the heart of the Cisco IOS Firewall. CBAC is essentially ACLs on steroids, providing the additional functionality of being able to perform stateful, dynamic packet inspection as well as being able to look deeper in the data.

The one caution that I want to address up front is using routers instead of firewalls for security. Although CBAC does provide better security than simple ACLs, at the end of the day, a router is a router, and it is designed primarily to route, not to function as a firewall. Consequently, I strongly recommend implementing an actual firewall instead of CBAC. Those circumstances, however, where you cannot implement a firewall (for example, the money layer of the OSI model) are a good environment for CBAC because it will provide you more security than simply applying an ACL (and because it is stateful, it is also much simpler to manage the traffic flow).

Five steps are involved in configuring CBAC:

1. Configure audit trails and alerts.
2. Configure global settings.
3. Define Port-to-Application Mapping (PAM).
4. Define the inspection rules.
5. Apply the inspection rules and ACLs to interfaces.

Configure Audit Trails and Alerts   The first step is to configure the router to write the CBAC audit trail and alert events to our previously configured syslog server. You can do this by running the following command from the global configuration mode of execution:

```
local-rtr(config)#ip inspect audit-trail
local-rtr(config)#no ip inspect alert-off
```

Configure Global Settings   The next step is to configure the CBAC global timeouts and thresholds. This step is optional because they all have default values. In general, all these settings influence the timeout and threshold values for the session state information.

In most cases, the default values are adequate. You could, however, change them (for example, if your system was being flooded with a SYN attack to reduce the SYN wait time).

Define Port-to-Application Mapping (PAM)   PAM allows you to specify a nonstandard port that an application is running on. For example, if you have a web server running on port 8000, you could use PAM to map port 8000 to HTTP for inspection purposes. In this example, the following command would configure the PAM:

```
local-rtr(config)#ip port-map http port 8000
```

Unless you are running applications on nonstandard ports, you should not need to make any PAM changes. For more information about the ports that are supported for PAM, see http://www.cisco.com/en/US/products/sw/iosswrel/ps1835/products_configuration_guide_chapter09186a00800ca7c5.html.

Define the Inspection Rules   The fourth step is to configure the application inspection rules. These allow you to configure CBAC to inspect the traffic specified to verify that it is not harmful. Application inspection is a mixed bag, however. First, CBAC will only inspect the traffic you configure it to. If you don't configure it to inspect HTTP traffic, it won't do so. Second, CBAC only inspects a subset of all the traffic out there. Although CBAC can inspect most of the common Internet protocols, such as HTTP, SMTP, and FTP, there are many protocols it is not capable of inspecting. Generally speaking, any traffic that you want to be permitted based on state must be inspected. For example, if you wanted to grant your internal users access to the Internet using HTTP, SMTP, FTP, as well as generic TCP and UDP, you would configure the following at the global configuration mode of execution:

```
local-rtr(config)#ip inspect name CBAC01 http
local-rtr(config)#ip inspect name CBAC01 ftp
local-rtr(config)#ip inspect name CBAC01 tcp
local-rtr(config)#ip inspect name CBAC01 udp
local-rtr(config)#ip inspect name CBAC01 smtp
```

In addition, if you wanted to generate an alert or audit trail in syslog, you could add the following option to the command: **alert on** or **audit-trail on**.

Apply the Inspection Rules and ACLs to Interfaces   The final step is to apply the inspection rules and any ACLs to the interface. Remember that CBAC only inspects the traffic you have defined, so if your ACL permits the traffic for the interface and CBAC is not configured to inspect the traffic, it will be allowed in without being inspected.

Applying the inspection rule is relatively straightforward. In our example of an Internet gateway, simply create an access list that denies all IP traffic. Next, change to the external interface and apply the access list and the CBAC inspect list:

```
local-rtr(config)#access-list 101 remark ACL to Protect Ext. Int.
local-rtr(config)#access-list 101 deny ip any any log
local-rtr(config)#interface Ethernet 0
local-rtr(config-if)#ip access-group 101 in
local-rtr(config-if)#ip inspect CBAC01 out
```

This allows all traffic permitted by the inspect list to exit the interface, and it permits the corresponding responses back because CBAC is stateful. It does this by dynamically modifying the ACL to permit the given traffic. You can see this by running the following command:

```
local-rtr#sh ip access-lists
Extended IP access list 101
    permit udp host 192.168.1.100 eq 389 host 192.168.2.10 →
eq 1201 (1 match)
    permit tcp host 192.168.1.100 eq 445 host 192.168.2.10 →
eq 1197 (6 matches)
    permit tcp host 192.168.1.100 eq 445 host 192.168.2.10 →
eq 1175 (14 matches)
    deny ip any any log (218 matches)
```

Flood Management

Another important role for a router is to control the flow of traffic through the router to protect against flood attacks (for example, DoS or DDoS attacks). One method of flood management that we have already discussed is the use of Cisco Express Forwarding (CEF), which uses a more efficient forwarding/switching path. Another feature to enable on your router interfaces is NetFlow. Not only does NetFlow provide a more efficient traffic-flow mechanism, but the data it collects can be used for security monitoring, network management, capacity planning, and application traffic-flow analysis. You can enable NetFlow on an interface by running the following command at the interface configuration mode of execution:

```
rtr-1721(config-if)#ip route-cache flow
```

Another traffic-flooding feature is to enable the nagle service by running the following command at the global configuration mode of execution:

```
rtr-1721(config)#service nagle
```

The Nagle algorithm is used to address small packet problems, such as with Telnet. Telnet sends each character as a single packet. Nagle establishes the initial session using a single packet and then collects the remaining Telnet packets and waits to submit them until it receives an ACK. At that point, it sends the collected packets as a second, larger packet, continuing to accumulate the data into larger chunks of data. It then paces the data out to the network, reducing the amount of CPU interrupts in the case of Telnet because each character is a single CPU interrupt.

Implement Committed Access Rate (CAR)   The committed access rate (CAR) has been traditionally viewed as simply a Quality of Service (QoS) tool that allows you to define what amount of bandwidth an application or protocol is guaranteed on the network. It has the pleasant side effect, however, of being able to be used as a rate-limiting tool to protect your network from attacks that rely on a certain protocol, such as ICMP, to function.

CAR functions by allowing you to define what portion of bandwidth should be reserved for critical traffic, forcing all other traffic to be dropped if it exceeds a certain amount of bandwidth. Although CAR is a very helpful feature for mitigating DoS attacks, it is not perfect. For example, if the attack is using a protocol that you have reserved for critical traffic (for example, HTTP traffic), CAR isn't going to help much because there is no method of differentiating between legitimate and illegitimate traffic. If, however, the attack is being waged using ICMP traffic, for example, CAR could insulate your HTTP traffic, ensuring that the router always provides a minimum amount of bandwidth to HTTP requests, as you defined.

You can define the CAR through the use of the **rate-limit** command. You can apply a rate limit to input and output traffic on the interface. The rate limit rule is broken into three distinct components:

- The first section defines whether the rule applies to input or output traffic. It can also be used in conjunction with an ACL to define the types of traffic to be managed by the rule.

- The second section defines what the token bucket parameters are. The token buckets represent the bit rate (in bps), the burst size (in bytes), and the burst excess size (in bytes). For more information about the token bucket parameters, see http://www.cisco.com/warp/public/732/Tech/car/index.html.

- The third section defines what should be done with the traffic that exceeds the CAR (for example, dropping it or continuing to transmit it).

For example, let's assume on your 10MB Internet connection that you want to define the following CAR rules for outbound traffic:

- HTTP traffic is reserved for 30 percent of the traffic.
- SMTP traffic is reserved for 10 percent of the traffic.
- ICMP echo and echo-reply (ping) is limited to less than 1 percent of the traffic.

You want to ensure that HTTP and SMTP always have the reserved amount of bandwidth available to them, and if more bandwidth is available, they can use it. For ICMP, however, you want to drop it anytime it exceeds the 1-percent reservation. To do this, you would run the following commands from the global configuration mode of execution:

```
rtr-1721(config)#access-list 170 remark ACL for HTTP CAR
rtr-1721(config)#access-list 170 permit tcp any any eq 80
rtr-1721(config)#access-list 171 remark ACL for SMTP CAR
rtr-1721(config)#access-list 171 permit tcp any any eq 25
rtr-1721(config)#access-list 172 remark ACL for ICMP (ping) CAR
rtr-1721(config)#access-list 172 permit icmp any any echo
rtr-1721(config)#access-list 172 permit icmp any any echo-reply
rtr-1721(config)#interface Ethernet 0
rtr-1721(config-if)#rate-limit output access-group 170 3000000 →
25000 50000 conform-action transmit exceed-action continue
rtr-1721(config-if)#rate-limit output access-group 171 1000000 →
25000 50000 conform-action transmit exceed-action continue
rtr-1721(config-if)#rate-limit output access-group 172 16000 →
8000 8000 conform-action transmit exceed-action drop
```

Implementing IPsec

As we have discussed in Chapters 3 and 5, using IPsec is the only real effective method of securing traffic that is otherwise insecure (SNMP, syslog, TFTP, and so on). You can configure IPsec on your routers in two scenarios:

- Establishing IPsec between two routers (or a router and other remote device such as a firewall or VPN concentrator) to encrypt all traffic traversing the network between the two devices
- Using IPsec for secure remote management of the device (for example, to tunnel Syslog, SNMP, or Telnet traffic in IPsec)

Configuring IPsec to a remote management station is covered in Chapters 3 and 10 of this book, so I am not going to repeat the process here. Instead, I will focus on how to configure IPsec on two routers to allow them to communicate securely with each other. The configuration differences between that and the remote administration scenario are relatively minor. If you can establish IPsec between two routers, you should not have any problems making the necessary changes for remote administration.

There are three steps to configuring IPsec on your router:

1. Configure common IKE authentication.
2. Configure the IKE security policy.
3. Configure the IPsec protection parameters.

Configure Common IKE Authentication

The first step is to configure the pre-shared keys that will be used by both routers. For example, let's assume that you have two routers connected via a serial line and you want all traffic traversing that serial line to be encrypted. One router is named local-rtr, and the other router is named remote-rtr. You would want to run the following command on local-rtr:

```
local-rtr(config)#crypto isakmp key 12345abcde address 192.168.254.1
```

You would run the corresponding command on the remote router:

```
remote-rtr(config)#crypto isakmp key 12345abcde address 192.168.254.2
```

Configure the IKE Security Policy

The next phase is to configure a common IKE security policy on both the routers. It is critical that you run the exact same commands on both routers because IPsec is a temperamental feature, and any difference between the two policies can cause the IPsec tunnel to fail. You want to run the following commands from the global configuration mode on both routers (only one router example is shown):

```
!-- You can assign any policy number
remote-rtr(config)#crypto isakmp policy 1
!-- 3DES is the most secure encryption, though you could use DES
remote-rtr(config-isakmp)#encryption 3des
!-- SHA is a more secure HASH method than MD5
remote-rtr(config-isakmp)#hash sha
remote-rtr(config-isakmp)#authentication pre-share
!-- Diffie-Hellman group 2 is more secure than group 1
remote-rtr(config-isakmp)#group 2
remote-rtr(config-isakmp)#lifetime 86400
```

Configure the IPsec Protection Parameters

The final step is to configure the IPsec tunnel characteristics. You will build the characteristics in three steps:

1. Configure the ACLs to define what traffic should be encrypted.
2. Configure the appropriate transform set.
3. Create the necessary crypto map.

Configure the ACLs to Define What Traffic Should Be Encrypted   In this case, you want all traffic to be encrypted by IPsec, so you will create an ACL on both routers that causes this to occur:

```
remote-rtr(config)#access-list 175 remark ACL for IPsec
remote-rtr(config)#access-list 175 permit ip any any
```

Configure the Appropriate Transform Set   Next, you want to configure the transform set with the appropriate encryption and authentication mechanism, and you want to set the tunnel mode on both routers:

```
remote-rtr(config)#crypto ipsec transform-set set1 esp-3des →
esp-sha-hmac
remote-rtr(cfg-crypto-trans)#mode tunnel
```

Create the Necessary Crypto Map   The final step is to create the crypto map that brings all the ISAKMP and IPsec information together to build the IPsec tunnel. Like the IKE security policy, both routers need to have exact matches of each other, with the exception of the peer value, which is configured with the neighbor router IP address:

```
remote-rtr(config)#crypto map pipe-1 1 ipsec-isakmp
% NOTE: This new crypto map will remain disabled until a peer
        and a valid access list have been configured.
remote-rtr(config-crypto-map)#match address 175
!-- Ensure that you specify the remote peer IP address, in this case
!-- the IP address of the local router
remote-rtr(config-crypto-map)#set peer 192.168.254.2
remote-rtr(config-crypto-map)#set transform-set set1
remote-rtr(config-crypto-map)#set security-assoc lifetime kilo 80000
remote-rtr(config-crypto-map)#set security-assoc lifetime sec 26400
```

Finally, you need to turn IPsec on for the appropriate interface. The best way to do this is to configure the remote side first, because as soon as you configure one side, you will not be able to communicate with the other router until IPsec is functioning. By configuring the remote side first, when you lose connectivity (and you will), the connection will automatically fix itself when you finish the configuration on the local router. Turn on IPsec on the serial interface of the remote router:

```
remote-rtr(config-if)#crypto map pipe-1
```

The link will not pass traffic until you turn on IPsec on the serial interface of the local router:

```
local-rtr(config-if)#crypto map pipe-1
```

At this point, all traffic passing across the serial interface should be encrypted by IPsec, as shown by the following command:

```
local-rtr#sh crypto isakmp sa
    dst             src            state          conn-id    slot
192.168.254.1   192.168.254.2   QM_IDLE           1          0
```

Hardening Switch Technologies

Switches are somewhat easier to harden than routers because switches do not perform as many functions or have as many features as routers do. Whereas with routers we focus on securing traffic flowing through the router and the routing protocols themselves, with switches we focus more on securing the connectivity to the network and the various layer 2 protocols that are run by the switches. In this section, we are going to look at the following topics:

- Harden VLANs
- Harden services and features

Hardening VLANs

Virtual LANs (VLANs) are used extensively in many environments. The primary benefit of VLANs is the ability to logically group systems regardless of their physical proximity to each other. As much as VLANs can assist us in providing a scalable and function network, they also introduce some security issues that we need to be aware of and implement measures to protect against.

One of the simplest things you can do is to ensure that you do not use the default VLAN (VLAN 1) anywhere in your production environment. This will ensure that, in conjunction with the other hardening steps in this section, any and all connections to network resource must come from systems that have the proper VLAN configuration.

VLAN Hopping

The most significant security issue related to VLANs is the tendency for a switch to allow traffic from one VLAN to "hop" to a different VLAN without being routed. This would potentially allow an attacker to gain access to resources by circumventing any routers or firewalls that have been put in place to control access to the target VLAN.

Unfortunately, there isn't very much software-wise we can do to prevent this because in many cases the exploit functions by leveraging a bug or design flaw in how the switch process packets. In those cases, we are really at the mercy of the vendor to fix the issue. You can mitigate this, however, by designing and implementing your VLANs wisely. The cardinal rule in VLANs is that you should never have a single switch housing VLANs from different security-level networks. For example, the DMZ housing your Internet servers should never reside on a switch that also contains internal network VLANs and connections. This is because the DMZ is a much, much less secure network segment by virtue of the fact that it is designed to provide services to Internet hosts.

One type of VLAN-hopping technique we can protect against is what is known as a *double encapsulated VLAN hopping attack*. This attack relies on the attacker being able to connect to a trunk port, which allows the hacker to appear to be a member of all VLANs because the hacker's system is connected as a trunk device.

The first way to mitigate this is to ensure that auto-trunking is disabled on all interfaces. In fact, you should disable trunking on all interfaces and then go back and enable trunking on the specific interfaces that require it. Although it is convenient to be able to just connect two switches together and have them automatically negotiate the trunk, this allows the attacker to do the same thing. You can disable auto-trunking on IOS-based switches by running the following command on all interfaces that should not be trunk ports:

```
switch02(config-if)#switchport mode access
switch02(config-if)#switchport nonegotiate
```

For your CatOS-based switches, you can run the following command:

```
Console> (enable) set trunk 3/1-24 off
```

For ports that must be configured as trunk ports, you should make sure you assign a native VLAN to the trunk port and that the native VLAN is not the default VLAN and is not the VLAN that the client systems connect to. You can do this on your IOS-based switches by running the following command at each interface that you want to configure as a trunk port:

```
switch02(config-if)#switchport trunk native vlan 777
```

For your CatOS-based devices, you can run the following command, specifying the port number of the trunk port:

```
Console> (enable) set vlan 10 3/2
```

Private VLANs

NOTE   You can only configure PVLANs if the switch is operating in VTP transparent mode.

Although traditional VLANs are used to provide layer 3 segmentation on your network, private VLANs take it one step further by providing layer 2 segmentation while allowing hosts to share a common subnet. You can configure three types of private VLAN ports:

■   **Promiscuous**   These ports can communicate with all ports in a private VLAN.

■   **Isolated**   These ports can only communicate with promiscuous ports.

■   **Community**   These ports can communicate among themselves and any promiscuous ports.

To create PVLANs, you will create one of three types of VLANs:

■   **Primary VLAN**   This VLAN is used to carry traffic from promiscuous ports to any other ports, including isolated and community ports.

■   **Isolated VLAN**   Also known as a *secondary VLAN*, this VLAN can only carry traffic from isolated ports to promiscuous ports.

- **Community VLAN** Also known as a *secondary VLAN*, this VLAN can carry traffic between community ports and promiscuous ports. Community VLANs are commonly used when you want some devices on a subnet to be able to communicate with each other, but not with devices that are not members of the community VLAN.

The primary VLAN is configured for all ports that need to communicate with all hosts on the VLAN (for example, switch uplink port and ports that servers are connected to). Isolated VLANs are configured for all other ports (for example, ports that a workstation connects to). Figure 6-1 illustrates a scenario where you might want to use PVLANs.

In this situation, you have two servers that do not need to talk to each other for any reason (perhaps they are on a DMZ and provide different services). For example, you would configure the primary VLAN as VLAN 11, and the servers would each be assigned to isolated VLAN 12. By making VLAN 11 a primary VLAN, you allow the servers to communicate with any hosts on those ports. Because VLAN 12 is an isolated VLAN, the servers are not able to communicate with each other, even though they are on the same subnet and use the same default gateway. The following commands illustrate how to configure this on CatOS-based switches:

```
Console> (enable) set vlan 11 pvlan primary
Console> (enable) set vlan 12 pvlan isolated
Console> (enable) set pvlan 11 12 3/9-10
Console> (enable) set pvlan mapping 11 12 3/15
Console> (enable) set pvlan mapping 11 12 3/14
```

Your lower-end IOS-based devices support PVLANs through the use of protected ports. With a protected port, the hosts connected cannot communicate with another protected port without going through a layer 3 device, but they can communicate with any other nonprotected ports, as normal. The following command will configure a protected port:

```
switch02(config-if)#switchport protected
```

VLAN ACLs (VACLs)

VLAN ACLs are implemented for the same reason you would implement any other ACLs. There is one significant advantage to VACLs over traditional ACLs, however. VACLs are configured at layer 2 on Catalyst 6000 series switches, which allows them to be applied without a router, although the switch needs a Policy Feature Card (PFC). This also allows the switch to process packets and enforce the VACL at wire speeds in hardware so that there is no performance impact on the traffic. It doesn't matter how large the VACL is, the forwarding rate remains unchanged.

Although VACLs can be deployed in a standalone fashion to manage traffic, they can also be deployed to support PVLANs. This would allow you to define a VACL on the secondary VLAN while leaving the traffic on the primary VLAN unfiltered, for example.

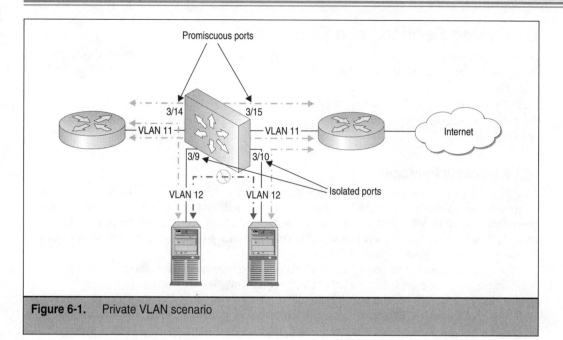

Figure 6-1.   Private VLAN scenario

Configuring a VACL on your CatOS-based switches is a three step process. First, you must create the VACL and add the access control entries (ACEs). The following commands demonstrate a VACL:

```
Console> (enable) set security acl ip vlan10acl permit tcp any →
host 172.20.10.4 smtp
Console> (enable) set security acl ip vlan10acl permit tcp any →
host 172.20.10.4 www
```

In this case, I have configured the VACL to permit SMTP and HTTP traffic from any host to 172.20.10.4. Because there is an implicit deny at the end of the VACL, all other traffic will be denied. The next step is to commit the VACL by running the following command:

```
Console> enable) commit security acl all
```

The last step is to map the VACL to a VLAN. This can be performed by running the following command:

```
Console> (enable) set security acl map vlan10acl 10
```

Hardening Services and Features

As with your routers, a number of services and features on your switches should be hardened. These include the following:

VLAN Trunking Protocol (VTP)	Auto-negotiation	Trunk links
Spanning Tree Protocol (STP)	Port security	Dynamic ARP inspection
Storm control		

VLAN Trunking Protocol

VLAN Trunking Protocol (VTP) allows the configuration of trunk links to be made at a central location and propagated to the rest of the switches in the VTP domain. One of the problems with VTP is that a malicious attacker could connect to the network posing as a VTP server and delete all the VLANs on the trunk ports throughout the network. There are two methods of handling this.

The first method is to configure VTP to operate in transparent mode. This allows VTP traffic to pass through a switch but prevents the switch from automatically updating the VLANs on the trunk ports. The obvious drawback, however, is that you will need to manually configure every trunk port in your environment anytime there is a VLAN change. You can configure your CatOS to operate in transparent mode by running the following command:

```
Console> (enable) set vtp mode transparent
```

For your IOS-based devices the command is

```
switch02(config)#vtp mode transparent
```

Another option to implement is a password for the VTP domain. This ensures that any systems that connect must know the VTP password in order to exchange information. You can configure the VTP password on you CatOS-based devices by running the following commands:

```
Console> (enable) set vtp domain mainoffice
Console> (enable) set vtp passwd <password>
```

For your IOS-based devices, the commands are

```
switch02(config)#vtp domain mainoffice
switch02(config)#vtp password <password>
```

The final VTP security issue is really more of a misconfiguration issue. You should ensure that all new switches are configured either as clients or in transparent mode to ensure that they cannot update the VLAN information if they are not configured properly.

Auto-Negotiation

Although technically not a security issue, it is a good design recommendation to hard-code your port speeds and duplex. This allows you to scale your bandwidth accordingly, providing more bandwidth to users the further away from the access port the network segment is. You should configure your access ports as 100 Mbps half-duplex ports. All interconnection ports (that is, switch to switch or switch to router) should be configured at the maximum speed allowed and for full-duplex operation.

You can configure the port speed and duplex on your CatOS-based devices by running the following commands:

```
Console> (enable) set port duplex 3/1 full
Console> (enable) set port speed 3/1 100
```

You can change the duplex syntax to half for half-duplex ports. In addition, like most other commands on the CatOS, you can specify a range of ports to configure with the single command. For your IOS-based devices, you will need to configure each interface individually by running the following commands:

```
switch02(config-if)#speed 1000
switch02(config-if)#duplex full
```

In this case, I have configured the interface to operate as gigabit full duplex.

Trunk Links

As you saw with the VLAN-hopping attack, you should control which ports are trunk ports. Unfortunately, many switches default to allowing all ports to auto-trunk—that is, ports will automatically negotiate to be trunk ports if the device connected is capable of being a trunk port. Because you should be planning each trunk port, there is no reason to allow ports to auto-trunk. You can disable auto-trunking as shown previously in the "VLAN Hopping" section of this chapter.

Spanning Tree Protocol

Spanning Tree Protocol (STP) is used to prevent layer 2 loops in the network. Although this is normally a good thing, attackers can force a root bridge to change, thus causing a DoS while the network converges on the new root. There are a couple of ways to prevent this from occurring. The first method is to simply disable STP. You can disable STP on your CatOS-based devices by running the following command:

```
Console> (enable) set spantree disable
```

For your IOS-based devices, you can disable STP by running the following command for each VLAN on which you want to disable STP:

```
switch02(config)#no spanning-tree vlan 10
```

In this example, I selected just VLAN 10. You can specify multiple VLANs by using a range, such as

```
1,3-5,7,9-11
```

The obvious problem with disabling STP is that if your network has loops, it could create the very problem you are trying to prevent. You can implement a couple features to protect the integrity of the STP root while still providing STP functionality on your network. These features are BPDU guard and root guard.

Implementing Root Guard   The root guard feature is used to configure ports to become designated ports so that no switch on the other end of the link can become a root switch. You can enable root guard on your CatOS-based devices by running the following command, specifying the ports on which you want to enable root guard:

```
Console> (enable) set spantree guard root 3/1
```

For your IOS-based devices, this can be done by running the following command on each interface on which you want to configure root guard:

```
switch02(config-if)#spanning-tree guard root
```

Implementing the BPDU Guard   The BPDU guard feature is used on ports that have been configured with portfast. portfast is typically implemented on access ports to allow a device to access the network without having to wait for the STP calculation to be performed. Unfortunately, portfast does not prevent hosts that connect from participating in STP, which can allow them to affect STP and the root placement. BPDU guard addresses this by disabling any port configured for portfast where a BPDU is detected. You can enable the BPDU guard feature by running the following command on your CatOS-based devices:

```
Console> (enable) set spantree portfast bpdu-guard 3/1 enable
```

For your IOS-based devices, you can enable BPDU guard by running the following command:

```
switch02(config-if)#spanning-tree bpduguard enable
```

Implementing BPDU Filtering   BPDU filtering prevents ports from sending or receiving BPDU packets. You have to be careful to ensure that you do not do this on trunk ports or any other port that may be looped. However, implementing BPDU filtering is an excellent prevention measure to ensure that a hacker cannot obtain a map of your network by processing the BPDU packets they receive. You can enable BPDU filtering on your CatOS-based switches by running the following command:

```
Console> (enable) set spantree portfast bpdu-filter 3/4 enable
```

For your IOS-based devices, you must configure the BPDU filter on each interface by running the following command:

```
switch02(config-if)#spanning-tree bpdufilter enable
```

Implementing UplinkFast   Some devices are intentionally configured with blocking ports to provide redundancy to the STP root. For these switches, typically access switches, it is recommended that you enable UplinkFast. This allows the backup port to begin passing packets immediately in the event of a failure with the primary connection instead of needing to wait the extra 30 seconds of convergence delay. You should implement UplinkFast on all switches in your environment that have blocking ports.

You can implement UplinkFast on your CatOS-based switches by running the following command:

```
Console> (enable) set spantree uplinkfast enable
```

You can implement UplinkFast on your IOS-based switches by running the following command:

```
switch02(config)#spanning-tree uplinkfast
```

Implementing BackboneFast   Like UplinkFast, BackboneFast is implemented to provide more rapid convergence times on STP networks. You should enable BackboneFast on all switches in your environment, unless your environment contains Catalyst 2900XL and Catalyst 3500 switches because they do not support BackboneFast.

You can enable BackboneFast on your CatOS-based switches by running the following command:

```
Console> (enable) set spantree backbonefast enable
```

For your IOS-based switches, the command is

```
switch02(config)#spanning-tree backbonefast
```

Port Security

Port security is one of the most fundamental security tasks that you can perform on your switches. Port security allows you to restrict the MAC addresses that can be associated with a switch. Port security should not be implemented on trunk ports because trunk ports potentially contain any number of MAC address associations; however, it is excellently suited for securing access ports.

You can configure port security to restrict MAC addresses in the following manners:

- **Restrict to learned MAC address**   This will configure the port to accept learned MAC addresses up to the limit of MAC addresses you have allowed.

- **Restrict to static MAC address**   This will configure the port to accept only packets with MAC addresses that you defined. Static port security should be implemented for all ports that connect to a router or to known servers that never move or change.

Restrict Using Learned MAC Address   Implementing port security using learned MAC addresses requires less overhead than manually assigning MAC addresses; however, it is also less secure. You can configure port security for learned MAC addresses on your CatOS-based devices by running the following command:

```
Console> (enable) set port security 3/1 enable
```

This will configure interface 3/1 to accept the first learned MAC address. You can configure the port to accept more than one MAC address; for example, you can allow five MAC addresses by running the following command:

```
Console> (enable) set port security 3/1 maximum 5
```

For your IOS-based devices, you can configure port security by running the following commands for each interface on which you want to enable port security:

```
switch02(config-if)#switchport port-security
switch02(config-if)#switchport port-security maximum 5
```

In both cases, if the port security is violated, the switch port will be shut down. Although this is the default behavior you can also configure the port to go into "restrict" mode. Restrict mode allows the port to continue to pass traffic, and only drops it from the offending MAC addresses. The following command will configure restrict mode on IOS based devices:

```
switch02(config-if)#switchport port-security violation restrict
```

Restrict to Static MAC Address   In addition to dynamically learning MAC addresses, you can configure the port with statically assigned MAC addresses. Although this is probably an overly cumbersome task for every port in your environment, you should implement static MAC address port security for all ports that connect to static resources (for example, routers and critical servers).

Configuring static MAC addresses is very similar to configuring learned MAC addresses. For your CatOS-based devices, you can run the following commands to configure static MAC addresses:

```
Console> (enable) set port security 3/4 maximum 5
Console> (enable) set port security 3/4 enable 00-00-56-02-11-23
Console> (enable) set port security 3/4 enable 00-00-56-02-11-25
```

For your IOS-based devices, you can run the following commands to configure static MAC addresses:

```
switch02(config-if)#switchport port-security maximum 2
switch02(config-if)#switchport port-security mac-address 0000.5246.1234
switch02(config-if)#switchport port-security mac-address 0000.5246.1235
```

Dynamic ARP Inspection

Dynamic ARP inspection (DAI) is a feature supported on certain Cisco switches, such as the Cisco Catalyst 4500 series of switches. DAI prevents MAC address spoofing and ARP cache poisoning by intercepting all ARP requests and comparing them against a

ONE STEP FURTHER

A more advanced form of port security is the use of 802.1x authentication for your switch ports. 802.1x port authentication is covered in more detail, including syntax examples, in Chapter 9.

known database that is obtained through DHCP snooping. Essentially, the switch will monitor DHCP broadcasts to see what MAC addresses and IP addresses are matched. Those addresses are added to the database of trusted MAC addresses. The following command will configure dynamic ARP inspection:

```
switch02(config)# ip arp inspection vlan 10
```

If you connect multiple switches that support DAI together, you will need to configure trusted ports for the ports that connect the switches together. For example, if interface FastEthernet 1/3 is connected to another switch running DAI, you will configure FastEthernet 1/3 as well as the corresponding port on the other switch as trusted ports, as shown here:

```
switch02 (config)# interface fa1/3
switch02 (config-if)# ip arp inspection trust
```

If you do not do this, the switches will block ARP requests originating from the remote switch, thus preventing communications.

Storm Control

Traffic storms typically occur when excessive broadcast and multicast traffic is present and can result in severe network performance degradation and even a DoS in extreme cases. You can control traffic storms, however, by specifying the percentage of bandwidth a given traffic type is allowed to use. This is known as *storm control* or *broadcast and multicast suppression.* The percentage listed ranges from 100%, which means no storm control (the traffic can use all of the bandwidth), to 0%, which means that all traffic of that type will be blocked (the traffic can use none of the bandwidth).

You can configure broadcast/multicast suppression by running the following command on your CatOS-based devices:

```
Console> (enable) set port broadcast 3/10-15 50%
```

In this case, we are limiting broadcast/multicast to 50 percent of the bandwidth for ports 3/10 through 3/15. For your IOS-based devices, you can configure storm control on each interface by running the following commands:

```
switch02(config-if)#storm-control broadcast level 50
switch02(config-if)#storm-control multicast level 50
```

In this case, we are configuring both broadcast and multicast levels at 50 percent of the bandwidth.

Summary

This chapter is easily one of the largest chapters in this book; however, it is also the most important. As I said when we started, routers and switches are your network infrastructure, and if you want to have a secure network infrastructure, you have to harden those devices.

As with all your other network devices, management, and more important secure management, is critical to maintaining a secure environment. You can have the most complex passwords imaginable, but if you are managing your device using Telnet, any decent hacker can gain access to that protected data. The most secure management mechanism leverages AAA for authentication, authorization, and accounting and reinforces AAA through the use of secure protocols such as SSL to gain remote management access.

The next security task to tackle is to harden all services, processes, applications, protocols, and features running on your network device. Unfortunately, our network devices ship with a bevy of services that, in theory, are there to simplify their implementation and function, but in many cases they can be exploited with equal simplicity. Turn off any services you don't need, and for the services you do need, leverage whatever means of authentication and encryption is available to protect the device.

Once you have secured your routers, it is time to secure the functionality your routers provide through the use of HSRP redundancy, authentication of your routing protocols, and traffic management. In particular with your routing protocols, implement static routing only for any insecure network segments, such as DMZ and perimeter networks. You should also use your routers to control the flow of traffic throughout your network, making extensive use of ACLs and CBAC to filter unwanted traffic while granting permitted traffic in as secure a fashion as possible.

Working down the OSI model, the next device group to harden is your switches. You want to ensure that your VLAN implementation is implemented in a secure fashion. Do not use the same switch for VLANs of different security-level networks (such as the internal network and the DMZ). Do not use the default VLAN (VLAN 1) in production anywhere on your network. Configure all your trunk ports to have native VLAN memberships that are on a different VLAN from the rest of your network devices. Finally, ensure that all switch ports are configured as access ports, and configure only those ports that should be functioning as trunk ports as trunk ports. As with your routers, you also want to restrict any unnecessary services, disabling what you can and implementing authentication for all protocols and services that support authentication. Finally, disable any unnecessary ports, not only on your switches but on your routers as well. If something isn't plugged into the port right now, it should require change control to get you to enable the port.

By following these procedures, you can greatly reduce the risk and threats to your environment.

Chapter 7

Securing the Network with Content Filters

- Internet Content Filtering Architectures
- Internet Content Filtering
- E-mail Content Filtering

When we talk about hardening network infrastructure, we often fall prey to looking at it from the perspective of keeping malicious users out of our network. We approach the subject with firewalls, access lists, and intrusion-detection/prevention mechanisms, which all do an excellent job of keeping people out of the network. However, we often overlook the value of hardening the network from the inside out.

Internet access is a way of life for many employees. It is something that is available to them that they often take for granted. For example, if they want to know what is happening in the world today, they can fire up their web browser and head over to www.cnn.com to get the latest news. Unfortunately, with equal ease the same employees can go to www.playboy.com, and suddenly the company finds itself in a situation where an employee's actions can result in financial liability on the part of the company. This type of misuse of resources can result in lawsuits due to the appearance that the company has created a hostile work environment. Even if things do not go to that extreme, this still results in a loss of bandwidth being available for legitimate resources. Thankfully, Internet content filtering can insulate our environment from these kinds of threats.

E-mail is also a way of life for many employees. In fact, for many companies, e-mail is a critical business resource that they cannot function without. At the same time, e-mail presents a huge potential for abuse. This abuse can come in many forms, but the most common are employees using e-mail resources for personal use, the influx of spam, and the ease in which viruses, Trojans, and worms can be spread via e-mail.

Instant messaging (IM) is another new aspect of Internet functionality that has quickly become an issues and needs to be addressed on corporate networks. On one hand, IM is instant access to people. It's like e-mail, but better. You need some information from someone? You can send them an IM and get a response faster than e-mail and without needing to make a phone call. For many sales organizations, IM is becoming a critical business process. At the same time, however, IM can be a pure timewaster as employees chat with their friends across the Internet (much to the relief of this book's author, I can assure you). IM also poses a distinct security problem because it is a very easy method for someone to share confidential information with external sources, and it's rapidly becoming a new source of viral infections, as evidenced by the recent Buddylinks AOL Instant Messenger worm.

A well-designed and implemented content-filtering solution provides us with a means by which we can mitigate all these threats and ensure that the Internet and e-mail do not represent a liability to the organization. In examining how to mitigate these threats, we are going to focus on the following content-filtering solutions:

- Internet content filtering
- E-mail content filtering

Internet Content Filtering Architectures

Three predominant content-filtering architectures are in use today: client, server, and gateway content filtering. Each architecture type has its own unique pros and cons that address items such as cost, effectiveness, and manageability.

Client-Based Content Filtering

Client-based content filtering is designed to be implemented at the client desktop. Client-based content filtering works by maintaining a database of blocked websites that the user can download updates to via the Internet.

One of the appeals of client-based content filtering is that the initial cost is usually cheaper than the alternatives, particularly for small-to-medium-sized businesses. Unfortunately, the long term costs are usually much higher because of the maintenance costs associated with trying to manage and maintain the software running on hundreds or thousands of desktops. Client-based content filtering is great for home users or very small shops, but it does not scale very well. Finally, because the software is running on the client, it is more susceptible to users not downloading updates or shutting down the service completely, which can render it ineffective. Although your acceptable-use policy (AUP) should prohibit this type of behavior in the first place, the reality is that the content-filtering software prevents access that is prohibited by the AUP, and you still need it. If people are willing to browse inappropriate content, they certainly won't have problems disabling software that prevents it.

Some examples of client-based content-filtering solutions are Zone Labs ZoneAlarm (http://www.zonelabs.com/store/content/home.jsp), NetNanny (http://store.netnanny.com/dr/v2/ec_dynamic.main?sp=1&pn=12&sid=53), and Cybersitter (www.cybersitter.com). In addition, many ISPs are starting to provide content-filtering solutions integrated into their client software. I do not recommend implementing client-based content filtering in most circumstances, but if your environment is small, it might be an option worth investigating.

Server-Based Content Filtering

Server-based content filtering provides a centralized mechanism for controlling content coming in and out of the network. Server-based content filtering is typically a two-part solution: the database server platform and the firewall or gateway. This is known as a *gateway integrated server-based content-filtering solution*. The database server platform is where the actual content-filtering software and database reside, and it contains the rulesets that define what will and will not be permitted. The firewall or gateway is then configured to query the content-filtering server when it receives an outbound request and will either forward the packet to the Internet or return an "access denied" page based on the content-filtering policy. Figure 7-1 details the topology for a gateway integrated server-based content-filtering solution.

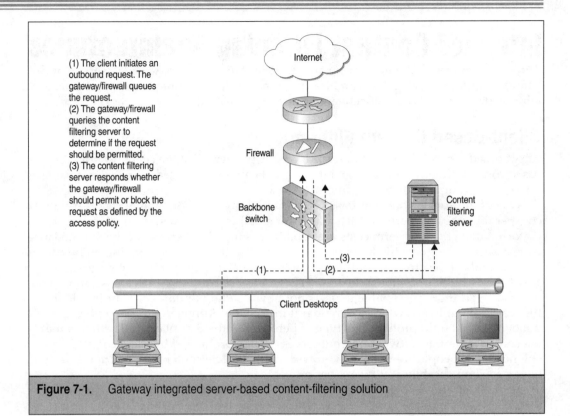

(1) The client initiates an outbound request. The gateway/firewall queues the request.
(2) The gateway/firewall queries the content filtering server to determine if the request should be permitted.
(3) The content filtering server responds whether the gateway/firewall should permit or block the request as defined by the access policy.

Figure 7-1. Gateway integrated server-based content-filtering solution

A variation of server-based content filtering does not include the integration of the content filter and the firewall or gateway. Instead, the content-filtering server is configured on the network so that it can observe all the traffic on a segment. The content-filtering server will then intercept the web requests and determine whether the content is permitted or denied. If it is permitted, it is passed on to the Internet. If it is denied, the content server responds with an "access denied" page. Figure 7-2 demonstrates the topology of this configuration.

ONE STEP FURTHER

For a content-filtering server to work in this fashion, it must be able to view every web request. Implementing a hub and connecting the content filter to the hub will not be a problem because the hub transmits the data signal to all ports. However, if you implement a switch, you will need to ensure that you have configured your switch with a monitor port for the content-filtering server to connect to, and this port must mirror all traffic to and from the Internet. If you do not do this, the content-filtering server will not be able to protect your network.

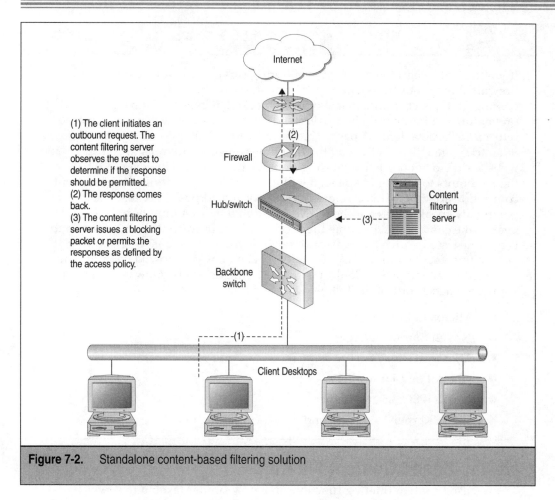

Figure 7-2.   Standalone content-based filtering solution

One of the benefits of a server-based content-filtering solution is that it is much easier to manage and maintain than a client-based solution. You merely need to update the server configuration and, by default, the clients are affected by the change. The server-based content-filtering solution also scales much better than a client-based solution because it is simply a matter of upgrading the server hardware in the event that the server begins having performance problems. A drawback of server-based solutions is increased cost. In addition to the cost of a firewall, these solutions typically require a dedicated server, and that server may need to be an extremely powerful server (or even a cluster of servers) in large environments.

Some examples of server-based content-filtering are Websense (www.websense.com), N2H2 (www.n2h2.com), and SurfControl (www.surfcontrol.com), all of which can operate in both modes.

I highly recommend server-based solutions; in fact, this chapter contains configuration examples for all three of these content-filtering solutions.

HEADS UP!

If you do not integrate your content-filtering server with your gateway or firewall, it functions by essentially sniffing the network to detect what traffic is passing. If it detects traffic that should be blocked, it generates a blocking packet, preventing the traffic from being received by the end-user system, and instead returns an "access denied" page. This is not a perfect situation, however, because often the page will initially load the first time someone attempts to connect to the website due to latency in the sniffing-to-blocking process. However, if the user then attempts to refresh the page, it will then be blocked, as will all subsequent connection attempts. This is referred to as "sneak and peek" because the user can potentially sneak access a website, even though they shouldn't be able to, and peek at the content the first time they connect. This only occurs when SurfControl is not integrated with a gateway or firewall. If you need to ensure that under no circumstances should a user be able to even view disallowed content, you will need to integrate SurfControl with one of the firewall/gateway devices it supports, such as one of the following:

- Microsoft ISA Server
- Novell BorderManager
- Microsoft Proxy Server
- Check Point Firewall-1
- Nokia IPSO 3.5 and higher
- Linux Kernel 2.4 of later and glib 2.2 or later

Gateway-Based Content Filtering

Gateway-based content filtering functions in a very similar fashion to server-based content filtering. It attempts to eliminate the drawback of server-based content filtering by removing the need for a dedicated external server and placing the content-filtering functionality into the firewall or gateway device. This can make for an even easier management task because the firewall and content-filtering functionality are centrally managed typically with the same management interface. The primary drawback of this type of system is that you are essentially placing all your eggs in one basket. If the content filter fails for some reason, you may need to take the firewall down to repair or replace it, which you would not have to do with a server-based solution. As a result, gateway-based content-filtering solutions are particularly suited for small-to-medium-sized environments and environments that cannot afford the cost of a server-based solution. However, if you require a separation of functions in your devices for either security or reliability reasons, a gateway-based content filter may not be the best choice.

Some examples of gateway-based content filters are Fortinet (www.fortinet.com), Symantec (www.symantec.com), and SonicWALL (www.sonicwall.com).

I recommend gateway-based content filters if you cannot afford a server-based solution or if you do not need the separation of resources in your gateway device.

Internet Content Filtering

Internet content filtering is essentially controlling everything going to and from the Internet with the exception of e-mail, which has its own unique filtering issues that we will discuss later in this chapter.

Although the Internet is a limitless pool of resources that can be used to research topics and provide a means for business-to-business communications, it is also a completely unmanaged and uncontrolled environment. I once heard the Internet referred to as the Wild West, and that is a pretty accurate representation. For all the good and value that it provides, a lot of danger seems to be waiting around the corner.

A good Internet content-filtering system can protect a network from numerous threats, including the following:

- Misuse of resources
- Preserving network bandwidth
- Hostile work environment
- Hostile web code (Java/ActiveX applets)

Misuse of Resources

Misuse of resources ranges from users surfing the Internet, to users frequenting newsgroups and chat rooms, to the rampant use of instant messaging software. Misuse of resources presents two distinct problems. First, it reduces an employee's productivity. Instead of working, employees will surf the Web and kill some time. Second, misuse of resources has the possibility of exposing the network to external threats through websites with active content or users downloading and installing software that is not permitted.

Preserving Network Bandwidth

The biggest culprit of bandwidth loss is the use of peer-to-peer file sharing applications such as Kazaa and Limewire. Streaming audio and video, for example, from people listening to Internet radio also can have a negative impact on Internet bandwidth. In addition, casual web browsing, if done enough, can have a detrimental effect on the company's productive Internet traffic.

Hostile Work Environment

The hostile work environment is perhaps the biggest problem that Internet content filtering needs to address. Companies can easily find themselves in the middle of costly litigation due to sexually explicit content that is on their network. Indeed, when you look at the numbers, it is really quite surprising what people are willing to do while at work and using work resources:

- Twenty percent of men and 12.5 percent of women admit to using their work computers to access sexually explicit content on the Internet—and these are just the ones that would admit it.

- Over 25 percent of workers say that they receive sexually explicit e-mails.

- Thirty-three percent of companies have terminated employees for abusing Internet access.

In today's litigious society, companies can and will find themselves liable for sexual harassment lawsuits due to a hostile work environment. In fact, one oil company paid a $2.2-million-dollar settlement as a direct result of content that was deemed to have created an unsafe work environment. This is especially true if it is found that the employer knew such activities were occurring and did nothing to prevent it.

Conversely, employers may establish an "affirmative defense" to a harassment claim by showing that they have an explicit policy concerning the use of corporate systems (an acceptable-use policy) as well as demonstrating that they have implemented a proactive system that seeks to prevent inappropriate content from appearing on corporate resources.

Hostile Web Code (Java/ActiveX Applets)

Since all Internet requests must go through the content filter to be permitted, your users can be protected from websites that may use Java or ActiveX applets to gain access to the user computer or surreptitiously install trojans or other applications.

Implementing Content Filtering

This section details the implementation of the following content-filtering solutions:

- SurfControl Web Filter Version 4.5 with Virtual Control Agent, using the Microsoft MSDE database engine on Microsoft Windows 2000 with Service Pack 3

- Websense version 5.1, integrated with Cisco Secure PIX Firewall version 6.3(1)

There are two primary objectives to implementing a content-filtering solution. The first is to block restricted content. You should approach blocking content as you do most security concepts, by taking a "deny all first, then permit only" position. By that you will design your initial blocking scheme to deny all traffic regardless of the source, the type, or who is attempting to generate the traffic. Once you have done that, you should go back and identify only the types of traffic you want to permit. For example, you might allow your administrators to access hacking-related sites while preventing your general user community from being able to do the same. You have to be prepared for configuring the initial ruleset to be a time-consuming process that involves making some mistakes. No matter how much you plan, you are going to block something that will need to be opened up. You need to set this expectation appropriately while at the same time planning as much as possible to minimize the chance of missing something.

The second objective is to be able to report on Internet usage. Although it is certainly nice to block access to restricted sites, you will also want to know what sites people are trying to go to. For example, do you have some people who are routinely trying to access blocked sites? If so, that could indicate a personnel problem that needs to be addressed. You also may have some people who are accessing permitted sites that your company may want to know about. For example, are people visiting a competitor's website? This may or may not be a problem, but either way it can be nice to know. Job-seeking websites are also good to track because this can indicate potential employee dissatisfaction, which might need to be addressed. If all the employees in a certain group seem to be looking for employment elsewhere, there might be something going on in that group that management needs to look into.

Unlike in most of the chapters in this book, because the configuration of these products is so unique, I am going to detail them in individual sections instead of detailing them inline with common concepts, as was done in other chapters.

SurfControl Web Filter Version 4.5

SurfControl is a server-based content-filtering architecture that does not require a firewall or gateway to be integrated with it to function. Because of this, SurfControl makes an excellent choice if you do not want a content-filtering solution that will tie you to a specific firewall or gateway.

The first step in installing SurfControl is ensuring that your network is configured properly to support monitoring. You can go about doing this in two ways. The first is to ensure that there is a hub that connects the firewall to the internal network. If that is the case, you can simply connect the SurfControl server to the hub, and it will be able to monitor all inbound and outbound Internet requests. However, if you have a switch that connects your firewall to the internal network, you need to configure the switch to mirror the firewall port to a NIC on the SurfControl server. This will allow the server to be able to monitor all activity. Because a mirrored port can only receive data, you will need a second NIC that connects to the switch so that the server can send any blocking packets and notify the user that their Internet access has been blocked.

You can configure mirrored ports, called *Switched Port Analyzer (SPAN)*, on a Cisco Catalyst 2950 series switch by running the following commands at the CLI:

```
switch02#configure terminal
Enter configuration commands, one per line.  End with CNTL/Z.
!- In this case I specified fastethernet 0/1 as the source port
switch02(config)#monitor session 1 source interface fa0/1
!- In this case I specified fastethernet 0/5 as the destination port
switch02(config)#monitor session 1 destination interface fa0/5
switch02(config)#exit
--! This line verifies that the SPAN has been configured correctly
switch02#show monitor
Session 1
```

```
---------
 Type         : Local Session
Source Ports:
    RX Only:       None
    TX Only:       None
    Both:          Fa0/1
Source VLANs:
    RX Only:       None
    TX Only:       None
    Both:          None
Source RSPAN VLAN: None
Destination Ports: Fa0/5
    Encapsulation: Native
Reflector Port:    None
Filter VLANs:      None
Dest RSPAN VLAN:   None
```

In this example, the firewall is connected on port FastEthernet 0/1, and the SurfControl monitoring NIC will be connected to port FastEthernet 0/5. Once you have completed this, the next step is to configure the filtering rules.

Filtering Content   SurfControl uses a basic ruleset to filter content and has three basic filtering levels:

- **Allow**   The traffic is permitted.
- **Disallow**   The traffic is blocked.
- **Threshold**   The traffic is permitted up to a threshold (either a certain amount of time or a certain amount of traffic). A threshold filter is good for allowing certain content through (for example, sports content), while only allowing a user to view that content for a certain amount of time in a 24-hour period.

In addition, you can filter traffic based on who is browsing, to where/what they are attempting to browse, and when they are attempting to browse. The combination of all three allows you to be extremely granular in what you will and will not permit in your environment. The rules are processed in a top-to-bottom fashion, so rules at the top of the list take precedence over any rules lower down in the list.

Creating a rule is a relatively straightforward process. Start the SurfControl Rules Administrator from the Start menu and click the Rule Wizard button. This will cause the Rule Wizard to start. At the first screen of the Rule Wizard, click Next.

At the Rule Type screen, select the type of rule you want to create—an allow rule, a disallow rule, or a threshold rule. In the following, I selected to create a disallow rule. Click Next to continue.

○ Allow Rule
    Create a rule that will allow people to go to certain web sites.

○ Threshold Rule
    Create a rule that will limit time spent online, or limit the amount of data downloaded.

◉ Disallow Rule
    Create a rule that will block people from going to certain web sites.

At the Who screen, select who to apply the rule to. You can select from six options:

- **Anybody** This rule will apply to anyone who attempts to access the Internet. This rule is good for restricting access for individuals who do not log into the domain, such as contractors. If you are unsure about whether everyone should be controlled by a rule, select Anybody. You can always change it later to be less restrictive if required.

- **Monitored Workstations** This rule will apply to any traffic coming from a monitored workstation. This is a good choice if you want to permit Internet browsing from kiosk systems (for example, in a break room) so that users can browse the Internet on their lunch hour or breaks.

- **Users, Groups, and Domains** This rule will apply to the users or groups that you specify. This is an excellent method of granting certain departments or groups of users access to Internet resources.

- **User Defined Objects** This rule will apply to any hostname, IP address, network name, MAC address, or subnet you define.

- **Who Lists** Using this option, you can apply the rule to groups of the previously mentioned objects. For example, you could create a group that contains domain groups and monitored workstations and apply the rule to that "who" group.

- **All Who Objects** Using this option, you can apply the rule to any combination of objects without needing to create a "who" list.

As shown next, I have decided to apply the rule to users, groups, and domains. When you're finished, click Next.

○ Anybody
    The rule will apply to anyone who tries to access the Internet.
○ Monitored Workstations
    Workstations monitored by SurfControl Web Filter.
◉ Users, Groups, and Domains
    Any Users, Groups or Domains on your network.
○ User Defined Objects
    A Host Name, IP Address, Network Domain, MAC Address, or Subnet.
○ Who Lists
    Customized groups of Who Objects.
○ All Who Objects
    Create a rule using any combination of the above.

At the Who Objects screen, select the appropriate "who" objects from the list on the left. The objects you can select are listed in the central list. When you select an object, the Add button becomes available. Click it to add the object to the Rule Members list. You can select multiple objects, which allows you to have a single rule apply to multiple users or groups of users. Here, I have selected to apply the rule to domain users. When you are finished, click Next.

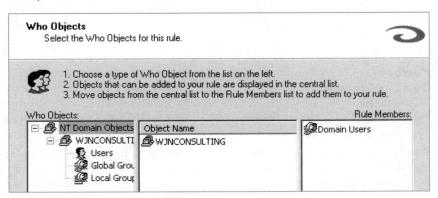

At the Where screen, you define where the rule will apply. You have the following six choices:

- **Anywhere**   This option will apply the rule to all traffic that the server monitors, both internal and external. For example, if the server was able to monitor traffic destined for an internal web server in addition to Internet traffic, selecting Anywhere would not only filter Internet traffic but would filter the traffic destined for the web server as well.

- **Monitored Sites**   This option will only apply the rule to all traffic going to or from websites that are monitored by the SurfControl web filter.

- **Categories**   This option will apply the rule based on traffic going to or from categories of websites. By default, SurfControl contains 39 categories of websites. Some examples of categories are Adult Content, Criminal Skills, and Drugs, Alcohol & Tobacco. You can find a comprehensive list of categories in Appendix A of the SurfControl Web Filter Administrator's Guide.

- **User Defined Objects**   This option will apply the rule on traffic going to or from a hostname, IP address, network domain, MAC address, or subnet that you define.

- **Where Lists**   This option will apply the rule on traffic going to or from groups of the previously mentioned objects. For example, you could create a group that contains monitored sites and categories and then apply the rule to that "where" list.

- **All Where Objects** This option allows you to apply the rule to any combination of objects without needing to create a "where" list.

As shown next, I have decided to apply this rule to traffic based on a category. When you're finished, click Next.

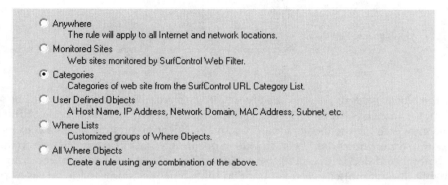

At the Where Objects screen, you can specify the "where" object you want to apply the rule to. Simply select the object name and click Add to add it to the rule membership. I have selected to apply the rule to Personals & Dating and Glamour & Intimate Apparel content in the screen shown next. I could also click New and create a new object that contains any one or multiple categories from the general list. When you are finished, click Next.

At the When screen, you can specify at what times the rule should be enforced. This is particularly valuable for filtering content that isn't offensive, but contributes to a loss of productivity. For example, sports websites can quickly erode employee productivity. However, you may want to permit that traffic during the lunch hour and after 6:00 P.M. for employees who want to check out the latest sports news on their lunch hour or when they are working late. Here, I have selected to apply the rule at all hours. Click Next to continue.

> **Anytime**
> The rule will be in effect at all times.
>
> **Set Date and Time Period**
> Create a new When Object or choose an existing object to define when the rule should be in effect.

At the Notify screen, you can specify whether an e-mail notification should be sent in the event that a rule is triggered. Notifications are an important part of content filtering because they provide the means for a proactive notification of questionable activities. At the same time, you should be judicious in deciding what rules to notify on so that you are not inundated with e-mails for relatively innocuous occurrences. For example, it probably doesn't matter if you get notified that someone attempted to access a sports website. However, you probably want to know if someone has attempted to access a sexually explicit website. Another good option to implement with notification is when you have developed a rule for a certain group. In those cases, you can add that group's manager as a notification recipient, allowing them to track and manage their employees and allowing yourself to take a hands-off approach. Here, I have selected Set Notification. Click Next when you're finished.

> **Nobody**
> No one will be notified when this rule is triggered.
>
> **Set Notification**
> Create a new Notify Object or choose an existing object to be emailed whenever this rule is triggered.

At the Notify Objects screen, you can add the list of e-mail addresses to notify by clicking New. That will open the SMTP Email Notification Properties dialog box, which allows you to create a customized notification, as shown next.

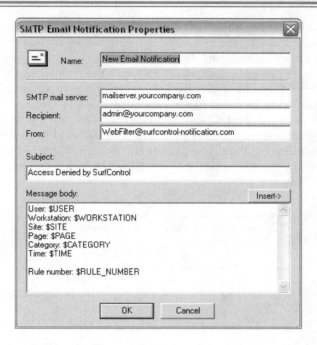

When you are finished with the e-mail notification, click OK. This will cause the new notify object to be created, as shown next. Select the object and click Add to add the object to the rule members list. When you are finished adding notify objects, click Next.

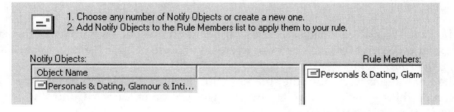

At the Http Deny Page screen, select whether you want to use the default deny page or to set a custom deny page. Here, I have selected the default deny page, though I have modified the HTML to add an explanation stating that the user can contact the helpdesk if they think they got this message in error. When you are finished, click Next.

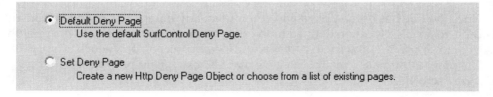

At the Rule Status screen, select whether you want to activate the rule immediately. If you select to make it active, the rule will be enforced as soon as you finish the wizard. When you are finished, click Next.

At the Rule Order screen, select where to apply the rule within the existing set of rules. Keep in mind that the rules are applied from the top down. If you have created a "disallow" rule, but you place it below an "allow" rule, the users will still be allowed to access the content. Conversely, if you create an "allow" rule and you place it below a "disallow" rule, the users will not be allowed to access the content. By default, the rule is placed at the top of the list and is highlighted. You can move the rule up or down using the Move Up or Move Down button, as shown next. When you are finished, click Next.

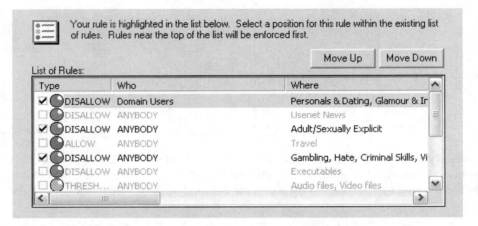

The Rule Wizard Finished screen will appear and present a summary of the rule. Verify that it is correct and click Finish to create the rule or click Back to go back and change the rule.

The final step is to commit the ruleset to the server so that it will be enforced. You can do this by clicking the Commit Changes button in the SurfControl Rules Administrator program, as shown here:

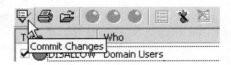

Once the rule has been applied and committed, any time a user defined in the rule attempts to access a location defined in the rule, the SurfControl server will apply the rule. For example, if I now try to access www.victoriassecret.com, which is a part of the Glamour & Intimate Apparel category that I blocked, I am presented with the following screen.

In addition, because I configured notification, I received the e-mail (shown at right) regarding the access attempt.

Although you will need to determine exactly what rules you should have in your environment, who they should apply to, and when they should be applied, I recommend that you start with the ruleset shown below. This ruleset will disallow most content that you do not need in your environment while providing access to certain leisure websites for up to 30 minutes per day. Finally, it will grant unrestricted access to other websites that rarely pose any threat to your network security or productivity.

SurfControl

Access Denied

Access to the requested URL has been denied by SurfControl

If you believe that you received this message in error or you do not

believe that this access should be blocked, contact the helpdesk.

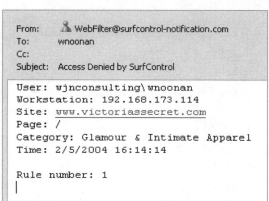

From: WebFilter@surfcontrol-notification.com
To: wnoonan
Cc:
Subject: Access Denied by SurfControl

```
User: wjnconsulting\wnoonan
Workstation: 192.168.173.114
Site: www.victoriassecret.com
Page: /
Category: Glamour & Intimate Apparel
Time: 2/5/2004 16:14:14

Rule number: 1
```

Type	Who	Where	When	Threshold	Notify	Http Deny Page	Comment
DISALLOW	ANYBODY	Remote Proxies, Glamour & Intimate Apparel, Usenet News, Personals & Dating	ANYTIME	NONE	NOBODY	DEFAULT	
DISALLOW	ANYBODY	Adult/Sexually Explicit, Sex Education, Hosting Sites	ANYTIME	NONE	NOBODY	DEFAULT	Disallow access to Adult materia
DISALLOW	ANYBODY	Games, Photo Searches, Streaming Media	ANYTIME	NONE	NOBODY	DEFAULT	Allow access to Travel material
DISALLOW	ANYBODY	Gambling, Hate, Criminal Skills, Violence, Weapons, Drugs & Alcohol, Hacking, Travel	ANYTIME	NONE	NOBODY	DEFAULT	Disallow access to inappropriate
DISALLOW	ANYBODY	Web-based Email, Chat	ANYTIME	NONE	NOBODY	DEFAULT	Disallow access to web- based (
DISALLOW	ANYBODY	Executables	ANYTIME	NONE	NOBODY	DEFAULT	Prevent the downloading of exe
DISALLOW	ANYBODY	MSN Messenger, Yahoo Messenger, ftp, nbsession, nntp, pop3, rlogin, telnet	ANYTIME	NONE	NOBODY	DEFAULT	Disallow access to Yahoo and M
THRESH...	ANYBODY	Audio files, Video files	Worktime	10Mbyte	NOBODY	Threshold	Limit multimedia activity to 10Mt
THRESH...	ANYBODY	Sport, Arts & Entertainment, Finance & Investment, Food & Drinks	Worktime	30 minutes	NOBODY	TimeExceeded	Limit access to Sports sites to 3
THRESH...	ANYBODY	Lifestyle & Cultures, Motor Vehicles, Religion, Real Estate, Shopping	Worktime	30 minutes	NOBODY	TimeExceeded	
ALLOW	ANYBODY	Computing & Internet, Education, Government & Politics, Health & Medicine, News	ANYTIME	NONE	NOBODY	DEFAULT	Give work related sites a higher
ALLOW	ANYBODY	Reference, Search Engines	ANYTIME	NONE	NOBODY	DEFAULT	Give Finance sites a lower priori

Reporting on Activity In addition to filtering content, you also need to be able to report on what the company Internet activity is. This allows you to determine who is trying to do what, and it also illustrates where you may need to add or remove rules or change your acceptable-use policy.

By default, SurfControl will monitor all users and sites with no additional configuration required by you. This allows you to quickly and easily generate reports on virtually any aspect of your company's Internet access.

You can generate reports by running the SurfControl monitor from the Start menu. Next, click the Reports button:

Reports

This will open the Reports screen, shown next. From the Reports screen, you can create virtually any type of report you may want. Some of the more valuable reports are the user activity, bandwidth analysis, and cost analysis reports, which can be used to provide detailed cost analysis of your Internet connectivity for the purposes of charging departments based on their portion of Internet usage.

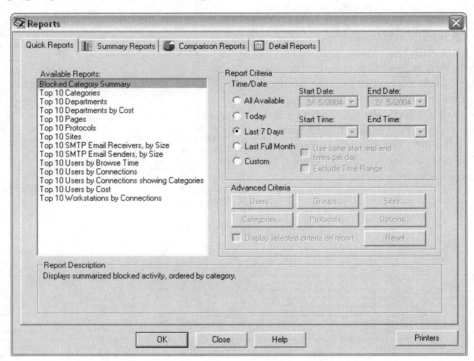

Websense Version 5.1 Integrated with Cisco Secure PIX Firewall

Websense integrates cleanly with the Cisco Secure PIX Firewall. The advantage of this type of implementation is that the firewall will not allow any traffic to pass to the Internet that has not been explicitly permitted. This prevents any chance of a sneak and peek occurring.

Once you have installed Websense, the next step is to configure the Cisco Secure PIX Firewall to use the Websense server for content filtering. This can be done by running the following commands at the CLI:

```
firewall# configure terminal
firewall(config)# url-server (inside) vendor websense host →
192.168.173.101 timeout 5 protocol TCP version 4
firewall(config)# filter url http 0 0 0 0
```

```
firewall(config)# filter ftp 21 0 0 0 0
firewall(config)# filter https 443 0 0 0 0
```

The first step is to configure the Cisco Secure PIX Firewall with the IP address of the Websense server and the interface that it is connected to, as just shown. The last three commands configure the firewall to filter all HTTP, FTP, and HTTPS traffic.

Once you have completed this, the next step is to configure the filtering rules.

Filtering Content   Websense uses a series of filter definitions for configuring its rulesets. The actual filter policies are contained in the Policies section. By default, there are three policies. The global policy is applied by default if no other filtering policy is specified. Websense determines which policy applies in the following order:

1. Policy assigned to the user
2. Policy assigned to the IP address of the machine being used
3. Policy assigned to groups that the user belongs to
4. The global policy

In the event that multiple group policies apply, Websense checks to see if they all have the same policy. If they do, Websense filters according to that request. If there is any difference between the policies, Websense filters according to the Use More Restrictive Blocking option at the server's Settings screen:

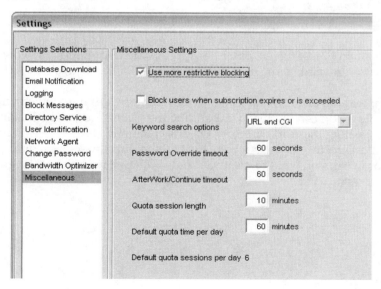

By default, this setting is unchecked. This means that if any group grants access, Websense will allow the connection. When the setting is checked, if any group denies access, Websense will block the connection. I recommend that you check this box for a more restrictive and secure content-filtering system.

Configuring content filtering for a new group of users is a fairly straightforward process. For example, let's assume that the Accounting group decides that they only want their users to be able to browse Business and Economy and News and Media sites (you can find a comprehensive list of all categories in Appendix A of the Websense Enterprise Version 5.1 Employee Internet Management Administrator's Guide).

The first step is to configure the Websense server to communicate with your directory service. This is done by right-clicking the server and selecting Settings. From the Settings screen, select Directory Service. Select the appropriate directory service (I selected Active Directory) and click Add:

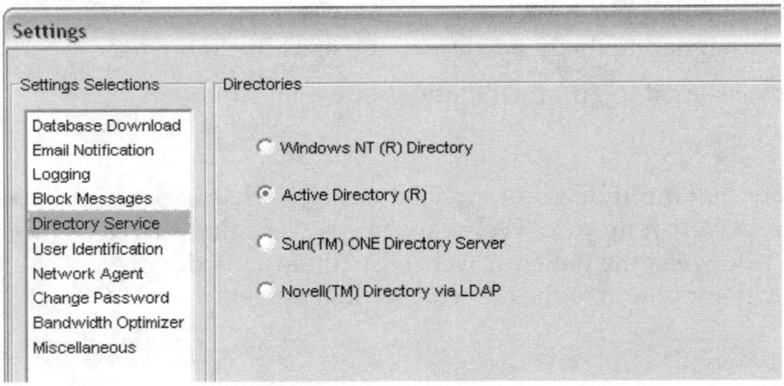

At the Domain Forest screen, enter the appropriate information to allow the Websense server to validate the domain and then click OK. Next, click OK to close the Settings screen.

Now you want to create a new client to represent the group to which you want to apply the policy. You can do this by expanding the Clients tree, right-clicking Directory Object, and selecting the Add Directory Objects command.

At the Add Directory Objects screen, expand the directory objects until you locate the group for which you want to create a client, as shown next. Select the group and click OK. The client will be created.

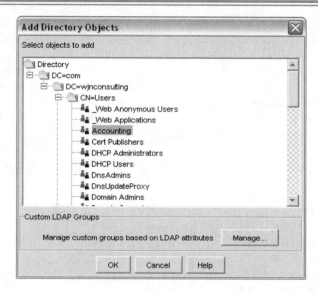

By default, the global policy is applied to the client. The next step is to create a new category set that contains the filtering rules you want to include in the policy. This can be done by right-clicking Category Sets and selecting Add Category Set.

When prompted, enter the appropriate category set name and click OK. When prompted for the category set model, select the category set to base the new category set on and then click OK. Next, select the new category set, as shown next, and click Edit. This will allow you to customize the category set.

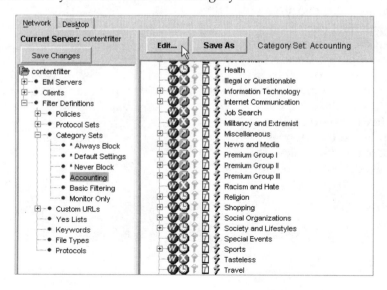

In the Edit Category Set screen, you can specify what traffic categories you will permit. In this case, we only want to permit Business and Economy and News and Media sites. First, select All Categories and select to block. The next step is to apply that setting to subcategories. This will cause all categories to be in a blocking state. Next, go back and permit the specific categories you want to grant access to by selecting them and clicking Permit. If there are subcategories, you need to select to permit them individually or select Apply to Subcategories, as shown here, to apply the setting from the parent value to all subcategories.

In addition to blocking sites, you should also click Block File Types and select Executables and Compressed Files. This will prevent people from being able to download any executables or ZIP files.

When you have completed editing the category set, click OK. The next step is to create a policy with the category set you want and apply it to the client. You can do this by expanding Filter Definitions tree and selecting Policies | Add Policy.

When prompted, enter a policy name and click OK. When prompted with the Policy Model screen, select the existing policy to base the new policy on or select Create Empty Policy to start from scratch. (For this example, I selected the latter option.) Click OK. Once the new policy has been created, click the top-left Edit button, as shown next, to edit the policy. This will open the Edit Policy screen.

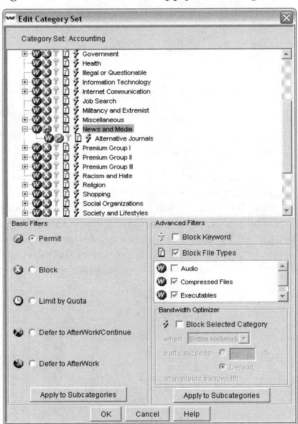

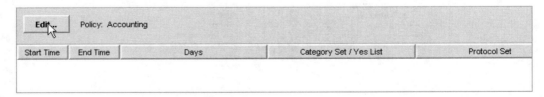

At the Edit Policy screen, enter a start and end time, the days that the policy should be applied, and the category set and protocol set to apply:

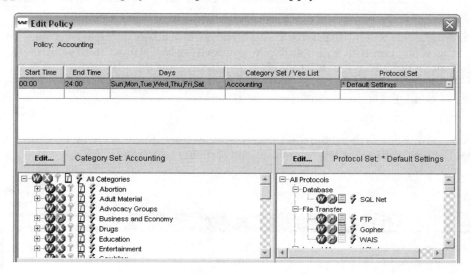

Next, you want to expand the client tree to select the client to which you want to apply the policy. Select the client and then select the policy from the Policy drop-down list:

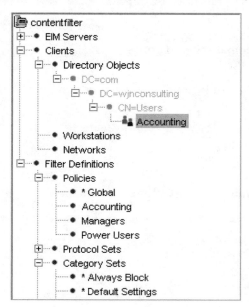

When you have made all the changes you want to make, click the Save Changes button to apply the changes to the Websense server.

HEADS UP!

The category Premium Group 1 contains a filter that controls whether advertisements will be displayed. If you do not permit advertisements, websites such as www.cnn.com will not display properly or will appear to have missing sections in the web page due to Websense filtering out the advertisements. This could create a usability issue or generate helpdesk tickets by confused users. Keep this in mind if you decide to filter advertisements.

Now, if a user to whom the filter policy applies attempts to access www.cnn.com, they will be permitted (notice the missing advertising banners):

However, if they attempt to access www.yahoo.com, they will receive an "access denied" statement:

Although you will need to determine exactly which policies you should have in your environment, to whom they should apply, and when they should be applied, I recommend that you start with the default category set shown here:

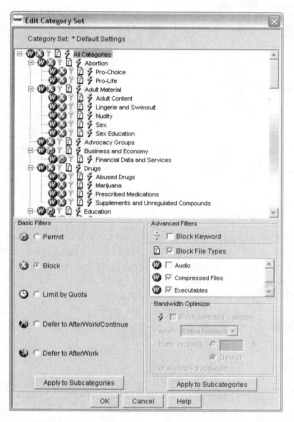

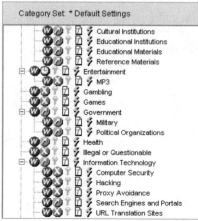

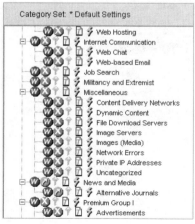

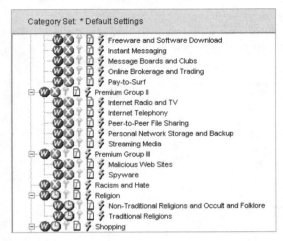
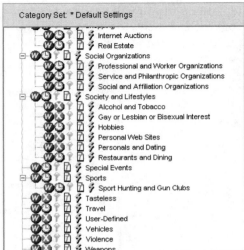

In this case, I am blocking all the content that could be considered harmful and setting a quota value for all casual or recreational browsing sites. The default quota time is 60 minutes per day in 10-minute session lengths. You can adjust this at the server's Settings screen, shown next.

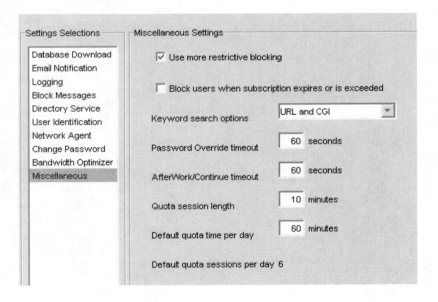

The last step of hardening your default policy is to restrict all protocols except HTTPS:

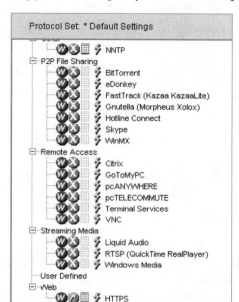

This policy will disallow most content that you do not need in your environment while providing access to certain leisure websites for up to 60 minutes per day. Finally, it will grant unrestricted access to other websites that rarely pose any threat to your network's security or productivity.

HEADS UP!

One easy method for trying to trick a content filter is to use URL obfuscation to mask the URL. This is typically done by trying to represent the URL in a format other than dotted decimal or DNS name. For example, one can convert the URL from dotted decimal notation to Hex, Octal, or Dword values and then use those values in place of the URL. An example would be using the URL http://0x40ec1074 to access www.cnn.com. When deciding which content filter you will use, make sure that people cannot use these methods to circumvent the content filter. For example, Websense is not susceptible to any of these types of URL obfuscation techniques.

Reporting on Activity   Like with SurfControl, in addition to simply filtering content, you need to be able to report on Internet usage with Websense. This can be done by installing the Websense Reporter program and then running the program from the Start menu. This will start the Websense Reporter:

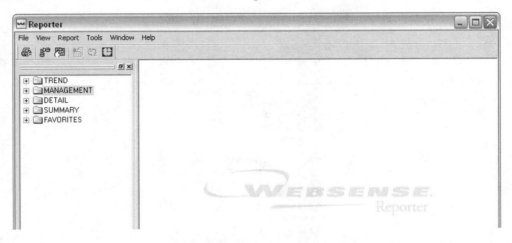

Websense uses canned reports for most circumstances to determine what kind of access is occurring on your network and who is responsible for the access. For example, if you wanted to determine what websites were being accessed, you could run the Top by Hits report under the MANAGEMENT | Category section:

Double-click the report and you will be presented with the Report Criteria screen, shown next. Specify the options you want to base the report on (by default, all options are enabled to create a full report) and click Generate.

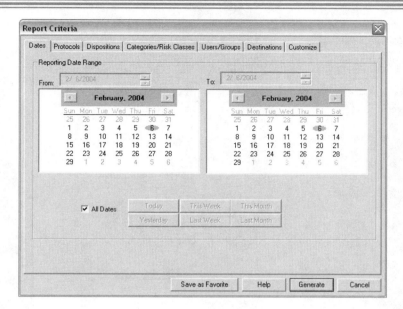

Figure 7-3 provides an example of what the Top Categories by Hits report looks like. If you notice that content such as "Adult Material: Adult Content" is frequently at the top of the list, you have a problem that needs to be addressed.

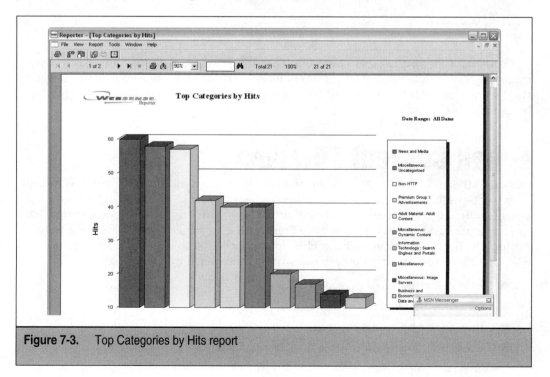

Figure 7-3. Top Categories by Hits report

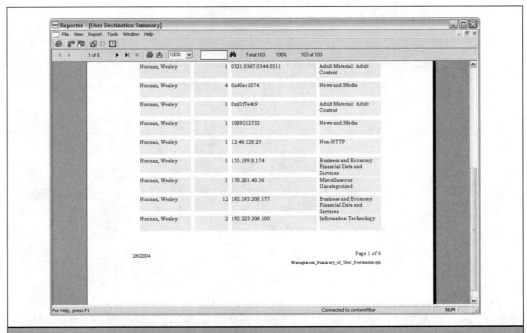

Figure 7-4. User Destination Summary report

You could then run a User Destination Summary report to determine which users might be responsible for the access, as shown in Figure 7-4. Notice how even though I tried using Octal, Hex, and Dword URL obfuscation, the attempts were still logged and blocked accordingly.

E-mail Content Filtering

Although the ins and outs of installing and configuring e-mail content filtering is outside of the scope of this book, there are a number of concepts and recommendations regarding e-mail content filtering we can discuss that will give you information you can take back to your e-mail administrators and have them look at as measures they can take to help protect the network infrastructure. Here are some of the things to consider when looking at how to protect your network from e-mail-based threats:

- Implementing virus protection
- Filtering attachments
- Implementing content filtering
- Implementing spam control

Implementing Virus Protection

E-mail is the predominant method of spreading viruses and worms today. Incidents such as the Melissa virus demonstrated that companies simply cannot afford to overlook having controls in place to prevent e-mail-borne viruses from entering their organization. There are two predominant techniques for addressing e-mail–based viruses and worms.

The first technique is to implement virus protection on the end-user systems. Typically, e-mail scanning on the end-user system is implemented as an overall component of the end-user system virus-protection software. For example, Network Associates VirusScan Enterprise has a component that will scan the client e-mail program (for example, Outlook) for viruses in addition to protecting the operating system against viruses. The benefit of this implementation is that you are getting e-mail protection without needing to actually implement anything special on the end-user system. In other words, because you need to be running virus protection on the end-user system anyway, it doesn't hurt anything to have that same product scan the e-mail users receive. There are a couple of downsides to this, however. First, it can be very difficult to update a large organization in the event of a new virus being spread by e-mail. The longer it takes to update your virus protection, the longer you will be susceptible to the threat. In addition, client-based virus scanning relies on the user receiving the e-mail *before* it can be potentially scanned for and cleaned. In many cases, e-mail–based viruses cannot be cleaned but rather wind up being quarantined where a user could potentially run them. Even with these downsides, you should run client-based e-mail virus protection as a component of your overall end-user virus security policy.

ONE STEP FURTHER

Many client-based e-mail antivirus products have the ability to e-mail the source of the infection to inform that person that they are infected with a virus. Unfortunately, this has become a case of "the road to hell is paved with good intentions." As is more and more the case, e-mail–based worms will spoof the e-mail address that the infected e-mail came from, which in turn causes the antivirus auto-response to go to someone who didn't actually send the e-mail. The net result is that the auto-response "you have been infected" e-mail messages increase the impact of the virus outbreak by clogging up e-mail gateways and mailboxes with essentially worthless junk e-mail. Therefore, you should turn this "feature" off.

In addition to implementing end-user antivirus protection, you should implement antivirus protection on your e-mail gateways. This mitigates the drawbacks of a client-only solution. First, you no longer need to update thousands of client systems in the event of a new virus, which decreases the amount of time it takes to be effectively protected. You simply update your gateways to gain the immediate protection you need; then you can update the client systems at a much more leisurely rate. Second, implementing virus protection on your e-mail gateways will catch and clean or quarantine the virus before it gets to the end users. This eliminates any chance of the users inadvertently launching the virus. Some examples of gateway-based virus protection are Network Associates GroupShield, Symantec AntiVirus Enterprise Edition (which contains e-mail gateway antivirus components), and GFI Mail Security.

In addition to you running antivirus protection on your e-mail gateway, many vendors are offering e-mail antivirus functionality integrated with the Internet gateway/firewall. For example, Netscreen and Fortinet both provide embedded antivirus protection in many of their firewall products. In addition, Check Point Firewall-1 and Microsoft ISA Server both accept the use of third-party plug-ins to provide antivirus capabilities at the firewall.

Filtering Attachments

Another effective method of preventing the spread of e-mail-based viruses and worms is to block certain attachments from being able to enter and exit your network. Simply put, some things just do *not* need to be e-mailed (for example, executables). At a minimum, Microsoft recommends that you block the following attachments on your e-mail gateways:

.{.	CLSID code	asd	Advanced Streaming Format Description file
asf	Active Streaming file	asx	Microsoft Windows Active Stream Redirector
ade	MS Access Project extension	adp	MS Access Project
bas	Visual Basic class module	bat	Batch file
chm	Compiled HTML Help file	cmd	Windows NT command script
com	MS-DOS application	cpl	Control Panel extension
crt	Security certificate	dll	Dynamic Link Library
exe	Application	hlp	Windows Help file
hta	HTML applications	hto	Hierarchal Tagged Objects
inf	Setup information file	ins	Internet communication settings
isp	Internet communication settings	js	JScript file

jse	JScript encoded script file	lnk	Shortcuts
mdb	Microsoft Access database	mde	Microsoft Access MDE database
msc	MS common console document	msi	Microsoft Windows Installer Package
msp	Microsoft Windows Installer Patch	mst	Visual Test source files
ocx	OLE Control Extension	pcd	Photo CD image, Visual Basic file
pif	Shortcut to MS-DOS programs	reg	Registration entries
scr	Screensaver	sct	Windows Script component
sh	Shell script	shb	Embedded shortcut
shs	Shell scrap object	url	Internet shortcut
vb	VBScript file	vbe	VBScript encoded script file
vbs	VBScript script file	vcs	Vcalendar file
wmd	Windows Media Download	wms	Windows Messaging System
wmz	Windows Media Skins	wsc	Windows Script component
wsf	Windows script file	wsh	Windows Scripting Host settings file

In addition, you should take a hard look at whether you need the following attachments to be permitted between your internal network and the Internet. Unfortunately, the business needs for many of these may preclude your ability to filter them.

doc	Microsoft Word documents	dot	Microsoft Word templates
mcw	Microsoft Word for Macintosh	xla	Microsoft Excel add-in
xls	Microsoft Excel spreadsheets	xlt	Microsoft Excel templates
zip	Compressed files		

Implementing Content Filtering

E-mail content filtering serves a number of roles in protecting your organization. First, it can detect whether content that is being sent or received is attempting to circumvent your existing anti-virus or e-mail security policy. For example, many users will attempt to rename an attachment that they want to send when they know that type of attachment will be filtered. Content filtering software is not susceptible to this because it does not rely on the file extension or file name to determine the file type. Instead, it examines the file headers to make a determination as to what the file is.

Second, content filtering can be used to scan for phrases, words, and other objectionable content for the same reasons that you filter Internet content. In addition, content-filtering software can prevent the use of HTML formatted, rich text font or other high risk e-mail formats. Some vendors of e-mail content-filtering software are SurfControl and GFI.

Implementing Spam Control

Spam control is a relatively unique aspect of network hardening in the sense that, in most cases, spam does not have the kind of impact that viruses or objectionable content do (although many times spam contains objectionable content). Spam is more in the realm of a nuisance than a real threat. This nuisance, however, can have a tangible financial impact on an organization. When you consider that estimates put the percentage of spam e-mail messages at 40–50 percent of all e-mail messages, the bandwidth cost of spam is substantial. Some estimates have placed the cost of spam on Korean Internet users and ISPs at $2.25 billion a year, and that is just Korea! In addition, the lost productivity of users dealing with spam is quite large. Some research has placed the cost of the time each employee wastes on e-mail at $4,000 a year. Although this does not exclusively refer to the cost of spam, the total cost in wasted productivity is roughly $130 billion, and even a conservative estimate would put the share of that cost in dealing with spam in the billions.

The single most important thing you can do to protect against spam is to ensure that your e-mail servers are not open relays. Spammers do not use their bandwidth for the sending of these e-mails. Instead, they attempt to locate open relays on the Internet and route the spam through them. You can test whether your system is an open relay at http://www.abuse.net/relay.html. For information about how to prevent your e-mail server from being an open relay, refer to your e-mail vendor's documentation.

Once you have taken steps to ensure that you are not part of the spam problem, the next step is to implement protection mechanisms to protect your systems from receiving spam. A common method of protecting from spam is through the use of DNS blacklists and open-relay database programs. These function by maintaining a list of IP addresses that spam is known to originate from (DNS blacklists) or a database of open relays (open-relay database programs). When an e-mail is received, the destination system queries an open-relay database server to see if it is listed as an open relay. If it is, the e-mail message is rejected. If it is not, the e-mail message is accepted. There are a number of well-known systems you can use for DNS blacklist and open-relay databases, including the following:

- **MAPS RBL**   http://www.mail-abuse.org/rbl/
- **ORDB**   http://www.ordb.org/

- **Spamcop**   http://www.spamcop.net/
- **Monkeys.com**   http://www.monkeys.com/upl/index.html
- **RFC- Ignorant**   http://www.rfc-ignorant.org/

Additionally, many content-filtering vendors are implementing content-based spam control by employing their content-filtering algorithms and heuristics to identify potential spam messages. Vendors that have spam-filtering software include SurfControl, SpamAssassin (http://www.spamassassin.org/index.html), and Network Associates (http://www.nai.com/us/products/mcafee/antispam/category.htm).

Summary

In a perfect world, you would simply tell your users what is and is not acceptable content, and you would never need to worry about it. You could tell your users not to download executables, and they wouldn't. Unfortunately, users don't tend to listen to us as much as we would like. To address this, you can implement content filtering on your network.

Internet content filtering provides the ability to very granularly control what kind of content will and will not be permitted in the environment. You can define which users can access what resources, even to the point of specifying when or how much of a resource they can access. In doing so, you can protect your company from litigation as a result of hostile work environment lawsuits, reduce productivity losses due to people browsing the Internet instead of working, and protect the company's network from external threats being passed in through the means of objectionable content. You can also report on the value of Internet content filtering by providing to management reports that demonstrate the tangible value content filtering provides by graphically demonstrating what content is being denied and what kind of content is being permitted. In addition, you can demonstrate what portion of bandwidth and, by extension, *cost* the permitted traffic represents.

In concert with Internet content filtering, you also need to implement e-mail content filtering. The most important e-mail content-filtering measure is to implement virus protection to ensure that e-mail–based viruses cannot threaten your organization. You also need to be able to filter and block certain attachments from being able to enter or exit your organization. Finally, you should implement content-filtering and spam-control measures to protect your organization.

Chapter 8

Hardening Wireless LAN Connections

- Banning WLANs Without IT/Management Approval
- Hardening Wireless Access Points
- Hardening Wireless LAN Connections
- Hardening Windows XP Wireless Clients

W ireless LAN (WLAN) connections represent the classic struggle between security and usability. On one hand WLANs were created and are used to simplify the ability of users to connect to and access network resources. With a wireless NIC, a user can connect to a network anywhere on a campus, in an office, or at any neighborhood coffee shop. On the other hand, WLANs are by their very nature insecure. The data is sent over the airwaves, where anyone can potentially receive it. In addition, an illegitimate user can often connect to a WLAN with the same ease that a legitimate user can if the WLAN is left in the default mode. Indeed, no one in their right mind who has any kind of security focus would allow a WLAN in their environment. However, it is not a lost cause. As you will see, there are many things you can do to secure your WLANs.

At the same time, you may already have a WLAN or are planning one. Does this mean you aren't concerned with security? Of course not. To the contrary, this illustrates how important it is to provide usability and functionality to your users. It also illustrates the simple reality that in the struggle between what users want and need and security, security frequently comes in second. This does not mean that we have to accept that we cannot secure our WLANs, though. Instead, it means that we need to take extra measures to ensure that we provide the access our users request while providing the security our network requires.

Banning WLANs Without IT/Management Approval

As mentioned in Chapter 1, wireless presents a unique problem to your networks. It is entirely too easy for someone to obtain a rogue WAP, connect it to your network (using DHCP to assign the WAP an IP address), and then allow anyone with a wireless client to be able to connect to your network, even though your wireless security policy should explicitly prohibit such actions.

Preventing Rogue APs

No good, bulletproof technical method exists to prevent a WAP from being connected to your network. By that I mean that if someone wants to bring a rogue AP onto your network, they are always going to have a chance of being successful. This doesn't mean that you should pack up the tent and head home, however. There are a few things you can do to prevent or greatly reduce the odds of a rogue WAP being successfully connected to your network:

■ *Implement a wireless security policy.* The first thing to do is to have a good wireless security policy. The problem of unauthorized WAPs is largely a people problem that requires a people solution in the form of enforceable security policies. Also, your wireless security policy is one that absolutely must have teeth. If someone brings a rogue WAP online, they need to be subject to termination of employment. Your wireless security policy also needs to define what the response to a rogue AP is. For example, will the AP be confiscated, and, if so, who is responsible for that?

- *Provide for physical security.* A WAP has a limited range. You should implement physical security measures that prevent someone from being able to get within range of a WAP running in your organization. Unfortunately, oftentimes this is not a practical measure, and it's useless in regard to people with unauthorized WAPs (they already aren't paying attention to the security policy, so they probably don't care about where they locate their WAP).

WLAN Modes of Operation and Components

Another aspect of your wireless security policy should define the mode of operation permitted for your WLANs. WLANs have two modes of operation. The first mode of operation is infrastructure mode, and it's the conventional WLAN configuration. Infrastructure mode entails the wireless clients being connected to the existing wired infrastructure by way of a WAP or wireless router. The second mode of operation is ad hoc mode, sometimes referred to as *peer-to-peer mode*. In ad hoc mode, multiple wireless clients are connected to each other in a peer-to-peer fashion, allowing small workgroups of computers to connect to each other without any other infrastructure. You should not allow ad hoc connections in your environment.

You also need to explicitly define the physical WLAN components you will allow in your network. This will assist you in detecting and identifying unauthorized wireless devices. The three primary WLAN components to define in your environment are the following:

- **Wireless access point (WAP)**   A WAP (sometimes referred to as a *base station)* is the device that wireless clients connect to. A WAP can typically connect hundreds of wireless clients and effectively operates like a bridge, allowing the client access to the physical LAN segment the WAP is connected to. WAPs are typically used in enterprise environments to provide wireless access.

- **Wireless router**   Wireless routers combine the functionality of a WAP with a router, allowing wireless clients to connect to the router and then be routed to other networks. Wireless routers often include firewall functionality and are typically used in small office/home office (SOHO) environments to provide wireless access.

- **Wireless client**   Wireless clients include any device that uses a wireless network card to communicate with a WAP or wireless router.

- *Provide a supported WLAN infrastructure.* If people want a WLAN and they don't have one, they might be tempted to implement one on their own. On the other hand, if you make sure you implement a WLAN that supports your users' needs, they will be much less likely to decide to go about it on their own. The truth is, most rogue WLANs are implemented by nonmalicious users who simply think that a WLAN will make their lives easier.

- *Implement 802.1x port-based security on your switches.* As we will discuss in Chapter 9, you should implement 802.1x port-based security to prevent any unauthorized connections to your network by requiring all connections to be authenticated. This includes preventing an unauthorized WAP from being able to connect.

- *Limit the number of MAC addresses per port to only one.* This will prevent switches from passing packets from rogue WAPs because the WAP and the client both have different MAC addresses. This is also a good measure if you want to prevent the users from plugging in a "rogue" switch or hub as well. You can implement this on many IOS-based switches by running the following command at the CLI:

```
switch02(config-if)# switchport port-security maximum <max addrs>
```

Rogue WAPs

I personally know of companies that have rogue WAPs that allow anyone on the freeway to access their internal production network, including potentially granting access to source code. A rogue WAP is a death blow to security because no matter how much you have hardened the perimeter, it has been instantly undermined by the WAP once it connects to your internal network.

Once you have undertaken procedures to prevent unauthorized WAPs, the next step is to implement procedures to detect unauthorized wireless connections.

Implementing WLAN Discovery Procedures

Just because we can't really prevent unauthorized WAPs from being implemented on the network doesn't mean we can't detect and remove them. It just means that we need to get a little creative in how we approach the problem.

You have two primary methods of detecting unauthorized WAPs on your network. The first method attempts to detect them wirelessly. The second method attempts to detect them from the wired network.

Detecting Unauthorized WAPs Wirelessly

The most effective method of detecting unauthorized WAPs is by simply using a wireless client and locating the WAPs broadcasting in your environment. A few caveats must be considered when employing this method, however:

- You have to be within range of the WAP in order to detect it.
- It is very difficult to detect a WAP that does not broadcast its SSID.
- It can be difficult to survey remote sites.

The good news is that because most unauthorized WAPs are not implemented by malicious users (and oftentimes are implemented by nontechnical users), the odds are high that the SSID broadcast has not been disabled. This leaves us with the problems of needing to be within range of the WAP to detect it and trying to survey remote sites. It is often impractical for someone in IT to spend the day walking around trying to determine if they can detect access points. One of the best solutions I have seen for this is to take advantage of someone who on a daily basis must walk around the environment—the mail delivery person. You can outfit this person with a laptop or handheld carrying extra batteries and while they make their normal rounds delivering the mail, the laptop can sit in the bottom of the mail cart quietly detecting any WAPs. A number of wireless analyzers can be used to detect the presence of unauthorized WAPs, including the following:

- Airdefense (http://www.airdefense.net/)
- Airmagnet (http://www.airmagnet.com/)
- Boingo (http://www.boingo.com/)
- Netstumbler (http://www.netstumbler.com)
- Kismet (http://www.kismetwireless.net/)
- Network Associates Sniffer (http://www.networkassociates.com/us/products/sniffer/home.asp)
- Wildpackets Airopeek NX (http://www.wildpackets.com/products/airopeek_nx)

Netstumbler provides one of the easiest methods for detecting a rogue AP over the wireless network. Once you install Netstumbler, the program automatically begins scanning for WAPs with no configuration required on your part (other than providing the wireless NIC, of course). For example, the screen shown next depicts what I was able to capture while driving down a major freeway in the Houston area. I captured 175 WAPs, of which 113 were running no encryption whatsoever, and none of which were running WiFi Protected Access (WPA). Instead, they were all using WEP.

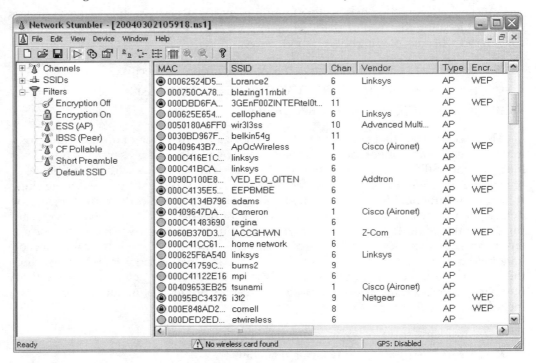

Detecting Unauthorized WAPs from the Wired Network

Detecting unauthorized WAPs from the wired network is generally not as easy a process as it is to detect them wirelessly. After all, it doesn't get much simpler than walking around with a laptop and a wireless card. At the same time, you can't really do much about the biggest problem with trying to detect a WAP wirelessly—namely—detecting a WAP that is not broadcasting its SSID.

Using a wired detection process can alleviate some of the disadvantages to trying to detect an unauthorized WAP wirelessly. For example, a wired detection process is not susceptible to missing WAPs that do not broadcast their SSIDs. In addition, a wired detection process can be used to survey remote sites and can even be scheduled and scripted to increase ease of use.

Unfortunately, there are some drawbacks to this method. It can be difficult to locate all the unauthorized access points. This is largely due to the lack of mature or specialized products for this task. Currently, most techniques rely on using MAC addresses (because all vendors are assigned a MAC address range) or OS fingerprinting to identify the WAP, both of which are an imprecise science. Here are two tools that can assist you in identifying an unauthorized AP by monitoring MAC addresses:

- **AP Tools (http://winfingerprint.sourceforge.net/aptools.php)**   AP Tools not only can discover an access point based on the MAC address, it can also attempt to check to verify that the access point is a WAP.

- **Arpwatch (http://www-nrg.ee.lbl.gov/)**   Arpwatch can monitor the network and maintain a database of MAC address and IP address pairings.

Here are some tools that can assist you in OS fingerprinting:

- **Nmap (http://www.insecure.org/nmap/index.html)**   Nmap can be used to identify the OS that a scanned host is running. For more information on using Nmap see Chapter 13.

- **Xprobe (http://www.sys-security.com/html/projects/X.html)**   Xprobe is similar to Nmap in its ability to identify the OS through the use of fingerprinting.

- **Nessus (http://www.nessus.org)**   Nessus is discussed in detail in Chapter 13. However, you can find an excellent whitepaper that details the process of using Nessus to detect rogue WAPs at http://www.tenablesecurity.com/wap-id-nessus.pdf.

Both of these methods share the common problem of generating false positives. For example, Nmap recognizes a Linksys WAP54G as a Linux device because it actually runs Linux for the OS. This can make it difficult to determine whether the device is indeed a WAP or just a Linux host running on your network. MAC address tools rely on identifying a device due to it having a MAC address that has been assigned to a wireless vendor. That can make it difficult to distinguish between a Cisco AP and a Cisco switch if the database of MAC addresses has not been accurately updated.

Detecting WAPs from the Wired Network

While I was writing this, I got into a discussion with a colleague about the inconsistencies and difficulties of detecting a rogue wireless AP on the network. He mentioned that he was testing an alpha version of Network Associates ePolicy Orchestrator (EPO; http://www.nai.com/us/products/mcafee/mgmt_solutions/epo.htm) that has the ability to detect rogue wireless APs. When I asked him how well it worked, he mentioned that he had tested EPO with a number of different wireless APs and that it detected all of them within 5–8 minutes of being brought online. The technology is definitely improving, and the accuracy of the detection algorithms is getting much better.

Removing Rogue WAPs

Once you have detected a rogue WAP, you have a couple of methods you can use to shut it down. One option is to attempt to physically locate and disconnect the WAP from the network. However, this can be both time consuming and prone to failure. The obvious difficulty in this method is that it can be very difficult to locate the WAP, usually through a trial-and-error process. (Is the WAP here? No. Is it here? No.)

Another option is to locate the switch port that the MAC address is connected to and shut that switch port down. Similarly, you can determine the IP address of the WAP and attempt to block the IP address. Personally, I recommend shutting down the switch port. In many cases, this will cause the person to seek you out, saving you the time and effort of trying to find them.

> **User:** Uh, yes, I can't access anything on the network anymore. I don't know what happened.

> **You:** No problem. We know exactly what is going on. What office are you in?

Hardening Wireless Access Points

Although all wireless access points have unique interfaces, they share common functions and processes that can be hardened. This section focuses on what you can do to harden the WAP itself. We will look at the following hardening steps:

- Hardening remote administration
- Configuring the Service Set Identifier (SSID)
- Configuring logging
- Configuring services
- Configuring wireless mode

It would be impossible to detail the procedures for hardening every type of wireless access point manufactured; therefore, I will illustrate the specific hardening steps for the following WAPs:

- Cisco Aironet 1200 running IOS version 12.2(13)JA2
- Linksys WAP54G running firmware version 2.06
- Dell TrueMobile 2300 running firmware version 3.0.0.8 in access point mode

HEADS UP!

Many of the configuration changes you make to the Dell TrueMobile 2300 require a restart before they take effect. This can make it difficult to make changes during production hours or while clients are connected to the WAP.

The instructions in this chapter assume that you have configured the device with an IP address that is relevant for your network and that you have already connected to the respective web-based management GUI and successfully logged on. In addition, the screen references refer to the menus you would need to click to access the given screen. For example, "go to the Security | Admin Access screen" means that you must click the Security menu and then the Admin Access menu to be presented with the screen in question.

Hardening Remote Administration

Like all our network devices, we should secure our WAPs against unauthorized remote administration. Unfortunately, unlike many network devices, virtually all WAPs fail miserably at providing secure remote administration. This is due to most of them providing only an unencrypted management protocol such as Telnet or HTTP for connecting to the device. Even with that gross oversight in security, certain steps can be taken to harden remote administration. The most important task is to change the default administrative username and to implement passwords that conform to your password security policy.

Changing the Default Administrator Name and Password

The Cisco Aironet 1200 implements a full IOS feature set. Consequently, it can be hardened for remote access by requiring all CLI connections to use SSH, as you do for your Cisco routers (refer to Chapter 6). In addition, out of the box the Cisco Aironet 1200 uses the default authentication mechanism of a global password (enable secret). You can change the password at the Security | Admin Access screen, as shown next. I recommend that you use an authentication server, where possible, and individual local users if an authentication server is not an option. By default, the WAP ships with a default username of Cisco and a default global password of Cisco. You should change both of these as well. Click Apply in each section when you are finished.

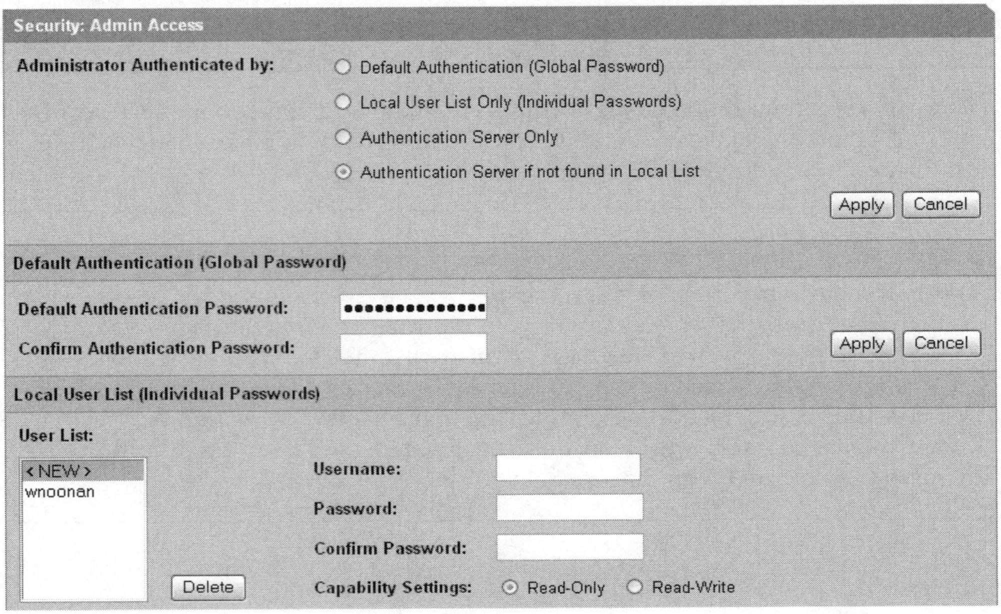

Security: Admin Access

Administrator Authenticated by:
- ○ Default Authentication (Global Password)
- ○ Local User List Only (Individual Passwords)
- ○ Authentication Server Only
- ⊙ Authentication Server if not found in Local List

[Apply] [Cancel]

Default Authentication (Global Password)

Default Authentication Password: ●●●●●●●●●●●●●●

Confirm Authentication Password: [ ]   [Apply] [Cancel]

Local User List (Individual Passwords)

User List:

< NEW >
wnoonan

Username: [ ]
Password: [ ]
Confirm Password: [ ]

[Delete]   Capability Settings: ⊙ Read-Only   ○ Read-Write

If you want to use an authentication server, you must first configure the WAP to use a RADIUS or TACACS+ server at the Security | Server Manager screen in the Corporate Servers section, as shown next. Make sure you scroll down to the Default Server Priorities section and select the newly added authentication server for the Admin Authentication setting. When you are finished, click Apply.

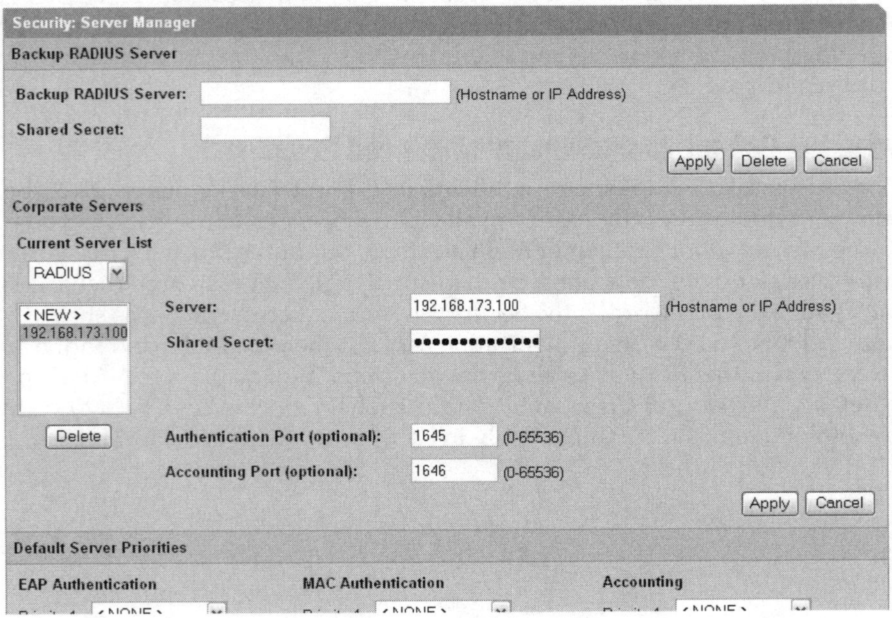

Security: Server Manager

Backup RADIUS Server

Backup RADIUS Server: [ ] (Hostname or IP Address)

Shared Secret: [ ]   [Apply] [Delete] [Cancel]

Corporate Servers

Current Server List

[RADIUS ▾]

< NEW >
192.168.173.100

Server: [192.168.173.100] (Hostname or IP Address)

Shared Secret: ●●●●●●●●●●●●●●

[Delete]   Authentication Port (optional): [1645] (0-65536)

Accounting Port (optional): [1646] (0-65536)

[Apply] [Cancel]

Default Server Priorities

EAP Authentication	MAC Authentication	Accounting
< NONE >	< NONE >	< NONE >

The Linksys WAP54G does not implement username and password security. Instead, it uses a password only. You can configure the password at the Setup | Password screen, as shown here. When you are finished, click Save Settings.

The Dell TrueMobile 2300 utilizes both a username and password. By default, the username is admin. You should change both the username and password according to your security policy. This can be done at the Advanced Settings | Administration Settings screen, as shown next. When you are finished, click Submit.

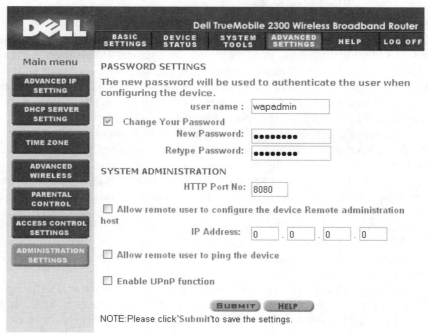

The system administration section shown here is used when the WAP is operating in router mode. The settings allow you to permit an external host (that is, across the Internet) to be able to make remote administration connections to the WAP. You should never enable this functionality because Dell does not support HTTPS for remote administration connections.

Securely Configuring the Service Set Identifier (SSID)

The service set identifier (SSID) is a unique identifier used in the packet header of wireless packets as a password for authenticating the client. The SSID is also known as the *network name*. By default, most WAPs will broadcast the SSID so that wireless clients can identify the WAP to which they should connect. This creates an obvious security vulnerability, however, because anyone with a wireless client can immediately determine a WAP is in the area by using a tool such as NetStumbler.

To address this issue, it is recommended that you disable the SSID broadcast.

HEADS UP!

In my experience, I have found that some wireless clients will not connect to a WAP that is not broadcasting the SSID. This is particularly true of Microsoft PocketPC 2003 devices using the SanDisk SDIO WiFi NIC (or any other NIC based on the Socket chipset and driver). I have, as of yet, been unable to determine why this is, though my suspicion is that it's due primarily to the immaturity of the SDIO cards and drivers.

Another problem with the SSID is that many people configure it with a value that makes it easy to locate where the WAP is physically located. This is both good and bad. It is good in the sense that it allows you to quickly identify where a WAP is. It is bad, however, in that it can let hackers know that they have connected to a WAP at their target company. As a result, when you configure the SSID, you should never include any information that might identify your company, location, or brand of WAP.

The last aspect of SSID hardening you should configure is the *beacon interval*, which is the amount of time that transpires before the WAP advertises the SSID via broadcast. By setting the beacon interval to its maximum setting, you increase the difficulty of performing passive scanning. It is important to understand that disabling SSID broadcast or increasing the SSID beacon interval is not an end-all security solution. In fact, Microsoft claims that this is not a security measure at all. This is due to the fact that even if the SSID is not broadcast, it can still be determined if someone is using a sniffer in the area where a WAP is in operation. Changing these settings is still an effective method of obscuring your WAP from casual threats, however. All these SSID settings can be configured as follows.

The Cisco Aironet 1200 uses a default SSID of "tsunami" in what is called *guest mode*, which means the SSID is broadcast in the beacon. The default SSID should be removed and replaced with a new one for your environment. This can be done at the

Security | SSID Manager screen shown next. If you want to make sure the SSID is not broadcast, ensure that no SSID is configured in the Guest Mode field in the "Global Radio0-802.11B SSID Properties" section of the SSID Manager screen. When you are finished, click Apply.

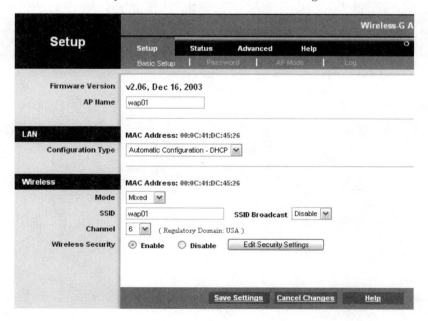

For the Linksys WAP54G, you can configure the SSID at the Setup | Basic Setup screen, shown next. When you are finished, click Save Settings.

The beacon interval can be configured at the Advanced | Advanced Wireless screen, shown next. When you are finished, click Save Settings.

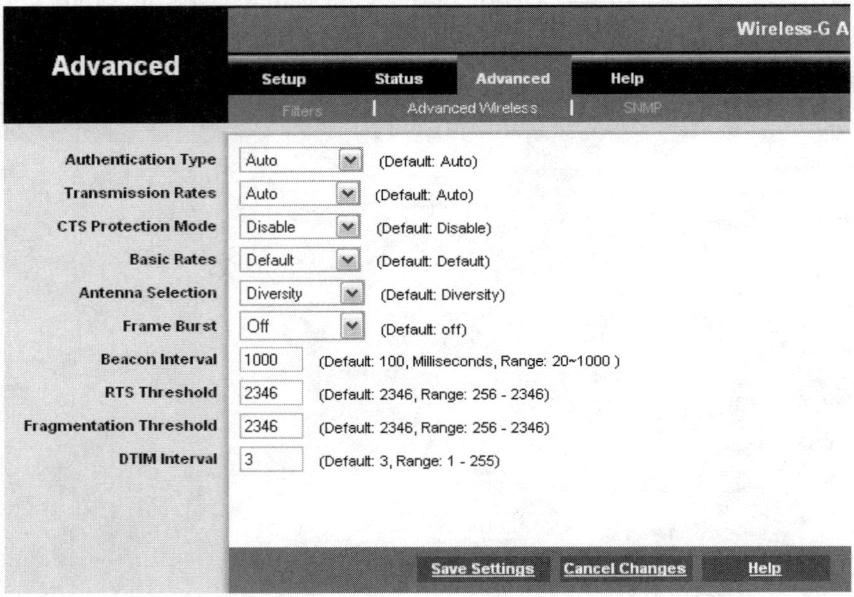

For the Dell TrueMobile 2300, you can configure the SSID and the beacon interval at the Advanced Setting | Advanced Wireless screen, as shown next. To turn off the SSID broadcast, check the box labeled Hide My Wireless Network. When you are finished, click Submit.

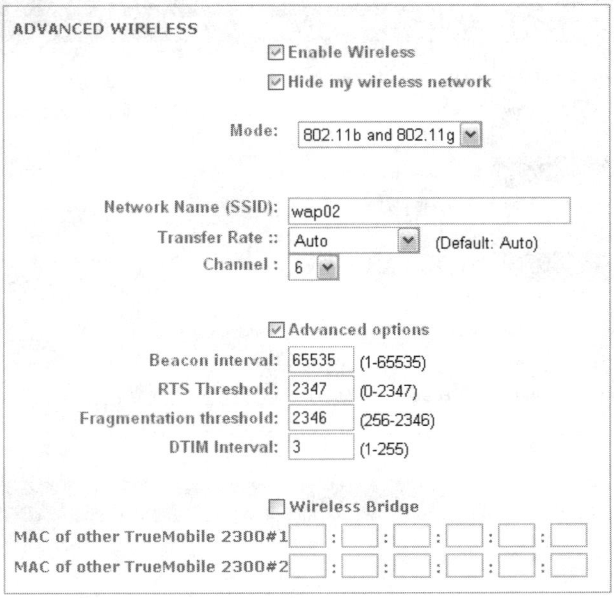

Configuring Logging

Like with your firewalls, it can be extremely beneficial to configure your WAP for logging. The objective is for the logging to show you what is going on with the WAP, particularly in regard to unauthorized access attempts. Cisco and Linksys support conventional syslog. Dell does not support any logging facility.

For the Cisco Aironet 1200, you can configure logging to a syslog server at the Event Log | Notification Options screen, shown next.

For the Linksys WAP54G, you can configure logging at the Setup | Log screen, shown next. Simple enable logging and enter the syslog server to which events should be sent. When you are finished, click Save Settings.

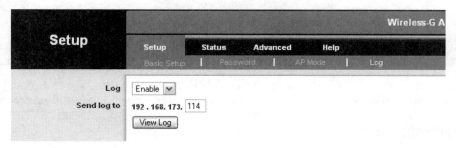

Hardening Services

Not many services need to be hardened for most WAPs, with the notable exception of Cisco. The most common services you might run across are as follows:

- Simple Network Management Protocol (SNMP)
- Network Time Protocol (NTP)
- Dynamic Host Configuration Protocol (DHCP)

Configuring SNMP

Cisco and Linksys support using SNMP for management of the WAP; however, neither supports using SNMPv3. Also, both SNMPv1 and SNMPv2 have no security features. Therefore, if you do not need SNMP, you should disable it.

By default, the Cisco Aironet 1200 ships with SNMP disabled. However, you can enable this service at the Services | SNMP screen.

You can configure SNMP support for the Linksys WAP54G at the Advanced | SNMP screen, shown next. Simply enable SNMP, specify a read-only and a read-write community string, and enter the appropriate information in the identification fields. When you are finished, click Save Settings.

HEADS UP!

Because the Linksys WAP54G displays the SNMP community strings in clear text, you should ensure that no one is looking over your shoulder while you are at this screen.

Configuring NTP

The Cisco Aironet 1200 supports the use of NTP primarily to facilitate accurate timestamps for the syslog facility. You can configure NTP at the Services | NTP screen, shown next.

Services: NTP- Network Time Protocol

NTP Server

Network Time Protocol (NTP):	⊙ Enabled ○ Disabled
Time Server (optional):	10.7.1.66 (Hostname or IP Address)

Time Settings

GMT Offset:	(GMT - 06:00) Central Time (US & Canada) ▼ (hrs)
Use Daylight Savings Time (United States only):	⊙ Yes ○ No
Manually Set Date:	2004/02/18 (yyyy/mm/dd)
Manually Set Time:	23:15:05 (hh:mm:ss)

Disabling the DHCP Server

Because the Dell TrueMobile 2300 is sold as a SOHO wireless access router, it is shipped with a DHCP server configured and active by default. You should disable DHCP at the Advanced Settings | DHCP Server Settings screen by unchecking Enable DHCP Server Functions and then clicking Submit.

Configuring Miscellaneous Services on the Cisco Aironet 1200

In addition to the previously mentioned services, the Cisco Aironet 1200 ships with a whole slew of additional services you need to be aware of. They can all be accessed at the Services screen, as shown next (in this case, the screen shows the default status of all the services after I disabled Telnet and permitted only SSH access, as previously recommended).

Services Summary	
Telnet/SSH: Disabled/Enabled	Hot Standby: Disabled
CDP: Enabled	DNS: Enabled
Filters: Enabled	HTTP: Enabled
Proxy Mobile IP: Disabled	QoS: Disabled
SNMP: Disabled	NTP: Enabled
VLAN: Disabled	ARP Caching: Disabled

As you can see, many of the services are disabled by default. In general, you should disable any service you do not need. The Cisco Discovery Protocol (CDP) and Domain Name Service (DNS) are two specific services you should consider configuring.

Cisco Discovery Protocol   As previously discussed, CDP is used by Cisco to locate other Cisco devices. Unless you are using a network management system that takes advantage of CDP, you should disable it. If you do require CDP, you should consider whether you need the CDP broadcasts to be sent over the WLAN. If you do not, you should disable CDP on the Radio0-802.11B radio, as shown next. Click Apply when you are finished.

Services: CDP-Cisco Discovery Protocol					
CDP Properties					
Cisco Discovery Protocol (CDP): ⊙ Enabled ○ Disabled					
Packet Hold Time (optional): 180 (10-255 sec)					
Packets Sent Every (optional): 60 (5-254 sec)					
Individual Port Enable:					
☑ Ethernet					
☐ Radio0-802.11B					
CDP Neighbors Table					
Device ID	Interface	Hold Time	Capability	Platform	Port ID
switch02.wjnconsulting.com	FastEthernet 0	171	S I	WS-C2950T-	FastEthernet 0/20
local-rtr	FastEthernet 0	140	R	2500	Eth 0

Domain Name Service DNS is used to allow the WAP to resolve names to IP addresses. It does not allow the WAP to operate as a DNS server. DNS is largely a service of convenience, allowing you to enter device names at various fields so that the WAP can automatically resolve and convert those names to IP addresses. Like all services, however, if you do not require this functionality, you should disable it. Remember, any running service is potentially vulnerable to current exploits as well as unknown future exploits.

Restricting Wireless Mode

Many WAPs support operating in 802.11a, 802.11b, 802.11g, or any combination thereof. If you do not need to support multiple wireless access modes, you should disable any unnecessary ones. For example, if you only need to support 802.11b in your environment, you should disable 802.11a and 802.11g. This will ensure that only individuals using the wireless mode you have defined have any chance of connecting to your environment.

The Cisco Aironet 1200 supports using multiple wireless modes through the implementation of multiple physical radio modules.

You can configure the wireless mode on the Linksys WAP54G at the Setup | Basic Setup screen, shown next. Simply select the access mode you want to use, or select Mixed to support both. Click Save Settings when you are finished.

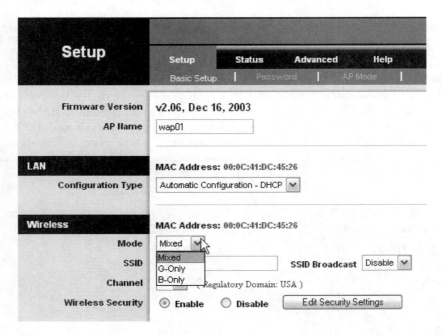

You can configure the wireless mode on the Dell TrueMobile 2300 at the Advanced Settings | Advanced Wireless screen, shown next. Simply select the wireless mode from the drop-down selection and click Submit.

```
ADVANCED WIRELESS
                                      ☑ Enable Wireless
                                      ☑ Hide my wireless network

                    Mode:     [ 802.11b and 802.11g  ▼ ]
                              [ 802.11b and 802.11g      ]
                              [ 802.11b                  ]
                              [ 802.11g                  ]
      Network Name (SSID):    wapu2
          Transfer Rate ::    [ Auto            ▼ ]   (Default: Auto)
                Channel :     [ 1  ▼ ]


                              ☑ Advanced options
           Beacon interval:   [ 65535 ]   (1-65535)
           RTS Threshold:     [ 2347  ]   (0-2347)
    Fragmentation threshold:  [ 2346  ]   (256-2346)
           DTIM Interval:     [ 3     ]   (1-255)


                              ☐ Wireless Bridge
   MAC of other TrueMobile 2300#1 [  ]:[  ]:[  ]:[  ]:[  ]:[  ]
   MAC of other TrueMobile 2300#2 [  ]:[  ]:[  ]:[  ]:[  ]:[  ]
```

Using MAC Address Filtering

One of the most valuable hardening steps you can undertake with your WAP is to implement MAC address filtering. MAC address filtering enables you to specify the MAC addresses that will be allowed to connect to the WAP. At that point, even if someone manages to obtain all the information necessary to connect to the WAP, if their MAC address is not permitted, they still cannot connect. The drawback to this method, however, is that it may require significant overhead for managing all the MAC addresses that may need to be permitted. In addition, MAC addresses can be spoofed, so it is not a panacea but rather another component of the hardening process.

The Cisco Aironet 1200 uses the well-documented Cisco access-list function to restrict/permit clients from establishing an association with the WAP. The first step is to build the access list. You can do this at the Services | Filters screen by selecting the MAC Address Filters tab, shown next.

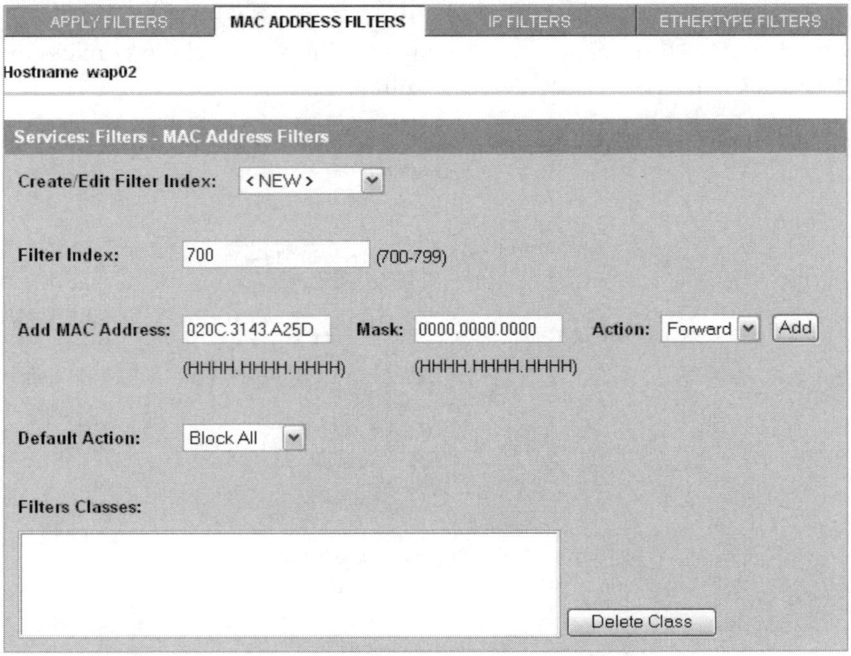

APPLY FILTERS	MAC ADDRESS FILTERS	IP FILTERS	ETHERTYPE FILTERS

Hostname wap02

Services: Filters - MAC Address Filters

Create/Edit Filter Index: `< NEW >`

Filter Index: `700` (700-799)

Add MAC Address: `020C.3143.A25D` **Mask:** `0000.0000.0000` **Action:** `Forward` `Add`
(HHHH.HHHH.HHHH) (HHHH.HHHH.HHHH)

Default Action: `Block All`

Filters Classes:

`Delete Class`

Enter the appropriate filter index (ACL number) for the MAC address filter. Next, enter the MAC address you want to specify and a wildcard mask. Keep in mind that for Cisco, a value of "0" in the mask means that the corresponding bit in the MAC address must precisely match the filter entry. A value of "H" in the mask means that the corresponding bit in the MAC address is ignored for the purposes of filtering. This can be used, for example, to grant all of a certain vendor's MAC addresses. Once you have entered this information, the next step is to decide whether the MAC address will be forwarded or blocked. My recommendation is to make the default action Block All and then configure a Forward action for the MAC addresses you explicitly want to forward. When you are finished, click Apply.

The next step is to apply that ACL to the WAP. You can do this at the Security | Advanced Security screen by clicking the Association Access List tab, shown next. Select the filter from the drop-down list and then click Apply.

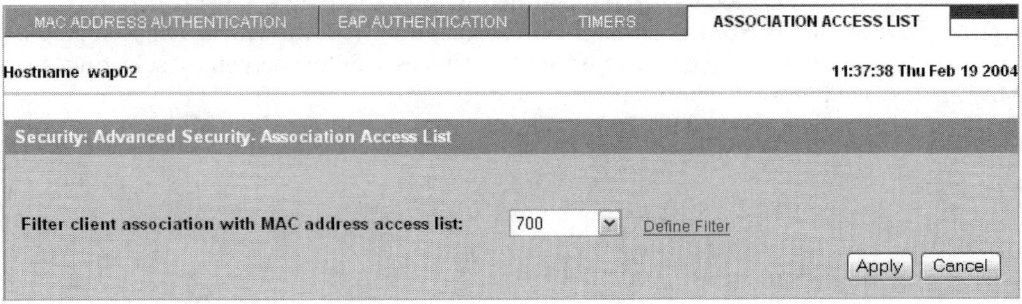

MAC ADDRESS AUTHENTICATION	EAP AUTHENTICATION	TIMERS	ASSOCIATION ACCESS LIST	

Hostname wap02   11:37:38 Thu Feb 19 2004

Security: Advanced Security- Association Access List

Filter client association with MAC address access list: `700` Define Filter

`Apply` `Cancel`

HEADS UP!

Once you have implemented this procedure on your Cisco Aironet 1200, you may find that wireless clients that are not permitted by the ACL still appear to associate with the WAP. Appearances are deceiving, however, because these wireless clients are unable to send and receive any data through the WAP.

You can enable MAC address filtering on the Linksys WAP54G at the Advanced | Filters screen, shown next. Simply select Enable from the drop-down box and specify how you want to perform the filtering. You can either filter to prevent the listed MAC addresses from being able to connect or to permit the listed MAC addresses to be able to connect. I recommend the latter in most circumstances, because it is generally easier to figure out who you want to allow to connect, as opposed to figuring out who you want to prevent. You can filter up to 40 MAC addresses by using the drop-down box to select MAC 21-40. When you have finished entering the MAC addresses to filter, click Save Settings.

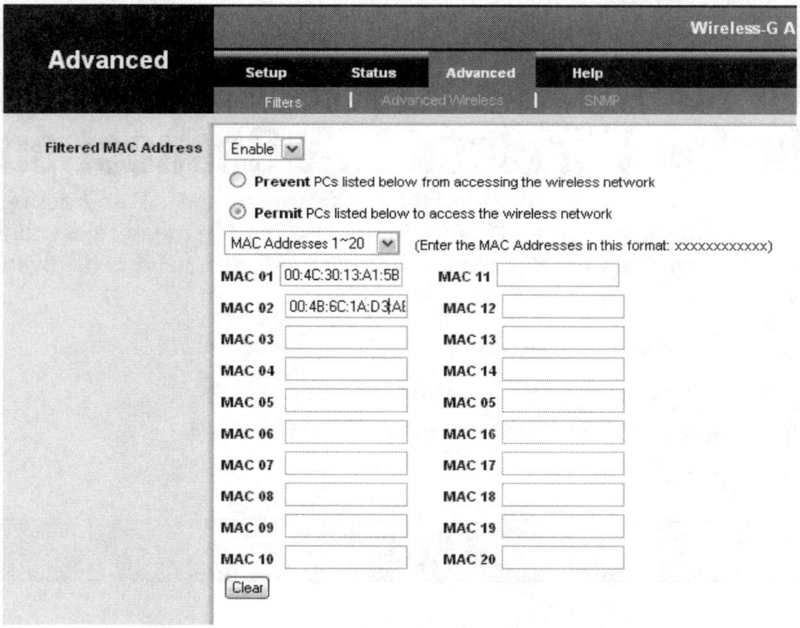

The Dell TrueMobile 2300 uses a simplified MAC filtering process. You simply enter the MAC addresses you want to permit to connect. This is done at the Advanced Settings | Access Control Settings screen, shown next. Check the box Enable MAC

Access Control and then add the MAC addresses you want to permit. When you are finished, click Submit.

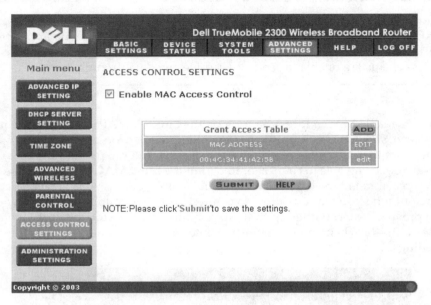

Hardening Wireless LAN Connections

All the hardening steps you have undertaken to secure your WAP and define who can connect to it are pointless exercises if you do not also harden the wireless connections themselves. The four main wireless connection methods you need to be aware of and know how to configure are as follows:

- Wired Equivalent Privacy (WEP)
- WiFi Protected Access (WPA) using pre-shared keys
- WPA using RADIUS
- Virtual private networks

HEADS UP!

A fifth type of wireless connection is the wide-open connection. This connection uses no form of authentication or encryption. Anyone with a wireless card can connect to the WAP and get access to the network. This type of connection is typically used for providing WiFi hotspots. By default, most WAPs ship configured in this manner. The recommendations that follow detail the methods you can use to harden the default configuration.

Hardening Wired Equivalent Privacy (WEP)

As the name implies, WEP was designed to provide privacy to wireless connections on par with a wired connection. WEP was part of the original 802.11 standard and is used by all three wireless standards. WEP was designed to prevent eavesdropping and data tampering and to prevent unauthorized access to the wireless network. WEP functions by utilizing the RC4 cipher stream and combining a 40-bit or a 104-bit WEP key with a 24-bit random number known as the *initialization vector (IV)*. This results in either a 64-bit or 128-bit encryption key. Because the IV changes with every message, a new encryption key is generated for each message. WEP functions by combining the encrypted data packet (known as the *ciphertext)* with the clear-text IV before transmitting. The IV is sent in clear text due to the destination needing to know the IV used to generate the encryption key. The receiver then uses the WEP key and attached IV to decrypt the packet.

Unfortunately, for all this effort, WEP has some significant security flaws that make it a very ineffective protocol. Although WEP is better than nothing, a hacker can crack WEP in 15 minutes or less, depending on the amount of traffic they can sniff. This is attributed to the following flaws:

- **WEP key recovery**   WEP uses the same WEP key and a different IV to encrypt data. The IV has a limited range of values (from 0 to 16777215) to choose from and eventually it uses the same IV over and over. By sniffing the wireless network and picking the same IVs out of the datastream, a hacker can gain enough information to figure out what the WEP key is.

ONE STEP FURTHER

RSA Security has developed a solution that addresses the weak WEP key methods. It is called the Fast Packet Keying Solution and utilizes a hashing mechanism to dynamically generate unique WEP keys for each packet, thus preventing a hacker from being able to determine the WEP key. You can find more information about this at http://www.rsasecurity.com/newsletter/wireless/2002_winter/feature.html and http://www.rsasecurity.com/rsalabs/technotes/wep-fix.html.

- **Unauthorized data decryption**   Once the WEP key is known, a hacker can transform the ciphertext into its original form and gain access to the original unencrypted data.
- **Violation of data integrity**   Once the original data has been decrypted, a hacker could potentially use the hacked WEP key to change the ciphertext and forward the changed message to the destination.
- **Poor key management**   WEP keys are typically static keys that, once configured on a device, remain the same from that point forward. The problem is exacerbated when an employee leaves the company because the WEP key really needs to be changed to ensure security. Unfortunately, this is not a

practical solution if your company has hundreds or thousands of wireless devices because they will all need to be configured with the new WEP key.

ONE STEP FURTHER

Some vendors address the key-management issue through the use of proprietary "dynamic WEP" mechanisms. This causes the systems to dynamically generate WEP keys that devices will use in conjunction with 802.1x authentication. Essentially, a new secret key is generated for each client that is authenticated. Although this can increase the security of WEP, because these are proprietary implementations, they are only practical if you use wireless devices that support the mechanism.

- **No access point authentication**   WEP functions by allowing the wireless clients to authenticate the WAP; however, the WAP has no means of authenticating the client. Consequently, a hacker can reroute the data to access points through an alternate and unauthorized path.

Although these flaws may seem to imply that one should not use WEP, this is not correct. If you have the ability to use a better protection mechanism, such as WPA or 802.11i, do so. If you can't, though, WEP is still better than nothing—even with the flaws.

For your Cisco Aironet 1200, you can configure WEP at the Security | Encryption Manager screen, shown next. Select WEP Encryption and choose Mandatory from the drop-down list. Enter the four 128-bit encryption keys and click Apply when you're finished.

For your Linksys WAP54G, the first step of configuring WEP is to enable wireless security at the Setup | Basic Setup screen. Next, you should click Edit Security Settings. This will present you with the Security Settings screen, shown next. Select WEP for the security mode. Select "128 bits 26 hex digits" for the WEP Encryption. Enter a passphrase that meets the requirements of your password security policy and click Generate. This will generate the WEP keys you will need to enter on your wireless clients. When you have finished, click Save Settings to close the Security Settings screen.

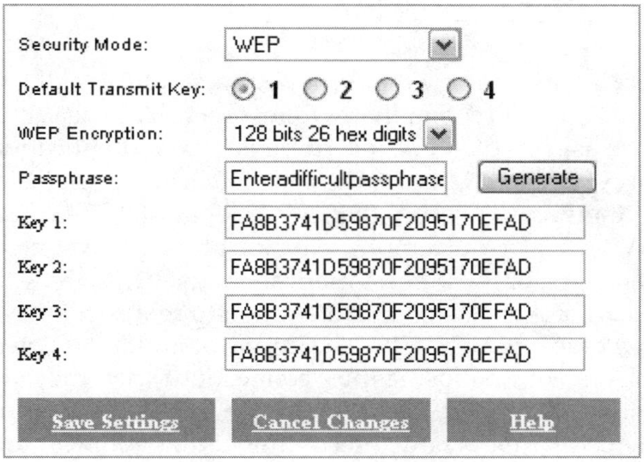

Security Mode:	WEP ▼
Default Transmit Key:	◉ 1 ○ 2 ○ 3 ○ 4
WEP Encryption:	128 bits 26 hex digits ▼
Passphrase:	Enteradifficultpassphrase [Generate]
Key 1:	FA8B3741D59870F2095170EFAD
Key 2:	FA8B3741D59870F2095170EFAD
Key 3:	FA8B3741D59870F2095170EFAD
Key 4:	FA8B3741D59870F2095170EFAD

[**Save Settings**]   [**Cancel Changes**]   [**Help**]

You can enable WEP on your Dell TrueMobile 2300 at the Basic Settings | Wireless Security screen. Once you check Enable Wireless Security and select WEP from the Network Authentication drop-down list, you will be presented with the WEP Settings section, shown next. Select "104 bits(13 characters)" for Key Length and enter a 13-character key value for all four keys that conforms to your password security policy. When you have finished, click Save & Apply. When prompted, click Save & Restart.

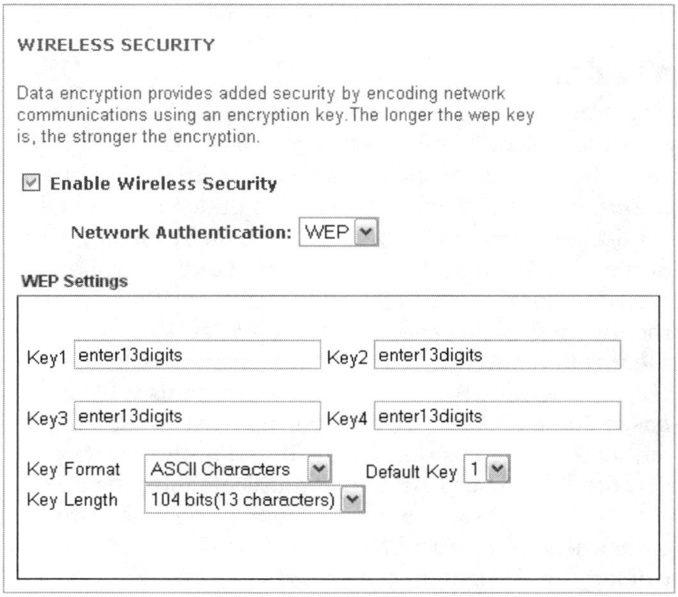

WIRELESS SECURITY

Data encryption provides added security by encoding network communications using an encryption key. The longer the wep key is, the stronger the encryption.

☑ **Enable Wireless Security**

Network Authentication: WEP ▼

WEP Settings

Key1	enter13digits	Key2	enter13digits
Key3	enter13digits	Key4	enter13digits

Key Format   [ASCII Characters ▼]   Default Key [1 ▼]
Key Length   [104 bits(13 characters) ▼]

Hardening WiFi Protected Access (WPA)

WPA is a subset of the 802.11i standard and was created to address the vulnerabilities of WEP.

802.11i

802.11i is an emerging technology that is designed to address all the security flaws related to WEP and is the direction that wireless security is heading. 802.11i incorporates all the aspects of WPA, including 802.1x authentication, Temporal Key Integrity Protocol (TKIP), and Michael Message Integrity Check (MMIC). In addition, 802.11i addresses a number of issues that WPA does not. 802.11i uses stronger encryption than WPA through the implementation of Advanced Encryption Standard (AES). This presents one of the biggest hindrances to 802.11i, however, because the processing overhead of AES is significant enough to require hardware upgrades to support it in many cases. 802.11i will also support roaming, which allows users to move between WAPs without losing their connection when they switch from the old WAP to the new WAP.

If you do not need wireless now, I recommend that you wait for 802.11i to be finalized and for 802.11i products to come out.

In fact, the hardening procedure for WEP is simply to use WPA instead. WPA is actually a combination of a few different techniques that mitigate the problems that WEP exposes. The first is the use of 802.1x authentication to address authentication issues. The second is the use of Temporal Key Integrity Protocol (TKIP) to address encryption issues. The final is a Michael Message Integrity Check (MMIC) to address message integrity. WPA is forward compatible with 802.11i.

802.1x Authentication

The 802.1x specification was originally defined for wired networks and provides a mechanism for allowing a client (known as a *supplicant*) to be authenticated by a network device such as a WAP (known as an *authenticator*) through the use of a RADIUS server (known as an *authentication server*). It is important to understand that the WAP does not perform the authentication; rather, it acts as a middleman by passing the client's credentials to the RADIUS server and letting it handle the actual authentication of the client.

802.1x uses a combination of the Extensible Authentication Protocol (EAP) and RADIUS for authenticating clients and distributing keys. RADIUS is used primarily for carrying the authentication and configuration information between the authenticator and the RADIUS server. RADIUS does not have a mechanism for using anything other than password-based authentication. To address this, EAP is used to provide the means to support authentication, such as public key–based authentication (that is, shared secret). Essentially, the WAP uses EAP to communicate with the client and RADIUS to communicate with the RADIUS server, encapsulating the data as required. EAP utilizes three common authentication means: EAP-MD5, EAP-TLS, and EAP-TTLS. In addition, Cisco has a proprietary implementation known as Lightweight EAP (LEAP). However,

LEAP uses a weaker authentication algorithm. This, combined with its proprietary nature, makes LEAP not a recommended solution. Finally, Microsoft has implemented Protected EAP (PEAP), which was designed to overcome some of the limitations and vulnerabilities of the other EAP methods. PEAP can use MS-CHAP-v2 authentication within the EAP-TTLS tunnel to actually authenticate the user based on Active Directory. Many vendors support PEAP, so much so that it is currently undergoing evaluation to become a standard.

Temporal Key Integrity Protocol

Although 802.1x addresses authentication problems with WEP, it does not address the security problems related to the weak encryption keys used by WEP and the ability for a hacker to determine what the WEP key is. TKIP fixes this. TKIP uses 256-bit long encryption keys that are generated through a more sophisticated procedure to provide a much stronger encryption key. TKIP functions by adding the client MAC address and a 48-bit IV to a 128-bit temporal key (which is shared among clients) to guarantee that the encryption key is unique. The temporal key is changed every 10,000 packets to further ensure that hackers cannot begin decoding all packets if they are able to ascertain the encryption key, thus strengthening the security of the network.

Message Integrity Check

WPA also uses a MIC that is known as Michael to verify message integrity. A 64-bit message is calculated using the Michael algorithm, which can be used to detect potential tampering of the message or data.

Hardening WPA Using Pre-shared Keys

WPA using pre-shared keys (WPA-PSK) is a very common method of configuring wireless connections. This is due to the fact that using pre-shared keys does not require an investment in any AAA mechanisms such as RADIUS. The drawback is the same as any other use of pre-shared keys—it does not scale as well in large environments as RADIUS does. Also, because the keys are human generated, they are more susceptible to cracking.

Configuring the Cisco Aironet 1200 for WPA-PSK is a multistep process. The first step is to configure TKIP as the cipher and to clear all encryption keys at the Security | Encryption Manager screen, as shown next. When you are finished, click Apply.

The next step is to configure the WPA-PSK settings for the SSID at the Security |
SSID Manager screen. First, select the SSID you want to configure. Next, scroll down
to the Authenticated Key Management section (shown next), select Mandatory, and
check WPA for Key Management. Enter the WPA Pre-shared Key value. When you
are finished, click Apply.

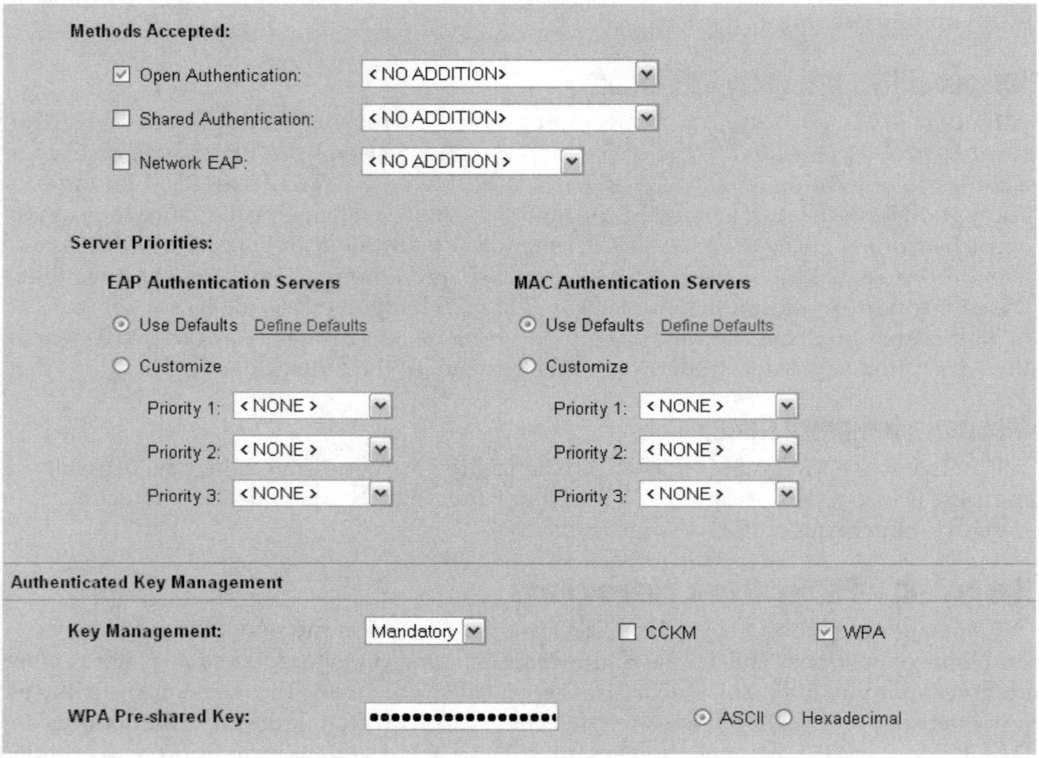

For the Linksys WAP54G, you configure the WPA settings at the Security Settings
screen (shown next), just like the WEP configuration. Simply select WPA Pre-shared
Key from the Security Mode drop-down box. For the WPA Algorithm setting, select
TKIP or AES. AES is more secure, but it can have a negative impact on performance
and is not supported by all wireless NICs. Next, enter the WPA shared key that should
be used. The shared key should conform to your password security policy. Finally,
enter the group key renewal time (default 300 seconds) and click Save Settings when
you are finished.

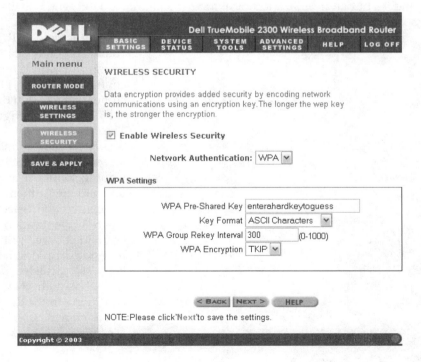

WPA
Pre-Shared Key

The Access Point supports 4 different types of security settings. WPA Pre-Shared Key, WPA RADIUS, RADIUS, and WEP. Please see the help tab for more details on the different types of security settings.

Security Mode: WPA Pre-Shared Key
WPA Algorithm: TKIP
WPA Shared Key: enterahardtoguesskey
Group Key Renewal: 300 seconds

Save Settings   Cancel Changes   Help

You can configure WPA using pre-shared keys on the Dell TrueMobile 2300 at the Basic Settings | Wireless Security screen, shown next. Simply check to enable wireless security and select WPA for the network authentication method. Enter the appropriate WPA pre-shared key and select the proper key format and WPA group rekey interval (default 300). Finally, specify whether to use TKIP or AES (Dell has the same limitations as Linksys). When you are finished, click Save & Apply and then click Save & Restart when prompted.

Configuring WPA Using RADIUS/802.1x

> **NOTE**   The Dell TrueMobile 2300 wireless access router does not support WPA and RADIUS/802.1x.

Using WPA with RADIUS/802.1x allows you to take full advantage of the benefits of the increased security that WPA provides while gaining the scalability that WPA with pre-shared keys does not provide. Before you can configure the WAP to use RADIUS, you need to make sure you have configured your RADIUS server to accept client connections from the WAP and have configured a shared secret. We will look at how to add and configure RADIUS clients in more detail in Chapter 9.

> **NOTE**   The Cisco Aironet 1200 WAP does not support WPA and RADIUS/802.1x without the use of a third-party supplicant such as the Funk Odyssey Client (http://www.funk.com) or the Meetinghouse Data Communications AEGIS client (http://www.meetinghousedata.com/). Refer to these vendors for the client-side configuration to support WPA and RADIUS/802.1x.

Configuring the Cisco Aironet 1200 to support WPA and RADIUS/802.1x is a multistep process. First, you need to make sure you have installed and configured Cisco Secure ACS on your network. We will cover installing and configuring the Cisco Secure ACS in detail in Chapter 9. Second, you will need to install a third-party supplicant on the wireless client. This is extremely important because Cisco devotes only one sentence to this—and it's buried deep in a technical note. If you don't do this, you will likely find yourself spending a couple hours thinking, "I've done *everything* that should make it work."

The actual WAP configuration is relatively straightforward. You need to configure the encryption cipher just like you did for the WPA-PSK configuration. The difference is at the Security | SSID Manager screen. Select the SSID you want to configure and scroll down to the Authentication Settings section. Select the Open Authentication check box and choose "With EAP" from the drop-down list. Next, select the Network EAP check box with <No Addition> in the drop-down list, as shown here. When you are finished, click Apply.

To configure WPA with RADIUS on the Linksys WAP54G, you will need to return to the Security Settings screen, shown here. Select WPA RADIUS for the security mode and specify the WPA algorithm. Enter the IP address and port number for the RADIUS server. Enter the shared key that is required to allow the WAP to authenticate with the RADIUS server and then specify the key renewal timeout. When you have finished, click Save Settings.

Hardening WLANS with Virtual Private Networks

Virtual private networks (VPNs) are not strictly wireless security protocols; however, they offer an excellent security mechanism for wireless networks right now. Because VPNs were designed to secure data in an inherently insecure environment (the Internet) and because WLANs are inherently insecure, VPNs make an excellent workaround to address WLAN security issues. Essentially, implementing a VPN over your wireless network requires your wireless clients to be running the appropriate VPN client software and the implementation of a VPN concentrator (for example, a Nortel Contivity Extranet Switch) that the WLAN connects to. The resources that the wireless clients need access to would reside on the other side of the VPN concentrator. Once the wireless client has connected to the WLAN, it simply uses the VPN client to connect to the VPN concentrator, and all the subsequent data is sent through the VPN tunnel. Implementing a VPN for all your wireless connections is as close to a bulletproof solution as you can implement. We will cover how to design a VPN for your WLANs in Chapters 11 and 12.

Hardening Windows XP Wireless Clients

Configuring your wireless connections on the WAP is only half the battle. You also need to properly configure the wireless NIC to allow the client to connect to the WAP. As with your WAP, you have three connection methods to configure:

- WEP
- WPA using pre-shared keys
- WPA using RADIUS/802.1x

Hardening with WEP

To configure WEP on a wireless NIC, open your network connections, right-click the wireless NIC, and select Properties. Then click the Wireless Networks tab, shown here:

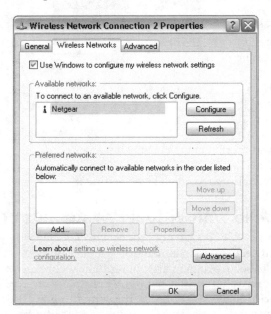

ONE STEP FURTHER

Notice that an available network is already listed. This is a WAP that belongs to one of my neighbors and is broadcasting its SSID. It's really just that easy to locate an open WAP. To illustrate how easy it is to connect to an open WAP, I have personally pulled over on the side of the road near a residential area to access the Internet and send an instant message to a buddy of mine when my cell phone battery died. You absolutely have to harden your wireless network if you are going to use wireless in your environment.

At the Wireless Networks tab, click Add to add a new wireless network. At the Wireless Network Properties dialog box, enter the SSID of the WAP to which you want to connect. These values must be the same on both the wireless client and the WAP. Select Shared for the Network Authentication field and WEP for the Data Encryption field. Uncheck the box The key Is Provided for Me Automatically and enter the appropriate WEP key, as shown next. When you're finished, click OK to close the Wireless Network Properties dialog box. Then click OK again to close the Wireless Network Connection Properties dialog box. In a few moments, the wireless NIC will authenticate with and connect to the WAP.

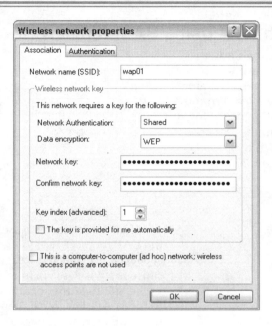

Hardening with WPA Using Pre-shared Keys

To configure WPA with pre-shared keys, you need to return to the Wireless Network Properties dialog box, as previously detailed. From the Network Authentication drop-down list, select WPA-PSK. From the Data Encryption drop-down list, select TKIP or AES, as required by your WAP configuration. Enter the pre-shared key, as shown here, and click OK to close the Wireless Network Properties dialog box. Then click OK to close the Wireless Network Connection Properties dialog box. In a few moments, the wireless NIC will authenticate with and connect to the WAP.

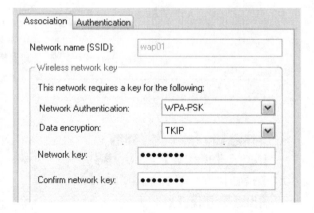

HEADS UP!

You need to obtain the WPA Wireless Security Update for Windows XP (Microsoft Knowledge Base Article 815485) at http://support.microsoft.com/?kbid=815485.

Hardening with WPA Using RADIUS/802.1x

To configure WPA using Radius/
802.1x, you need to return to the
Wireless Network Properties dialog
box, as previously detailed. From the
Network Authentication drop-down
list, select WPA. From the Data
Encryption drop-down list, select
TKIP, as shown at right.

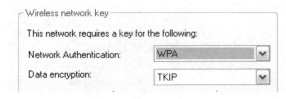

Next, click the Authentication tab to specify
the EAP method, as shown at left. For the EAP
type, select Protected EAP (PEAP). This will
cause the wireless client to use WPA and PEAP
as the 802.1x authentication method to connect
to the WAP. The WAP then encapsulates the
user authentication passed using MS-CHAP-v2
into a RADIUS datagram and sends the
authentication request to the RADIUS server.
The RADIUS server responds with the
authentication response, and the WAP either
permits the connection, if the user was
authenticated, or denies the connection, if the
user was not authenticated.

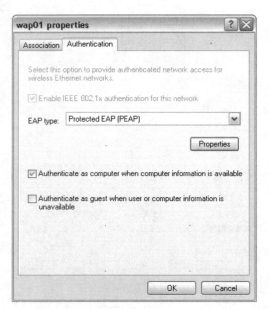

Using the Funk Odyssey Client Version 2.28.0.798 to Support WPA and RADIUS/802.1x

Once you have installed the Odyssey
client, select the Odyssey Client
Manager from the Start menu. This
will cause the Odyssey Client
Manager to open, as shown here.

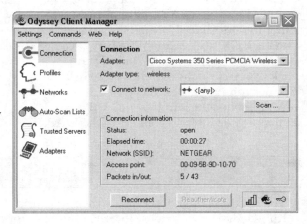

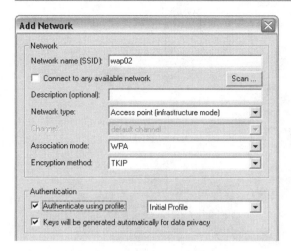

In the column on the left, select Networks and then click Add. Enter the appropriate SSID and select WPA for the association mode and TKIP for the encryption method, as shown at left. In the Authentication section, select the profile to use. When you are finished, click OK.

The next step is to configure the profile you specified in the network's configuration. Select Profiles and click Properties to edit the initial profile. Select the Authentication tab and click Add to add EAP/PEAP, as shown at right. When you are finished, click OK.

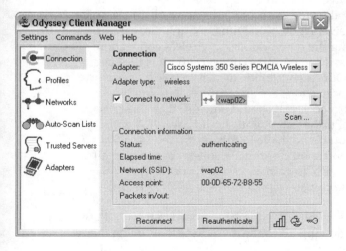

The last step is to click Connection and select the network you configured from the drop-down list, as shown at left. As soon as you do this, the client will begin authenticating.

When the authentication has successfully completed, your screen should look something like this:

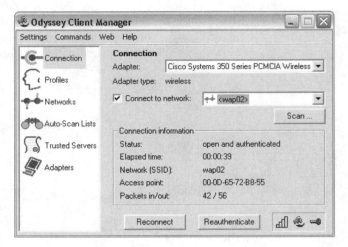

Summary

The term "wireless network" is perhaps the ultimate oxymoron when discussing network security. You want your network to be as secure as possible, but by its very nature the wireless data is transmitted over radio waves that can be captured by anyone within range. On the surface one would think that trying to secure your network and provide wireless access would be mutually exclusive. At the same time, though, the ease of connectivity and the flexibility of accessing the network over a wireless connection are causing more and more networks to include wireless connectivity. It is the classic challenge of functionality versus security. Our responsibility, then, is to take the necessary precautions to ensure that our wireless connections are as secure as they can be.

Because WEP is effectively a broken protocol, you should only use it as a last resort. If your devices support WPA, use WPA. Furthermore, you should use WPA with RADIUS/802.1x authentication so that you do not have to rely on shared keys for authentication. If you have to use WEP, you should seriously consider requiring all WEP-based wireless connections to use a VPN to gain access to the production/ wired network resources. We will look at how you can design this VPN network architecture in Chapter 12.

Once you have decided on the wireless protocol, you need to harden the WAP. By default, most vendors ship their WAPs allowing all connections as well as using many default settings that you'll need to change. The first step is to harden your remote administration capabilities by changing any default usernames and implementing passwords that conform to your password security policy. Next, you should disable

SSID broadcasts to keep the WAP from advertising itself to unknown users. If someone is going to connect to the WAP, they should know the SSID already. You also need to implement whatever logging facilities are supported so that you can better monitor the connections being made and, more important, the connections being denied. You also need to disable or harden all services that the WAP is running, paying special attention to ensuring that you do not leave the default SNMP community strings in place. Next, you should explicitly define the wireless mode that the WAP should operate in. If you know that all your users will connect using 802.11g, you should configure the WAP to only allow 802.11g connections. Although this does not necessarily prevent someone from connecting, it at least ensures that they have to have a NIC that supports the wireless mode you have specified. The last step is to implement MAC address filtering to explicitly permit only those MAC addresses you want to be able to connect to your network and denying everything else.

If you follow these hardening steps for your WLAN, you will greatly mitigate the risk related to offering wireless network access to your users.

Chapter 9

Implementing AAA

uthentication, Authorization, and Accounting (AAA) is one of the most overlooked methods of hardening networks, particularly in small and medium-sized networks. A couple of factors contribute to this. First, many companies don't think about controlling access to their network infrastructure resources like they should. Companies fall prey to thinking of network devices as "just a switch, so what does it really matter if someone gains access to it?" Second, many network administrators are accustomed to using shared passwords for access to network equipment. After all, they were almost all taught that method. Third, many companies just don't realize that they can restrict access to many of their network devices with a degree of granularity similar to how they restrict access to their server resources.

However, AAA is really a necessity for all networks. Authentication allows you to determine the identity of a user. Authorization allows you to determine what the user is permitted to do. Accounting allows you to determine what a user did while logged in. At the very minimum, you need to implement an AAA scheme that allows you to use stringent access control for the administrative sessions on your network devices. In addition, AAA enables you to provide granular management access through the use of authorization, which allows you to break away from the all or nothing administration that is so prevalent on today's networks (that is, you either know the enable secret or you don't). You can specify read-only or diagnostic commands for some users, while allowing other users less restrictive access. You can then verify the use and function of your AAA implementation by configuring accounting, allowing you to determine who did what and when they did it. Having this record can be an invaluable resource in legal proceedings, in addition to letting you know who is doing what on a day-to-day basis.

This chapter explores how we can implement an AAA framework to control who is allowed to access the network and what they are allowed to use once they have access. The first step is to look at not only how we can leverage authentication as a management access control mechanism, but also how we can use it to control access to the network in general. Next we will look at how we can control what an authenticated user can do through the use of authorization. After that, we will look at using accounting to provide a means to show what was done for auditing purposes. We will finish up by looking at how we can implement 802.1x to require authentication of all systems attempting to connect to the network.

AAA Mechanisms

Two primary technologies are used to provide AAA for our network infrastructure:

- Remote Authentication Dial-In User Service (RADIUS)
- Terminal Access Controller Access Control System (TACACS+)

Remote Authentication Dial-In User Service (RADIUS)

RADIUS was developed as a client/server architecture that allows a remote access server to authenticate user connections against a centralized database of user credentials. RADIUS also provides a means of authorizing access to the resources that the user has requested. Finally, RADIUS provides a means of accounting that allows you to track what a user did once she was authenticated and authorized. Because RADIUS is a de facto industry standard, most vendors support RADIUS as a means of providing authentication for their network devices.

You can use a couple of different RADIUS servers in your environment. Microsoft ships RADIUS as a component of Microsoft Windows 2000 and 2003, known as Internet Authentication Service (IAS). A benefit of using Microsoft IAS for your RADIUS services is that it is designed to integrate seamlessly with Active Directory for credentials. We will use IAS on Microsoft Windows 2000 SP4 for this chapter.

Funk Software also produces the most widely used RADIUS server, known as Steel Belted RADIUS (SBR). The benefit of Funk SBR is that it is not tied to a Microsoft architecture and can be installed on NetWare and Solaris in addition to Microsoft Windows.

Terminal Access Controller Access Control System (TACACS+)

TACACS+ is similar to RADIUS in function and use. In addition to authentication and authorization, TACACS+ provides a means of accounting that allows you to track what a user did once he was authenticated and authorized. While TACACS+ is similar to RADIUS, it has a couple of distinct differences. First, TACACS+ uses TCP for data delivery instead of UDP (what RADIUS uses). Second, TACACS+ separates the authentication and authorization operations. This means that a single user can have separate and distinct authentication and authorization options, which grants more granular control over user access, while RADIUS relies on a single profile for both authentication and authorization. The big drawback to TACACS+ is that since it is a protocol that was developed and pushed largely by Cisco, most other vendors offer little to no support for it, opting instead to use the more open RADIUS protocol. We will use Cisco Secure ACS version 3.2 for the TACACS+ server in this chapter.

Authentication and Access Control

Access control is a critical aspect of your network security. When we talk about access control in regards to our network infrastructure, we want to control not only the access to the devices themselves, but potentially access to the network itself. Authentication is the process of providing access control by ensuring that the user is who he or she claims to be by examining username and/or password credentials.

Authentication as a component of an AAA architecture relies on the use of external servers running RADIUS or TACACS+ to validate the user's credentials, not local user accounts or shared passwords. In turn, these RADIUS and TACACS+ servers are typically configured to use additional account databases such as Microsoft Active Directory, Novell NDS, or LDAP for user account validation, although they can also use their own local user databases. The benefit of this type of system is the ability to use a centralized authentication authority throughout your enterprise that can not only authenticate management sessions but user network access sessions as well.

AAA Authentication on IOS-Based Equipment

Access control on IOS–based equipment is used to control who has management access to the device. Four basic steps are involved in configuring AAA authentication on IOS-based equipment:

1. *Enable AAA.* This configures the device to use AAA.

2. *Configure the authentication server network parameters.* This defines the AAA server or server group to use for authentication.

3. *Define one or more method lists for AAA authentication.* This defines the AAA authentication methods that will be used.

4. *Apply the method lists to a particular interface or line (this is an optional step).* This allows you to use unique method lists for each line or interfaces.

Method lists simply define the authentication methods that will be used for AAA and the order in which they will be attempted. When you define a method list, you must apply that method list to a line or interface before it will be used. The sole exception to this is the default method list, which is used for all lines and interfaces. You want to implement method lists so that you have a backup authentication method in the event that the initial authentication method fails.

Server groups are used in conjunction with method lists to define a group of TACACS+ or RADIUS to use for AAA authentication. The primary benefit of server groups is in providing redundancy and failover. For example, if authentication server 1 fails, the other authentication servers in the group will be queried before undertaking the other authentication methods defined in the method list.

Login Authentication Using RADIUS (Microsoft IAS)

Configuring login authentication using Microsoft IAS as the RADIUS server has two main tasks. First you must configure the appropriate IAS settings. Then you must configure the appropriate AAA settings on the IOS-based device. I recommend that you use windows global security groups to identify the users that you want to grant login access. By specifying a group of users, as you will see in the configuration steps, you can restrict who can connect to the equipment.

IAS Installation Procedures

IAS is not installed by default in a Microsoft server installation. For more information about the installation prerequisites and procedures for IAS, see http://support.microsoft.com/default.aspx?scid=kb;en-us;317588.

Configure the IAS Server   The first step is to configure the appropriate user groups and IAS with the RADIUS settings that you need in your environment.

1. Ensure that you have created the appropriate users and groups in the Microsoft Windows domain. You can do this by running the Active Directory Users and Computers MMC administrative tool.

2. Run the Internet Authentication Service MMC administrative tool. Right-click the Clients container and select New and then Client. This will start the New Client Wizard.

3. At the Add Client screen, enter the host name of the RADIUS client and select RADIUS as the protocol. When you are finished, click Next.

4. At the Add RADIUS Client screen, enter the IP address of the RADIUS client. This is the IP address of the network device on which you want to configure AAA, for example the Cisco router. Select RADIUS Standard as the client-vendor and specify a shared secret. The shared secret can be up to 255 characters in length and is case sensitive. The longer the shared secret value the better the security it will provide and the less susceptible it will be to brute force hacks. As a result, I recommend that at least 22 random alphanumeric/special characters be used. The shared secret will be used later on when we configure the router to use this RADIUS server. Uncheck the box Client Must Always Send The Signature Attribute In The Request. When you are finished, click Finish.

5. The next step is to configure the remote access policy that will determine which clients will be authenticated. Select the Remote Access Policies container and remove any existing remote access policies. This is very important, because by default Microsoft IAS grants access for any clients that have dial-in permissions enabled in their user account properties. You should start with a blank slate of remote access policies, because IAS will apply the remote access policies in order. As soon as a match is made, the IAS server stops processing the remaining rules. As a result, if you are going to configure multiple rules (for example, if you want to grant a certain privilege level to some users and a different privilege level to others) you need to make sure that they are listed in the order that you want them processed.

6. Right-click the Remote Access Policies container and select New Remote Access Policies. This will start the New Remote Access Policy Wizard. Enter a name for the access policy. In this example, we will create a policy for users that should have privilege level 15 access, so we will name it CiscoPriv15Policy. When you are finished, click Next.

7. At the Conditions screen, click Add to add a new condition. At the Select Attribute screen, select Windows-Groups, as shown here, and click Add.

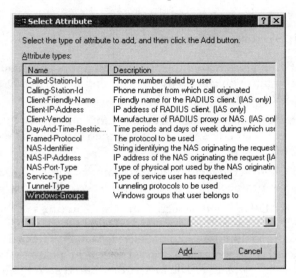

8. At the Groups screen, click Add to select the user group from Active Directory that you want to use for authentication. Select the group from the Select Groups screen and click Add. When you are finished selecting groups, click OK to return to the Groups screen, and then click OK again to return to the policy wizard. When you have finished adding all of the conditions, click Next.

9. At the Permissions screen, select whether to grant or deny access based on the policy. In this case, we want to select to grant access. When finished, click Next.

10. At the User Profile screen, click Edit Profile. This will present you with the Edit Dial-in Profile screen. Click the Authentication tab and select only Unencrypted Authentication (PAP, SPAP) as shown next. Cisco does not support any of the encryption methods, but it will use the shared secret to encrypt the password, so make sure that you use a long and difficult shared secret to provide a stronger level of encryption. As previously mentioned, you should use a shared secret of at least 22 alphanumeric/special characters in length.

11. Click the Advanced tab and remove any existing attributes. Once you have done that, click Add to add the vendor specific attributes that will be used by the remote access policy. Scroll down and select Cisco-AV-Pair and click Add.

12. At the Attribute Information screen, click Add and enter **shell:priv-lvl=15** in the Attribute Value box, as shown next. When you are finished, click OK two times to return to the Add Attribute screen.

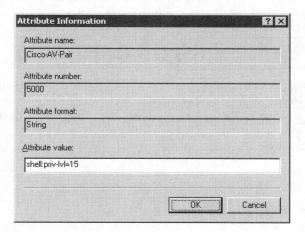

13. Repeat steps 11 to 12, this time selecting Service-Type as the attribute with an attribute value of Login, as shown next. When you are finished, click OK and then Close to return to the Edit Dial-in Profile screen. Click OK to return to the access policy wizard. You may be prompted to decide whether you want to review the corresponding help file. Select Yes or No, as appropriate.

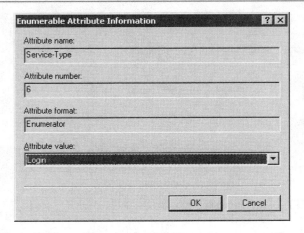

14. At the User Profile screen, click Finish. This will create the remote access policy that allows members of the group you specified to be able to log in to the network device and access the privileged mode of operation. If you wanted to create another remote access policy that granted only user mode access (for example to your help desk or network design team), you could repeat steps 6 to 13, selecting to set the value in step 12 to **shell:priv-lvl=1**.

HEADS UP!

Remember that remote access policies are applied in order. As soon as a match is found, the RADIUS server stops processing. So, for example, if you have a user that is a member of the network admins group (privilege 15) and the help desk group (privilege 1), if the remote access policy for the help desk group is first in the order, the user will never be able to gain privilege level 15 access.

Configure AAA on the Network Device   Once the IAS server has been configured correctly, the next step is to enter the AAA commands on the IOS-based device to configure it to use RADIUS for authentication. The following steps detail this process:

1. Use the AAA command to configure the AAA authentication on the device. At the global configuration mode, enter the following:

```
local-rtr(config)#aaa new-model
local-rtr(config)#aaa authentication login default group radius local
```

This will configure the device with a default method list that uses RADIUS as the primary authentication and the local user database as the backup.

2. Configure at least one local user as a backup user in the event that the RADIUS server is unavailable. This can be done by entering the following command at the global configuration mode:

```
local-rtr(config)#username backupadmin privilege 15 password →
difficultpass
```

3. Now configure the device with the RADIUS server settings by running the following commands at the global configuration mode. Make sure that you specify the exact RADIUS key that you used when you added the client to the RADIUS server in step 4 in the previous section.

```
local-rtr(config)#radius-server host <radiusserverIP> auth-port 1812 →
acct-port 1813
local-rtr(config)#radius-server key <theradiuskeyfromabove>
```

At this point, you should be able to connect to the device using RADIUS authentication. However, this is only part of AAA. While the user will be authenticated, you will still need to use the enable password to enter the privileges mode of execution until you complete the authorization steps detailed in the section "Hardening Your Network with Authorization." The final step is to save your configuration when you are finished by running **copy running-config startup-config** at the command-line interface (CLI).

Login Authentication Using TACACS+

Like configuring login authentication using RADIUS, TACACS+ requires two steps. The first step is to configure the Cisco Secure ACS server properly. The second step is to configure the IOS-based device properly.

Configure the Cisco Secure ACS Server   Configuring the Cisco Secure ACS server includes first configuring the server to authenticate using a Microsoft Windows user database. The benefit of this system is that your administrators can connect to and manage the network equipment using the same username and password that they use to log in to the Microsoft workstations. The steps to configure Cisco Secure ACS are as follows:

1. Connect to the Cisco Secure ACS server and click External User Database in the navigation bar. This will bring up the External User Database screen.

2. Click Database Configuration, and at the next screen click Windows Database. The Database Configuration Creation table will appear:

3. Click Create New Configuration. Enter the name for the new configuration for windows and click Submit.

4. In the External User Database Configuration table, click Configure.

5. This will present you with the Windows User Database Configuration page. By default, Verify Grant Dialin Permission To User Has Been Enabled is checked. Check or uncheck this as appropriate in your environment. If you are not sure, leave it checked and make sure that the users that you want to authenticate with TACACS+ have that setting checked in the user properties in Windows 2000.

6. Scroll down to the Configure Domain List table and select the domains that you want Cisco Secure ACS to try in the event that the username is not qualified by a domain (for example, if it is not in the domain\username format).

7. Scroll down to the MS-CHAP Settings and Windows EAP Settings tables and enter the appropriate values for your environment. If you are unsure of what to use, leave them at their default values.

8. When you are finished with the configurations, scroll down and click Submit.

The next step is to configure an unknown user policy. This tells the Cisco Secure ACS server what to do in the event that it can not authenticate the user using the local database. For example, you can use this to tell the Cisco Secure ACS server to attempt to validate the user against the domain that you just added.

1. In the navigation bar, click External User Databases, and then click Unknown User Policy.

2. In the Configure Unknown User Policy table, select Check The Following External User Databases and move the appropriate external database to the selected databases field, as shown next. When you are finished, click Submit.

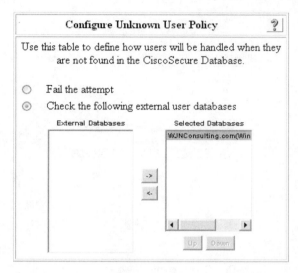

Next, configure the database group mappings that will define what access will be permitted by the user.

1. You can do this by clicking External User Databases in the navigation bar, and then clicking Database Group Mappings.

2. In the Unknown User Group Mappings table, click the name of the external user database that you want to configure.

3. In the Domain Configurations table, click New Configuration.

4. This will take you to the Define New Domain Configuration table. Select the domain that you want to configure and click Submit.

5. You will be returned to the Domain Configurations screen, where two entries should appear. The \DEFAULT entry is used to define what to do with any users not explicitly matched to a group. By default, they are made members of the Default Group. The other entry is the domain that you just added. Click it.

6. In the Group Mappings for Domain <YOUR DOMAIN> table, click Add Mapping to add a new NT group to CiscoSecure group mapping.

7. This will take you to the Create New Group Mapping for Domain <YOUR DOMAIN> table. Select the NT group that you want to map to the CiscoSecure

group and click Add To Selected. Once you have added all of the NT groups, select the CiscoSecure group that you want to map from the drop-down list, as shown next. When you are finished, click Submit.

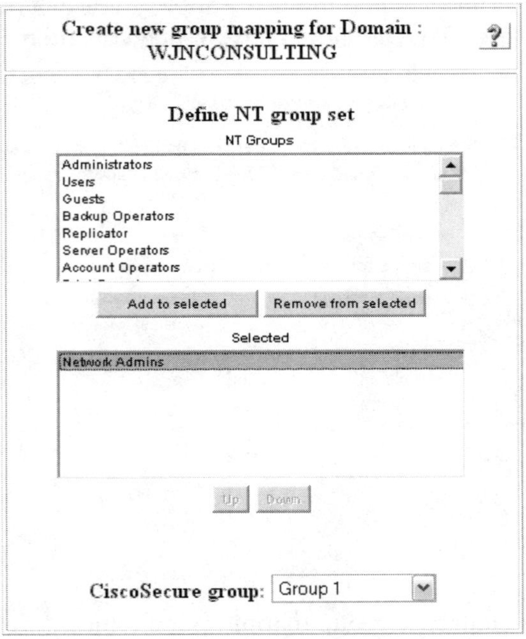

The next process is to configure the CiscoSecure groups with the appropriate permissions. You want to configure at least two groups. The first group is the default group. By default, all users that are not mapped to another group are members of the default group. Because this group could potentially grant anyone access to your resources, I strongly recommend that you configure the group with access restrictions that do not allow connections at any time. This will ensure that no one can accidentally connect to your equipment. You can do this by performing the following steps:

1. Click Group Setup in the navigation bar. Select 0: Default Group in the Group drop-down box and click Edit Settings.

2. In the access restrictions table, check Set As Default Access Times and click Clear All, as shown next. This will prevent any user who is a member of the Default Group from being authenticated. When you are finished, click Submit.

3. You will be returned to the Group Setup screen. Select the group that you configured for the group mapping and click Edit Settings.

4. Scroll down to the TACACS+ table to configure the TACACS+ settings. Check the values for Shell(exec) and Privilege level. For the privilege level, specify 15, which will grant the users of this group full access to the network device. While this is not required for authentication, it will be used for authorization when we discuss that. When you are finished, click Submit + Restart.

The next step is to configure the Cisco Secure ACS server to allow the network device to authenticate against it. This is similar in function to adding the client to the RADIUS server, which you did previously.

1. Click Network Configuration in the navigation bar.

2. In the AAA Clients tables, click Add Entry.

3. In the Add AAA Client table, enter the hostname, IP address, and preshared key that should be used, and select Authenticate Using TACACS+. When you are finished, click Submit + Restart.

HEADS UP!

Because Cisco does not hide the key value, make sure that people are not watching over your shoulder when you configure the key value.

Configure AAA on the Network Device   Once you have configured the Cisco Secure ACS server properly, the next step is to enter the AAA commands on the IOS-based device, configuring it to use TACACS+ for authentication. The following steps detail the process:

1. Use the AAA command to configure the AAA authentication on the device. At the global configuration mode, enter the following commands:

```
local-rtr(config)#aaa new-model
local-rtr(config)#aaa authentication login default tacacs+ local
```

   This will configure the device with a default method list that uses TACACS+ as the primary authentication and the local user database as the backup.

2. Configure at least one local user as a backup user in the event that the TACACS+ server is unavailable. This can be done by entering the following command at the global configuration mode:

```
local-rtr(config)#username backupadmin privilege 15 password →
difficultpass
```

3. Now you want to configure the device with the TACACS+ server settings by running the following commands at the global configuration mode. Make sure that you specify the exact TACACS key that you did when you added the client to the TACACS server in step 4 in the "Configure the Cisco Secure ACS Server" section.

```
local-rtr(config)#tacacs-server host 192.168.173.100
local-rtr(config)#tacacs-server key tacacskey
```

At this point, you should be able to connect to the device using TACACS+ authentication. This is only part of AAA, however. While the user will be authenticated, you will still need to use the enable password to enter the privileges mode of execution until you complete the authorization steps detailed in the section "Hardening Your Network with Authorization." The final step is to save your configuration when you are finished by running **copy running-config startup-config** at the CLI.

AAA Authentication on PIX Firewalls

Configuring access control using AAA on a PIX firewall is similar to configuring your IOS-based devices. The first step is to configure the TACACS+ or RADIUS server as follows:

1. Configure the appropriate users/groups.

2. Add the PIX firewall as a new client.

3. Define the remote access policy (RADIUS).

These steps are the same as those for configuring your IOS-based devices. What is unique are the commands that must be run on the PIX to configure it to use RADIUS or TACACS+. Those are the final steps required to configure the PIX to use AAA authentication.

Configuring the PIX to Use RADIUS for Administration Sessions

The first step in configuring the PIX to use RADIUS authentication is to run the following commands:

```
firewall(config)# aaa-server RADIUS protocol radius
firewall(config)# aaa-server RADIUS (inside) host 192.168.173.100 →
radiuskey timeout 10
```

These commands configure the PIX to use the AAA server that you have specified.

The next step is to configure the PIX to use RADIUS for all of the connection methods as follows:

```
firewall(config)# aaa authentication serial console RADIUS
firewall(config)# aaa authentication telnet console RADIUS
firewall(config)# aaa authentication ssh console RADIUS
firewall(config)# aaa authentication http console RADIUS
```

Configuring the PIX to Use TACACS+ for Administration Sessions

The steps to configure the PIX to use TACACS+ are almost identical to the RADIUS configuration. First you configure the PIX to use the appropriate AAA server, and then you configure authentication on the various connection methods.

```
firewall(config)# aaa-server TACACS+ protocol tacacs+
firewall(config)# aaa-server TACACS+ (inside) host 192.168.173.115 →
tacacskey timeout 10
firewall(config)# aaa authentication serial console TACACS+
firewall(config)# aaa authentication telnet console TACACS+
firewall(config)# aaa authentication ssh console TACACS+
firewall(config)# aaa authentication http console TACACS+
```

Authentication of Users Through the PIX

In addition to being able to authenticate users for administrative sessions on the PIX, you can also use AAA to authenticate users through PIX. This is an excellent method of controlling who can and cannot access Internet resources if you cannot afford a content filtering solution.

ONE STEP FURTHER

The PIX does not grant access to the privileged mode to users, as do your IOS-based devices. Instead, you will still need to use a local username and password, the AAA user password, or the enable secret password, to enter privileged mode. The command **aaa authentication enable console <server_tag>** can be used to provide an extra level of security by requiring the user to be authenticated to enter the enable secret password.

To configure PIX enable authentication, perform the following steps:

1. At the Cisco Secure ACS server, go to the Interface Configuration | TACACS+ (Cisco IOS) screen.

2. Scroll down to the Advanced Configuration Options table, and check Advanced TACACS+ Features. When you are finished, click Submit. This will enable the Advanced TACACS+ Settings table in the User Setup.

3. Go to the User Setup screen and enter the name of the user you want to manage. Click Add/Edit.

4. Scroll down to the Advanced TACACS+ Settings table and set the Max Privilege for any AAA Client to Level 15. Next, select To Use External Database Password and select the appropriate user domain. This will allow the user to enter privileged mode by entering his password (not the enable secret password). When you are finished, click Submit.

5. The last step is to configure enable authentication by running the following command:

```
firewall(config)# aaa authentication enable console TACACS+
```

Once you have taken care of the previously mentioned pre-configuration tasks on your AAA server and configured the PIX to use AAA, the next step is to run the appropriate commands to configure the authentication. Two methods can be used, though you should never mix their use.

Authenticating Using AAA Authentication Include   The first method is to run the command **aaa authentication include <svc> <if_name> <l_ip> <l_mask> [<f_ip> <f_mask>] <server_tag>**for each service that you want to authenticate. For example, if you wanted to authenticate all HTTP traffic at the inside interface using TACACS+, you would run the following:

```
firewall(config)# aaa authentication include HTTP inside 0 0 0 0 TACACS+
```

Any user that attempts make an HTTP connection from the inside will be prompted for a username and password. If the user is authenticated, the HTTP traffic is permitted. If not, the HTTP traffic is denied. While the example provided here covers all traffic, you could also specify certain internal or external addresses that must be authenticated to access, while allowing others to pass without authentication.

Authenticating Using AAA Authentication Match   The second method allows you to leverage any investment that you have made in access control lists (ACLs) by configuring the PIX to authenticate traffic that matches an existing ACL. For example, if an existing ACL defined the traffic that could pass through the interface, and the ACL was named "101," you could run the following command:

```
firewall(config)# aaa authentication match 101 inside TACACS+
```

The benefit of this method is that since the ACL has already been created, it takes a single command to apply authentication to it.

Hardening Your Network with Authorization

Authorization is the second step in AAA, and it is the natural progression from authentication. Authorization allows you to define what commands and processes the user is authorized to run and perform, giving you granular control over your network devices. For example, you can authorize certain users to be able to run commands in the user and privileged modes but prevent them from making any configuration changes, while granting other users full unrestricted access.

Authorization on IOS-Based Devices

AAA authorization can be configured for the following methods:

auth-proxy	Allows you to control what traffic can pass through the router by configuring the router to authenticate the user when she attempts to pass certain traffic
commands	Allows you to authorize commands that are associated with a given privilege mode
configuration	Can be used to download the configuration from the AAA server
exec	Used to authorize the execution of an EXEC shell

Before you can configure authorization, you must first enable AAA on the device, configure AAA authentication, and configure the RADIUS or TACACS+ server with the appropriate users or groups as previously detailed. Let's look at how to perform EXEC and command authorization.

EXEC Authorization

EXEC authorization is the most common method of authorization. If you recall when you configured your RADIUS remote access policy and your TACACS+ group settings, you specified the privilege level. This is used during EXEC authorization to define the EXEC shell that the user is authorized to run. So if you have configured some users at privilege level 1 and others at privilege level 15, you can run the following commands to authorize their ability to start the appropriate EXEC:

```
local-rtr(config)#aaa authorization exec default group tacacs+ →
if-authenticated
local-rtr(config)#privilege exec level 2 enable
```

The first command specifies that AAA authorization should occur and defines TACACS+ as the AAA mechanism to use. If you wanted to use RADIUS, you would type **radius** instead of **tacacs+**. The second command ensures that you must be in EXEC mode with a privilege of at least 2 to run the **enable** command. This is an important step, because if you do not do this, a user that is authorized at privilege level 1 can run the **enable** command and attempt to brute force or guess the enable secret password and thus gain access to the privileged mode of execution.

Commands Authorization

Commands authorization allows you to be even more granular than EXEC authorization by configuring the router to authorize all commands that are being run at the specified privilege level. You can define the commands that belong to a certain privilege level by running the **privilege exec level <priv lvl> <command>** command. For example, if you wanted to allow certain users who are configured through the AAA server to run at privilege 7 to be able to run the show interface and show version commands, you would run the following commands at the CLI:

```
local-rtr(config)# privilege exec level 7 show interface
local-rtr(config)# privilege exec level 7 show version
```

The users will be able to run all of the privilege level 7 commands, as well as the two commands that you specified.

```
local-rtr(config)#aaa authorization commands 15 default group tacacs+ →
if-authenticated
```

HEADS UP!

Command authorization is much easier to implement when using TACACS+; therefore, I recommend that you use TACACS+ instead of RADIUS if you want to do AAA command authorization. If you have to use RADIUS authorization, use the command **aaa authorization commands 15 default if-authenticated**.

Authorization on PIX Firewalls

You can configure authorization on your PIX firewalls for the same reasons and benefits as configuring authorization on your IOS-based devices. One benefit to configuring authorization on the PIX is that it uses a much more robust command set. For example, you can view what privilege level all commands run at by running the following command:

```
firewall# show privilege all
```

Most of the commands are set to privilege level 15, though some are set at privilege level 0.

NOTE   RADIUS authorization is not supported on PIX firewalls. Instead, you must use TACACS+ for authorization

---

Like your IOS-based devices, the prerequisites for authorization on the PIX are that you must enable AAA on the device, configure AAA authentication, configure AAA enable authentication, and configure the TACACS+ server with the appropriate user or group settings as previously detailed.

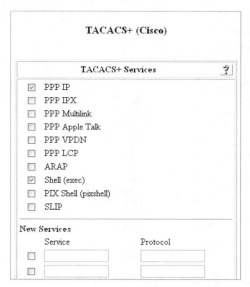

Command Authorization on PIX Firewalls

Command authorization for the PIX is actually configured as a property of the user or group in the Cisco Secure ACS server. To configure command authorization, perform the following steps:

1. Verify that the Shell (exec) TACACS+ Service has been enabled by clicking Interface Configuration in the navigation bar and then clicking TACACS+ (Cisco IOS). Verify that Shell (exec) is checked in the TACACS+ Services table, as shown here. When you are finished, click Submit.

2. Click Group Setup in the navigation bar. Select the group that you want to configure and click Edit Settings.

3. Scroll down to the Shell Command Authorization Set settings and select Per Group Command Authorization.

4. If you want this user to be able to run all commands, select Permit under Unmatched Cisco IOS Commands:

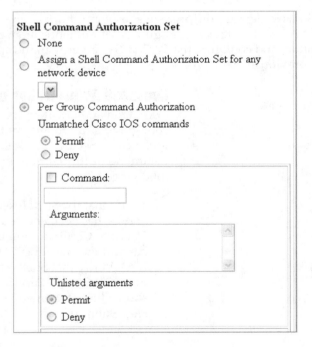

Two methods can be used for determining how to perform the command authorization. The first method is to select the option in step 4 that will permit all commands and then specify the commands that you want to deny. The other method is to deny all the commands and then specify the commands that you want to permit. This latter method is a more secure method and is the method detailed next.

5. Under Unmatched Cisco IOS Commands, select Deny.

6. Check the Command button and enter the command that you want to permit. In the Arguments field, enter the command arguments that you want to permit (for example, **running-config** for the **show** command).

7. Under Unlisted Arguments, select Permit. This will authorize the user to be able to run the command that you defined as well as permit unlisted arguments. If you do not want to authorize running unlisted arguments (for example, you want the user to be able to run the commands show version and show interface but no other show commands), select Deny under Unlisted Arguments. The following shows a configuration that permits the user to run the commands **enable**, **show interface**, **show version**, and **exit** (not shown) while denying them the ability to run any other commands.

```
☑ Command:
enable
Arguments:

Unlisted arguments
⦿ Permit
○ Deny
☑ Command:
show
Arguments:
permit interface
permit version

Unlisted arguments
○ Permit
⦿ Deny
```

8. To enter additional commands, click Submit and then return to this screen. You can check a new command entry to repeat the process. When you are finished with all of your configurations, click Submit + Restart.

9. The last step is to enable AAA command authorization on the PIX by running the following command:

```
firewall(config)# aaa authorization command TACACS+
```

10. When you are finished, make sure that you save your configuration.

Authorization of Users Through the PIX

While authorization of users, for example to control what websites users access, is certainly able to be implemented, due to the nature of HTTP and the fact that it uses multiple connection for a single website request, in addition to the fact that a single website might have multiple IP addresses it is probably a much more feasible solution to implement content filtering, as discussed in Chapter 7. You can configure authorization (for example, for HTTP traffic) by running the following command:

```
firewall(config)# aaa authorization include HTTP inside 0 0 0 0 TACACS+
```

Hardening Your Network with Accounting

Once you have configured authentication and authorization, the last component of AAA to configure is accounting. Accounting is designed to allow you to track what servers a user is accessing, what commands a user is attempting to use (successful or not), as well as the amount of network resources that they are using. This information can then be analyzed and used for network management decision-making, client billing, as well as auditing.

AAA Accounting on IOS-Based Equipment

Enabling AAA accounting is going to be a familiar process at this point, because it is largely the same process that you followed for authentication and authorization. Indeed, authentication and authorization is a prerequisite if you want to perform accounting.

Accounting uses method lists similar to our other AAA processes and supports five different types of accounting:

Network	Allows you to configure accounting for all PPP, SLIP, or ARAP sessions
EXEC	Provides information about the EXEC terminal sessions that a user creates
Commands	Allows you to provide accounting information about all commands that a user issues
System	Provides accounting for system-level events
Resource	Provides start and stop records of all calls that have been authenticated as well as provides records of all calls that fail to authenticate

We will look at enabling EXEC and command accounting, though all of the accounting methods use the same fundamental commands with a slightly different syntax.

EXEC Accounting Using TACACS+

Enabling EXEC accounting is a straightforward process if you have already configured the rest of AAA properly, as we have done previously in this chapter. If you want to enable EXEC accounting using TACACS+, you can run the following command at the global configuration mode:

```
local-rtr(config)#aaa accounting exec default start-stop group tacacs+
```

You can view the accounting reports on your Cisco Secure ACS server by clicking Reports And Activity in the navigation bar and clicking TACACS+ Accounting. Next, select the TACACS+ Accounting file that you want to view. The following shows an example of the accounting file, including the EXEC shell being started (when the user connects) and stopped (when the user disconnects).

TACACS+ Accounting active.csv								
Date ↓	Time	User-Name	Group-Name	Caller-Id	Acct-Flags	elapsed time	service	byte
02/26/2004	16:02:55	timc	Group 2	192.168.173.114	stop	12	shell	..
02/26/2004	16:02:43	timc	Group 2	192.168.173.114	start	..	shell	..
02/26/2004	15:48:57	wnoonan	Group 1	192.168.173.114	start	..	shell	..

Commands Accounting Using TACACS+

Commands accounting can be enabled by running the following command at the global configuration mode:

```
local-rtr(config)#aaa accounting commands 0 default start-stop group tacacs+
```

Repeat this command for privilege levels 1–15 by replacing the "0" with the appropriate privilege level number. These commands specify that all commands running at any privilege level be logged for accounting. While most commands are going to run at privilege level 0, 1, or 15, I recommend implementing all privilege levels to ensure that you do not inadvertently miss something. To view the command accounting reports on the Cisco Secure ACS server, click Reports And Activity in the navigation bar and click TACACS+ Administration (not TACACS+ Accounting). Next, click the report that you want to view.

NOTE   AAA accounting using RADIUS leaves a lot to be desired. As a result, I recommend that you use TACACS+ for accounting if at all possible.

AAA Accounting on PIX Firewalls

You can configure accounting of your user connections through the PIX by running the following command after configuring the previous AAA configuration prerequisites (that is, authentication):

```
firewall(config)# aaa accounting include any inside 0 0 0 0 TACACS+
```

This will cause the PIX to log any traffic passing through the PIX to the TACACS+ accounting log. As previously mentioned, however, AAA authorization and accounting of user connections through the PIX, while useful, is not anywhere near as robust and reliable as content filtering. I recommend that you consider implementing a content filter before you implement authorization and accounting.

HEADS UP!

Command accounting is not supported on the PIX. The PIX by default logs everything that occurs in a syslog format. You can get the same functionality by reviewing the syslogs that you get by enabling command accounting on your IOS-based devices.

802.1x Port-Based Authentication

As we saw in Chapter 8 when we talked about wireless LANs (WLANs), 802.1x can be used to authenticate users attempting to connect to the WAP. 802.1x actually predates WLANs, however, and was originally designed for function in a wired network environment.

802.1x functions by requiring the client to authenticate before being able to access any network resources. Until authentication has occurred, the switch will only allow Extended Authentication Protocol over LAN (EAPOL) traffic to pass. Once the client has been authenticated, however, normal traffic can pass through the switch.

802.1x port-based authentication on your access switches can prevent anyone who can not be authenticated from being able to connect to your network. This is a paradigm shift from many LAN technologies, however. For example, DHCP and auto-negotiation has created an environment where we almost take for granted that we can connect a computer to the network and gain access to resources. This is a double-edged sword, however, because as easy as it is for that consultant to plug into your network and start helping you with network management issues, he can just as easily plug his laptop that is infected with a worm into your environment and begin infecting your systems.

802.1x Network Device Roles

Before we can configure 802.1x port-based authentication, we have to take a look at the network devices and their roles in an 802.1x deployment. Figure 9-1 shows the 802.1x device roles.

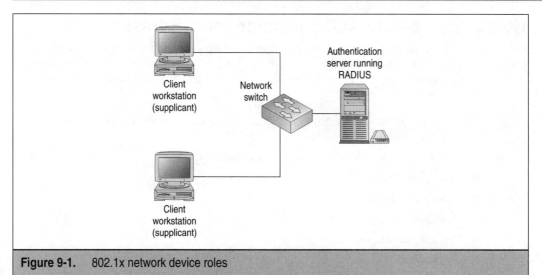

Figure 9-1.   802.1x network device roles

- **Client**   The client workstation, also known as the supplicant, is the device that requests access to the LAN. The client also responds to any requests from the switch. In order for the client to participate in 802.1x authentication, it must be running an 802.1x-compliant operating system or client software. Windows XP is 802.1x compliant.

HEADS UP!

Microsoft Windows XP uses display balloons to notify the user that she needs to log on for 802.1x authentication. If you experience problems with Microsoft Windows XP not properly displaying the 802.1x notifications, refer to the following Microsoft Knowledge Base article for a potential resolution: http://support.microsoft.com/default.aspx?scid=kb;en-us;303597.

- **Switch**   The switch can be either a LAN access switch or a wireless access point and is responsible for controlling the client access to the network. The switch effectively acts as an intermediary or proxy for the client by receiving the client authentication request via EAP and passing that information to the authentication server via RADIUS.
- **Authentication server**   The authentication server is running RADIUS and is responsible for the actual client authentication. The authentication server is responsible for validating the client and informing the switch that the client is authorized to access the network.

Configuring 802.1x Authentication for IOS-Based Switches

By default, 802.1x authentication is not enabled. For your IOS-based switches, configuring 802.1x requires the implementation of AAA to facilitate the authentication of the client workstations. You should be aware of some important caveats before you do this, however:

- When you enable 802.1x, the ports must be authenticated before any other layer 2 features will be enabled.
- 802.1x is not supported on the following port types:
  - Trunk ports
  - Dynamic ports
  - Dynamic-access ports
  - EtherChannel ports
  - Secure ports
  - Switch Port Analyzer (SPAN) destination ports
- It is imperative that only one client be connected to any switch port that is configured with 802.1x. The command **dot1x multiple hosts** run on an interface will allow multiple hosts to connect; however, only one of the hosts is actually authenticated, while all of the rest of the hosts will be permitted to access the network. This creates a security hole that allows unauthenticated access to your network.

Enable 802.1x Authentication

802.1x authentication is configured on a per-interface basis. Before you can do this, however, you must enable AAA on the switch. The following steps detail the process of enabling 802.1x authentication on a Cisco 2950 switch running software version 12.1(20)EA1.

1. Enable AAA on the switch by running the following command at the global configuration mode:

   ```
   switch02(config)#aaa new-model
   ```

2. Enable AAA authentication using **dot1x** and RADIUS:

   ```
   switch02(config)#aaa authentication dot1x default group radius
   ```

3. Globally enable 802.1x on the switch by running the following command:

   ```
   switch02(config)#dot1x system-auth-control
   ```

4. Enter the interface configuration mode that you want to configure (in this case **fastethernet 0/4**):

```
switch02(config)#interface fastethernet 0/4
```

5. The next command is optional; however, since by default most IOS-based switches configure all ports to be dynamic ports, I recommend that you run it just to be safe. This will configure the port as an access port only.

```
switch02(config-if)#switchport mode access
```

6. The final step is to configure the 802.1x port control. There are three options: auto, force-authorized (default), and force-unauthorized. Auto enables 802.1x. Force-authorized is the default setting and forces the port to operate in an authorized mode without exchanging any 802.1x authentication data (essentially it disables 802.1x). Force-unauthorized prevents the port from authorizing a user under any circumstances. The following command will enable 802.1x:

```
switch02(config-if)#dot1x port-control auto
```

NOTE Make sure that you save your configuration when you are done.

At this point, the switch and interface have been configured to use 802.1x authentication.

Configuring the Switch to Communicate with the RADIUS Server

Once 802.1x has been enabled and configured, the next step is to configure the switch to communicate with the RADIUS server. The following command can be run at the global configuration mode to do this:

```
switch02(config)#radius-server host 192.168.173.100 auth-port 1812 →
acct-port 1813 key radiuskey
```

In this case, I have configured the switch to communicate with a RADIUS server running at 192.168.173.100 with a key of *radiuskey*.

Configure the Microsoft IAS Server and Windows Domain

Once you have configured the switch properly, the next step is to configure the IAS server and the Microsoft Windows domain information to allow the client to connect.

First you must add a new IAS client on your IAS server using the same credentials that you specified on the switch. Next you want to create a new remote access policy to be used for 802.1x authentication. The following steps detail policy creation:

1. Open the IAS MMC, right-click Remote Access Policies, and select New Remote Access Policy. Enter an appropriate name and click Next.

2. At the Conditions screen, click Add to add a new condition. I recommend the Day-And-Time-Restriction, specifying the appropriate days and times. When you are finished, click OK and then Next.

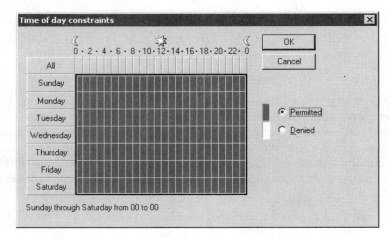

3. At the Permissions screen, select to grant remote access permission and click Next.

4. At the User Profile screen, click Edit Profile. Select the Authentication tab and check Enable Authentication Protocol; then select MD5-Challenge from the drop-down menu, as shown here:

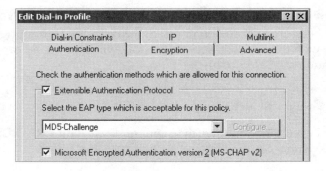

5. Select the IP tab and check Client May Request An IP Address To Support The Use Of DHCP. When you are finished, click OK and then Finish.

6. The next step is to configure Active Directory to support reversible encryption format for EAP-MD5. Two methods can be used to accomplish this, however both introduce a significant security vulnerability to your Microsoft Windows servers. Steps 7 and 8 detail the process of enabling reversible encryption on

your entire domain. If you do this, you do not need to perform step 9. Likewise, if you decide to do step 9, you do not need to perform steps 7 and 8.

7. Open the Active Directory Users And Computers administrative tool, right-click the domain name, and select Properties. From the Properties screen, select the Group Policy tab. Highlight the Default Domain Policy and click Edit. This will open the Group Policy administrative tool.

8. Navigate to Computer Configuration\Windows Settings\Security Settings\Account Policies\Password Policy, double-click Store Password Using Reversible Encryption, and select Enable, as shown next. When you are finished, close the Group Policy administrative tool. You do not need to perform step 9 if you have performed steps 7 and 8.

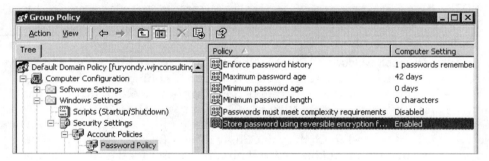

9. If you decided not to perform steps 7 and 8, the final step is to enable Dial-In access and Password Reversible Encryption for all of your user accounts. This can be done by selecting Allow Access on the Dial-in tab of the user account and checking the value Store Password Using Reversible Encryption on the Account tab, as shown here:

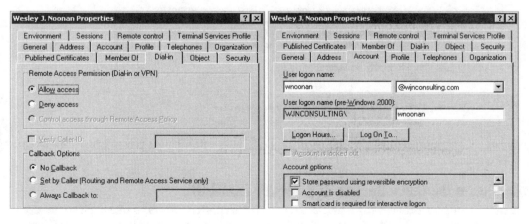

HEADS UP!

Enabling reversible encryption is a huge security risk on your Microsoft server. It significantly weakens the security of the user accounts passwords, allowing them to be easily compromised by anyone who gains access to your server. As a result, it is highly unlikely that your server administrators will allow this change to be made. If that is the case, the only alternative is to use TACACS+ or a third-party RADIUS server instead of Microsoft IAS.

NOTE If you are changing existing user accounts, you need to reset or have the user change his password to enable the reversible encrypted password format.

Configure the Microsoft Windows XP Client   Now that the switch, IAS server, and Active Directory have been configured properly, it is time to configure the Microsoft Windows XP Client. Open the properties of the network connection that you want to configure and select the Authentication tab. Check the value Enable Network Access Control Using IEEE 802.1X and select MD5-Challenge for the EAP Type, as shown next. Select the General tab and check the value Show Icon In Taskbar When Connected. This will allow the pop-up bubble that will prompt the user for the authentication credentials. When you are finished, click OK.

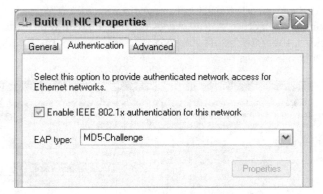

At this point, the user will be prompted for a username and password for network authentication.

Configure the Cisco Secure ACS Server (RADIUS)

A much simpler process for using 802.1x with Cisco switches is to use a Cisco Secure ACS server as the RADIUS server. The first step is to add a new client on your Cisco Secure ACS server using the same credentials that you specified on the switch.

The second step is to ensure that you have users defined in the Cisco Secure ACS database that have been granted network access using any of the previously mentioned methods. That's it!

Configure the Microsoft Windows XP Client   The last step is to configure the Microsoft Windows XP Client. The real beauty of this method is that you can configure the Microsoft Windows XP Client to use transparent authentication. To do this, edit the properties of the network connection and select the Authentication tab. Check Enable IEEE 802.1x Authentication For This Network and select Protected EAP (PEAP) for the EAP Type:

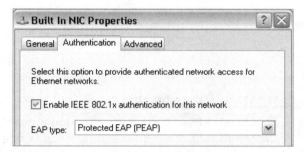

Click Properties and verify that Secured Password (EAP-MSCHAP v2) is the selected authentication method:

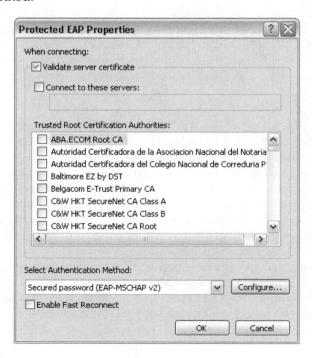

Click Configure and make sure that Automatically Use My Windows Logon Name And Password (And Domain If Any) is checked, as shown next. Click OK three times to close the network properties. The system will automatically authenticate using the current user's logon credentials without prompting the user.

802.1x Authentication Drawbacks

You should be aware of the fact that 802.1x authentication can make it difficult to manage systems, because until the client is authenticated, it will not be able to obtain an IP address via DHCP, since the switch will not allow traffic other than EAPOL, Cisco Discovery Protocol, and Spanning-Tree Protocol in Cisco switches. This can also prevent login scripts from running and group policy updates, since the client system may authenticate the user using cached credentials. Be aware of these caveats before you deploy 802.1x through your environment.

Summary

AAA is a necessity for all networks. At the very minimum, you need to implement a AAA scheme that allows you to implement stringent access control for the administrative sessions on your network devices. In addition, AAA enables you to provide granular management access through the use of authorization, which allows you to break away from the all-or-nothing administration that is so prevalent on today's networks. You can specify read-only or diagnostic commands for some users, while allowing other users less restrictive access. You can then verify the use and function of your AAA implementation by configuring accounting, allowing you to determine who did what and when they did it.

AAA is about more than just managing administrative access to your network devices, however. Through the use of 802.1x port authentication, you can also control who can physically connect to your network by ensuring that they have to authenticate before they are granted access to network services and resources.

Chapter 10

Hardening Your Network with Network Management

- Fault Management
- Configuration Management
- Performance Management
- Accounting or Asset Management
- Security Management
- Configuring IPsec on Microsoft Windows 2000

Network management applications and programs are often overlooked tools for hardening your network infrastructure. Reasons for this include the following:

- Traditionally, network management has not really been considered a security mechanism. This is even evident in the design of many of the management protocols we use; many of them have no authentication or weak authentication and no encryption of data.

- Network management is often considered an afterthought in network design and implementation.

- As network administrators, we wind up spending so much time reacting to problems and incidents that we rarely find the time to really consider network management and what we can accomplish with it. Sure, we all know we need it and we know we want it—but we don't always know what we want to accomplish with it. You can see this put into practice with industry reports that put over 60 percent of network management implementations as failed projects or as projects that did not live up to expectations.

In this chapter, we are going to look at two aspects of network management. The first aspect is an examination of how you can use network management tools to increase the security of your network and ensure that your network management implementation accomplishes the goals and objectives you define. The second aspect is an examination of the network management protocols and utilities that exist and how you can secure them.

Implementing a Network Management System (NMS)

There is more to hardening your network than merely implementing firewalls, ACLs, and virus protection. No matter how secure your network is, if it isn't functional and reliable, all your efforts are an exercise in futility. A too-often thrown around buzzword in our industry is "proactive." We all want to be proactive instead of reactive; however, very few of us manage to accomplish that goal. Instead, we spend our days (and nights) reacting to security incidents and technical failures, and "proactive" becomes an almost utopian term that is beyond our grasp. It does not have to be that way, however.

A network management system, if properly implemented, not only can help us achieve a goal of proactive management of our network, but it can also help us to secure our network by providing insight into how it operates. Fundamentally, all networks have identifiable patterns or habits. In fact, I often refer to networks as having a personality. In a sense, they are very much like children. For example, many parents seem to have an almost instinctual knowledge as to what is going on with their kids. The reason for this is pretty simple really: As a parent, you are so in tune with your children that you just know when things are not "normal." You know your child's personality and habits, and you know when things aren't in line. This doesn't necessarily mean that what happened is a bad thing, but you know that something is up that warrants further investigation.

A well-implemented NMS can provide the same insight as to the habits and personality of your network. If you spend enough time observing and learning the way your network works, it becomes very easy for you to detect when something is occurring that is out of the ordinary. This does not necessarily mean that something wrong has occurred, but it lets you know that something is up that warrants further investigation—and at that point you make the turn from being reactive to being proactive.

The International Organization for Standardization (ISO) defined five functional areas for network management to help network administrators understand what to do and how to manage their networks. The acronym FCAPS is used to represent these five areas:

- Fault management
- Configuration management
- Performance management
- Accounting or asset management
- Security management

We are going to look at each functional area and at how we can use it to increase not only the security but also the reliability of our network infrastructure.

Fault Management

Fault management is the process of trouble detection, trouble logging, trouble notification, and trouble correction. Fault management is probably the most widely implemented area of network management because it provides the functionality we all want—it informs us of a fault or failure that is causing downtime. Most of us do not have the time or desire to spend all day watching screens to tell us if we have experienced a failure somewhere in the network that could be the result of a security incident or could contribute to a security incident. Instead, we want fault management to be an almost transparent process that is used to monitor the network on our behalf and to alert us in the event that something occurs that requires human intervention.

Two primary mechanisms are used for fault management. The first is the use of proactive polling systems to detect a fault. The second is the use of log monitoring to detect that a noteworthy event has been logged.

Using Polling to Detect Faults

Polling is the classic "Is it up or is it down?" method of fault management. Most products that do polling use ICMP pings or SNMP polling to detect whether the device being monitored is available. If the monitoring station receives a response, the device is considered up. If it does not, the device is considered down. A number of products are available that you can use to poll your network:

- Ipswitch WhatsUp Gold (http://www.ipswitch.com/products/network-management.html)

- HP OpenView (http://www.openview.hp.com/index.html)

- Solarwinds Orion (http://www.solarwinds.net/)

- Micromuse Netcool (http://www.micromuse.com/sols/ent_net_man.html)

Using Ipswitch WhatsUp Gold for Fault Management   Ipswitch WhatsUp Gold is one of the leading fault management products and, in fact, is bundled with CiscoWorks to provide fault management functionality for CiscoWorks. Using WhatsUp Gold to monitor your network is surprisingly easy.

The first step to using WhatsUp Gold to monitor your environment is to build a network map. Once you have started WhatsUp Gold from the Start menu, click File | New Map Wizard to start the New Map Wizard. At the Device Discovery Information screen, select Discover and Map Network Devices and then click Next.

At the Device Discovery Methods screen, select either Discover Your Network with SNMP SmartScan or Discover Your Network Using ICMP. If your network supports SNMP, I recommend that you use it (and this example will use it). Otherwise, use ICMP. When you are finished, click Next.

At the SNMP SmartScan screen, enter the appropriate SNMP root device, as shown next. The root device is typically the backbone router from which you want to begin the scan. Enter the SNMP communities you want to use. Also, review the scan depth—setting this value too large will cause a scan to take a very long time in large networks. Under Active Discovery, select whether you want to keep your network maps current with the latest devices. This will cause WhatsUp Gold to automatically scan the network to update the network map with new devices that come online. If you select Scan at Intervals, the discovery will happen at the specified scan interval (the default is 1440 minutes). If you select Scan at Distributed Intervals, the discovery will be spread throughout the scan interval to minimize the network impact. When you are finished, click Next.

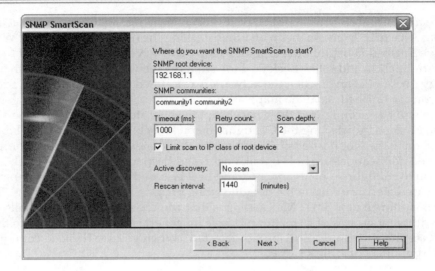

HEADS UP!

Because automatically scanning will add network devices to your map, this can cause the placement of objects on the map to change. If you do not want the discovery of new devices to change the placement of existing devices, make sure you lock the devices in the map properties while in edit mode. You can do this by right-clicking the devices in the edit map and selecting Lock Position from the menu.

At the TCP/IP Service Scan screen, select the services you want to attempt to scan for and discover. At a minimum, you should scan for interfaces. When you are finished, click Next.

The scan will begin. When the scan is completed, you will be presented with the Scan Results screen. Uncheck the devices you do not want to be added to the map and click Finish.

Once the devices have been added to the map, the next step is to configure the map and save the settings. You can rearrange the layout of the devices on the map by clicking the Edit tab. You can reposition the devices by simply clicking and dragging to move them around. You can link devices together by right-clicking an object and selecting Attach To from the menu and then clicking the device to connect to. When you have finished laying out the topology map the way you want it, select all the objects, right-click, and select Lock Position from the menu. This will ensure that the topology does not change when the network is rescanned or new devices are added. When you are finished, save the map.

Once you have configured the device map, the next step is to configure the alerts. This can be done by selecting the Configure menu and clicking Notifications Library. This will open the Notifications Library screen, shown next. The most commonly configured notifications are SMTPMail, Pager, and Beeper. As the names imply, they allow you to configure e-mail- , pager- , and beeper-based alerts. You can configure e-mail–based alerts by editing the default setting or adding a new mail setting. The benefit of adding a new SMTPMail setting is that you can create custom e-mails to send to different groups of users (for example, to generate an alert that goes to the firewall admins when a firewall fault is detected). When you are finished configuring your alert notifications, click Close.

The next step is to configure the devices to send alerts based on fault detection. Select the device (or devices), right-click, and select Properties from the menu. This will open the Properties screen for the devices you selected, as shown next. Click Alerts in the navigation bar and click Add. Select the notification you want to use and specify a Trigger value. The Trigger value is how many failed checks must occur before an alert is generated. Although you may have a desire to select 1, keep in mind that fault management uses ICMP, and therefore a low value here could cause false positives for any of a number of reasons. When you are finished configuring the alert, click OK. Repeat the process for the other alerts you want to configure for the device (or devices). When you are finished, click OK.

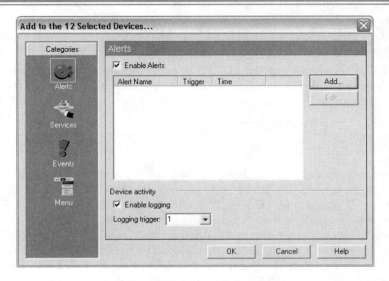

WhatsUp Gold also provides web-based management, which is particularly useful because it does not require you to be sitting at the machine running WhatsUp Gold to get your network status. By default, the web server is not enabled, but you can change this by clicking the Configure menu and selecting Web Server. This will open the Web Server Properties screen, shown next. Under the General category, check the value for Enable Web Server.

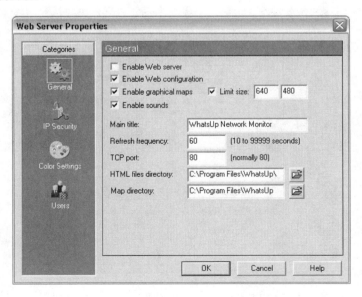

HEADS UP!

WhatsUp Gold does not support HTTPS as a management protocol; therefore, you might not want to allow this traffic to traverse insecure networks, or you might want to encapsulate the management console traffic in IPsec, as detailed later in this chapter.

Like any time you configure a device to be remotely accessible, you need to take steps to secure the device. The first step to securing your WhatsUp Gold web server is to configure the IP security by clicking IP Security from the navigation bar. Select to deny access to all computers, except those listed, and add the IP addresses of the systems that you want to be able to connect to the WhatsUp Gold web server. The next hardening step is to configure the users who will be allowed to log in by clicking Users in the navigation bar. First, delete the guest user by right-clicking it and selecting Delete. Next, delete the admin user. The next step is to add the users you want to be able to connect. I recommend that you use individual user accounts for each user who will be granted permission. Click Add User. At the Add User screen, enter the username and password and select the maps you want this user to be able to view. When you are finished, click OK. When you have returned to the Users category, select the user and configure the appropriate user security settings, as shown next.

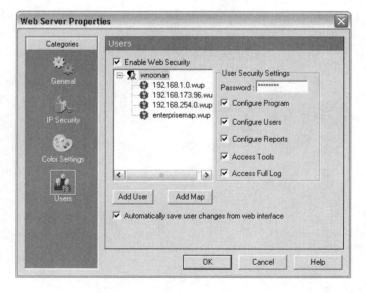

In this case, I have granted the user full access to all aspects of WhatsUp Gold. Next, select a map and configure the Map Level Security Settings area, as shown next.

Again, in this case, I have granted the user full rights to the map. Repeat this step for each map that the user has access to. When you are finished adding users, click OK.

The final step of getting WhatsUp Gold set up and running with basic functionality in your environment is to configure it to automatically load maps on startup and to start automatically. You can configure the maps to open on startup by selecting the Configure menu and selecting Program Options. In the Startup category, select Open Maps on Startup and add the maps you want to open, as shown next. When you are finished, click OK.

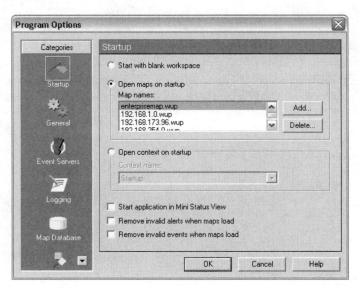

Next, configure WhatsUp Gold to run as a service (this is not enabled by default). Open a command prompt, change to the WhatsUp Gold program directory, and then enter the following command:

```
wugsvc -install
```

This will install WhatsUp Gold as a service and start the service. If you do not do this, you have to run the WhatsUp Gold application in order to monitor your devices.

At this point, you can safely close the WhatsUp Gold application, and it will continue to monitor your environment. If you need to manage WhatsUp Gold, you can simply so from a web browser, as shown here:

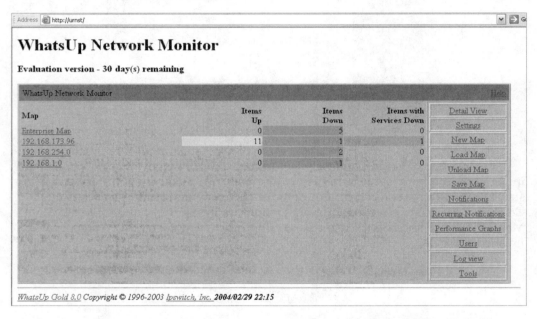

Notice that there are devices in alert right now. For example, I can click 192.168.173.96 to drill down and look at what device is down (in this case, the device local-rtr), as shown next.

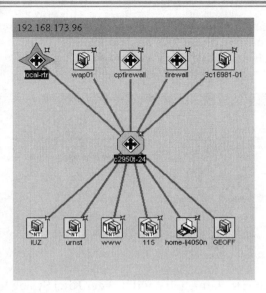

Using Logging to Detect Faults

In addition to using tools to detect up/down faults on your network, you can use logging to detect faults or error conditions. This is most effectively done through the use of syslog. We covered the fundamentals of how syslog works and how to configure devices to use syslog in their respective chapters, and now we are going to take a look at how you can configure the syslog server to provide you with the information and alerts you require. We will be doing this using Kiwi Enterprises Syslog Daemon 7.0.3 (Build 174).

Using Display Filters   The Kiwi Syslog Daemon supports using up to ten displays. These displays come in particularly handy in allowing you to separate the output of your syslog messages by logging levels. For example, you can send all your debug-level (level 7) messages to Display 7 and send all your informational-level (level 6) messages to Display 6.

Like much of Kiwi Syslog's advanced configuration, this can be accomplished through the use of rules. The steps to configure a display rule are as follows:

1. Run the Kiwi Syslog Service Manager and select File | Properties.

2. You will notice a default rule. This rule causes all messages to be displayed to the Display 0 output, and it logs all data to a file. You can create a new rule by right-clicking Rules in the tree view and selecting Add Rule. Assign the rule a name, as shown here (in this case, I named it Display 7):

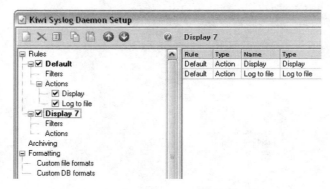

3. Configure a filter to define what will trigger Kiwi Syslog to use this rule. Right-click Filters under the new rule and select Add Filter. Then name the filter accordingly.

4. In the Field drop-down list, select Priority. In the Filter Type drop-down list, select Priority. Next, select Debug for all the logging facilities. When you are finished, the screen should look like this:

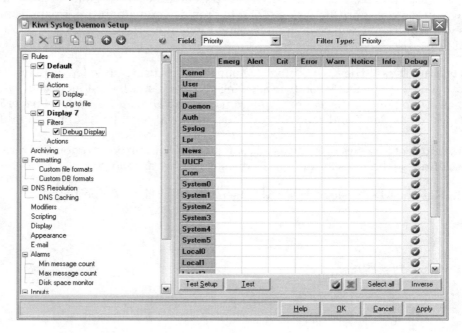

5. Right-click Actions in the tree view under the rule you created and select Add Action. Then name the action appropriately.

6. In the Action drop-down field, select Display.

7. In the Display Number field, select Display 07, as shown here:

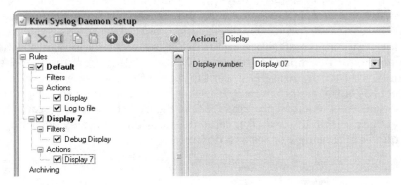

8. When you are finished configuring the rule, click Apply.

Display 07 should display only debug-level values in the Display 07 output (while continuing to display and log debug-level values according to the default rule). Now if you want to look only at debug-level messages, you can select Display 07, as shown next. Repeat this process for each display you want to customize.

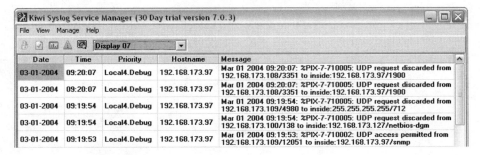

Sending Alerts   Although display filters provide an excellent method of separating data to make it easier to locate messages, you probably don't have the time to sit in front of your syslog server waiting for important messages to scroll by. Thankfully, Kiwi Syslog provides alerting functionality that allows you to use rules to define a filter and attach an e-mail alert action. The following steps detail this process:

1. Open the Kiwi Syslog Service Manager properties as previously detailed.

2. Right-click Rules, select Add Rule, and name the rule accordingly.

3. Right-click Filters, select Add Filter, and name the filter accordingly.

4. In the Field drop-down list, select Message Text. In the Filter Type drop-down list, select Simple or Complex. Simple filters are simple one-line filters. Complex filters allow you perform complex include/exclude matching.

5. In the Include field, enter the text string for which you want to search. Wherever possible, I like to use syslog event severity levels. For the Cisco PIX Firewall, Cisco maintains a list of all the messages at http://www.cisco.com/en/US/customer/products/sw/secursw/ps2120/products_system_message_guide_chapter09186a00801582af.html. For example, if you want to filter for invalid logon attempts, the severity ID is 6-605004 (information level-event number). Enter the string you want to search for, enclosing it in quotes, and select [C] or [S], as shown next. Pressing [C] tells the filter that the string is case sensitive, whereas pressing [S] tells the filter that the data can appear anywhere within the text. You can enter multiple strings by enclosing each in quotes and using a space as a delimiter.

6. Right-click Actions in the tree view and select Add Action. Then name the action accordingly.

7. In the Action field, select E-mail Message.

8. Enter the appropriate information for the e-mail, as shown here:

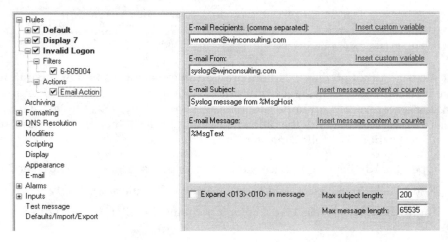

9. The last step is to configure Kiwi Syslog to use an SMTP server. This can be done by clicking E-mail in the tree view.

10. Configure Kiwi Syslog with the appropriate SMTP mail server and a valid "from" address. If your SMTP server requires it, configure a username and password. You can also configure the syslog server to send an e-mail in the event that the syslog server itself experiences an alarm condition (this is not the same as configuring an e-mail action in a rule). For example, if the syslog server experiences low disk space, it could send an e-mail. You can also configure the syslog server to send a daily statistics e-mail. I highly recommend configuring this so that you can start to get a feel for the amount of daily syslog events the server logs. Finally, configure the e-mail logging options, as shown next. When you are finished, click Apply.

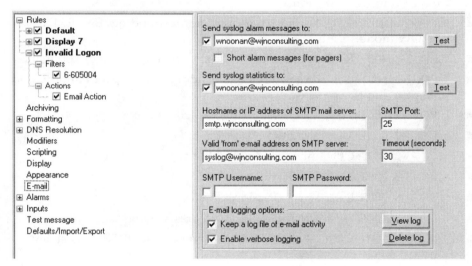

At this point, any time this event occurs, the syslog server will send an e-mail, as shown here:

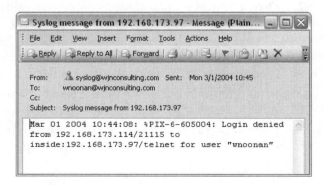

Simply repeat this process for any other events for which you want to send messages. I recommend that, at a minimum, you configure e-mail alerts for the following Cisco PIX syslog messages:

- All Severity Level 1 messages (use the string "%PIX-1" for the filter)
- %PIX-2-106016: Deny IP spoof from (IP_address) to IP_address on interface interface_name.
- %PIX-2-106017: Deny IP due to Land Attack from IP_address to IP_address
- %PIX-2-106018: ICMP packet type ICMP_type denied by outbound list acl_ID src inside_address dest outside_address
- %PIX-2-106020: Deny IP teardrop fragment (size = number, offset = number) from IP_address to IP_address
- %PIX-2-304007: URL Server IP_address not responding, ENTERING ALLOW mode.
- %PIX-2-304009: Ran out of buffer blocks specified by url-block command
- %PIX-2-316001: Denied new tunnel to IP_address. VPN peer limit (platform_vpn_peer_limit) exceeded
- %PIX-3-201008: The PIX is disallowing new connections.
- %PIX-3-211001: Memory allocation Error
- %PIX-3-211003: CPU utilization for number seconds = percent
- %PIX-3-302302: ACL = deny; no sa created
- %PIX-3-304003: URL Server IP_address timed out URL url
- %PIX-3-304006: URL Server IP_address not responding
- %PIX-3-315004: Fail to establish SSH session because PIX RSA host key retrieval failed.
- %PIX-3-710003: {TCP | UDP} access denied by ACL from source_address/source_port to interface_name:dest_address/service
- %PIX-4-106023: Deny protocol src [interface_name:source_address/source_port] dst interface_name:dest_address/dest_port [type {string}, code {code}] by access_group acl_ID
- %PIX-4-209003: Fragment database limit of number exceeded: src = IP_address,dest = IP_address, proto = protocol, id = number
- %PIX-4-209004: Invalid IP fragment, size = bytes exceeds maximum size = bytes: src = IP_address, dest = IP_address, proto = protocol, id = number
- %PIX-4-209005: Discard IP fragment set with more than number elements: src = IP_address, dest = IP_address, proto = protocol, id = number

- %PIX-4-401004: Shunned packet: IP_address ==> IP_address on interface interface_name

- %PIX-4-402103: identity doesn't match negotiated identity (ip) dest_address= dest_address, src_addr= source_address, prot= protocol, (ident) local=inside_ address, remote=remote_address, local_proxy=IP_address/IP_address/port/ port, remote_proxy=IP_address/IP_address/port/port

- %PIX-4-407001: Deny traffic for local-host interface_name:inside_address, license limit of number exceeded

- %PIX-5-111001: Begin configuration: IP_address writing to device

- %PIX-5-111003: IP_address Erase configuration

- %PIX-5-111004: IP_address end configuration: {FAILED | OK}

- %PIX-5-111005: IP_address end configuration: OK

- %PIX-5-111007: Begin configuration: IP_address reading from device.

- %PIX-5-111008: User user executed the command string

- %PIX-5-199001: PIX reload command executed from telnet (remote IP_address).

- %PIX-5-304001: user source_address Accessed {JAVA URL | URL} dest_ address: url.

- %PIX-5-304002: Access denied URL url SRC IP_address DEST IP_address: url

- %PIX-5-500001: ActiveX content modified src IP_address dest IP_address on interface interface_name.

- %PIX-5-500002: Java content modified src IP_address dest IP_address on interface interface_name.

- %PIX-5-501101: User transitioning priv level

- %PIX-5-502101: New user added to local dbase: Uname: user Priv: privilege_ level Encpass: string

- %PIX-5-502102: User deleted from local dbase: Uname: user Priv: privilege_ level Encpass: string

- %PIX-5-502103: User priv level changed: Uname: user From: privilege_level To: privilege_level

- %PIX-5-612001: Auto Update succeeded:filename, version:number

- %PIX-6-109006: Authentication failed for user user from inside_address/ inside_port to outside_address/outside_port on interface interface_name.

- %PIX-6-109008: Authorization denied for user user from source_address/ source_port to destination_address/destination_port on interface interface_name.

- %PIX-6-109009: Authorization denied from inside_address/inside_port to outside_address/outside_port (not authenticated) on interface interface_name.

- %PIX-6-109015: Authorization denied (acl=acl_ID) for user 'user' from source_address/source_port to dest_address/dest_port on interface interface_name
- %PIX-6-308001: PIX console enable password incorrect for number tries (from IP_address)
- %PIX-6-309002: Permitted manager connection from IP_address.
- %PIX-6-315011: SSH session from IP_address on interface interface_name for user user disconnected by SSH server, reason: reason
- %PIX-6-605004: Login denied from {source_address/source_port | serial} to {interface_name:dest_address/service | console} for user "user"
- %PIX-6-605005: Login permitted from {source_address/source_port | serial} to {interface_name:dest_address/service | console} for user "user"
- %PIX-6-606001: PDM session number number from IP_address started
- %PIX-6-606002: PDM session number number from IP_address ended
- %PIX-6-610101: Authorization failed: Cmd: command Cmdtype: command_modifier
- %PIX-6-611101: User authentication succeeded: Uname: user
- %PIX-6-611102: User authentication failed: Uname: user
- %PIX-6-611311: VNPClient: XAUTH Failed: Peer: IP_address
- %PIX-7-111009: User user executed cmd:string

Archiving Data   It is not good enough to simply log events in your environment. You have to be able to archive the data, and you have to be able to archive the data in such a manner as to ensure data integrity in the event that the data is needed for future legal actions or reasons. Kiwi Syslog includes an archival system that you can expand to provide for long-term archiving and data integrity. It can be accessed via the Kiwi Syslog Daemon Setup properties, as previously detailed. Right-click Archiving, select Add New Archive Schedule, and name the new archive schedule accordingly. By default, the archive schedule is set to occur every 24 hours. You can select a different schedule if you so desire. Specify the source and destination folders for the logs. For the matching file mask, enter the extension used for your log files. By default, this should be .txt. Kiwi Syslog will archive all files that match the extension you enter. Specify the date format and any file/folder options. If you select to use dated folder names, the archives will be stored in folders based on date. If you select to use filenames, the filename will be prefaced with the date format information.

The last step is to configure the archive system to provide for data integrity. This can be done by running an external program that will calculate a hash file based on the log file contents. At a later date, you can verify the data integrity by checking the hash value through recalculating the hash and verifying whether the two values match (for example, by running the command **fsum –c <hash file>** against the original hash file generated). If the hash value does not match, the file has been manipulated or changed. If the hash does match, the data integrity of the file is ensured. This can be of critical importance for the legal admission of these files into court. The easiest way to generate the hash value is through the use of a batch file. Although you can use any of a number of command-line hash utilities, I will use Slavasoft FSUM (http://www.slavasoft.com/fsum/). For the batch file to work, fsum.exe must be copied to your path. I recommend copying it to *%systemroot%\system32*. You also need to create a batch file (I called it shahash.bat) that contains the following lines:

```
@echo off
fsum -sha1 C:\progra~1\syslogd\Dated1~1\%1 >
C:\progra~1\syslogd\Dated1~1\%1.sha
```

This will cause FSUM to generate an SHA-1 hash for the file that is fed to it via the command-line arguments from Kiwi Syslog:

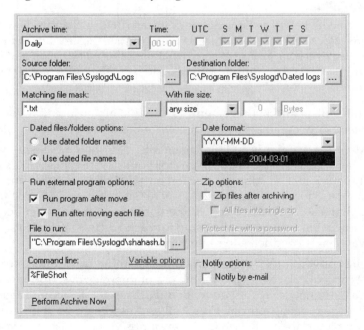

Don't forget to encapsulate the file that you want to run in parentheses. In addition, if you do not use the *%FileShort* command-line variable, you will need to edit the batch file accordingly. At this point, you can archive the files to tape or CD-R with the hash file, and as long as the values precisely match when you run the **fsum –c** command, you can be confident that the log data has not been changed or tampered with.

Configuration Management

Configuration management is the process of providing consistency in your device configurations and having a mechanism to verify if any changes have occurred. Configuration is largely a process of best practices, with some tools and utilities to help enforce those best practices. Here are the five steps to implementing a successful configuration management system in your environment:

1. Create standards.
2. Implement standards.
3. Maintain documentation.
4. Validate and audit compliance.
5. Review standards.

Creating Standards

Standardization is the key to a stable network infrastructure. Standards will not only reduce the network complexity, but they will also reduce the amount of unplanned downtime because everyone knows exactly what they should be doing and how devices should be configured. At a minimum, you need to have the following standards in your organization:

- **Version control and management** This will help ensure that you are running consistent software images in your environment.

- **IP addressing standards and management** You should break up your address space and assign ranges of addresses for your device types. For example, you might require that all subnets function on a /24 address space and reserve .1–.2 for routers, .3 for HSRP addresses, .5–.9 for switches, and .10–.254 for DHCP. This will make troubleshooting your environment much easier because you will know what to expect to be using for each address. You also should subnet in a way that is conducive to route summarization.

- **Naming conventions** You should define naming conventions for all your devices and interfaces, including the use of interface descriptions. This will make it extremely easy for you to identify the exact device and interface that may be experiencing a problem as well as providing a good description of what that interface's function is. For example, you might define your routers using a convention that concatenates the location, building, and floor with the router number—for example, houb02f14rtr01 to refer to Houston, Building 2, Floor 14, Router 1.

- **Standard configuration** The vast majority of your devices can probably share between 75–90 percent of their configurations, with the only unique aspects being advanced features, such as certain access lists and interfaces, or device-specific configuration settings. This allows you to copy the standard configuration to any new devices, providing only the unique device settings, to ensure that the devices have a consistent configuration. For example, you should specify full duplex operation for all your network devices except your access devices. Access devices should be configured for half-duplex operation. By default, most switches operate in auto-detection mode. By making a change such as this to part of your standard configuration, it makes it much easier to ensure the change is made on all the devices that are implemented. Using standard configurations will also greatly assist in troubleshooting by allowing you to compare configurations between "known good" and malfunctioning equipment to determine whether the problem is related to a simple misconfiguration.

■ **Configuration upgrade procedures** You need to put all these practices into effect by building configuration upgrade procedures that define how to plan, test, and implement changes in your environment. We will explore change control and upgrade procedures in much greater detail in Chapter 14.

Implementing Standards

Once you have defined the standards that should be used in your environment, you have to implement them. Don't have standards simply for the sake of having them or so that your auditors can check a box on their audit form. Ensure that all the systems that are implemented actually follow the defined standards. This will help ensure that your systems are less susceptible to security threats, because your standards should define the most secure methods of implementation and configuration.

Maintaining Documentation

I have mentioned this throughout this book and will not belabor the point again. You need to maintain documentation of every aspect of your network environment. In fact, you should not allow any changes to be made to your network without accompanying documentation, including the following:

■ Inventory documentation

■ Configuration version control

■ AAA configuration logs

■ Network topology documentation (both physical and logical)

■ Security policies and procedures

Validating and Auditing Compliance

Once you have taken the time and effort to define, implement, and document the configurations that should be used in your environment, you should periodically audit your environment to ensure compliance. The objective is to verify that the configuration of your devices complies with the standards you have defined. You can follow a number of methods to verify your configurations and audit your network devices, including using vendor tools and utilities (some very expensive) as well as using homegrown scripts that download and diff the configurations (much cheaper, but time consuming to write and test the scripts). Here's a list of some vendor tools for automated configuration management, compliance, and auditing:

- Cisco CiscoWorks (http://www.cisco.com/en/US/customer/products/sw/cscowork/index.html)
- OPNET Netdoctor (http://www.opnet.com/products/modules/netdoctor.html)
- AlterPoint DeviceAuthority (http://www.alterpoint.com/products/index.html)
- Ecora Enterprise Auditor (http://www.ecora.com/ecora/products/jump/auditor1.asp)
- Visonael Network Audit (http://www.visionael.com/products/info/network_audit.pdf)
- Cisco Router Audit Tool (http://www.cisecurity.org)

NOTE Sample scripts for downloading configurations are provided in Chapter 14.

In addition to implementing tools and utilities that will audit your environment and verify your configurations, you can also use syslog to proactively alert you in the event that an IOS-based device or Cisco PIX firewall configuration has changed. You can do this by configuring rules for Kiwi Syslog, as previously demonstrated, using the following syslog values:

- %SYS-5-CONFIG: Configured from [chars]
- %SYS-5-CONFIG_I: Configured from [chars] by [chars]
- %SYS-5-CONFIG_NV: Nonvolatile storage configured from [chars]
- %SYS-5-CONFIG_NV_I: Nonvolatile storage configured from [chars] by [chars]
- %PIX-5-111007: Begin configuration: IP_address reading from device.
- %PIX-5-111008: User user executed the command string

For example, you could parse for "configured from" as the search string for all your IOS-based devices and "5-111007" and "5-111007" for your PIX firewalls.

Reviewing Standards

Like all aspects of security, you should periodically review your configuration management policies to ensure not only that they remain current and address recent security issues and updates, but that they are indeed functional standards and are being adhered to.

Performance Management

Performance management is an often-overlooked aspect of hardening your network infrastructure. This is largely due to the fact that many folks look at performance management as being something that is only really useful in ensuring that the network meets the appropriate service-level agreements. Although this is certainly the major reason for implementing performance management, performance management has the additional ability to be a precursor to future potential network problems.

In addition, as you'll recall, I mentioned earlier that learning the habits and personality of your network can help you "know" what is going on with your network. Performance management is how you learn those habits.

A proper performance management system will monitor, measure, and report on all aspects of your network infrastructure. This is typically done through the use of the following protocols:

- Simple Network Management Protocol (SNMP)
- RMON
- Cisco NetFlow
- Cisco IOS Service Assurance Agent (SAA)

Using SNMP for Performance Management

SNMP is the conventional method of providing performance-related data on your network devices. A number of SNMP MIB values are particularly valuable for providing security information, including (listing OID shortnames) the following:

- **SysUpTime**   This value provides information about how long the system has been up. It can indicate a compromise or failure condition that caused a reboot.

- **ifInOctets and ifOutOctets**   These values provide the total number of octets received or transmitted on the interface, including framing characters.

- **ifSpeed**   Although not of particular use by itself, ifSpeed provides the bandwidth of the interface, which can be used to calculate bandwidth utilization. For an example of how to do this, see http://www.cisco.com/en/US/tech/tk648/tk362/technologies_tech_note09186a008009496e.shtml.

- **ifInDiscards and ifOutDiscards**   These are packets that were discarded even though no errors had been detected. They can indicate a problem with the device input or output buffers being full. This can be a symptom of a denial of service attack.

- **ifOutQLen**   This value represents the length of the output queue, and it can indicate a problem with the buffer getting full, which can be a symptom of a denial of service attack.

Some Cisco-specific MIB values to monitor are listed here:

- **locIfInputQueueDrops and locIfOutputQueueDrops**   These values represent the number of packets dropped because the input or output queue was full. They can indicate a potential denial of service that is attempting to flood the network device.

- **locIfarpInPkts and locIfarpOutPkts**   These values represent the ARP traffic that is being seen by the device. It is normal to see this value increment as devices ARP for resources. If these values make a marked increase or remain consistent (that is, they never increase), this could be a symptom of a denial of service.

- **busyPer, avgBusy1, and avgBusy5**   These values list the CPU busy percentage for the last five seconds, one minute, and five minutes, respectively, and can be an indicator that something is causing excessive CPU utilization. This was a symptom of CodeRed and many of the worms that resulted in ARP-based denial of service attacks.

You can use a number of network management systems to monitor your network devices using SNMP, including the following:

- Multi Router Traffic Grapher (MRTG) (http://people.ee.ethz.ch/~oetiker/webtools/mrtg/)

- PATROL DashBoard (http://www.bmc.com/products/products_services_detail/0,,0_0_0_22,00.html)

- Concord eHealth (http://www.concord.com/solutions/ent/network/)

- HP OpenView (http://www.openview.hp.com)

- Micromuse Netcool (http://www.micromuse.com/sols/ent_net_man.html)

Using RMON, Cisco NetFlow, and SAA for Performance Management

RMON, Cisco NetFlow, and SAA pick up where SNMP leaves off. SNMP does an excellent job of showing you what is happening on a device or an interface. RMON, Cisco NetFlow, and SAA take it a step further and display the traffic flows throughout the network enterprise. This allows you to correlate the network traffic so that you can view the entire conversation between two hosts throughout your network. For example, you can identify a host that is attempting to communicate with all the hosts on your network by seeing that multiple traffic flows are coming from this single host. This can be a symptom of a worm attempting to replicate throughout your network. With the exception of MRTG, all the previously mentioned tools will display RMON, Cisco NetFlow, and Cisco SAA data. In addition, BMC Software offers PATROL Visualis to provide topology mapping to support these protocols, and in the open-source arena you have NTOP (http://www.ntop.org/) as the counterpart to MRTG.

Accounting or Asset Management

Accounting or asset management is the process of measuring your network usage so that individuals or groups of users can be charged appropriately based on their share of the network utilization. Although not a traditional security process, the same Cisco NetFlow and IP Accounting data (as detailed in Chapter 8) can be used as a very basic indication of what your users are doing. Some vendors of accounting software include the following:

- Evident Software (http://www.evidentsoftware.com/)
- Amdocs XACCT Solutions (http://www.xacct.com/)
- NetScout nGenius Probes (http://www.netscout.com/products/probes_home.asp)

Security Management

Security management is really what this entire book has focused on. From hardening your network devices to implementing AAA to controlling network access through the use of access control lists, security management is the goal and objective. I will refer you to any of the other chapters of this book for more security management information.

Hardening Your Network Management Protocols

You will use a number of network management protocols on your network, including Cisco NetFlow, RMON, SNMP, syslog, TFTP, and Cisco Discovery Protocol (CDP). All these protocols share some common flaws, including the lack of any kind of data encryption or integrity mechanisms. In a number of the chapters in this book, we took a look at what can be done to secure or turn off these protocols for each device type, including firewalls, routers, and switches. With the sole exception of SNMP, there isn't much you can do with the protocols themselves to secure them. It's the old catch-22 of how to secure an insecure protocol. Well, the good news is that we can do something, at least for those protocols that utilize TCP/IP (which includes Cisco NetFlow, RMON, SNMP, syslog, and TFTP), and that is to encapsulate the traffic in IPSec. Although this technically does nothing for the protocols themselves, it at least ensures that the data is transmitted via a secure mechanism, effectively providing the kind of security you need for your network management traffic. We are going to look at how to configure IPsec on a Microsoft Windows 2000 server to allow it to communicate with your network devices. The device-specific IPsec configurations are covered in their respective chapters (see Chapter 3 for firewalls and Chapter 6 for routers and switches).

Configuring IPsec on Microsoft Windows 2000

IPsec is configured on Microsoft Windows 2000 systems through the use of the local security policy. The following steps detail how to configure the Microsoft Windows 2000 system to send all traffic to and from the given network device via IPsec.

The first step is to create the IPsec policy:

1. Open the Local Security Policy administrative tool.

2. Right-click IP Security Policies on Local Computer and select Create IP Security Policy. This will start the IP Security Policy Wizard. At the Introduction screen, click Next.

3. At the IP Security Policy Name screen, enter the appropriate name and description. When you are finished, click Next.

4. At the Requests for Secure Communication screen, uncheck Activate the Default Response Rule and click Next.

5. At the Finish screen, leave the Edit Properties box checked and click Finish.

The next step is to configure the filter list from the Microsoft Windows 2000 host to the device that will be managed:

1. At the NMS Security Policy Properties screen, clear the Use Add Wizard check box and click Add.

2. At the IP Filter List tab, click Add.

3. At the IP Filter List screen, enter the appropriate filter list name and description, as shown next. Clear the Use Add Wizard check box and click Add.

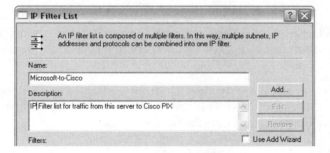

4. At the Filter Properties screen on the Addressing tab in the Source Address section, select A Specific IP Address and enter the IP address of the server. In the Destination Address section, select A Specific IP Address and enter the

IP address of the device you want to communicate with. Finally, clear the Mirrored check box. The following is an example of what the screen should look like:

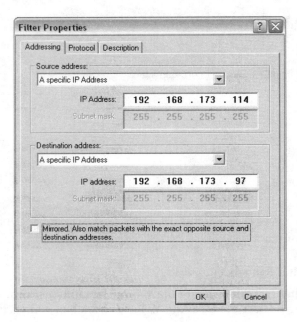

5. Click the Protocol tab and verify that Any is selected.

6. Click the Description tab and enter an appropriate description. You can copy the description from step 3. When you are finished, click OK and then click OK again.

The next step is to configure the filter list from the device that will be managed to the Microsoft Windows 2000 host. This process is an almost duplicate of the preceding process, switching the source and destination addresses:

1. Click Add at the IP Filter List tab.

2. At the IP Filter List screen, enter the appropriate filter list name and description, as shown next. Clear the Use Add Wizard check box and click Add.

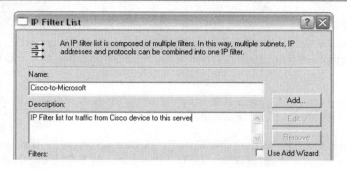

3. At the Filter Properties screen on the Addressing tab in the Source Address section, select A Specific IP Address and enter the IP address of the device you want to communicate with. In the Destination Address section, select A Specific IP Address and enter the IP address of the server. Finally, clear the Mirrored check box. The following provides an example of what the screen should look like:

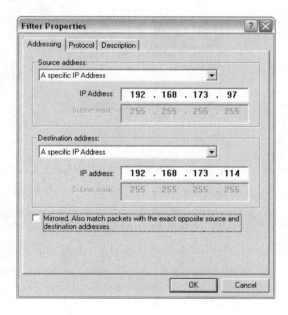

4. Click the Protocol tab and verify that Any is selected.

5. Click the Description tab and enter an appropriate description. You can copy the description from step 2. When you are finished, click OK and then click OK again.

The next step is to configure a rule for the tunnel from the Microsoft Windows 2000 server to the device that will be managed:

1. You should still be at the New Rule Properties screen with the two new IP filter lists you created displayed on the IP Filter List tab. Select the first filter list that you created (that is, Microsoft-to-Cisco) and click the Tunnel Setting tab.

2. Select the option The Tunnel Endpoint Is Specified By This IP Address and then enter the IP address of the remote device, as shown here:

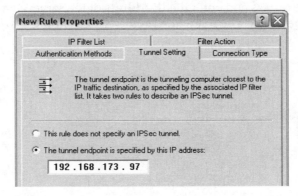

3. Click the Connection Type tab and select All Network Connections.

4. Click the Filter Action tab, clear the Use Add Wizard check box, and click Add.

5. Click the Negotiate Security option and click to clear the setting Accept Unsecured Communication, But Always Respond Using IPSec. Click Add.

6. At the New Security Method screen, select Custom and then click Settings.

7. At the Custom Security Method Settings screen, enter the appropriate Data Integrity and Encryption settings. I recommend using SHA-1 and 3DES for the highest level of security. If the remote device will be configured with session

key settings, enter them here, as shown next. When you are finished, click OK and then click OK again.

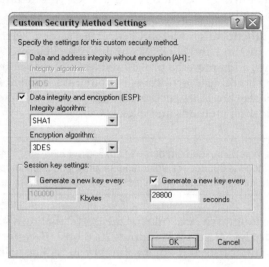

8. At the New Filter Action Properties screen, click the General tab and enter the appropriate name and description, as shown next. When you are finished, click OK.

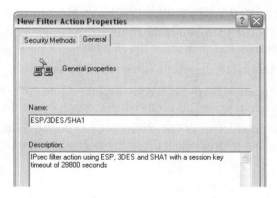

9. At the Filter Action tab, select the filter action you created.

10. Select the Authentication Methods tab and click Add to add a new authentication method.

11. At the New Authentication Method Properties screen, select the appropriate authentication method and click OK. In this case, I clicked Add, selected pre-shared keys, and entered a pre-shared key for ease of implementation. However, you should use certificates in your environment if possible because certificates are more secure and will scale better. Remove any other authentication methods and click Close.

NOTE   See http://support.microsoft.com/default.aspx?scid=kb;en-us;253498 and http://www.microsoft.com/windows2000/techinfo/planning/security/ipsecsteps.asp for information about how to add a certificate for use in IPsec on Microsoft Windows XP, 2000, and 2003 systems.

The last step is to configure a new rule for the traffic that flows from the device that will be managed to the Microsoft Windows 2000 host. Because you have already configured most of the filter lists and other settings you will be using, the process is much shorter:

1. At the Security Policy Properties screen, click Add to create a new rule.

2. At the IP Filter List tab, select the filter list for the traffic from the device that will be managed to the Microsoft Windows 2000 host.

3. At the Tunnel Setting tab, select the option The Tunnel Endpoint Is Specified By This IP Address and then enter the IP address of the server.

4. At the Filter Action tab, select the filter action you created.

5. At the Authentication Methods screen, add the same authentication method you previously configured and remove any other authentication methods.

6. When you are finished, click OK. Your security policy should look something like the screen shown next. Click Close to finish creating the new security policy.

The final task is to assign the IPSec security policy that you created by right-clicking the security policy and selecting Assign, as shown here:

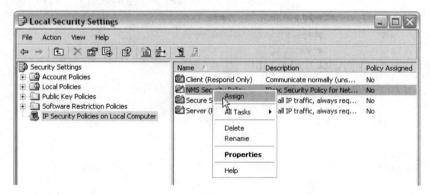

At this point, you can configure the remote host to use IPsec. It is important to make sure the various components of IPsec match exactly on both clients. Table 10-1

	Cisco PIX	Microsoft Windows
Peer Settings	192.168.173.114 (Microsoft server)	192.168.173.97 (Cisco PIX)
Transform Set/Filter Action	ESP, 3DES, SHA	ESP, 3DES, SHA
IPsec Authentication Method	Pre-shared Key	Pre-shared Key
IPsec Encryption Method	3DES	3DES
IPsec Integrity Method	SHA1	SHA1
Key Lifetime	28,800 seconds	28,800 seconds
Diffie-Hellman Group	Group 2	Group 2
IKE Encryption Method	3DES	3DES
IKE Integrity Method	SHA1	SHA1

Table 10-1. Matching IPsec Settings

shows how I have configured the settings on both the Cisco PIX firewall and the Microsoft Windows XP host in this chapter.

For example, if the remote host was a Cisco PIX firewall, I could run the following commands (based on how I configured the Microsoft Windows 2000 server earlier):

```
access-list secure-nms permit ip interface inside host 192.168.173.114
sysopt connection permit-ipsec
crypto ipsec transform-set ESP-3DES-SHA esp-3des esp-sha-hmac
crypto map secure-nms 30 ipsec-isakmp
crypto map secure-nms 30 match address secure-nms
crypto map secure-nms 30 set peer 192.168.173.114
crypto map secure-nms 30 set transform-set ESP-3DES-SHA
crypto map secure-nms interface inside
isakmp enable inside
isakmp key presharedkey address 192.168.173.114 netmask 255.255.255.255
isakmp policy 10 authentication pre-share
isakmp policy 10 encryption 3des
isakmp policy 10 hash sha
isakmp policy 10 group 2
isakmp policy 10 lifetime 28800
```

As Figure 10-1 shows, all the traffic between hosts 192.168.173.114 and 192.168.173.97 is being encapsulated in ESP IPsec packets (in this case, that traffic is syslog and Telnet traffic). This allows the server and the remote host to communicate with each other only using IPsec, thereby encapsulating all the insecure TFTP, syslog, SNMP, RMON, and any other traffic in the secure IPsec tunnel.

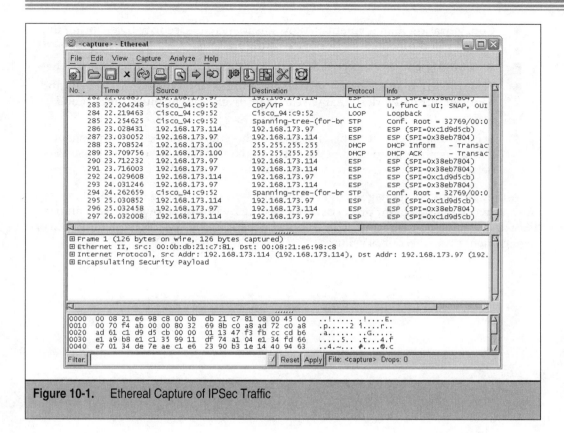

Figure 10-1.   Ethereal Capture of IPSec Traffic

Summary

A network management system can be more than just a tool that reports the health and status of your network. It can be used as a security tool, providing insight into potential security risks before they reach a crisis stage. You should implement an NMS to provide insight into the habits and patterns of your network, which will allow you to better judge and forecast when events may be occurring that need to be examined in more detail.

The five areas for network management that provide us with the information we need are as follows:

- **Fault management**   Allows us to identify and address faults that occur in the network.

- **Configuration management**   Allows us to increase security by ensuring the integrity and function of our device configurations.

- **Accounting management**   Allows us to determine what our users are doing.

- **Performance management**   Allows us to understand the traffic patterns and habits of our network so that we can identify exceptions much quicker and easier.

- **Security management**   This is the goal of this entire book. Security management allows us not only to harden the network devices themselves, but to use those network devices to harden the infrastructure in general.

Although network management is required to effectively run a network of any size, most network management protocols are insecure by design. However, we can use IPSec as an option to secure any TCP/IP-based network protocols, including the network management protocols our NMS uses.

Chapter 11

Implementing a Secure Perimeter

A network is a Twinkie. I have heard numerous people make that reference, and it is a pretty accurate, albeit entertaining, reference. Much like a Twinkie, the good stuff in a network is on the inside, and you want to protect that stuff with a tough outer shell—the network perimeter.

This chapter builds upon the device-hardening methods we have talked about in the previous ten chapters and looks at how we can use that information and those devices to provide a secure, hardened perimeter to protect our interior network.

The best methodology for hardening the perimeter that I have found is the Cisco SAFE blueprint (http://www.cisco.com/safe), and this chapter follows and builds on that methodology. We will look at a number of aspects of the network perimeter, including the following:

- **DMZ implementation methods**   The different techniques of implementing secure access to resources in the network perimeter

- **Internet access module**   The collection of devices that provides Internet connectivity

- **VPN/remote access module**   The collection of devices that provides virtual private network (VPN) and remote access connectivity

- **WAN access module**   The collection of devices that provides wide area network (WAN) connectivity

- **Extranet access module**   The collection of devices that provides extranet connectivity to external partners

- **Wireless access module**   The collection of devices that provides wireless network connectivity

- **E-commerce access module**   The collection of devices that provides e-commerce services

DMZ Implementation Methods

The demilitarized zone (DMZ) is a common element of most perimeter modules. In concept, the DMZ is pretty simple: you need to place a barrier between your internal network and any external hosts that ensures that no requests that originate from the external network can be directly passed to your internal network. In practice, however, the DMZ can be a rather complex component of your network, because a number of different types of DMZ implementation methods can be used. We are going to look at the pros and cons of the following DMZ designs:

- Multi-homed firewall
- Dual firewall

In addition, we'll take a look at an often raging debate in the security world: the use of virtual local area networks (VLANs) for your DMZ.

Using a Multi-homed Firewall for Your DMZ

Using a multi-homed firewall to create your DMZ architecture is a relatively common DMZ implementation. It is sometimes known as a "DMZ on a stick." Figure 11-1 illustrates how it functions.

Traffic can pass to and from the DMZ and the Internet. Traffic can also pass to and from the DMZ and the internal network. Finally, traffic can pass from the internal network to the Internet. The most important point, however, is that no traffic can pass directly from the Internet to the internal network. Instead, those requests must all pass to a proxy in the DMZ, and the proxy can then issue the request against the internal resources on behalf of the external client. Figure 11-1 illustrates this with dotted lines representing the direction in which traffic can be initiated. Reply traffic is assumed to be allowed and is not indicated on the diagram. An excellent example of this would be using a Simple Mail Transfer Protocol (SMTP) proxy for passing Internet-based e-mail to your internal e-mail services. This buys you the protection of ensuring that external traffic can never directly access internal hosts and resources.

An often overlooked aspect of DMZ filtering is the application of filtering at the external router. By implementing filtering at an external router, you can add a layer of security, ensuring that the firewall needs to concern itself only with traffic related to the services and resources being offered at the DMZ. You should implement filtering at the external router for all DMZ designs.

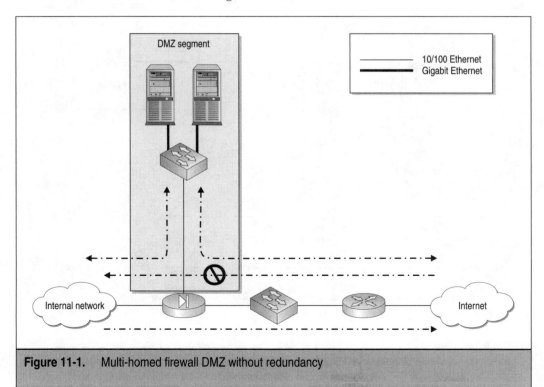

Figure 11-1.   Multi-homed firewall DMZ without redundancy

While Figure 11-1 shows only a single DMZ, you can create additional DMZs by simply adding more interfaces to the firewall. This would allow you to create task-specific DMZs—for example, having one DMZ exclusively for VPN and remote access connections and another DMZ for Internet-based traffic and requests (such as SMTP or HTTP traffic). The only real limitation on the number of DMZs that you can have is the number of interfaces your firewall supports.

The next progression of the DMZ on a stick design is to introduce redundancy into the design. The objective of redundancy is to ensure that no single failure will cause a loss of functionality. This design specifies that you have multiple firewalls, switches, and routers that connect to separate Internet service providers (ISPs). By simply ensuring that both firewalls have a connection to the switch in the DMZ, you gain the full benefits of the DMZ regardless of which firewall is functioning. Figure 11-2 illustrates a multi-homed firewall DMZ with redundancy.

The benefits of this type of DMZ design are as follows:

- **Simplicity** The design is pretty simple: you add an interface to your firewall and configure it accordingly.

- **Cost** This design does not require as much additional hardware as other DMZ design solutions.

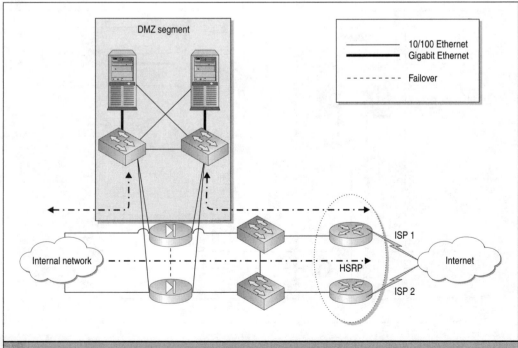

Figure 11-2. Multi-homed firewall DMZ with redundancy

ONE STEP FURTHER

If possible, you should use separate providers for the local loop and keep power for the primary and secondary loops on separate uninterruptible power supplies (UPSs) and power grids.

The primary drawback of this type of DMZ design is that you are relying on a single device, in this case the firewall, for handling all of the traffic. If the firewall can be compromised, your internal network could be left completely unprotected. Even with this drawback, the DMZ on a stick design is a good design for a cost-conscious company.

ONE STEP FURTHER

When implementing firewall failover using in-band heartbeat (the heartbeat is sent via the network instead of a dedicated failover cable), you may need to change the design slightly to account for latency in the heartbeat network. This is especially true in cases where the DMZ spans multiple buildings or locations, where the loss of heartbeat could cause a failover due to faulty cabling.

Using Dual Firewalls for Your DMZ

The use of dual firewalls is the natural progression of the router and firewall DMZ design. Through the use of dual firewalls, all of the drawbacks of the router and firewall design are mitigated. In addition, the use of dual firewalls provides even more security than any other design through the use of two different firewall vendors' products, ensuring that in order to access internal resources, someone would need to compromise both types of firewall. Figure 11-3 depicts a dual-firewall DMZ.

As you can see in the figure, the DMZ is bordered by two firewalls. The first firewall protects the DMZ and internal network from Internet-based threats. The second firewall protects the internal network not only from Internet-based threats, but from any potential threats that originate from the DMZ as well. This type of system is commonly implemented with faster packet filtering or hybrid firewalls at the Internet side and more advanced application proxies or application-level gateways at the internal network side. This facilitates access to DMZ resources from the Internet while requiring a more thorough examination of data attempting to pass through to the internal network.

Like all of our DMZ designs, you can implement redundancy to provide fault tolerance, as shown in Figure 11-4.

The primary benefit of this type of DMZ design is security. The primary drawback is cost. As a result, dual-firewall DMZ is commonly implemented in environments where security is critical at any cost—for example, in banking and finance organizations.

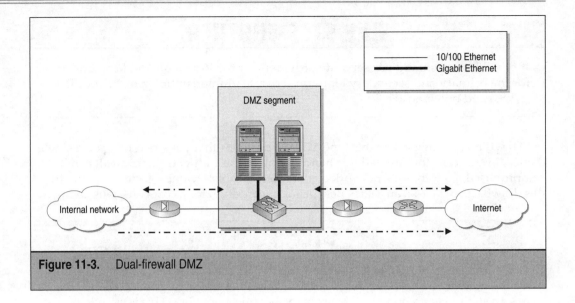

Figure 11-3. Dual-firewall DMZ

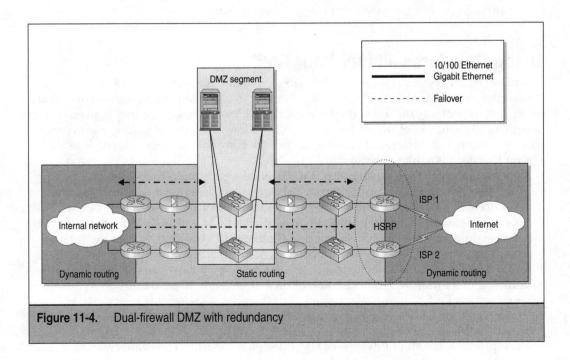

Figure 11-4. Dual-firewall DMZ with redundancy

ONE STEP FURTHER

Many people think that because resources that reside in the DMZ are frequently accessed by Internet-based hosts, the resources must use real IP addresses, but this is not correct. You can implement Network Address Translation (NAT) at the firewall or routers in front of the DMZ and use private addresses on your DMZ. At that point, you can simply advertise the DMZ resources on the firewall using routable IP addresses and map those addresses back to the private addresses that the DMZ hosts are using. In fact, this is generally the recommended approach to use.

HEADS UP!

Using a router in place of a firewall in the DMZ design is a common occurrence. The drawback of this approach is that your router isn't a firewall and generally speaking should not be used as a firewall. This type of DMZ design should not be used and should be replaced in your environment if it is in use. If you must use it, however, you should harden your router as if it was a firewall and include, but not be limited to using, a firewall software feature set.

VLANs and DMZs

A discussion of the use of VLANs in DMZs frequently results in a heated debate. The logic is pretty sound: You have a relatively big switch and you are not using all the ports on it. You also need a few ports to create a DMZ. You have two options—you can either buy an additional switch, which takes power, connectivity, and rack space, or you can simply create a VLAN on the switch for the ports that you want to use for the DMZ.

No good answer exists as to which solution is the "best" solution because "best" is a subjective term. Let's take a look at some of the pros and cons, though, so that you can be better informed on which solution will work in your environment. Using VLANs is advocated because you can use equipment that already exists on your network. The biggest argument against using VLANs for your DMZs is that traffic can inadvertently pass from one VLAN to another in some circumstances. Many of the vulnerabilities that exist with VLANs is covered in depth in a whitepaper at http://www.sans.org/rr/papers/38/1090.pdf.

I can make one recommendation, however: you should never implement VLANs on the same switch for networks with differing security levels. For example, you should never VLAN a switch between your DMZ and your internal network. This will ensure a few things. First, someone won't accidentally plug internal resources into the DMZ and vice versa, because the ports are on the same device. Second, if there is a chance that the traffic can be passed inadvertently between the VLANs, someone at a lesser security level won't potentially be able to gain access to resources that they shouldn't. Third, there isn't a chance that the switch gets configured incorrectly, inadvertently putting the wrong device in the wrong VLAN. Last is the administration considerations. While VLANS aren't incredibly complex, if you have a 48-port switch with 18 different VLANS in it, it can get messy. This increases your odds of a misconfiguration, which could result in a security risk. It also makes troubleshooting much more difficult down the road if something needs to be reconfigured or upgraded.

When I consider whether or not to use VLANs, I tend to keep one thing in mind: the goal of a DMZ is security. Consequently, I don't want to do anything that could possibly be a security vulnerability for something for which I require stringent security. Therefore, I don't recommend using VLANs. The only way that VLAN vulnerabilities can be exploited is if you use VLANs. With the low cost of many switches today, I can't justify the security exposure for the savings that using an existing switch might provide.

Internet Access Module

The Internet module houses the devices that provide Internet connectivity to the organization. The Internet module is essentially a hub of connectivity, providing access between the following modules:

- Internal network and the Internet
- VPN/remote access module and the Internet
- Extranet module and the Internet
- E-commerce module and the Internet

Figure 11-5 depicts a fully redundant Internet module. The first component of your Internet module is the use of redundant routers connecting to separate ISPs using Border Gateway Protocol (BGP) for Internet routing. The routers connect to separate switches and use Hot Standby Router Protocol (HSRP) to advertise a virtual router as the gateway. In addition, you should implement the first layer of filtering on these routers. You should implement an IDS/IPS at the switch to interrogate all traffic coming from the Internet to the firewalls. The firewalls are configured with two DMZs on a stick. One DMZ provides access to public services such as SMTP, DNS, FTP, and HTTP. The other DMZ provides content filtering functionality for the firewalls to ensure that no unauthorized or objectionable content is permitted to or from the internal network. Both DMZs follow the redundant design implementing dual switches with an IDS/IPS implemented on the public services DMZ to interrogate all traffic sent to and from the DMZ. Finally, the firewalls connect to the internal network, again implementing an IDS/IPS to interrogate all traffic sent to and from the internal network.

Traffic Flow Through the Internet Module

In a properly implemented Internet module, the only traffic that actually passes between the internal network and the Internet are the web requests that are sourced from the internal network and must be permitted by the content-filtering server and firewall.

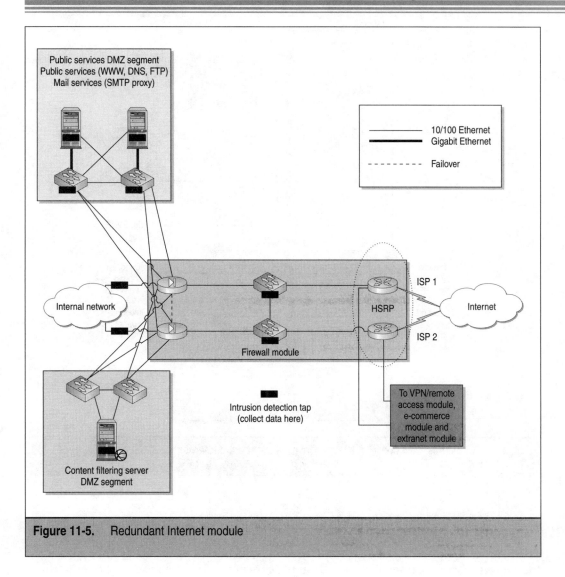

Figure 11-5.   Redundant Internet module

All other traffic uses proxies in a DMZ for connectivity. Figure 11-6 depicts the traffic flow using this system. For example, SMTP e-mail from the Internet goes to an SMTP server on the DMZ, which then forwards the e-mail to the internal network. By ensuring that all traffic that enters the internal network must go through a proxy or must be a response to an outbound Internet request, you protect your internal network from external threats. You should never allow traffic to be initiated inbound directly from the Internet.

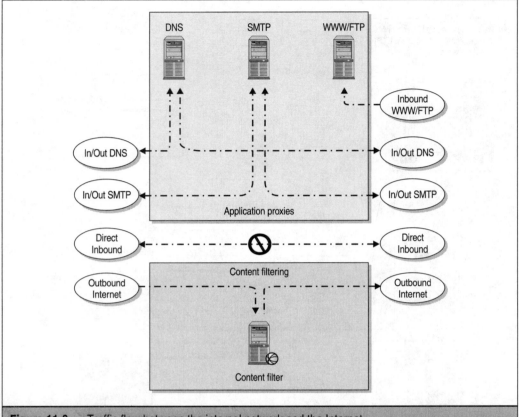

Figure 11-6.   Traffic flow between the internal network and the Internet

Firewall Implementation

The heart of the Internet module is the firewall system. The firewall system consists of the routers, switches, firewalls, and IDS at the core of the Internet module. I refer to this as a *firewall system* because I believe that the concept of a standalone firewall providing security is a flawed design. Security is achieved in layers, and the firewall system uses layers at the external routers, the IDSs, and finally the firewalls themselves to provide perimeter security.

External Router Configuration

Your external router is the first line of defense in your firewall system, and consequently it is at your external router that you should implement basic spoof mitigation and filtering of traffic that is entering your network. The following task list details the hardening steps to undertake on your external router:

- Implement RFC1918 (Private Address Space), RFC2827 (Network Ingress Filtering), and bogon Filtering (filtering unassigned address spaces).

- Drop fragmented traffic.

- Implement Authentication, Authorization, and Accounting (AAA).

- Implement management console access restrictions using AAA and ACLs.

- Harden the routing protocols.

- Implement ACLs to restrict SNMP access.

- Implement flood management through the use of traffic shaping, Quality of Service (QoS), and Weighted Fair Queuing (WFQ) on routers that support it.

- Remove all unnecessary services.

- Implement logging with syslog, SNMP traps, and accounting.

- Drop directed broadcasts.

- Implement anti-spoofing. Don't allow your internal IP range to be the source address of packets arriving on the external interface.

- Prevent source routing.

- Prevent ICMP redirects.

- For your Cisco routers, implement Cisco Express Forwarding (CEF) to handle SYN floods.

- Ensure that you are running the latest stable software version to prevent being susceptible to threats that have been patched or updated.

- If your router has the horsepower to support it, implement the first line of traffic filtering to allow only traffic that should be traversing the network edge through the use of ACLs, or in the case of Cisco routers running the IOS firewall feature set and using Context Based Access Control (CBAC).

IDS/IPS Configuration

The IDS/IPS configuration depends largely on where in the module the IDS/IPS is implemented. For the IDS/IPS located at the public edge, you should implement a more broad analysis. This is because at this point any alarms do not represent an actual breech of the network; rather, they merely represent potential attempts.

As you get closer to the internal network, you need your IDS/IPS to take a more focused approach to traffic analysis. For example, on the public services DMZ, you know exactly what traffic is permitted, allowing you to focus the alarms for the network-based IDS/IPS (NIDS/NIPS) on traffic matching those patterns. In addition, you need to implement host-based IDS/IPS (HIDS/HIPS) on the servers in the DMZ to protect against operating system–level tampering.

The IDS/IPS implemented between the firewall and the internal network is where you need to undertake the most stringent analysis. This is because any suspicious traffic that has been able to make it this far is inside your perimeter defenses. Very few attacks should be detected at this point, and every attack detected should be treated with the utmost of importance.

Firewall Configuration

The actual firewalls are the core of your firewall system. The firewalls are ultimately responsible for filtering permitted traffic to the specific hosts while ensuring that nonpermitted traffic is blocked accordingly. This is typically done through the use of ingress and egress filtering.

Implementing Ingress Filtering   Ingress filtering is the traditional method of filtering traffic to your network resources that is sourced from the Internet. For Cisco PIX firewalls and IOS-based network equipment, ingress filtering is implemented through the use of ACLs. For Check Point firewalls, ingress filtering is implemented as part of the ruleset with the appropriate source (Internet) and destination (DMZ) addresses.

An example of implementing ingress filtering with a Cisco PIX firewall uses the following steps:

1. Implement an ACL.
2. Implement a static mapping or internal and external resources.
3. Apply the ACL to an interface.

Implementing an ACL is a straightforward process. You can run the following commands at the global configuration mode to implement an ACL for basic Internet functionality:

```
access-list 100 permit tcp any host 1.1.1.10 eq www
access-list 100 permit tcp any host 1.1.1.10 eq ftp
access-list 100 permit udp any host 1.1.1.11 eq domain log
access-list 100 permit tcp any host 1.1.1.12 eq smtp
```

In this example, you are permitting any traffic to access the web server and FTP server on IP address 1.1.1.10, the DNS server at 1.1.1.11, and the SMTP server at 1.1.1.12. If you wanted to log all traffic that matches these entries, you could add the syntax **log** at the end of the ACL, as shown in the third line. This would cause the connections that match the traffic to be logged via syslog. These four services are the most commonly implemented services that Internet-based hosts need to access and in many cases are the minimum required ingress filters that most companies need.

The next step is to implement a static mapping that correlates the external address to the internal address of the server that provides the services that are being used. There are two schools of thought about how to implement the static mappings. The first is simply to create a static mapping from one IP address to the other IP address. The problem with this implementation is that if someone misconfigures an ACL, the traffic would be able to access the protected resource since the static mapping already permits all traffic. The other school of thought is to configure the static mapping to support only the explicit traffic that you want to map. This is the configuration that I recommend, since to cause a security breach, it would take someone misconfiguring not only the ACL but the static mapping as well. The following example is an illustration of static mappings that map the explicit ports and services to correspond with the ACL from the previous example.

```
static (DMZ01,outside) tcp 1.1.1.10 www 192.168.1.10 www netmask →
255.255.255.255 0 0
static (DMZ01,outside) tcp 1.1.1.10 ftp 192.168.1.10 ftp netmask →
255.255.255.255 0 0
static (DMZ01,outside) udp 1.1.1.11 domain 192.168.1.11 domain netmask →
255.255.255.255 0 0
static (DMZ01,outside) tcp 1.1.1.12 smtp 192.168.1.12 smtp netmask →
255.255.255.255 0 0
```

The final step is to apply the ACL to an interface using the **access-group** command. The following example illustrates how to apply the ACL to the outside interface for all inbound traffic:

```
access-group 100 in interface outside
```

Implementing Egress Filtering   Egress filtering is the filtering of traffic that is sourced from protected networks such as DMZ segments or the internal network to external resources. Egress filtering is often overlooked because folks inadvertently focus on controlling what is entering their network, not what is exiting their network.

Part of what probably contributes to the lack of use of egress filtering is a little bit of confusion as to how egress filtering functions in regard to a stateful firewall. For example, if I implement a firewall with ingress filtering as previously described and then implement egress filtering that blocks all traffic from the DMZ segment, many folks believe that will prevent the servers on the DMZ from being able to respond to external requests. However, this is not correct. Remember that the whole point of being a stateful firewall is its ability to remember the state of all conversations so that valid responses can be passed through the firewall accordingly. So the servers would still be able to respond to all external requests; however, they could not originate any packets through the DMZ interface. This is particularly valuable in ensuring that hosts on the DMZ cannot pass traffic back to the Internet in the event that they are compromised.

The following code example illustrates how to implement an egress filter that permits only SMTP and DNS traffic that is sourced from the servers on the DMZ in the previous example. This allows you to use the DNS server in your DMZ as a DNS forwarder for your internal hosts as well as the SMTP server as the SMTP relay for both incoming and outgoing e-mail, while preventing all other traffic that is sourced from the DMZ servers from being passed by the firewall:

```
access-list 200 permit tcp host 192.168.1.12 any eq smtp
access-list 200 permit udp host 192.168.1.11 any eq domain
access-list 200 deny ip any any log
static (inside,DMZ01) tcp 192.168.1.12 smtp 172.16.1.12 smtp netmask →
255.255.255.255 0 0
access-group 200 in interface DMZ01
```

No good baseline is available for implementing egress filtering since the traffic that should be permitted to exit the network largely depends on the resources that are located on that network segment. The best approach is to allow the absolute minimum traffic required.

Content-Filtering Configuration

The content-filtering DMZ should be restricted by egress filtering to permit only the content-filtering traffic between the content-filtering server and the firewall. All other traffic is unnecessary and potentially unsafe. In addition to filtering the traffic at the firewall, you should implement an HIDS/HIPS to alarm and prevent any attacks that might traverse the firewall.

VPN/Remote Access Module

The VPN/remote access module exists to perform three functions:

- Terminate remote access VPN connections
- Terminate site-to-site VPN connections
- Terminate dial-in remote user connections

A number of different types of VPN/remote access module design methods can be used, but Figure 11-7 depicts the most hardened method in a large enterprise environment. This can be scaled back in smaller environments, for example by terminating the VPN connections on the firewall instead of separate VPN concentrators.

At the core of this module are the firewalls that provide a different interface for each type of connection to access the internal network. One obvious missing element is full redundancy for interface connections. This is because many VPN termination devices lack redundant interfaces by design, relying instead on software features such as Virtual Router Redundancy Protocol (VRRP) for redundancy. In addition, if you are going to use certificates for your VPN connections, it is necessary that a certificate authority be available for both sides of the VPN connection, though this is best implemented in the public services DMZ of the Internet module.

This module has two entrances. This first is for the VPN traffic and comes from the corporate Internet module. This connection should be filtered at the Internet gateway router to allow only IPsec traffic through to the VPN/remote access module. At a minimum, you should permit the following ports and protocols:

- UDP port 500–ISAKMP
- IP Protocol 50–Encapsulated Security Payload

In addition, you might need to permit the following ports to do IPsec NAT traversal over TCP or UDP:

- UDP Port 4500
- UDP Port 10000
- TCP Port 10000

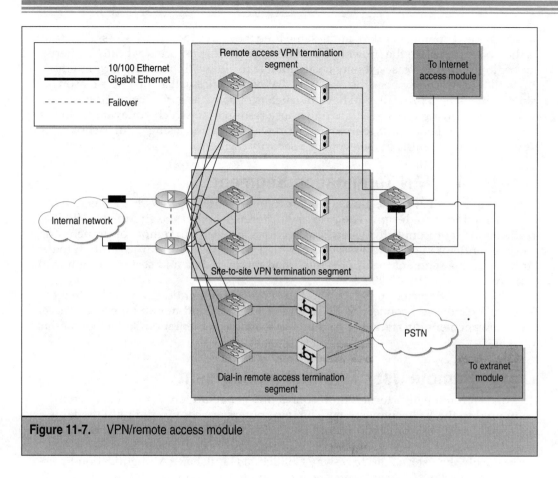

Figure 11-7. VPN/remote access module

The second entrance is through the Public Switched Telephone Network (PSTN) for dial-in users. We will look at each connection type individually.

Remote Access VPN Termination Segment

The remote access VPN connections are used for client-based remote access—for example, a user with a laptop connecting with a VPN client. The users are terminated at a pair of VPN concentrators that provide all of the authentication and validation required to permit the traffic. What is not depicted in the diagram but is used to authenticate and validate the VPN connections is a connection between the VPN concentrator and the AAA server via a management interface that connects to the management module on the internal network.

Once the connection has been validated, the VPN configuration is provided to the remote user, specifying such things as IP address and name servers as well as employing hardening measures such as preventing remote users from employing split tunneling to access the corporate network at the same time they have local LAN access. The traffic is then passed back to the firewall in an unencrypted format, where it can be filtered accordingly. In some cases, it may be acceptable to allow all the traffic through the firewall. This of course begs the question, "Why use a firewall at all"? The reason is simple. By using a firewall, you have the means of being as explicit and granular as you want, allowing users to access only those resources to which you want them to be able to connect. In addition, employing a firewall gives you a single quick choke point at which to block traffic in the event of a security incident.

Site-to-Site VPN Termination Segment

The site-to-site VPN connection is similar to the remote access VPN connection in form, function, and design. The primary difference is that the site-to-site VPN connections represent "always on" connections, typically to remote or branch offices. Consequently, it may be necessary to permit a wider range of traffic through the firewall to this segment to support the broad range of data and services that may be required.

What is not depicted in Figure 11-7 but is used to authenticate and validate the VPN connections is a connection between the VPN concentrator and the AAA server via a management interface that connects to the management module on the internal network.

Dial-in Remote User Termination Segment

The dial-in remote user termination connection is a relatively simple connection compared to the VPN connections. The two routers are configured with modems for analog or ISDN connections, and once the initial physical connection has been established by virtue of the user calling the router, the router uses AAA to authenticate the user using three-way Challenge Handshake Authentication Protocol (CHAP). As in the VPN segments, a connection to the internal AAA server is used for this authentication.

NIDS/NIPS Deployment

As with all of the perimeter modules, you need to deploy NIDS/NIPS to analyze the traffic and generate alarms. In the VPN/remote access module, you first need to deploy an NIDS/NIPS for the traffic coming from the Internet module primarily to detect reconnaissance traffic targeting your VPN termination devices as well as to detect any non-IPsec traffic on the segment. Because of the filtering to allow only IPsec traffic, if the NIDS/NIPS detects any other traffic it signifies a potential compromise or misconfiguration of the devices on that segment.

In addition, you should deploy an NIDS/NIPS behind the firewall to monitor and analyze all traffic that has made it through the module and onto the internal network.

WAN Access Module

The WAN access module is an often overlooked aspect of the perimeter, because the remote connection is part of the overall protected network. Most WAN connections are in the form of leased lines such as T1 and T3 lines, packet-switched networks such as frame relay, and cell-switched networks such as ATM. Figure 11-8 depicts a hardened WAN module.

At the core of the security for the WAN module is the implementation of firewalls to provide security to the enterprise network from the remote location. In Figure 11-8, the firewalls are external to the routers; however, the filtering capabilities could easily be bundled into the routers themselves through the use of firewall feature sets, ACLs, and CBAC for Cisco-based equipment.

Redundancy is provided through the use of technologies such as Hot Standby Router Protocol (HSRP) for fault tolerance. For businesses that are particularly concerned with security, IPsec can be implemented on the routers at each end of the WAN connection to provide data integrity and security over the public or private service provider network.

In addition, like all of our perimeter modules, NIDS/NIPS are implemented behind the firewall to monitor and analyze the traffic traversing the module to the internal network.

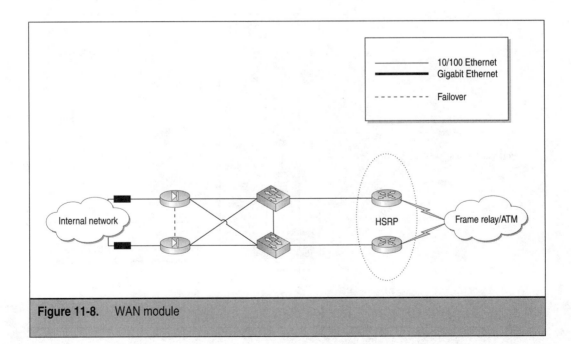

Figure 11-8.   WAN module

Extranet Access Module

The extranet access module is almost a hybrid of the Internet access module in the sense that this module exists primarily to allow external hosts to access services and resources in your network. The difference lies in to whom that access is granted. For the Internet access module, virtually anyone on the Internet is allowed to access the public services that you make available. For the extranet access module, the only systems that can access the resources are the external partners to which you explicitly grant access. All other hosts will be denied access.

This is accomplished by placing the application servers that are required in a DMZ using the firewalls on the external edge to control access to the servers for external hosts and placing firewalls on the internal edge to restrict further access to the internal network. A variation on this design also uses VPN connectivity to terminate the external partner connections securely. The systems in the application server DMZ should contain all of the information required by your extranet partners, or they should be configured as proxies to access information from the internal network (for example, data that resides on a mainframe or in a database server) on behalf of the extranet partner. Like the Internet access module, no traffic should be able to pass from the external network to the internal network without going through a proxy. This design is illustrated in Figure 11-9.

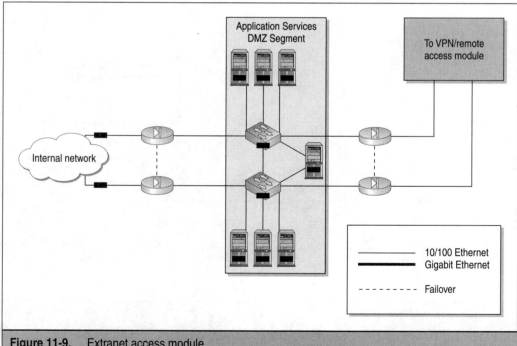

Figure 11-9.   Extranet access module

As is customary for all of our perimeter modules, NIDS/NIPS are deployed on the application services DMZ to analyze and monitor traffic to ensure that no unauthorized traffic is being passed. In addition, the servers should each be running an HIDS/HIPS to protect the server against operating system–level tampering. Finally, an NIDS/NIPS is deployed behind the internal firewall to monitor and analyze the traffic traversing the module to the internal network.

Wireless Access Module

As we have investigated in Chapter 8, wireless presents some significant security problems when used on a corporate network. So much of this insecurity is due to the fact that it can be easy for an unauthorized user to gain access to your WLAN. This presents a huge security risk if the WLAN is directly connected to the internal network, since that user has now effectively circumvented all of your perimeter protections, exposing the soft underbelly of your internal network. Using our Twinkie example, the user is now in the creme filling.

Perhaps the best method to mitigate this security issue is to implement your WLAN not as a module of your internal network but as a module of the perimeter of your network. Figure 11-10 illustrates how to design the wireless access module.

In this configuration, security is provided through the use of VPN connections for the wireless clients. This is performed in addition to any wireless-specific security that is implemented such as Wired Equivalent Privacy (WEP), WiFi Protected Access

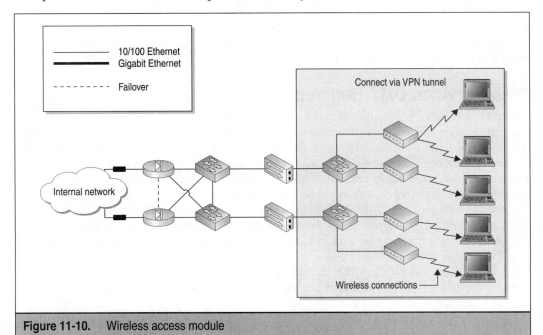

Figure 11-10.   Wireless access module

(WPA), or 802.1x. Once the users are able to establish a wireless connection properly, the users must then use the appropriate VPN client to establish a connection with the VPN concentrators. Only after the VPN has been established will unencrypted traffic be allowed to pass from the concentrator to the firewall. At the firewall you need to implement ingress and egress filtering as in the other modules to ensure that the wireless clients are able to access only the specific resources to which you want to grant access.

E-Commerce Access Module

E-commerce security is a bit of an oxymoron. The primary objective of e-commerce is to allow customers to access your online facilities to do business. At the same time, one of the primary objectives of network security is to keep people out of the network and systems. Building an e-commerce module requires that you strike a balance between access and security. While this section focuses on how to build an infrastructure to support a secure e-commerce implementation, you cannot overlook the requirement of having the application developers design the applications to support such an infrastructure. If they do not, you simply cannot use this design.

The e-commerce access module is built on a three-tier model. At the first tier are the web servers that function as the front end for the e-commerce applications and are accessible to the end users over the Internet. The middle tier represents the middleware applications that process the requests from the first tier and request data from the third tier. The third tier represents the data itself, typically housed in database servers. Figure 11-11 illustrates the e-commerce access module design.

In this system, three DMZs are designed primarily to control and regulate what data can pass from one tier to the next.

Web Services DMZ Segment

The web services DMZ segment is the only segment that is accessible from the Internet. The firewall on the external perimeter should be configured with ingress filtering that allows traffic from the Internet to the web services DMZ segment only. The DMZ services segment interface should be configured with egress filtering that allows no traffic to the Internet and ingress filtering that allows only the required traffic to the application services DMZ segment that is required by the e-commerce application. The interface on the application services DMZ segment should be configured with egress filtering that blocks all traffic in the direction of the Internet or, if required, permits traffic only from the servers in the application services DMZ segment to servers in the web services DMZ segment.

NIDS/NIPS and HIDS/HIPS should be deployed on this segment and on the servers themselves to monitor and analyze the traffic traversing this segment and to detect operating system–level tampering.

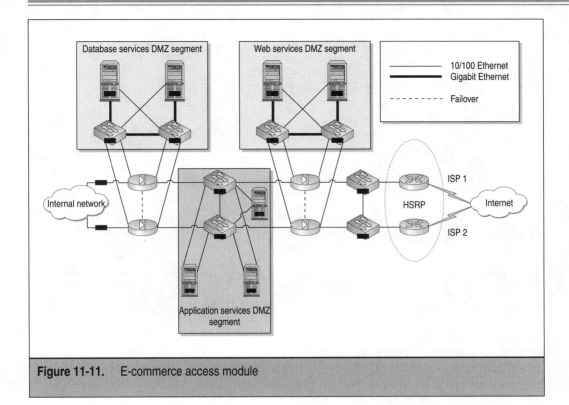

Figure 11-11.   E-commerce access module

Application Services DMZ Segment

The application services DMZ segment is designed to allow traffic in two directions. First, traffic from the web services is allowed to access the servers on the application services DMZ segment only as previously detailed. Second, the firewall on the interior perimeter is configured with ingress filtering that allows only e-commerce–related traffic from the application servers to the database servers on the databases services DMZ segment.

NIDS/NIPS and HIDS/HIPS should be deployed on this segment and on the servers themselves to monitor and analyze the traffic traversing this segment and to detect operating system–level tampering.

Database Services DMZ Segment

The database services DMZ segment is the final tier in the e-commerce access module and is the most protected of all the segments, because this is where the actual data resides. The firewall interface on this segment should be configured with egress filtering that blocks all traffic in the direction of the Internet or, if required, permits traffic only from the servers in the database services DMZ segment to the servers in the application services DMZ segment. The firewall interface should also be configured with ingress

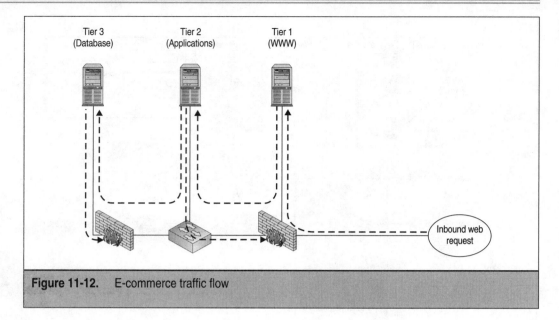

Figure 11-12. E-commerce traffic flow

filtering that blocks all traffic to the internal network, with the exception of any traffic required for the e-commerce application.

NIDS/NIPS and HIDS/HIPS should be deployed on this segment and on the servers themselves to monitor and analyze the traffic traversing this segment and to detect operating system–level tampering.

If implemented properly, your e-commerce access module creates the traffic flow shown in Figure 11-12.

Traffic can flow from the Internet to the web servers, and only to the web servers. The firewall blocks all other inbound traffic from the Internet. Traffic can flow from the web servers to the application servers, but the first firewall blocks it from flowing anywhere else. In this sense, the web servers are functioning as proxies on behalf of the user. Traffic from the application servers can flow to the database servers, but the second firewall blocks it from flowing anywhere else. In this sense, the application servers are functioning as proxies on behalf of the web servers. Finally, traffic from the database servers can flow nowhere. The database servers are either responding to requests from the application servers (dynamically permitted due to stateful packet inspection) or they don't communicate. This ensures that external users must breach at least two levels of security before gaining access to any data, and with luck your IDS/IPS deployment will have triggered an alarm on the suspicious activity long before that happens.

Summary

Your network perimeter is the most important part of your network to harden. This is because it serves as the barrier between your valuable internal resources and a bevy of external hackers, crackers, and criminals looking for something to exploit.

A fundamental aspect of your network perimeter is the proper use of DMZs to provide restricted external access to resources. The most effective DMZ configurations are either the DMZ on a stick deployment or the dual-firewall deployment.

The perimeter of your network plays host to a number of unique needs and requirements. The most effective method of granting secure access for these different needs is to employ a modular design approach, building modules specific to the perimeter task and functionality required. Six modules are commonly implemented:

- **Internet access module**   This module serves primarily to provide external Internet access to your internal users as well as to provide external access to common public services such as SMTP, WWW, and DNS services. In addition, the Internet access module serves as a hub for other access modules that require Internet connectivity. Security is provided through the use of firewalls and IDS/IPS.

- **VPN/remote connectivity access module**   This module serves primarily to provide IPsec-based VPN access for remote hosts and site-to-site connections. In addition, this module provides dial-in and ISDN access for remote users. Security is provided through the use of VPN concentrators, firewalls, and IDS/IPS.

- **WAN module**   This module serves primarily to provide access to remote sites via leased line, packet-switched, or cell-switched service provider networks. Security is provided through the use of firewalls or IPsec tunnels between locations.

- **Extranet access module**   This module serves to provide remote access to strategic business partners and vendors, allowing secure access to shared systems through the use of firewalls, IDS/IPS, and sometimes VPN concentrators.

- **Wireless access module**   This module serves to provide wireless access to users of your corporate network. Security is provided through the use of wireless security protocols such as WEP, WPA, and 802.1x and by requiring authenticated wireless clients to establish a VPN connection to gain access to internal resources. Firewalls and IDS/IPS can also be deployed to control the traffic to and from the wireless clients.

- **E-commerce access module**   The e-commerce access module is the most complex of all of the modules, functioning as a hybrid somewhere between the Internet access module and the extranet access module. This module is designed in a three-tiered architecture that uses firewalls to ensure that external connections can be made only to the first-tier devices, that first-tier devices can connect only to second-tier devices, and that second-tier devices can connect only to third-tier devices. All other communication is blocked, and IDS/IPS are extensively deployed to monitor and analyze the traffic in this module.

Chapter 12

Implementing a Secure Interior

- Using Virtual LANs (VLANs) to Segment the Network
- Designing the Enterprise Campus
- Hardening Branch/Remote Offices

ollowing our Twinkie analogy, the interior network is the creamy filling, the good stuff so to speak. And much like a Twinkie, the interior network is often completely unprotected. The real problem presents itself in a couple of different ways.

First, the majority of security incidents occur from the inside of the network. Now on the surface one might think, "OK, so why harden the perimeter?" The reason that so many incidents occur from the internal network is *because* we have hardened the perimeter. We have done such a good job of separating our internal network resources from the external world that it is difficult for an external attacker to exploit the network. This does not mean, however, that we can stop worrying about the perimeter, but it does mean that we need to start focusing more resources on hardening the internal network.

Second, there is a predominance of worms that wreak havoc on many corporate networks. The sad reality is that most of the people reading this book (including this author) have worked at a company that experienced a worm outbreak that had a negative impact on the network. In my case, I worked at a company that had its network effectively crippled for almost three days, with lingering effects for another two days, as a result of CodeRed. Worms such as this one are able to decimate our networks because in many cases we have designed the networks like the Internet: open access is the order of the day, which means that any system can communicate with any other system anywhere in the network.

This chapter is going to build upon the device-hardening methods that we have discussed in previous chapters to look at how to design a hardened interior network. Like Chapter 11, this chapter is going to follow and build upon the Cisco SAFE design methodology. To that end, we are going to look at the following topics:

- Using Virtual LANs (VLANs) to segment the network
- Designing the Enterprise Campus
- Hardening Branch/Remote Offices

Using Virtual LANs (VLANs) to Segment the Network

Coming off the heels of the previous chapter you might be thinking, "VLANs must not be a good thing for security." Nothing could be further from the truth, however. Like many things, how something is used ultimately defines the value. If you are using VLANs to separate critical resources (such as internal resources) from highly insecure resources (such as the Internet or a DMZ), then VLANs are not a wise choice. When used to separate resources within a common security zone (for example, separating resources on the internal network), then VLANs can really excel at making your network more secure.

Trust Model Enforcement

A *trust model* simply defines who needs to talk to whom and what kind of traffic should be permitted. A flaw in many interior network designs is the fact that all systems can potentially communicate with each other. On the surface that sounds great, but when you look at it in more detail, there are a number of flaws in this design.

Most of the resources that a host needs to access are located on servers that are controlled and managed by IT. This creates a trust model that requires client systems to be able to communicate with the server systems. For example, if all of the servers are located in a server module, the trust model dictates that communication is required from the client systems to the server module, but not necessarily among client systems.

The first flaw then is that many interior network designs lack anything that prevents two clients from being able to communicate with each other directly, even though there is no valid business justification for such functionality. In addition, even in environments that subnet their server resources onto dedicated segments, traffic is still allowed to pass between subnets that do not contain resources that need to be accessed. For example, if you have a remote location in Austin and the enterprise campus in Houston, is there a need for the Austin users to be able to access the Houston client systems or just the Houston servers on the server subnet? These breaches in the trust model create an environment that is vulnerable to exploitation by things like worms that spread by infecting peer systems. VLANs can be used to effectively enforce a proper trust model in your network.

Using VLANs to Enforce Trust Model Among Subnets

Traditionally, VLANs can be used to enforce the trust model among subnets by requiring that all communications among subnets go through a layer 3 device, making that traffic susceptible to filtering and access control lists (ACLs). While you can achieve this same effect through the physical segmentation of your network, it is often a cost-prohibitive undertaking due to the requirements of so many different switches. In addition, through the use of VLANs, you can remove the physical limitation of requiring hosts that need to share a common subnet to maintain a physical proximity, giving you much greater flexibility in assigning hosts to a subnet.

The use of VLANs to enforce a trust model among subnets is very simple. At the layer 3 device, you implement an ACL that controls what traffic can pass to any given subnet. This allows you to be incredibly granular in determining the traffic that can enter and exit a subnet, for example, allowing a single host or range of hosts access while denying all other access. You can also implement restrictions based on source or destination port numbers, for example, preventing destination UDP port 1434 from entering any segments that do not contain SQL servers (an effective method of mitigating the SQL Slammer worm). For more information about how to implement ACLs, see Chapter 6.

As is always the case, all this additional security is not free. There is additional expense in providing the extra router ports needed to interconnect all the VLANs. Also, there will be expense in the form of administrative costs associated with properly configuring the VLANs.

Using Private VLANs (PVLANs) to Enforce Trust Model Among Hosts

A relatively new method of enforcing the trust model among hosts is through the use of PVLANs. As we saw in Chapter 6, PVLANs allow you to create a scenario by which hosts share the same subnet; however, they can communicate only with systems that are connected to promiscuous ports or are connected to common community ports. Figure 12-1 illustrates how this functions.

In this example, the port that the router is connected to is a promiscuous port and a member of the primary VLAN. Hosts A and B are connected to the isolated VLAN (lightly shaded area). When hosts A and B communicate, the traffic goes on the isolated VLAN and is accepted only by hosts connected to promiscuous ports on the primary VLAN (for example, routers or servers). Host A and B cannot communicate with each other even though they are members of the same VLAN and are connected to the same subnet. Additionally, hosts A and B cannot communicate with hosts C and D, even though they are on the same subnet. Hosts C and D are connected to the community VLAN (darkly shaded area). They can communicate with all hosts on the primary VLAN and they can also communicate with each other since they share a common community VLAN with each other.

Effectively, the primary VLAN bundles one or more secondary VLANs, allowing promiscuous ports to communicate with hosts on any VLAN. Secondary community VLANs can communicate with promiscuous ports, as well as with other ports that share the same community VLAN. Isolated VLANs can communicate with any promiscuous ports but are prevented from communicating with any other ports, even if they share the same VLAN.

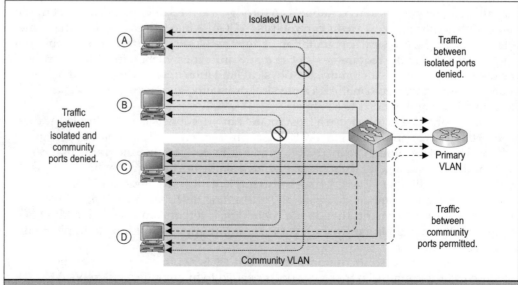

Figure 12-1.   Private VLANs

There is a limitation to the use of PVLANs, however, and that is the ability for a router to forward traffic back on the same interface that it was received on, effectively circumventing the purpose of implementing PVLANs. This can be mitigated, however, through the use of VLAN ACLs (VACLs) on the primary VLAN, configured to drop traffic originating from the same subnet and routed back to the same subnet.

Using VLANs to Isolate Systems

Another effective use of VLANs to segment your network is to isolate systems with administrative VLANs, particularly as an element of incident response. I like to refer to these VLANs as jail segments. When a system is suspect or believed to be compromised, it can be a tremendous undertaking to physically locate the system so that it can be patched or updated. However, if you have properly deployed NIDS throughout your environment, the odds are high that you know either the IP address or MAC address of the suspect system. You can use this address to rapidly locate the switch port that the system is located on, and then place that switch port in a VLAN that prevents it from being able to communicate anywhere else on your network. This buys you time in responding to an incident, enabling you to focus on preventing an expansion of an incident without needing to spend as much time worrying about whether compromised systems can infect the network. Once the system has been fixed by technical support, it can be quickly moved back onto an operational VLAN.

Designing the Enterprise Campus

The most effective method to design a secure infrastructure is to employ a modular design principle. By employing a modular design, you gain the benefit of being able to plan and implement the security requirements of each module on a module-by-module basis, instead of trying to address the security needs of the network as a whole, which can be a daunting task. You also gain the ability to group common network devices into easier-to-manage modules, and then address the security relationship among the modules as opposed to among the individual devices.

In the broad sense, there is a three-tiered design model that should be used when planning and implementing the enterprise campus infrastructure. At the top of the design model is the core network layer, which is designed explicitly to facilitate communications throughout the entire enterprise. In the middle is the distribution network layer, which exists primarily as the location within the network where traffic and security are controlled and managed. As the name implies, the distribution layer is responsible for coordinating the traffic to and from end systems. At the bottom of the model is the access layer, which is where the users connect to the network itself. Figure 12-2 illustrates the relationship among the three layers.

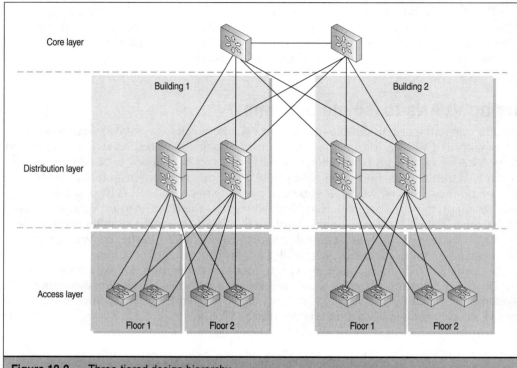

Figure 12-2.   Three-tiered design hierarchy

In this example, the core layer is used to connect the distribution layer devices that provide network access to two buildings. The access layer devices are connected to the respective distribution layer devices, providing network access for clients on each floor in the building.

As previously mentioned, the most effective method of putting the three-tiered design model into practice is through a modular design process. We are going to take a look at the following design modules and how they interconnect:

- **Core module**   This module exists to facilitate communications among all of the other modules in the design.

- **Server module**   This module exists to provide end user services and applications.

- **Building distribution module**   This module exists to provide data services to the building access module and to connect the building access module with the rest of the network.

- **Building access module**   This module exists to provide end user connectivity to the network.

■ **Management module**   This module exists to facilitate the secure management of your network resources.

■ **Lab module**   This module provides a safe and secure method for testing unsecured and new applications and services.

Figure 12-3 illustrates the interaction of the various network modules.

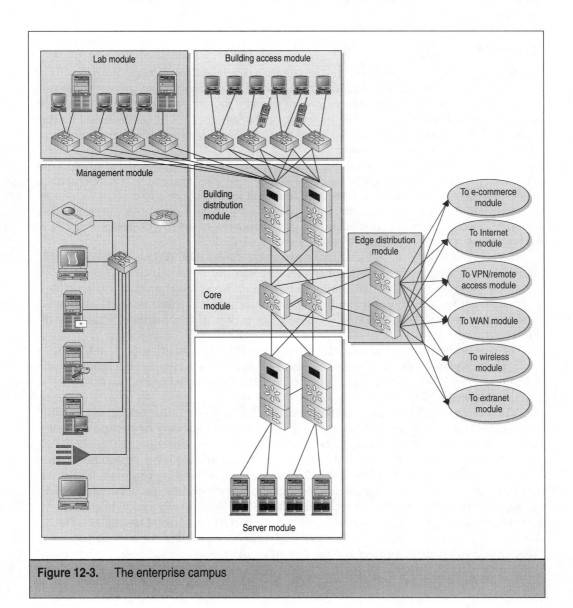

Figure 12-3.   The enterprise campus

Core Module

The core module is a relatively simple module from a security perspective because there is no real security within its structure. The devices in the core module exist exclusively to transmit data among distribution layer devices and other modules in the fastest fashion possible. Because all traffic in the core module has to originate from somewhere else in the network, the security requirements are implemented at those other modules.

Server Module

The server module houses those resources that the user community requires access to. The server module contains the file servers, authentication servers (domain controllers), name resolution servers, e-mail servers, departmental servers, application servers, and similar devices. While in principle the servers should be hardened by their respective administrators, there are steps that can be taken at the network level to increase the security of these devices.

Perhaps the most important thing to do at this level is to exercise stringent ACLs to control who has access to a given resource. Because of the nature of server resources, it may be easier to deny access to resources than it is to grant access to resources, which is contrary to the minimalistic security approach employed throughout the rest of the network. The ACLs can be implemented as components of layer 3 switches, routers, or firewalls that control access to the devices in this module.

The server module should also make extensive use of IDS/IPS for the network connections as well as the hosts themselves. Throughout the enterprise the most valuable resources are invariably going to be located here, which makes this module a prime target for attack. Implementing IDS/IPS throughout this module to analyze traffic and generate alarms on suspicious activity is critical to ensuring the security of these resources.

The server module is also an excellent location for implementing private VLANs to control which servers can access each other. This establishes a trust model that ensures that if one server is compromised, it would be difficult for it to be used to attack the remaining servers in this module.

While the most effective design requires that the server module is a separate component from the core module, in smaller environments it may be cost prohibitive to separate these functions. Figure 12-4 details the server module.

At the entrance to the server module is a pair of redundant layer 3 switches with firewall and NIDS functionality. These devices can be replaced by routers with firewall functionality in smaller environments. Within the server module, servers that require increased bandwidth can be connected directly to the layer 3 switches, while other servers are distributed across access layer switches in the module. This can also be done to reduce the cost of additional access layer switches. All of the servers run HIDS/HIPS software to protect against operating system level exploits.

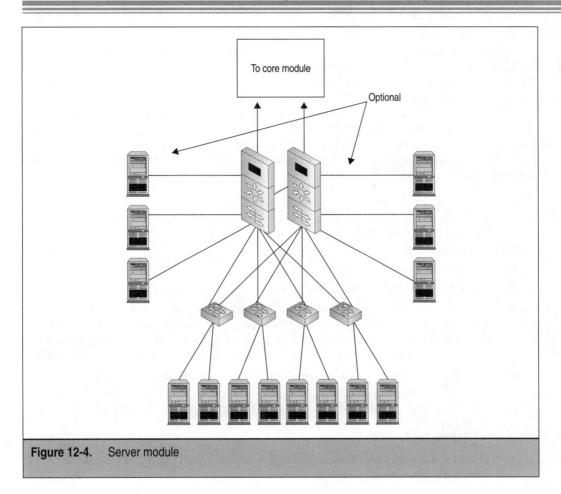

Figure 12-4. Server module

Building Distribution Module

Although it lacks the name, the building distribution module is truly the core of the
security infrastructure. The building distribution module ties the access layer devices
(particularly those in the building access module) to the rest of the enterprise through
the core module. The building distribution module is designed to handle all packet
manipulation such as routing, access, and Quality of Service (QoS), as well as all
security functions such as access control, filtering, and packet inspection through
the use of firewalls or firewall modules. While the building distribution module can
have some intrusion detection functionality, that is usually reserved for the modules
containing resources that are probable targets, such as the server, Internet, or remote
access modules.

The building distribution module provides a location that can act as the first line of defense in protecting the rest of the infrastructure against internally sourced attacks. This protection is implemented through the use of VLANs and PVLANs to segment the network and prevent hosts from being able to access other hosts without explicit permission being granted.

The building distribution module is typically built around powerful, fast layer 3 switches, although in smaller environments the building distribution and core modules may be merged. Because the building distribution module is designed around a switched infrastructure, it is critical to employ switch hardening methods, as detailed in Chapter 6.

- Disable any unused ports and place them in a VLAN that is not in use (such as a jail VLAN, as described in the earlier "Using VLANs to Isolate Systems" section). This will prevent accidental access to resources by incorrectly connecting new devices to the switch.

- Use a dedicated VLAN ID for all trunk ports.

- Implement dynamic ARP inspection to protect against ARP poisoning attacks.

- Implement PVLANs to isolate traffic from devices that do not need to access each other. For example, you can place the access module for one floor into one PVLAN and place the access module for another floor into a different PVLAN, effectively preventing end user stations from communicating with each other.

- Hard code the port speed, duplex, and trunk mode to prevent dynamic connections and mitigate the ability for an attacker to spoof as another switch in trunking mode, thereby gaining access to more data than they would have otherwise.

- Do not use VLAN1. This is the default VLAN for all devices, and by using VLAN1 you allow any device the ability to potentially connect to and communicate throughout your network.

- Deploy port security where possible, specifying which MAC addresses are allowed to connect, as well as implementing 802.1x port authentication where supported.

- Enable spanning tree protocol attack mitigation to prevent a hacker from spoofing the root bridge and executing a denial of service or man-in-the-middle attack.

- Restrict the use of Cisco Discovery Protocol to only where it's required.

- Implement VLAN Trunking Protocol (VTP) passwords to force authentication of all VTP advertisements.

- Implement firewalls or firewall modules in the switches to provide more granular packet inspection and filtering.

Building Access Module

The building access module exists primarily to provide network access and services to end user systems such as PCs and telephones. The building access module is the largest module in terms of connections because all end user connections terminate into this module. Unlike the building distribution and server access modules, which may employ layer 3 network functionality, the building access module almost exclusively provides layer 2 functionality. As a result of this we are limited in just how much hardening we can undertake at this layer, relying instead on the building distribution module for the majority of the security enforcement. However, this does not mean that there is nothing that we can do.

The majority of the hardening steps that can be taken in the building access module are going to be the responsibility of the desktop administrators. For the network equipment, we can undertake the same steps as we did for our building distribution module switches.

Management Module

The management module is the only module that does not show a clear connection to any other module. This is due to its very nature and purpose. The management module exists to facilitate the secure management of all of the devices within an enterprise. As a result, the management module is best implemented as a dedicated network that connects all of the network devices but does not connect to any other network segments.

The management module should be implemented as a dedicated subnet that is not advertised or accessible from the production network, thus providing a secure out-of-band management network from which to manage all the devices in the enterprise. Out-of-band management simply means that the network management traffic does not occur on the same subnet as the production data traffic that is being carried by the network device. If the device that needs to be managed does not support out-of-band management or does not have enough interfaces to support the connection to the management network, the management module provides the ability to connect via IPsec to a firewall that allows the remote management traffic to enter the management subnet, while also providing outbound SSH, SSL, and SNMP management traffic. Once again though, this should be implemented only in cases where out-of-band management is not supported. Figure 12-5 illustrates how this all comes together for the management module.

Because the information contained in this module is so critical (for example, device passwords, logging data, and SNMP community strings), it is critical that this module be protected from access from the internal network through the use of a firewall to segment it from the rest of the network. The firewall should accept only IPsec

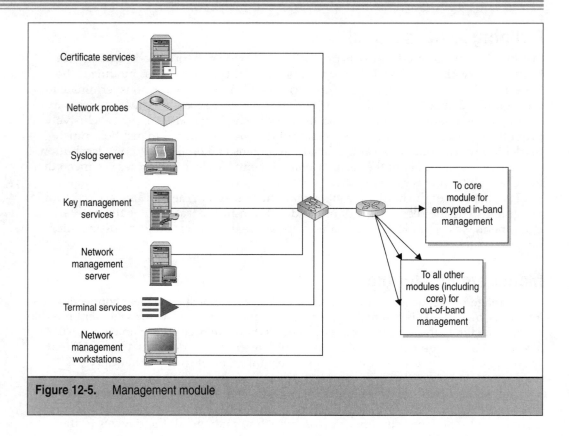

Figure 12-5. Management module

connections, and only from those network devices that require in-band management. All other connection methods should be dropped with ingress filtering. Similarly, you should employ egress filtering that allows access to the production network only when using defined management protocols such as SSH, HTTPS, SNMP, and TFTP, and then provide such access only to defined network devices. Everything else should be dropped.

Lab Module

The corporate lab module represents one of the largest internal threats to our network security due to the fact that so many of the devices in the lab environment are not adequately patched and updated. As a result, I highly recommend that the lab module be physically disconnected from the production network or be treated as a hostile DMZ network.

The Hazard of Connecting the Lab Module to Your Network

I worked at a company that connected their lab environment directly to the corporate network with no access restrictions. When CodeRed hit, over 1,000 unpatched systems in the lab became infected and generated so much ARP traffic as a result of the worm propagation methodology, that it effectively executed a denial of service attack on the network by filling the interface queues on routers throughout the enterprise. The painful lesson that was learned is that no matter how badly R&D claims that they need access to the production network from the lab, they probably don't need it as much as they think they do (i.e., checking e-mail, and so on). Try to find solutions that will allow them to perform the tasks they require while still providing the level of security that is required. For example, you might be able to set up a webmail system and grant access from the lab to that system and that system alone, allowing users in the lab to use the webmail system to check their e-mail.

Being a realist, however, I recognize that you may not be able to keep the lab module disconnected from the rest of the network. The next step then is to mitigate the risks associated with connecting the lab module to the rest of the network by implementing stringent access controls for all traffic passing to and from this module. You should be especially careful about allowing routing information out of the lab environment and into the rest of your production network where it could be propagated and cause problems.

Hardening Branch/Remote Offices

Branch and remote offices are often overlooked for security because they fall prey to the "out of sight, out of mind" syndrome. Because many IT organizations maintain staff at the enterprise campus, the enterprise campus stays at the front of everyone's mind when discussions about network security arise.

The good news is that hardening the branch/remote offices is no different than what you are going to do on the enterprise campus; you just perform it on a smaller scale. Branch offices will generally connect to your enterprise campus in one of two ways. The first method is via the Internet using a site-to-site VPN connection through the VPN/Remote Access module on the enterprise perimeter. The second method is via a WAN connection through the WAN module on the enterprise perimeter. You should secure these connection methods as detailed in Chapter 11.

Regardless of which type of connection the remote office uses, the internal network of the remote office should be hardened in the same fashion as you would the campus enterprise, again just on a different scale. You should take advantage of VLANs, packet filtering, NIDS/NIPS, HIDS/HIPS, and content filtering and inspection. Finally, you should configure your enterprise such that remote branches only have access to the subnets in the campus that they require. For example, your remote branches almost certainly do not require access to the building distribution or building access modules in your network. Consequently, you should implement filtering, preferably at each end of the WAN connection, to keep unnecessary traffic off the WAN link and block all unnecessary traffic from being passed to the remote offices.

Summary

The interior network is the most vulnerable part of our network infrastructure. While implementing a secure perimeter goes a long way to keeping the interior network secure, we must undertake a number of design steps on the interior network to secure it against internal threats.

The most important aspect to remember in designing your internal network is the need for trust model enforcement. You need to define what systems can talk to each other and build your network within that trust model. The most effective method of doing this is through a modular design process. Within the interior network, we have the following modules to consider:

- **Core module** This module exists to facilitate fast communications among all of the other modules in the design. Security is not provided at this level, relying instead on security at the other modules to protect the network.

- **Server module** This module exists to provide end user services and applications. Security is provided through the use of firewalls and ACLs to control the access to this module, and PVLANs to further segment the resources and prevent them from communicating with each other. Because the most valuable resources in the enterprise likely reside in this module, extensive use of IDS/IPS is employed to analyze and monitor the traffic.

- **Building distribution module**   This module exists to provide data services to the building access module and to connect the building access module with the rest of the network. This module effectively ties everything in the campus together, acting as the intermediary connection between the access devices and the rest of the network. Security is provided through the use of VLANs and PVLANs, as well as through extensive firewalling and filtering, to ensure that communications can only occur between authorized and permitted hosts.

- **Building access module**   This module exists to provide end user connectivity to the network. Security is provided through the use of layer 2 security features such as port authentication and MAC address filtering to ensure that only authorized systems are permitted to connect to the network.

- **Management module**   This module exists to facilitate the secure management of your network resources. This module is effectively a network within the network, connecting to all of our network devices for out-of-band management, while using firewalling and filtering methods to provide secure in-band management as required.

- **Lab module**   This module provides a safe and secure method for testing unsecured and new applications and services. Security is provided by ensuring that this module is not connected to the rest of the campus network, or if a connection is required, by implementing firewall and filter controls to explicitly permit the minimum-required network access while denying everything else.

- **Branch/remote module**   This module is a scaled-down version of the rest of the modules, suited for smaller remote and branch offices. For branches that have their own Internet connection, a firewall and IDS/IPS are required to provide perimeter protection on scale with the enterprise campus Internet module. For branches that use WAN connections, firewalls or IPsec can be implemented to provide perimeter protection as well as data protection across the WAN connection. Otherwise, the remote and branch office module is treated like the rest of the interior network modules, employing VLANs, PVLANs, IDS/IPS, firewalls, and filtering, as required.

Part III

Once Is Never Enough!

Chapter 13

Auditing: Performing a Security Review

- Reviewing Your Security Policy
- Reviewing Your Security Posture
- Auditing Your Environment

So you have read the first 12 chapters and have implemented the changes on your network. You fought political battles over your security policy, fought technical battles trying to configure your equipment in a manner that hardens your network, and are thinking, "Boy, am I glad that is done." Unfortunately, I have some bad news for you…you aren't done. In fact, truth be told, you will never be done with the systematic hardening process on your network.

Remember when I said that your security policy needs to be updated and reviewed periodically? This is where that comes into play. We are going to take a look in Chapter 13 at how you should review not only your security policy but your overall security posture. We will also look at how you should go about auditing your networks and discuss some tools and options available to assist you in this endeavor.

One of the "nice" things about security is that as soon as you have finished hardening your systems and protecting your resources, they aren't protected anymore. What's that you say? Did Wes just lead me in an exercise in futility? Well, not quite. The problem is that new exploits and threats are constantly being developed for your network equipment. This means that you can't update your systems once and expect them to be protected. Instead, you have to have a policy and procedure in place for patching and upgrading systems both to address security issues and to simply upgrade or enhance functionality. So now that you have the bad news—that you will have to periodically change, update, and upgrade your systems as part of the systematic hardening process—we need to take a look at how you can safely plan and execute those changes. This is where Chapter 14 comes into play. Chapter 14 will look at how to implement a patch and upgrade policy including defining a change control policy that allows you to update your systems without outdating your documentation, policies, and procedures.

If you recall, in Chapter 2 I stated that it should become habit for you to design and implement technologies and processes on your network using the guidelines defined in your security policy. Reviewing your security policy and posture is a part of those habits.

The threats that exist against your network infrastructure are constantly changing and evolving. As a result, your security policy and posture must change and evolve to account for those new and different threats. At the same time, you have to ensure that your security policy is functioning as intended and providing the kind of protection you expect from it. From policies that aren't being followed to policies that don't adequately address their security issues, you have to verify that your overall security policy addresses the threats it was intended to address.

One of the most effective methods to ensure that your security policy is performing as expected and that new threats are being adequately addressed is to implement an audit policy. A good audit policy will cover a spectrum of issues, including verifying technical, procedural, functional, and personnel issues to ensure that your security policy and posture are functioning as intended. This chapter covers the following aspects of security policy and posture review:

- Reviewing your security policy

- Reviewing your security posture
- Auditing your environment

Reviewing Your Security Policy

It cannot be stated enough that security is a process, not a goal. There is no endgame in hardening your environment; rather, you will be constantly updating and changing your security policies to address new threats that exist against your network infrastructure and new technologies that expand and change your network infrastructure.

Your security policy is a living document and, as such, should adapt to the changing needs of your organization. As best practices change, your policy needs to be checked against the best practices to make sure it is up to date. You should review your policy against each vendor's recommendations as well as check the SANS (www.sans.org) and CERT (www.cert.org) resources for tips, practices, and security updates and alerts that you can incorporate into your policy.

When you review your security policy, you want to focus on the following objectives:

- Is your security policy being adhered to?
- Does your security policy address all known threats to your environment?
- Do you have adequate prevention and enforcement of your security policy?

Is Your Security Policy Being Adhered To?

On the surface, this task may seem pretty simple to address: if your security policy isn't being adhered to, it may be time for some serious enforcement, such as employment termination. However, the situation probably requires a more detailed examination to determine why the security policy isn't being adhered to instead of just a knee-jerk reaction of "This is what we said to do, now do it." There are a number of reasons why your security policy might not be adhered to:

- **Lack of knowledge** This is the old "I didn't know" situation. People may not know that a policy is in place that they need to adhere to. You can address this through education and training. Although classes are certainly an effective method of informing your users, you can employ additional training methods to further cement the users' understanding of what the security policy is. When you have a new employee, you should make sure that part of their employment indoctrination covers the aspects of your security policy that apply to them. In addition, you should ensure that an explanation of the security policy is a component of their annual review to reinforce their knowledge of old policies and introduce them to any new or changed policies. Another very effective form of education (at least from a legal standpoint) is the use of banners. For example, you can have a banner that pops up when a user logs on or accesses the Internet explaining the acceptable-use policy, including a link to the actual full-text policy on your intranet. You could also have a banner that pops up when a user accesses their e-mail detailing the acceptable-use policy for e-mail, including a link to the actual full-text policy on your intranet. Banners and messages of the day (MOTD) make it very difficult for someone to claim they didn't know about a certain policy, especially if they had to click to get past that information. Finally, make sure you use e-mail and intranet websites to inform your users of the security policies they need to be aware of. Ignorance can only be an excuse if you give your users the opportunity to be ignorant about the subject.

■ **Policy interferes with business processes** This is the most difficult situation to address because it generally becomes a very politically charged issue. Because your security policy is often at odds with the easiest way to do something, people may decide to simply not follow the policy. In some cases, this is going to require upper management support and strict enforcement of the policy to effectively force the users to adhere to the policy. In other cases, the policy will have to be changed, sometimes providing weaker security in the process, so that the policy truly matches the work environment and what is being done there. For example, you might really want to use only 3DES encryption for increased security, but due to export regulations, you may have to run DES encryption at some locations. Pick your battles and be willing to compromise on issues that require it.

■ **Policy is ineffective** This is a case of a policy sounding really good on paper, but in practice it falls short of the expectations. Consequently, your security policy will need to be reevaluated to ensure it meets the expectations set forth in the design phase. An example of this might be a security policy that requires a certain type of VPN software to be used, even though not all operating systems in use support that type of VPN software. This problem commonly occurs when policies are tested by administrators using administrator-level accounts. Make sure your policies are always tested by all the types of users the policies are supposed to apply to.

A policy that isn't being adhered to is simply a waste of time and resources because it merely provides a feel-good measure with no tangible benefit. However, this does not mean you should simply change or remove any policies that aren't being adhered to. Review the reasons why the policy isn't being adhered to and make the appropriate adjustment. Sometimes this will simply involve educating your users. Other times it may require you to implement some kind of control that enforces the policy. In other cases, you may have to change the policy to better fit the business process, or you might need to change the policy because, in practice, it fell short of expectations. For example, if you have a password policy that requires a minimum of eight characters using uppercase letters, lowercase letters, and numbers, and you find that your users aren't adhering to the policy, don't just remove the password policy completely. Take a look at whether you simply need to educate your users. If so, take care of that so your users start doing what is expected of them. This might even require you implementing software that enforces the policy and requires your users to select an appropriate password.

Does Your Security Policy Address All Known Threats to Your Environment?

It sometimes seems that certain vendors have new security bulletins on a daily basis, even though this is not the case. Although it is common to point to Microsoft as the biggest culprit here, the truth of the matter is that every single vendor has security bulletins that they release, and you only need to watch the SecurityFocus BugTraq mailing list (http://www.securityfocus.com/archive/1) to realize this. The most difficult part of writing an effective security policy isn't defending against the threats you know about but rather trying to defend against the threats you do not yet know exist. For example, you cannot possibly know what vulnerabilities might be discovered for the various services and applications your network infrastructure equipment runs; however, if your security policy requires that all unnecessary services be disabled, you can effectively protect yourself from exploits directed at those services.

Protecting Yourself from Future Exploits

In July of 2003, Cisco announced a security vulnerability (Cisco IOS Interface Blocked by IPv4 Packets) that affected virtually every version of IOS prior to 12.3. This security vulnerability would block an interface, preventing it from sending and receiving any data. The vulnerability was based on the interface receiving traffic with protocol types of 53 (SWIPE), 55 (IP Mobility), 77 (SunND), and 103 (Protocol Independent Multicast – PIM). Keep in mind that these are not port numbers, but protocol numbers. Although I had heard of some of these protocols, I had never actually seen them in use anywhere I had worked. Ever. In fact, after reading the RFCs and related documentation about these various protocols, I can think of very, very few environments where they would likely be needed. And yet I had never thought to disable those protocols at my border routers for sure, and my interior routers in most cases—and, frankly, apparently most everyone else had never thought of this either. Consequently, many tens of thousands of systems were vulnerable to an exploit for protocols that in 99.999 percent of the cases no one actually used. The lesson to be learned here is simple: If you don't need something, turn it off. This is the most effective method of protecting yourself from future exploits.

Although protecting from unknown future exploits by disabling unnecessary services is key to ensuring that all known threats are addressed by your security policy, you also have to protect against those new threats that come out for the services you do require. In an almost-perfect world, the only vulnerabilities would be against services that we do not use or do not need. Unfortunately, security threats exist against protocols such as SSH (which you should require in your environment) that force us to address them to ensure that our systems are not left vulnerable.

Even Secure Protocols Can Be Insecure

As we have discussed, SSH provides encryption of data, which makes it an excellent candidate for providing remote management capabilities for your devices. This doesn't mean that SSH is not vulnerable to being exploited, however. For example, in September of 2003, Cisco released a security bulletin detailing vulnerabilities in the SSH server software of a number of network devices. Even so, given that SSH is more secure than Telnet will ever be, it doesn't make sense to disable SSH in your environment because the net effect would be to weaken your overall security posture—even more than the vulnerability does. As of November, all affected systems had a corresponding fix or workaround that should have been applied. See Cisco Document ID 45322 for further information regarding the status of this issue.

The most effective method to recognizing and addressing new threats is to keep your pulse on the industry and be aware of what is happening. By that I mean you have to make every effort to be as personally informed about the discovery of new threats, patches, and upgrades as you possibly can. A number of resources are available to assist you in this endeavor:

- **BugTraq**   BugTraq is a mailing list maintained by SecurityFocus (http:// www.securityfocus.com/archive/1) that tracks bugs and vulnerabilities for virtually every product and vendor on the planet. Subscribe to this mailing list.

- **NTBugTraq**   Modeled after BugTraq, NTBugTraq according to its website (http://www.ntbugtraq.com/) "is a mailing list for the discussion of security exploits and security bugs in Windows NT, Windows 2000, and Windows XP plus related applications." Subscribe to this mailing list.

- **Full Disclosure**   Run by Netsys, Full Disclosure is a mailing list that grew because of the perception that other mailing lists delay information until the vendors have had a chance to build a response, thus delaying the ability for you and me to know about potential threats. Although there is much bluster and hot air behind this, there is a grain of truth to it. Also, be aware that unlike the other mailing lists I have mentioned, this one is not moderated. On the surface that may sound like a good thing—open access to information without any interference—but in practice it sometimes means that you don't always get accurate information, and you might even find yourself receiving attachments or links to harmful data in addition to witnessing a significant amount of flame wars between Linux and Microsoft purists. Use caution if you decide to subscribe to Full Disclosure. You can subscribe to this mailing list at http://lists.netsys.com/mailman/listinfo/full-disclosure.

- **Vendor mailing lists**   Many of your vendors have mailing lists or notification processes to inform their customers of new security-related issues.

- **The CERT Coordination Center**   Located at http://www.cert.org, the CERT®/CC serves as a central information-reporting center and clearinghouse of security-related information (see Figure 13-1). You should make it a habit to check this website regularly. Personally, I check it a couple of times a day for new events and information.

- **Virus software vendor websites**   Many virus-scan vendors maintain websites with up-to-date information regarding new viruses and worms. Because so many of these programs can affect your network infrastructure, you should make it a point to check your favorite virus software vendor's website a few times a day. Personally, I check with Symantec at http://www.sarc.com/ (shown in Figure 13-2) and Network Associates at http://www.nai.com/us/security/vil.htm.

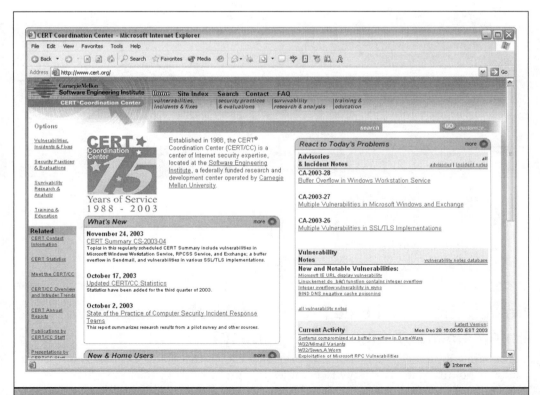

Figure 13-1.   The CERT website's main page

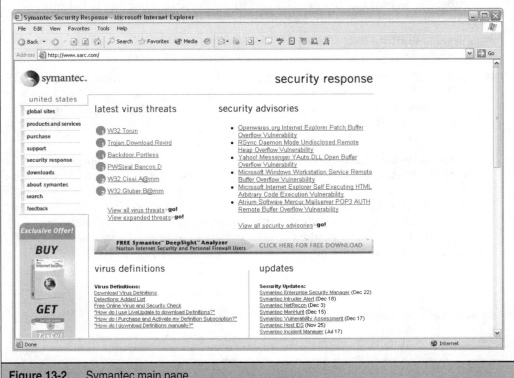

Figure 13-2.   Symantec main page

ONE STEP FURTHER

Here's a daily checklist of information sources:

1. Monitor BugTraq and NTBugTraq mailing lists.
2. Monitor vendor mailing lists.
3. Check www.cert.org for any new advisories.

Do You Have Adequate Prevention Mechanisms and Enforcement of Your Security Policy?

We all know the adage that an ounce of prevention is worth a pound of cure. Your security policy is no different. You have two angles from which to approach prevention—preventing threats and preventing noncompliance with your security policy.

The best security policy is one that focuses on preventing exploits from occurring, not simply defining what the threats are or what to do once an exploit has occurred. You can ensure your security policy focuses on preventing threats by ensuring that when you identify a threat, you also identify how to protect against that threat.

You will also want to prevent your security policy from not being adhered to. In many cases, you can prevent noncompliance by implementing the appropriate hardware and software. For example, if you have a password security policy that requires certain password characteristics, you can implement software that ensures that all user passwords adhere to the policy you've defined.

Like prevention, there are two angles to enforcement. The first is to ensure that your security policy enforces the recommendations it makes. You can do this by adopting procedures, software, and hardware that force whatever your recommendation is to occur. For example, if you require that only IPsec VPNs can be established, you can enforce this by ensuring that all your VPN concentrators only support IPsec VPN connections. This, in turn, forces the users to adhere to the policy, whether they want to or not.

The second aspect of enforcement is a much more political situation in that it defines what the response will be for violations to the security policy. You absolutely must involve your human resources and legal departments in these discussions because, in almost all cases, you will be dealing with personnel issues. You must ensure your users sign the security policy at employment and review time to verify that the users understand what is expected from them and what acceptable use is as defined by the policy. This is where your legal department plays a major role in ensuring that the policies are legally enforceable and do not expose your company to litigation. Once the users understand the security policies and expectations, you need to have a method of addressing security policy violations with some kind of punitive enforcement. Common methods of enforcement include verbal or written warnings, incident records attached to employee personnel files, wage garnishment, suspension, and even employment termination in the most egregious of offenses. For example, attempting to run a port scan on your network may justify a simple warning in either verbal or written form, whereas surfing porn sites should be grounds for immediate employment termination.

Be Aware of the Legal Liabilities

I worked for an employer who had an employee who liked to surf porn. This individual worked the night shift and also had a habit of showing the porn to other members of the staff. This was, obviously, a bad thing. Once this was discovered, we recommended that the individual be immediately terminated from employment. For reasons that to this day I still don't understand, the employer chose not to do this. Because of the legal liabilities related to a sexual harassment lawsuit, the IT department consequently drafted a document that stated that the company did not adhere to the IT recommendation and therefore IT was not liable for any future liabilities that might result from this individual's action. Although this might seem like overkill, we thought that in light of the severity of the policy violation, it was necessary.

Reviewing Your Security Posture

Many people confuse reviewing a security posture with reviewing a security policy. When you review your security policy, you are focusing on the policy itself and how it addresses the threats and requirements that have been documented. Reviewing your security posture is a review of how well you and your organization are positioned in regard to your security policy. For example, if you have defined that only IPsec VPNs are allowed, have you actually implemented the changes required to enforce this? If you haven't, your security posture is not in line with your security policy, and one of the two must change.

Reviewing your security posture is also where practice comes into play. You should practice to ensure that your organization is prepared to address any security incidents that occur. We will discuss incident response in much more detail in Chapter 17; however, as part of reviewing your security posture, you should validate that your incident response plan performs as expected. You should schedule and perform drills to test the security staff and ensure that everyone knows what their responsibilities are and what they need to do when a violation is detected. Although having notice of a drill is worthwhile, it is also important to have unannounced drills periodically. It's kind of like the part in the movie *Heartbreak Ridge*, where the troops are complaining that they always ambush the other platoon at the same place. That's when Clint Eastwood says, "Kind of makes it easy to get out of an ambush when you know when and where it is happening." Apply the same philosophy to your security posture review. These drills will further assist in illustrating any gaps in the policies, processes, and procedures that need to be addressed and corrected.

As part of reviewing your security posture, you should make sure you evaluate the following areas:

- Review your security policy against what you are actually doing. If they don't match, you need to either change your policy or change what you are doing.

- Review the technical controls you have put in place to enforce your policies. For example, if you have implemented software to require a certain password methodology, make sure the control is working as defined in the security policy.

- Review your users' behavior in regard to your security policy. Make sure your users are adhering to the security policy. For example, if your password policy states that your users should never give out their password to anyone, call some users and ask for their passwords.

- Review the administrators' behavior in regard to your security policy. Make sure your administrators are performing tasks as defined by your security policy. For example, if your security policy defines that event logs should be reviewed on a daily basis, make sure that task is actually being performed.

Auditing Your Environment

The most effective method of validating your security policies and posture is through the use of audits. Your audit process should include not only an examination of your policies to ensure that they are accurate and well written, it should verify that technical controls are in place that enforce them. It should also contain an active test of your systems and applications to test not only compliance with the security policies but also vulnerabilities to threats. The active testing of security controls and vulnerabilities is commonly known as *penetration testing* or *vulnerability assessment*. These guidelines cause a good security audit to be composed of three distinct components:

- **A checklist of items composed from your policy and from industry best practices**   This checklist is used to verify and validate that everything contained in your policy is indeed occurring in your environment and that you are adhering to industry best practices. For example, if your security policy states that certain ports should be blocked at your external firewall, the audit would verify that those ports are indeed blocked.

- **A vulnerability assessment (VA)**   A VA comprises testing your systems for common vulnerabilities to determine what potential exposure an organization might have. For example, a VA might test your Cisco routers to see if they are vulnerable to various denial of service attacks.

- **A penetration test**   A penetration test is similar to a VA test with one major difference. Whereas a VA seeks to identify vulnerabilities, a penetration test seeks to exploit those vulnerabilities in an attempt to bypass your defenses and gain access to your systems. For example, a penetration test might attempt to brute-force guess what a VPN pre-shared key is, allowing the attacker to establish a VPN connection to your network.

One thing to understand about an audit is that just because someone claims they have performed a security audit doesn't mean that is what they actually did. What they might have done is performed a security review, which is a little different. The term "security audit" has a very distinct meaning, and it is becoming more important for a company to understand that meaning as a result of laws being enacted to ensure the security of critical information. A security audit should only be performed by someone who is a certified auditor. What constitutes a certified auditor often depends on the laws and regulations that govern your business; however, you can find some general references about certified security auditors at the following websites:

- International Register of Certificated Auditors (http://www.irca.org/index.html)
- Information Systems Audit and Control Association (http://www.isaca.org/)

There are two primary methods of auditing your environment. The first is an internal audit, where either your internal audit team or you and your staff will audit your policies and test your infrastructure. The second is an external audit, where you have an external company come in and perform an audit of your policies and environment.

Performing an Internal Audit

The primary benefit of an internal audit is that it is a relatively low-cost endeavor because you will be using local resources. Many companies' organizational charts maintain a separate audit staff from the IT or security staff. This is the best method of performing an internal audit because you have a clear separation of audit and technical resources, thus alleviating any appearance of impropriety. In addition, a dedicated audit staff is generally more trained and specialized in performing the kinds of testing required for an effective audit than your normal IT or security staff.

There are a couple of drawbacks, however, that you need to consider when performing internal audits. First, if the audit is being performed by the people involved in hardening your network infrastructure, they are susceptible to overlooking issues. This is not an intentional issue in most cases. However, because they know what should be occurring, they are vulnerable to assuming certain things occur. It's kind of like that Internet brain teaser where you are given a sentence to read and asked how many times a certain word occurs. Upon rereading it, however, you find that the word was never used, but because you are so used to reading that word in the phrase, your mind assumed it was there. Your internal auditors who are also members of the IT or security team may do the same thing, assuming that certain procedures are being followed because they are expecting that to be the case. The second drawback is that if you don't have dedicated internal auditors, they may lack the expertise of knowing exactly what and how to test for issues. This is not a condemnation of your internal personnel's, yours, or my skills, but the reality is that most of us are not hackers. We do not have the time to be hackers. Instead, we have to spend the vast majority of our time working on issues that facilitate the corporate goals and objectives as part of the daily IT or security grind. You simply need to be aware of the limitations that exist in undertaking an internal audit.

Common Auditing Tools and Documentation

Here's a list of some tools and documentation available for those of us who aren't hackers that can assist us in auditing our environments for most of the basic threats and vulnerabilities:

- **The Open Source Security Testing Methodology Manual (OSSTMM)**   This manual, by Pete Herzog (http://www.isecom.org/projects/osstmm.shtml), is an excellent reference for providing a security testing methodology for the following six security areas: information security, process security, Internet technology security, communications security, wireless security, and physical security.

■ **Insecure.org** This site maintains a list of the top-75 security tools, based on a poll of the subscribers of the nmap-hackers mailing list (http://seclists.org/#nmap-hackers), at http://www.insecure.org/tools.html. I will point out a couple of tools of particular value in auditing your environment.

■ **Port scanners** These tools try to connect to a system on many different ports in an attempt to identify the ports on which a system will respond. This can assist a hacker in determining what the target system is or what types of exploits to attempt against a target. A number of commercial and open-source port scanners are available on the market:

   ■ **Nmap 3.48 and Nmapwin 1.3.1** These are both simple port scanners that can be used to determine the open network ports on which a device is responding. Nmap works on Unix/Linux systems, whereas Nmapwin is designed for Microsoft Windows systems. Both are free products that can be obtained from http://www.insecure.org/nmap/index.html. I highly recommend either version of Nmap.

   ■ **GFI LANguard Network Security Scanner (N.S.S)** This is a commercial hybrid port scanner and rudimentary vulnerability-assessment tool. It can be obtained at http://www.gfi.com/lannetscan/.

   ■ **netcat** This tool has been described as a TCP/IP Swiss army knife. Although technically not a port scanner, netcat is an excellent tool when used in conjunction with a port scanner to connect to the open ports in an attempt to determine exactly what program is actually running on the port. netcat for Windows and Unix can be obtained at http://www.atstake.com/research/tools/network_utilities/.

■ **Vulnerability analyzers (VA) and assessment tools** These products use a database of signatures or scripts to detect whether a system is vulnerable to a certain exploit. By running a VA program against a device or network, you can determine what vulnerabilities your infrastructure equipment is susceptible to. Be advised, however, that VA programs are not a vulnerability-assessment panacea. Many provide false positives—and, more important false negatives—that can give you an inaccurate picture in regard to your security posture. Here are the five main VA tools on the market today:

   ■ **Nessus 2.0** This is an open-source vulnerability-assessment tool provided for free on Unix/Linux systems. Also, a retail version is available for Windows. One of the benefits of Nessus is that its scripts are constantly being updated by members of the open-source community, which generally results in a quicker ability to detect new vulnerabilities. You can obtain Nessus at http://www.nessus.org. I highly recommend Nessus.

   ■ **Internet Security Systems' (ISS) Internet Scanner 7.0** This retail product can be obtained at http://www.iss.net.

- **eEye Digital Security's Retina 4.9.145**   This retail product can be obtained at http://www.eeye.com/html.

- **Symantec's NetRecon 3.6**   This retail product can be obtained at http://enterprisesecurity.symantec.com/products/products.cfm?ProductID=46.

- **SAINT's SAINT 5.0**   This retail product that can be obtained at http://www.saintcorporation.com/.

HEADS UP!

Because many VA tools are actively attempting to exploit systems, you should use extreme caution in running them against production equipment. For example, if a particular vulnerability will render a device unusable due to a denial of service attack, running the VA program could well have the same effect. Nessus is particularly notable for its ability to crash systems, in some cases to the degree of requiring a complete rebuild to recover.

- **Packet sniffers**   These are simply invaluable in performing a security audit, as well as for daily network administration tasks. The reason for this is simple: Only with a packet sniffer can you directly observe exactly how systems are communicating with each other. You can decode and translate the conversations occurring on your network, giving you insight into precisely what your network devices are doing. For example, we all know what a TCP three-way handshake is. Document after document explains that it is used by two devices to negotiate a TCP conversation. This simple expression is great from an esoteric theory perspective, but it doesn't tell us how it works. It is only by decoding and viewing the establishment of a TCP three-way handshake that we can truly understand what is occurring and precisely how network communications work. For example, Figure 13-3 shows the TCP three-way handshake and session negotiation (packets 21, 22, and 23) occurring before an SSH connection is established between two systems.

  - **Microsoft Network Monitor 2.0**   This retail product is a component of Microsoft System Management Server. A free version ships as a component of Microsoft's Server class operating systems; however, it will only monitor traffic that is sourced or destined for the server. Microsoft Network Monitor 2.0 only runs on Windows platforms, though the full version can capture any packets on the network. I highly recommend Microsoft Network Monitor. You can obtain it by purchasing Microsoft SMS at http://www.microsoft.com/.

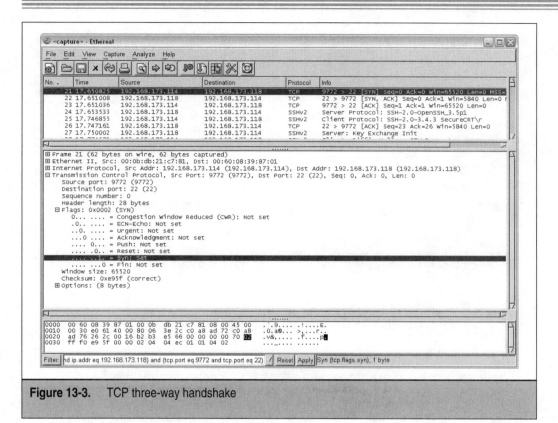

Figure 13-3. TCP three-way handshake

- **Ethereal 0.10.0**   This freeware product runs on Unix/Linux and Windows platforms. Although I like the interface in Network Monitor 2.0 better than Ethereal's, Ethereal is a very robust packet sniffer with the particularly useful feature of replaying TCP conversations, which allows you to see the output of a conversation on your screen, as opposed to having to manually piece it together from the packet decodes. You can obtain Ethereal at http://www.ethereal.com. I highly recommend Ethereal.

- Figure 3-4 demonstrates why packet sniffers are so valuable and dangerous. Although I sanitized the image by removing any addresses and names, this was a capture I ran while chatting with the tech editor for this book. Notice how easy it is to view the entire conversation. Indeed, clear-text communication is not really that top secret if you have a sniffer that can capture and decode the conversation.

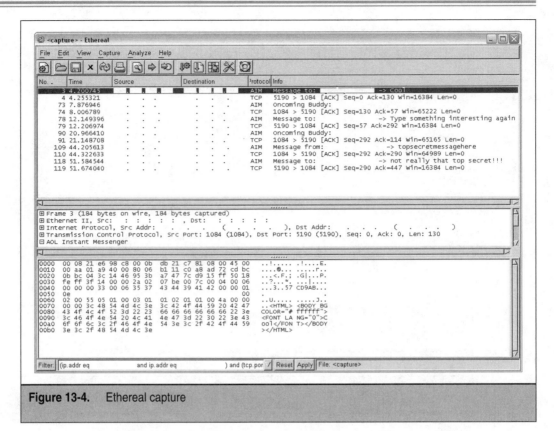

Figure 13-4.   Ethereal capture

- **Network Associates Sniffer Distributed and Netasyst Network Analyzer**   These retail products run on Microsoft Windows platforms only. Sniffer Distributed is a two-component solution consisting of the actual sniffer probe that you capture traffic with and a separate management console that you decode and view the captured traffic with. Netasyst is the replacement product for Sniffer basic, which is designed to run on a local system and capture traffic like Ethereal or Microsoft Network Monitor. You can obtain either product at http://www.nai.com.

The Value of a Sniffer

I once had a customer that was experiencing connectivity problems between their web server in a DMZ and their SQL server on their internal network. The systems could not communicate with each other when the firewall was in place, but they worked fine when the firewall wasn't in place. This was a particularly troubling issue, and no logging on the firewall gave any indication of the problem. It was not until we put a sniffer on the network and monitored the conversation that we realized the programmers were causing the web server to initiate a TCP three-way handshake on one port and then switch to another port for the data conversation to occur. Normally, a stateful firewall has an entry in its state table that keeps track of incoming and outgoing communications, so the firewall can determine which responses should be automatically allowed to pass. Switching the port numbers in use had the effect of causing the firewall to drop the data conversation because it did not have an entry in its state table for the conversation, which in turn caused a nonstop cycle of initiating a three-way handshake and attempting to send data, resulting in the initiation of another three-way handshake, and so on. In addition, the system was making a name resolution call that would fail when the firewall was in place but generated no errors. Without using a packet sniffer to see exactly how the systems were communicating, we would have found it much more difficult to diagnose the problem. The solution in this case required the programmers to change the SQL configurations and the network team to configure the firewall to permit the DNS request.

HEADS UP!

All of these tools, and especially a packet sniffer, are a real gift if a hacker can find them installed on your network, ready to be used. As a result, you should not install packet sniffers, or any of the other tools, on your servers and desktops in general. Like all applications, only install them when and where you need them, and remove them when you are done.

Using Nmap and Nessus to Perform a Basic Security Review

Two tools you should have in your security toolkit are Nmap and Nessus. Although both originated as Linux/Unix only utilities, Nmap now runs native on Windows as well, and Nessus has a Windows client that you can run against the Nessus server on Linux/Unix. For someone who does not have a Linux/Unix background, these tools may seem like they are more of a hassle than they are worth, but nothing could be further from the truth. In fact, it was my desire to run both of these tools that caused me to decide to learn Linux a number of years ago.

A note of caution needs to be mentioned before we start, because I do not want to give you the impression that running these two tools will give you an accurate security audit, vulnerability assessment, or penetration test of your systems. They will not do this. However, if you have never run any kind of tests against your systems, running these two tools will give you a good starting point on things to look at and tasks to perform before you invest the money in a formal security audit. Likewise, these two tools can help you identify any issues involved if you are looking for a quick-and-dirty answer to the question, Is there anything blatant I have overlooked? It is far more efficient and cost effective to become proficient in these tools and clear up the easy stuff yourself and leave the high-dollar penetration testers to find the hard stuff. We will start by looking at Nmap and what it can do; then we will look at Nessus and what it can do.

Port Scanning with Nmap

Nmap is a basic port scanner. It works by trying to connect to a remote host using TCP or UDP ports in an attempt to determine what applications and services might be responding on the system. Although this does not provide a guarantee that a certain service is running, it is usually a safe bet that it is. For example, if someone were to decide to run an SMTP server on TCP port 80, which is normally reserved for HTTP servers, a port scanner will simply state that port 80 is open. The safe assumption is that it means that an HTTP server is running on that port. However, only by performing a vulnerability assessment or penetration test will you know for sure. The value in a port scanner is the ability to identify whether ports are open that you did not intend to be open. For example, if you have configured your firewall to only allow TCP ports 25 (SMTP), 80 (HTTP), and 110 (POP3) to be open, when you run your port scan, you should not see any other open ports. If you do, this is an indication that something might be running that you did not plan to have running.

Nmap has two interfaces: a command-line interface and a GUI. The command-line interface generally provides more options for running Nmap in different configurations than the GUI does, though the GUI really just runs the command-line Nmap executable in the background. The two primary types of scans are TCP scans and UDP scans. As the names imply, a TCP scan is used to detect open TCP ports, and a UDP scan is used to detect open UDP ports.

A UDP scan is a relatively straightforward process, although it can provide inconsistent results. This is due to the nature of how UDP works. Because UDP is a connectionless protocol, there isn't a good way to know whether a UDP is closed. Nmap functions by sending a 0-byte UDP packet to each port on the target system. If an ICMP "port unreachable" message is received, the port is closed. In all other cases, the port is assumed open. The problem with this is that there are many systems that will not respond with an ICMP "port unreachable" message because they are trying to mask the fact that anything exists on the target IP address. This is commonly known as operating in "stealth" mode, because you can't really tell if something does or doesn't exist on that IP address. Consequently, you need to take your UDP port scan results with a grain of salt. If Nmap is reporting that virtually all UDP ports are open, the system you are scanning is probably operating in stealth mode.

Running a UDP scan is pretty easy using the GUI. Simply start Nmapwin from your Start menu, and you will be presented with the main Nmap screen. Leaving everything else as their defaults, enter the name or IP address of the host or the range of IP addresses you want to scan in the Host field and then select UDP Scan in the Scan

Mode section. When you are ready to initiate the scan, simply click Scan. Nmap will begin scanning the target, as shown here:

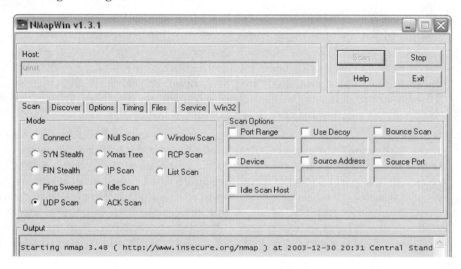

Notice how the actual **nmap** command to run the exact same scan is shown at the bottom of the screen:

```
nmap -sU -PT -PI -O -T 3 urnst
```

If you wanted to run Nmap at the command line, that is what you would type. Once the scan has completed, you will be presented with output, as shown here:

```
Output
Warning:  OS detection will be MUCH less reliable because we did not find at least 1
Interesting ports on URNST (  .  .  ):
(The 1469 ports scanned but not shown below are in state: closed)
PORT      STATE SERVICE
123/udp   open  ntp
137/udp   open  netbios-ns
138/udp   open  netbios-dgm
161/udp   open  snmp
445/udp   open  microsoft-ds
500/udp   open  isakmp
712/udp   open  unknown
713/udp   open  unknown
1028/udp  open  ms-lsa
Too many fingerprints match this host to give specific OS details
Nmap run completed -- 1 IP address (1 host up) scanned in 13.800 seconds
```

Looking at the results, it is probably a safe bet that the system scanned was a Microsoft Windows–based system. It is responding on most Microsoft NetBIOS–based port numbers, but we can see that it is also responding on NTP and SNMP ports. If you have a policy that SNMP should not be run on the target system, running a port scan is a quick way to determine whether the machine is in compliance.

Running TCP scans is a little more difficult than running a UDP scan because of the options available for TCP. Unlike UDP, which really only has one scanning option, there are five primary TCP port scanning methods:

- **Connect scan**   This is the most basic form of TCP scanning, and it uses the connect() system call provided by the operating system to open a connection to every port specified. This is essentially the normal three-way handshake. If a connection can be established, the port is open. If it can't, the port is closed. This type of scan has the advantage of requiring no special privileges in order to run, but it's generally very easy to detect in target host logs.

- **SYN stealth**   This is the most common scanning method and is often referred to as "half-open" scanning because Nmap will send a SYN packet as if it were trying to establish a session and wait for a response. If it receives a SYN | ACK response, the port is open. If it receives an RST response, the port is considered closed. If a SYN | ACK is received, Nmap will immediately send an RST to tear down the connection. The advantage of this type of scan is that fewer systems will log this type of connection, but the drawback is that it requires root privileges on the scanning system (not the target) to build this type of custom SYN packet.

- **FIN stealth, Xmas tree, and Null scan**   These scanning methods are all designed to be as clandestine as possible when compared to a SYN stealth or connect scan. Because more firewalls have been designed to watch for open SYN connections, these advanced scanning methods can sometimes pass unnoticed by a firewall. The concept behind these scans is that closed ports are required to reply to a connection attempt with an RST response, whereas open ports are supposed to ignore the packets in question. A FIN scan uses a FIN packet to "surprise" the target because there is no corresponding SYN | ACK that preceded it. An Xmas tree scan will turn on the FIN, URG, and PUSH flags, whereas a Null scan turns off all flags. The drawback of this type of scan is that many systems, including Microsoft, Cisco, BSDI, HP/UX, MVS, and IRIX, do not respond appropriately to a FIN probe against an open port. They all respond with an RST when they should, according to RFC (RFC 793), simply drop the packet. As a result, you may only use these types of scans in special circumstances.

In most cases, you will only need to use a connect or SYN stealth scan for your testing. Personally, I tend to run SYN stealth scans because they are faster than a connect scan. Performing a connect scan is as simple as selecting Connect in the Scan Mode section and clicking Scan. Shown next is the result of a connect scan.

```
Scan │ Discover │ Options │ Timing │ Files │ Service │ Win32 │
┌─Mode──────────────────────────────────┐  ┌─Scan Options──────────────────────────────┐
│  ⦿ Connect      ○ Null Scan     ○ Window Scan  │  □ Port Range      □ Use Decoy       □ Bounce Scan │
│  ○ SYN Stealth  ○ Xmas Tree     ○ RCP Scan     │  ┌──────────┐    ┌──────────┐     ┌──────────┐ │
│  ○ FIN Stealth  ○ IP Scan       ○ List Scan    │  □ Device          □ Source Address  □ Source Port │
│  ○ Ping Sweep   ○ Idle Scan                    │  ┌──────────┐    ┌──────────┐     ┌──────────┐ │
│  ○ UDP Scan     ○ ACK Scan                     │  □ Idle Scan Host │
│                                                │  ┌──────────┐ │
└────────────────────────────────────────┘  └────────────────────────────────────────────┘
```

```
┌─Output────────────────────────────────────────────────────────┐
│ Warning:  OS detection will be MUCH less reliable because we did not find at least 1 ▲│
│ Interesting ports on URNST (    .    .    .    ):                                      │
│ (The 1650 ports scanned but not shown below are in state: filtered)                   │
│ PORT      STATE SERVICE                                                                │
│ 135/tcp   open  msrpc                                                                  │
│ 139/tcp   open  netbios-ssn                                                            │
│ 445/tcp   open  microsoft-ds                                                           │
│ 710/tcp   open  unknown                                                                │
│ 711/tcp   open  unknown                                                                │
│ 1025/tcp  open  NFS-or-IIS                                                             │
│ 3389/tcp  open  ms-term-serv                                                           │
│ Device type: general purpose                                                           │
│ Running: Microsoft Windows 95/98/ME|NT/2K/XP                                           │
│ OS details: Microsoft Windows Millennium Edition (Me), Windows 2000 Professional or A ▼│
│ Nmap run completed -- 1 IP address (1 host up) scanned in 418.991 seconds              │
│ ◄            IIII                                                              ►        │
└────────────────────────────────────────────────────────────────┘
```

ONE STEP FURTHER

In order to understand what type of TCP port-scanning method to use, we have to first review how TCP communications occur and define some terms. Two hosts communicate over TCP by first establishing the manner in which the conversation is going to occur. This is known as a *TCP three-way handshake*. During the handshake, the systems negotiate the sequencing and windowing of the data. The initial connection request is known as a *synchronization (SYN) request*. The responding host then responds with a SYN and an acknowledgement (ACK) segment to acknowledge the original synchronization request. The originating host then responds with a final ACK that signifies that a session has been established (EST). TCP supports some other commonly used control bits, each having a distinct meaning:

- **FIN** Short for "finished," the FIN control bit is used to tell the hosts to clear the connection because there is no more data to be sent.

- **RST** Short for "reset," the RST control bit is used to tell the hosts to reset the connection, typically due to errors in the sequence numbers. For example, if a host expected to receive sequence 301 and actually received sequence 589, it would issue an RST to force another three-way handshake so that the sequencing could be renegotiated properly.

Shown next is the result of a SYN stealth scan. Notice that although the exact same number of ports were detected, it took only 3.085 seconds, compared to 418.991 seconds (almost 7 minutes) for the connect scan.

Although plenty of other options are available for running Nmap in a more advanced scanning configuration, these are the basic tasks you'll use for 99 percent of your port-scanning needs. Nmapwin ships with a really nice help file that contains very detailed information about all the options, how they work, and how to configure them.

Performing a Basic Vulnerability Assessment with Nessus

Whereas Nmap is a fairly straightforward port-scanning tool, Nessus is a little bit more complex to initially set up and configure. This is due to a combination of factors. First, it is much more robust and complex compared to Nmap. Second, the Nessus server component can only be installed on a Linux/Unix system.

Installing Nessus is fairly straightforward. First, you need to be logged in as root. You will need to install and configure the following components to support Nessus if you do not already have them:

- **GTK** The Gimp Toolkit version 1.2. You can obtain GTK from ftp://ftp.gimp.org/pub/gtk/v1.2.

- **OpenSSL** Although not required, OpenSSL is recommended because it is used for remote client connections to the Nessus server. You can obtain OpenSSL from http://www.openssl.org.

I recommend downloading and installing the nessus-installer.sh standalone installation package for the simplest installation routine. This eliminates the need to compile the binaries and the related tasks that make Linux not so user friendly. You can begin the installation by typing the following:

```
[root@keoland nessus]# sh nessus-installer.sh
```

The installer will begin and prompt you to press ENTER to continue:

```
--------------------------------------------------------------------------
                    NESSUS INSTALLATION SCRIPT
--------------------------------------------------------------------------
Welcome to the Nessus Installation Script !
This script will install Nessus 2.0.9 (STABLE) on your system.
Please note that you will need root privileges at some point so that
the installation can complete.
Nessus is released under the version 2 of the GNU General Public License
(see http://www.gnu.org/licences/gpl.html for details).
To get the latest version of Nessus, visit http://www.nessus.org
Press ENTER to continue
```

Once you press ENTER, the nessus-installer will prompt you for where to install the files. Accept the defaults:

```
--------------------------------------------------------------------------
              Nessus installation : installation location
--------------------------------------------------------------------------
Where do you want the whole Nessus package to be installed ?
[/usr/local] <enter>
--------------------------------------------------------------------------
                 Nessus installation : Ready to install
--------------------------------------------------------------------------
Nessus is now ready to be installed on this host.
The installation process will first compile it then install it
Press ENTER to continue
```

Once you press ENTER, the nessus-installer will begin installing and configuring Nessus on the system. When it is finished, you will be presented with the "Nessus Installation: Finished" screen:

```
--------------------------------------------------------------------------
                   Nessus installation : Finished
--------------------------------------------------------------------------
Congratulations ! Nessus is now installed on this host
. Create a nessusd certificate using /usr/local/sbin/nessus-mkcert
. Add a nessusd user use /usr/local/sbin/nessus-adduser
. Start the Nessus daemon (nessusd) use /usr/local/sbin/nessusd -D
. Start the Nessus client (nessus) use /usr/local/bin/nessus
. To uninstall Nessus, use /usr/local/sbin/uninstall-nessus
. Remember to invoke 'nessus-update-plugins' periodically to update your
  list of plugins
. A step by step demo of Nessus is available at :
        http://www.nessus.org/demo/
Press ENTER to quit
```

Once you have pressed ENTER, it is time to run the post-installation configuration steps. The first step is to generate a certificate for Nessus to use. This is done by changing to the /usr/local/sbin directory and running the nessus-mkcert program. A wizard will walk you through the creation of the SSL certificate:

```
[root@keoland nessus]# cd /usr/local/sbin
[root@keoland sbin]# nessus-mkcert
/usr/local/var/nessus/CA created
-------------------------------------------------------------------------
                  Creation of the Nessus SSL Certificate
-------------------------------------------------------------------------
This script will now ask you the relevant information to create the SSL
certificate of Nessus. Note that this information will *NOT* be sent to
anybody (everything stays local), but anyone with the ability to connect to your
Nessus daemon will be able to retrieve this information.
CA certificate life time in days [1460]: <enter>
Server certificate life time in days [365]: <enter>
Your country (two letter code) [FR]: US
Your state or province name [none]: TX
Your location (e.g. town) [Paris]: Houston
Your organization [Nessus Users United]: <enter>
-------------------------------------------------------------------------
                  Creation of the Nessus SSL Certificate
-------------------------------------------------------------------------
Congratulations. Your server certificate was properly created.
/usr/local/etc/nessus/nessusd.conf updated
The following files were created :
. Certification authority :
   Certificate = /usr/local/com/nessus/CA/cacert.pem
   Private key = /usr/local/var/nessus/CA/cakey.pem
. Nessus Server :
    Certificate = /usr/local/com/nessus/CA/servercert.pem
    Private key = /usr/local/var/nessus/CA/serverkey.pem
Press [ENTER] to exit
```

The next step is to add a user to Nessus who is allowed to run the program. This can be done by running the nessus-adduser program from the /usr/locl/sbin directory. A wizard will walk you through the user-creation process:

```
[root@keoland sbin]# nessus-adduser
Using /var/tmp as a temporary file holder
Add a new nessusd user
----------------------
Login : wnoonan
Authentication (pass/cert) [pass] : pass
Login password : <password>
User rules
----------
nessusd has a rules system which allows you to restrict the hosts
that wnoonan has the right to test. For instance, you may want
```

```
him to be able to scan his own host only.
Please see the nessus-adduser(8) man page for the rules syntax

Enter the rules for this user, and hit ctrl-D once you are done :
(the user can have an empty rules set)
<CTRL+D>
Login             : wnoonan
Password          : password
DN                :
Rules             :
Is that ok ? (y/n) [y] y
user added.
```

The next step is to run the nessus-update-plugins command to update to the latest version of the plug-ins. The plug-ins contain the information that Nessus uses to test for vulnerabilities. As new vulnerabilities are written, new Nessus plug-ins are written to test for those vulnerabilities. You can run the command from the /usr/local/sbin directory as follows:

```
[root@keoland sbin]# nessus-update-plugins
```

The final step is to start the Nessus server in daemon mode. Nessus is a client/server vulnerability-assessment tool. The Nessus server running on Linux/Unix is where all the testing is performed. The Nessus client is used to connect to the Nessus server and configure it to perform the configured tests. The client and server can be running on the same system, or the client can be running on a remote system (even running Microsoft Windows if the NessusWx client is used) that connects to the Nessus server over the network. The command to start Nessus in daemon mode is

```
[root@keoland sbin]# nessusd -D
```

You can verify that the Nessus server is functioning by running the ps –ef | grep nessusd command as follows:

```
[root@keoland sbin]# ps -ef | grep nessusd
root      29470      1  0 21:46 ?         00:00:00 nessusd: waiting for
ncoming connections
root      29474   3438  0 22:02 pts/1     00:00:00 grep nessusd
```

Now that Nessus is installed and configured and the Nessus server is running, the next step is to run the Nessus client by running "nessus" at the command line, as follows:

```
[root@keoland sbin]# nessus &
```

Typing **&** after the command allows you to return to the command line to run other commands while the GUI client is running. The first step is to log on to Nessus using the user account you specified with the nessus-adduser command, as shown here:

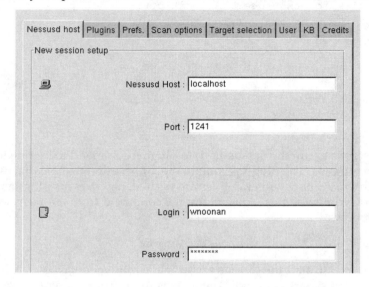

You will be prompted for your SSL setup options. Select the option you prefer and click OK:

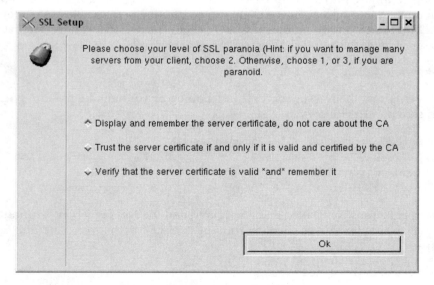

Depending on the option you selected, you will be prompted with certificate validation information. Click the appropriate button for your screen to continue. Option 1 will display and remember the certificate without worrying about whether or not the CA is a trusted CA. This is not a secure method of using SSL. Option 2 will only accept the server certificate if it is valid and certified by a trusted CA; however, it will not remember the certificate. This is a more secure and recommended method of configuration. Option 3 is similar to option 2; however, it remembers the server certificate. This will allow you to detect whether the certificate has changed. This is more secure than option 2 because if the certificate changes for some reason, you will be prompted and notified of the change.

Once you have been logged on, you will receive a pop-up message stating that plug-ins that have the ability to crash services have been disabled. Keep in mind that running certain tests can and will crash systems you are testing against. Enable them with caution.

Once you have been logged on to Nessus, you will be presented with the Plugins tab. There are literally hundreds of Nessus plug-ins you can choose to run (or not to run). However, if you want to run the most thorough test possible, you should select to enable all plug-ins:

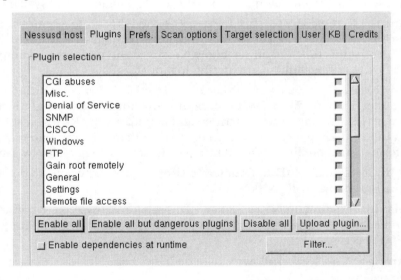

CAUTION Enabling all plug-ins could cause the target host that is being tested to crash or have other unexpected results. For example, when I run a Nessus scan against my HP LaserJet 4050N printer, it causes the printer to start printing nonstop garbage pages and eventually causes an EIO error that requires me to physically reboot the printer. In my small lab, that is no big deal, but if you were to do this to hundreds of printers in your enterprise, I would bet that you would have a lot of unhappy people. Be very careful about enabling all your plug-ins to make sure that no critical business systems will be affected if you test a system with all plug-ins enabled. You can mitigate this to some degree by specifying the hosts that you want to scan, ensuring that your critical systems are not scanned until the risk associated with the scan is acceptable (for example, scanning during nonbusiness hours). Unfortunately, if you don't test with all plug-ins enabled, you will not get a complete and accurate vulnerability assessment.

Next, you will need to configure the Nessus preferences from the Prefs tab. Nessus uses Nmap to perform port scans, and this screen allows you to define what Nmap options to use. In addition, you can configure the following preferences:

- **Timing Policy**   This defines how fast you want Nessus to run its tests. This is useful if you are trying to scan a system but want to take your time so as to not generate a bunch of log entries that would cause an administrator to discover that something is trying to exploit the system. Something to be aware of in setting the timing policy is that it can be used to try to scan a system without generating alerts that might notify an admin that something potentially harmful is occurring on the network. In some cases, you are going to want to scan systems in this manner, trying to avoid detection. You should only do this with the appropriate authorization, however. A benefit of slowing down the scanning rate is that if it does happen to start crashing systems, at least it is not doing it at breakneck pace, and hopefully it would give someone time to respond and shut down the scan before affecting too many systems.

- **Ping the Remote Host**   This defines how and whether to attempt to ping the remote host. Many firewalls will no longer respond to an ICMP echo request, so turning this function off can allow Nessus to run under the assumption that the host is online without attempting to ping it.

- **Libwhisker Options**   Libwhisker is used for HTTP server security testing, and these options allow you to configure how libwhisker should function under Nessus. Libwhisker is written and maintained by Rain.Forest.Puppy, a fairly well-known hacker and security consultant. You can find more information about libwhisker at http://www.wiretrip.net/rfp/lw.asp.

- **SMB Use Domain SID to Enumerate Users**   This allows you to define Microsoft domain SID options to use in testing.

- **Misc Information on News Server**   This section allows you to define news server connection settings for testing Network News Transport Protocol (NNTP) servers.

- **Services**   This section allows you to define various Nessus service connection settings.

- **HTTP NIDS Evasion**   This section allows you to configure settings for evading detection by a network intrusion-detection system (NIDS) while you are testing HTTP servers and services.

- **Web Mirroring**   This section allows you to define how many web pages Nessus should mirror if it finds a web server running on the target host.

- **FTP Writable Directories**   This section allows you to define how to test for FTP writable directories.

- **Brute Force Login (Hydra)**   This section allows you to define how hydra should be configured for performing brute-force password cracking. Hydra is a tool developed by "The Hackers Choice" at http://www.thc.org/.

- **SMTP Settings**   This section allows you to configure SMTP testing options.
- **NIDS Evasion**   This section allows you to configure different techniques to evade detection by an NIDS.
- **HTTP Login Page**   This section allows you to configure settings for HTTP login.
- **SMB Scope**   This section configures Nessus to attempt to gain information about your Windows domain.
- **SMB Use Host SID to Enumerate Local Users**   This allows you to define Microsoft host SID options to use in testing.
- **Login Configuration**   This section allows you to specify usernames and passwords for various services that may request login authentication.

As you can see, there are a lot of options you can configure that will change how Nessus attempts to test a system. For simplicity, you can leave these settings at their default values until you get more comfortable with them, with the exception of the Nmap settings, which I would configure to use SYN stealth scanning to speed up the scanning process:

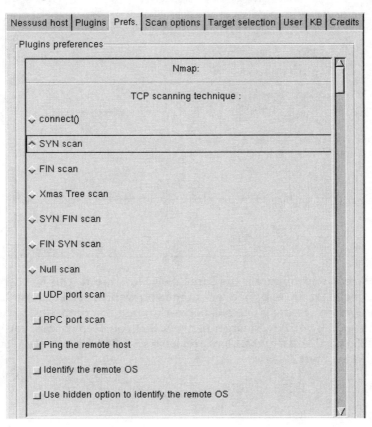

The next screen to configure is the Scan Options screen. Like the Prefs screen, it offers a number of options that will define how Nessus performs the scanning. I recommend leaving most settings at their default values until you get more comfortable with them, with the exception of turning off Connect Scanning and turning on Nmap and SYN Scan in the Port Scanner window:

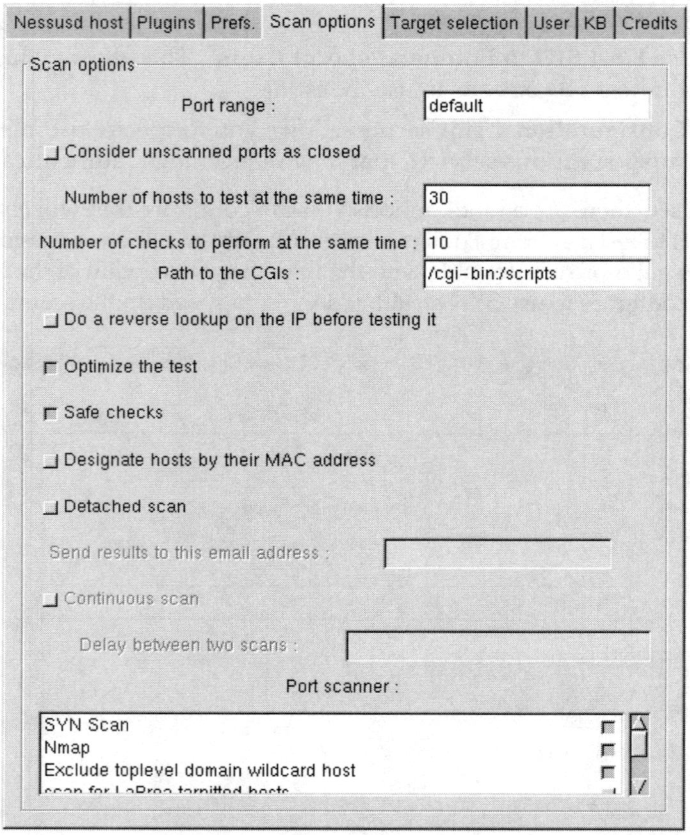

| Nessusd host | Plugins | Prefs. | Scan options | Target selection | User | KB | Credits |

Scan options

Port range :	default
☐ Consider unscanned ports as closed	
Number of hosts to test at the same time :	30
Number of checks to perform at the same time :	10
Path to the CGIs :	/cgi-bin:/scripts

☐ Do a reverse lookup on the IP before testing it

☐ Optimize the test

☐ Safe checks

☐ Designate hosts by their MAC address

☐ Detached scan

Send results to this email address :

☐ Continuous scan

Delay between two scans :

Port scanner :

SYN Scan	☐
Nmap	☐
Exclude toplevel domain wildcard host	☐
scan for LaBrea tarpitted hosts	

The next screen to configure is the Target Selection screen. This is where you specify the name, IP address, or network range you want to scan against. In general, I recommend only scanning a Class C network range at a time, due to time and performance issues. If you have a larger network that you need to scan, you should scan it in Class C (255 host) size chunks. Once you have specified the target(s), you can begin the scan by clicking Start the Scan.

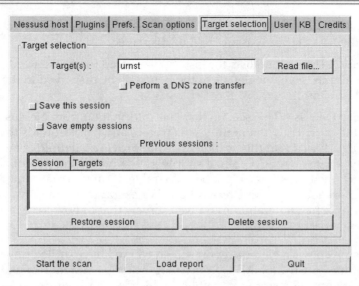

Nessus will display a scanning progress screen, as shown next. You can stop the scan at any time by clicking the Stop button. Be advised that depending on how many hosts you are trying to scan and how powerful the Nessus server is, it could take hours to complete a single scan. Nessus begins by performing a portscan (if you selected this option) before it begins running attack tests.

Once the scan has completed, you will be presented with a report screen that details the results of the scan. The report screen is separated into five sections:

- **Subnet**   This section shows the subnet or range of hosts that were scanned. If you scanned a single host, it will be listed here as well. Once you select the subnet value, the list of hosts on that subnet will be displayed.

- **Host**   This section is where the individual hosts from the subnet section are listed. This allows you to select a single host to view the vulnerabilities of just that system. Once you select the host to view, the list of open ports on that host will be selected.

- **Port**   This section lists the ports detected as being open. Once you select a port, the list of severity issues will be displayed.

- **Severity**   This section lists the issues discovered for the selected port. Once you select an issue, the details of the issue will be displayed in the Severity Details section.

- **Severity Details**   This section displays information from Nessus regarding what the potential vulnerability is as well as any workarounds that may exist. Be advised that this section does not provide a definitive answer of exactly what is wrong. Often, it simply gives you a list of potential problems to which the target host might be vulnerable. Be aware that sometimes Nessus will report a false positive report here. For example, I commonly see Nessus report Apache vulnerabilities on web servers that I know for a fact are not running Apache.

The following shows a Nessus report screen where I have drilled down to select a security hole for port 161 (SNMP). Notice that the target system responded to the default SNMP community string of "public," which is a cardinal sin and a no-no for all systems on the network, because every hacker and script kiddie is automatically going to attempt to connect using default community strings (public, private, security, and monitor).

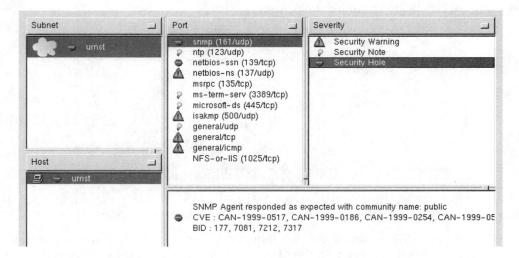

The CAN number listed in the security details section represents a list of common vulnerabilities and exposures (CVEs) that are maintained at http://cve.mitre.org. For example, CAN-1999-0517 is the CVE candidate that refers to having a default, null, or missing SNMP community string.

If you want to save the report for future viewing, you can click the Save Report button. Although you can save your reports in a number of different file formats, I am particularly fond of HTML with Pies and Graphs, because I can store the reports on a web server in a format that is generally well liked by upper management due to the pretty graphs. This screen shows how you would save the report:

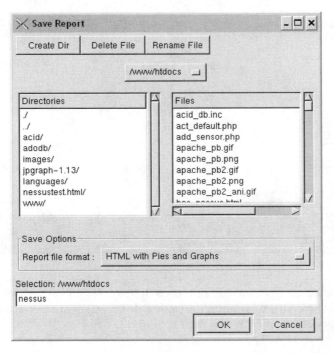

Figures 13-5 through 13-8 provide some examples of what the HTML reports look like. As you can see, the information is presented in a number of different formats, making it easy to cater not only to the technical folks but also to your upper management. When the reports are used for scanning multiple systems, the graphs in particular provide a very good representation of what protocols, services, and systems pose the greatest risk to your environment.

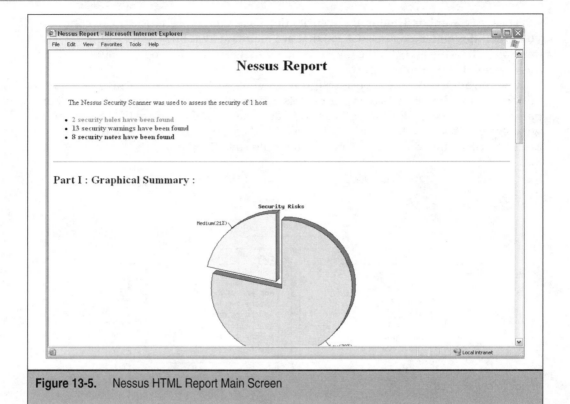

Figure 13-5. Nessus HTML Report Main Screen

Although Nmap and Nessus are not tools that you should solely rely on to gauge your security posture, like a hammer and screwdriver, they are two tools that every security professional should have in their toolbox.

Performing an External Audit

The primary benefit to having an external audit performed is the fact that the audit is (or should be) performed by a company that has expertise in specifically auditing and testing an organization's security policies for compliance, function, and vulnerabilities. They should also be able to provide a certified audit report that you can use to prove that you are meeting whatever legal requirements (such as HIPAA or Sarbanes-Oxley) your organization is governed by. However, a caveat emptor to an external audit is the fact that if the company auditing your environment is simply running the previously mentioned tools, frankly, they aren't really adding any value beyond what you could probably do on your own—and it is coming at a substantially higher price than what it would cost to perform an internal audit. To address the issue of competence on the

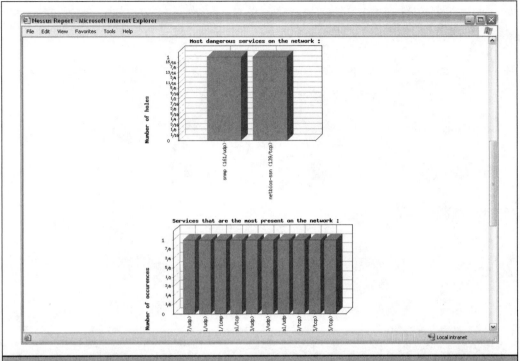

Figure 13-6.   Nessus HTML Report Statistics

part of your external auditing company, you should make sure you select a reputable and known company for testing your systems. You also should define whether the company in question is expected to provide all three components of an audit. For example, an auditing firm may not be able to provide an effective VA or penetration test. Instead, you might need an auditing company to handle strictly the audit side of the house while you use a specialized security firm for providing your VA and penetration testing. Although each component will give you a little bit of information, only by having all three components can you get the full picture as to the validity of your security policy and posture.

Many companies that provide financial auditing services have a dedicated practice that can perform security auditing at the same time. Here's a list of some of the better known companies that can perform a security audit:

- Deloitte Touche Tohmatsu (http://www.deloitte.com)
- PricewaterhouseCoopers (http://www.pwcglobal.com)
- Accenture (http://www.accenture.com)
- Ernst and Young (http://www.ey.com)

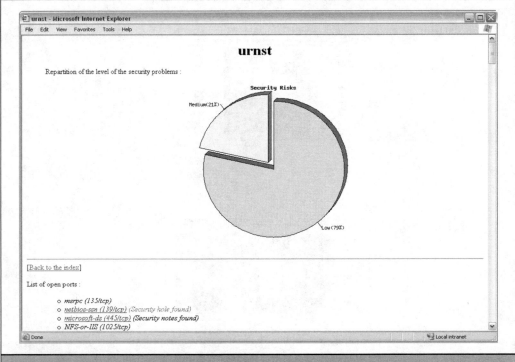

Figure 13-7. Nessus HTML Report Security Risk Proportion

In addition, here are some of the better known companies that can perform VA and penetration testing:

- Foundstone (http://www.foundstone.com/)
- Symantec (http://www.symantec.com)
- @stake, formerly L0pht Heavy Industries (http://www.atstake.com/services/)

Perhaps the most important aspect of an external audit, however, is the fact that the information contained in the audit can go a long way toward validating the security direction of your organization as well as provide political capital to lobby for additional resources in achieving your security goals.

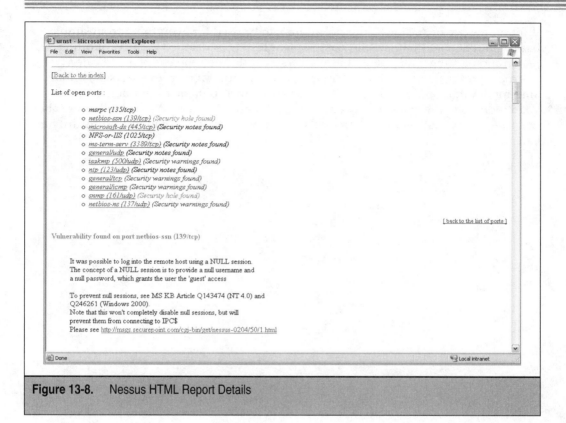

Figure 13-8.   Nessus HTML Report Details

Summary

There is no goal or conclusion to the security policies and procedures involved in hardening your network. Security is a process that has no end. As a result, your security policy should be a living document that is reviewed on at least an annual basis to ensure that it adequately addresses the security threats and exploits that exist against your network infrastructure. You should ensure that your security policy is being adhered to and that it puts forth an effective solution to the security issues in your environment. You also should test and verify that your organization's security posture is in line with the expectations your security policy defined. A simple and effective method of validating and reviewing your security policy and posture is through the use of auditing. Internal audits can be used for everything from simple, basic validation and vulnerability-assessment testing to detailed security auditing, penetration testing, and vulnerability assessment through the use of a dedicated internal auditing staff. On the other hand, external audits can provide a substantial amount of information that can be used as an agnostic outside recommendation and validation of your organization's security goals and objectives. We will talk more about this last point when we look at methods to justify the expense of increased security in Chapter 15.

Chapter 14

Managing Changes to Your Environment

- Implementing Change Control
- Implementing a Patch and Update Policy

O ne of the most difficult aspects of hardening your network infrastructure is managing the changes that are going to occur on your network. Regardless of how well you plan, you are going to have to make changes to your network to address security updates, technology updates, and even acquisitions and employee moves. All these changes can undermine—or improve—the security on your network.

In this chapter, we are going to look at how you can manage the changes that will inevitably occur on your network while ensuring that you maintain your security posture at an acceptable level. We are also going to look at how you can implement a patch management strategy to address not only security patches and updates, but also general patches and updates in your network.

Implementing Change Control

Your change control process has two fundamental areas. The first is planning for changes. This is often called the *change planning process*. This is the step where you want to identify the risks involved in the change and build the change planning requirements to ensure that the change is successfully implemented. Before any changes are made, you should take a look at the key tasks required to ensure the success of the potential changes. The second step is managing the change. This area is often called the *change management process*. This is where you need to define the process that approves and schedules the changes to ensure that there is adequate notification and minimal user impact as a result of the change.

The most effective way to implement a successful change control policy is to define a process flow that identifies the key steps and requirements of the change control process, as shown in Figure 14-1.

We will refer to this flowchart as we discuss how to plan and manage changes in the next sections. First, however, we need to look at who manages the changes in our environment.

Defining the Change Management Team

Before you can begin effecting any changes in your environment, you need to define who is responsible for managing those changes. Defining the change management team is another one of those political endeavors you will need to undertake in your enterprise. You need to identify all the people who will be involved in accepting or denying change management requests. Your change management team does not need to be made up exclusively of technical experts. In fact, it shouldn't be made up exclusively of technical experts. This is because the goal of the change management team is not to investigate the technical accuracy of the changes being proposed. To achieve this, your change control team should be made up of a mix of people from all your major business units and organizations so that they can provide the necessary business impact information to properly judge the change request. At the same time, you need to try to keep your change control group as small as possible; otherwise, it becomes very difficult to coordinate all the members. If there are too many people, it can be difficult—if not impossible—to have effective change control meetings.

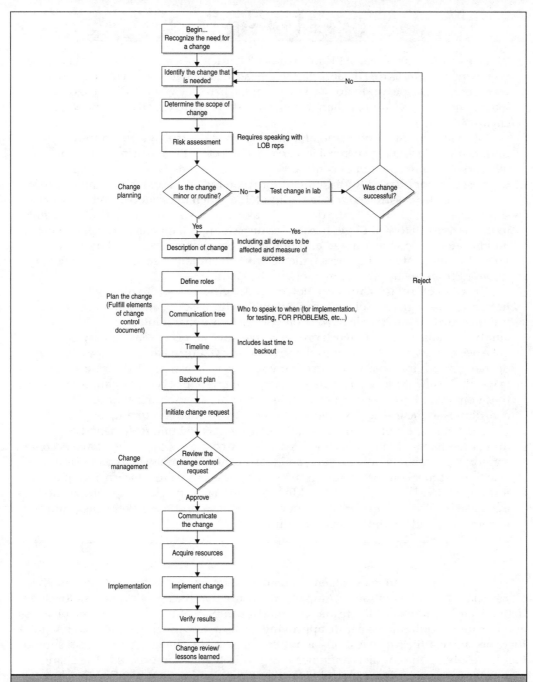

Figure 14-1.   The change control process flow

ONE STEP FURTHER

Change control can be one of the most difficult hardening steps you can implement on your network. This is due in large part to the fact that change control often interferes with the ability of people to do what they want, when they want to do it. No one likes to be told no, and yet change control is there to do exactly that in some circumstances.

At the same time, the value of a good change control system cannot be underestimated. Change control is a critical component in ensuring that your network does not spin out of control. We have all seen networks that are in some degree of shambles. Did the administrators plan for the network to be an insecure, unmanageable mess? Of course they didn't, but much like that old Talking Heads song "Once in a Lifetime," one day they wake up, look at their network, and think to themselves, "How did I get here?" Because changes happened on the network, and because no one evaluated and managed these changes to make sure they knew and understood the impact, the network eventually became something very different from the network they thought they had.

Change control isn't all good, however. As critical as it is to managing your network, if change control isn't implemented with wisdom and planning, it can become such an intolerable burden on your network that it interferes with your ability to manage your network properly. We have all heard—and many of us have been a part of—change control horror stories, where making even the simplest of changes requires so much effort that you start to question whether the change is worth the effort required. In these cases, change control ceases being something that helps you harden your network and becomes something that ultimately contributes to the greater likelihood of a security incident occurring.

The final aspect of change control to consider is the human element. People don't like change. Many folks are threatened by change because they have become comfortable with how things work, and they are afraid that when a change is made it will upset that comfort factor. In some cases, this is a valid concern, but in others it is not. In an ideal world, we wouldn't need to make any changes—but we don't live in an ideal world. In our world, new technologies and security threats continue to come out, and we must react accordingly.

The goal of the change management team is to review each change to ensure that all associated documentation is complete, to ensure that the appropriate risk levels are defined, and then to investigate and evaluate the impact of the change on the business and business requirements before approving or disapproving the requested change. If there are any conflicts or questions about the request, the change control team should handle resolving the conflicts and questions so the change can proceed. The change management team is also responsible for scheduling and communicating the change to all affected parties.

ONE STEP FURTHER

One of the difficulties of involving the line of business (LOB) on the change management team is that the LOB representative may be inundated with changes that do not affect their LOB and therefore they don't care about them. You have a couple of ways in which you can approach this problem.

One thing you can do is to involve the LOB representative only in the change control meetings that directly affect them. The other thing you can do is to remove the LOB representative from the change management team; however, you must ensure if you do this that you still engage the LOB in discussions and ensure that they sign off on the risks and changes.

You will need to determine which method is the most effective to use in your environment.

A specialized role within your change control team is the change controller. Your change controller is generally a member of your IT team who acts as a project manager for all the change process details. Some organizations will attempt to have the change controller role shared with other roles within IT, but if you are in a large environment, this really needs to be a dedicated person to keep track of and manage the status of all potential requests in your organization. If the volume of changes is large enough, you may need to go a step further and divide this role up among several controllers, with responsibilities divided by geographic region. The change controller should be responsible for the following elements of the change control process:

- Accepting and reviewing all change requests to ensure completeness and accuracy. Your change controller needs be a central point of contact to properly manage all this information.

- Managing and running all change control meetings. (I recommend weekly or biweekly meetings.)

- Presenting the completed change requests to the change review board for approval or disapproval.

- Preventing any scheduling conflicts by maintaining the calendar and schedule of all changes as well as business-related scheduling data (such as holidays, company all-hands meetings, and so on).

- Publishing all meeting notes and helping to communicate all changes to the relevant implementation teams and user groups, possibly distributing a calendar of changes to LOB leads.

- Ensuring that only authorized changes are implemented and that all changes are implemented in a timely fashion in accordance with business requirements and technology standards.

- Providing after-action reports to ensure that the changes were indeed successful and had no negative impact on any business processes.

- Providing all required metrics and data requested by management regarding the status of the change control team. This can include the volume of changes, average turnaround time, number of changes accepted and rejected, number of backouts, number of changes that generated new incidents, number of changes that did not produce the appropriate results, number of emergency changes, and the degree of client satisfaction.

The Change Planning Process

The change planning process is where you do all the legwork before the change is implemented in your mainstream environment. I've said it before, but it bears repeating: Proper prior planning prevents poor performance. If you do not plan your changes before you make them, you will rapidly lose control of your environment. To help ensure that you plan your changes appropriately, you should make sure you perform the following six steps:

1. Recognize the need for a change.
2. Identify the change that is needed.
3. Define the scope of the change.
4. Perform a risk analysis.
5. Test the change.
6. Plan the change.

Recognize the Need for a Change

The first step of your change control process is to identify the need for a change. Within a security context, this can be done by following the principles laid out in Chapter 13. Keep informed of new security exploits and, by extension, the potential need for changes in your environment by strictly adhering to a daily checklist, as follows:

1. Monitor the BugTraq and NTBugTraq mailing lists.
2. Monitor vendor mailing lists.
3. Check www.cert.org for any new advisories.
4. Check your virus software vendor's website for any new advisories by subscribing to vendor mailing lists.

Identify the Change That Is Needed

In many cases, there isn't just one way of addressing an issue. There might be multiple solutions that will achieve the same result. During this phase, you need to identify the change that makes the most sense for your environment. Make sure you know and understand all the alternatives so that you can select the most effective solution. At the same time, be prepared to return to this phase to try the alternatives in the event that the original change doesn't work.

Identify the Scope of the Change

The next step is to identify what the intent and purpose of the change is. You need to define what systems and users are affected by the change, including not only the end users but the administrators who are responsible for implementing the change. When you define the change, you should make sure you include a complete technical definition of the change and the reason for the change. During this phase, you should answer the following questions:

- *What is the nature of the change?* Consider what the change is going to address and how the change is going to address it.

- *What systems are impacted by the change?* Consider not only the direct systems you may be changing but also incidental systems that could be affected. For example, if you are making a change on your external firewall, the ability for devices on the DMZ to communicate with systems on the internal network could be impacted.

- *Who is affected by the change?* Define the users who will be affected by the change. This is primarily so that you know who needs to be notified of the potential change to make sure you take into account their schedule. For example, if you need to make a change that will impact your accounts receivable department, and it is the end of the month, this might not be a good time for this particular change.

Perform a Risk Assessment

Once you have identified the potential need for a change, you need to perform a risk assessment. There are actually two parts to the risk assessment that you need to perform.

The first risk assessment is actually defining the level of risk associated with the threat the change seeks to mitigate. This is an important step because the level of risk a change mitigates is critical in identifying how quickly a change needs to be made. Low-risk changes can likely be made at a much more leisurely pace, perhaps being addressed at the regularly scheduled change control meetings and on the regularly scheduled days identified for making changes. Medium-risk changes may or may not be able to wait for a predefined change schedule. High-risk changes might require immediate action that occurs outside the traditional change control mechanism.

The second risk assessment is defining the level of risk associated with making the change in question. The objective here is to understand what the potential negative impacts of making the change are. On the surface, it is easy to look at a security issue and say, "We must make this change." Practically speaking, however, we have to make sure that the changes we make will not cause even more problems than they solve. Examining the risk involved in the change will allow you to judge the worst-case scenario to ensure that you have looked at all the pros and cons associated with the change before you actually make the change. This will also assist you in identifying the level of testing and validation to undertake before making the change. You can use the following five general risk levels to assign the risk of making the change:

- **High potential impact to a large number of users or business-critical resources due to the introduction of new products, technologies, or features**   The change will involve expected network downtime.

- **High potential impact to a large number of users of business-critical resources due to a change in the existing environment**   This change could involve increased network traffic or involve enterprise-wide changes (such as backbone router changes, routing protocol changes, or access list changes). There may be some network downtime involved in the change.

- **Medium potential impact to a smaller number of users because of a nonstandard change**   The change may involve new or changed products, technologies, and features. The change may also involve some network downtime.

- **Low potential impact involving a minimum amount of users**   This change will generally involve bringing new locations and services online that are not yet used by the general user community. This level can also be used to define higher-level changes that have been tested in your production environment.

- **No service or user impact**   This level generally defines making standard configuration changes, such as changes to passwords, banners, descriptions, SNMP community strings, and so on, that present no expected network downtime.

ONE STEP FURTHER

Although this chapter focuses on changes for security-related reasons, these concepts also apply to any other type of change you would make in your environment. For example, changes due to increased functionality, failed hardware, end-of-life hardware, business acquisitions, and so on, should all go through a change control process and risk assessment before you make them.

Test the Change

The next phase of the change planning process is to test the change that will be made. Testing the change can be made in a lab or with controlled users in your production environment. For example, if you need to make a change to your routers, you might test the change first on a router that is not heavily used, that does not control critical business processes, or that is only used by a small group of users and work with those users to make sure that they can still do what they need to after the change has been implemented.

ONE STEP FURTHER

One of the things you can do to help identify how much testing you should perform on a change is to identify the types of changes and then define the level of testing expected for each change. For example, the following changes should be tested in a test environment if at all possible:

- System image changes
- Updates to critical resources
- Routing configuration changes

Other changes might be OK to test in a controlled production environment, depending on the circumstances. Here are some examples:

- Access list changes
- Virus signature updates
- Content filtering updates
- Device configuration changes

The most important aspect of testing the change is to make sure your test, as near as possible, mimics the environment and the method of the change you will make. For example, if your change is updating an access list on a router and you test that change while physically consoled into the router, you may find that when you make that change in production on a remote router, the access list blocks your Telnet access, something that you would not have discovered in your test.

Another testing gotcha you should be aware of is that you test the change as all users who will be impacted by the change. In testing, make sure you test as every type of user who could be affected by the update. If you only test an update as an administrator, you can almost bet on your regular users having a different experience. I have lost count of how many changes I've tested by rolling the changes to the IT staff first, only to discover that once they were rolled out to the general user population, their access rights did not allow for the changes to occur.

This brings up an important point: Be careful to make sure when testing with your IT staff that you do not do things that may prevent your IT staff from working. In fact, I recommend that you try to identify users across your environment who are willing to test changes that need to be made. These people are easy to identify. They are your users who are geeks like you and me. They like technology and like being involved in technology, and using them to help you test changes is a good way to give them their technology fix in a more productive manner than them deciding on their own to "help" you in your environment.

If the test is successful, you are ready to plan the change for the production environment and submit the change control request. If the test was not successful, however, it is time to return to the change identification phase (step 2) and attempt a different change, or make changes to the current change in an attempt to achieve success.

Plan the Change

This step is where you bring all the prep work you have performed together to build a change plan that will subsequently be submitted to your change control management team prior to rolling out on your network. Your overall goals during the change planning step are to ensure that the following points have been addressed:

- *Make sure that all resources required for the change have been identified and put in place.* Answer the question, who needs to perform the change? This will help ensure that everyone required for the change is aware of the change.

- *Ensure that a clear goal has been defined for the change.* Answer the question, why are we making this change? This will help ensure that everyone understands why the change is being made.

- *Ensure that the change adheres to all your organization's standards and procedures.* Answer the question, are we following the security policy and any relevant procedures that have been defined? If no procedure has been defined, this is also an excellent opportunity to write one. This helps ensure that any changes will conform to your current architecture or engineering design guidelines or constraints.

- *Create a backout procedure.* Answer the question, how do we undo the change if it doesn't work, or if it doesn't go well? This will help ensure that if things go wrong or don't work out the way you expected, you have a structured plan for reversing the changes.

- *Define any necessary escalation paths.* Answer the question, who do we contact if we run into any problems? This helps ensure that you know who to talk to in the event that you run into a problem. This could include internal or external technical support resources as well as any key line of business (LOB) representatives.

- *Define the affected users and any downtimes required for notification purposes.* You should have identified the users during the scope process. At this point, you should take that information and make sure you have a notification process for informing those users of the change. This will help ensure that your users are not caught by surprise by the change. If the impacted users are a critical LOB, you probably want signoff from the LOB on a change before implementing it.

- *Update all network documentation.* Make sure that all relevant network documentation and diagrams are updated and ready to be submitted at the time you make the change control request. This is so important because, as you know, if you don't make sure your documentation is updated at the time of the change, it will quickly be forgotten. In fact, any change control request that does not contain this information should be rejected. This helps ensure that your network documentation is always an accurate reflection of your network.

When you plan the change for your network, you also need to generate the change control request you will be submitting. Your change control request should contain the following information:

- Name and contact information, including phone number, e-mail address, pager, cell phone, and department of the person making the request.

- Date the request is being submitted.

- Target date for implementing the change.

- The change control number. This number should be generated by a central authority, such as the change control project manager or the change controller.

- Helpdesk tracking number (if applicable).

- Description and security bulletin information of the vulnerability the change addresses (if applicable).

- Type of change being requested. Software (OS, application, service pack), hardware (processor, memory, disk), network (router, switch, WAN, LAN) and security are good general types you can use.

- Description of the change. Be as informative as possible here, in particular, making sure that you explain the positive impact of making the change and the negative impact of not making the change.

- Risk level of the change, including any potential service interruptions and the number of users impacted by the change.

- System name, IP address, and location for all affected devices.

- User group contacts (if applicable and available).

- Whether the change has been tested.

- How the change was tested.

- Completed test plan, including the exact procedure for making the change. This should include any code or configuration examples as well as information regarding how the change will be deployed, whether a reboot is required, and whether the change can be uninstalled. Include planned timelines and milestones (for example, bring up and test T3 links by 1 A.M.).

- Backout plan. Include timelines for backout and what the cutoff time is, after which there is no backout. For example, if the change window is 1 A.M. to 4 A.M., and backout will take two hours, your cutoff time is 2 A.M. If it doesn't work by then, you must decide to back out or get signoff and plow forward.

- Whether this change will be migrated to other locations.

- Any prerequisites or assumptions required for the successful implementation of the change.

When you generate your change control request, you need to approach it from the perspective of "there is no such thing as too much information." Make sure you include any of the following components as a part of your change control request: current and updated topology and configuration, physical rack layouts, hardware and hardware modules, software versions, software configuration, cabling requirements, network topology maps, port assignments and addressing, device naming and labeling, name resolution updates and changes, circuit identifiers and assignments, network management update requirements, out-of-band management requirements, solution security information, and exact change procedures.

The Change Management Process

Whereas the change planning process was about preparing for a change, the change management process defines the approval and scheduling of the change to ensure that the correct level of user notification and impact occurs. During the change management process, you want to focus on undertaking steps directly related to the actual rollout and implementation of the change in your environment. There are six phases of the change management process:

1. Review the change control request.
2. Communicate the change.
3. Acquire resources.
4. Implement the change.
5. Verify results.
6. Review the change.

Review the Change Control Request

The first step of the change management process is to review the change control request to determine whether the change should be approved or rejected. During the review process, you should compare the change against documented standards and best practices to ensure that the change complies with your business and security policies. You also need verify that all related documentation that will need to be updated as a result of the change has been updated and submitted as a part of the change control request. If this does not happen, the change should be rejected due to lack of documentation. You should also verify with the affected LOB that the change is acceptable to them and that the change schedule does not conflict with any other changes or previously scheduled tasks. For example, if the change affects the accounting group and is scheduled for the last weekend of the month when accounting is frequently working overtime to complete end-of-month transactions, the change should be rejected or at the very least the schedule should be adjusted.

If the change is rejected, the process returns to the change identification phase. This does not necessarily mean that a new change needs to be identified. For example, if it is merely a scheduling conflict, the same change can be kept, with all the related testing and preparation, and the scheduled date and times are merely changed when the request is resubmitted.

Communicate the Change

Once a change has been agreed upon, the next phase is to communicate this change to all users in your organization. Communication is one of the most effective means to ensuring the success of your changes, and the success of IT in general. If you doubt me, sit down with some of your users and ask them what the one thing IT does that annoys them to no end, and most will tell you, "They don't tell us what is going on."

Because the nature of the changes you are making can be so complex, you should build a matrix to help define who will be affected by the change and any downtime that might result from the change. This is also important because different groups may require different degrees of information related to the change. For example, if you are upgrading your corporate DHCP servers, your users probably only need to know that they will not be able to connect to any network resources during the change. Your support staff probably needs to know exactly what change you are making that is causing the users to not be able to connect to any network resources during the change.

At a minimum, your communications process should address the following points:

- *Set realistic expectations.* An old mentor of mine used to tell me, "under-promise and over-deliver." You should set the appropriate expectations not only of what to expect during the change, but what to expect after the change.

- *Identify support resources.* Identify who is responsible for making the change and who should be contacted for any questions or problems related to the change.

- *Communicate operational requirements.* Make sure you define what applications and systems are being changed or affected by the change.

- *Inform your users.* Make sure every person who could be affected by the change is notified about the change. When in doubt, notify them anyway. Make sure you choose a notification mechanism that is not going to be affected by the change. For example, if you are going to be making a change on the e-mail server, you might not want to use it as your primary notification mechanism.

ONE STEP FURTHER

One method of communicating changes to your user community is to use some sort of simplified impact rating for informing users of changes. For example, you could designate that green changes mean if everything goes properly, they will never know anything has changed. Orange changes mean they will see something different, but it shouldn't impact the way they work. Red changes mean they will work differently due to the change. This lets users not get so many notices they simply start ignoring them. It also illustrates the changes (that is, red changes) the users need to pay attention to.

Acquire Resources

Now that the change has been communicated, it is time to acquire the resources necessary to implement the change. These include not only hardware and software resources, but people resources as well in the form of the implementation team. The implementation team is responsible for having the technical expertise and skills necessary to make the change. In many cases, this will be the people who submitted the change request in the first place. The implementation team should be involved in the planning phase to contribute in the design and development of all aspects of the change that is being requested. The implementation team is primarily responsible for ensuring the change then goes off without a hitch while adhering to any and all organizational standards, policies, and requirements. To assist in this, your implementation team needs to be able to answer the following questions:

- How and how thoroughly are they going to test the change?
- How will the test and change be rolled out?
- How long will testing and rollout last?
- How can the change be removed?
- What is the backout criteria?

The final requirement of the implementation team is to make sure that all results and deviations from the submitted change control request are documented and submitted to the change controller when the change has been completed.

HEADS UP!

The person or group that performs changes to the network should not be the person or group that approves those changes. There should be a separation of duties—to remove the possibility of someone wanting to do something they shouldn't and then approving themselves. In some environments, there could be legal regulatory requirements to keep these entities separate.

Implement the Change

After all the preparation work has been completed, the request has been submitted, the change control team has approved the change, the implementation team has been identified, and the users have been notified, it is time to actually make the change. During the change implementation phase, the implementation team should be monitoring and verifying that all the steps defined in the implementation plan are being followed. During this time, the implementation team should also be routinely and regularly testing the change to ensure that all systems that were supposed to be affected by the change have indeed been affected. Some of the testing and verification steps that can be performed to validate the change are as follows:

- **Connectivity testing through the use of extended pings and performance monitoring tools**   For example, you can run the command **ping –t <ipaddress>** and it will continue sending out ping requests until you disable it by pressing CTRL-C.

- **Traceroutes to verify network routing functions**   For example, you can run the **tracert** command on Windows or **traceroute** on Unix or Cisco IOS–based devices. You can also run **show ip route** on your routers to output the active routing information on your routers.

- **End-user desktop and application testing**   For example, if you changed a router that exists between the users and their e-mail server, have the users attempt to send and receive e-mail to make sure everything is still working.

- **File transfers or traffic-generation methods to verify network performance**   For example, you can run programs such as UDPFlood or Blast from Foundstone (www.foundstone.com) to generate traffic.

HEADS UP!

Many of these traffic-generation tools are detected as denial of service programs in modern virus-protection software. You may need to add exclusions on the systems that you want to run these programs on to prevent the virus-protection software from detecting and deleting the traffic-generation software.

- **Bit error rate testor (BERT) testing for new circuits**   You will likely need your provider to run this test, or you can use a BERT tester such as the Harris TS-350 Test set.

HEADS UP!

BERT testing interrupts network services, so make sure you schedule the time to run the BERT test to ensure that the network outage is acceptable.

- **Interface statistics monitoring**   For example, you can run the **show interface** command and look for values that are not what was expected:

```
local-rtr#show interface e0
Ethernet0 is up, line protocol is up
  Hardware is Lance, address is 0050.736b.fec3
(bia 0050.736b.fec3)
```

```
Internet address is 192.168.173.99/27
MTU 1500 bytes, BW 10000 Kbit, DLY 1000 usec,
   reliability 255/255, txload 1/255, rxload 1/255
Encapsulation ARPA, loopback not set
Keepalive set (10 sec)
ARP type: ARPA, ARP Timeout 04:00:00
Last input 00:00:00, output 00:00:00, output hang never
Last clearing of "show interface" counters never
Queueing strategy: fifo
Output queue 0/40, 0 drops; input queue 1/75, 0 drops
5 minute input rate 0 bits/sec, 0 packets/sec
5 minute output rate 0 bits/sec, 0 packets/sec
   22743 packets input, 3233863 bytes, 0 no buffer
   Received 21345 broadcasts, 0 runts, 0 giants, 0 throttles
   0 input errors, 0 CRC, 0 frame, 0 overrun, 0 ignored
   0 input packets with dribble condition detected
   30152 packets output, 2835588 bytes, 0 underruns(0/0/0)
   0 output errors, 0 collisions, 17 interface resets
   0 babbles, 0 late collision, 1 deferred
   0 lost carrier, 0 no carrier
   0 output buffer failures, 0 output buffers swapped out
```

- **Log file verification**   For example, if you implemented a change to block traffic on a certain port, you can check your system logs to see if the traffic is actually being blocked. This can be done by reviewing syslog or even the console logging capabilities through the use of the **terminal monitor** command on your IOS-based routers.

- **Viewing system configurations**   For example, you can compare your previous configuration to the new configuration to verify that the changes have been made.

- **Enterprise management station availability and verification**   For example, you can verify that the network device is still being monitored by your enterprise management station and is performing as expected.

Verify Results and Update All Network Documentation and Enterprise Management Applications

Once you have performed the change, the next phase is verifying that the results were successful and that all network documentation and enterprise management applications have been updated to reflect the change. You should also back up the configuration from all relevant devices to reflect any new configurations. Some specific items to verify are listed here:

- Visio or other physical and logical network diagrams.

- Network policies and procedures.

- Security policies.

- Name resolution (DNS and so on) works against the device loopback address and adheres to corporate naming standards.

- Name resolution (DNS and so on) works against the device interface addresses and adheres to corporate naming standards.

- Removal of any old DNS entries or enterprise management objects from the network.

- Standard enterprise management (SNMP, RMON, and so on) on the device.

- Fault management tools are updated according to the change.

- Inventory management tools are updated.

- All network management scripts, databases, and spreadsheets are updated.

- IP address number plans and assignments are updated.

- Out-of-band management access maps, phone numbers, and documentation are updated.

- VLAN numbering plans are updated.

- Software code and hardware device matrixes are updated.

- Protocol and packet filters and ACL documentation are updated.

- Routing protocol standards and configurations are updated.

- DHCP server reservations are updated.

In addition, you should keep all the change documentation in the event that you experience a problem that may be related to the change, or have to make a change in the future that the current documentation could assist in the planning and implementation of.

Review the Change

The final phase of the change management process is to perform an after-action report on the change. The goal of the after-action report is first to ensure that the change met the goals and objectives used for the justification for the change. If it does not, you need to ask and answer the question, why? You also need to review whether all tasks required by the "Update All Network Documentation and Enterprise Management Applications" phase were completed to the satisfaction of the change management team. Finally, you should review any and all problems encountered—especially if you had to roll back the change—to see if there is anything that could have been done to improve the process. This is helpful in developing a "lessons learned" document that will help make sure future changes go more smoothly.

How to Ensure a Successful Change Control Process

As you have read through this chapter, you might find yourself thinking, "OK, this sounds great in the perfect world where I am in control of everything, but in the real world, this process seems like it is overbearing." In fact, a common response to implementing proper change control is often, "Whoa, that seems like way too much." The good news is that it doesn't have to be that way. If you want to be successful in implementing a change control process in your organization, you need to consider the following:

- You absolutely must have upper management support. If you do not have it, you will fail.
- Your change control process must be flexible.
- Change control is a learned habit.

Gain Management Support

A reality of all businesses is that everyone has their territory. The network guys are in charge of the routers, the server guys are in charge of the servers, the desktop guys are in charge of the client PCs, and so on. Each group takes ownership of their territory. To the network guys, these are their routers. It doesn't matter that they are really the company's routers; the network guys don't usually see it that way. This creates a built-in problem when we talk about change control because change control has the potential to work across multiple groups' territories, acting in many ways as a central control. The psychological issue then becomes having an outside group that has the appearance and, in some cases, the effect of telling other people what to do with what they perceive as their resources. This is a recipe for disaster that has to be addressed with two things.

First, you have to have tact in dealing with these groups. They don't want to feel like they are giving up control, so your job is to convince them that they are not doing that. I had a mentor who used to call it "finding your champion." You should identify individuals in all the groups you are going to have to work with who want to work with you. Then, instead of you fighting the battles to get things done, you can empower that person to do it. Why? Because they are already a part of the group. They can say the same thing you would and have it be accepted much more readily than if you were to say it. They become your champions, fighting the battles that you can't win.

Second, you have to have strong upper management support. When push comes to shove and when tact and diplomacy have failed, you must have upper management support. They can step up to the plate and say, "We are doing it this way because change control said so." You want to use this support as little as possible, though, because it is going to leave a bitter taste in some folk's mouths. Choose your battles wisely, and, most important, you should ask yourself, "Can I make a compromise here instead of having to force the change?" If you can, then compromise.

Make Your Change Control Process Flexible

Another step in making your change control process successful is to implement a flexible change control process. The strongest process is one that is flexible when it needs to be, yet rigid when required. In addition to being open to compromise where possible, you have to understand that not all changes are the same, and therefore not all changes require the same change control flow. There are generally three types of changes you will need to make on your network:

- Immediate, critical, or high-risk changes
- Urgent, important, or medium-risk changes
- Nonurgent, routine, or low-risk changes

The type of change should dictate how you engage the change control process. Your change control process should define a regular and routine time to meet and discuss the changes that need to be made—perhaps every week or every two weeks. In addition, you should have a regularly scheduled day for most changes to occur. For example, you could say that all changes must occur on Thursdays. The benefit of this is that it allows you to make changes part of your regular activities so that they become less of an intrusion and more of a normal occurrence in your environment. It also allows your various groups to get into a routine for how they approach making changes so that they include the change control process as part of their planning, and not as an afterthought.

However, not all changes can wait for a regularly scheduled meeting. This is why you must also build a process that can account for immediate or urgent changes in addition to your nonurgent and routine changes. You need to ensure that your change control process has a mechanism defined for meeting and planning changes in a much quicker fashion than your routine and regularly scheduled process. This is commonly referred to as *emergency change management*.

Emergency change management does not abandon the concept of change control; it merely expedites it. For example, let's say a new virus is released in the wild that you are going to be highly susceptible to. You do not have time to wait for your regularly scheduled meeting and then until the next Thursday to roll out new virus signatures. You need to make a change now. To this end, you must identify the type of situations that warrant an emergency change and who is authorized to make those changes. This creates a limited change control process flow, as illustrated in Figure 14-2. Many of these steps are simply lightweight counterparts to the full change control process we previously defined.

Change Control Is a Learned Habit

Remember that change control is a learned habit. You are going to have to educate your users—but more important, your IT staff—of the requirements and responsibilities of change control. Do not assume just because you have technical gods on your staff that they understand what is necessary for change control. Set their expectations and responsibilities so that they know what is expected and what they need to do to meet those expectations. Finally, show them the value in adhering to change control. The knee-jerk reaction is going to be, "This is just making my job more difficult." You need to make sure it's understood that although it may be more difficult in planning and implementing the actual changes, managing the changes appropriately will make their day-to-day jobs as well as troubleshooting much easier.

Implementing a Patch and Update Policy

As we have established, new threats and exploits are constantly coming out that impact your network infrastructure. Some reports have stated that the number of new exploits has increased 90 percent a year, every year since 1992. No matter how much we wish that vendors would release bug-free code, it is never going to happen. We have to accept that we will need to patch and upgrade our systems regardless of which vendor or product we are using, and each of these patches or updates represents a change we will need to make in our organization.

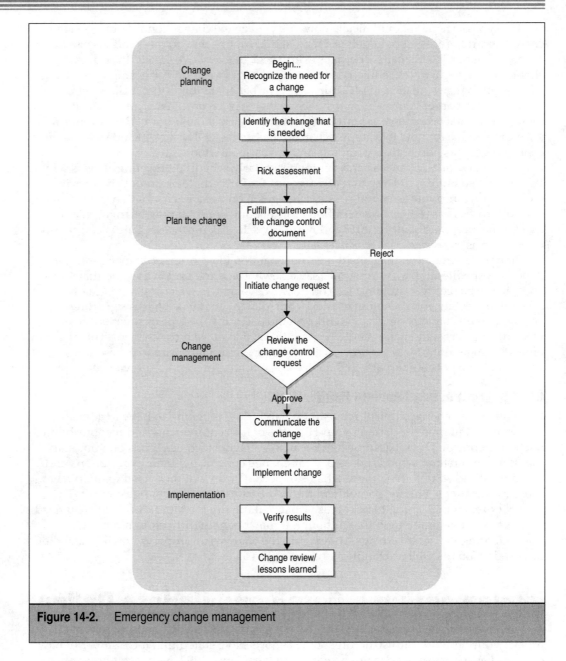

Figure 14-2. Emergency change management

A lot of folks like to focus on Microsoft as being the problem with buggy code and patches, and although no doubt Microsoft has a cross to bear here, anyone who seriously pitches Linux or anything else as a better solution solely due to patches or security is approaching the subject with entirely too much naivety. The same can be said with your network infrastructure devices. Do not think that by using a certain vendor you will be protected from having to routinely patch and upgrade your systems. As times change and other vendors and new products displace the market share of the leading vendors and products, those new products will become more and more commonly exploited. You have to accept and be prepared to apply patches and updates for all software and hardware you receive from all your vendors.

Now I have to be careful here, because I am not saying to only buy Microsoft or only buy Cisco. I'm also not saying not to buy Microsoft or not to buy Cisco. Instead, I am saying that you must be aware of all the conditions that lend themselves to a particular product having an exploit before you decide whether to use that product. If all you are doing is saying, "Well, they seem to have fewer exploits than product X," you probably are not looking at enough information. Information is the key here, and you have to cut through the FUD (fear, uncertainty, and doubt) and religion (see the upcoming sidebar) to make an intelligent and informed decision that weighs not only how buggy a product might be, but also the functionality that product contains, the needs it addresses, the level of support the product has (including responsiveness to bug reports), the interoperability with your existing systems, and the usability of the given product or solution. Simply put, look at the totality of the circumstances before you make a decision on how to proceed.

The Religious Layer of the OSI Model

I often refer to the top three layers of the OSI model as being the political, religious, and monetary layers, because those are the three layers that dictate most decisions an organization makes. The debate over bugs and patches is largely a religious debate. Simply put, you have advocates on all sides who believe with an almost religious fervor in a particular solution, and there is often nothing you can say or do that can change their thinking. They bleed IBM blue, Novell red, or Microsoft rainbow, and that is just the way it is. Fortunately, we can all choose to remain as agnostic as possible and judge a particular solution on its technical merits. If you do this, you will often find that your organization's security policy and posture will be greatly enhanced by your openness to selecting best-of-breed solutions that meet your needs.

When to Use a Workaround, Hotfix, Patch, or an Upgrade

Vendors employ four major methods to deal with a particular bug, exploit, or issue. These are to use a workaround, employ a hotfix, release a patch, or release an upgrade. Each of these terms carries a distinct meaning that you need to be aware of so that you can decide which solution is appropriate for your circumstances.

A workaround is something the vendor will recommend to address a problem without the vendor needing to release any new code to the public. Workarounds generally require you to make configuration changes to the product so as to protect against a given exploit. One of the major drawbacks of many workarounds is that often the workaround will interfere with needed functionality. An example of this might be a vendor stating that in order to protect yourself from an exploit in their web server, you should disable the web server. Although this may be a very effective workaround, if you require the use of the web server for your remote management functionality, the workaround is probably no longer valid for your environment.

Hotfixes and patches are often treated as the same thing, though there is (or should be) a subtle difference between the two. Hotfixes are generally made available to vendor technical support without going through exhaustive or detailed quality assurance testing. Consequently, many companies require that customers explicitly request a hotfix so that they can track who has this relatively untested and possibly unstable code. You should avoid hotfixes of this nature unless you are susceptible to the problem the hotfix addresses, and even then I would only apply it to my high-risk resources.

Patches, on the other hand, generally go through a more detailed and exhaustive quality assurance testing process before they are made available to the general public. The benefit of this is that there is a much smaller chance of a patch causing a problem on your systems compared to a hotfix. The drawback, however, is that patches often take more time to be made available to customers, which can leave your systems vulnerable to an exploit for a longer period of time compared to a hotfix or workaround. Even with this drawback, it is a best practice to not widely deploy an update to your systems unless that update is at least of patch quality.

Whereas workarounds, hotfixes, and patches generally address a specific issue, upgrades are designed to address multiple issues. In fact, upgrades are often a combination of multiple hotfixes and patches, potentially with some new functionality included as well. The big benefit of an upgrade is that it has often undergone significant quality assurance testing to ensure as best as can be done that the upgrade will not adversely affect an environment. The drawback of upgrades is twofold. On one hand, it generally takes months for upgrades to be released due to the development and testing that must be performed. On the other hand, upgrades are often not free like many hotfixes and patches are.

Staying Informed of Workarounds, Hotfixes, Patches, and Upgrades

One of the most difficult processes of dealing with patches and upgrades is knowing when patches and upgrades are available. If anyone is unsure of this fact, consider that Microsoft had a hotfix for Code Red almost two months before Code Red was released in the wild. Code Red was 100-percent preventable, yet so many companies and users had not applied a fix that was two months old that Code Red was still able to devastate numerous networks and the Internet in general. Using many of the same resources I mentioned in Chapter 13 is the best method for staying aware of the patches and upgrades your vendor has:

- **BugTraq**   BugTraq is a mailing list maintained by SecurityFocus (http://www.securityfocus.com/archive/1) that tracks bugs and vulnerabilities for virtually every product and vendor on the planet. Subscribe to this mailing list.

- **NTBugTraq**   Modeled after BugTraq, NTBugTraq, according to its website (http://www.ntbugtraq.com/) "is a mailing list for the discussion of security exploits and security bugs in Windows NT, Windows 2000, and Windows XP plus related applications." Subscribe to this mailing list.

- **Full Disclosure**   Run by Netsys, Full Disclosure is a mailing list that grew because of the perception that other mailing lists delay information until the vendors have had a chance to build a response, thus delaying the ability for you and me to know about potential threats. Although there is much bluster and hot air behind this, there is a grain of truth to it. You can subscribe to this mailing list at http://lists.netsys.com/mailman/listinfo/full-disclosure.

- **Vendor mailing lists**   Many of your vendors have mailing lists or notification processes to inform their customers of new security-related issues.

- **The CERT Coordination Center**   Located at http://www.cert.org, the CERT/CC serves as a central information reporting center and clearinghouse of security-related information. You should make it a habit to check this website a couple of times a day for new events and information.

- **Virus software vendor websites**   Many virus scan vendors maintain websites with up-to-date information regarding new viruses and worms. Because so many of these programs can affect your network infrastructure, you should make it a point to check your favorite virus software vendor's website a few times a day. Personally, I check with Symantec at http://www.sarc.com/ or Network Associates at http://www.nai.com/us/security/vil.htm.

If you are not able to stay on top of when vendors release a hotfix, patch, or upgrade, you can almost pack up the shop and call it a day because your regular routine is going to consist largely of dealing with the fallout related to an exploit or frantically implementing a patch when you could have worked it into the regular change management schedule instead and thus preventing the exploit from affecting you in the first place. Make sure you stay informed of patches and updates at all costs.

Purchasing Maintenance and Support Agreements

An unfortunate reality with many corporate hardware and software vendors is the use of paid maintenance and support agreements to allow their users to download hotfixes, patches, and upgrades. Although in a perfect world all vendors would make available for free all patches and fixes for the software and hardware you have purchased, many vendors do not do this. The level of support without paying for a maintenance or support agreement differs from vendor to vendor, but in many cases upgrades are only provided to customers who either have purchased a maintenance and support agreement or buy the upgrade outright. Patches and hotfixes are generally made available for free in many, but not all, cases. The more high profile a particular threat is, the greater the likelihood that the hotfix, patch, and sometimes even the upgrade is made available for free.

Another issue that maintenance and support agreements address, in addition to providing access to software updates, is the ability to contact the vendor regarding potential security or technical support issues. Without a valid maintenance and support agreement, many vendors require you to pay for each support call you place. In some cases, they will refund the call if you are the first person to report a valid vulnerability, but that is not always the case. Although maintenance and support agreements on the surface may seem to be just another method vendors use to make more money off of you, when you consider the access to vendor technical support and "free" software updates, it is probably a good investment to make for your critical business resources at the very least.

Defining a Change Control Patch Policy

It is paramount that you define a policy and procedure that will ensure the application of updates in a rapid fashion, while leaving the network insulated from untested updates as much as possible. Your patch update policy should be defined in accordance with your change control policy, and the process for applying a patch should follow your change control process flow. They should complement each other, with your patch policy addressing issues that are unique to addressing patches and your change control policy dictating the process for applying the patch in your environment. To do so, follow these steps:

1. Define a timely method for identifying and applying patches and updates. If you are waiting months between when updates are released and when you apply them, you are inviting problems. Shortening the time period between availability of a patch and the time you implement it is even more critical when updates are high risk. Remember, in many cases, the patch that corrected the vulnerability exploited by a major worm was available many months before the worm was released. For example, the vulnerability that Code Red exploited was patched two months before Code Red was released. Apply updates in a timely fashion.

HEADS UP!

It is just a matter of time before we have a zero-day exploit (in other words, an exploit that occurs within a day of a particular vulnerability being discovered). Because you will likely not be able to patch your systems fast enough to address a zero-day exploit, you have to build a security policy on your network that follows the security principles and practices in this book. For example, if a zero-day exploit comes out that uses port 1433 to spread, but you are blocking all unnecessary ports (including 1433) at your firewall, you can reduce the likelihood that the exploit can infiltrate your network.

2. Specify how to determine which workarounds, hotfixes, patches, and upgrades are relevant to your environment. You are not going to be susceptible to every exploit that is out there, so you do not want to spend time worrying about issues that aren't relevant to your environment. For example, if a Microsoft Outlook exploit is made public but you don't use Microsoft Outlook in your environment, you don't need to worry about patching your systems.

3. Require explicit identification of the systems that need to be upgraded. This serves a couple of purposes. First, it allows you to identify whether any critical resources are susceptible to a given exploit. Second, it allows you to identify the scale of the task that it will take to update your systems. If you only have five systems that the update is applicable to, applying the update will probably be a relatively easy process. However, if you have identified that all 20,000 desktops in your environment are susceptible, the scale of the task just got much more difficult because you will probably need to rely on scripting or deployment software to apply the update.

4. Detail the implementation process. Once you have identified the relevant upgrades and the systems affected, you should proceed through the change control process to begin the planning and implementation of the patch or update. Depending on the severity of the issue with the patch or update, you might follow your standard change control process or you might need to invoke your emergency change control process. Regardless of which process you follow, you should always adhere to your change control process.

Writing Patch and Update Procedures

The most important aspect of patching and upgrading your systems is to define the patch and upgrade process and procedures. For the vast majority of your network infrastructure products, you may need to make three types of changes as part of your patch and update process:

- The first type of change is to upgrade the actual system image. For example, Cisco may release a new version of the IOS that addresses the relevant security issues or provides new features that you require. In turn, this requires you to upgrade your existing IOS version to a new version. This type of change is commonly applied to the actual network infrastructure hardware, such as routers, switches, hardware-based firewalls, and intrusion detection/ prevention systems.

- The second type of change is to upgrade or change the configuration of the network device. During a configuration change, the actual system image is not going to be touched in any fashion, but rather you will simply reconfigure the device to address the security issue you are concerned about. This type of change can be applied to all your network infrastructure devices because they all support some kind of configuration mechanism.

- The third type of change involves upgrading an application that is running as part of your network infrastructure. For example, your content-filtering system typically is installed as an application on an existing network operating system such as Microsoft Windows or Linux. You may need to install a vendor-supplied patch to upgrade or replace the application to address the security issue you are concerned about.

Although each method of change has unique characteristics, there are some common elements that we should consider to allow us to safely and effectively apply these patches and upgrades in our environment. They are listed here:

- *Plan the change.* You have to plan the change in order to identify any potential problems before you decide to deploy the change. Proper planning will ensure the success of your change.

- *Make backup images before and after a change.* You should have a central TFTP server to send images and configuration files to and from. When you make backups, make them of the running and startup configuration both before and after the changes. In addition, back up any old OS images prior to upgrading by whatever means that device has. Many times, the running configuration and startup configuration don't match, which means when the device gets rebooted, something is broken or undone because someone made changes to the running configuration and didn't save them.

- *Test the upgrade.* You have to test the change as much as possible. You do not want to deploy a change to your environment that has not been tested. Where possible, you should test the change in a controlled environment, such as a lab. If you lack those resources, however, you should at least test the change against noncritical production resources, where the negative impact of the change would be minimal, before you deploy it widely in your environment.

- *Adhere to your change control process.* Above all else, you must adhere to your defined change control process. It exists for a reason, and this is that reason. By strictly adhering to your change control process, you gain a methodical and structured approach to the change, which will ultimately cause the change implementation to occur much smoother.

Changing the System Image

One of the most delicate changes you can make in your environment is changing the system image of a device. This is due in large part to the fact that if you incorrectly or improperly change the system image, you could be looking at a very laborious and time-consuming remedy that may even require travel to a remote location. At the same time, however, if you have planned and tested your system image change, the upgrade process can be very simple and straightforward.

Because the system image typically is stored in flash (non-volatile memory), you can change the system image while the device is still running, without impacting the

Planning Your Patch Response

I worked at a company that did not plan before they reacted to the Nachia/Blaster worms. When they realized that it was using port 135 to spread, they blocked port 135 at all their internal and external routers within their infrastructure. On the surface, this sounded like a good way to isolate the worm on subnets; however, they did not consider the fact that virtually all Microsoft communications require the ability to communicate on this port; therefore, because their Exchange server was on a dedicated segment away from the user segments, all e-mail, in addition to file and print and many database functions, ceased working. They had effectively implemented a denial of service against their users in an attempt to control the spread of the worms. Had they done even the most basic of planning and testing before distributing this change in their environment, they would not have spent hours trying to undo a change in the middle of a security incident, and they would have been able to spend more time focusing on more effective methods of controlling the worm.

currently running system image. You can then reboot the device at your leisure, and upon reboot the device will read and load the new system image into RAM and begin functioning based on the new system image.

So how exactly can we change the system image? A few methods are available that work for most of the network hardware that is out there:

- *Use vendor-supplied tools to change the system image.* Tools include Cisco's CiscoWorks and Nortel Networks Optivity network management software.

- *Manually change the system image.* You can manually connect to and run the commands to perform the change.

- *Automate the manual process for changing the system image.* You can use Perl, VBScript, or another scripting language as well as SNMP to make the changes.

HEADS UP!

Many times people make changes to the running configuration and never save those changes to their startup configuration, which causes the device to lose whatever changes had been made when the device is rebooted. This happened at a location where I used to work. They had changed their routing to use an Internet gateway at a new location, but they didn't save that change in their core router. They had to reboot the router due to a hardware problem, and when they did, suddenly no one could get to the Internet anymore. This was due to the fact that the router was trying to send Internet-bound traffic to the old gateway, which was trying to send it right back to the core router.

Because the vendor-supplied tools provide an abundance of documentation regarding how to use them to make changes in your environment, I am going to focus on the second and third methods.

Manually Changing the System Image

Manually making changes to the system image is an effective, albeit time-consuming, method of updating the system image on your network devices. Virtually all vendors use the same method of upgrading their systems through the use of Trivial File Transfer Protocol (TFTP). The obvious drawback to TFTP is the lack of any encryption or authentication mechanism, and although some vendors can allow you to define the TFTP server that the device is permitted to use to obtain software and updates from, this is still a highly suspect security practice because of the underlying lack of encryption or authentication.

The actual implementation process tends to be rather straightforward. Most vendors use a command-line interface (CLI) that is very similar to the Cisco IOS CLI, or they use a menu-driven CLI. For a menu-driven CLI, the upgrade process is as simple as navigating to the appropriate menu and entering the IP address of the TFTP server and the full path and name of the file to retrieve. The file is then transferred and will typically overwrite the previous system image. The final step is to simply reboot the device, allowing the device to read and process the new system image.

NOTE   Although this procedure focuses on the actual commands and uses command examples from a Cisco device running IOS, it is largely the same for all IOS-based CLIs, such as those by Extreme Networks, Nortel Networks, Dell, and Foundry Networks.

From the IOS CLI, the process is very similar, although you often have additional options to consider. The most noteworthy difference is the ability to decide whether you are going to overwrite the existing system image or install the new system image in addition to the existing system image. The biggest benefit of this choice is that if you decide not to overwrite the previous system image, you can quickly and easily roll back to the previous system image in the event of a problem. You can do this by specifying the boot file to use in the device configuration and setting the configuration register appropriately:

```
local-rtr#configure terminal
Enter configuration commands, one per line.  End with CNTL/Z.
local-rtr(config)#boot system flash c2500-jk8os-l.122-1d.bin
local-rtr(config)#config-register 0x010F
local-rtr(config)#exit
local-rtr#copy running-config startup-config
```

In this case, I have specified to boot using the file c2500-jk8os-l.122-1d.bin. If I wanted to boot using the file c2500-jk8os-l.113-1.bin, I would simply replace that value in the configuration, and my device would roll back to booting on the previous system image.

The decision to overwrite your previous system image is generally going to be defined by whether you have enough storage for both system images in flash. If you do, I recommend that you keep the most recent running system image and the new system image at a minimum for backup purposes. If you don't have enough storage for both, it is OK to overwrite the existing system image if you are sure the new system image will work. Although you can usually recover from an incorrectly installed system image, the process is laborious and may require physical access to the device in order to be performed.

The first step of manually upgrading your system image is to make sure the system image file exists on your TFTP server, as shown here:

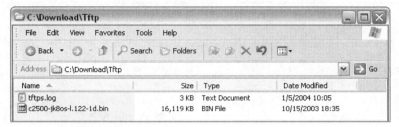

The next step is to ensure that your TFTP server is running and operational. If you are using a TFTP server application, make sure that the application is running and that the TFTP server is using the same directory your system image file exists in, as shown here:

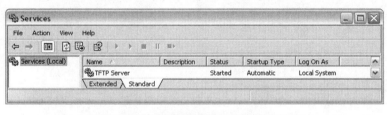

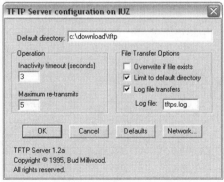

At this point, it is time to connect to the network device and run the commands that will upgrade the system image. You should first verify that you can connect to the TFTP server by running a ping from the network device. The next step is to simply copy the system image file to the flash on the target device. When doing that, you can choose whether to erase the contents of flash (to not erase the contents of flash, type **n** when prompted). The file will be copied to the device, and upon completion and checksum verification, you can simply reboot the device for the new system image to be loaded.

HEADS UP!

If you select to erase the contents of flash, you will erase *all* the contents of flash. Make sure you do not have any other files in flash that you need to save. You can check this by running the command **show flash** at the privileged mode to view the contents of flash.

Here's an example of upgrading the system image while erasing the contents of flash:

```
Local-rtr#copy tftp://192.168.1.254/c1721-y-mz.122-1.bin flash
Destination filename [c1721-y-mz.122-1.bin]? <press enter>
Accessing tftp://192.168.1.254/c1721-y-mz.122-1.bin...
Erase flash: before copying? [confirm] <press enter>
Erasing the flash filesystem will remove all files! Continue? [confirm]
<press enter>
Erasing device...
eeeeeeeeeeeeeeeeeeeeeeeeeeeeeeeeeeeeeeeeeeeeeeeeeeeeeeeeeeeeeeee ...erased
Erase of flash: complete
Loading c1721-y-mz.122-1.bin from 192.168.1.254 (via Serial0):
!!!!!!!!!!!!!!!!!!!!!!!!!!!!!!!!!!!!!!!!!!!!!!!!!!!!!!!!!!!!!!!!!!!!!!!
...
!!!!!!!!!!!!!!!!!!!!!!!!!!!!!!!!!!!!!!!!!!!!!!!!!!!!!!!!!!!!!!!!!!!!!!!
[OK - 3491304/6981632 bytes]
Verifying checksum...  OK (0xB352)
3491304 bytes copied in 430.392 secs (8119 bytes/sec)
```

Here's an example of upgrading the system image without erasing the contents of flash:

```
Local-rtr#copy tftp://192.168.1.254/c1700-y-mz.122-1.bin flash:c1700-y-
mz.122-1.bin
Destination filename [c1700-y-mz.122-1.bin]? <press enter>
Accessing tftp://192.168.1.254/c1700-y-mz.122-1.bin...
Erase flash: before copying? [confirm]n
Loading c1700-y-mz.122-1.bin from 192.168.1.254 (via Serial0):
!!!!!!!!!!!!!!!!!!!!!!!!!!!!!!!!!!!!!!!!!!!!!!!!!!!!!!!!!!!!!!!!!!!!!!!!!
...
!!!!!!!!!!!!!!!!!!!!!!!!!!!!!!!!!!!!!!!!!!!!!!!!!!!!!!!!!!!!!!!!!!!!!!!!!
[OK - 3491304/6981632 bytes]
Verifying checksum...  OK (0xB352)
3491304 bytes copied in 439.576 secs (7952 bytes/sec)
```

Automate Changing the System Image

The obvious drawback to manually changing the system image is the time it takes to manually connect, log into, and run the commands required to update the system image. The alternative is to automate the change. There are two predominant methods for automating the upgrade procedures of the system image on your network infrastructure devices, depending on what your vendor supports:

- Use SNMP and scripting to perform the upgrade. (Not all vendors support using SNMP for performing this change.)

- Use a management client, such as Telnet or SSH, that supports scripting to automate the manual commands. (Not all management clients support scripting.)

If your network device supports using SNMP to upgrade the system image, you can script the necessary SNMP commands that will enable this functionality. Foundry Networks supports doing this on both their management processors and their switching processors. The steps to using SNMP to upgrade the system image are as follows:

1. Configure the device with a read-write community string. You can run the command **snmp-server community <string> rw** to configure a read-write string.

2. Disable the password checking for SNMP set requests. This is a proprietary measure that must be done only if you are using a third-party (non-Foundry) SNMP management application. The command to run is **no snmp-server pw-check**.

HEADS UP!

Disabling the password-checking option will reduce a proprietary security measure that Foundry uses to protect against unauthorized SNMP set requests. When you attempt to issue an **snmpset** request to a Foundry device, it expects you to provide the privileged password in the SNMP request. If you use a Foundry SNMP tool, you can enter the password and you don't need to disable the password checking functionality. However, if you use a third-party SNMP tool that does not support passing this data, you have to disable this functionality. If you do disable this functionality, I strongly recommend that you reenable it after you have performed the required functions.

---

3. For your management process, run the following command:

```
snmpset -c <rw-community-string> <device-ip-address>
1.3.6.1.4.1.1991.1.1.2.1.5.0 ipaddress <tftp-ip-address>
1.3.6.1.4.1.1991.1.1.2.1.6.0 octetstringascii <image-file-name>
1.3.6.1.4.1.1991.1.1.2.1.7.0 integer <command-integer>
```

The supported command integers are the following:

20	Download the flash code into the device's primary flash area.
22	Download the flash code into the device's secondary flash area.

For your switching processors on a chassis device, run the following command:

```
snmpset -c <rw-community-string> <device-ip-address>
1.3.6.1.4.1.1991.1.1.2.1.5.0 ipaddress <tftp-ip-address>
1.3.6.1.4.1.1991.1.1.2.1.6.0 octetstringascii <image-file-name>
1.3.6.1.4.1.1991.1.1.2.1.56.0 integer <module-type>
1.3.6.1.4.1.1991.1.1.2.1.57.0 <slot-number> 1.3.6.1.4.1.1991.1.1.2.1.7.0 →
integer <command-integer>
```

<module-type> is one of the following values:

2	VM1 module
3	OC-3, OC-12, and OC-48 non–Network Processor Architecture (NPA) POS modules
4	OC-48 NPA POS modules
5	ATM module

<slot-number> is the slot that contains the module you are upgrading. To upgrade all slots, you can enter **0** (zero).

For <command-integer>, enter one of the following values:

24	Download the flash code into the device's primary flash area.
25	Download the flash code into the device's secondary flash area.

You could then write a script that runs the appropriate **snmpset** commands for each device in your network that you want to change.

If your device does not support using SNMP to automate upgrading the system image, you can attempt to script the manual commands, provided you have a Telnet or SSH application that supports it. For this purpose, I recommend SecureCRT by VanDyke Technologies (http://www.vandyke.com). SecureCRT supports using a variant of VBScript as their scripting language. The steps to script an upgrade of the system image on a Cisco IOS–based router are as follows:

1. Create a new session in SecureCRT for each device you will be connecting to. The script will use these session names to define which devices to connect to. Do not use spaces in the folder or session name. For example, in the following screen I have created a folder named "Routers" and created seven sessions to connect to router1 through router7.

2. Write a script that performs the following functions:

   ■ Provides the required login information. You can either script the login as part of your session creation, as shown next, or you can have the script prompt for the appropriate login information. For simplicity, I placed the login information in the session creation.

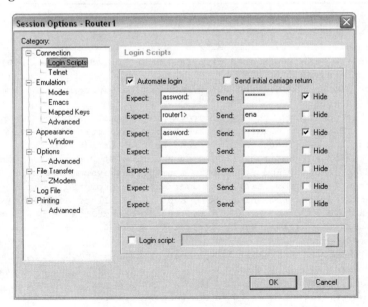

   ■ Defines the TFTP server that the system image is located on.
   ■ Defines the system image source filename.

- Defines an array containing all the devices you want to connect to. In the example, I have defined an array of seven values to connect to router1 through router7.
- Defines a subroutine that contains the input and output you will pass through SecureCRT to the device.
- Provides a logging mechanism so that you can verify the success of all functions.
- Provides error-handling capabilities as required.

In the following sample script, I have created seven sessions for seven different routers in SecureCRT. I am using the SecureCRT session login scripts to log into the routers. The script will connect to a TFTP server located at 192.168.1.45 and copy a new system image file named c1700-y-mz.122-1.bin. If the copy result is successful, it will simply be logged into a file and will proceed to the next router in the array until all routers have completed. If there is an error with the TFTP server or system image name, it will prompt the user to find out whether they want to enter a new TFTP server name or IP address and system image name. If the user selects no, the script logs the error and exits. If the user selects yes, the script will attempt to reconnect using the new information.

NOTE Due to page width limitations, some lines in this code will be wrapped.

```
#$language = "VBScript"
#$interface = "1.0"
'========================================================================
' VBScript Source File -- Created with SAPIEN Technologies PrimalSCRIPT(TM)
' NAME: IOS_update.vbs
' AUTHOR: Wes Noonan , WJN Consulting, LLC. wnoonan@wjnconsulting.com
' DATE   : 01/14/2004
' COMMENT: This script is used by SecureCRT to automate a process. While it
' is based on VBScript, it is customized to run in SecureCRT as evidenced
' by the first 2 lines above. See www.vandyke.com for more info.
' This script will automatically login to a series of Cisco switches/routers
' as defined in an array and attempt to upgrade the system image file from a
' TFTP server. If the copy fails, the user will be prompted whether to
' continue updating the remaining systems or exit. All transactions will be
' logged to a file so that the admin can verify the status of the copy.
'========================================================================
' dim variables
' change the number to represent the number of values in the array below
dim SwitchArray(4)
dim SessionName, DisconnectString, Switch, Start, Append, loginpass
dim enablepass, tftpservername, sourcefilename, result, errorresult
dim exitresult, logfile, errorornot, screenrow, datetime
' Define constants
Const ICON_STOP = 16              ' display the ERROR/STOP icon.
Const ICON_QUESTION = 32          ' display the '?' icon
Const ICON_WARN = 48              ' display a '!' icon.
Const ICON_INFO= 64               ' displays "info" icon.
```

```
Const BUTTON_OK = 0                    ' OK button only
Const BUTTON_CANCEL = 1                ' OK and Cancel buttons
Const BUTTON_ABORTRETRYIGNORE = 2      ' Abort, Retry, and Ignore buttons
Const BUTTON_YESNOCANCEL = 3           ' Yes, No, and Cancel buttons
Const BUTTON_YESNO = 4                 ' Yes and No buttons
Const BUTTON_RETRYCANCEL = 5           ' Retry and Cancel buttons
Const DEFBUTTON1 = 0         ' First button is default
Const DEFBUTTON2 = 256       ' Second button is default
Const DEFBUTTON3 = 512       ' Third button is default
' Possible MessageBox() return values
Const IDOK = 1                 ' OK button clicked
Const IDCANCEL = 2             ' Cancel button clicked
Const IDABORT = 3              ' Abort button clicked
Const IDRETRY = 4              ' Retry button clicked
Const IDIGNORE = 5             ' Ignore button clicked
Const IDYES = 6                ' Yes button clicked
Const IDNO = 7                 ' No button clicked
' set variables to allow logging. Change as needed.
Start = true
Append = true
Logfile = "C:\Test.log"
' This variable sets the date/time variable to ensure that the config file
will be unique
Datetime = Month(Date) & Day(date) & Year(Date) & "-" & Hour(time) &
Minute(time) & Second(time)
' prompt for variables to be used in the script
' remove the comment on the next 4 lines if you want to be prompted for the
information
' and comment the last two lines out. Otherwise leave as is for logging on
using session
' login scripts and statically defined tftp server and source system image
names
'loginpass = crt.Dialog.Prompt("Enter the login password:", "Login
Password", "", True)
'loginpass = ""
'enablepass = crt.Dialog.Prompt("Enter the enable password:", "Enable
Password", "", True)
'enablepass = ""
'tftpservername = crt.Dialog.Prompt("Enter the name or IP address of the
TFTP server:", "TFTP Server", "Enter the TFTP Server Name or IP Address")
'sourcefileame = crt.Dialog.Prompt("Enter the name of the system image
source file:", "Source File Name", "Enter the name of the system image
source file")
tftpservername = "192.168.1.45"
sourcefilename = "c1700-y-mz.122-1.bin"
' define the array of devices to configure.
' These should be the hostnames of the devices you want to update
' you will need to change the array values as you add/remove devices
SwitchArray(1) = "Routers\Router1"
SwitchArray(2) = "Routers\Router2"
SwitchArray(3) = "Routers\Router3"
```

```
SwitchArray(4) = "Routers\Router4"
' change the numbers to reflect the min/max value of the array defined above
For Switch = 1 to 4
     SessionName = SwitchArray(Switch)
     for each object in SwitchArray
          If SessionName <> "" then
               ' turn on synchronous mode so we don't miss any data
               crt.Screen.Synchronous = True
               ' connect using SecureCRT session names
               crt.session.Connect("/s " & SessionName)
               ' log the results to review for success
               crt.Session.LogFileName = LogFile
               crt.Session.Log Start, Append
               ' run login subroutine do not use if you are using session
login scripts
               'login
               ' Send a command to display the date/time for the log
               crt.Screen.WaitForString "#"
               crt.Screen.Send "show clock" & vbCr
               ' run tftpconnect subroutine
               tftpconnect
               ' Check to see if there was an error updating. If so, give
the option to exit the script
               crt.Screen.WaitForString "#"
               screenrow = crt.screen.CurrentRow - 1
               errorornot = crt.Screen.Get(screenrow, 1, screenrow, 6 )
               If errorornot = "%Error" Then
                    errorresult = crt.Dialog.MessageBox("There was an
error updating the system image for: " & VbCr & VbCr & SessionName & VbCr &
VbCr & "Check the log at " & LogFile & " for the error output." & VbCr &
VbCr & "Select OK to continue, CANCEL to end the script.", "Error Backing Up
Configuration!!", ICON_WARN or BUTTON_CANCEL )
                         If errorresult = IDCANCEL then
                              exitresult = "1"
                              ExitDialog
                         End if
               End If
               ' Wait for copy to end then disconnect from device
               crt.session.Disconnect
               ' Set the SessionName variable to nothing to cause the
               ' script to run through each session in the array
               SessionName = ""
               ' turn off synchronous mode to restore normal input
processing
               crt.Screen.Synchronous = False
          end if
     next
next
ExitDialog
' subroutines used in script are listed below
' This subroutine contains the logon functions
```

```
Sub login
      ' Wait for a string that looks like "password: " or "Password: "
      'crt.Screen.WaitForString "Password: "
      ' Send your username followed by a carriage return
      'crt.Screen.Send loginpass & VbCr
      ' Send the command to enter priviledged mode
      'crt.Screen.Send "ena" & VbCr
      ' Wait for a tring that looks like "password: " or "Password: "
      'crt.Screen.WaitForString "Password:"
      ' Send your password followed by a carriage return
      'crt.Screen.Send enablepass & VbCr
End Sub
' This subroutine contains the commands to connect to the TFTP server
' and copy the system image to flash
Sub tftpconnect
      ' Copy config from TFTP
      crt.Screen.Send "copy tftp flash" & VbCr
      ' wait for the prompt for the tftp server name
      crt.Screen.WaitForString "]?"
      crt.Screen.Send tftpservername & VbCr
      ' wait for the prompt for the source image name
      crt.Screen.WaitForString "]?"
      crt.Screen.Send sourcefilename & VbCr
      ' this line accepts the default name (the original source image name)
      crt.Screen.WaitForString "Destination filename [" & sourcefilename &
"]?"
      crt.Screen.Send VbCr
      ' this line confirms to erase the flash
      ' this will also detect if there was a tftp error
      If crt.Screen.WaitForString ("[confirm]",20) = True Then
            errorornot = ""
            crt.Screen.Send VbCr
      else
            tftperror
      End if
      ' this line reconfirms to erase the flash
      crt.Screen.WaitForString "[confirm]"
      crt.Screen.Send VbCr
End Sub
' This subroutine checks for an error connecting to the TFTP server
Sub tftperror
      screenrow = crt.screen.CurrentRow - 1
      errorornot = crt.Screen.Get(screenrow, -1, screenrow, 1 )
Do While errorornot = "%"
      ' If there was an error, see if the user wants to continue or exit
      If errorornot = "%" then
            errorresult = crt.Dialog.MessageBox("The server name " &
tftpservername & " or system image name " & sourcefilename & " was invalid."
& VbCr & VbCr & "Do you want to enter a new server name and source system
image name?" & VbCr & VbCr & "Select YES to enter a new name and continue."
```

```
                 & VbCr & VbCr & "Select NO to end the script.", "TFTP Server Name
         Unknown!!", ICON_WARN or BUTTON_YESNO )
                     if errorresult = IDNO then
                             exitresult = "1"
                             Exitdialog
                             else if errorresult = IDYES then
                                     tftpservername = crt.Dialog.Prompt("Enter the name
         or IP address of the TFTP server:", "TFTP Server", "Enter the TFTP Server
         Name or IP Address")
                                     sourcefilename = crt.Dialog.Prompt("Enter the name
         of the source system image file name:", "System Image Name", "Enter the name
         of the source system image name")
                                     tftpconnect
                             End if
                     End if
             End if
         Loop
         End Sub
         ' This subroutine exits the script and closes SecureCRT
         Sub ExitDialog
             If exitresult = "1" then
                     result = crt.Dialog.MessageBox("There was an error and the
         script was stopped." & VbCr & "Please check the log at " & LogFile & " for
         more details.", "Copy Failed!!", ICON_STOP or BUTTON_OK )
                     Else
                     result = crt.Dialog.MessageBox("Please check the log at " &
         LogFile & VbCr & "to verify that all the devices have upgraded.", "Upgrade
         Complete", ICON_INFO or BUTTON_OK )
             End If
             crt.quit
         End Sub
```

Changing the System Configuration

System configuration changes are perhaps the most common patch/upgrade
procedure that you will do. This is due to the fact that if a new system image that
addresses the problem does not exist or if you cannot upgrade the system image for
some reason, you may have a workaround available by simply changing the system
configuration to address the specific concern.

The methods of changing your system configuration are virtually the same as
changing your system image. Changing your system configuration can be performed
via a vendor-specific configuration management tool such as CiscoWorks or Nortel
Optivity. This can be manually performed or can be automated in some fashion.

Manually Changing the System Configuration

Manually changing your configuration is as simple as connecting to your device
via a GUI, Telnet, or SSH and running the appropriate commands. In the case of
CLI-based products, you can often simply copy and paste the configuration commands

from a text file into the CLI. For example, if I wanted to change the SNMP community strings and add an access list entry that restricted the systems that could connect via SNMP, I would need to run the following commands after logging into a Cisco IOS–based router and accessing the privileged mode:

```
configure terminal
access-list 10 remark Access List for SNMP Access
access-list 10 permit host 192.168.1.45
snmp-server community readonlystring RO 10
snmp-server community readwritestring RW 10
exit
write memory
```

So what I could do is simply list the commands in order in a text file, copy the contents of the file as shown here, and connect to each device I needed to update. Then, as soon as I logged in, I could simply paste the commands into the CLI. The router would run each command and finish by saving the active configuration. In a sense, you somewhat automate the configuration update process by doing this in this manner. If you want to fully automate the process, you must either use SNMP and scripting or script the commands necessary to upgrade the configuration in a fashion similar to upgrading the system image.

Automate Changing the System Configuration

Updating your configuration is much simpler to do than upgrading your system image. This is due to the fact that your configuration is really just a batch file of commands to run. Consequently, you can build a configuration file that contains only the commands that you want to run and then load it on your device. This will cause the router to parse the new configuration file, making it part of its active configuration, at which point you can choose to either save the configuration or not. For example, let's say that I wanted to make the previously mentioned changes on a Cisco IOS–based router using SNMP. I would need to perform the following steps:

1. Build a text file containing the commands I want to run on my router. For example, I could put the following commands in a text file:

   ```
   access-list 10 remark Access List for SNMP Access
   access-list 10 permit host 192.168.1.45
   snmp-server community readonlystring RO 10
   snmp-server community readwritestring RW 10
   ```

2. Store the configuration file on a TFTP server (for example, as "snmpupdate").

3. Run the following command to tell the router to copy the source file from the network:

   ```
   snmpset -v 2c -c <read-write-community> <router-ip-address> →
   1.3.6.1.4.1.9.9.96.1.1.1.1.3.12 int 1
   ```

4. Run the following command to tell the router to copy the destination file to the running configuration:

```
snmpset -v 2c -c <read-write-community> <router-ip-address> →
.1.3.6.1.4.1.9.9.96.1.1.1.1.4.12 int 4
```

ONE STEP FURTHER

Cisco uses the following integer values for copying from and copying to:

1	Network File (from a TFTP server, for example)
2	iosFile
3	Startup Configuration
4	Running Configuration
5	Terminal

You can change the integer to reflect the kind of copy that you want to perform. For example, if you wanted to copy from the running configuration to the startup configuration, you would specify integer 4 for the source file and integer 3 for the destination file.

5. Run the following command to tell the router the IP address of the TFTP server:

```
snmpset -v 2c -c <read-write-community> <router-ip-address> →
.1.3.6.1.4.1.9.9.96.1.1.1.1.5.12 a <tftp-ip-address>
```

6. Run the following command to tell the router the name of the configuration file to use from the TFTP server:

```
snmpset -v 2c -c <read-write-community> <router-ip-address> →
.1.3.6.1.4.1.9.9.96.1.1.1.1.6.12 s <config-file-name>
```

7. Run the following command to tell the router to initiate the copy:

```
snmpset -v 2c -c <read-write-community> <router-ip-address> →
.1.3.6.1.4.1.9.9.96.1.1.1.1.14.12 int 1
```

8. Because I updated the running configuration, the next step is to copy the running configuration to the startup configuration to make the changes permanent. First, however, I must clear the row status of the previously entered values:

```
snmpset -v 2c -c <read-write-community> <router-ip-address> →
.1.3.6.1.4.1.9.9.96.1.1.1.1.14.12 int 6
```

9. Run the following command to tell the router to copy the source file from the running configuration:

```
snmpset -v 2c -c <read-write-community> <router-ip-address> →
.1.3.6.1.4.1.9.9.96.1.1.1.1.3.12 int 4
```

10. Run the following command to tell the router to copy the destination file to the startup configuration:

```
snmpset -v 2c -c <read-write-community> <router-ip-address> →
.1.3.6.1.4.1.9.9.96.1.1.1.1.4.12 int 3
```

11. Run the following command to tell the router to initiate the copy:

```
snmpset -v 2c -c <read-write-community> <router-ip-address> →
.1.3.6.1.4.1.9.9.96.1.1.1.1.14.12 int 1
```

12. The final step is to clear the row status one final time to remove the existing values:

```
snmpset -v 2c -c <read-write-community> <router-ip-address> →
.1.3.6.1.4.1.9.9.96.1.1.1.1.14.12 int 6
```

I could then write a script that ran the appropriate snmpset command for each device in my network that I wanted to change.

I can also script the updating of my configuration by using the manual commands at the CLI using SecureCRT. The steps to script an upgrade of the running configuration on a Cisco IOS–based router are as follows:

1. Build a text file containing the commands that I want to run on my router. For example, I could put the following commands in a text file:

```
access-list 10 remark Access List for SNMP Access
access-list 10 permit host 192.168.1.45
snmp-server community readonlystring RO 10
snmp-server community readwritestring RW 10
```

2. Store the configuration file on a TFTP server (for example, as "snmpupdate").

3. Create a session in SecureCRT for each device that I want to connect to, as previously described.

4. Write a script that performs the following functions:

- Provides the required login information. I can either script the login as part of my session creation, as previously described, or I can have the script prompt for the appropriate login information. For simplicity, I place the login information in the session creation.

- Defines the TFTP server that the configuration file is located on.

- Defines the configuration file source filename.

- Defines an array containing all the devices I want to connect to. In the example, I have defined an array of seven values to connect to router1 through router7.

- Defines a subroutine that contains the input and output that I will pass through SecureCRT to the device.

- Provides a logging mechanism so that I can verify the success of all functions.

- Provides error-handling capabilities, as required.

In the following sample script, I have created seven sessions for seven different routers in SecureCRT. I am using the SecureCRT session login scripts to log into the routers. The script will connect to a TFTP server located at 192.168.1.45 and copy the configuration file snmpupdate to the running configuration. If the copy result is successful, the router will save the running configuration to the startup configuration, log the success into a file, and proceed to the next router in the array, until all routers have completed. If there is an error with the TFTP server or configuration filename, it may prompt the user to determine whether they want to enter a new TFTP server name or IP address and configuration file. If the user selects no, the script logs the error and exits. If the user selects yes, the script will attempt to reconnect using the new information.

> **NOTE**   Due to page width limitations, some lines in this code will be wrapped.

```
#$language = "VBScript"
#$interface = "1.0"
'===========================================================================
' VBScript Source File -- Created with SAPIEN Technologies PrimalSCRIPT(TM)
' NAME: tftpupdate.vbs
' AUTHOR: Wes Noonan , WJN Consulting, LLC. wnoonan@wjnconsulting.com
' DATE  : 01/11/2004
' COMMENT: This script is used by SecureCRT to automate a process. While it
' is based on VBScript, it is customized to run in SecureCRT as evidenced
' by the first 2 lines above. See www.vandyke.com for more info.
' This script will automatically login to a series of Cisco switches/routers
' as defined in an array and attempt to update them by using TFTP. If the
' update fails, the user will be prompted whether to continue updating the
' remaining systems or exit. All transactions will be logged to a file so
' that the admin can verify the success/failure of the updates.
'===========================================================================
' dim variables
dim SessionName, DisconnectString, SwitchArray(4), Switch, Start
dim Append, loginpass, enablepass, tftpservername, configfilename
dim result, errorresult, exitresult, logfile, errorornot, screenrow
' Define constants
Const ICON_STOP = 16                    ' display the ERROR/STOP icon.
Const ICON_QUESTION = 32                ' display the '?' icon
Const ICON_WARN = 48                    ' display a '!' icon.
Const ICON_INFO= 64                     ' displays "info" icon.
Const BUTTON_OK = 0                     ' OK button only
Const BUTTON_CANCEL = 1                 ' OK and Cancel buttons
Const BUTTON_ABORTRETRYIGNORE = 2       ' Abort, Retry, and Ignore buttons
Const BUTTON_YESNOCANCEL = 3            ' Yes, No, and Cancel buttons
Const BUTTON_YESNO = 4                  ' Yes and No buttons
Const BUTTON_RETRYCANCEL = 5            ' Retry and Cancel buttons
Const DEFBUTTON1 = 0         ' First button is default
Const DEFBUTTON2 = 256       ' Second button is default
Const DEFBUTTON3 = 512       ' Third button is default
' Possible MessageBox() return values
Const IDOK = 1               ' OK button clicked
```

```
Const IDCANCEL = 2          ' Cancel button clicked
Const IDABORT = 3           ' Abort button clicked
Const IDRETRY = 4           ' Retry button clicked
Const IDIGNORE = 5          ' Ignore button clicked
Const IDYES = 6             ' Yes button clicked
Const IDNO = 7              ' No button clicked
' set variables to allow logging. Change as needed.
Start = true
Append = true
Logfile = "C:\Test.log"
' prompt for variables to be used in the script
'loginpass = crt.Dialog.Prompt("Enter the login password:", "Login
Password", "", True)
'loginpass = ""
'enablepass = crt.Dialog.Prompt("Enter the enable password:", "Enable
Password", "", True)
'enablepass = ""
'tftpservername = crt.Dialog.Prompt("Enter the name or IP address of the
TFTP server:", "TFTP Server", "Enter Server Name or IP Address")
tftpservername = "192.168.1.45"
'configfilename = crt.Dialog.Prompt("Enter the name of the config file to
download from the TFTP server:", "Config File", "Enter Config File Name")
configfilename = "snmpupdate"
' define the array of devices to configure.
' These should be the hostnames of the devices you want to update
' you will need to change the array values as you add/remove devices
SwitchArray(1) = "Routers\Router1"
SwitchArray(2) = "Routers\Router2"
SwitchArray(3) = "Routers\Router3"
SwitchArray(4) = "Routers\Router4"
' change the numbers to reflect the min/max value of the array defined above
For Switch = 1 to 4
     SessionName = SwitchArray(Switch)
     for each object in SwitchArray
          If SessionName <> "" then
     ' *** If you want the config file to change on a per device basis
remark the configfilename
     ' *** variable on line 79 and unremark the lines below. This will
allow you to save the
     ' *** config for each router/switch in a unique name based on the
session/host name.
     ' *** The msgbox line is for debugging purposes
     'configfilename = SessionName & "-config"
     'msgbox configfilename
               ' turn on synchronous mode so we don't miss any data
               crt.Screen.Synchronous = True
               crt.session.Connect("/s " & SessionName)
               ' log the results to review for success
               crt.Session.LogFileName = LogFile
               crt.Session.Log Start, Append
               ' run login subroutine
```

```
                        'login
                        ' Send a command to display the date/time for the log
                        crt.Screen.WaitForString "#"
                        crt.Screen.Send "show clock" & vbCr
                        ' run tftpconnect subroutine
                        tftpconnect
                        ' Check to see if there was an error updating. If so, give
the option to exit the script
                        crt.Screen.WaitForString "#"
                        screenrow = crt.screen.CurrentRow - 1
                        errorornot = crt.Screen.Get(screenrow, 1, screenrow, 6 )
                        If errorornot = "%Error" Then
                                errorresult = crt.Dialog.MessageBox("There was an
error updating system: " & VbCr & VbCr & SessionName & VbCr & VbCr & "Check
the log at " & LogFile & " for the error output." & VbCr & VbCr & "Select OK
to continue, CANCEL to end the script.", "Error Updating System!!", ICON_WARN or
BUTTON_CANCEL )
                                If errorresult = IDCANCEL then
                                        exitresult = "1"
                                        ExitDialog
                                End if
                        End If
                        ' run writechange subroutine
                        writechange
                        ' Wait for copy to end then disconnect from device
                        crt.session.Disconnect
                        ' Set the SessionName variable to nothing to cause the
                        ' script to run through each session in the array
                        SessionName = ""
                        ' turn off synchronous mode to restore normal input
processing
                        crt.Screen.Synchronous = False
                end if
        next
next
ExitDialog
' subroutines used in script are listed below
' This subroutine contains the logon functions
'Sub login
        ' Wait for a string that looks like "password: " or "Password: "
        'crt.Screen.WaitForString "Password: "
        ' Send your username followed by a carriage return
        'crt.Screen.Send loginpass & VbCr
        ' Send the command to enter priviledged mode
        'crt.Screen.Send "ena" & VbCr
        ' Wait for a tring that looks like "password: " or "Password: "
        'crt.Screen.WaitForString "Password:"
        ' Send your password followed by a carriage return
        'crt.Screen.Send enablepass & VbCr
'End Sub
' This subroutine contains the commands to connect to the TFTP server
```

```
Sub tftpconnect
     ' Copy config from TFTP
     crt.Screen.Send "copy tftp run" & VbCr
     crt.Screen.WaitForString "Address or name of remote host []?"
     crt.Screen.Send tftpservername & VbCr
     If crt.Screen.WaitForString ("Source filename []?",3) = True Then
          errorornot = ""
          entertftpfile
     else
          tftperror
     End if
End Sub
' This subroutine contains the commands to enter the TFTP file to use
Sub entertftpfile
     crt.Screen.Send configfilename & VbCr
     crt.Screen.WaitForString "Destination filename [running-config]?"
     crt.Screen.Send VbCr
End Sub
' This subroutine checks for an error connecting to the TFTP server
Sub tftperror
     screenrow = crt.screen.CurrentRow - 1
     errorornot = crt.Screen.Get(screenrow, -1, screenrow, 1 )
Do While errorornot = "?"
     ' If there was an error, see if the user wants to continue or exit
     If errorornot = "?" then
          errorresult = crt.Dialog.MessageBox("The server name " &
tftpservername & " was invalid. Do you want to enter a new server name?" &
VbCr & VbCr & "Select YES to enter a new name and continue." & VbCr & VbCr &
"Select NO to end the script.", "TFTP Server Name Unknown!!", ICON_WARN or
BUTTON_YESNO )
          if errorresult = IDNO then
               exitresult = "1"
               Exitdialog
               else if errorresult = IDYES then
                    tftpservername = crt.Dialog.Prompt("Enter the name
or IP address of the TFTP server:", "TFTP Server", "Enter the TFTP Server
Name or IP Address")
                    tftpconnect
               End if
          End if
     End if
Loop
End Sub
' This subroutine writes the changes to the startup-config
Sub writechange
     ' Copy the running config to startup config
     If errorornot <> "%Error" then
          crt.Screen.Send VbCr
          crt.Screen.Send "copy run star" & VbCr
          crt.Screen.WaitForString "[startup-config]?"
          crt.Screen.Send VbCr
```

```
              crt.Screen.WaitForString "#"
              crt.Screen.Send VbCr
       End if
End Sub
' This subroutine exits the script and closes SecureCRT
Sub ExitDialog
       If exitresult = "1" then
              result = crt.Dialog.MessageBox("There was an error and the
script was stopped." & VbCr & "Please check the log at " & LogFile & " for
more details.", "Update Failed!!", ICON_STOP or BUTTON_OK )
              Else
              result = crt.Dialog.MessageBox("Please check the log at " &
LogFile & VbCr & "to verify that all the devices have been configured.",
"Update Complete", ICON_INFO or BUTTON_OK )
       End If
       crt.quit
End Sub
```

Changing the Application

Although the previous sections defined managing changes and applying patches and updates to your network infrastructure's hardware (such as routers and switches), some of our network infrastructure is actually an application running on a server. For example, Check Point Firewall-1 is an application that can run on Solaris, Windows, or Linux. Content-filtering software may run on Windows or Linux. In the case of applications, our options available for performing and automating patches and updates are limited largely by what the vendors provide as an installation mechanism. Some vendors support using tools such as Microsoft SMS for the deploying of updates and patches. Others may support scripting the installation routing through the use of InstallShield or other installation mechanisms. Unfortunately, however, the majority of your application changes will likely have to be manually performed by you on each system that needs to be updated.

Summary

Change is a necessary evil in our environments. No matter how well we plan, there are going to be exploits against our software and hardware, and the product vendors are going to release new software to address those exploits. The key to managing these changes is to implement an effective change control policy.

We need to plan for changes before we make them. This can be done by identifying the need for a change, defining the scope of the change, identifying the change that will be made, performing a risk analysis, planning the change, and then testing the change. Once the change-planning process is complete, we are ready to manage the change. This can be done by defining the change management team, communicating the change, defining the implementation team, updating all documentation and diagrams, and finally reviewing the change for effectiveness.

Change control will only help us if we make sure we have upper management support before undertaking the change control process. We must then ensure that we build a flexible change control process that addresses the different types and degrees of importance and timeliness of changes in our environments. Finally, we have to remember that change control is a learned habit, and it takes time, training, and patience before it becomes a part of our normal routine.

The most common changes we will make in our environments are applying patches and updates from vendors to address security and other issues. Before we apply a patch, however, we have to identify and understand the terminology our vendors use to identify how to address an exploit or vulnerability. We also must remain informed not only of new vulnerabilities and exploits, but of new updates to address any existing or potential vulnerabilities and exploits. If necessary, we need to budget and plan for purchasing a maintenance or support agreement to ensure we have timely access to software updates. We must define a policy and procedure for updating our systems as well as ensure that all changes go through change control to minimize the risk of updating our systems. Finally, we must apply updates to our systems in a timely fashion to ensure that our systems are as protected as quickly, and safely, as possible.

Part IV

How to Succeed at Hardening Your Network Infrastructure

Chapter 15

Setting Perceptions and Justifying the Cost of Security

■ Setting User Perceptions and Expectations

■ Setting Management Perceptions and Expectations

■ Risk Analysis

As we have seen, hardening your network infrastructure can be a very long and laborious process. After you've put forth the effort to harden your network, however, the last thing you want is to see all of your effort and work fail, and yet many companies find themselves in this situation. They did everything that they thought they needed to do. They bought the hardware, and they bought the software. They brought out the auditors, they wrote their policies. Yet they still fell short.

The inevitable question is "why"? In Part IV we seek answers to that question, and by doing so provide you with tools and information that you need to ensure that you can succeed at hardening your network infrastructure.

In this section we shift our focus from some of the technical aspects of hardening your network and look at some of the soft skills involved. In this chapter we take a look at how to set perceptions and examine methods to get the money required for succeeding at hardening your network infrastructure. In Chapter 16 we look at staffing and training issues and focus on how to address those issues to ensure that you have the appropriate staff as well as the appropriate training and education, not only for your administrators but for your users as well. Chapter 17 wraps up with the aspect of hardening your network infrastructure that no one wants to see but everyone needs to expect and be prepared for—handling a security incident with effective incident response policies.

Throughout this book, the focus has been primarily on technical solutions for hardening your network infrastructure. In this chapter we shift our focus and look at some of the more esoteric requirements for hardening your network infrastructure. This does not mean that this chapter is any less important than learning how to harden your firewalls or routers and switches. In fact, this chapter can be key to ensuring the success or failure of your infrastructure hardening efforts, because it looks at the two things that are most likely to contribute to the success or failure of efforts: setting the appropriate expectations and getting the money needed to undertake the effort.

Throughout this chapter, it may seem like some of the information is directed more at management personnel. That isn't quite correct. While it is critical that management understands and supports the concepts and recommendations put forth, the technical folks must also understand the impact that they can have with the user community through their words and actions. Even those ideas that are key to management are important for the technical folks to be aware of and understand.

Setting Perceptions and Expectations

In virtually all aspects of life, individual perceptions mean no two people see things in exactly the same way. Perception is like that old team-building exercise, where you tell a story to someone in the group and he tells someone else, and she tells someone else, and so on, until the last person retells the story—inevitably, the story changes as it goes from person to person, and the retelling is never the same as the original.

Perception contributes to an individual's expectations. Your perception is your filter on reality. The old expression "perception is reality" is true. It doesn't really matter what actually occurred; what matters is what people perceive occurred. On the other hand, expectation is what you think will happen. This is where perception and expectation cause problems with security and technology in general. Two people or groups of people undertake a technical project with a different expectation of what the effort and end result should be. This virtually ensures that at least someone is going to be disappointed by the end result, because it likely is not going to be what he or she expected. The perception then has the potential to be "technology and IT failed."

You can address this, however, by looking at how properly to set the perceptions and expectations of all the people involved, so that everyone shares a common perception and expectation of what will be accomplishing by hardening your network infrastructure.

Setting User Perceptions and Expectations

Your users are one of the most important groups to set perceptions and expectations with. A user is anyone who is going to be using the technologies and systems that you are implementing. While it can be somewhat entertaining to look upon our users and think "what do they really matter, they are just users after all," the truth of the matter is that the whole existence of technology and by extension security is based on supporting the users' needs.

For example, let's say you decide that it is time to implement a content filtering system. The technical goals of this project are to help reduce malicious content from entering your network as well as to prevent access to websites with questionable content that could expose the company to litigation. Your perception, then, is that this will be a good investment in technology, and the expectation is that your network will be more secure as a result of implementing the new system. Your users may look at this same situation from a completely different perspective. Their perception might be that IT is trying to monitor what they are doing in a sort of Orwellian fashion—Big Brother, if you will. Their expectation, then, is that this project will merely make their lives more difficult by preventing them from accessing websites of content they might want or think they need. Whether or not this occurs, the users' perception and expectations have already been molded. Your responsibility is to make sure that you adjust the users' expectations to be more in line with reality. This is turn will contribute to a different and better perception on the part of the users. The end result is that your job will become easier and your users will start trusting you, especially if you accurately deliver based on their new expectations.

Technology evolved not so that we would have cool things to mess with, but so that those users could be more effective in performing their jobs and businesses could run more effectively. The goal never was and never should be to make the user a technical expert. The goal is to make that user better at his or her job. You want your sales force to be able to sell more. You want your accountants to be able to manage the cash flow more effectively. You want your engineers to be able to design more.

This is a key point to understand, because many users do not comprehend what it means to be more secure. Sure, they understand it in general terms, but they don't know what that *really* means to them. They don't understand what impact it will have on their daily routines, and that lack of understanding often leads to fear. This is all human nature. People routinely fear things when they don't understand how it will affect them. For example, if your users get told that IT is monitoring the network, they may get the impression that IT is monitoring them. It goes right back to that perception that IT is on some Big Brother mission to know what every user is doing every minute of the day. You can then adjust what your users perceive and expect by providing them more information about what monitoring the network means. Perhaps you are merely trying to monitor the bandwidth utilization on some network segments. Let your users know that so that they understand exactly what you mean by "monitoring the network." Your responsibility is to set the users' expectations on security so that they understand what security means to them and, more important, how it will affect them.

You can do five things to help set your users' perceptions and expectations:

- Eliminate user fear.
- Earn your users' trust.
- Communicate with your users.
- Find champions.
- Be realistic.

Eliminating Fear

Fear, uncertainty, and doubt (FUD) can undermine just about anything, including an attempt to harden your network. FUD creates an environment of fear and uncertainty in your user community due in large part to confusion, misunderstanding, and rumors about the goal of network security. While FUD can be a powerful factor in contributing to the failure of a hardening project, the good news is that FUD can easily be countered through a strategy of education and communication.

One method of eliminating FUD with your users is to set the appropriate perception of your users. Unfortunately, many people look at network security with a Big Brother type of fear. This often comes from a mistaken perception that increased security and reduced privacy are the same thing. They are worried that someone is watching them, just waiting for them to slip up and view that personal e-mail or go to that non-work-related web site. Make sure your users understand that this is not the goal or objective. While you certainly may be and should be tracking your users' online activities, and they need to know that you are doing this, you need to make sure that they understand *why* you are doing this. For example, let's say that you run reports that show who is visiting online employment web sites. The knee-jerk reaction on the part of the users when they discover this might be that you are trying to monitor whether they are looking for other employment so that the company can fire them or give them bad references. In fact, you might be monitoring this solely for use by human resources so that they can determine whether a morale problem needs to be addressed. In an example like this, it is important to set the users' perception accordingly. Let them know that in this case there are no adverse consequences related to their online activities. This can often be handled through the use of an acceptable use policy that stipulates what kind of Internet access is acceptable.

Gaining User Trust

An often overlooked aspect of setting user perception is the need to gain the trust of your users. This because, much as we may have our preconceptions about users, users have their preconceptions about us. Many users have had that fateful run-in with someone in IT when they were made to feel stupid by virtue of how they were talked to or treated. While the user may or may not have been justified in feeling that way, all that matters is the perception of that user. As long as he believe that he was talked down to, then he was. As a result of these kinds of interactions, many users view IT as a bunch of snobby geeks who can barely be tolerated, much less trusted.

This general lack of respect undermines trust, but it is not the only reason that a lack of trust exists. Things like the network being down frequently or a slow/lack of response from the help desk, or even a response from the help desk that doesn't help— all contribute to the lack of trust by causing your users to lose faith in the abilities of IT.

You have to overcome this lack of trust if you want to be successful at hardening your network. If your users trust you, they will work with you. If they don't, they will work against you. The easiest method to earn their trust is simply to talk to them, treat your users as equals, and mitigate any feeling of threat. Make sure that they understand and believe that you are here to support their needs, not to spy on them or tell their boss if they make a mistake. If you show your users respect, they will return it in kind. That will earn their trust, making it much easier for you to get them to make the changes necessary to make your network more secure.

Communicate with Your Users

By far the best method to set your users perceptions and expectations is to communicate effectively with them. You can shape and mold what a user perceives by telling her what is going on. At the same time, you need to use some caution. Too much information can be a bad thing, especially if the users do not understand the information you are providing.

Different Communication Methods

I worked at a company that had two managers who required a dramatically different level of communication when we made network changes. One manager really needed to know the gritty details of what we were doing. Anything less than that left the manager very uncomfortable, which often translated into difficulty in getting him to sign off on making changes. The other manager wanted to know none of the technical details. If you could provide an analogy that he would understand, then great. Otherwise, we could simply tell him that we were making things better, and he was happy. Identify the level of communication required for each group of users you have to deal with, and attempt to find common communication levels that you can use across your environment.

Some methods of communication that can help you set the perceptions of your users are listed here:

- Build a newsletter of tips and tricks that is distributed via e-mail or intranet. If your users know of more secure methods to perform tasks, they will often use them.

- Be willing to explain "why." No one likes being told to do something without being given an explanation. You can address this before it is an issue by making it a point to always answer the question "why" without your users needing to ask it.

- Explain the benefits and drawbacks of the security measure or practice. The key here is making sure the users know what to expect in advance. You have to address the benefits *and* the drawbacks, however, especially if the users can no longer do the things they used to be able to do. It is important not to gloss over the drawbacks or you will lose user trust.

- Ensure that all communications are phrased and presented as if between equals. Make sure that you don't inadvertently speak down to your users.

- Communicate with your users on a schedule other than "when it hits the fan." You want to make sure that your users do not begin to see you as the bearer of bad news. Make sure that you are the periodic bearer of good news as well. For example, if you are able to prevent a new virus or worm from affecting the company, take the time to send a notice to the users commending them for adhering to your e-mail or virus protection security policies.

- Get and keep your users involved in the process. Make all your users a part of the security process, not just those who are most affected by the security process. The more involved your users, the more aware they will be. You can do this through the use of regular "lunch and learns" and scheduling training sessions on new products and technologies with which the users will be frequently interacting.

Using Lunch and Learns to Earn Trust

"Lunch and learns" can be about topics other than just work-related tasks. Eric, the technical editor of this book, has hosted some lunch and learns on how to buy a new PC, and comparing and explaining DSL to cable modem and dial-up Internet access. While the lunch and learns didn't really relate to work, the users liked them, and it allowed some of the users to get to know some of the technical people a little better, and in a positive light. Be creative when coming up with lunch and learn topics.

Find Champions

In my younger days, I had a mentor who one time told me "Wes, you fight too many battles. You need to learn how to let other people fight some of your battles." In the days of old, the king wouldn't always compete in the joust. Sometimes he would find his best knight and sent him out to fight on his behalf. This was because the king recognized that the knight stood a better chance at winning than he did. The reasons for finding champions today have not changed.

Rewarding Champions

The best knights were chosen as champions and were often greatly rewarded for their services. You need to make sure that when you find your IT champion you continue that policy. Make sure that she gets the recognition that she requires with the people that matter. This in turn will make her much more willing to work with you in the future, because she knows that she will personally receive a reward for her actions.

In many cases, IT is an outsider in an organization. IT isn't a part of HR or accounting. So often when IT makes recommendations to other organizations, they are viewed as trying to come in and change things without understanding the organization. This can make your security steps more complex because you must first overcome that perception before you can begin the actual hardening process. For example, if you want to implement a firewall between the accounting resources and the rest of the company, it may require your changing how accounting accesses the network or what resources they have access to. This might be necessary in order to secure the accounting resources effectively. If this means that the accounting folks can no longer access something that was not required for their job but they frequently accessed anyway, you can almost bet money that the change is not going to be well received. To eliminate this issue, attempt to find a champion who can fight on your behalf. Try to identify the people who have bought into your message and who want to see the changes happen. Then empower those people to convince the rest of the organization that what you are trying to do is a good thing. Let them convince the accounting folks that the benefits of the more secure operating environment will ultimately benefit everyone in the long run.

We have all run across the secretary who has been with the company longer than anyone else, and we will follow that person in any decision. Focus on that secretary and have him lead the rest of the group in the direction necessary to secure your environment. Let's face it; your users may not trust you very much to begin with. But the secretaries do trust the executive secretary who has been there 20 years and says that this is a good thing to be doing. Let him become your champion.

ONE STEP FURTHER

One frequent question is, "Who can I make my champion?" While each environment will have unique characteristics, some common folks usually make good candidates for champions:

- **Executive secretaries/administrative assistants** It is said that an army travels on its stomach. Well, a company works through its secretaries, and invariably they look to the executive secretaries for guidance.

- **Auditors** Internal or external auditors can be some of the best champions that you can find, because they bring with their recommendations an impartial perspective. You may fight for months to try to convince management to do something that an auditor needs to mention once to make happen.

- **Finance executives/management** From the CFO to a VP of finance, the people who control the money wield tremendous influence over what will or will not be done. Convince them that something makes financial sense and you have won half the battle.

- **People with tenure** These are often the natural leaders of the organizations. They are the folks with the "been there, done that" t-shirts. People look to their experience as an indicator of whether something makes sense or not. If you can convince them, then like all good leaders they can convince their followers.

Be Realistic

Be realistic in dealing with your users. It is not possible to prevent every security incident from occurring. You are going to have security failures. For example, you can implement the most stringent anti-virus measures, and you still may get hit by an e-mail virus that adversely affects your users. Be realistic when you approach your users, and make sure that they do not get the mistaken impression that if you implement some security measure, everything will be completely safe.

Your users need to be prepared for a security incident for two reasons. First, they must be ready to accept some temporary pain related to trying to correct a security incident. For example, if a worm is spreading via e-mail, users may need to be ready to live without e-mail while the e-mail system is being patched, and they need to understand the reason for this. Second, users have to be aware and on the lookout for suspicious activity. If they know that a possibility exists that a security incident may occur, they will be more alert to strange occurrences, phone calls, and e-mails and will be more likely to let someone know about it.

Setting Management Perceptions and Expectations

You must also set the perceptions and expectations of management. The reason for this is simple. If management does not buy off on what your are trying to do with respect to security, you will not be successful. If management does not support you, the first time someone "important" goes to management and says "I don't want to do this because it makes my life difficult," management will cave in. The odds of a cave-in are directly related to the amount of revenue that person is responsible for. The key to setting the management perceptions and expectations is to make sure that management understands the goals and benefits of the security measures that you are taking so that managers are not swayed by influential people in the company.

As with your users, you should set management perceptions and expectations by doing the following:

- Communicate with management.
- Gain the trust of management.
- Demonstrate the value proposition.
- Be realistic.

Communicate with Management

The most important task to undertake as part of your network infrastructure hardening process is to communicate with management. Why is this? Without management support, you will not succeed at hardening your network. Sure, you may be able to do certain things, but ultimately you will fail. You have to gain management support if you want to succeed.

The only way to gain upper management support is to communicate with them. Your goal here is different than it is with communicating with your users. In this case, you need to educate your management as to the repercussions of *not* securing your environment. You should not embellish the risk; you need to provide factual and accurate information to management so that they can make the decisions that must be made with the most information possible. Security costs money, as we will see in a moment when we look at some methods to justify the cost, and you have to be able to communicate the value that will result from the cost expenditure to management.

One item to be cautious about is not to inundate management with technical information. While some managers may want all of this information, in most cases they do not have the time to learn all of the technical details of a security implementation. A great method to eliminate this issue is to present all of your information to management in an executive summary format. Focus on the main points and communicate by sticking to answering the following:

- **Who** Who is affected by the change?
- **What**   What is the change supposed to fix or prevent?
- **Why** Why is the change necessary?
- **What if**   What are the repercussions for not making the change?

For example, let's say that you want to implement an intrusion detection/prevention system between your firewall and your production network. In communicating the need for this device, you might build an executive summary as follows:

The implementation of an intrusion detection/protection system will affect all users in the organization, although it should be a transparent effect that is generally unnoticed. This device is recommended so that IT can gain a notification/prevention mechanism to alert IT to suspicious network traffic that needs to be evaluated and prevent said traffic in the case of an intrusion protection system. In addition, this device will provide a much better insight into the kind of traffic that is being passed between the internal network and the Internet. This device will allow IT to be more responsive to potentially threatening traffic as well as provide a measure of defense in preventing unauthorized traffic from entering the production network. As you may recall, we were infected by Code Red traffic through the VPN connections at the firewall. An intrusion prevention system could have prevented that from occurring at all, while an intrusion detection system could have provided an early warning, allowing us to respond much quicker to the threat and thereby reducing the impact and cost. If this device is not implemented, we will continue to remain more susceptible to unauthorized traffic entering the network without the knowledge of IT. This can lead in turn to more downtime and expense while we recover from a security incident.

While the above is a brief example of an executive summary, it sets the tone for the kind of communications you need to have with management.

Gain the Trust of Management

A critical part of setting the perception and expectations of management is gaining the trust of management. If management trusts in your skills and advice, they are going to be far more willing to undertake the spending expenditures required to harden your network infrastructure properly. You will gain their trust by demonstrating the effectiveness of the solutions that you have implemented as well as by being honest and forthright with them. One of the most self-destructive things that you can do is attempt to "hide" information from management because the information may not be what management wants to see. Often this is done with the best of intentions. It is what I call "protect the president" syndrome. We have all seen it in the movies and TV, where someone doesn't give the president information because they think they are protecting him by not divulging the information. This never works in the movies, and it never works in real life. The odds are far greater that eventually the information will come to pass, and you will likely have lost whatever trust and confidence you had attained as a result.

Demonstrate the Value Proposition

One of the great debates in security is the question of security versus money. On one hand, you have folks who will argue that the cost of implementing a hardening measure is too expensive to do. On the other hand, you have folks who will argue that the cost of not implementing a hardening measure is too expensive not to do. The fact of the matter is sometimes each group is correct. In a perfect world, money would not be an issue when it comes to security. In our world, money is always the issue when it comes to security. Far too often, the cost of security will be paid only after an incident has occurred and management has realized the cost of not being protected. Our responsibility then is to be able to demonstrate not only the cost of implementing a security solution, but, more important, the potential cost of not implementing it. We will look at some of the methods of cost justification in the next section.

Be Realistic

As you do with your users, you need to be realistic when dealing with management. You have to present realistic scenarios and realistic solutions at all times. This is critical in maintaining the trust of management. However, the most important statement that you can make to management is that even if they take all of the steps outlined in your security plan, you still may be vulnerable to an incident. Security is not an exact science, and in many cases the ability to mitigate a threat is based in large part on the ability to be informed of a threat and take countermeasures before it can infiltrate your organization. With a proper security plan, and if you undertake the recommendations in this series, you can mitigate most current and future threats; however, you cannot guarantee that you will mitigate all of them. Management has to understand this, and they have to accept this as one of the risks involved in doing business.

Justifying the Cost of Security

The first step of hardening your network infrastructure is to justify the cost of the hardening measures you want to take. Without the money, it doesn't matter what you want to do, because you probably are not going to be able to do it. Security is not a cheap endeavor. Unfortunately, almost all of the security tasks fall well within the category of being a cost center, not a revenue center. One of the best methods to get the money required to implement these security practices is to demonstrate the expenses that exploits and security failings will cost the company. This is known as performing a risk analysis. For example, if your network is down for one day as a result of viruses, how much money was lost as a result of employees not being able to work? Knowing or being able to demonstrate this cost can be the best method to justify spending the money one time to prevent the situation from occurring. Even this is not a perfect method, however. Unfortunately, sometimes the best way to get the money needed to fix security problems is after an exploit has cost money and caused pain to the company.

Risk Analysis

A *risk* is the probability of a threat or exploits occurring in your environment. Risk analysis is a method assigning a cost-effective, relevant, and timely response to those threats. Because of the complexities involved in hardening your network infrastructure, it is easy to fall victim to applying too much, too little, or the wrong type of security in your environment. By performing a risk analysis, you can more effectively and efficiently mitigate those threats.

Risk analysis and risk assessment are two similar functions, but with some key differences. In the risk assessment, the objective is to define what level of risk something may have. The risk analysis builds upon the risk assessment with the objective being to demonstrate the security value of implementing the technology that mitigates the risk.

Risk analysis is vital to demonstrating the return on investment (ROI) of the security practices that you are undertaking. This section will provide the information that you need to justify the cost of the firewall or intrusion detection system that you want to implement. Without an effective risk analysis, it can be nearly impossible to justify spending the money that you require.

There are three main goals to performing a risk analysis:

- *Identify risks and threats.* You need to identify the risks that exist to your environment. For example, if you are transmitting confidential data to an external partner, there is a risk involved in that data becoming compromised.

- *Quantify the impact of threats.* You need to determine clearly and concisely the impact of a given threat. The overall impact is a combination of the financial and environmental impacts of a threat.

- *Define the balance between the cost of the impact and the cost of the security measure.* You need to qualify and provide a comparison of the cost of an impact versus the cost of the prevention or countermeasure to the impact. For example, if the cost of an impact is $50,000 and the cost of the solution is $200,000, it might not make financial sense to implement the solution.

Like so many other objectives in this book, performing a risk analysis requires management support. If management will not support and act upon the results of the risk analysis, there really isn't a point in performing one. It's like installing locks on doors that no one ever bothers to lock.

Two predominant risk analysis calculation methods are used: quantitative risk analysis and qualitative risk analysis. Each method contains a distinct process to determine the risk. Both methods share some common elements, however—namely, the identification of threats, determining the value of assets and information, and the data gathering requirements.

Threat Identification

As I mentioned in Chapter 2, a threat is simply the possibility of an exploit or security incident occurring in your network. In order to analyze the risk of a threat, you have to identify the nature of the threat. This is because each threat carries with it a unique vulnerability method and associated risk result. Table 15-1 illustrates some common threats and their respective vulnerability methods and risk results. You need to evaluate your environment and identify all of the threats, vulnerability methods, and risk results that exist.

Threat	Vulnerability Method	Risk Result
Hacker	Open services and application	Unauthorized access to information
User	Misconfigured access permissions	Unauthorized access to information
Worms and virus	Lack of anti-virus software	Virus infection
Attacker	Lack of firewall protection	Potential to access data or conduct a denial of service
Contractor	Lax access security mechanisms	Can gain access to trade secrets
Attacker	Poorly written applications and services	Conduct a buffer overflow to gain privilege escalation
Remote user	Lack of filtering and intrusion detection/prevention mechanisms	Ability to infect corporate network with worm/virus
Remote user/business partner	Lack of data encryption	Allows intermediary parties to gain unauthorized access to information
Users	Lack of content filtering software	Exposes company to litigation from inappropriate content and allows unauthorized software to be downloaded

Table 15-1. Common Threats

Once you have identified the risk result, you need to determine the loss potential. Loss potential is simply what the company would lose if a risk was realized. This loss can be anything from corrupted data to destruction of systems and data, unauthorized access and disclosure of confidential or protected information, and a loss of productivity in your user community. Not all loss is immediate, however. Some loss is considered *delayed* loss. Delayed loss defines the negative effects of a risk over time as a result of the risk. For example, if a network outage resulted in enough loss that the company could not pay other bills and expenses, this would be a delayed loss.

Determine the Value of Assets and Information

Another common element to all risk analysis methods is the need to determine and assign a value to all assets and information. This is critical since the company needs to understand the value of the information and assets they are trying to protect, so that they can determine how much money is an appropriate amount to spend on protecting it. The easiest method for determining the value of assets and information is to identify the costs that it takes to acquire, develop, and maintain. The cost is not simply a matter of saying "Well, it would cost $3000 to replace the firewall if it was destroyed for some reason, so the value must be $3000." You need to evaluate not only the actual asset repair or replacement costs, but also the cost in lost productivity, the value of any data that might be lost as a result of the incident, and the labor costs associated with shipping, installing, configuring, and testing the new device. The total of all of these costs represents the true value of the asset and the information.

When assigning a value to information, you should consider the following:

- *What is the cost to acquire or develop the asset?* This includes not only the purchase price, but the salary of all the man hours for research and development.

- *What is the cost to maintain and protect the asset?* This includes the cost of maintenance contracts and the salaries for the man hours spent maintaining the asset.

- *What is the cost to replace the asset if lost?* This includes not only the actual purchase price, but the cost of the implementation in salary and man hours.

- *What is the value of the asset to the owners and users?* This is a more intangible value that represents how critical the asset is to the owners and users responsible for the asset.

- *What is the value of the asset to a competitor?* This is a representation of the value that the intellectual property would have in the hands of a competitor. For example, if you are developing a new product and the data was compromised, it could have tremendous value to a competitor by allowing the competitor to see your product strategy and direction, enabling them to develop competitive solutions.

- *What are the liability issues if the asset is compromised?* This is a representation of the legal and monetary liability that your company could be held for in the event of the asset being compromised. For example, how much could the company potentially lose in a lawsuit related to the asset?

- *What is the usefulness of the asset?* This is an examination of how useful the asset is in regard to increasing productivity and/or revenue. For example, if you lost a server that allowed you to process twice as many orders as normal, the asset would be extremely useful.

The objective of assigning the value of the asset and information is to allow you to determine a value related to the cost associated with not protecting the asset. This allows you to answer the question "How much would it cost if we didn't protect the asset?" The answer to this question allows you to determine the amount of money that might be able to be justified to protect the asset.

Data Gathering

The data gathering step is the most time-consuming aspect of risk analysis. This is because it requires you to perform a significant amount of research and calculations to gather the appropriate information needed for the risk analysis. You need to identify the following components for the risk analysis:

- Estimate and assign the values to all assets and information that is to be protected.
- Identify each threat and corresponding risk.
- Estimate the loss potential.
- Estimate the frequency of the threat.
- Identify and recommend the relevant remedial measures.

Quantitative Risk Analysis

A quantitative risk analysis uses real numbers in an attempt to assign a value to the costs of a threat and the cost of the security measures to protect against the threat. Each aspect of the risk analysis is quantified and assigned a value that is then used to determine the total and residual risks. This method has the benefit of attempting to determine the real costs associated with the threats and security measures so that management can make its determinations based on the actual costs. The downside of a quantitative risk analysis is that the very nature of security is a qualitative one. It is extremely difficult, if not impossible, to assign accurate numbers to all aspects of the risk analysis, which in turn can reduce the value and accuracy of a purely quantitative risk analysis.

Qualitative Risk Analysis

Unlike a quantitative risk analysis, a qualitative risk analysis does not attempt to assign a cost to the threats, losses, and security measures that can be implemented. Instead, it assigns degrees of severity, probability, potential loss, and effectiveness of a solution in an attempt to define the impact of threats and responses. Qualitative risk analysis is a much more subjective method of risk analysis that relies on judgment, intuition, and experience as its risk analysis formula.

In general, you will gather together a team of specialists, who will examine a given scenario. Based on the scenario, each team member will assign a rank, for example from 1 (least severe) to 5 (most severe), to the threat and the vulnerability of assets based on the severity of the threat. Next each team member will assign a rank based on the probability of the threat occurring. After that, each team member will assign a rank to the potential loss to the company due to the threat. The final step is to assign a rank based on the protection mechanisms that can be used to mitigate the threat. This information is calculated and used to determine the relative severity, probability, and loss due to the threat. In addition, the recommended countermeasures are reviewed to determine the most effective countermeasure identified by the risk analysis team. For example, the team could evaluate the threat of an outside hacker gaining access to a web server. They would assign ranks to the severity of this threat, the probability of occurrence, and the potential loss to the company. Next, they would assign ranks to the effectiveness of various solutions—for example, implementing a firewall, IDS, and honeypot. Each individual's results would be calculated to determine the overall degree of risk the team assigns to the threat as well as the most effective countermeasure for the threat. This information could then be used by management to determine whether they want to take the countermeasures recommended or not based on the relative risk of the threat.

Because it is less precise than a quantitative risk analysis, a qualitative risk analysis tends to lend itself more to prioritization of risk than anything else. Table 15-2 provides a detailed breakdown of the difference between quantitative and qualitative risk analysis.

Perform the Quantitative Risk Analysis Calculation

All of the preparation and planning of a quantitative risk analysis can be identified in a six-step process that should happen in every risk analysis and assessment. This is where we tie the identification of threats, the value of assets and information, and the data that we have gathered into a formal procedure that will allow us to determine the results of the risk analysis.

Attribute	Quantitative	Qualitative
Requires complex calculations	X	
High degree of guesswork		X
Can be automated	X	
Provides a cost/benefit analysis	X	
Uses objective metrics	X	
Uses subjective metrics		X
Shows clear losses associated with threat	X	

Table 15-2. Differences Between Quantitative and Qualitative Risk Analysis

Risk Analysis Terms and Definitions

Before we perform the steps required for the risk analysis calculation, we must define some terms:

- **Exposure Factor (EF)**   The EF is the percentage of loss an incident can have on an asset.

- **Annualized Rate of Occurrence (ALO)**   The ALO is a value that represents the estimated possibility of an incident occurring within a year. The range for the ALO is 0.0 (never) to 1.0 (always). The ARO can be determined by performing the following calculation:

  1 / number of years = ARO

  For example, if an incident is expected to occur every 100 years, the ARO would be 0.01, or it would have a 1 percent chance of occurrence every year.

- **Single Loss Expectancy (SLE)**   The SLE is the dollar amount that is assigned to a single event that represents the company's potential loss if an incident were to occur. The SLE is determined by performing the following calculation:

  Asset value × EF = SLE

  So if the asset is valued at $100,000 and an incident would result in an estimated 25 percent loss (the EF), the SLE would be $25,000.

- **Annualized Loss Expectancy (ALE)**   The ALE is the dollar amount that is assigned to a risk on an annual basis. The ALE is determined by the following calculation:

  SLE × ARO = ALE

  So if the SLE is $25,000 and the ARO is 0.5 (once every two years), then the ARE would be $12,500. The ALE value is what a company can use to determine the amount of money that it makes sense to spend on an annual basis (in this case, $12,500) to provide protection from the incident occurring.

The steps of a quantitative risk analysis are as follows:

1. Assign the asset or information value as defined above.
   a. What is the value of the asset to the company?
   b. What is the maintenance cost?
   c. For how much profit is the asset responsible?
   d. What is the value of the asset to the competition?
   e. What would the cost be to recover or re-create the asset?
   f. What is the cost to acquire or develop the asset?

2. Estimate the potential loss per risk.

   a. What is the cost of physical damage?

   b. What is the cost in lost productivity?

   c. What is the cost of confidential information being disclosed?

   d. What is the cost of recovering from an attack?

   e. What is the SLE for each risk scenario?

3. Identify the threats.

   a. Determine the likelihood of each risk occurring and where the threat may come from.

   b. Calculate the probability of an occurrence for each risk.

   c. Calculate the annualized rate of occurrence for each risk.

4. Determine the overall loss potential for each risk.

   a. Combine the potential loss and probability.

   b. Calculate the ALE using the information previously gathered for the SLE and ARO.

5. Identify the methods to mitigate each risk.

   a. Can you implement new hardware or software?

   b. Do you need to redesign your network?

   c. Do you need to change or improve procedures?

   d. Do you need to implement a training and education program?

   e. Do you need to implement some kind of detection methods to minimize the impact of the risk?

6. Reduce, assign, or accept the risk.

   a. **Risk reduction**   Implement changes and/or spend money to reduce the risk occurrence.

      i. Install the new hardware or software.

      ii. Change the network environment.

      iii. Improve your procedures.

      iv. Implement a training and education program.

      v. Implement an intrusion detection mechanism to identity the risk.

   b. **Risk assignment**   Transfer the liability for the risk to other parties.

      i. Purchase insurance to transfer some or all of the risk.

   c. **Risk acceptance**   Accept the possibility of the risk while undertaking no actions to reduce or assign the risk.

Keep in mind that while we are attempting to provide quantitative values associated with risk and risk loss, we are relying on forecasting the potential of future events occurring. This is not an exact science, however, and while we do our best to provide as much accurate and correct information as possible, we cannot accurately predict the future. This is a level of expectation that you must set with upper management.

Determining the Value of Protection

Now that we have performed the risk analysis and identified the cost associated with a given threat, we need to determine the value of the protection and countermeasures to the threat. This allows us to determine the effectiveness of the security mechanisms that were implemented.

At the end of the day, whatever security mechanism you implement must be cost effective and the benefits must outweigh the cost. To determine whether this is the case, we can perform a cost/benefit analysis against the security mechanism. The calculation for this is

(ALE before implementing security mechanism) – (ALE after implementing security mechanism) – (annual cost of the security mechanism) = value of the security mechanism

For example, if the ALE of hacking a web server is $10,000 and after a firewall implemented to protect the web server the ALE is $2500 and the cost of maintaining and operating the firewall that is protecting the web server is $1000, then the value of the firewall is $6500. If this number is less than the ALE before implementing the security mechanism, which it is in this case, we have a cost effective security mechanism because it is saving us more than it would have cost us not to have it.

When you calculate the cost of the security mechanism, you have to be careful that you do not underestimate the full cost of the security mechanism. To ensure that this does not occur, make sure that you consider the following:

- **Product costs**   The raw product cost from the invoice.

- **Design and planning costs**   The costs associated with designing and planning a solution.

- **Testing and implementation costs**   The costs associated with testing and implementing the solution.

- **Modifications that need to be made to the environment**   The costs associated with needing to change the operating environment to support the solution—for example, needing to purchase an additional switch.

- **Compatibility with other security mechanisms**   The costs associated with integrating the security mechanism with your existing environment—for example, purchasing additional enterprise management plug-ins.

- **Maintenance costs**   The costs associated with maintaining, repairing, replacing, or updating the security mechanism.

- **Operating costs**   The costs associated with the operating and support of the security mechanism, which also includes training for the new mechanism.

- **Effects on productivity**   The costs associated with downtimes and outages related to the implementation of the security mechanism.

Not all of these costs occur on an annual basis. Some of these costs will occur only once, during the first year of implementation, causing the value of the security mechanism to increase in subsequent years. For example, if the ALE of a web server is $10,000 and the ALE after implementing a firewall is $2500 and the total cost of the firewall is $9000 ($4000 to purchase, $500 to design and plan, $500 to test and implement, $1000 for modifications to the environment, $1000 in maintenance costs, $1000 in operating costs, and $1000 in lost productivity for the implementation) for the first year, the cost/benefit analysis is a loss of $1500. However, in subsequent years the costs associated with the purchase, design and planning, testing, modifications to the environment, and lost productivity for the implementation are no longer relevant. This means that the total cost of the firewall for the second year is only $2000. This means that the cost/benefit analysis for the second year is a value of $5500, and that over the course of two years the cost/benefit analysis is a value of $4000 and will only increase as more time goes by. This is commonly referred to as the return on investment (ROI).

Provide the Risk Analysis Results

Once you have conducted your risk analysis calculations, you need to present that information to management to determine what measures, if any, will be taken for a given risk. The objectives of the risk analysis results are to provide the following information:

- The value of the assets

- The list of all threats

- The likelihood of occurrence of each threat

- The loss potential of each threat on an annual basis

- The recommended safeguards, countermeasures, and actions and the costs associated

You should be prepared to present this information in two formats. First, you need a detailed analysis that addresses all aspects of the risk analysis. Second, you need an executive summary that can be used by upper management to help them understand the issues and costs.

When you submit your risk analysis results, you need to make sure that you identify the residual risk as a mechanism of setting the appropriate expectations. We know that we cannot prevent 100 percent of threats and incidents 100 percent of the time. Residual risk is simply the amount of risk left over even after all the security mechanisms have been put in place.

Summary

Setting the appropriate level of perception and expectations can be a critical element in ensuring the success or failure of your network infrastructure hardening efforts. If people do not know what they are to expect as a result of the security measures you will be implementing, it is a relative certainty that they will not be pleased with the results. To remedy this, you need to set the appropriate level of perception and expectation of your users by doing the following:

■ Eliminate user fear.

■ Earn your users' trust.

■ Communicate with your users.

■ Find champions.

■ Be realistic.

Setting the expectations of management is another critical element in ensuring the success of your network infrastructure hardening efforts. The reason for this is simple. If management does not buy off on what you are trying to accomplish, you will not be successful. To do this, you should do the following:

■ Communicate with management.

■ Earn the trust of management.

■ Demonstrate the value proposition.

■ Be realistic.

The most effective method to demonstrate the value of implementing security is to perform a risk analysis. The three goals of risk analysis are

■ Identify the threats and risks.

■ Quantify the impact of the threats.

■ Define the balance between the cost of the impact of a threat and the cost of the security measure.

You can accomplish these goals through the use of a quantitative or qualitative risk analysis. You should first assign a value to the asset that you will be protecting. Next you need to estimate the potential loss for each risk and the threats to the assets. This will allow you to determine the overall loss potential for each risk. After that you need to identify the methods to mitigate each risk and then make a determination of whether the risk should be reduced, assigned, or accepted.

Chapter 16

Addressing Staffing and Training Issues

- Increasing Staff Headcount
- Utilizing Contractors
- Outsourcing
- Recruitment and Retention
- Individual Roles and Responsibilities
- Organization/Group Roles and Responsibilities
- Knowledge Management
- Training Resources
- Implementing a Lab Environment

The requirement to harden one's network infrastructure is a very broad and very deep requirement. Expertise is required on a multitude of products and technologies. This creates a problem because it is nearly impossible to find someone with the breadth and depth of knowledge that an organization requires. It is simply too much information for one person to know.

You can address this need in one of two ways. The first method is to bring in the expertise that you need through hiring additional personnel or using contractors/consultants. The second method is to train your people for the relevant skills that your environment requires. In this chapter, we are going to look at how to address those staffing and training issues to ensure that you have the necessary skills to succeed at hardening your network infrastructure.

Staffing Issues

If you want to succeed at hardening your network infrastructure, you must have a competent and qualified staff that can properly plan, implement, and maintain your environment. In small environments, staffing may not be an issue because you can have a single person fulfilling multiple roles, and the requirements for those roles are generally much simpler. In larger and more complex environments, however, there arises a need for multiple people to address the various roles and responsibilities. This is due to the fact that people have a finite amount of time they can spend working on things. If there is more that needs to be done than they have time for, either tasks will get overlooked or you will need to augment your staff to address any issues that are not being handled. Here are the three predominate schools of thought regarding how to augment your staff:

- *Increase staff headcount.* This involves hiring new employees to be members of the IT organization.

- *Utilize contractors.* This involves bringing in outside expertise to address your staffing needs on a temporary or long-term contract basis.

- *Outsource.* This involves bringing in an external company to handle some or all of the IT responsibilities.

Increasing Staff Headcount

Adding headcount is simply increasing the number of staff employees by recruiting and hiring new ones. One of the benefits of increasing your staff headcount is that these workers become members of the company and, in theory at least, have more loyalty to the company than the other choices. A drawback of adding to your staff, however, is the increased overhead of having to provide for employee benefits, such as health care and retirement.

Utilizing Contractors

Utilizing contractors to augment your staff is a very viable option. You can use contractors temporarily to help when you have a lot going on, and you can cut back when things slow down again. One of the big benefits of utilizing contractors is that you have the ability to pick and choose a specific expertise much more readily than is typical with staff employees. Many contractors are able to gain a specialization more easily than a staff employee, who tends to need to be an expert at many things. Another benefit is that the company does not have the overhead of providing benefits to the contractor, as compared to a staff employee. A drawback, however, is that the contractor is not an employee of the company and therefore you don't know where this person's loyalties lie—with their employer or with their customer. Another drawback is that not all contractors live up to expectations, though you can often address this issue by having a good screening process before you hire a contractor.

Outsourcing

Outsourcing is one of the more controversial methods of augmenting your staff. It involves using an external source for some or all of your IT staffing needs. This is typically done in one of two fashions. The first method is for the company to hire an external company that handles all IT responsibilities. The benefit to this is that it allows the company to focus its resources on corporate objectives without needing to concern itself with IT objectives. The outsourcing firm can handle those responsibilities. The drawback, however, is that the company is no longer in control of IT, which can make it very difficult to accomplish technology goals, especially if those goals are not defined in the outsourcing contract.

The second method is to outsource certain parts of the IT organization, typically the helpdesk and related functions. Although this has the same benefit as the prior method, the drawbacks include the previously stated reason as well as the fact that the outsourced personnel reside offsite or even in a foreign location. Outsourcing also has the potential for political backlash caused by user/employee resentment if it's not handled properly.

Recruitment and Retention

Recruitment and retention are two of the most difficult staffing issues you will have to face. First, you have to identify a method to find good people for your organization. Then you have to try to keep them so that you do not lose that investment in their skills and knowledge. You need to make wise choices in both regards if you want to have an effective staff that can properly manage and maintain your environment.

Recruitment

Recruiting good people for your organization is the first step in being successful at hardening your network infrastructure. If you can't find the right people to do the jobs that need to be done, you will not be able to begin, much less succeed.

You can use many methods of recruitment to identify good candidates for your organization. In some cases, the education of the candidate may be important. The proper candidate must have a college degree, preferably in a discipline that complements the goals and objectives of the position they will fill. In other cases, experience may be what matters. You need someone who has been there and done that, and can identify the pitfalls and prevent your organization from falling into them. And in yet other cases, certification may be the key. You need someone who carries the credentials of a vendor or organization that identify this individual as being skilled in the products or technologies you require.

One aspect of recruitment to not overlook is the possibility of moving someone into the position or promoting people internally. Although the candidate might not be technically as proficient as someone else, it is a great morale booster and an excellent reward for employee loyalty. It sends the message that the company is willing to help those employees who have done right by the company.

Each method has its pros and cons. In seeking candidates with a college degree, you can identify folks who have gone through a formal education process and, in the case of business majors, can bring a good amount of business acumen into a field that struggles sometimes to align technology and business objectives. At the same time, by restricting yourself to only recruiting candidates with degrees, you might overlook someone who has the experience you need—and experience can be more valuable than any degree in some cases. In seeking candidates with certification, you can identify folks who have demonstrated at least a basic degree of competence in a specific product or technology. However, certification is a double-edged sword. It is so easy today to simply braindump the required information to obtain certification that often it is hard to really know how competent someone might be based on their certification.

Keeping the Bar High for Certifications

Some certifications have taken steps to ensure, as best as can be done, that candidates can back up the certification with the relevant skills. Some certifications, such as the Cisco Certified Internetwork Expert (CCIE), rely on practical application labs to ensure that candidates can demonstrate the required degree of knowledge. Other certifications, such as the International Information Systems Security Certification Consortium (ISC) Certified Information Systems Security Professional (CISSP), rely on peer recommendation and verifiable experience to ensure that candidates can demonstrate the required degree of knowledge.

This leaves us with what I believe is the most important aspect of any prospective candidate—experience. Although having a degree or certification certainly has its value, experience is really king, especially for your mid- and senior-level staff. You need to have people who have done what you are trying to do or accomplish, or have enough industry experience that they can identify the proper methods of hardening your network infrastructure if you want to be successful.

The Technical Interview   One of the most overlooked steps of identifying a solid candidate is the technical interview. Many times people look at technical interviews from the perspective of "I don't have time to spend an hour or an afternoon with someone." However, if this person is someone you may be trusting your enterprise to, I would ask, how could you not have the time to spend to find the right candidate?

The Lost Art of the Technical Interview

In all the positions I have interviewed for (roughly 30), I have only had two technical interviews that I considered tough interviews. The first was with a software development company, where I spent over four hours interviewing with eight different people. The second was with a consulting company, where I spent an entire afternoon interviewing with four different people, ranging from pure technical interviews to one interview regarding business decisions, politics, interpersonal skills, and how to handle difficult customers—and that was after three phone interviews. Good technical interviews are invaluable in identifying the best candidates.

In designing a good technical interview, you should approach the subject from multiple angles. On one hand, you want to ask directed questions, such as "What commands would you run to enable OSPF routing on a Cisco router?" These allow you to more readily gauge the breadth and depth of a candidate's knowledge for those times when you truly need an expert who knows a product inside and out. These very specific questions, however, are not the end-all-be-all of interviewing. In fact, they are probably not nearly as important as some other types of questions you could ask, such as scenario-driven and troubleshooting questions. These are perhaps the most valuable of all questions because they allow you to get a feeling for how the candidate solves problems. They also demonstrate the candidate's logical thought process. As part of my technical interviewing process, I also like to ask a troubleshooting scenario question. Although the goal is to see if the candidate can determine the proper solution, the most important objective is to allow me to see how the candidate deals with unknown or uncertain situations. It is easy to demonstrate something that you know, but it is far more difficult to figure out something that you don't know—and that is a skill I have always prized in candidates because so much of the time technical folks are fixing things that they might not fully know or understand. Finally, give the candidate an opportunity to detail something that they have done. This grants them the comfort factor of being able to describe something they are comfortable with, and it allows you to see how well they can articulate solutions—a valuable skill for building executive summaries and gaining management support.

Background Checks   In addition to identifying the type of candidate that will properly fill a position and performing a solid technical interview, you should also check the background of a potential candidate. At a minimum, you should verify the references of any prospective candidate. Again, in my personal experience, my references have only been checked about 25 percent of the time. Although references are not a guarantee of quality, they at least provide some measure of validation of a candidate's credentials and employment history.

Limitations of Employer References

Most large companies now only verify employment because they are very afraid of lawsuits due to revealing any info about former employees. Consequently, many companies do not allow reference checks. In fact, my last employer was one of these companies. Be aware of this limitation when you check references, especially references from former employers.

Some environments require strict background checks. This is particularly true in regard to banking and federal contracts. Indeed, when you consider that many network administrators, helpdesk personnel, and security professionals will be privy to sensitive corporate information, it is a worthwhile investment to verify the criminal and credit history of your candidates. Practically speaking, someone who has administrator-level access to your network effectively has access to all the data that flows across it.

A couple of methods are available for performing a background check. With the Internet, one of the easiest ways to find out about someone is to simply "google" them. You can do this by going to www.google.com and entering the person's name in the search field. Although there is no guarantee that something will turn up, it is a good free method of checking someone out before you pursue more costly alternatives.

If your company subscribes to LexisNexis (www.lexisnexis.com), you can use it to research just about anything, including people. LexisNexis maintains an online legal database of virtually every person and company in the world. The only real drawback of LexisNexis is that it can be a costly solution.

Also, several online background-check firms can perform the background check for you and provide you with the results. Here are some of the better known firms:

- US Search (www.ussearch.com)
- Employment Screening Resources (www.esrcheck.com)
- American Background (http://www.americanbackground.com)

Security Clearances   In conjunction with performing background checks, it may be necessary to obtain security clearances for your employees. This is especially true if you are going to be trying to obtain any government contracts. You need to be aware of the three common levels of security clearance:

- **Level 1 (Top Secret)**   Top-secret clearance requires candidates to profile their lives for the previous ten years and requires a periodic reinvestigation every five years. The cost of qualifying for top-secret clearance can cost tens of thousands of dollars and take up to a year to process.
- **Level 2 (Secret)**   Secret clearance requires candidates to profile their lives for the previous five years at the same level of detail as top-secret clearance. Secret clearance also requires a periodic reinvestigation every ten years. The cost of qualifying for secret clearance can cost thousands of dollars and take up to a year to process.
- **Level 3 (Confidential Clearance)**   Confidential clearance requires a much lower level of detail than secret and top-secret clearance. This is the lowest level of clearance and must be reinvestigated every 15 years.

For government contracts/employees, all security clearances are investigated by the Defense Security Service (DSS). You can find more information about the DSS at http://www.dss.mil. The process for obtaining a security clearance involves submitting an electronic personnel security questionnaire (EPSQ), which as a Microsoft Word document is 31 pages in length and involves providing information regarding personal information, citizenship, locations lived, education history, employment history, personal references, spouse and family members' information and citizenship, military history, records and history of foreign dealings, medical records, police records, drug activity, alcohol activity, investigation records, financial records, civil court records, and personal and professional association memberships. Upon the completion of this form, the DSS will then investigate the background of the candidate. Clearly this is a very time-consuming process.

Bonded and Insured   In addition to all the background checks and security clearances that may be required for a candidate, once you hire someone, it may be necessary to obtain bonded insurance for the employee. This is especially true for contractors and consultants. The reason for obtaining bonded insurance is to protect your company and your employee from liability in the event that something they do causes the company to lose money.

Bonding and Background Checks

Bonding companies will not just bond anyone. For the cost of bonding, you can often get a little bit of a background investigation as well, provided by the bonding company.

Retention

Now that you have hired a good candidate, the next step is keeping them. Even in a tough job market, people can and will find other opportunities. Money is always a potential issue. People simply have to be paid a competitive wage. In addition to that, however, here are some other things you can do to help keep good employees:

- *Provide a casual work environment.* Although there are times when it is appropriate to dress in a coat and tie, the ability to come to work dressed casually cannot be overlooked as an excellent quality-of-life measure for retaining good people.

- *Provide a technically challenging environment.* By and large, people are in this industry because they enjoy the challenge. Although this does not mean you need to be a bleeding-edge technical company, it behooves you to maintain a technically challenging environment by constantly looking at new things that can be done. Otherwise, your employees may get bored and move elsewhere.

- *Provide flexible hours.* Flexible work hours come in many forms. In some cases, it means allowing an employee to come in early or late to avoid the hassle of rush hour. In other cases, it means allowing the employee the opportunity to telecommute or work from home from time to time. Depending on the position to be filled, some jobs really don't need the person to be physically present to effectively perform their duties.

- *Provide the proper tools.* One of the most frustrating things on the job is being asked to do something without having the proper tools (hardware or software). Although sometimes it is not feasible to provide everything an employee wants, when at all possible, you should provide them with the tools they need to do their jobs in an efficient fashion.

- *Provide a good career path.* You should provide a solid career path that allows the employee to grow with the company. One of the best things you can do is provide a technical career path in addition to a management career path, allowing your employees to decide the direction they believe best suits them.

- *Provide positive feedback.* Although not limited to technical staff, if employees only ever hear from their managers when something is broken or to complain about the quality of work being delivered, it makes for low morale and employees who will monitor the classifieds hoping something better will come along. Be sure to take notice when projects are completed early and come in under budget.

Individual Roles and Responsibilities

Before you can determine which candidate is the most appropriate for a given position, you need to identify the roles and responsibilities required in your organization. This allows you to identify exactly what it is you are looking for in a candidate. Although I will break each role down individually, you may be able to have multiple roles handled by a single person, provided the workload is not too much; likewise, you might need to have multiple people handling the responsibilities of high-workload roles:

- **Chief Security Officer (CSO)**   This role is responsible for managing all security personnel and projects in an organization.

- **WAN Administrator**   This role is responsible for implementing, managing, and maintaining all WAN equipment, protocols, and technologies.

- **LAN Administrator**   This role is responsible for implementing, managing, and maintaining all LAN equipment, protocols, and technologies.

- **Firewall Administrator**   This role is responsible for implementing, managing, and maintaining all firewall hardware, software, and technologies.

- **VPN Administrator**   This role is responsible for implementing, managing, and maintaining all VPN hardware, software, and technologies.

- **Public Key Infrastructure (PKI) Administrator**   This role is responsible for implementing, managing, and maintaining all PKI hardware, software, and technologies.

- **Intrusion Detection/Prevention Administrator**   This role is responsible for implementing, managing, and maintaining all intrusion detection/prevention system hardware, software, and technologies.

- **Internal Security Auditor**   This role is responsible for testing and auditing the security policies, procedures, and posture of an organization.

- **Change Controller**   This role is responsible for managing all aspects of the change-control process. Your change controller is one role that should not share responsibilities with any other positions. This will eliminate any potential conflicts of interest with regard to network changes that need to occur.

- **Network Architect**   This role is responsible for designing all aspects of the organization's network infrastructure.

- **Virus Software Administrator**   This role is responsible for implementing, managing, maintaining, and updating all virus software in the organization.

- **Capacity Planner**   This role is responsible for monitoring bandwidth usage and network performance and uses that information to project the sizing of circuits and determine the necessary bandwidth capacity required to effectively pass the required levels of data.

- **Security Tester**   This role often works in concert with the Internal Security Auditor and is responsible for performing penetration and vulnerability tests to validate the actual security level of the network.

- **Incident Response Team Leader**   This role is primarily responsible for managing and coordinating incident-response activities.

Organization/Group Roles and Responsibilities

As with the individual roles and responsibilities in your organization, it is helpful to identify the organizational/group roles and responsibilities, which allows you to group individuals in easily managed teams:

- **WAN Management Team**   This group consists of WAN Administrators and WAN Architects and is responsible for all aspects of WAN design, planning, implementation, administration, and maintenance.

- **LAN Management Team**   This group consists of LAN Administrators and LAN Architects and is responsible for all aspects of LAN design, planning, implementation, administration, and maintenance.

- **Security Team**   This group consists of all Firewall Administrators, VPN Administrators, PKI Infrastructure Administrators, and IDS/IPS Administrators and is responsible for all security-specific devices, software, and technologies.

- **Virus Software Management Team**   This group consists of all Virus Administrators and is responsible for all aspects of virus-protection software, from the desktop to e-mail servers to gateway virus protection.

- **Change Management Group**   This group consists of individuals from every other information technology group as well as representatives from the respective line of business (LOB) groups, as required. This group is responsible for approving and managing all changes that occur in the environment and preventing implementation conflicts.

- **Audit/Vulnerability Assessment/Penetration Testing Group**   This group consists of all security auditors and penetration testers and is responsible for testing the environment to ensure that it complies with all policies and procedures. In addition, this group should actively test the security posture of the organization by periodically attempting to compromise security on the network. This group should not contain members of any of the groups they will be testing, to avoid any potential conflicts of interest.

- **Incident Response Team** This group consists of individuals who are responsible for handling security incidents. The incident response team is detailed in more depth in Chapter 17.

Knowledge Management

Knowledge management is one of the most crucial staffing issues you will need to address. There was a time when an individual who knew everything about the network or about their responsibilities, even if no one else did, was considered a tremendous benefit to a company. That is no longer the case. An individual who knows how something works when no one else does is no longer a benefit. Instead, they are a liability—and a large liability at that. In today's environment, people have to share knowledge with each other. Being the only person who knows how something works should not be allowed to be considered job security. In fact, you need to make it clear that being in such a position makes for an even more insecure job. The reason for this is simple: the more that an individual knows without sharing that knowledge with their peers, the greater the difficulty you'll have trying to replace that person if they leave the company. You are better off to have that happen sooner than later.

This does not mean you necessarily need to let folks know they will be fired for not sharing information. Instead, you need to build a culture and environment that encourages and rewards the sharing of information, in addition to letting them know that it is not acceptable to withhold information. You can make this happen in a number of ways:

- *Have regular team meetings.* You should have regular team meetings to ensure that, at the very least, everyone is aware of what everyone else is doing, even if they might not necessarily know how to perform those tasks.

- *Require documentation of all changes.* You should require as a component of your change-control process that all changes must have the appropriate documentation created or updated prior to these changes being approved. If the network diagrams have not been updated, for example, the change should be rejected.

- *Encourage mentoring.* Encourage your senior personnel to mentor and teach your junior personnel. This has the twofold benefit of helping your senior personnel develop career skills that will benefit them in the long run as well as helping your junior personnel develop skills and expertise by learning from your best and brightest.

- *Have regular chalk-talk sessions.* A chalk-talk session is simply an informal training session. These should not take up more than an hour or so and are a great way to share concepts and show employees what each other is doing. For example, you might have a chalk-talk session that demonstrates how the router ACLs are configured and what traffic is being permitted and denied.

- *Provide a central data repository.* Provide a central, secured location such as an SSL-protected website for your employees to share data, information, whitepapers, and technical notes as well as all the policies, procedures, and documentation related to the network. This provides an easy-to-locate and easy-to-navigate method for people to find information related to how the network is designed and functioning.

- *Cross-train people.* Not only will individuals benefit from knowing more, and thus becoming more flexible in their career both in and outside the company, but the company will benefit from the increased number of people who know different areas of the network.

- *Move people around.* Letting someone stay in the same job for years is not good for them or good for business. As technologies change, they may find themselves obsolete. Also, moving people around merges knowledge and skills. This does not mean that people are arbitrarily moved into areas they know nothing about; it simply means that they have opportunities to work in other areas. Moving people around is also a good security measure, because it is harder for someone to defraud the company, and fraud is more easily discovered.

Training Issues

Once you have recruited and determined how to retain your staff, the next step is ensuring that your staff remains as technically competent as possible. This is where training comes into play. It is in the best interest of the company and its employee to take the time and set aside the money to continue to train the employees on any new technologies and products that will be implemented on the network.

The company IT Cortex has a study on failed IT project statistics and rates located at http://www.it-cortex.com/Stat_Failure_Rate.htm. The findings identified that between 50 and 75 percent of IT projects ultimately fail either in terms of not functioning properly or exceeding budget. This means that, on average, more projects fail than succeed. When reasons for the failures were examined, a common thread was identified. People didn't understand how the project or product was supposed to help them in their jobs or benefit the company. Training and education are the only ways you can address this problem.

Training Resources

Many avenues of training are available that allow you to ensure that employees stay sharp, ranging from instructor-led classroom-based training to self-study resources and books. We will look at all of these and examine the pros and cons of each.

Training is not a one-way street, however. The best training requires the employee to be self-motivated. After all, it is in the employee's best interest to be trained as much

The Value and Cost of Training

When I worked for an enterprise management software company, one of the biggest reasons that implementations would fail at customer locations was directly related to training. The software was incredibly complex, and it needed to be so that it could meet all the requirements. Unfortunately, many companies viewed it as being technically no more difficult or complex than implementing the next version of Microsoft Office. They thought they could just perform a typical install and everything would work properly. Unfortunately, that was rarely the case. Although some of the problem was certainly software related, a significant portion of the problem was simply that the customers lacked the knowledge they really needed to properly implement and utilize the product, and they did not budget or plan for training on the product when they purchased it. Whenever you decide to purchase a new piece of hardware or software in your environment, you need to ask whether it will require training of the staff to properly implement and manage it. If it will, you need to factor that training cost into the planned expense for the product.

as it is in the company's best interest to train them. Not only is it usually cheaper, with the employer only paying for literature and/or testing fees in the case of self-study, it lets you know who in your group is motivated enough to find the time and get the training done, which, as you and I know, is not an easy thing to do. It's a good indicator of who is really motivated at advancing their technical knowledge and being a productive member of your team.

Instructor-Led Training (ILT)

ILT is the classic training model. With ILT, you have an instructor who is available to teach the students the relevant concepts in a classroom-based setting. The advantage to this method is that the students have someone available who can answer their questions and teach them the right way to do things the first time. One of the drawbacks to ILT is cost. In addition to the course cost, ILT will often include costs associated with travel or taking time away from work to participate in the class. This can sometimes be mitigated by finding a local community college or training center that offers evening classes, but that now cuts into the employees' personal time, which might not be acceptable. Another drawback to ILT is that it is generally only as valuable as the instructor is capable. Unfortunately, many instructors lack real-world experience that is critical to providing value to corporate students. Use discretion when deciding who to use for your ILT, and don't hesitate to ask for references and work experience of the instructors.

Computer-Based Training (CBT)

CBT is a training concept that allows a student to learn at their own pace. Some CBT is application based, requiring you to install and use CD-ROM media for the training materials. Other CBT is Internet based, allowing the student to connect to Internet-based resources for the training materials. The benefit of this is that the student can connect to and continue their lesson from anywhere. Many CBT programs, especially online CBT, actually have instructors who are available, can answer student questions, and deliver lectures via streaming media. One of the benefits of CBT is that it tends to be cheaper than ILT and can oftentimes be shared among multiple people, thus providing even more bang for the buck. A drawback of CBT, however, is that many students do not do a very good job of retaining information learned in this manner.

Technical Seminars

Technical seminars are an excellent method of learning about a specific product or technology as opposed to ILT or CBT, which tend to focus more on broad topics and concepts. Many vendors schedule regular technical seminars for products and technologies that are in the middle of a marketing push. Consequently, technical seminars are often free of charge, which is a great benefit. In addition, technical seminars are commonly a half day in length, which makes it much easier to find the time to participate, as opposed to ILT, which might require anywhere from 3–5 days. The only downside is that there is often quite a bit of marketing literature that one must endure, and sometimes the technical content is woefully lacking.

Technical Conferences

Technical conferences such as Networld+Interop, Cisco Networkers, Microsoft Tech Ed, SANS, Black Hat, and Def Con are all great opportunities to not only participate in technical seminars but also take a look at the new technologies and products many vendors will be releasing. One of the biggest benefits of technical conferences, however, is not purely educational. Because many of these conferences occur in nice tourist destinations, they also provide a good way to reward your employees by sending them to a place that not only allows them to learn, but allows them to relax and get away from the office. There are a couple of downsides to conferences, however. Sometimes the technical sessions can be very hit or miss in terms of value and content. In addition, it can be costly in terms of not only registration, but travel and time away from the office.

Vendor Training

Vendor training has some of the best return on investment (ROI) because it is often targeted to the products and technologies you will be using. This allows employees to participate in targeted education that more accurately matches the information they will need to perform their daily functions. Instead of getting a general education based on how something works, they can get a very specific "this is how you should do this based on your environment" explanation. The cost of vendor training varies, with some vendors making it free as part of the product deal, and others charging explicitly for the training beyond any other costs (the truth is, you are always going to have to pay for it one way or the other). In many cases, vendor training can be performed at your location, reducing the travel cost of sending employees to a remote location for training in addition to making it much easier for multiple people to attend the training. There are not really any downsides to vendor training beyond any costs associated with having to pay for or send people to the training.

Self-Study Resources

Self-study resources cover a wide range of sources; however, they all have a single common element: the user of the resources is responsible for study and learning at their own pace, generally by themselves or with a study group. Here are some examples of self-study resources:

- **Certification training books**   These books are focused on providing the relevant information required to pass a certification exam.

- **Technical books**   These books, such as the ones in this series, do not focus on any given exam but instead focus on providing technical content related to some product or technology.

- **Whitepapers**   These are reports or treatises that have been developed to educate individuals on a specific topic. Some examples of whitepapers are the Cisco High Availability Whitepapers located at http://www.cisco.com/en/US/tech/tk869/tk769/tech_white_papers_list.html, the NSA Security Recommendation Guides located at http://nsa1.www.conxion.com/, and the information listed at the SANS Reading Room http://www.sans.org/rr.

Implementing a Lab Environment

A lab environment is traditionally considered a location to test products, technologies, and changes before implementing them in an organization. However, a good lab environment actually has substantial training and education value as well. This is especially true when used in conjunction with self-study resources from the previous section. For example, if someone has read about how to configure OSPF with authentication, they may be able to utilize lab equipment to perform hands-on configuration and learn how to actually implement what they have read about.

An important point to make on lab equipment is that it does not necessarily need to exactly match your production equipment to be effective. Although that is certainly the best-case scenario, it is often a cost-prohibitive undertaking. In many cases, however, you can get by for testing and learning by using similar but cheaper equipment. For example, if I have redundant PIX-535 firewalls in production, I probably don't have the money to duplicate that in a lab. However, if I want to test how various ACLs or protocols might work with the PIX, I can use a PIX-501 as a very cost-effective solution that will allow me to validate 99 percent of the commands and configurations I might need to test or learn.

A lab, in addition to the traditional benefits, can be one of the best investments you can make.

ONE STEP FURTHER

As a rule, a lab should never be allowed to connect to the production network in any way. If, however, you must allow a connection, that connection should be firewalled, filtered, and treated like any other external network connection.

Summary

Two of the most important aspects of hardening your network infrastructure are to ensure that you have adequately addressed any staffing or training issues and to ensure that you have the personnel and expertise required to be successful.

There are three predominant methods of adding personnel:

- Increasing staff headcount
- Utilizing contractors
- Outsourcing

In dealing with staffing issues, you want to make sure you identify and recruit the right candidates for the position and your environment. The first step is to identify the type of candidate you need. The next step is to engage in a sound technical interview to gauge how well a candidate will truly fit the position. Some positions may require background checks, security clearances, or for the candidate to be bonded and insured, so you need to be prepared for these possibilities.

Once you have identified a candidate, you need to keep them. You can do a number of things to help retain candidates, including making sure they are paid a competitive wage, making sure they are technically challenged, and providing a flexible and friendly work environment.

Another aspect of dealing with staffing issues is to identify the various roles and responsibilities for both individuals and groups. This allows you to clearly define what everyone is expected to do as well as to ensure your entire environment has someone who is responsible for managing and maintaining it.

The final staffing issue to consider is knowledge management—ensuring that employees share information among each other. Do not allow an employee to become the only person who understands some aspect of your network. As good as that person might be technically, they are a liability in such circumstances. Instead, build an environment that encourages and rewards data sharing through the use of regular meetings, requiring documentation for all changes, mentoring, and the use of a central repository for data storage and access.

One you have recruited and retained the people you need, the next phase is keeping them sharp. This is where training comes into play. You have numerous training resources at your disposal that can help ensure your staff stays sharp and on top of the products and technologies required in your environment. These include instructor-led training, computer-based training, technical seminars, technical conferences, vendor training, self-study resources, and a lab environment where employees can test and learn new technologies.

Chapter 17

Incident Response

I used to ride motorcycles and have many family members who still ride. When I first started riding, one of my uncles told me, "There are two types of motorcycle riders: those who have hit the ground, and those who will." That statement translates to security administrators. There are two types of security administrators: those who have had a security incident, and those who will.

No matter how hard you plan and prepare, sooner or later there will be a security incident that you will need to respond to. Even if you follow every best practice that has been recommended in this series, you will not be 100-percent protected. As a result, it is fitting that the final chapter in this book examines what to do when everything else you have put in place to prevent a security incident has failed, and you must now address and recover from the security incident.

Building an Incident Response Plan

As we have established, no matter what you do to try to prevent an incident from occurring, you cannot guarantee that one will not occur. As a result, you have to plan for how you will handle a security incident when it happens. Incident response is like a fire drill for network security. You have fire drills so that, in the event of an actual fire, you have a methodical and structured method of evacuating the building, and at least in theory, everyone knows what that method is. You do this because if you don't, with the smoke and fire there is a much greater likelihood that confusion could result in a catastrophe.

Incident response is no different. During an actual security incident, emotions are going to be running so high that there is a much greater likelihood of confusion, and that is the last thing you need in an already stressful situation. The more confused and ill prepared you are in dealing with an incident, the greater the potential for damage as a result of the incident. Therefore, you want to plan in advance for your incident response so that when an incident occurs, you will have a methodical and structured method of addressing it.

A number of aspects of incident response must be performed, including the following tasks:

- Assembling a computer incident response team (CIRT)
- Developing an incident response plan
- Discovering incidents
- Handling incidents
- Reporting incidents
- Recovering from an incident

Assembling a Computer Incident Response Team (CIRT)

One of the most effective tasks you can undertake as part of your incident response policy is to build a CIRT. It is important to understand that a CIRT does not exist solely to deal with incidents after they have occurred. In fact, a well-developed CIRT should actually exist to attempt to prevent an incident from occurring in addition to being able to address an incident after it has occurred. A CIRT exists primarily to confront security incidents that might occur, are occurring, or have occurred. The objective is to prevent an incident from becoming a crisis, and the sooner a CIRT can react, the greater the success rate at accomplishing this objective.

The overriding mission of a CIRT is to provide the guidance and direction required for a company to effectively prepare for and respond to any security incidents that may occur on the network. Because these incidents include such different things as viruses, worms, intrusions, and unauthorized system access, a good CIRT comprises many different specialties. Simply put, a CIRT needs to be able to handle a myriad of different types of incidents and must do so with skill and expertise regarding the subject.

Forming a CIRT

A CIRT can be built in a couple different ways, depending on the needs of the company. One method is to establish a static group of people as members of the CIRT. These folks are sometimes referred to as *core team members*. The benefit of this method is that you always have a defined group that is responsible for incident response. The drawback of this method is that it can be very costly, so much so that it is cost prohibitive in many environments.

Another method is to define a dynamic group of people to address a specific issue or to deal with a specific incident. These folks are sometimes referred to as *support team members*. This is a much more common method of operating because it reduces the overhead of maintaining a dedicated incident response staff. You simply grab the people who are best suited for a problem and give them the authority and direction to handle it. For example, if you have a new worm that has to be addressed, you might identify who in the IT department is going to be responsible for dealing with the issue at that time and direct them to respond to the incident. The drawback of this method, however, is that because the components of the CIRT may change depending on the incident, it can take longer to mount an effective response.

One of the most effective methods of building a CIRT is to apply components from both of the previous methods in building a kind of hybrid CIRT. You will have certain individuals who are part of the core membership of the CIRT. They are always components of the CIRT and are available to respond to any incident that may occur. Then, when a specific incident arises, they may identify individuals with specific skills who need to be brought in to respond to the incident. In this manner, you really get the best of both worlds in that you have a dedicated group that can quickly respond to any incident while remaining cost effective because a mechanism is provided to augment the CIRT as the situation requires. This is the method I recommend and will detail in the rest of this chapter.

CIRT Membership

Once you have identified the need for a CIRT, the next step is to identify who needs to be a member of the CIRT and what their responsibilities are. A number of roles are identified within the CIRT, including whether these people are core members or are support members who are brought in as the situation requires.

This list is not exhaustive. In addition to the CIRT members we will identify, you may periodically involve team members from outside of your organization. For example, law enforcement, vendors, business partners, and consultants could all be necessary CIRT members in the appropriate circumstances.

CIRT Team Leader   This person is a core member of the CIRT and is primarily responsible for managing all the other members of the CIRT in respect to their CIRT responsibilities. The team leader is responsible for determining the relative threat any incident has and mobilizing the proper resources and personnel to address the incident.

Security Staff   The security staff includes both information and physical security personnel. These people are core team members and are primarily responsible for handling any issues related to the direct contact of your systems as a result of the incident. For example, if there was a physical breach of security, the physical security staff would be the people responsible for responding to the incident. Your security staff is frequently the group that interacts with law enforcement and may even consist of retired or off-duty police officers.

Forensics Staff   Your forensics staff is composed of core team members and is primarily responsible for determining what has happened as a result of the incident. The primary objective of the forensics staff is to investigate the incident in such a manner as to be able to provide evidence and establish facts that can be used for the prosecution of any crimes as a result of the incident.

IT Staff   Your IT staff can be either core or support team members, depending on the circumstances. For example, you might have members of your IT staff who are involved in all incidents that may occur, or you might have members of your IT staff who only get involved when an incident occurs that affects them. Because of the cost of maintaining permanent roles in the CIRT, I recommend the latter approach as part of the hybrid method described earlier. Identify who in the IT staff the CIRT should involve for any given incident type and have those personnel provide the required level of support that the CIRT needs.

Risk Manager   The risk manager is a core team member who is primarily responsible for identifying and assessing the level of risk an incident has. As previously mentioned in Chapter 2, this can typically be done by assigning a threat rating to your network resources. The risk manager can then evaluate any incidents and determine the level of risk associated with an incident so that the CIRT team leader can determine the appropriate response.

Disaster Recovery   Disaster recovery is composed of support team members who are primarily responsible for coordinating incident response in regard to recovering from incidents that have resulted in a catastrophic failure on the same level that a disaster would have. For example, if you have a system that is responsible for all your business continuity (for example, SAP or PeopleSoft) and it is compromised to the point that it is rendered inoperable, this is an incident on the same level as a natural disaster, rendering the system inoperable. In these circumstances, disaster recovery can work to get the company back up and operational through the use of previously defined mechanisms, such as an offsite failover location.

Legal Staff   Your company's legal staff is composed of support team members who are primarily responsible for addressing and advising the CIRT in regard to legal advice and issues. The legal staff ensures that any evidence collected during the incident response is usable in the event that the company decides to take legal action. The legal staff is also responsible for providing legal advice to address any liabilities in the event that the incident affects customers, vendors, or the general public.

HEADS UP!

Under some circumstances, failure to notify law enforcement can be a crime in itself (child pornography, specifically). Your legal staff can advise you of these situations.

Human Resources   Human resources personnel are support team members who are primarily responsible for addressing any personnel issues related to an incident. Unfortunately, many incidents do not involve external threats but rather internal employees. Human resources provides the necessary advice on how to properly handle any situation that involves employees to ensure that the company does not violate any employment laws.

Public Relations   Public relations, particularly in regard to security and security incidents, can have a large impact on the damage an incident causes. One need only look at Microsoft for an example of that. Microsoft has regularly and routinely been taken to task in the media due to the perception that Microsoft is weak on security. This has had the result of causing many people to dismiss Microsoft products as not capable of operating in a secure environment. For example, many folks still will not acknowledge that Microsoft ISA Server is a genuine firewall. Public relations includes support team members who are responsible for providing advice and guidance on how best to handle that most delicate of security issues—the public perception. Public relations is also critical in helping to address stockholder concerns related to a security incident.

Financial Auditor   Financial auditors are support team members who are responsible for assigning a monetary value to the cost of an incident. This is a critical requirement for most insurance companies as well as being necessary if you decide to press charges under the National Information Infrastructure Protection Act.

Defining the CIRT Charter and Responsibilities

Now that we have defined what a CIRT is and who should be a member of the CIRT, the next step is to define the role and responsibilities of the CIRT. For a CIRT to be effective, it must have a clearly defined charter or mission statement. The charter should define not only the philosophy, policies, and practices that will shape the role of the CIRT, but also the goals and the level of authority the CIRT has within an organization. Like so many other things, for a CIRT to be effective, it must have management support and recognition, and the CIRT charter should be an embodiment of that support.

As mentioned previously, the objective of a CIRT is ultimately to prevent an incident. If this cannot occur, however, the CIRT has the responsibility of defining the pre-established response to an incident, thus minimizing the potential impact and keeping the incident from reaching crisis proportions.

ONE STEP FURTHER

You can see an example of why you need an effective CIRT by examining what happened with SCO and the MyDoom/Norvarg worm on February 1, 2004. The MyDoom/Norvarg worm carried a payload that launched a denial of service (DoS) against www.sco.com. Although it can be difficult to combat a DoS, you can undertake steps to mitigate it. One method is to engage filtering at your upstream neighbor routers where they have the bandwidth capacity to handle the traffic load. Another option is to increase the bandwidth capacity of the network connections to deal with the increased load. A third option, in the event that the DoS is so significant that nothing can effectively be done to prevent it, would be to change the DNS records of, in this case, www.sco.com to 127.0.0.1 or remove the www.sco.com DNS entry so that at the very least the traffic does not affect the Internet in general. It is during a scenario such as this that you need a CIRT to examine the consequences and determine the most effective course of action that allows the company to respond accordingly and quickly. Can you afford the cost of increasing your bandwidth? Does your upstream provider have the capacity to attempt to filter the attack? Your CIRT can manage the options and determine the most efficient and effective course of action. Ultimately, in this case, SCO removed the DNS entry, thereby addressing the incident in a manner that was appropriate for them.

In addition to the broad responsibilities of preventing and handling incident response, the CIRT has some specific responsibilities. These include the following:

- Development and maintenance of an incident response program and the related documentation, including the integration of lessons learned from any incidents that may occur.

- Defining and classifying incidents.

- Determining the necessary tools and technologies to be used for detecting incidents, such as intrusion detection software and hardware.

- Determining which incidents should be investigated and to what degree the investigation should be undertaken. This includes determining whether law enforcement should be involved and what forensics work is necessary to investigate the incident.

- Securing the network in response to an incident.

- Conducting follow-up interviews and reviews to provide after-action reports that can be used to prevent subsequent incidents.

- Promoting incident awareness throughout the organization as a preventative measure.

HEADS UP!

Be advised that while the CIRT should determine whether law enforcement needs to be involved and what degree of investigation should be taken, bringing in any external authorities should only be performed after consulting with management. The corporate officers are who may or may not be liable as a result of a security incident. Accordingly, you should obtain explicit instructions from management to involve legal authorities based on the CIRT recommendation. Conversely, you should document if the CIRT has recommended to involve the legal authorities and management made the executive decision not to. (Remember, in some cases, it is not management's call. If you find kiddie porn on the company server, you are breaking the law if you don't report it. But that doesn't mean you shouldn't engage management and be a good corporate citizen also.)

Planning for Incident Response

This first step of planning for incident response is to determine what the organization's incident response needs are. Once you have done that, the next step is to build the policies and procedures that will be used in the event of an actual incident. Finally, a critical step of planning for incident response is to practice what needs to be done to effectively minimize the impact an incident will have on the organization.

Determining the Organization's Incident Response Needs

The easiest method of determining what services, applications, and devices need to have an incident response plan is to perform an assessment of the resources that need to be protected. This rather simple statement is an incredibly complex process, however. This is due to the fact that it is virtually impossible for a CIRT to be able to identify every resource that needs to be addressed.

You can approach this issue in a couple of ways to make it a more practical undertaking. One method is to distribute questionnaires to the relevant individuals and groups and get them to identify what their needs are. The drawback of this method is that these questionnaires are frequently not returned or are not returned in a timely fashion.

Another option, and the more successful method, is to personally approach the relevant individuals and groups to discuss what their needs are. There are a number of benefits to this approach. The most important benefit of this approach is that it allows you to establish and maintain the personal contacts that can be critical to leverage in the event of an incident. In addition, people are generally more open to discussing things and usually provide more information when they are given an opportunity not only to answer but also to ask questions regarding the process. It allows them to feel more involved, and the more involved someone is in a process, the more they care about the success of that process. Another benefit is that it gets exposure to the computer incident response team, providing an excellent avenue for marketing the value of the CIRT throughout the organization.

In performing the assessment, you should at a minimum involve the following individuals to better ensure that you have properly defined all the critical resources that need an incident response plan and the type of incident response plan that is required:

- **Department managers**   You need to talk to the department managers of all the departments in an organization to ensure that you identify all the resources that they use and can assign a threat level to each of them.

- **IT staff**   One of the best groups for identifying resources that need an incident response plan is the IT staff. This is due to the fact that the IT staff, by and large, already knows and is responsible for most of the critical technology resources in the organization.

- **Helpdesk staff**   The helpdesk staff is a critical group for identifying the high-risk resources in an organization. This is due to the fact that any time there is a problem with any technology resource, it is a virtual certainty that the helpdesk will be called about it. This allows the helpdesk to quickly be able to determine what is and is not important within an organization.

- **HR staff**   So many critical resources are components of an organization's HR resources that speaking with the HR staff is a critical component of identifying what resources require an incident response policy and the degree of policy necessary.

- **Risk management**   Because risk management is responsible for determining the level of risk associated with resources within the organization, it is an important group to meet with to help identify what resources require an incident response policy and the degree of detail that policy requires.

- **Users**   Although it is impractical to meet with all the users in an organization, it can be worthwhile to identify specific users or user groups to meet with to discuss what resources they believe need to be protected.

Building an Incident Response Policy

Like in other aspects of hardening your network infrastructure, it is necessary to design written incident response policies that provide the guidance necessary to define how to respond to an incident. The reason for this is simple: It is much easier to react to an incident when you have defined how to react, as opposed to trying to make it up in the midst of an already stressful situation. Your incident response policy contains those definitions.

RFC2350, located at ftp://ftp.rfc-editor.org/in-notes/rfc2350.txt, is the definitive best-practices standard on how to handle incident response and, in particular, how to build your incident response policies. RFC2350 details the necessity of your incident response policy documenting the types of incidents as well as the level of support that will be provided for these incidents. I recommend that you take this a step further and generate a unique incident response policy for each type of incident you identify. This is because each incident may require a different level of response, and maintaining this information in separate documents will make it much easier to determine what the appropriate response for any given incident is. Another item you should ensure your incident response policy contains is an explanation of who the CIRT routinely interacts with and the degree of cooperation that the various groups in your organization will have. This is not to define whether cooperation should occur as much as it is to reduce the chance of misunderstandings or duplication of efforts between groups. Finally, your incident response policy should detail the level of communication and disclosure that will occur as well as the appropriate mechanisms for communication and disclosure. This is to ensure that only the information the organization wants to be disclosed is disclosed and that it is done so in the appropriate manner, such as through the use of press releases.

The best way to approach an incident response policy is in the same manner you would a security policy. In fact, an incident response policy is really just a very specific security policy, and like a security policy there are sections that every incident response policy should contain, including the following:

- Overview
- Incident identification
- Incident classification
- Incident response process flow
- Communications
- Reporting
- Definitions
- Revision History

Overview   The overview section should contain a brief explanation of what the incident policy addresses. This section could also include background information regarding the technology or resources the incident response policy will address. Details of how to handle the incident are left for further explanation in the other sections. This section is where you briefly explain what the incident response policy will address and what the objectives of the policy are.

Differences Between Security Policy and Incident Response Policy

One of the biggest differences between a security policy and an incident response policy is how they are written. Security policies are often passive documents that prescribe how systems should be used and what should be put in place to prevent something from occurring. On the other hand, incident response policies are action oriented. They focus on what to do, how to do it, when to do it, and who to notify.

Incident Identification   The incident identification section is where you explicitly define the incidents that the policy covers. In addition to identifying the incidents, you need to define the types of incidents. For example, computer fraud and computer abuse are two different types of incidents that require a different kind of response.

It is also a good idea to provide examples of the incidents in the incident identification section. This will not only help people better understand what incidents the policy applies to, but it can also help to identify where you are missing or overlooking security incidents that need to be addressed with a policy.

The incident identification section is used to determine what needs to be documented in the other sections of the policy.

Incident Classification   Because not all incidents require the same level of response, you need to define an incident classification system. The incident classification section is where you will define the degree of urgency and priority that incidents addressed by the incident response policy will be handled with.

Incident Response Process Flow   The incident response process flow section is where the feet hit the pavement. This section concerns itself with what to do when an incident has been identified and classified. This section is where you document what to do for the incident the policy addresses. For example, if the policy addresses a compromise of your external firewall, this section should detail the steps to be followed in addressing the incident, including stating whether it is acceptable to disconnect the firewall from the network, thus terminating all Internet connectivity, or whether the firewall must be kept operational while the incident is being addressed. In addition to defining whether business continuity must be maintained, this section should also define what is required to restore business continuity after an incident. For example, your policy may dictate that before a compromised system can be brought back online and put into operation, it must be completely scrubbed and rebuilt from scratch.

A formal incident response process flow system will be discussed in more detail in the "Handling Incidents" section later in this chapter.

Communications   The communications section is where you document who to contact regarding an incident and how to contact them. The communications section should also detail the escalation path to be used for the incident so that the appropriate people can be notified at the appropriate time.

Reporting   The reporting section is where you document the kind of data that will be collected, how the data will be reported, and who the data will be reported to. This section is also where you define how much information will be released to the customers/partners/general public and who is responsible for doing so.

Definitions   The definitions section is where you define any terms or concepts you used in the incident response policy to ensure that everyone understands what was meant. You should also use this section to clarify any acronyms used in the policy.

Revision History   The revision history section is where you track all updates and changes made to the incident response policy. You need to document not only the current date and version of the incident response policy, but also a brief explanation of the changes made to the incident response policy and who made those changes.

Practicing for an Incident

The last step of planning for incident response is to practice for an incident to occur. The reason for this is simple: If you have undertaken the hardening steps in this book, the likelihood of you having an incident is going to be greatly reduced. If you don't periodically review what needs to be done in the event of an incident, you just might be caught with your proverbial pants down. In addition, the more you practice, the more natural it will be to react to an incident. Incident response will become second nature, and instead of spending time thinking about what you need to do in the middle of an incident, you will find yourself falling back on your practice and simply doing what needs to be done without spending a lot of time thinking about it.

The best way to practice is to simulate going through an incident. Have the CIRT respond as if an actual incident is occurring and go through the processes and procedures that you have documented as part of your incident response plan. In addition to making sure that everyone knows what they need to do, this will also show you where your incident response plan fails so that you can fix it before a real incident occurs.

Discovering Incidents

Discovering incidents is a critical part of incident response. After all, how can you respond to an incident if you don't know that an incident exists? Incident discovery really entails two separate processes. The first process is discovering incidents before they occur in your environment. The second process is discovering incidents after they occur in your environment. Each process has its own unique characteristics.

Discovering Incidents Before They Occur

Because the best incident response is to prevent an incident from becoming a crisis, the best way to discover incidents is before they occur in your environment. The best method for doing this is to monitor different vendors' and organizations' websites for incident reports. Table 17-1 details some common websites to monitor on a regular basis.

Organization	Website
CERT Advisories	http://www.cert.org/advisories/
SecurityFocus	http://www.securityfocus.com
Microsoft	http://www.microsoft.com/security/
Cisco	http://www.cisco.com/security/
Check Point	http://www.checkpoint.com/securitycenter/index.html
Red Hat	https://www.redhat.com/solutions/security/
Symantec Anti-Virus	http://www.sarc.com/
Network Associates	http://www.nai.com/us/security/vil.htm

Table 17-1.   Websites to Monitor for Incident Reports

In addition to checking vendor websites, you should subscribe to a number of mailing lists for incident notification, as detailed in Table 17-2.

Discovering Incidents in Your Environment

Discovering incidents in your environment can be a much trickier proposition than monitoring websites and mailing lists for vendor advisories. This is due to the fact that in many cases you don't know exactly what to look for. There are a few things that you can do to help with this, however.

Event Monitoring   Virtually all your network devices support some kind of event-logging functionality. Most support some form of syslog notification. This is important because most incidents are precipitated by some kind of event. If you monitor your event logs for these events, they can tip you off that there might be an incident happening or about to happen.

Organization	Subscription Website
NT Bugtraq	http://www.ntbugtraq.com/
Buqtraq	http://www.securityfocus.com/archive
Full Disclosure	http://lists.netsys.com/mailman/listinfo/full-disclosure (Be advised that Full Disclosure is an unmoderated mailing list and frequently becomes filled with religious wars between Linux advocates and pretty much everyone else.)
SecurityFocus Incidents	http://www.securityfocus.com/archive
CERT Advisory Mailing List	http://www.cert.org/contact_cert/certmaillist.html

Table 17-2.   Mailing Lists to Subscribe to for Incident Reports

One of the biggest problems with event monitoring is the sheer volume of events. This makes it an almost impossible task to try to review your event logs. To help with this, you can use products that filter through your event logs and alert you whenever an event you have stipulated is logged. One of the products you can use to help you isolate events is Kiwi Syslog Daemon from Kiwi Enterprises (http://www.kiwisyslog.com/). Although a freeware version is available, the retail version supports configuring e-mail notification when certain administrator-configured events are logged. Another product that scales much better in large enterprises is NetIQ VigilEnt Log Analyzer (http://www.netiq.com/products/vlm/default.asp). In addition to robust alerting capabilities, VigilEnt Log Analyzer also supports very robust log archival and reporting functionality. Event monitoring has been covered in more detail in Chapter 10.

Helpdesk Ticket Tracking One of the most underestimated methods of recognizing that an incident might be occurring in your environment is monitoring the helpdesk tickets being generated. No matter how well you try to monitor your environment, one group of people will monitor your network better than you—your end users. Your end users will almost always notice a problem with something that they use before you do. In many cases, they will call the helpdesk to report the problem. You can use this information to your advantage to try to stay on top of potential issues in your environment.

Intrusion Detection Systems Intrusion detection systems can also inform you of potential incidents by identifying any unusual traffic patterns and notifying you when they detect one. For example, many worms have a distinct signature of what their network traffic looks like. Your intrusion detection system can be loaded with that signature and be configured to alert you in the event that the traffic pattern is identified. Intrusion detection is covered in more detail in Chapter 4.

Bandwidth Monitoring Applications A somewhat unusual event-identification system is conventional bandwidth monitoring. Many of today's worms will cause a significant increase in network traffic as they attempt to spread. If you have a bandwidth-monitoring application running on your network, it can help to identify unusual traffic spikes that could indicate that an incident is occurring. One of the better freeware products you can use to monitor your bandwidth is the Multi Router Traffic Grapher (MRTG), which can be obtained at http://people.ee.ethz.ch/~oetiker/webtools/mrtg/. In addition, BMC Software, Inc., makes two very good network-monitoring applications. PATROL DashBoard is a report-driven web-based GUI similar to MRTG. PATROL Visualis takes monitoring a step further, providing a 3D graphical topology display that can show you real-time bandwidth on a per-link basis. The benefit of this type of system is that you can actually see what network segments are being inundated with traffic so that you can isolate where the incident might be occurring. Both PATROL DashBoard and PATROL Visualis can be obtained at http://www.bmc.com/products/products_services_detail/0,,0_0_0_22,00.html.

Change Monitoring Another method you can use to determine if an incident is occurring on your network is the use of change-monitoring applications and processes. In the case of many Cisco devices, you can actually monitor for changes by using syslog because

Cisco will generate a syslog message any time that the configuration is changed. In addition, Tripwire makes a product known as Tripwire for Network Devices (http://www.tripwire.com/products/network_devices/) that can also monitor your network devices for configuration changes. For the servers in your environment, you can use another Tripwire product, Tripwire for Servers (http://www.tripwire.com/products/servers/).

Handling Incidents

Incident handling is the most important part of any incident response plan. Incident handling is where you put all the planning, preparation, and practice into effect and attempt to minimize the impact an incident has on your environment. Figure 17-1 details a process flow for implementing an incident response plan.

There are four phases to handling incidents. The first phase is incident discovery. The second phase is incident handling. The third phase is incident reporting, and the final phase is incident recovery.

Incident Discovery

The entrance into the incident response flow is the discovery of an incident. Although the actual discovery methods have been previously discussed, from the perspective of the incident response flow, incident discovery is the process of determining what needs to be done once the incident has been identified.

Once a potential incident has been identified, you must observe and monitor the situation so that you can assess what is happening based on the available information. The important thing at this phase is to determine whether this is a real incident that needs to be addressed. This will prevent the CIRT from having to jump through hoops for a false alarm. At the same time, you need to make sure that what you are observing is the actual problem and not merely a symptom of the problem or simply a ruse that is designed to divert attention from the real problem.

After you have established that this is indeed an incident that requires a response, you need to define the urgency and priority of the incident. This will allow you to coordinate the appropriate resources for the problem at hand. For example, if the incident is deemed a low-risk, low-priority incident that is mitigated by existing protection mechanisms, the decision might be made to do nothing further for the incident and to merely monitor the systems to ensure that it does not become a bigger issue. An example of a low-risk, low-priority incident might be one that does not result in any data loss or data compromise or an incident that affects an extremely small percentage of your environment. Medium-risk, medium-priority issues may require action, but they do not require any special efforts to begin the incident-handling process. An example of a medium-risk, medium-priority incident might be an exploit that affects a web browser and has the potential to grant privilege escalation. Although the exploit needs to be addressed, the likelihood of occurrence is relatively low (a user must visit a website that exploits the flaw) and can be addressed through routine change-control and patching procedures. On the other hand, high-risk, high-priority incidents may require the CIRT

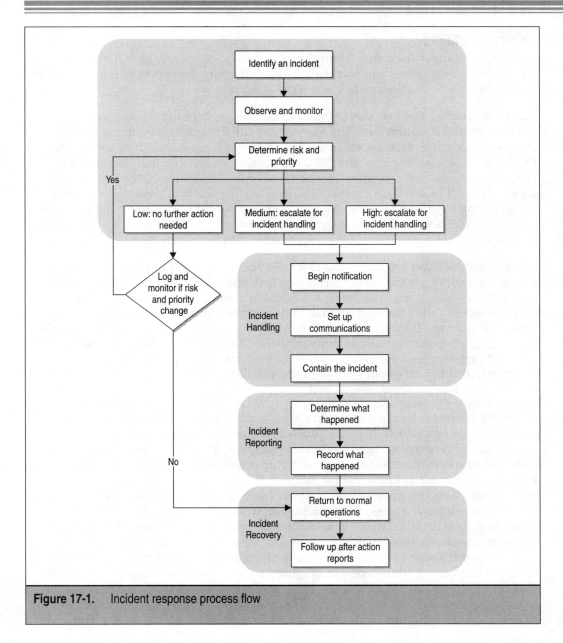

Figure 17-1.   Incident response process flow

to stop whatever it is that they are doing and to focus exclusively on the incident at hand. An example of a high-risk, high-priority incident might be a worm that has begun infecting your internal resources and must be addressed immediately to prevent subsequent damage.

Incident Handling

Incident handling is the actual "doing" phase of the incident response flow. During the incident-handling phase, you want to identify and notify the appropriate resources and undertake the necessary steps to contain the incident.

Begin Notification   The first step of incident handling is to notify the appropriate individuals in the organization and identify the CIRT that will need to contain the incident. This is the phase in which the relevant on-call personnel should be notified. During the notification phase, the CIRT team leader will ensure that the previously defined processes and procedures for addressing the incident begin being put into action. The CIRT team leader should also decide if the incident meets the requirements for involving legal authorities or if it meets requirements to make notifying the legal authorities mandatory. It is important at this phase that the CIRT team leader has the necessary authority to carry out the response that has been identified.

Set Up Communications   Because the CIRT members may span multiple sites and physical locations, or they may be running here and there trying to respond to the incident, it is important to establish a method of communication so that all the CIRT members can communicate their status, actions, and responses. This is also critical in ensuring that there is no duplication of effort or, even worse, that people start unintentionally undoing things that other CIRT members did. You also need to establish communications with management so that you can keep them apprised of the situation, and you might need to notify public relations so that they can begin drafting a public response as required.

Contain the Incident   Incident containment is simply the process of limiting the scope of an incident as much as you can. Incident containment will often require the application of vendor patches to address security holes that contributed to the incident. This type of containment is best applied before the security hole has been exploited in your environment as a preventative measure. If you cannot do this, however, remember that patching a compromised system can still leave a back door in place and operational. Although a patch can address the security hole, it often does not address the results of the security hole. In many cases, incident containment will also require the disconnecting of systems from the network or the Internet to prevent the spread of the incident and to make it easier to recover systems. You have to weigh this against the need to catch an intruder, however. If the incident in question is a new worm, it probably isn't worth the effort to try to catch who you got the worm from; instead, you want to isolate the infected systems and remove the worm. However, if the incident is someone attempting to gain access to your internal database of customer financial records, you will probably need to weigh very carefully whether it is more important to contain the incident right now, or if the incident can be allowed to proceed a little longer in an attempt to determine who is responsible.

Incident Reporting

After you have successfully contained the incident, the next phase is to prepare to report the incident to the necessary organizations. In some cases, that will be law enforcement. In other cases, it will be internal management resources, and in yet other cases, it might be an ISP.

ONE STEP FURTHER

The National Infrastructure Protection Center (NIPC) maintains an excellent incident-reporting form in both online and PDF format that provides a good example of the kind of information you need to gather and be prepared to present when reporting an incident. This form can be accessed at http://www.nipc.gov/incident/incident.htm. Some common elements to include in your incident response form are listed here:

- Point of contact information.

- Date and time of the incident.

- Whether the affected system is business critical.

- Nature of the problem. (Was it an intrusion, a website defacement, a worm, and so on?)

- Suspected method of intrusion/attack. (Did it use a trap door or Trojan horse, or was there a vulnerability that was exploited? If so, what was the vulnerability?)

- Suspected perpetrators or motivation for the attack.

- Whether any spoofing appears to have been used.

- The apparent source of the incident.

- What systems (hardware and software) were affected.

- Whether there was a loss in data, and the level of sensitivity of the data loss.

- What actions have been taken to mitigate/resolve the incident.

Determine What Happened   The first step of incident reporting is to determine exactly what happened, why it happened, and how it happened, and then to identify the steps necessary to prevent it from happening in the future. It may be necessary to involve an internal or external forensics team to assist in trying to determine what occurred. It is important at this step to remember that there is no magic in computing. Computers and networks do exactly what they are programmed to do every time. Even when systems crash, they are doing so because they were programmed to do so. In determining what happened, do not leave things to chance, guesswork, or gut feelings. Although those are all potentially valuable in helping to determine what happened, you need to deal in facts at this stage of the game. In addition to figuring out what happened, you also need to identify who was or is still involved in the incident. This might be an internal or an external person or group.

Record What Happened   Next, you should document everything about the incident. No detail is too small, especially if there is any possibility that there might be litigation or criminal prosecution as a result of the incident. A critical component of recording what happened is maintaining a verifiable chain of custody. The chain of custody is simply the ability to ensure that at no time has any evidence been tampered with. To establish a chain of custody, you must be able to prove the following:

- No information has been added, charged, or deleted.
- A complete copy was made.
- A reliable copy process was used.
- All media was secured.

You can obtain more detailed information about chain of custody and the federal rules on evidence at http://www.usdoj.gov/criminal/cybercrime/usamarch2001_4.htm or by speaking with your legal department and ensuring that they help to develop your chain of custody process.

In addition to simply documenting the incident, it may also be necessary that you make a backup of all the damaged/tampered with systems so that they can be submitted for legal purposes.

Incident Recovery

The last step is to recover from an incident. Incident recovery is typically the most important step of all of incident response as far as management is concerned. The sooner that an incident has been addressed, the sooner the company can get back to business. This desire often puts an incredible strain on the CIRT that might influence the team to perhaps not spend as much time investigating the incident or containing the incident before they attempt to bring the resources back online. At all costs, this desire must be resisted, and you need to make sure you follow all the steps of the incident response flow to ensure that you have effectively addressed the incident and have not done anything that could ultimately harm the company in a desire to get things running again.

In addition to simply restoring the operation of systems, recovering from an incident also includes ensuring that all the vulnerabilities and points of penetration used to exploit the systems have been properly patched or corrected. You should ensure that you did not go through all these efforts just to have the incident repeat itself again in the future.

Unfortunately, often the only way to recover from an incident is to wipe the system out and reinstall. This is particularly critical if you even suspect that the incident may have enabled an intruder to install any kind of software (such as a Trojan horse or key logger) on the system. Although it may be easier to say, "But we found the Trojan so everything must be OK," the truth of the matter is that you have to approach it from the perspective of "If they did this, there is no way to know what else they might have done." You need to be prepared to accept this consequence as a result of a security incident.

The last thing to do after you have returned to normal operations is to have a formal review process and perform an after-action report on the incident. The goal is twofold: First, you want to understand everything that conspired to cause the incident to occur so that you can make sure you addressed any of the issues to ensure that this never happens again. Second, you want to review how the CIRT performed and how well the incident response policies and procedures worked in containing and recovering from the incident. This will help you identify areas that need to be changed or improved to ensure a more effective process the next time an incident occurs—because there will be a next time.

Summary

One of the worst fears of any security organization is that a security incident will occur that they will have to address. Unfortunately, the reality is that sooner or later it is going to happen. Planning for incident response is a necessary function to ensure that your organization is prepared to deal with any incident that may present itself. The incident response flow can help you determine what to do in the event of an incident. The first thing you need to do is to develop a computer incident response team (CIRT) to deal with any incident that may arise.

Next, you should plan for incident response and begin getting prepared to deal with incidents before they occur. Once you have discovered an incident, you need to observe the situation to determine exactly what is going on before deciding what the best method of handling the incident is. During incident handling, you should notify all the affected personnel of what is occurring as well as establish a method for the CIRT to communicate while they contain the incident. After you have properly contained the incident, you should gather the necessary information required for you to report the incident to the relevant groups and organizations, including law enforcement. The last step is to recover from the incident by patching and repairing any systems that were compromised as well as closing/fixing whatever means were used to exploit the system. Remember, you cannot prevent all incidents. It is never going to happen. You have to be prepared to handle those incidents that you cannot prevent to allow your organization to become fully operational again in the most rapid and reliable fashion possible.

Index

■ M

■ N

Z

INTERNATIONAL CONTACT INFORMATION

AUSTRALIA
McGraw-Hill Book Company
Australia Pty. Ltd.
TEL +61-2-9900-1800
FAX +61-2-9878-8881
http://www.mcgraw-hill.com.au
books-it_sydney@mcgraw-hill.com

CANADA
McGraw-Hill Ryerson Ltd.
TEL +905-430-5000
FAX +905-430-5020
http://www.mcgraw-hill.ca

**GREECE, MIDDLE EAST, & AFRICA
(Excluding South Africa)**
McGraw-Hill Hellas
TEL +30-210-6560-990
TEL +30-210-6560-993
TEL +30-210-6560-994
FAX +30-210-6545-525

MEXICO (Also serving Latin America)
McGraw-Hill Interamericana Editores
S.A. de C.V.
TEL +525-1500-5108
FAX +525-117-1589
http://www.mcgraw-hill.com.mx
carlos_ruiz@mcgraw-hill.com

SINGAPORE (Serving Asia)
McGraw-Hill Book Company
TEL +65-6863-1580
FAX +65-6862-3354
http://www.mcgraw-hill.com.sg
mghasia@mcgraw-hill.com

SOUTH AFRICA
McGraw-Hill South Africa
TEL +27-11-622-7512
FAX +27-11-622-9045
robyn_swanepoel@mcgraw-hill.com

SPAIN
McGraw-Hill/
Interamericana de España, S.A.U.
TEL +34-91-180-3000
FAX +34-91-372-8513
http://www.mcgraw-hill.es
professional@mcgraw-hill.es

**UNITED KINGDOM, NORTHERN,
EASTERN, & CENTRAL EUROPE**
McGraw-Hill Education Europe
TEL +44-1-628-502500
FAX +44-1-628-770224
http://www.mcgraw-hill.co.uk
emea_queries@mcgraw-hill.com

ALL OTHER INQUIRIES Contact:
McGraw-Hill/Osborne
TEL +1-510-420-7700
FAX +1-510-420-7703
http://www.osborne.com
omg_international@mcgraw-hill.com